LADY GREGORY

JUDITH HILL is an architectural historian and writer. Her previous books include *The Building of Limerick* (1991), *Irish Public Sculpture: A History* (1998), and *In Search of Islands – A Life of Conor O'Brien* (2009). She has taught Irish cultural history, written for the *Irish Arts Review*, *The Irish Times* and *Times Literary Supplement*, and featured on RTÉ television and radio. She lives in Limerick.

For Kathleen and Peter

LADY GREGORY
AN IRISH LIFE

JUDITH HILL

The Collins Press

FIRST PUBLISHED IN IRELAND IN 2011 BY
The Collins Press
West Link Park
Doughcloyne
Wilton
Cork

First published in hardback by Sutton Publishing Limited in 2005

British Library Cataloguing in Publication data
Hill, Judith.
Lady Gregory : a life.
1. Gregory, Lady, 1852-1932. 2. Women authors, Irish—19th
century—Biography. 3. Authors, Irish—19th century—
Biography. 4. Women authors, Irish—20th century—
Biography. 5. Authors, Irish—20th century—Biography.

I. Title
822.9'12-dc22

ISBN-13: 9781848891104

Typesetting by Red Barn Publishing
Typeset in Sabon
Printed in Ireland by Sprintprint

Cover photographs:
Front: Portrait of Augusta, Lady Gregory by Antonio Mancini (1908).
Collection: Dublin City Gallery The Hugh Lane
Back: as per photo pages

Contents

Acknowledgements

My greatest debt is to the libraries and their unfailingly helpful staff: Mary Immaculate Library, Limerick; University of Limerick Library; Noel Kissane and Elizabeth Kirwan, Department of Manuscripts and Colette O'Flaherty, National Library of Ireland; Trinity College Library; Mary Boran, The Special Collections and Kieran Hoare, archivist, National University of Ireland, Galway; Catherine Farragher and Mary Quilter, Galway County Libraries; The Kiltartan Museum; Raymond Refaussé, The Representative Church Body Library, Dublin; Mary O'Doherty, The Mercer Library, Dublin; Richard Mills, The Royal College of Physicians, Dublin; Mairead Delaney, The Abbey Archive; Kathy Shoemaker and Stephen Enniss, Robert W. Woodruff Library, Emory University, Atlanta; Rodney Phillips and Isaac Gewirtz, The Berg Collection, New York Public Library; The British Library.

Entering a field of great scholarship, I am indebted to the work of many scholars, including Roy Foster, Adrian Frazier, Nicholas Grene, John Kelly, David Krause, Dan Laurence, Lucy McDiarmid, Daniel Murphy, Christopher Murray, James Pethica, Ann Saddlemyer.

Several people agreed to be interviewed and shared their memories of Lady Gregory with me: the late Martin Hehir, the late Catherine Kennedy, Anne de Winton.

I received great encouragement and help from a number of people who gave me specialist advice: Brian Coates, Mary Coll, Patricia Conboy, Maura Cronin, Sheila Deegan, Sister Mary de Lourdes Fahy, Terry Devlin, Roy Foster, Caroline Hill, Kathleen Hill, Madeleine Humphreys, Declan Kiberd, John Logan,

Patricia Lysaght, Maurice McGuire, Philip McEvansoneya, Deirdre McMahon, G.D. Mulroney, Jane Murray Brown, Máire Ní Neachtain, Sheila O'Donnellan, Lionel Pilkinton, Pat Punch, John Quinn, Veronica Rowe, Colin Smythe, Monica Spencer, Lois Tobin.

The Royal Irish Academy very generously awarded me two Eoin O'Mahony bursaries, which allowed me to travel to New York.

I am very grateful to my agent, Sara Menguc, who has been encouraging at the worst times; to my excellent editor at Sutton [publishers of the hardback edition], Jaqueline Mitchell; to my editors at The Collins Press who allowed me to make some minor adjustments, my understanding children, Lily and Helena; and to Mark Davies, who is a rock.

Finally, I would like to acknowledge the Berg Collection of English and American Literature, the New York Public Library Astor, Lenox and Tilden Foundations for permission to quote from Lady Gregory and Edward Martyn correspondence in their collection; the Foster-Murphy Collection Manuscripts and Archives Division, the New York Public Library Astor, Lenox and Tilden Foundations for permission to quote from material in their possession; Special Collections and Archives, Robert W. Woodruff Library, Emory University, for permission to quote from material in the Gregory Family Papers; National Library of Ireland for permission to quote from Lady Gregory correspondence; A.P. Watt Ltd on behalf of Michael B. Yeats for permission to quote from the published prose and poetry of W.B. Yeats; the Society of Authors on behalf of the Bernard Shaw Estate for permission to quote from George Bernard Shaw's letters; the Catholic University of America Press, Washington DC for permission to quote from the letters of Seán O'Casey; Pan Macmillan UK for permission to quote from Seán O'Casey's autobiography.

Preface

Lady Gregory lived a full life, very different from the one mapped out for the daughter of a Galway landowner, born in mid-nineteenth-century Ireland. She founded the Abbey Theatre, Dublin, supplied it with a steady stream of plays and directed it through controversy and war. She was a close friend, patron of, and artistic collaborator with the poet W.B. Yeats. She was a pioneering folklorist. She made Coole Park, County Galway, a home of the Irish Literary Revival, and was an influential commentator on Irish culture. She supported her nephew, the art collector Hugh Lane, in his desire to establish a modern art gallery in Dublin, and fought tirelessly for his pictures to be returned to Ireland from Britain. She loved her husband, her son, Robert, her three grandchildren, her numerous friends, and she had two lovers. She suffered too; most heartbreakingly when Robert and Hugh were killed in the First World War.

It was not, as might be anticipated, a straightforward life. There were many intriguing contradictions. She gradually gained an empathy with those from whom she was separated by birth, education, culture, habit, dress, manner of speaking and family allegiance, to become a nationalist. Yet she remained a landowner, collecting twice-yearly rents, grooming her son to take up his inheritance. She was ambitious to succeed as a writer, and could be forceful when trying to get her own way in the Abbey. But she believed that women should put men first, or at least be seen to, and so she concealed some of her successes and made her presence felt indirectly. She made no public statements about the role of women in society, and lived her life as though there was no need for change. Yet in several of her plays she demonstrated an interest in questioning traditional female roles, and she explored the lives of strong women. There were hidden contradictions, too. She seemed the epitome of an emotionally restrained person; she had married pragmatically, and after her husband's death her forty years of widow's black proclaimed a lack of interest in re-marriage. Yet she had two passionate affairs, and her letters and diaries reveal the depth of her love for her son and grandchildren. She was extremely secretive about her private life. However, several of her plays contain surprisingly significant autobiographical seeds. She is a fascinating character, at once a product of her class and time, and a rebel against circumstance.

For much of the time since her death in 1932, Augusta Gregory has held a secure but distinctly minor position on the stage of the Irish Revival. Yeats is the dominant figure, their male contemporaries take second place and Lady Gregory stands somewhat to the side. The image of the influential, successful woman had already been tarnished before her death by some of the men she knew: Joseph Holloway characterised her as the formidable autocratic ruler of the Abbey Theatre to whom others were meekly acquiescent; the writer George Moore named Yeats as the instigator of her folklore and legends; the surgeon-poet St John Gogarty suggested that Yeats had written most of her plays. After her death, Yeats's image of her as an aristocratic patron was hugely influential, while most scholarly assessments concentrated almost exclusively on her plays. These plays continued to be performed at the Abbey until the early 1970s, and even longer by amateur groups, but most of them were out of print by the early 1950s.

There was a scholarly revival of interest in her work in the early 1960s when Elizabeth Coxhead wrote her delightful *Literary Portrait*. This initiative was reinforced in the early 1970s by Colin Smythe's monumental effort to publish the complete works in his *Coole Edition*. This work continues. In 1970 critics acknowledged the legitimacy of this project, but without enthusiasm. At the time Lady Gregory's reputation was suffering from the fact of her Ascendancy background, which was popularly deemed to outweigh her nationalist credentials. Meanwhile, scholars continued to reassess her plays, and Ann Saddlemyer and Hazard Adams found much in them to support their claims that she was a significant creative figure. An attempt to get behind the façade of her image and to evaluate her in her own terms without constant reference to her colleagues was made by Mary Lou Kohfeldt in her full-length biography, *Lady Gregory, the Woman Behind the Irish Renaissance*, published in 1985. This was soon followed by an inspirational series of essays, *Fifty Years After*, published in 1987 in which her roles as wife, lover, mother, and her friendships were systematically explored. Behind the scholarship the tone was celebratory, and George Bernard Shaw's assertion that she was 'the greatest living Irishwoman' suddenly began to have some resonance. In 1995 Penguin published a selection of her writings, including folklore, poetry, journals, translations and autobiography, convincingly presenting the variety and complexity of her work in a single volume. In 1996 James Pethica edited the diaries she wrote after her husband's death, when she was becoming involved in the Irish Revival. And the spring/summer 2004 edition of the *Irish University Review* reveals that she is an inspiring subject for many contemporary scholars.

She is now emerging as a writer who was embedded in the many preoccupations and initiatives of her time, and who had a significant influence. The recent publication of comprehensively researched biographies of her contemporaries – J.M. Synge, George Moore, W.B. Yeats, George Yeats, Seán O'Casey – in which the interaction of this remarkable group of people is repeatedly spelt out from different angles, has helped to redraw the terrain of the Irish Revival. Instead of being perceived as a group of competing artists of varying degrees of ability, waiting to be ranked, they now appear as a diverse, ambitious, often conflicting, but more often collaborative group of people who, existing at a time of great change and sensing the emerging importance of Ireland on the world stage, lived intensely, with a great desire to serve Ireland, influence events and realise their creative potential.

There are many ways to reassess Augusta Gregory's achievements and set her in her rightful place in the history of the Irish Revival. In the literary field current interest in the context in which works of art and journalism are produced, and in the way they are received, means that minor stars can take their place without the tone of special pleading; Yeats's genius, still recognised, can no longer effortlessly outshine his contemporaries in an account of the Irish Literary Revival. One aim of this biography is to situate Augusta Gregory's plays in her life so that they can be reassessed without the pressure to prove that they are great literature. Lady Gregory was neither a stylistic innovator nor a writer who aimed primarily to explore the human condition. Her subject was society, and most particularly the social and cultural values of her Galway neighbours as she understood them through her empathetic folklore. If she is judged according to traditional literary values she fails, though not absolutely. She needs to be understood as a cutting-edge folklorist, who realised the need to present the voices of her interviewees in as unmediated a way as possible, and as a writer who was able to translate this into plays. Her achievement emerges as an ability to present the values of a dying society to the metropolitan stage. Thus she made a decisive impact on Irish cultural nationalism. Arguably, her plays are still a largely untapped source for understanding this society.

Current interest in a fuller picture of human endeavour has drawn our attention to many abilities that tended to be obscured when the focus was on genius. Now the ability for organisation, diplomacy, management and propaganda in many different situations are also seen as important and interesting. These were all talents that Augusta Gregory had in abundance. Post-colonial studies have drawn attention to the wider issues of colonialism, so that Lady Gregory's early experience of the British Empire from two very different angles – as a consort of a politician and administrator, and as a champion of Egyptian nationalism – is now of crucial interest.

An important focus of a modern biography of Augusta Gregory is to bring her out from behind the shadow of Yeats where, admittedly, she had deliberately put herself. What exactly was her role in their collaborative writing, especially their plays? To what extent was Yeats the making of her? Did being Yeats's patron mean that her own work suffered? In order to answer these questions the relationship between these two formidable personalities has to be drawn with care, a not altogether impossible task because of the hundreds of letters that they sent each other whenever they were apart in the 40 years they knew each other. Assessing the influence of others, such as the folklorist and Gaelic

League president, Douglas Hyde, Augusta's frequent support in Abbey crises, the playwright J.M. Synge, the New York patron and Augusta's particular friend and lover, John Quinn, the writer and nationalist Edward Martyn and Augusta's lover and lifelong friend, the poet Wilfrid Scawen Blunt, all help to give a more rounded picture of Augusta's achievements.

One of the fascinations of Augusta Gregory is the way in which she was able to bypass the alternatives of her contemporary politics, and to work with her own vision of an independent Ireland, which encompassed both nationalist ideals and an aspiration for the Anglo-Irish. When this book was originally written, Ireland seemed to be experiencing a political coming of age, evinced in, for example, the Northern Ireland peace process, economic vitality, the divorce referendum, all of which were neutralising the enchantment of opposing ideologies. Now, despite recession and the revelation of serious political and economic incompetence, that framework of consensus remains. These contemporary parameters more nearly reflect Augusta Gregory's dream of Ireland. It is an environment in which her non-sectarian spirit can finally expand and her many-sided life be fully appreciated.

ONE

Roxborough

. . . the youngest daughter of the house was weighted with a many syllabled 'Isabella Augusta', borrowed from a never to be seen godmother, a Miss Brown of Bath.

Seventy Years

Two things about her birth, on 15 March 1852, would haunt Isabella Augusta Persse. The first, she learnt as a young child from her nurse. Her mother, who had already given birth to four boys and four girls, was hoping for another son. Disappointed by the girl, she initially ignored her, so that the baby nearly died.[1] The second, Augusta discovered for herself much later reading Shakespeare's *Julius Caesar*. She had been born at midnight between the 14th and 15th, the ides of March. 'Beware the ides of March,' the soothsayer warns in the play. If the first discovery told her that she was dispensable, the second suggested that she was in some sense marked out. As Augusta's mother went on to have another four boys, and as boys were given preference over girls, Augusta's overwhelming experience as a young child was that she was unimportant and should know her place. She would only gradually come to realise that she had much to offer the world.

To the thirteen children of Augusta's parents – Dudley Persse and Frances Barry, married in 1833 – must be added

Dudley's three children from his first marriage to Katherine
O'Grady.[2] This large family fell easily into separate groups.
Of Katherine's children, only the youngest daughter, Maria,
remained at home. The son, Dudley (b. 1829), was an army
captain who had fought in the Crimean War and been
severely wounded at Alma in 1854. Having quarrelled with
his father he rarely visited Roxborough, and Augusta hardly
knew him. The other daughter, Katherine, also a hazy
presence for Augusta, had married and left home when
Augusta was ten.[3]

Augusta's mother's elder sons – Richard, William Norton,
Edward and Algernon – and two of her daughters –
Elizabeth (Eliza) and Adelaide – were old enough to be
distant for the most part to the child Augusta. When
Adelaide, twelve years older than Augusta, was a beautiful
young woman being presented at the Viceregal Court in
Dublin, Augusta thought of her excitedly as a fairytale
princess.[4]

Augusta, a slim, vivacious child with soft dark eyes and
lustrous brown hair, spent most of her time with her two
slightly older sisters, Gertrude and Arabella.[5] She could be
quiet and shy with adults and relied on these lively sisters to
take her part. Gertrude, a happy child, had a steady
character, and Augusta later felt she had been her moral
mentor.[6] Arabella was quick to laugh, irreverent, a mimic.
Augusta thought that she had more natural ability than
herself, but that as an adult she failed to develop her talents,
preferring to surround herself with uninspiring people.
Together the girls would spend hours devising and
performing elaborate charades, Augusta directing.[7]

Unlike her sisters she envied the freer outdoor life of her
four younger brothers, Frank, Henry, Gerald and Alfred.
Exuberant and high spirited, they were allowed to hunt
foxes, trap rabbits and birds, and a blind eye was turned to

their passion for playing tricks. Occasionally Augusta persuaded them to include her in their antics, and as she got older they shared money earned shooting pests with her, and lent her books. She was particularly attached to Frank, just two years younger than her, a kind boy, with 'a dancing light in his eye'. They shared a corner of the garden, where one year the children built a summer house with the boys' French tutor. When Frank died in 1928 Augusta recalled one particular moment when they were out riding, Frank on his horse, Twilight: 'He had lost his hat in the run, his fair hair was shining; as they passed the M.F.H. [Master of Foxhounds], Burton Persse [a distant relative] called out "tell your mother I'm prouder of Frank than if he wrote the Bible!"'[8] The children formed a large crowd, constantly jostling for attention, quick to criticise each other. Such a family encouraged both Augusta's introverted and extroverted tendencies; she kept quiet about her passions, and she learnt to stand up for herself.

Augusta's father, Dudley, the 'Master', was autocratic, self-indulgent and profligate. He had gout – the result of excessive eating and drinking – and was paralysed from the waist down.[9] But, with plenty of servants to call on to propel him from donkey cart to horse to wheeled chair, his mobility was unaffected and he effortlessly maintained his authority in the estate yard, demesne fields and over family gatherings. Augusta summed this up dryly by observing that being paralysed never interfered with his duties or his pleasures. A miniature painted of him when young shows a dark handsome man of upright bearing and arrogant expression.

By the time Augusta knew him he was a man who lived for hunting and had little sympathy for the books that would become Augusta's passion, and the religion that would preoccupy his wife and several daughters. He dealt with his tenants with unthinking domination. A Galway farmer vividly remembered him as a grotesque figure, 'a fierce-looking man to look at. He had two big jaw-bones and wore side whiskers and he had big teeth in his head and they were nearly as long as my thumb. He was a big strong man in his day.'[10] Augusta hardly mentioned him in her autobiography, *Seventy Years*. The impression is that Dudley had very little to do with his youngest daughter, and she reciprocated by having little curiosity about him or affection for him. Yet he set a standard of male authority that she never seriously questioned, even though she would chafe against it.

Augusta had far more to do with her mother – an heiress when she married Dudley, the only daughter of Colonel Richard Barry of Castle Cor in County Cork. But there was a singular lack of affection between them, expressed in the distant tone in *Seventy Years*. This derived from Frances, who was an emotionally withdrawn mother who put great value on courtesy and good manners.[11] Augusta remembered her being called the 'Mistress' by the children as well as the servants. She was tall, handsome and fashionably dressed – as a young married woman she had worn the tiny waisted, full dresses and ringletted hair of the 1840s – and Augusta admired her style. She remembered her in black velvet and diamonds standing at the door to welcome a newly-arrived tutor with unforgettable friendliness.[12] She sentimentally imagined that the source of her mother's fine manners was her French Huguenot relative, Frances Aigoin (in fact an Irishwoman who had married into a Huguenot family), whose late seventeenth-century Bible her mother bequeathed to Augusta who treasured it.[13] Courtesy was the cornerstone of a well-bred woman's persona in the mid-nineteenth century, and Augusta would accept it without question. Although she would grow up to be a very different person from her mother, capable of showing great warmth, love and kindness to her son and grandchildren, and having an enormous capacity for friendship, she did adopt her mother's courtesy, and even close friends such as Yeats sometimes found it hard to penetrate the façade of her impeccable manners. But, whereas for her mother good behaviour towards others was a matter of form, for Augusta it had the force of a moral creed; she saw it as part of the duty of privilege to accommodate the emotional and physical needs of others who were less fortunate.

According to Christopher Redington, a neighbouring landowner, Augusta also inherited her mother's robust sense of humour and enjoyment of the ridiculous. It is likely, however, that Frances's humour was directed against her daughter. Frances's daughters came second to her sons. She accepted the social convention that boys were more important than girls. Boys would earn a living, whereas wealthy marriageable men had to be found for girls otherwise they remained a burden. Her prejudice was expressed in all sorts of ways – fires were lit later in the autumn in the girls' schoolroom and their education was scantier, while the boys were indulged, and they were given no sense of their responsibilities. This attitude reinforced the message given by Dudley's autocratic ways. It was a particularly virulent form of the Victorian assumption that women were subject to men, and Augusta would persist in seeing women as 'the weaker side' despite her own obvious force of character and strength of purpose.[14]

As a small, unshowy and not always docile girl, Augusta was regarded as a failure by her mother. She repeatedly drew attention to her diminutive height and discouraged her from expecting that she would ever be attractive. '. . . I was not to think myself the equal of beautiful Adelaide, of tall gay musical Gertrude or agreeable Arabella.'[15] But Augusta's lively intelligence, most discernible in her bright dark eyes, was vividly apparent to her neighbour and future husband, William Gregory, who saw her as a child and told her incredulous mother that she was her prettiest daughter.[16]

Frances was narrow-minded and unimaginative, and she imposed an extremely restrictive regime on her daughters. Her narrowness was cripplingly evident in her limited educational aims for the girls in which any significant mental and physical development was absent. 'Religion and courtesy, and holding themselves straight, these were to her mind the three things needful. French perhaps also' (learnt from their brothers' French tutor), and the painful practice of scales on the piano. Literature had no foothold in this regime; in fact the Mistress was clear, she 'did not consider book learning as of any great benefit to girls'.[17] Augusta would rectify much of this, but she always felt deficient in arithmetic and was unable to teach her grandchildren even when they were quite young. Like other girls of their class, the Persse girls had governesses. Forced to earn a living at a time when earning a living was, for women, deemed to be a failure, governesses were often ill-equipped to teach. The Persse governesses, described by Augusta as 'a procession of amiable incompetent [women]', were no exception.

The school books were the potted and 'improved' histories and grammars of which Pinnock was the great exponent. They used Pinnock's *Greece* and it is not unlikely that they also read his *Catechisms*; slight books with the question and answer formula of the religious catechism and the similar claim to be definitive, they seemed to be designed to constrict rather than develop a desire for knowledge.[18] Memory was the only skill that might be expected to be honed in this intellectual environment.

This regime was particularly hard for the intelligent Augusta who from an early age displayed a distinct bias towards literature. But she was a resourceful child who found stimulation in the few illustrated books of romantic literature – Thomas Moore's oriental tales, anthologies entitled *Books of Beauty*, English ballads, Wordsworth's poems – that were displayed on the drawing-room table and to which she had access on long winter evenings when, after prayers, the family sat in their allotted places around the fire in silence.

Frances Persse's intellectual narrow-mindedness and emotional coldness were exacerbated by her religious beliefs. She was a Church of Ireland evangelical, a product of the growing influence of evangelicalism in Ireland in the 1820s and 1830s. She was devastated by the disestablishment of the Church of Ireland in 1869 – the loss of power for Protestants. Her assumption of Protestant superiority over Catholicism influenced Augusta deeply.[19] But Augusta would come to despise her simple evangelicalism, which put faith above (Catholic) good works, and stated that however virtuously you had lived, you were destined for hell unless you believed in God and were 'washed in the blood'. Frances, according to Augusta, interpreted this to mean that if you had faith and lived the narrow prescribed life (reading religious books, going without entertainment) you could be 'greedy, untruthful, uncharitable, dishonest – in moderation' – in the knowledge that you would be saved.[20] This moral vacuum was condemned by Augusta. She was particularly critical of her mother's failure to prevent her wilful husband from installing a sawmill, cutting down Roxborough timber and denuding her step-brother Dudley of his inheritance (it was the sawmill that had alienated Dudley). Frances remonstrated so mildly with her husband that he could either ignore her or pacify her. Augusta, good Victorian that she was, assumed that it was the woman's duty to provide a good moral influence in the family, and she blamed her mother's unwillingness to emphasise the need to live a virtuous life for her father's selfishness.

Even as a child Augusta observed that religious bias clouded her mother's judgement of character: she encouraged the children to be priggish and she favoured pious servants.[21] When Augusta was older she scorned her mother, who found it hard to accept that any detail in the Bible was not literally true, for not rising to the intellectual challenge posed by Charles Darwin's *Origin of Species* (1859). Augusta tartly observed in her autobiography, 'repeated rumours and then authoritative statements of geologists at last forced the Mistress to give up the six days creation of the world in favour of six periods', although 'she refused other concessions'.[22]

Frances imposed an intensely religious upbringing on her children: twice daily family prayers, a daily answering of Biblical questions on an Old Testament reading, a weekly Bible verse, and Sundays dedicated to worship and religious tracts. This at least had a positive effect on Augusta, laying the foundations for a solid belief and giving her an intimate knowledge of the Bible, which she valued as a well-spring of her imagination, belief and susceptibility to language.

Her mother's religious tuition and example were complemented by Augusta's experience of Killinan, the barn-shaped demesne church with its stumpy tower, unwhitewashed walls of 'respectably grey hue', damp interior and informal ways, which served the Persses and local Protestants – squires, gamekeepers, police.[23] For much of her childhood, the kind, liberal Revd William O'Grady, a brother of Katherine O'Grady, was the archdeacon. He encouraged Catholic girls to attend to augment the singing, cultivated his garden with passion, often wore a shooting coat and intimidated no one, allowing extempore comments in the service. After Disestablishment (and the end of sinecures) he was succeeded by the less high-born, more ideological and hard-working Archdeacon Burkett, who supported the Mistress's ban on dancing lessons and amateur dramatics.[24] Augusta expressed great affection for this institution in her autobiographical sketch, 'An Emigrant's Notebook' of 1883, finding piety in O'Grady's regime and appreciating that post-establishment clergy had to live more like their Catholic counterparts. Membership of the Church of Ireland was to be a cornerstone of Augusta's definition of herself as Irish, and she remained faithful to the institution throughout her life.

Augusta, always reluctant to discuss her feelings, gives us little idea how her mother's dogmatism, restrictiveness and unwillingness to understand her daughter affected her emotionally. The indication is that by being outwardly obedient to someone she could not fully respect and who displayed little affection for her, Augusta gradually lost her filial love. She made hardly any effort to understand her mother in her autobiography, and once she was mature she seemed to return her mother's coldness, inevitably referring to the Mistress in dry detached tones, intent only on performing her duty towards her.

The emotional and intellectual deprivation of her childhood may have contributed to Augusta's marked self-reliance. From an early age she followed her own instincts and gave the impression of being self-contained. Her family accused her of pride. 'Where is the pride for which I once was blamed?' she wrote in a sonnet when she was 31.[25] Yeats, too, would describe '. . . all that pride and that humility'.[26] It was a salient characteristic and a key to her achievements.

Although Augusta never fell out irrevocably with her family, and her life would continue to be bound up with many of her siblings and their children, she would, with two exceptions – Hugh Lane (Adelaide's son) and John Shawe-

Taylor (Eliza's son) – be emotionally detached from them. She described her childhood self in the third person in *Seventy Years*, and she showed little interest in Persse family history, a marked omission in someone who would write extensively about the Gregorys. Had she learnt as the bookish child in an unbookish house that to preserve the fragile sense of her own identity she must keep herself, and especially her imagination, free of her family? She was so adept at distancing herself from the Persses as a married woman in London that George Moore, who knew some of her relatives, would describe her as someone he imagined being without family, '*sans attaché*'.[27] She once remarked to Yeats that relations did not mind one's opinions, only one's independence.[28] She cherished her independence; it was the precondition of her life as a writer, campaigner, theatre director and patron.

Augusta's background, against which she had no thought of rebelling, defined her. The Persses belonged to the Anglo-Irish Ascendancy, a small, powerful elite of diverse origins – Gaelic aristocrats, twelfth-century Norman barons and adventurers, sixteenth- and seventeenth-century English planters. This elite owned most of the land and was, by the nineteenth century, predominantly Protestant. The Anglo-Irish exercised power within the British-controlled system of local and central government, as justices of the peace, sheriffs, Lord Lieutenants and Members of Parliament, sitting, since Union in 1800, at Westminster. The British sovereign was present in Ireland in the person of the Viceroy, who came to Dublin with his court while Parliament sat, residing in the palatial Viceregal Lodge in Phoenix Park near his Irish administrator, the Under-Secretary, while conducting business and hosting the glittering early spring Season in the palace-cum-government office of Dublin

Castle. Ascendancy social life rippled out effortlessly from the person of the Viceroy, establishing hierarchies and a cultural consensus.

The Ascendancy was set apart from their impoverished neighbours not only by their religion, but by their English culture. It was absorbed for some at Eton, Harrow, Oxford, Cambridge, reinforced by travel, the habit of wintering in London, by commissions in the British army, employment in the colonial civil service and associations with British institutions, marriage and, for the wealthiest, through their English estates. It earned them the epithet Anglo-Irish and gave them a hybrid identity. Like any other class their cultural homogeneity was challenged by individuals who in their private lives or with public gestures ensured that there was no simple relationship between the ruling Anglicised elite and the ruled Gaelic majority. Wolfe Tone and Lord Edward Fitzgerald led the revolutionary United Irishmen in the late eighteenth century, and it was from the Anglo-Irish that the painters, archaeologists, antiquarians and historians of Gaelic Ireland, forerunners of the Irish Revival, emerged in the early nineteenth century.

The Persses, originally clergymen, came with the seventeenth-century planters, but by the turn of the eighteenth century they were landed gentlemen.[29] Cregarosta, later re-named Roxborough, had been acquired by Dudley Persse (1625–1700), Archdeacon of Tuam and Dean of Kilmacduagh in 1662, who was granted over 4,000 acres in County Galway and County Roscommon by Charles II and James II.[30] Roxborough became the focus of the estate when Dudley's eldest son, Henry (d. 1733), bought nearly 600 acres around the house in Galway and sold peripheral lands. Later, more acres were acquired, until, at its peak, the estate comprised nearly 12,000 acres.[31] Augusta's father inherited about 9,800 acres, the rest

(Castleboy) passed to his younger brother; an inheritance which Dudley contested successfully in 1852 in the courts, but at great expense.[32]

Roxborough estate lay on rising ground on the eastern edge of the broad fertile plain of the Owenshree River, between the moorland of the Slieve Echtge mountains, which rise to over 1,000ft to the east, and the quiet inlets and stony wastes of Galway Bay to the west. With his 9,800 acres Augusta's father entered the category which the historian Mark Bence-Jones has described as 'landlords of consequence not in the magnate class'.[33] The Persses were manifestly rooted in County Galway, and although younger sons might enter the army, be called to the Bar or marry Englishwomen, this did not disturb the provincial temper of the main family; the sons were educated in Dublin, they did not aspire to high-ranking posts in politics, the judiciary and the colonial civil service and they had no English estates. Since Henry Persse became High Sheriff in 1701, the Persses held local public offices; Augusta's father was a justice of the peace and a Deputy Lieutenant, performing the duties of magistrate and local official, involved in decisions about infrastructural changes and the administration of central government acts.

Provincial though they might be, the Persses were not untroubled by outside changes and conflicts, nor by idealism and generous spirits within the family. William Persse (1728–1802), standing out as public spirited and liberal, was a moderate Irish patriot who formed the first Volunteers in Connaught, in 1777, as part of the landed proprietors' strategy to defend Ireland from possible invasion by France and Spain when the regular garrison was in America.[34] He supported Volunteer efforts to secure commercial and constitutional reform, and when, in 1782, the Irish Parliament and courts acquired the right to make and administer laws for Ireland, he built a bridge in the demesne inscribed 'In Memory of Ireland's Emancipation from Foreign Jurisdiction'. As a child, Augusta, ignorant of Irish history, found this puzzling. When she was beginning to get an insight into the role the Ascendancy had played in Irish history she remembered her great-grandfather, and wrote wistfully, 'I might have learned this change of class tradition and one at least of its causes by an object lesson at my old home.'[35] She also proudly recalled the fact that her great-grandfather had corresponded with the American President, George Washington. Her father showed bravery as a young man in 1821, but it was in the defence of Roxborough with the aid of garrison soldiers against a night-time attack by Ribbonmen, members of a secret, oath-bound society which traced its lineage to the radical United Irishmen.[36]

The young Augusta was surrounded by other Persses whose provincial character resembled that of her own family. Dudley's younger brother, Robert Henry, and his growing family lived at neighbouring Castleboy. Relations with this family were fraught, for throughout Augusta's childhood Robert Henry would periodically reassert his claim to Castleboy. Burton Persse, a distant cousin, lived at Moyode Castle, Athenry (much grander than Roxborough, now a ruin), sat on the local bench with Dudley and was a Deputy Lieutenant and High Sheriff. Persses lived at Glenarde, Spring Garden and in Galway City. When Augusta was 12, Eliza married Walter Shawe-Taylor of Castle Taylor (a tower house with Gothic-style nineteenth-century block, now gone), at Ardrahan. The frequency with which the Persses visited the Shawe-Taylors is conveyed by Augusta's observation in *Seventy Years* that the books she loved were, with her sister's marriage, transferred to the Castle Taylor drawing-room table, but still accessible to her.

En masse, the Persses convey the strong impression of an Anglo-Irish stereotype: vigorous, earthy, uncultivated, rooted in their locality. In *Dramatis Personae* W.B. Yeats wrote: 'Free State Ministers were fond of recounting the adventures of Lady Gregory's "Seven Brothers", who, no matter who objected to their rents, or coveted their possessions, were safe "because had one been killed, the others would have run down and shot the assassin".'[37] He set this against the sober, nineteenth-century evangelism of Augusta's mother and sisters. The impression of an absence of culture was bluntly reinforced: 'The house contained neither pictures nor furniture of historic interest.'

The character of the estate as Augusta knew it had been greatly influenced by the ruthless reaction of her father to the Great Famine, which started in 1845, the effects of which were waning just before her birth in 1852. The Persses had done little to help their starving tenants, who had died or been forced or encouraged to emigrate, with the result that in the 1850s the estate was largely cleared of the poorest.[38] Before her father regained Castleboy, he held about 7,000 acres in fee, comprising the demesne and the meadows on the lower slopes of Slieve Echtge, which were grazed by sheep and cattle (a more profitable option than tillage) and herded by labourers who inhabited cabins and cottages on tiny plots in the hills, or in the village of Kilchreest. They formed the 'long array' of men recalled by Augusta in *Seventy Years*, who arrived each morning in the Roxborough yard. The remaining 2,800 acres of the estate were divided between substantial tenant farmers, some renting as much as 400 acres, others only 12 acres. The atmosphere was notably tranquil. As a child Augusta could perceive no tragedy in the post-famine calm of Roxborough, where landless labourers without expectations had replaced the poorest tenants. Instead, as a young woman in 1883, when the Land War was irrevocably souring relations between landlords and tenants, she would, in 'An Emigrant's

Notebook', look back nostalgically to this time when doors and windows were left unlocked, she was allowed to wander freely in the demesne, and there was trust between the Persses, their tenants and servants.

Augusta's great delight as a child was to be outside at Roxborough in the three-acre walled kitchen garden filled with fruit and vegetables, with its view of the bare purple slopes of Slieve Echtge, an ever present reminder that Roxborough was a protected oasis. She went alone onto the mountains, looking for deer, straining to see the distant, biblically barren, layered slopes of the Burren mountains to the south-west. Or she would go to the river which threaded the demesne, the backbone of her childhood games. As an adult, Augusta appreciated this sensual enjoyment of Roxborough as 'romance of river and hillsides', a phrase which evokes the love of place (rather than abstract love of country) that inspired many literary, imaginative Anglo-Irish with a muted patriotism. Augusta identified with Roxborough and it was the well-spring of her identification with Ireland.[39]

Augusta did not extend her romanticism to the house. 'The old house, our home was not beautiful – quite the reverse.'[40] Set back from the river and connected to the road by a long drive, Roxborough was a two-storey house of steeply pitched roofs, tall chimneys, two projecting wings and relatively small rooms. When it was first built in the late seventeenth century it would have stood out among the castles and tower-encrusted houses as a go-ahead undefended 'mansion house'.[41] However, beyond the installation of regularly spaced sash windows and a fanlight over the hall door, it had never been remodelled to give the classical space and elegance that had subsequently become *de rigueur* for the Anglo-Irish. But the Persses had aggrandised the demesne, adding a serpentine lake and trees to create, sometime in the eighteenth century, an informal, picturesque landscape. A battlemented and turreted Gothic fantasy gateway had been built by the river in the early nineteenth century.[42]

Between the house and the river was a vast complex of stone buildings and yards. Here were stables full of hunting and carriage horses, kennels for Gordon setters, retrievers and greyhounds, cow houses, coach houses and dairy. This, the hub of the estate, was haunted by the children who were alert to the daily rhythm of activity, and who found entertainment and occupation among the people working there. Roxborough was one of those self-sufficient estates, providing food (fish, venison, woodcock, pheasant, fruit, vegetables, mutton, beef, dairy products), drink, fuel (turf and timber), leisure and distraction for a sizeable family, and supporting large numbers of retainers on low wages. Dudley's steam-powered sawmill employed carpenters, engineers and turners, mostly Protestants brought over from England, and was the major source of cash, used by him for the Castleboy law suit.[43] Much of the available surplus – cash or produce – tended to be channelled into outdoor male pursuits, such as fox hunting (there was a thatched hunting lodge, Chevy Chase, in the Slieve Echtge hills) and fishing (there was a fishing lodge on Lough Corrib). They also held the traditional balls and parties associated with the annual sheep shearing, and seasonal shooting and fishing expeditions. This consumption of wealth locally for convivial pursuits was typical of many Anglo-Irish families whose estates were centred on or confined to Ireland. All the buildings at Roxborough are now ruined and although the site is designated a national monument, it is an integral part of a farm, its former connections with the outside world severed and the order and hierarchy of buildings and gardens destroyed. Nothing is as it was in the place where Augusta was born and brought up, except the view from the walled garden of the still largely barren and often bleak Slieve Echtge mountains.

Persse heritage gave Augusta her place as part of the ruling elite. But being the daughter of an Irish landowner also gave Augusta the opportunity to form relationships with the country people who lived and worked on the estate, for, despite the intellectual restrictions imposed on the girls, there was a strong element of benign neglect. For the boys the servants and estate workers were shooting companions or the easy butt of a joke, for some of Augusta's sisters they were Catholics to be converted. But for the curious, sympathetic, observant Augusta, eager for friendship, they provided great interest and in some cases gave her the chance to show affection. She never forgot their faces, clothes, characters, words or songs, incorporating some of these things in her early short stories and later plays. When she looked back on her childhood with nostalgia in 1883 it was her relations with these people which gave her most pleasure. She discovered much about their lives, and developed a sympathy for them. It was a folklorist's apprenticeship.

The young Augusta could not always assume that her position would confer automatic authority. In mid-nineteenth-century Ireland servants were not expected to be discreet, polite, invisible. The steward would not automatically ask the carpenter to make a window for the windowless room of the herdsman's dying daughter, Margaret Mulbern, because Augusta requested it, and Pat Glynn, the carpenter, had his own business independent of the estate and was unwilling to undertake unprofitable jobs.[44] Augusta had to learn to consider their priorities.

Persse tenants sometimes sang together at lunch time or at social events, inadvertently stimulating Augusta's lifelong interest in songs. She appreciated the way the audience encouraged the singer with a 'raise it!' 'more power!', and became aware that many of the songs referred to rebellion and oppression, about which she had little knowledge and which she suspected they did not wish her to hear. The drawing-room, where guests would occasionally sing the sentimental ballads of Thomas Moore, also roused her interest in patriotic Irish songs.[45] Realising that her family disliked nationalist ballads published as broadsheets or in collections (*The Harp of Tara*, or *The Irish Song Book*), discovering they could be bought in the nearby town of Loughrea and wishing to provoke her sisters she bought the cheap collections with sixpences earned from reciting Bible verses, one eye on the reaction of her touchy English governess.[46]

Augusta advanced in this assault on household sensitivity by requesting *The Spirit of the Nation* for her birthday, poems written by members of the romantic nationalist group, Young Ireland, many of whom were Protestant. Her sister Arabella responded with satisfying sarcasm, inscribing the book with a quotation from Dr Johnson: 'Patriotism is the last refuge of a Scoundrel.' Tellingly, Augusta observed, 'It is not likely that the idea of her [Augusta] having any thoughts or sympathies different from their own had ever entered the mind of any of the elders of the house.'[47] Augusta now looked down on the Roxborough songs, described condescendingly in 'An Emigrant's Notebook' as 'local compositions', comparing them unfavourably with the Young Ireland songs, particularly those of Thomas Davis: 'I think they are not satisfied with their simple beauty but seek something of a more sensational kind.' She would later develop an ear that was finely attuned to 'local compositions'. Augusta requested Irish lessons from a parish Scripture reader. This may have been inspired by her Irish-speaking relative, Standish Hayes O'Grady, or made in a spirit of provocation, or because she already felt her facility with languages. She feared mockery, but her request was turned down. Later she felt it was a lost opportunity to become an Irish scholar, 'and not as I am imperfect, stumbling'.[48]

It is unlikely that Augusta's relationships with the tenants and servants was untroubled. The famine had left a legacy of distrust and guilt which developed into Fenianism, a movement calling for violent revolution that emanated from those who had emigrated to America and which was launched in Dublin in 1858 by James Stephens. The distrust and secrecy engendered by this movement touched many with relatives in America; for a time it prevented those unable to read from asking the Persses to read their letters to them, and inevitably tarnished relations with the tenants in the early part of Augusta's childhood. Then in February and March 1867, when Augusta was 15, there was the Fenian rising, culminating, for the Persses, in periodic alarms and 'ungrounded rumours of an American-Irish army coming to land in Galway Bay & likely to march through the country . . .' But, Augusta remembered in 1883, 'these were imaginary scares & only seemed to lend a little excitement to our life & then all grew quiet & tranquil again'.[49] Fenianism inspired new rebel songs, adding to those the tenants tried to keep from her.

Of all the people Augusta encountered at Roxborough, the one she knew best and who had the greatest influence on her was her nurse, Mary Sheridan. She had come to Roxborough in the late 1830s from the large Ascendancy household of the United Irishman, Rowan Hamilton. By the time Augusta knew her she was an proud, elderly woman who kept her distance from other servants and 'professed to take the aristocratic side'.[50] She had an unwavering loyalty and intense concern for her charges, but this was counterbalanced by unselfconscious displays of her own values and independent interests, which kept the children riveted. In adult life Augusta still vividly recalled her nurse's overwhelming grief when her daughter, who had died suddenly, failed to accompany her senile aunt home from America on a passage paid for by Dudley Persse.

Mary Sheridan seemed to possess the loving authority that Frances Persse lacked. At the end of 'An Emigrant's Notebook' Augusta evoked an image of children resolving the day's quarrels at a mother's knee to convey the idea of a country where different interests could co-exist peacefully. Such an image was surely inspired by an involved and understanding Mary Sheridan, rather than by the dogmatic Frances Persse. Augusta loved her nurse, and saw her as an integral part of the family. Describing her death in the late 1870s, just before that of Gertrude, Richard and her father, she wrote that it was 'the first that had taken place in our house in all that generation'.

All the young Persses asked 'the nurse' for fairy stories. She responded with European tales, Irish fairy stories, or reminiscences of and 'half-revealed sympathy' for the time of the United Irishmen when the French landed in Killala Bay in 1798 and she had been among a theatre audience that had shouted and clapped support. Augusta clearly remembered Mary Sheridan telling the children about the escape of the United Irishman Hamilton Rowan, imprisoned in 1794. He was identified by a boatman who said, 'We know you very well Mr Rowan and the reward thats on your head, & there is no fear that we will betray you.' The story emerged in her play *The Rising of the Moon* in 1907.

Mary Sheridan once, memorably, startled Augusta, and helped to set seeds that would develop into a passion for folklore. Like many who become intimate with the people of 'the big house', Mary Sheridan was quick with displays of superiority towards people such as beggars who in different circumstances she would have treated more sympathetically. So, catching her proud nurse absorbed in conversation with a white-haired beggar at the hall door steps, Augusta was curious to know what they were talking about, and discovered that this woman, too, remembered the landing of the French. What stayed with Augusta was the spectacle of Mary Sheridan's social pride forgotten in the desire to hear the woman's stories about a past event which they both valued, and the importance of the relating of stories in the absence of books and the ability to read.

The age of 15 was a personal watershed for Augusta. It was from this time that she had, she wrote nearly thirty years later, her 'first *real* recollections' of herself.[51] In the next few years her awkward sense of not belonging would be transferred to a number of interests that would define her more satisfactorily as different. However, her first transforming experience seemed on the surface to be firmly within the Persse tradition: she had a religious conversion. After a severe bout of anxiety about whether she would ever believe in God sufficiently to be saved, she woke one morning, in the Lough Corrib fishing lodge, 'at peace with God'.[52] This led, not to proselytising, which was practised zealously by Katherine and Eliza (Katherine had once struggled physically with a priest over a disputed child), but to philanthropy. The good works were a challenge to her mother, but they were more in tune with later nineteenth-century Protestantism.[53] She took food and medicines to the poorest village on the estate, Illerton, taught at Sunday School, and engaged a sewing teacher for the estate girls, much to the discomfort of the priest who suspected proselytising motives.[54]

Her religious conversion temporarily overlay her budding interest in Irish ballads and English literature. However, religious literature – George Herbert's poems, Thomas à Kempis's *Imitation of Christ* – would pull her back to an appreciation of the power of language. After that, with Chambers's *Encyclopaedia of English Literature* from which to make lists, she obtained the well-loved poetry of her day – Alfred Lord Tennyson (the Pre-Raphaelite edition), Robert Burns, Arthur Hugh Clough, John Keats and Robert Browning – as well as the essays of Matthew Arnold and Montaigne, Malory's *Le Morte d'Arthur*, and Walter Scott's novels. Her delayed access to literature combined with her innate receptiveness to words, her youthful impression-ableness and her need to escape from the constraints of her family life meant that her adventure into literature was particularly poignant and significant. Books soon became indispensable; her love of poetry, novels, essays, words, images, the rhythm of sentences a badge of identity. She had become a bookworm and an object of curiosity and ridicule for a family that never quite rid itself of the belief that her interest was a pretence.

There were few opportunities to share her quiet passion with other people. But she met her distant relative, the elderly poet Aubrey de Vere, one time friend of Wordsworth and Tennyson, who lived at Curragh Chase in County Limerick, and whose poetry was suffused with the myths and atmosphere of Ireland. And there was brief contact with another distant relative, the civil engineer Standish Hayes O'Grady (1832–1915), who had learnt Irish and translated Gaelic poetry, and introduced her to the world of Gaelic scholarship.[55]

The teenage Augusta remained on good terms with her brothers. They now went deer hunting and shooting, chased women and drank copiously. They still gave Augusta money and books, and encouraged her to ride with them. While riding across country was tolerated, hunting was frowned on for girls at Roxborough, in line with other evangelical households. Augusta managed at least one 'triumphant run' with the foxhounds which ended on Roxborough lawn in front of her astonished father.[56] Augusta persuaded her parents to let her learn to shoot when the threat of a Fenian rising encouraged them to teach the younger boys, although, as she ruefully pointed out, 'my gun was never loaded with anything more weighty than a copper cap'.

As a young woman, Augusta, for whom, as the youngest Miss Persse, there was no coming-out ball in Dublin, lacked all confidence in her appearance. This was exacerbated by a lisp. Although commented on by her contemporaries it was only the playwright Seán O'Casey, who visited her when she was in her seventies, who has given us an idea of how she spoke.[57] She mixed something of the local accent ('ting' for 'thing', 'dere' for 'there') with a reluctance to pronounce the initial g ('dood' for 'good', 'detting' for 'getting'), v ('berry' for 'very'), and c ('tandels' for 'candles'). O'Casey was prone to exaggerate accents in his plays and may have overdone her lisp. There were inconsistencies in his account: she also said 'come' and 'cold'. It is difficult to know what the effect of her lisp was and whether it varied with circumstance. It would have sounded different in an elderly woman with a formidable reputation; idiosyncratic by then, part of her established personality, a welcoming touch of weakness, homely. In a young girl it would be perceived as a defect, most painfully by the girl herself, keeping her quiet when she would have liked to talk, a sign perhaps that she would not be marrying and leaving home.

Augusta's shyness prevented her from forming the light, socially flirtatious relationships that could lead to marriage. However, when Henry Hart, one of Frank's undergraduate friends from Trinity College, a handsome boy with an interest in literature, an athlete and rather 'wild' (all qualities that would attract Augusta in later life), visited Roxborough when Augusta was 18, they had intense evening discussions about Shakespeare's sonnets.

> One or two things happened. He had come to sit near me in the drawing-room one evening. I think they had been racing at a fair that day, and after a minute or two Frank came and touched him and took him out. Frank told me the next day that H.H. was very penitent and asked to apologise. Though I had not noticed it, he had too much to drink. I felt sorry for him and after a day or two, chancing to meet him in the garden we sat down and talked of the violets which I had in my hand.[58]

The next day Augusta was sent to Castle Taylor; her father had objected to the tête-à-têtes. Years later she learnt that Henry had written to her, that Archdeacon Burkett was asked to open the letter and that it had contained a friendly note 'giving the authorship of a once discussed quotation'. Augusta had been glad to find someone to talk to about her new enthusiasm; she was not given the opportunity to fall in love with him.

Marriage began to loom as an issue as her sisters and brothers gradually married and left home. Most memorable, coming when Augusta was 18 and sensitive to her own potential fate, was Adelaide's marriage. Having rejected illustrious suitors at the Dublin Castle balls, Adelaide fell for James Lane, an ambitious divinity student at Trinity, destined for the church, but, to the family's horror, 'the son of an *attorney*'.[59] After categorically rejecting the marriage the family agreed that it could take place after three years, although the couple were married after two years when Lane had been ordained. But the family would not allow the marriage to take place in the estate church. James and Adelaide had been deeply in love, but once they were married they discovered that they had both been living with illusions; James had expected Adelaide to bring more money to the marriage, and Adelaide had not realised how humble her social position would be as the wife of a curate.[60] Goodwill between them would slowly crumble. It was clear to Augusta that marrying for love was neither easily accepted by her family nor necessarily wise.

Marrying pragmatically was more acceptable, as she discovered when her closest sister, Gertrude, married a widower, Edward Beauchamp, in 1873. Edward was fifteen years older than Gertrude and already had a young daughter. But Gertrude's experience was not happy either; she suffered a series of difficult pregnancies (she had three girls) before dying in 1876. Augusta visited her several times in those three years at her home in Cornwall, and suffered greatly when she died.

In 1875 it was decided that her elder brother, Richard, now tubercular, should spend the winter in Cannes on the French Riviera. Augusta, 23, was chosen to accompany him. They did this for the next four years. The pursuit of health in southern Europe was a relatively new idea (the Persses may have been encouraged by their neighbour Mrs Gregory's annual visits to the Riviera), and Cannes had only recently been converted from an obscure fishing village to a resort for the rich by the construction of the palm-fringed promenade, La Croisette, thirteen years earlier.

Richard was not a good companion for Augusta. Nearly twenty years older than her, they had never been close. She had suffered from his sarcasm as a child, and he now had little sympathy for her intellectual interests. She missed Roxborough and disliked their dull life – the quiet hotel, the monotonous walks, their predominantly elderly English fellow guests concerned only with health or pleasure. And she did not warm to Cannes: 'Cannes was not France, it had no history, no national life, no language but a patois, few inhabitants . . .'[61]

In the spring they went to the resorts – Bellaggio, Pallanza – on the Italian lakes. Augusta was happier here where Italian culture flourished, and, instead of wondering whether she was destined to spend her life at the service of others, she realised that she had a measure of freedom and began to enjoy it. In Pallanza she explored the old town on her own, and visited a priest who she engaged to teach her Italian.[62] Once she could read Dante in Italian, she translated it with the help of a French version. Cannes became bearable in 1876 when she found a tutor to improve her French. It was a new life.

In the summer of 1878, Augusta was back at Roxborough nursing Gerald who had pleurisy. One night in September she overheard some servants saying they had heard the banshee, a signal that a death was imminent '. . . and though I had not thought of such warnings being attributed to our family, or being anything but an idle tale, I felt a sudden dread'.[63] She assumed it referred to Gerald, but going out onto the landing she saw her father's servant coming slowly up the stairs. It was her father who had died.

For all his excesses and short-sighted selfishness, Dudley had presided over a kingdom of magnificent proportions, apparently solid structure and abundant life. 'To those of his children still living under the roof, it seemed as if all had been shattered around them.'[64] His eldest son, Dudley, unmarried, was now in possession of the estate, and the rest of the family had to disperse. Augusta's mother bought 2 Merrion Square in Dublin for herself and the unmarried Persses, and Augusta accompanied Richard to Cannes for the fourth time. When Augusta returned to Roxborough in the late spring of 1879 she discovered that Dudley, far from taking on his inherited responsibilities, was still living his old bachelor life, drinking with Dublin club friends and, worse, was displaying the symptoms of alcoholism. Augusta, now regarded as the sensible, unmarried sister, was asked to help Algernon in the running of the estate. 'Yet another brother needed my care. I was tied as before.'

Although Augusta, accepting that men were freer to follow their own interests and that her interest in literature, so consistently devalued by her family, would have to be an evening pastime, acquiesced in her duties, she did 'fret', as she put it. At the gathering after Richard's funeral (he died in September 1878) she nearly fainted, to Eliza's alarm; 'Oh, Augusta, you must not break down!'[65] She did not, and shortly afterwards summoned the necessary resolve to send Dudley to Dublin to see a doctor.

Together with Algernon she reformed the running of the estate.[66] Agricultural prices had fallen and, after a particularly poor harvest in the summer of 1879, many tenants were in arrears with their rents. Augusta and Algernon reduced the consumption of meat and beer in the house and tried to protect the tenants from undue expenditure by sending a cricket tent to Ballinasloe fair to provide an alternative to the public houses. They opened a shop in the steward's lodge on Friday afternoons so that the labourers who had just been paid could buy tea, sugar, flour, bacon at reasonable prices, instead of paying the exorbitant credit rates for poor quality goods at the local shops. This rationalising and paternalistic organising, together with her continued philanthropy, set Augusta alongside other energetic women of means, who combined a strong practical streak with a healthy conscience, but whose limited education and lack of power did not enable them to make more radical changes.

Meanwhile her reading was expanding into new areas: Pope's *Iliad* and *Odyssey*, a translation of *Don Quixote*.

Within the dutiful sister there seemed to be an inner buoyancy. Towards the end of her life she remembered her young self: 'It surprises me now I did not fret more than I did, I seemed to be convinced that a pretty full life awaited me, and in this world too.'[67] In the spring of 1880, she was enjoying Ruskin's *Stones of Venice* 'without much prospect,' she remarked, 'of ever seeing Venice itself.'[68] A year later she had not been to Venice, but she had visited Paris, Rome, Athens, Constantinople, and dined and danced in the best society. She was no longer a chaperone, but the wife of Sir William Gregory.

TWO

Becoming Lady Gregory

... & triumphal arch with 'Cead Mile Failthe' [*sic*] (a
hundred thousand welcomes) at the gate of Coole ...
29 July [1880], autograph diary

It happened that at the Roxborough cricket match in the
summer of 1877, to which Sir William Gregory had been
invited, Augusta wore a fashionable dress bought at Bon
Marché in Paris, and a black and white straw hat decorated
with corn ears and poppies, so that the usually plain, quiet,
girl was noticeable and pretty. William was late, arriving
when the guests were seated at the long dining-room table
for lunch. He was shown to the only available place, at the
head of the table.[1]

Sir William Gregory (1817–92) was 60, 35 years older
than Augusta, and a wealthy widower.[2] He was not a
handsome man. He was stout with a heavy face and thin
hair. With his mutton-chop whiskers, firmly set mouth and
the upright posture of the habitually and unselfconsciously
authoritarian, he looked like a classic Victorian male.[3] But
there is a surviving photograph that indicates a melancholy
or introspective aspect to his character: his shoulders droop,
his necktie is skewed, he looks away from the camera with
a distracted expression. Add to this his contemporaries'
observations that he was a humorous and warm man, with

an interest in literature, and an urbane manner, and it seems less improbable that the shy girl should find herself discussing Ceylon with him (one of her brothers was about to go), and later show him the gardens.[4] She met him several times that summer and found him attentive. On one occasion she was invited with Richard to his estate at Coole, about eight miles to the south-west of Roxborough, to dine and stay the night. William took them for a drive in the woods, showed them treasures from Ceylon and gave her a pearl ring.[5]

While Roxborough was associated with hunting and rowdiness, Coole was civilised and scholarly. An elderly friend of Augusta's, who gave her books, came to see her one day from Coole extolling its 'fine intellectual tradition' and the rich collection of books in its library. He observed, mischievously, 'That is the only house I have seen in the county that would make a right setting for you.'[6] If Coole, nearby but largely unvisited, had a somewhat mythical character for Augusta, its master, often absent, a man of the world, of whom a number of stories were told, must have had a certain glamour.

William's privileged youth had encompassed a Harrow and Oxford education and a grandfather who was Under-Secretary to the Viceroy and who provided him with the contacts to become MP for Dublin at the age of 25 through vote purchasing and patronage, not unusual for the period.[7] Old Mr Gregory also ensured that his grandson became a protégé of Robert Peel, then Prime Minister; Peel's door, including the door to his study, was always open to William. When William's old schoolfriend, Anthony Trollope, an insecure and poorly connected assistant surveyor for the Post Office in Ireland, visited William in 1844 he was impressed by his achievements and is said to have based his eponymous hero, Phineas Finn, on him.[8]

In fact, William was squandering his magnificent advantages, mainly at the racecourse where he was becoming a serious gambler. He lost his seat in 1847 – the year his father died and he inherited Coole – and in the next ten years he lost his fortune. He had to sell half of the estate in the Encumbered Estate Court in 1857.[9] William had been unemotional and pragmatic about the sale, engaging a businessman to push up the prices at the auction, but unfortunately his financial problems were not resolved and he still had a substantial debt. More land was sold, and in 1867 he had 5,000 acres of the 15,000 he had inherited.

His only political legacy from his first term in Parliament was the notorious Gregory Clause, an amendment to the Poor Law Bill of 1847, enacted during the famine, which made those tenants occupying more than a quarter of an acre ineligible for relief.[10] It was designed to reduce the numbers of people with tiny holdings, but in proposing it William displayed a profound insensitivity to the vulnerability of the poorest in Ireland, for, as it was pointed out in the Parliamentary debate, the poorest, who had to relinquish their lease to gain relief in a workhouse, effectively had to chose between having a home or receiving sustenance. His father died from typhus caught trying to relieve the distress of his tenants, so that William was soon confronted with the horror of their situation, and he was haunted by their suffering until the end of his life. Yet when he came to write his autobiography he still stood by his policy as a necessity for Ireland.

In his autobiography, William adroitly distanced himself from the disastrous effects of the Gregory Clause by painting a picture of himself as a good landlord. It was true that, unlike some landowners, he had not used the clause as a way of getting rid of tenants who were in arrears; he had, he claimed, never evicted a tenant. But his was a paternalistic care, typical of his time, that prided itself on the trust that existed between tenant and landlord, but which neglected to ensure that tenants' positions were formally defined. He did not raise rents if tenants improved their holdings, but equally he did not grant secure leases so that if he sold land, which he did, the tenants were not protected from a more unscrupulous landowner.

Augusta saw enough of his practical concern and his involvement to realise that he was a far superior landlord to her father. However, the shortcomings of paternalism would become more obvious in 1879 when the Land League would initiate the demand for tenant rights. Later, Augusta, as a nationalist, would have a far greater insight into the needs of the tenants than William ever had. Yet, apologist of the Gregorys as she would also become, she never shook off William's romanticism about the trust that could exist between tenant and landlord. Even in 1915 she could write a play where that relationship is exhibited without irony.

Keen to atone for his wasted youth, William Gregory re-entered Parliament in 1857 as an MP for Galway, supported by the Catholic Church, to studiously address the economic and social needs of the west of Ireland. As high office eluded him he set his sights on the governorship of Ceylon (now Sri Lanka), a position that was secured for him in 1872 by his friend Lady Frances Waldegrave. He flourished there for five years, exercising his landowning and political skills in the expanded arena of a colony. He returned to Ireland with a knighthood.

He also returned to a lonely house. His mother, whom he admired for being religious, but unprejudiced and broadminded, had died two years previously. Worse, Elizabeth Temple Bowdoin, the woman he had loved for years and married when her husband died in 1872, had died just seventeen months later in June 1873 of fever in

Ceylon.[11] She had been his ideal companion, intelligent, fond of art and travel, a good linguist, well read. William, who inherited an annual life income of £1,200 from her, had been devastated by her death.[12] But, much as he missed her, only four months after her death he did consider remarriage. 'Of course I never can feel as I felt for my late dear wife,' he wrote to his mother. 'Still I could have a warm regard and respect for a woman who suited me and that would be enough.'[13] Once at quiet Coole in 1877 the ready attention and engaging eagerness of Augusta emerging from the convivial atmosphere of Roxborough may well have revived thoughts of the desirability of marriage.

As the 25-year-old Augusta wheeled her brother about the promenades of Southern Europe her thoughts often turned to marriage. Should one marry for love or was affection and mutual respect enough? Should one marry at all? At Bellaggio on Lake Como she translated Heine's poem, *Bad Dream*, from German and was swept up by his vision that only those who find something to admire in each other should marry.[14] But at Pallanza, full of couples on honeymoons, Augusta could only see the disadvantages of marriage where couples seemed reticent with each other and isolated from other people. She exulted in her own comparative independence.

After their encounters in Galway in the summer of 1877, William and Augusta met frequently during the next few winters. William, in Cannes, would call at her hotel; Augusta later recalled how on his last day in 1878 he came three times, 'and three times the porter, Henri, had told him I was out, as porters do. I had got to like him very much.' Augusta was delighted to find someone who loved literature – he was also familiar with the Greek, Roman and Singhalese classics – and was prepared to share his enthusiasm with her, copying his favourite poems and prose extracts into little books. She could enthuse about Italian writing, and he could tell her about art. On 10 April he acknowledged her interest in Dante by giving her a terracotta head of the poet.[15]

Augusta admitted in *Seventy Years* that the idea of marrying him soon presented itself to her: 'I lived in too large and irreverent a family for [the] detachment of mind [not to think of marriage].' They were not in love, but she was satisfied that they had interests in common and plenty to talk about. William was the first person she had met who offered her something: 'He cared for the things I cared for, he could teach me and help me so much.' Back at Coole she was given the run of the library, and soon there were six books of her own choice in his will. Choosing the titles was a challenge that remained with her, so that periodically throughout her life she wondered what her six books would be.[16]

The Persses were slow to perceive that William and Augusta were finding mutual enjoyment in each other's company. Richard was bemused by the way William talked to Augusta rather than to him, and her mother was preoccupied by William's kindness to herself, not realising that he was habitually attentive to women. They were not going to smooth the way for the couple, and in the early spring of 1879, when Richard's condition worsened, Augusta's duties increased. William, concerned that Augusta was being marked down for the life of a spinster, visited her mother in Dublin to object to the increased demands for self-sacrifice.[17]

As her patient improved in the warm spring of 1879 Augusta wrote from Cannes to tell William. His reply from Rome to 'my dear Miss Persse' warmly rejoiced in the slackening of her duties. He had not thought that Richard would die, 'but I did fear that he was likely to fall, as it were, into a lower stage of health and the more thrown on your constant care.'[18] William had recently met an old friend, Robert Tighe, 72 years of age, about to be married to a girl of 27 who hated parties and loved art as he did. William had been doubtful about pursuing the much younger Augusta, wondering if he looked foolish. Later he would justify his choice to his closest friend, Henry Layard, by pointing out that she was mature 'in thought and habits', clever, well-informed and shared his interests.[19] He felt encouraged by Tighe, and described the couple to Augusta, conveying a hint of his intentions.

But that was the summer that Augusta, when she returned to Ireland, was expected to help run Roxborough. Marriage seemed more remote than ever. For Christmas William lent her a copy of Henry James's first novel, *Roderick Hudson*. When he came to Roxborough before going abroad in January 1880, Augusta noted that he looked ill 'and was, I thought, depressed, and when he said good-bye I felt sad and lonely'.[20] Her instinct was sure, for in a letter written to Sir Henry Layard on 15 February William confided: 'I have found myself of late so lonely especially when in the country and by myself that my spirits and health were giving way and I could no longer live without a companion. It is all very well when you are young, but solitude is bad for the old, and last winter tired me terribly.'

When she returned the copy of *Roderick Hudson* to William in early January 1880 Augusta included an oblique indication that she was willing to think of marriage. Unfortunately Augusta's letter is lost and we only know this from William's reply on 25 January: 'I have read over many times the letter which you wrote to me a fortnight since when returning *Roderick Hudson*. Am I too presumptuous in thinking that there is something more in it than a mere critique of that book?'[21] Cautiously he laid his cards on the table: 'I have thought over & over again on the subject, and have at length determined to ask you if I may write freely to you on the most momentous question affecting man's & woman's life?' Fearful that she would refuse him and cause him to lose face he gave her the opportunity to withdraw before he formally proposed, and ended rather coldly, 'and I ask also this favour that until I hear from you . . . you will refrain from communicating the purport of this letter to *any one.*'

She replied immediately, and a few days later, sifting through the post before she led household prayers, she saw a sealed letter (they were usually unsealed) from William. Once her duty was performed she opened the letter and read a proposal of marriage beginning 'Dearest Augusta'.[22]

Here, without illusion, he set out the character of their marriage: affectionate companionship based on similar tastes. There was no mention of love, but 'I have too deep an affection for you to try & influence you to take such a step as marriage with me without the deepest consideration'. He described the positive aspects: 'We know something of the character of each other, though I know far more of you than you of me. We can both live quietly, if we think fit, without yearning for balls and dissipation. It is great happiness no doubt to see this beautiful world in the companionship that is the most congenial one can select.' But, on the other side, he warned, '*pray pray remember* that I am old enough to be your father.' There was the possibility of illness: 'Your life has not been very bright. Think what it would be if you had an invalid again thrown upon you. All I could offer you would be affection, a small consolation.' He told her that he had been devastated by the death of his first wife and dreaded another big public wedding ('feast, & toasts & gossip') in Castleboy or Dublin. He was investigating a quiet, unheralded wedding in Tooting,

London, though it was up to her (or, more likely, her mother).

Augusta matched his measured tone of good sense and clear-eyed expectation in the description of her reaction in *Seventy Years*: 'I felt extraordinarily happy and serene, happy in the thought of being with him, of serving him, of learning from him. And I was happy also in the thought of not leaving the country, the neighbourhood which I loved.' It was, in fact, an offer that lay close to her well-prepared heart. In an early draft of her memoirs written in later years she compared herself to Dorothea in George Eliot's *Middlemarch*: 'It seemed to me that her [Dorothea's] feelings for her idealised Casaubon (before she realised them!) were something like mine.'[23] She admired William and hoped to lead a better, more meaningful life with him. He also needed care and attention. Where duty and a measure of self-fulfilment had formerly been at odds, now they could be reconciled in a life lived with Sir William Gregory. But above all she was making an escape from constricting circumstances. That desire for self-fulfilment was as yet muted, but it might not always be so subdued. The self-effacing, reliable, responsible, quietly intelligent girl that William deemed a suitable companion for his declining years lacked opportunities rather than innate spirit. And now, here was the first opportunity, heralded by William's direct and insistent question: 'Will you be my wife?' 'Will you marry me at once?'

With the marriage established Augusta was, with eye-opening speed, freed from her duties at Roxborough; an uncle's widow and daughter were found to take her place. The Persses, true to their consistent misunderstanding of Augusta, greeted the marriage with a mixture of astonishment – 'How did that little thing get the big man?' – pleasure, when they thought of the benefits to themselves

– uninterrupted shooting from Castle Taylor to Coole – and sadness, when they realised that her valuable contribution would cease. The only one who seemed as though he would miss her was Algernon.[24]

As the couple immersed themselves in the preparations for their new life Augusta's rise in status was palpable. William engaged a lady's maid for her.[25] There were financial arrangements. Augusta brought a modest dowry: £800 from her parents and £1,100 in stock, all of which remained in her name, as was usual by that time.[26] William sent her a letter which introduced her to her new role as wife of the master of Coole, emphasising her obligation to respect and maintain the trust that existed between himself and his tenants.[27] He still worried about her age: '. . . you looked quite in your early teens when you appeared in your sealskin & hat the other day, and I am dreadfully afraid that the Society for the Suppression of Vice will seize & prosecute me for abducting a girl below the proper age . . .' he wrote on 16 February.

If clothes, worn, regretted, planned for oneself or observed on others are an indicator of states of mind, then Augusta's attitudes and feelings during the flurry of her wedding and honeymoon emerge from their not infrequent mention in letters and in her *Seventy Years* account. She easily acquiesced to the need for morning and evening dresses, but the habitually self-effacing girl, further constrained by the bare month for her wedding preparations, demanded no wedding dress. And for the travelling dress, which she wore for her wedding, she chose grey, unwilling to change to colours after eighteen months of mourning for her father and brother. She had no desire to sever the bonds with her family. William did nothing to encourage Augusta to step out of her serious-minded apparel, affectionately describing her as a 'Jenny Wren' among more fashionable 'birds of plumage'. Later Augusta would regret not entering into the spirit of her wedding as she periodically looked at photographs of herself in her wedding dress and black bonnet, wincing as the hat became increasingly unfashionable until, in 1922, the style was only to be seen 'on a charwoman in an omnibus'.

There is a surviving photograph of this girl, soon to be 28. She stands in a neat silk dress with doll-like stiffness, uncertainly touching an elaborate vase on a heavily carved table, objects that were meant to endow gravitas, but which have the effect of emphasising her appearance of extreme youth; she does not stand confidently or proprietorially in the world of the vase and table yet. Her hair is centrally parted and drawn tightly back behind her ears so that a strong jaw is prominent. This contributes to the plain appearance that her family saw, though her obvious shyness exacerbated this effect. A portrait taken in Milan on her honeymoon reveals the heaviness of Augusta's young features: her lips are full, her eyes dark, uncertain, watchful.[28] She is dressed in a black-buttoned bodice, a severe costume which emphasises the restraint in her face. She has obviously still to come to terms with her new position.

They were married on Thursday 4 March at St Matthias Church on Hatch Street in Dublin.[29] St Matthias, although a popular Ascendancy church, was relatively new and on the edge of fashionable Dublin; a society wedding would have taken place in St Patrick's Cathedral or St Peter's. They were married by licence, dispensing with the calling of banns, perhaps to limit advertisement of the wedding (although it was announced in *The Times*) or, more likely, so that they could get married quickly and avoid fuss. William and Mrs Persse had compromised: it was Dublin, but quiet. Algernon – Algie, now to William – was a witness, and after dinner the Gregorys went straight to the steamer at Kingstown (now Dun Laoghaire) and spent the night in Holyhead before proceeding to London.

❖ ❖ ❖

William's emphasis in his letters on a quiet life was inspired by the fear that that was the life illness would compel him to live. In fact, he relished social events, and the honeymoon, originally intended as a tour of Italy, soon became an opportunity for him to introduce his bride to the aristocratic European society in which he moved so easily. It demanded a more adventurous wardrobe for Augusta and they visited the court dressmaker, Madame Durrant in Bond Street – she made Augusta a violet silk evening dress decorated with a panel of Augusta's own point lace – and corset-makers, Sykes, in Hanover Square.[30]

It was now that Augusta began to enjoy herself, much to William's surprise and amusement: 'I am hardly recovered as yet from the surprise which my marriage has caused me,' he wrote to Layard. 'My wife, who was quite a student, is now plunged among *chiffons* and *modistes*, and I am bound to admit that she bears the infliction with a resignation which is rather alarming and ominous, excusing her new-fangled interest in dress on the grounds of pleasing me.'[31]

Augusta's first priority was to prepare for her presentation as a newly married woman to Queen Victoria at one of the Queen's 'Drawing Rooms', for which she needed a dress with a train, a veil and plumes of feathers. When the event took place it was Disraeli, standing in the background behind the Queen, 'a diamond star glittering from his black velvet', who particularly attracted Augusta's attention in the bewildering crush of the presentation. Knowing he had at one time been a friend of William's, she wanted an introduction to hear 'some finely phrased compliment', but William had a meeting about newly uncovered frescoes in Rome and, the audience with the Queen over, they hurried away, William's concerns taking priority over his wife's romantic hopes.[32]

Had she known it, she met, in those packed and no doubt

confusing ten days, some of the people who would form the circle of friends that closed comfortingly around her after William's death twelve years later. They lunched and dined with Arthur Haliburton, a War Office official. She met Albert Gray, who had been with William in Ceylon, and his wife, who took her out driving in Hyde Park. There was an alarming meeting with the difficult, reticent director of the London National Gallery, Frederic Burton (1816–1900). An Irishman who, in the 1840s, had made his name painting the rural poor of Kerry and Galway, Burton had left Ireland in 1851. Augusta disarmed him with a naive comment which burst out of her shyness as they examined a painting, and felt that his delighted laughter signified that she had broken through his hauteur.[33] They visited the studio of the fashionable sculptor, Edgar Boehm, who was casting a bronze statue of Sir William for Colombo in Ceylon. She lunched with the celebrated society beauty, Lady Virginia Somers, and with the wife of a neighbouring landlord in Galway, Lady Redington. She may have been quiet, but she was not uncritical, immediately taking against Henry Singleton for abusing Irish landlords.[34]

After two social days in Paris, there were twelve days alone with William in small Italian towns, the first real test of their compatibility. Augusta had started a terse diary on the day of her wedding, dominated until Turin by lists of new acquaintances and engagements. Now this was replaced by brief descriptions and much approval of paintings and churches as Augusta became the willing pupil. Cautiously, the comments on these works of art expanded, and by the time she got to Perugia, Augusta was appreciating an early Raphael, finding Perugino exquisite, noting a fine façade 'showing the transition to the classical style'.[35]

In Rome they were quickly absorbed into the flourishing society of semi-resident Europeans and Americans. She met

Comte Florimond de Basterot (1836–1904), the wealthy and sophisticated descendant of a Frenchman who had bought a house at Duras, not far from Coole on Galway Bay. In his youth de Basterot had travelled dangerously and written books about it. Now, paralysed from the waist down, he surrounded himself with writers and artists, and took the Gregorys to the lavishly decorated villas of his friends.

Augusta also met the novelist Henry James. In his late thirties, James had made his name with *Daisy Miller*, published the year previously. This, together with his consistently courteous, thoughtful manner spiced by a sharp wit had given him easy access to the salons that Augusta was just entering. In later years Augusta and James would become friends, but on this occasion Augusta could only marvel at William's urbane reference to the role *Roderick Hudson* had played in their courtship, while she herself remained dumb.[36]

At the centre of this society was the British Embassy and the British ambassador who invited them to dinner to meet the Crown Princess of Prussia, Queen Victoria's daughter. She went to her first ball, and the newly married Gregorys were received by the Pope, Leo X, at the Vatican, where Augusta presented rosaries given to her by country people at Roxborough for him to bless. Then they sailed to Greece and met Heinrich Schliemann, the archaeologist who dominated the profession at that time, having claimed the sole credit of discovering Homeric Troy (in Turkey).

It was in Constantinople (now Istanbul), where Sir Henry Layard (1817–94) was British ambassador, that Augusta really began to enjoy herself. As the embassy launch took them away from the din of the quays through the Bosphorus to the summer residence of the ambassador, Augusta felt that she was now participating in one of those adventurous journeys that so many of William's friends had undertaken as young men. Henry Layard had been one of these, becoming an archaeologist in Iraq and discovering Nineveh before becoming an MP and then a diplomat. He had come to Constantinople with his young wife, Enid, in 1877. However, his career was about to end abruptly, for, arriving with the Gregorys was a telegram from the Prime Minister William Gladstone recalling him to discuss Layard's indiscreetly expressed distrust of the Sultan.[37]

Enid, a good looking blonde woman, nine years older than Augusta, had proved to be a stoical and resourceful diplomatic wife, enjoying gossipy embassy society and developing her interest in painting and sewing. She was an obvious role model for Augusta, and would become that rare thing for her, a close female friend. On this occasion, however, they both kept their distance. Enid was 'Lady Layard' in Augusta's diary, while Enid remarked in a detached way in her diary that Augusta was 'about 21 . . . plain but intelligent looking'.[38] While Enid stayed at home, Augusta accompanied William and Henry sightseeing. As ever, Augusta was easy in all-male company, especially as the stout and genial Henry had taken her on by extending to her the humorous grumbling manner he used with Enid. As a house guest Augusta could relax and enjoy her co-guests, including the traveller Laurence Oliphant, talking volubly about a scheme to settle Palestine with Jews.

After seven days at sea the Gregorys reached London in June, the middle of the summer season. They took up residence in William's recently acquired house, 3 St George's Place (now demolished), in an enclave off Hyde Park. This was Augusta's entry into what would become a significant part of her life, for William belonged to that group of aristocrats who annually left their country estates for the May-to-July season in London. The Gregorys joined the vivacious, exhausting and compact social world revolving around the luncheons and dinners, balls, salons, private views and Sunday afternoon calls of the social elite of late Victorian Britain, which climaxed with the Marlborough House garden party hosted by the Prince of Wales. John Buchan recalled this London in his memoirs, describing it as still preserving 'the modes and rites of aristocracy'; it was 'friendly and well-bred', 'secure and self-satisfied', despite the social changes of the late nineteenth century.[39]

Among the lists of people that now filled her diary some were familiar from home – her sister Adelaide, Aubrey de Vere – some she had met recently, others new to her – Arthur Birch, Lieutenant Governor of Ceylon when William was Governor, Arthur Clay, a barrister-painter related to William's first wife, William Lecky, the Irish historian, the elderly Robert Browning – 'pleasant and agreeable . . . but so unlike his poetry' – and Lady Lilford, Lady Margaret Beaumont and Lady Stanley, three formidable hostesses who lionised William. By the time the Marlborough House garden party arrived on 13 June, Augusta could mingle among people whose names she at least knew.

Although delighted by these acquaintances, she was also daunted, for society welcomed, even required, wit and character, while Augusta was shy and inexperienced. And society and William were not willing to make allowances: 'I found it hard to plunge into the Bethesda pool. And he [William], half vexed, half amused, would quote what was said of Goldsmith as a talker, that he had a thousand pounds in the bank but not a penny of small change in his pocket. It was not all my fault, for when he took me to see or dine with old friends, they would, after a kindly greeting to me, turn to him as was natural, and ask his opinion on this or that and gather round him to listen.'[40] Gregory, knowledgeable and authoritative, consistently charming and even-tempered in company (Gladstone pronounced him 'the most agreeable I have ever known'), was a formidable consort for his young wife.

The experienced William and gauche Augusta appeared in the novelist George Moore's mischievous pre-First World War memoirs.[41] Moore inaccurately described Augusta as having a 'Protestant high-school air', implicitly associating the intellectual impression of her exposed forehead with a young lady's formal education. But his experience of her as anxious 'to say or do nothing that would jar', echoed Augusta's own admission, as did his memory that 'on the whole it was pleasant to pass from her to William, who was more at his ease, more natural'.[42]

In an attempt to shine socially, she did allow herself the odd daring comment, and the gambit of asking people she admired to sign her fan, which had a band of white signature-sized sections. Moore, not initially asked to sign the fan, was critical and felt that William found it an embarrassingly tactless project. Augusta would first make her mark socially in Egypt, over a year later, when she found subject, style and passion, so that one evening, 'coming from a small dinner at Sir Edward Malet's, where I had held my own, my husband made me very happy by saying he was content'.[43]

They returned to Coole on 29 July 1880 for the traditional welcome for the bride of an Anglo-Irish landlord: 'Received at Gort by [the] Canon and Father Shannon & a mob, the temperance band playing, town decorated, a bonfire at the gate, & triumphal arch with "Cead Mile Failthe" at the gate of Coole,' she wrote in her diary.[44] While this display of respect and loyalty for the family from the tenants was in all probability planned and executed in a spirit which both tenants and Gregorys felt to be fixed, there were covert voices of dissent, and a new temper, just discernible before their marriage, was hardening into opposition. But this was as yet no concern of Augusta's as she was plunged into a round of local visits to be congratulated on her marriage.

The Coole Park that Augusta was brought to in the summer of 1880 has substantially gone. The estate was sold to the Land and Forestry Commission in October 1927, and the buildings, allowed to fall into ruin, were later sold to a building contractor for £600 (the price of the stone) who demolished the house in 1941. A new Coole has come into being. At the centre is the carefully preserved footprint of the house – a neat, low rectangular platform. A short flight of wide limestone steps which once rose to a terrace in front of the house now rises inconsequentially. To the right are the ruins of the dairy and laundry, while to the left the coach house which faced the stables and barns across a great cobbled yard, have been converted into a visitor centre. Two walled gardens survive. One, between house and stables, is stripped of its fruit and vegetables. The other, beyond the dairy, circumvented by box-lined gravelled paths, maintains the tranquillity of a garden sheltered from salt winds, and is still home to the often photographed autograph tree (witness to Augusta's continuing passion for collecting signatures of those she considered significant), a copper beech, now inaccessible to would-be inscribers. The garden once housed vineries protected by yew, and a vast Catalpa tree, and here Augusta would plant flowers. It still harbours, under a mass of ivy, the colossal white marble bust of Maecenas, the only remnant of the cultural presence of the Coole that greeted Augusta.

Traces of the ordering of approach remain: gateposts on the road, a gate lodge, a curving drive through fields, the plunge into overarching Ilex trees, but not the opening out to a sunny lawn overlooked by a white-painted, welcoming house. Most memorable are the trees; the specimens brought back from the East, many by William, and the 'seven woods' that Yeats named in 'The Shadowy Waters', some wild, some planted, that Augusta would tend with passion – Shan-walla, Kyle-dortha (the dark wood), Kyle-na-no (the nut wood), Pairc-na-lee (the calves' field), Pairc-na-carraig (rock field), Pairc-na-tarav (the bull field), Inchy Wood. They distinguished Coole for everyone, farmers and neighbouring landowners, and visitors. Today, with Forestry Commission pines planted on lawns and in the older woods, the formerly demarcated spaces have merged, and the silence of the whole place is the silence of the forest, broken by calls of blue tits and rustles in the undergrowth.

Beyond this is the river which, having risen from an underground cavern, runs into the turlough, a lake that rises with the winter rains and drops with the summer drought. The water was once visible from the house through the winter trees of Pairc-na-carraig. Now the wild stoniness of the place is only discovered on emerging from the wood.

Coole was the creation of many generations.[45] The core of the estate – Coole and Kiltartan – was bought by Robert Gregory (1727–1810) in 1768.[46] He had made a significant fortune in the East India Company and had followed a successful political career in England. At Coole he built a modest, square six-bay house like many others of the period, with three storeys to the front and two to the back facing the turlough and distant Burren Hills.[47] The only gesture to architecture was a tripartite Venetian window under a semi-circular Diocletian window designed to light the staircase and decorate the front elevation. Inside, the three main rooms – library, dining-room and drawing-room – had the view. The entrance floor contained a gun room, small dining-room, breakfast room, informal rooms to which tenants could be admitted, and which had easy access to the kitchen, servants' hall and stores half a floor below in the basement. The house, rising half-floor by half-floor, which gave views up and down onto other landings, achieved light and spaciousness with economy.

Robert planted trees, set out the front and back lawns, constructed a high stone wall about the demesne, introduced modern cultivation techniques, stocked the library and commissioned Nathaniel Dance to paint his portrait and Joseph Nollekens to produce his bust.[48] In the 1780s, his fortune exhausted, he sold his two English estates, thus re-orienting the Gregorys towards Ireland. His eldest son Richard added books, Italian sculpture – including a copy of the statue of the Venus di Medici which stood in the drawing-room – the Victorian bay windows to the rear and a less than elegant porch to the front.[49]

Where Robert had endowed the Gregorys with landed wealth, his youngest son, William Gregory (1762–1840), as Civil Under Secretary to the Viceroy from 1813–31, gave them status among the Ascendancy.[50] At Coole he contributed neo-Classical marble busts, priceless porcelain, books on India and Egypt and early nineteenth-century Celtic studies, and his prints of politicians and Lords Lieutenants hung in the dim gold breakfast room.[51] His son, Robert (1790–1847), Sir William's father, inherited in 1841 and after his death in 1847, his wife lived there a further thirty years.[52] William and Augusta added furniture, books, pictures and the subdued richness of William Morris wallpaper.

Photographs taken of Coole interiors in the early twentieth century show that the successive acquisitions of the previous 100 years were put together to make a comfortable, full, eclectic house. Georgian decorum just won over Victorian clutter, but Coole did not stand on ceremony; it was an enveloping house. It would not be difficult for Augusta to insert her paintings – many by her son, many of Coole – and books, which she put on shelves made from gilded picture frames in the drawing-room which would become a richly personal room.

Like Roxborough, the estate at Coole was a thriving, self-sufficient enterprise. Its water was supplied by a horse-drawn pump from the turlough. Cows, sheep and pigs grazed on the front and back lawns, in the fields nearer the road, and in 40 acres beyond the river.[53] They were housed in haggards and piggeries behind the barn complex. There were fewer servants living in the house than at Roxborough. Some lived over the dairy and laundry. There were also eight houses set singly in the demesne beyond the woods, for the game keeper, steward, coachman and farm servants.[54]

Within a month of arriving at Coole Augusta was pregnant. Surviving letters written before their marriage do not mention children, but as Augusta was young and an heir to Coole desirable children may well have been in their minds. For people of their class children did not have to interfere with the travelling and intellectual companionship they had planned.

In his biography of W.B. Yeats, R.F. Foster repeated a Gort legend that the father of Augusta's son was not the elderly Sir William, but a young blacksmith, Seanín Farrell, who had been approached to father the child and then helped to emigrate to America.[55] We will never know whether this is true or not. As a rumour it is provocative, for it cuts into Lady Gregory's image of the Gregorys as liberal landowners, throwing up a more archaic impression of absolute power. As a story it has a strong element of wish fulfilment for people long overshadowed by the Gregorys who were too beneficent to be hated yet indisputably in charge. Augusta was adept at keeping secrets so that no hint of this, if it was true, was transmitted to her son or grandchildren. Yet, it may have added fuel to her life-long championing of the Gregorys, and deepened her desire to defend William against the possible charges of posterity. And in the diary she kept after William's death, in which she occasionally mentioned the help she gave to local people, 'old Farrell' does have a puzzling prominence. Overall though, it is unlikely to be true, not least because Augusta was pregnant so soon after her arrival at Coole, and because William, apparently unprepared for fatherhood, reacted with such irritated intolerance to the changes pregnancy made to Augusta's life in the next nine months.

By the end of October Augusta was ill and needed rest. William was self-pitying, worried about his own health and impatient to visit the warm south as they had planned. 'People congratulate me on the prospect of being a father which I dread and detest,' he complained to Layard. 'My wife is so poorly that she cannot do anything at present and so as I am likely to be detained at Coole much longer than I intended I have left her there with her sister and come to London.'[56] It would, from a modern perspective, be reasonable of Augusta to be severely disappointed by this lack of support from her husband, but it is questionable whether a late Victorian wife would have expected much sympathy. She was stoical, and her sister Arabella, still unmarried, was on hand to help her.

The disconsolate William went off to Southern Italy as planned in the autumn, without her. But he spent New Year in Dublin with her and they returned to Coole on 2 January. By March he was back in Dublin and she was at Roxborough. On the anniversary of their marriage he wrote cursorily and a shade dutifully, 'Let me send you many words of love and esteem,' before plunging into details about his plans and present experiences, although he did express concern about her reading material.

It was then, in the third trimester, when morning sickness has usually worn off, that Augusta became seriously ill. Realising that William found her pregnancy 'unpleasant and distasteful' she forbade anyone to tell him of her danger, and he only discovered it when she had improved.[57] Cancelling his plans to travel south again, William came back, penitent, to Coole. After that Augusta's condition improved so that they spent May together in London, and on the day, 20 May, when the doctor pronounced her confinement to have begun, she felt able to proceed with the luncheon party for eight guests that they had already planned.

Her baby was born at 9pm that evening. He was later christened William Robert at fashionable St George's Church, Hanover Square, where William had married Elizabeth Bowdoin. The christening was not recorded in Augusta's still very terse diary. Was this an oversight or had Augusta not quite come to terms with the fact of the new baby? As was the custom 'baba' was immediately handed over to a wet nurse. Within a month he had gone to Dublin, and Augusta was back in society, attending the Queen's ball, spending a country weekend with Lady Molesworth, the Gladstones, Lord Northbrooke, 'etc, etc', as she wrote in her diary. Even by the standards of a society that prioritised dancing over a prolonged confinement, this was a quick recovery, no doubt encouraged by William.

Augusta was extremely reticent in her diary and letters about her feelings as a mother for Robert, although less so once he became a schoolboy. Stray comments over the next few years about being reunited with 'baba' when she returned from travels abroad with William tell us that she missed him. In *Seventy Years* she once quoted a letter from 1909 in which she stated categorically, though in parenthesis, that she suffered from the frequent breaks with him: 'The London life and that abroad with my husband (but for the constant pain of leaving Robert) went by swiftly and delightfully.'[58]

Whatever her maternal feelings for her baby son Augusta was required to think first of William. He had no qualms about farming out the baby, writing grumpily to Robert's godfather, Henry Layard, when Robert was five months old, 'I wish to heavens he could be shut up . . . till he reaches the age of 7 *at least*.'[59] William insisted that they resume their travelling, that Augusta become again an engaging and interested companion who would put her husband's needs, particularly his uncertain health, first. It was the call of duty, familiar from Roxborough, and Augusta was well able to stow away her own feelings and respond ungrudgingly to her husband's demands. The price she paid was that she was rarely close to Robert as an infant, and he remained 'baby' or 'baba' for at least two years. It was perhaps a point of tension between herself and William, a hidden source of resentment or dissatisfaction. Augusta would never formally criticise her husband, but a generalisation she later made about marriage is revealing: 'The weak point in marriage is that it legitimises selfishness.'[60] This disappointment may have made her more alert to the idealistic generosity of the much younger Wilfrid Blunt when she met him a year later.

There was another aspect to Augusta's motherhood. Robert was the heir to the Coole estate and, as his mother, Augusta had augmented her social position. Even her own mother could not quibble, and recognised that of her five daughters only plain Augusta and Eliza of Castle Taylor had produced heirs to substantial estates. Augusta was now one of her more successful daughters.

Something of Augusta's buried discontent was evident, though not to William, on their month's tour of Belgium, Holland and Germany in summer 1881. The two-month-old

Robert had been taken to Dublin (probably to her mother's house) on 18 June and they left London five weeks later. William was cock-a-hoop, feeling life was back on its proper course again: 'We have had a charming tour. Fortunately Lady G— is as fond of pictures and architecture and works of art as myself,' he wrote to Layard, listing the places they had visited and their associated artists – Cologne, Cassel (Rembrandt), Brunswick (Jan Steen), Hildesheim.[61]

These names had a different resonance for Augusta, who was recording the pictures in her diary 'that I might remember them to please W. more than for my own pleasure'.[62] She was diligent, and the detailed descriptions, occasional comparisons, comments on an artist's handling of paint, notes on artistic influences and quality in her diary all speak of long evenings without the distraction of friends, and a continued determination to be a well-informed companion. But her heart was not engaged as it had been the previous year. Some entries are brief: 'Museum again'. There was one entry, squashed at the top of the page, which described a painting of a baby in a cradle over which a girl stooped, smiling at him, which suggests a secret longing to be with her own baby. It was with relief that she received a 'good account of baby' on 21 August. They were back in London two days later, and then it was 'Coole & baby'.

During Augusta's courtship, marriage, pregnancy and early motherhood relations between tenants and landlords in Ireland began to deteriorate as low agricultural prices caused tenants to fall into arrears with their rents and landlords to respond with evictions.[63] William, cushioned by his first wife's legacy, could afford to give a 10 per cent abatement for rents after the poor harvest of 1879, and, although he raised his rents the following year when the harvest was good, it was not to earlier levels. Coole tenants were apparently content.[64]

Where landlords had evicted, tenants began to agitate, and nationalists responded by forming the Land League in October 1879 to resist rack renting and unjust evictions. This was done peacefully at first, but later with violent attacks on landlords and by boycotting those who evicted tenants for refusing to pay a rent regarded as too high. The balance of power was shifting on many estates as the tenants pulled away from the unspoken pact of the past, whereby they gave respect, allegiance and loyalty in return for accepting the care of the landlord. Landlords began to fear that their power at Westminster and on their estates was slipping from them and that eventually their land would be confiscated.

William was horrified and distraught by what he heard. When he returned to Coole with his new wife in the late summer of 1880 he was relieved to find his tenants unaffected by the League. He tried to pre-empt such disruption at Coole with warnings, and gifts of dinner and dancing. In early 1881 he also produced a pessimistic pamphlet predicting ruin for Ireland and loss of power for Britain, which was widely read in political circles.[65] He discussed his fears with Augusta, and in one letter, which he asked her to burn, he told her of his hopes that the Liberal, John Bright, would stand up to the League.

In 1881 the government alienated the tenants with a Coercion Bill, and the landlords with a Land Act. This latter aimed at securing tenant rights – the often referred to three F's (fair rents, fixity of tenure and free sale) and the provision for a land commission to set rent levels. Some landlords welcomed this as a moderate move to secure peace, which in the event it was. But the ageing Gregory was despondent and negative, believing that landowners had lost all power to deal with recalcitrant tenants. In October, his pessimism seemed justified for, despite good crops and excellent prices, his goodwill gesture of a 10 per cent abatement in rents was rejected. He would, he claimed bitterly, fight them now, then, if necessary, leave Coole.[66]

Her husband's inability to stay level-headed when faced with the first stirrings of opposition from the tenants made for an uneasy introduction to Coole for Augusta. It is not surprising that she did not immediately put down roots. But she had little opportunity to find her place there for the time being as William was impatient to go south for the winter.

THREE

Egypt and Wilfrid Scawen Blunt

> We talked over her early married life . . . Sir William did
> all the talking then and her marriage though he was quite
> kind to her was always more or less the continuance of an
> act of condescension on his part.
>
> W.S. Blunt, unpublished memoirs

Egypt, exotic and inexpensive, seemed a good idea for the
winter of 1881–2. For Augusta it would be momentous;
she would fall in love, and she would discover the pull of
nationalist politics. Egypt would mark her for life. This time
Augusta sent her five-month-old baby to stay with her
unhappily married sister, Adelaide, and her growing family
in Redruth, Cornwall, where James Lane had been given a
parish in 1877. He left on 19 October. The next day Augusta
and William sailed for Calais.

They stopped in Venice en route for Egypt to visit the
Layards who now lived in a magnificent palace, Ca' Capello
on the Grand Canal. Sir Henry Layard had furnished it with
his books and treasures, and with Enid he would entertain
royalty, Ruskin and 'all the English in Venice'. Enid, sociable
and light-hearted, still did not see eye to eye with the more
serious-minded Augusta. Where Enid rejoiced in music and
cribbage for the evenings, Augusta tried to circumvent cards
by reading; whereas Sunday 6 November, a foggy day in

which they were confined to the house, was '*Dies non*' for Augusta, for Enid it was a relaxed, jolly day in which, as they sat about 'roaring over a joke', she rolled cigarettes for Henry.[1] Enid was preoccupied as a hostess, while Augusta inevitably accompanied William and Henry to churches and galleries. But there was one afternoon in which Enid took to her room with a headache and Augusta sat with her; such behaviour suggested that they were beginning to find things to talk about.

The Gregorys, arriving in Cairo on 18 November, went to Shepheard's Hotel, one of those delightful French-colonial buildings in which wide balconies cut cool dark bands into the light plaster of the façades. Delicate wrought iron railings, spindly chairs and an almost overwhelming profusion of palms, oleander and hibiscus completed the picture. William was dismayed by the disappearance of old Arab quarters in Cairo since his visit with Elizabeth nine years earlier.[2]

Augusta was not very interested in Cairo, but she was immediately intrigued by what people thought of Arabi Bey, a young Egyptian nationalist.[3] Under William's guidance she had been reading Egyptian history and following recent political developments in the newspapers. Egypt was not a fully fledged colony, but Augusta, following *The Times*, wrote in her notebook that she thought it should become one. Later, she would scribble underneath, 'My salad days, when I was green in judgement.'[4]

Egypt was in fact a colony under the Sultan of Turkey, administered by a viceroy, the Khedive, who lived in the legendary Ezbekiya Palace in Cairo.[5] In recent years the extravagant and ambitious Khedive, Ismail Pasha, had attempted to modernise Egypt and put the country in debt. After the building of the Suez Canal in 1869, providing a conduit for ships sailing to India, Egypt had become of vital economic and strategic interest to England and France. So, when Europeans purchased nearly half the shares of the Suez Canal from the impecunious Khedive, there was very little to stop the English and French asserting their strength, which they did in 1876 under what was termed 'Dual Control'. This was reinforced when Britain sent a Commissioner of the Debt, Sir Evelyn Baring (a friend of William's), to Egypt. He had established a strong and privileged European administration whose personnel could avail of tax exemptions and other perks. When the Gregorys arrived the British advisers to the Khedive were Auckland Colvin, the Controller-General, and Sir Edward Malet, the Consul, both well-seasoned, cautious-minded, imperial civil servants.

There had been responses from two very different quarters to this intensified Europeanisation in Egypt. The Khedive's attempt to restrict European influence through constitutional means under the prime minister, Sherif Pasha (personally Europeanised, but moderately keen to reassert the Muslim character of Egypt), had resulted in Ismail's replacement with his more amenable, though weak, son, Tewfik, in April 1879. However, an inchoate nationalist movement that by early 1881 had solidified around the courageous and committed figure of Ahmed Arabi Bey had had more success.

Arabi was a *fellah* or peasant who had become a colonel in the Egyptian army in which officers were usually drawn from the ruling Turkish-Circassian class. He was a committed Muslim who always appeared in public wearing a tarboosh (the Egyptian fez) and carrying his ceremonial sword. Arabi maintained a stern demeanour, spoke with authority on the Koran in Arabic, and was conscious of the increasing need to assert Egyptian culture. He had challenged the army to observe Ramadam, and, having discovered the Khedive's plot to murder him, had led 2,500 men into open confrontation with the government outside the Abdin Palace on 9 September 1881. He had demanded the replacement of reactionary ministers with men sympathetic to the nationalists. Sherif Pasha had been reappointed to the ministry, and Arabi, at the forefront of a pandora's box of potential trouble, was widely regarded as the most powerful man in the country.

The Gregorys slipped effortlessly into Egyptian colonial society in which Turkish princesses rubbed shoulders with British officials. Enid had facilitated Augusta's entrée into Middle Eastern aristocratic society by giving her a bracelet for the Princess Nazli Khaman, whom Augusta found 'fat [and] rather pretty'.[6] She also visited the Franco-Turkish Madame Sherif Pasha and the Khedive's sister and was fascinated by their style; all smoked, wore Paris fashions and spoke frankly and intelligently about everything from childbirth to the current situation.

William and Augusta dined with Malet and met many officials and ex-pats, such as the worldly, erudite and witty former politician, Lord Houghton, known among his male contemporaries for his collection of pornography, and Sir Gerald FitzGerald, the Director General of Public Accounts in Egypt.[7] Augusta listened carefully and wrote down anything that touched on Arabi: one diplomat thought him 'honest but too powerful . . .'; Colvin was cautiously optimistic that the situation could be kept under control. But he and Malet were also tense; if there was to be any trouble with the Egyptians, their ability to negotiate a compromise would be severely reduced by more jingoistic British public opinion looking for decisive action against foreign troublemakers.

William was rejuvenated by the fluid political situation and by the fact that, with his experience of the East, his opinion was soon sought. Before arriving in Egypt he had accepted

The Times' opinion that Arabi was a 'mutinous rascal' and that British intervention would be legitimate.[8] But, fortified by an habitual distrust of the French and the Turks and an inclination towards the Arabs, he now saw that British interests would be served by a national government led by Arabi, whom he found to be an honest, intelligent, noble-minded liberal, rather than a fanatic, and whose movement he hoped to 'guide and moderate'. He wrote several letters to *The Times* to assure readers that the nationalists had respectable support.[9] 'I have fought for England first,' he wrote to Layard in May 1882, 'and for Egypt also.'

In the months that followed, this was no doubt apparent in his habitually careful choice of words and discreet, diplomatic manner. Temporarily though, at the dinner-tables of official residencies and in hotel restaurants where he and Augusta found themselves in dispute with the British representatives in Egypt, he was bracketed with one who was an ardent and ideological supporter of the Egyptian nationalist cause and his opposite in nearly every way.

Wilfrid Scawen Blunt, as Gregory observed to Layard, 'fought for Egypt alone'. He had arrived in Egypt with his wife, Lady Annabella King-Noel, the granddaughter of Byron, shortly before the Gregorys.[10] Blunt, now 41, a Catholic and the second son of a Sussex landowner, had entered the diplomatic service in 1858. It had been a modest career of lowly office in safe locations, enlivened by a series of love affairs which the tall, well-dressed, handsome Blunt, self-consciously modelling himself on Byron, easily fell into. They had inspired a number of poems, *Sonnets and Songs of Proteus*, which were published in 1875. By then he had inherited the family estate of Crabbet in Sussex and his daughter, Judith, had been born. A career as a flamboyant and self-regarding country gentleman and connoisseur of love seemed to be mapped out for him. However, he was also passionate about Arab culture and had no desire to stay rooted in England.

He had married a quiet, talented, unshowy woman 'who', according to Blunt, 'thought herself plainer than she was'. She shared his love of riding and adventure, his desire to establish a stud of Arab horses at Crabbet, and his fascination with Arabic culture. She also brought him the wealth to live the self-indulgent life he craved.[11] After the birth of Judith, Blunt resolved 'to act my own part of hero'. So in a spirit of adventure Lady Anne and Blunt travelled across the Arabian desert riding camels and sleeping in tents, enjoying the rigour of sparse food, privation and danger. They had observed the oppressiveness of Turkish imperialism and learnt Arabic. Politics seemed to have replaced love for Blunt, though subjective poetry still had a place.[12] Courage and spontaneity (or at least a kicking against convention) were his watchwords in life and art. Having left England for Arabia in 1881, the Blunts were diverted to Egypt when the September revolt of the colonels, coming hard on the heals of the establishment of a French Protectorate in Tunis, made Blunt smell the bloodless, anti-imperialist, anti-Christian, spiritually-based movement he was looking for. By early December they were in residence at the Hotel du Nil, and on 2 December lunching with Gerald FitzGerald where they met the Gregorys.

Augusta, just back from a modest adventure at Sakkarah with William, riding donkeys, visiting the pyramids, and full of enthusiasm for ancient Egypt, perhaps confirmed Blunt in his idea that he could expect little intellectual stimulation from the Gregorys.[13] However, William was interesting – he remembered the young Blunt courageously facing a bull in Madrid, complemented him on his articles on the future of Islam, gave him his views on Arabi and encouraged Blunt, who had never actually intervened in politics before, to write to *The Times*. But while William talked, Blunt studied his young wife. He later recorded his first impressions of Augusta in his unpublished 'Secret Memoirs', written in 1913–14: '[she was] a quiet little woman of perhaps five and twenty years, rather plain than pretty, but still attractive, with much good sense and a fair share of Irish wit; hardly more than two years married to a husband greatly older than herself and kept by him rather in the background.'[14]

Augusta did not record her first impressions, but the ebullient and emotionally volatile Blunt, whom she would see frequently oscillating between despair and 'radiance', was in conspicuous contrast to her restrained husband. She admired him for being outspoken, however awkward for himself: 'You will never be afraid to speak the truth, & that will be a comfort,' she wrote seven months later.[15] This could easily put William's more calculating and diplomatic habits in the shade for someone like Augusta who had only recently come out into the world and was perhaps at her most idealistic. She herself learnt from Blunt to have the courage of her opinions, but she was instinctively cautious and her methods would always be more diplomatic. Poetic Blunt, advocating that she read *The Arabian Nights*, also compared favourably with more prosaic William.

Lady Anne, more level-headed than Blunt, preferring the desert to elegant hotel balconies, carefully recording the political developments in her own diary, and without the literary interests of her husband, claimed less attention and, judging by her absence from Augusta's diary, was less interesting to her.[16] But Augusta's letters reveal that she respected her opinion and liked her. Over the next two months, as the political drama unfolded, the couples were frequently together, and Augusta was exposed to Blunt's sexual magnestism in an arena where there was no competition (except for Anne), for, as their support for

Arabi increased, that of the British colony waned. But the only hint of the arousal of Augusta's interest is in the marked reticence of many of her references to Blunt in her diary.

After Blunt had met Arabi he came to Shepheard's Hotel full of a plan to publish the nationalists' programme in *The Times*. When Malet, fearful of alienating the Sultan, reacted angrily to this, Blunt was again at Shepheard's, distressed that his plan was condemned as 'interference'.[17] The letter, though, was sent. When *The Times* assumed the letter was from Arabi, Augusta, again in her rooms, received an agitated Blunt: 'Wilfrid rushes in from Helwan in despair, writes a letter to *The Times* explaining the situation & renouncing Egyptian politics, but is persuaded to go and see Arabi before sending it – Returns radiant in the evening. Arabi sticks to his guns & authorises a telegram to *The Times* acknowledging the authenticity of the letter,' wrote an unusually forthcoming Augusta in her diary, forgetting to put the date.

On 6 January a small time bomb was dropped on the already nervy and fragile administration in Cairo. Dual Control sent a provocative 'Joint Note' threatening armed intervention if the nationalists caused a disturbance. The Gregorys went away for a three-week cruise up the Nile. During that time the nationalists responded by demanding points that France and Britain would never concede without a struggle. On their return the Gregorys stepped off the train in Cairo to find battle lines drawn: Blunt supporting (and covertly encouraging) the nationalists; Colvin entertaining the annexation of Egypt to Britain. The Gregorys soon found themselves in the middle, with Colvin asking them to restrain the troublemaking Blunt, who in turn complained piteously that everyone was against the nationalists.

On 2 February, when the Egyptian-dominated Chamber finally refused to yield on the proposed budget, Wilfrid appeared at Shepheard's Hotel in full Bedouin costume and told Augusta he was hopeful that the dispute would escalate. Augusta looked at him critically. 'He is becoming impracticable,' she wrote afterwards, 'says the Chamber is right in holding out, that if England intervenes there will be a bloody war but that liberty has never been gained without blood.' But, demonstrating that her social skills were now carefully honed, she humoured him when Villiers Stuart came in to talk of mummies. 'Wilfrid sat looking unutterably disgusted & I gave him the *Arabian Nights* & some bonbons to console him. He left in the lowest depths, Wm's moderate counsels & the discovery that his letters to *The Times* had not been published being too much for him.'

It looked as though the cautious, peace-preferring Gregorys and the revolutionary-advocating Blunts might be starting to drift apart as conflict seemed inevitable. However, two days later the Gregorys were at Heliopolis outside Cairo where the Blunts had bought a 37-acre walled estate, Sheykh Obeyd, eating nougat and boiled lamb with the Blunts, Lord Houghton and Mrs FitzGerald while incense burned. The moderate Sherif had resigned. And, when a pro-Egyptian ministry was formed with Arabi as Minister of War, venerated by a passionate crowd, William began to hope again for a peaceful solution.

Augusta, no longer content to watch from the sidelines, entered the fray by asking Malet to speak to Arabi about the abolition of the slave trade.[18] This was an issue that was peripheral to the present crisis but fundamental to the nationalists' agenda and one which all parties could agree on. Augusta also made a modest effort to make her own contact with Arabi by writing to him for a signed photograph. On 17 February she met him accidentally in the hotel foyer and was formally presented. A few weeks later the Gregorys received him at Shepheard's; he kissed a photograph of baby Robert, and they spoke about a return visit to Egypt.[19] Augusta was impressed by his quiet authority as he spoke simply about the Egyptians' desire for equality with the Europeans, and, as he countered rumours that the nationalists were preparing for battle, the Gregorys' perception of him as responsible and reform-minded was reinforced. Augusta had not lost her focus on Arabi, and would later candidly admit that she was far more interested in Arabi than in Egyptian nationalism, something that William would condescendingly smile at.[20]

Augusta's passionate attachments to men of vision or genius – Arabi and Blunt can be seen as forerunners of Yeats – would be remarkably productive for her. In Arabi's case she was inspired to meet his wife and family. Visiting with Anne Blunt as her interpreter, Augusta discovered a hybrid culture with a curious mixture of the luxurious and simple – hard chairs and photographs of Arabi set in diamonds – a mother dressed in the clothes of a country woman, and an articulate wife in a European dress with a long train (disapproved of by Arabi for its cultural resonance) who revealed she was Arabi's third wife (he was twice divorced) and who uninhibitedly told her that the last wife had been 'big and fat – just a bit of meat'.[21] His wife was also keen to get a political message across, stressing the mutual need of Christian and Muslim, and the desirability of peace.

On a second visit, with a different interpreter, Augusta played with Arabi's 4-year-old son, and both his wife and mother revealed their anxieties about Arabi's safety. Augusta would later use these experiences as a basis for her own, extended, letter to *The Times*, 'Arabi and his Household', in which she argued Arabi's case.

Meanwhile, at the dinner-table discussions of European Cairo the Gregorys and Blunts increasingly found themselves alone in their defence of Arabi, as the officials continued to be fearful of Turkish reprisals and under pressure to consider military intervention by Britain and France. It was now that Augusta began to sparkle socially, for, informed and opinionated, she could make her own mark, and found she could be witty and sophisticated. She conducted 'good-humoured quarrels', based around her open support for Arabi, provoking Gerald FitzGerald to 'threaten to come in return [for their support of Arabi] and wave the green Land League flag at the gates of Coole.' Lord Houghton, on hearing of Arabi's appointment as Minister of War, teased her to give Arabi up. 'I said, "no," I supported him when he was down in the world and I can't forsake him now he is gone up.'"[22] Augusta's reply has the casual society tone, the unwavering witty rejoinder, though her message was the less fashionable one of loyalty.

Augusta reveals one charged moment with Blunt in her diary. When he called to tell her that he and Anne were leaving Cairo to go to England to set public opinion right, he stayed some time while the newly confident, flirtatious Augusta tried to whittle secrets out of him. But there was no indication that their delight and interest were anything other than high-spirited friendship and complicity in intriguing political events.

The Blunts left Cairo on 28 February. The Gregorys stayed another month while the situation deteriorated, then left for Sicily. She had been away from baby Robert for four months but her diary as usual reveals nothing of her feelings. Perhaps it was an awareness of what she seemed to be laying aside that had made her particularly sensitive to Arabi's domestic life. On 8 May they heard about the Phoenix Park murders in Dublin in which the newly appointed Chief Secretary to Ireland and the Under-Secretary had been assassinated near the Viceregal Lodge. Ten days later they were back in London.

Blunt took precedence over Robert, for, on arrival, Augusta went straight to his house in St James Street, and the next day she was at Crabbet Park, Blunt's fine four-square neo-Georgian house in Sussex (designed by himself and Anne to replace the ancestral Tudor manor) set among a wilderness of ancient woodland and untended lawns. 'Arab horses & Egypt!' she wrote with a hint of emotion in her diary. William had declined to go, vaguely telling Blunt that his movements were 'uncertain owing to Irish news'.[23] Two weeks earlier, writing from Paris about being forced to stay – 'or there would be a great outcry' – because of Augusta's wishes, William had hinted to Blunt that he would indulge Augusta's youthful sociability where it exceeded his as long as decorum could be retained; he valued society's good opinion above his own comfort or inclinations.[24] On 22 May, four days after her return, Augusta travelled with excited anticipation to Redruth to pick up Robert.

At Crabbet she had been pitched back into the political situation. A plot to murder Arabi had occurred only days before the Phoenix Park murders, fuelling popular belief that Irish and Egyptian nationalism were mysteriously linked, and strengthening the hand of the Marquis of Hartington, a brother of one of the Phoenix Park victims, as he tried to persuade Gladstone's cabinet that Arabi should be deposed. British and French fleets set sail for Alexandria ready to intervene in the increasingly volatile situation, and Blunt organised an anti-aggression league meeting for 19 May in London.

It was at this point that William suddenly began to distance himself from Blunt's schemes. Partly, William now regarded his case as hopeless; Arabi was being increasingly alienated by British aggression and could not hope to be influenced by them. But Blunt was a firm outsider, a wild card, described succinctly by Lord Houghton as 'Arabi

Blunt', and William had no wish to draw the hostility Blunt was attracting to himself.[25] Later, he privately admitted that if he wanted another foreign appointment (he had not ruled one out) 'my former connection with him wd have told thoroughly against me'.[26] Blunt, scathing about his defection, guessed that he was nursing his reputation among official people.[27] But it was not really as black and white as Blunt maintained, for William continued in sympathy for Arabi, and would deplore British violence in Egypt. Augusta, though, never wavered in her public support for Arabi, and at various moments in the coming year found herself with Blunt and against William. She was not secretive about her continued allegiance to Arabi, but the sense of participating in a conspiracy, with William depicted as 'gone over to the enemy' (although she was not as quick to condemn William as Blunt was), was a secret she had with Blunt.[28]

On 25 May Malet sent an ultimatum to the Egyptian nationalists – Arabi to go into voluntary exile under threat of force. Blunt was in agony, for it seemed to be the end for the nationalists. The next day, Augusta was with Blunt: 'To the New Cut. Thought myself a very ridiculous little creature.'[29]

Both Augusta and Blunt tell, in quite different ways, that this was the moment when they first kissed. Later, in his 'Secret Memoirs' Blunt, the practised sensualist, coolly assessed this affair with Augusta, associating it with their work in England for Arabi.

> . . . with a woman's constancy [she] remained untouched by the decline of [Egypt's] fortunes, and as far as lay in her power served its interests still. This naturally drew us more closely than ever together, and at the climax of the tragedy by a spontaneous impulse we found comfort in each other's arms. It was a consummation neither of us, I

think, foresaw, and was a quite new experience in her quiet life. It harmonised not ill with mine in its new phase of political idealism and did not in any way disturb or displace it. On the contrary to both of us the passionate element in our intercourse at this time proved a source of inspiration and of strength.[30]

Blunt's view was conventional: love was regarded as the primary event of her life (a woman), a sideline for him (a man). For, although Blunt stated that passion gave them both inspiration for other things he spelt this out as being political for him, whereas for Augusta he suggested that it fortified her life more generally. It was true that the tenor of Augusta's private life was irrevocably changed, but her affair with Blunt also awakened her literary ambition and political sensibilities in a way that her marriage to William, though influential, had not.

Neither Blunt nor Augusta ever made direct reference to a sexual relationship between them. It was Blunt in his 'Secret Memoirs' who hinted most strongly (twice) that they had a sexual liaison. But, intriguingly, the more forceful suggestion was a later amendment: 'we found comfort in each other's arms' was an alteration of 'we found comfort in each other's affection'; a reference to Augusta staying at Crabbet was also added later.[31] It is possible that in rewriting this diary he was inspired to evoke a sexual intimacy that had not existed. However, the depth of Augusta's feelings of guilt which were not called forth by a jealous husband, suggest that she and Blunt did sleep together.

Augusta's account is found in twelve sonnets which she wrote in a disguised hand for Blunt.[32] According to Blunt they made a pact in the summer of 1883 to replace their passionate relationship with 'one of a saner and less intimate kind'. It is likely that this was proposed by Blunt. He was not deeply in love and his involvement in Egyptian politics, which would go hand-in-hand with his affair with Augusta, was over by that time, and it no doubt seemed right to him that he should also withdraw emotionally. The morning after their last night in Crabbet she gave the sonnets to him as they parted. For him they were 'a farewell to our passion'.[33] Blunt included them, slightly altered, with her cautiously given consent, in the 1892 Kelmscott Edition of *Proteus*, under the title, 'A Woman's Sonnets'. Augusta's authorship of the sonnets and the affair were only discovered when Blunt's 'Secret Memoirs' were opened in 1972 at the Fitzwilliam Museum, Cambridge, England.[34]

They are not great poetry, but they were written straight from the heart of a woman in love. For her they were an attempt to say what she had, for the last year, found unsayable. She was not looking back on a pleasurable and receding experience; she was still in the throes of her passion.[35]

> If the past year were offered me again,
> And choice of good and ill before me set
> Would I accept the pleasure with the pain
> Or dare to wish that we had never met?
> Ah! could I bear those happy hours to miss
> When love began, unthought of and unspoke –
> That summer day when by a sudden kiss
> We knew each other's secret and awoke?
> Ah no! not even to escape the pain,
> Debate and anguish that I underwent
> Flying from thee and my own self in vain
> With trouble wasted, till my strength all spent
> I knew at last that thou or love or fate
> Had conquered and repentance was too late.[36]

Here is her voice telling us that she had fallen in love with a passion that she had never felt before, and there is no reason to disbelieve her. She does not mention Egypt and the mingling of love and political excitement. Yet it is striking that these two heady experiences came to her simultaneously. Her impulsive embracing of both seems so radically at odds with the girl who had read William Gregory's proposal with such calm happiness over two years previously. Yet she had not entered marriage without a certain amount of personal ambition, and the opportunities presented in Egypt were in part a realising of that ambition. Here she had found a cause and in Egypt she had discovered what it was to fall in love. She had someone wholeheartedly to admire. It was a fulfilment of expectations awoken by her marriage and escape from Roxborough.

Augusta, though, was not single-mindedly ambitious for self-fulfilment. As she wrote in her first sonnet, at the moment when she kissed Blunt and realised she could become his lover the intense pleasure she felt was scored by guilt and fear. She stepped back, overwhelmed by the danger of loving a man who had loved so easily and so often, vividly aware that her moral universe would be overturned if she embarked on deceit and forbidden love. The following two months was a period of protracted agony in which her solitary struggle with temptation was bizarrely mirrored by the dipping and soaring of Arabi's fortunes in Egypt, while Blunt rode with practised exhilaration on the sexual and political currents which he could feel he had called forth.

On 29 May there was news of a popular rising in support of Arabi in Cairo, and three days later Gladstone finally spoke against Arabi in Parliament. On 11 June there were riots in Alexandria. Arabi was accused of incitement, and the scene was set for British intervention to restore law and order. Blunt unleashed a long-considered open letter to Gladstone in *The Times* arguing against armed intervention. Arabi refused to surrender the forts of Alexandria, and on 11 July British naval guns finally bombarded Alexandria. Augusta (and William) found themselves isolated in gloom at parties at the Admiralty and Lady Waterford's. But on 13 July news that the Egyptians had massacred and burnt the garrison in retaliation sent Imperial Britain, at the Marlborough House garden party, into depression while Blunt rejoiced.[37]

Augusta was torn and confused. She had been at Blunt's side when he wrote to *The Times*. But she was unprepared for bloodshed. '[He] says,' she wrote in her diary, 'there must be bloodshed before things come right.' She sounds bemused and unconvinced. Then, overwhelmed by the feeling that everything had got out of hand, she fled, on 18 July, to Roxborough.

There she hoped she could reconnect herself with the innocent girl she had been and so gain the power to resist Blunt. 'It is good for me to be here & my brothers are glad to have me – Having come without husband child or maid I can hardly believe I am not "Miss Augusta" again!' she wrote to Blunt on the 24th.[38] She hoped she would soon return to London 'quite cured of all weakness'.

Strikingly for a woman of Augusta's religious background there was no mention in her letters or sonnets of God. Instead she focused on an idealised view of her Roxborough self, a woman with a mother and sisters who loved and trusted her, and a woman who assumed that right would prevail, and that life could be lived without deceit. Her Christian morality was mediated by her feelings about her childhood experiences and these were her touchstone at this moment of crisis. Notably, her struggle to do the right thing was not motivated by a sense of responsibility to her husband: 'Sought my own soul to save, sought my own peace.'[39] She felt that if she embarked on an affair the moral wrong would strike at the core of her own sense of personal worth. There is an element of self-assertion here that is not normally associated with Victorian woman, although the stress on moral virtue in a woman was common enough.

Although Augusta did desire to live her life according to the high moral standards she had learnt as a child, she failed. She could not give up Blunt. And she was unrepentant. Several times she wrote that faced with the same choice again she would choose Blunt. Her greatest fear became discovery. If no one found out, she could bear to lead a double life; she would atone by fulfilling her duties and hoping for peace. If she was discovered, 'I must die'. She could secretly despise herself for her weakness – that was sustainable – but shame and dishonour in the world's eyes she felt she could not bear. She already knew that she was dependent on the good opinion of others.

This element of her character would become a pronounced part of her, and later, in the 1920s among the more self-questioning Bohemian writers and artists that she was associated with, it would look rigidly old-fashioned and be construed as a lack in her. However, Augusta's fear of discovery was a legitimate fear in the 1880s for, although there was a laxer moral atmosphere in society instigated by the Prince of Wales, discreet affairs among the aristocracy were only permitted as long as they never became public. Should this happen it was understood that this was temporarily disastrous for a man, permanently so for a woman.[40]

'In French romances,' Blunt wrote to her on 29 July, 'one always hears of people being cured by their "natal air", and so it will be with you – Only let the cure be quickly made and come back to this busy world.'[41] By 9 August, feeling defeated, drained, excited, compelled, knowing it was 'a losing game', Augusta returned to him.[42]

But first she attempted to grasp for another lifeline. It was at Roxborough that she finally sat down to write her own defence of Arabi, before the annexation of Egypt became a *fait accompli*. The act of writing and the setting of her own stamp on a confusing situation would, she instinctively knew, be therapeutic. The article was an attempt to present English readers with an Arabi who was incapable of cold-blooded violence and treachery. He was neither Sir William's ally for Britain against Turkish ambition nor Blunt's Muslim freedom fighter. Instead he was a champion of the weak, and the victim of misapprehension and slander. The theme of righting a reputation was, of course, also painfully close for someone who was dreading the possible discovery of an illicit affair.

On 24 July, Augusta asked Blunt whether he knew of any magazine that would take it. He was encouraging, 'You write so well, & something of that sort would be more likely to touch the public than any argument.'[43] She wrote freely, claiming the immunity of her sex, and adopting the tone of a society lady – with imperfect access to information (although she later checked the accuracy of her stories in the Parliamentary Blue Books), but privileged to have been admitted to Arabi's home. It allowed her to use descriptions of the domestic and personal to appeal to her readers' broad humanity and so influence public opinion; an idea that may have been suggested to her by the even greater segregation between the public and domestic in Arab culture than in Europe. Her tone is epitomised by her implication that Arabi's objection to his wife's European dress was merely because he disliked its elaborate train. 'I think,' she added with the hint of a smile, 'there are English husbands who, in this grievance at least, will sympathise with Arabi.' This tactic, judiciously utilising the woman's voice (empathetic, balanced, domestic, personal, constrained) to make a serious point in the masculine world of politics or letters, was one that she would use time and again. It matched her personal aspiration; she would work within the status quo using force of character and intellect. She had little sympathy for larger female claims for equality.

At Roxborough Augusta was given first-hand experience of the fear and brutality generated by the Land War which had intensified in the aftermath of the Phoenix Park Murders. Men patrolled the grounds, armed soldiers kept guard in the hall at night, some tradesmen had been rounded up as suspects, many landlords had left.[44] She soon absorbed their fear: 'Who could say the danger was exaggerated when within a few miles might be seen the spots where murder had been attempted or committed?' she would write a year later in 'An Emigrant's Notebook'. Ironically, in Ireland she was on the receiving end of nationalist violence and was not (just yet) particularly interested in the cause or its leaders.

The experience may have given her some insight into her husband's current state of mind, for he was morbidly pre-occupied with what he saw as a tragedy unfolding at Coole. While the Gregorys had been in Egypt, William's relations with his tenants had soured considerably, for under the influence of the League, the tenants were refusing to pay rents until the estate had been re-evaluated. On 1 May 1882 William had written to Father Shannon (acting as mediator with the tenants) in bitter despair at the breakdown of his relationship with his tenants, reiterating his threat to leave Coole.[45] In June the tenants responded to the threat by paying their rents, but, receiving League abuse for this in the *Tuam News*, they soon stopped.

Landlord–tenant relations would reach their nadir at Coole in December 1882 when William went pessimistically to Ireland 'to shoot or be shot at', and was met by tenants demanding a substantial rent reduction as the price for reconciliation. Police protection was even felt to be needed. Most humiliating of all for Gregory, however, were the small signs of a deepening lack of respect, such as the failure to touch a cap, which proved to him that the old order was irretrievable.

Augusta returned to London in early August 1882 and was reunited with Robert: 'Baby hopping about in his nightdress and blue shawl.'[46] On 9 August she visited Blunt alone and conspiratorially at Crabbet: '. . . stayed to dinner & talked treason'. Augusta began to advise Blunt more forthrightly on his campaign. Commenting on an article he had sent her on Egypt intended for the prestigious journal *The Nineteenth Century*, she complimented him on his style, but advised him not to attack Gladstone or Granville, because he would only alienate them, whereas if the situation changed they may come to him for advice.[47] She also thought his explicit over-enthusiasm for Egypt ('not greater than mine,' she noted with some asperity) would alienate his readers. Blunt wisely took heed of this.

Augusta was acting as a restraining influence on Blunt (she would later play a similar part for Yeats). Her authority with Blunt was partly due to her striking ability to imagine the possible outcomes of an event and weigh up the likely consequences, an ability that people tend to develop at a later stage in life, with more experience. The impetuous Blunt later acknowledged his reliance on Augusta's shrewd political sense and calm judgement: 'It was under [the influence of that affair] that I was able to carry on that hardest public battle of my life, the rescuing of Arabi from the vengeance of his enemies – she working with me and advising and encouraging.'[48] Elsewhere in the diaries he described her as 'my secret and most trustworthy ally, the consequent confidante of my political joys and sorrows'.[49] In 1913 he remarked in his diary, 'She is the only woman I have known of real intellectual power equal to men's.'

On 21 August Augusta was in Ems, Germany, with William who was at the spa to cure his eczema. She was impatient with this enforced holiday; they planned to go on to Vienna and Venice and, she wrote to Blunt, 'not be home until October – I hope Sir Wm will have had enough wandering then & stay quietly in London for part of the winter. I can have baby with me then!'[50]

She was trying to arrange for the publication of her article on Arabi before General Wolseley attacked an entrenching Arabi; she hoped that it just might have an effect. William, surprisingly (she noted to Blunt), did not object to her publishing it under her own name, and Blunt sent it to the liberal *Pall Mall Gazette*.[51] But on 13 September Arabi's troops were massacred by Wolseley at Tel-el-Kebir and Arabi was taken prisoner. Augusta's article supporting Arabi now seemed redundant, and William told her he '[did] not wish [it] to appear . . .'[52] There was no question of publishing it behind his back. She was devastated, and wrote emotionally to Blunt, full of apology; she was not angry with William, but guilty that she had caused Blunt so much trouble and had not been able to support Arabi in his hour of need. She felt she had been a coward.

They had failed. Egypt was occupied by Britain (though never annexed), and a year later Evelyn Baring would be appointed Consul-General. The Gregorys, who had discussed Arabi amicably in Germany, were worried that he would not receive a fair trial. In London they found Blunt was resolved that Arabi should have a fair trial.[53] He opened a public subscription for the defence (though paid most of it himself) and Augusta, resourceful, practical, unhesitating about string-pulling, became his indispensable assistant.

She wrote much of Blunt's initial letter to *The Times*, translating verses from Dante for it, and she persuaded Lord Elcho to ask a question in the House of Commons. She researched reports of Parliamentary sessions for his question early one morning at the University Club before the members arrived and could object to the presence of a woman on the premises.[54] Her vigorous petitioning of journalists and politicians for Blunt's scheme gave her a higher social profile. She even attracted the attention of the notoriously aloof Gladstone, both of them concealing a steadiness of purpose with a lightness of tone: Augusta single-mindedly requesting a fair trial for Arabi; Gladstone persisting in scepticism of Arabi's motives.

Aware that public opinion would influence the outcome of Arabi's trial, she now submitted her article, with William's approval, and it was published as a letter on 23 October in *The Times*.[55] Many gratifying compliments were sent to Augusta via William from his club, the Athenaeum. It was agreed that it played its part in ameliorating opinion; even Gladstone was touched.[56] Arabi was tried in November and, although Blunt had to consent to Arabi pleading guilty to rebellion, the resulting death sentence was commuted to banishment. Gregory contacts ensured that exile was in Ceylon.

With Arabi's fate decided Blunt began to think of visiting India and of concluding his passionate relationship with Augusta. Her letters and activities during the spring and early summer of 1883 successfully concealed the mounting distress that fill the sonnets. But there is a hint that she was becoming more demanding, behaving more like a woman in love. At Easter time she visited Portugal with William and, among others, Sir Evelyn Baring. They travelled in trains and mule-driven carriages from Lisbon to Braga, and she made detailed notes on architecture and customs which she would later use for an article. She wrote regularly to Blunt. Her letters to 'My dear Mr Blunt' were relentlessly light-hearted, but with an occasional window into her soul: 'I thought of you very much at Cinhua & had an oak stick cut for you in the woods, but it is such a club you will never be able to use it but must hang it up as a trophy.'[57]

When she returned to London on 13 May she wrote flirtatiously to Blunt asking him to come and see her, evoking herself as needing 'all the attention' because 'baby has not come back yet'.[58] Nine days later Blunt sent an extravagant box of bluebells and marsh mallow: 'It is such a long time since I have had such . . . fresh country flowers in my hands. I could have cried over them!' she wrote emotionally. She then begged him to come and see her while William was at Ascot.[59]

Meanwhile William, who seems not to have visited Crabbet yet, was remaining resistant to invitations: 'As I anticipated Sir Wm says that though he shd like very much to go & see your stud he is not ready to leave town just yet,' she wrote on 17 May. But that did not prevent her from going to Crabbet or having lunches alone with Wilfrid at St George's Place. She also ostentatiously disparaged the Khedive, siding with Blunt against William, who deplored a stand that went against the government's interests.

The rest of the time Augusta could play the immaculate society hostess, overseeing the marriage of a cousin, attempting to find a husband for Arabella, organising a formal photograph of Lady Anne and Wilfrid. There was one recorded moment of social tension. Frederic Burton, the painter and Director of the London National Gallery, complained to William that once, finding her with Blunt, he felt '*de trop*'. But Burton always was over sensitive and Augusta could reassure herself that they had made every effort to entertain him.[60]

The woman of the sonnets was a quite different creature. It was clear to her now that she loved more than she was loved:

> Thou wert my all dear, and too soon I knew
> How small a part I could be in thy life –[61]

She pleaded that they remain lovers a little longer. She observed the loved one adopting a light tone to keep intensity at bay. She dreaded the emotional barrenness of life without him, while trying to steel herself to endure an existence plagued by shame, the fear of discovery and of seeing him with another woman.

However, towards the end of the sonnet sequence her tone changed as she painted herself as a victim. Whereas in the early sonnets Augusta wrote directly of her feelings, and evoked a woman concerned to be true to herself, in the later sonnets she apologised for tempting her lover, and wrote that his life had greater value than hers. This could express altered feelings, but a suspicion creeps in that she was trying different ideas and attempting to find a literary expression for her experience. Writing the Arabi article Augusta had discovered that writing could be therapeutic. It had also given a shape to her vague ambitions, revealing to her that she could be a writer, one complimented and encouraged by Blunt. Part of Augusta may have written the sonnets to impress him.

Blunt, who admired the poems and now regarded Augusta as a poet, nevertheless rewrote parts of the sonnets to make them conform more neatly to established precepts before he published them. He ironed out the emotion and turmoil with a few unhesitating conjunctions and abstract nouns. He also banished the impression that she had been engaged in a moral struggle.

> Their peace I seek, and though my soul be rent
> With the hard conflict, I will not relent.[62]

This was dimmed by him by replacing 'soul' with 'life', which suggested that it was her daily existence rather than her moral being which was involved.[63] Thus he superimposed his pleasure-loving perspective, incorporated his theories about 'Love' and added the gloss of a more conventional poetic vocabulary.[64]

Finally, the last night proposed by Blunt arrived, and waking the next morning in the room over the (distinctly Victorian) bay window at Crabbet, Augusta gave Blunt the sonnets, keeping no copy for herself. Three days later Lady Anne, loyal, supportive and in love, gave Blunt a more sombre document: '. . . all keen interest I have in life is gone past recall,' she wrote, 'the cause, the shock of discovering that I have spent many years under a false impression.' Her despair was the culmination of years of turning a blind eye to his affairs, more recent unhappiness about the cessation of their sex life and (she was now 45) their failure to have an heir, all brought to a head by his involvement with Augusta. Her statement was unspecific and, undiscussed, misapprehension would fester between them.[65]

It is not clear whether William knew about the affair with Blunt, or what he thought of it. Augusta lived the rest of her life as if the secret was intact. William did not indicate that he even suspected; he was not upset by her growing friendship with Blunt in the late spring of 1882, his letters to Augusta remained affectionate, and he did not break off with Blunt. However, it is highly likely that he did suspect the affair (Augusta's behaviour was markedly different during that time) but, as it was not known, he pretended to ignore it. For someone who valued the world's opinion it would be a safe strategy not to acknowledge that which was not known and so ensure that there was no chance of it leaking from the private domain. It is also quite possible that he was not jealous. He read Blunt's love poetry, and, making no effort to keep Augusta and Blunt apart, he allowed their intimacy to grow.[66] Maybe he reasoned that he was too old to keep his young bride. However, he no doubt received her back with relief, and in the immediate aftermath of the affair he encouraged her in her writing, perhaps realising that she needed some outlet for her energies. He would become a demanding though consistently affectionate companion.

Augusta returned to London to pack for Ireland and a self-imposed period of secluded reflection and writing. She needed time to recover. She and Blunt had decided to maintain their friendship, which they did for thirty-nine years, until Blunt's death. From the start of this period Augusta was able to write him friendly, chatty, newsy letters, largely unpunctured by intimacy. It was done with great effort at the beginning; she did send him iris bulbs to remember her by, and she did not write as frequently as Blunt had expected.[67] But the longevity of their correspondence is a tribute to their shared interests, and particularly to Augusta's talent for friendship with men; Blunt was far less adept at friendship with women.

Augusta found Coole, away from Blunt and politics, quiet. A lull in Land League activity was partly responsible for the calm, a state of affairs that would continue the following summer. There was still tension at Roxborough and a police presence.[68] But Augusta was relieved to find that domesticity in Ireland need not mean complete detachment from political excitement: 'It strikes me curiously,' she told Blunt, 'after England, how in paying a morning visit to a neighbour, the conversation naturally turns on politics, Gladstone's views on Home Rule and the strength of the English Radical party.'

Augusta did not accompany William to London in September, nor on his eight-month journey to Ceylon in 1884, though he had tried to persuade her to go. Instead she lived a life of distractions and duties; a partridge shoot in

September, her mother's first visit to Coole, the daily overseeing of staff. She still had her maid, Revol, a woman of some character whose opinions Augusta recounted to Blunt and whom William valued for not having ideas above her station.[69] Augusta was at last reunited with Robert, now two, and 'delighted with the cows and chickens and country sights and sounds'.[70]

It may have been because of Robert that she stayed at Coole in August 1883. But, still disorientated by her affair, she also wanted to sit down in her 'summer room' and write articles and a memoir.[71]

'Through Portugal,' published in *Fortnightly Review* on 1 October 1883, was a competent piece of travel writing in which Augusta nicely balanced authoritative references to architecture, plants and food with personal reactions and idiosyncratic details, carefully gauging the interests of her audience. She wrote confidently, occasionally with panache, but with the well-meaning condescension of the time. She received £5 and the possibility of a mild journalistic career of regular, slightly quirky, topical articles perhaps presented itself. 'I feel rather proud of myself just now,' she told Blunt, 'it being my first earned money. I feel very proud even of being valued at a quarter of you.'[72] William was proud too: 'What a little puffy, round, feathered out Dir I shall find you,' he wrote fondly, though he concluded plaintively, 'I wish you wd flatter me sometimes as I flatter you.'[73]

As the boat taking him to the Middle East in January 1884 pitched and tossed on stormy Mediterranean seas, he steadied himself with thoughts of Augusta, and wrote her a caring, appreciative letter:

I am glad you have begun the netting, it is a good thing to have something 'for idle hands to do', but I shd like to hear that you are employing your mind also. Why do you not write a concerted vindication of Arabi and the national party? It has never been done yet – or why not turn to something else? I think you have the power of writing well & piquantly.[74]

Her next article, on Sudan, the new theatre of Arab nationalism, paraphrased a contemporary anthropologist and provoked criticism from William; he thought she should do original work.[75] She was also writing down anecdotes of her Roxborough childhood and her early visits to the Continent. She called it 'An Emigrant's Notebook', suggesting that she felt like a refugee from her past. She was returning to the idea that there was a barrier between her present worldly self and the innocent girl she had been pre-Blunt, and trying to distract herself from troubling thoughts by reconnecting herself with a time when 'love joy duty were one thing'.[76]

She soon realised that her personal Eden was also a collective Eden. The Anglo-Irish, and many of the tenants, could look back on the relative harmony of the years before the Land War with nostalgia and the conviction that it could never be recovered. Her personal fall had mirrored the experience of Ireland. Might not an account of this Ireland without the heroes and villains thrown up by the Land War, but showing people 'possessing like feelings with ourselves and needing sympathy', find a market among those who value Irish romances? she asked herself.

When she had finished, Augusta, thinking more seriously of publication, rewrote 'An Emigrant's Notebook' almost immediately, omitting direct references to public figures, taking out the potentially politically inflammatory and accounts of personal motivation.[77] In this version the Land War stood alone as the barrier between the present and the past. Beyond simple nostalgia she was now hoping that the sympathy between classes could be restored if the landlords did not judge 'too harshly those who are against us'.

Ignoring the fact that differences in race and religion had a class basis, she depicted Ireland as a heterogeneous country and argued that diversity did not preclude harmony. It was the old paternalism for new times; the paternalism that Sir William was struggling to recover within himself.

In a second part she considered her future by relating stories about marriage and motherhood. She recalled a friend's dissolute son. Some stories provided ascerbic observations on marriage. But the balance was tipped in favour of dutiful marriage and physical security. She ended in true Victorian fashion with a light-hearted ditty on the theme that love and duty each have their time.

'An Emigrant's Notebook' was never published. Maybe William thought it was too personal, or too topical. Maybe Augusta thought it was too self-indulgent. She put away her writing for four years and, atoning for her affair, resolved to be a dutiful wife, diligent mother and effective mistress of Coole. This converting of a sense of shame into a purposeful life was typical of Augusta's spirit. It was also an heroic resolution, for in the first three years of her marriage she had discovered much in herself that did not square easily with such a life. She could write fluently and challengingly. She was interested in national self-determination, and found that her voice – her arguments and opinions – could have weight with those in power. She had discovered sexual passion. Most of this had to be suppressed. Instead of honing these skills, rising to challenges, having some small influence on a public stage, all must be kept for her domestic circle, and in public she must confine herself to being William Gregory's wife.

It was not going to be easy. But she had two advantages. She was the sort of person who, once convinced that she was doing the right thing, would be able to keep to what had become her duty. And she was actively trying to fulfil the idealistic role allocated to a Victorian woman. It is depicted in many of the most compelling (and still absorbing) stories of the period, where women are shown to understand the supreme importance of loyalty and love and living for others and to have the courage to act according to their knowledge. There would be moments of frustration for Augusta, but the life she had decided upon had sufficient meaning for her to live it wholeheartedly. Although she did not realise it – she was not prone to self examination – she was a woman with two conflicting impulses: towards the passionate and the socially conventional. When the time came she would find that what she had largely denied was still there waiting to be used.

FOUR

Mistress of Coole

> If I had not married I should not have learned the quick
> enrichment of sentences that one gets in conversation . . .
> Company gave me swiftness in putting thought into a
> word, a sentence.
>
> *LGJ,* II

There was nothing browbeaten about the chastened
Augusta. Instead, she emerges from William's letters to
her as self-willed, strong-minded, responding unpredictably
and forcefully to him. 'Is it not strange that instead of a deep
& durable resentment my heart should yearn to a little
"spiriting devil" who has so ill treated me that I should
constantly miss her, and even at times wish she was coming
out with me,' William wrote to her from Ca' Capello in early
January 1884, before setting off for Ceylon.[1] He had been
struck by the way Enid Layard let her querulous husband
nag her without apparently noticing it, 'in a way that you
would not stand for a second'. If he even remonstrated very
feebly with her about some misconduct, he continued
affectionately, she would tell him that he was teaching his
wife and child to dislike him.

William's appreciation of Augusta's feistiness settled into
a fantasy that he was still evoking in his letters four years
later: 'Dearest little Dir, . . . I have half a mind not to send

any money in order to make my arrival more rapturous.' Or, on 7 August 1888, 'Now good-bye, you little rough 'un. Don't you wish you had the chance of coming in to fight me – I give you full leave to ask yr friends, all the boys in the county.'

William still worried that the disparity in their ages told against him, and that Augusta's playful baiting concealed a lack of affection for her elderly husband. 'The following question was put to me the other day,' he wrote to her with careful light-heartedness in July 1889, '"Is it true that you are ever wooing Lady G as ardently as you did before your marriage?" I replied it was quite true and that in order to get rid of this importunate affection you constantly send me away from home for short periods.'[2]

This worry no doubt underlay his humorous allusions to any attention either of them received from the opposite sex. He remarked on Augusta's susceptibility to the advances of 'the elder Lyall' (a friend of William's that Augusta met in India in 1885), while emphasising the 'dreadfully affectionate' letters of his *grande dames* – Lady Molesworth, Lady Rothschild and Lady Lindsay. He lost no opportunity to keep his end up. 'Lady Tweeddale gave me a lift in her brougham – rather compromising was it not?'[3] He would write freely about the charms of young women he met on country house weekends (he admired the full-bosomed, quietly-spoken, intelligent, warm, pretty; he could almost, though not quite, excuse a woman who 'squares her shoulders' and 'squeals,' if she was pretty), eliciting expressions of jealousy from Augusta.[4]

On the other hand, this epistolary ragging also indicates that whatever the shortcomings of the relationship there was a sufficiently solid and satisfying base. The core of trust and affection with which they had started was intact, and now encompassed their shared life as parents, and guardians of

Coole: '. . . you know well enough how deep is my affection for you, how steadfast my trust in your honour & right judgement, how confident my expectation that under your guidance our boy will grow up to be a credit to the name which has not been wanting in men of some mark.' William wrote this on 4 January 1884, as he finally set sail for Ceylon, afraid that he might not return. Still raw with guilt, Augusta took this injunction to heart and never forgot it.

It is hard to know what Augusta's feelings were for William as her side of the correspondence has not survived. She certainly became very fond of him. Shortly after he died she told Comte Florimond de Basterot that she would increasingly miss 'that bright, many sided companionship I appreciated so much.'[5] She was always loyal to his memory and treasured his gifts; she often wore the sapphire ring that he gave her for Christmas 1883, and it appears in Gerald Kelly's portraits of her.[6] She looked after him with anxious concern when he became ill, and her diary indicates that when he was dying she was distraught. But odd comments about the selfishness of married people and the lost opportunities of her married years – 'We both had energy – & love of Ireland . . . we might between us have done some big thing' – betray a dissatisfaction, as do comments in her diary.[7]

That Augusta made a great effort to put the interests of her husband (and her son) before her own is illustrated by a practical joke that William played on her in the early years. Discovering that she had secretly arranged to take 15 poor boys to the Natural History Museum, he pretended that he had arranged a dinner for some old friends, telling her, 'I want it to be a pleasant one', while watching her reaction. She was gratifyingly horrified at the conflict. The joke worked on a person who was keen to do her duty; it was conceived by a person who, roused by the spectacle of his wife's independent action, was not averse to pointing to where her duty lay.[8]

The impression is that the marriage, loving, but skewed towards William's needs, was fulfilling for him, but rather less so for the self-denying Augusta. But, sustained by her self-imposed task to perform her part dutifully, and by her conviction that a good marriage need not be passionate, only companionable and affectionate, she could, most of the time, effectively suppress her frustrations and present the face of contentment. She also had many outlets for her energy, love and interests.

Not least of these was Robert. He had a nurse, Nana, but when he was ill (twice with croup) Augusta looked after him. Unlike William, who retained his dislike of the noise and disruptiveness of small children, Augusta was patient and sympathetic. She allowed herself to be drawn into Robert's games and his love of animals. 'Robert has now a pig which he calls Wideawake, and a puppy which he calls Pompey, and is very happy,' she reported to Blunt in May 1885, just after Robert's fourth birthday.[9] He was a contented child, 'bright enough for two and as happy as the day is long . . .'[10]

Inadvertently, Robert breathed new life into her relationships with the Persses. He was Mrs Persse's favourite grandchild. She first came to Coole in October 1883 to see him: 'I shall feel like a child again and expect scoldings,' Augusta wrote to Blunt, barely disguising some anxiety, 'though whereas she scolded me very often when I was young and a model of goodness, now that I am not particularly good she never finds fault with me.'[11] When Augusta travelled, Robert, accompanied by Nana, would be passed from house to house – Roxborough with Dudley and Gerald, Castle Taylor with Eliza, her husband Walter and their children Fanny and John (older than Robert), The

Croft, Taylor's Hill just outside Galway where his grandmother lived with Arabella, Glenarde with a distant cousin, Henry Sadleir.

William's urbane readiness to take on Persse problems and personalities also helped Augusta to make the transition into an independent, but closely involved member of her family. He was unfailingly complimentary to Augusta's mother and encouraged her to visit Coole. He responded to news of Gerald's alcoholism in October 1886 with sympathy for Augusta's sadness and sound advice, and he was an admirer of Eliza's 'serenity'.[12]

Augusta's brothers, Gerald and Algernon, acted as agents for Coole farm. Frank, who married four months after William and Augusta, had had a wild youth. Seven years later, working diligently for an architect in London, and living economically, he seemed a reformed character: 'One should despair of no one after this,' Augusta noted in her diary.[13] In 1889 William commissioned him to design a new schoolhouse at Kiltartan. A stone building set on high ground at Kiltartan Cross it is, with its red tiled roofs, open loggia and brick decoration, still an eye-catching sight, and an interesting application of Arts and Crafts ideas to the local vernacular. It is now the Kiltartan Gregory Museum.[14] Thus the families became increasingly interdependent.

When William returned from Ceylon in the spring of 1884 they settled into an annual pattern of late spring in London for the Season, summer at Coole, the autumn and winter abroad (often Italy; it was cheaper than Coole and William preferred it for his health) and usually Coole in the spring. William could not stand long periods at Coole and he frequently left Augusta there while he went to London, or spent weekends in English and Scottish country houses.

Augusta did not settle down easily to life at Coole, and in her diary she admitted to boredom: 'the trivial round, the common task'.[15] Its main attraction was that to arrive at Coole was to be reunited with Robert. She wrote a poem on her way back from India in 1886 about her 'bright haired child' waiting at the open door, and her experience of homecoming when she had her arms about him again.[16] It was in this way that she gradually came to a love of the place.

William was keen to give her responsibility in the running of the household and estate, but this conflicted with his anxious interest in the day-to-day details, manifest even during his absences in his letters. He gave her a monthly allowance of about £5 and free rein over interior decoration, but only once he had decided what could be afforded. And his letters were full of instructions – sort out rooms in the stables and coachhouse for the servants, make sure Algernon gets the sawmill going at Roxborough. Further, the staff wrote to him with problems and William would communicate possible solutions to Augusta. When Augusta discovered that the cook, Mrs Egan, who had been given a glowing report by William, drank, William advised her to be tolerant: 'It is far better to endure an occasional tantrum than to go through a crowd of cheats, drunkards & poisoners.' But Augusta had underplayed her tribulations, and when they proved intolerable William was given the full picture. The cook was denounced as 'that odious woman' and he arranged for her to be dismissed. 'I shall certainly never again expose you to such annoyances,' he wrote contritely.[17] He advised her to be alert for servants who put their own interests first, but generally advocated 'toadying', 'it is the only way to make life go on smooth wheels'.[18] Apart from the difficulties with servants there were other frustrations, recounted to Blunt, including the need to entertain friends and relatives of William's who felt slighted by his marriage to her, and the 'unprofitable chat' of social events.[19]

Augusta soon developed strategies to stave off boredom and make her own mark. On 9 September 1884 one particular litany of woes to Blunt ended on a new note: 'But to make up the average of human happiness I have had all the Gort Workhouse children out to spend the day, and the poor little things who had never been asked outside the walls before managed to enjoy themselves very much.'[20] Entertaining the workhouse children two days a year – boating, roaming in the woods, having a picnic – would become a life-long tradition and she was careful never to disappoint them.

It was a form of philanthropy, a well-worn track to redemption. Augusta had practised it in Roxborough, but with the popularity of Thomas Carlyle's advocation of the 'Gospel of Labour', and the high profile example of the beautiful Lady Warwick, a lover of the Prince of Wales and a friend of the Gregorys, there was particular pressure to have a social conscience in the late nineteenth century.[21]

Augusta soon discovered that there were plenty of other opportunities at Coole for philanthropy, responding to requests from tenants or itinerants for medicines, food or clothing. In the spring of 1885 she began to make more regular visits locally. In March, recently returned to Coole, she wrote to Blunt, 'I was so tired by travelling and unpacking that I have not yet recovered my energy, but half dormant take up my old occupations and buy flannel and make cough cures for old women.'[22] She did not always find the transition to Coole easy: 'What did I do? What did I care for when I was here before? How did I fill my days?' she wondered in June 1887, fresh from the social delights of London.[23]

Augusta viewed her work as the necessary duty of the privileged. After a ball in honour of the Prince and Princess of Wales at Dublin Castle in April 1885 she visited, she told

Blunt, 'our own poor people as an antidote'.[24] But it was no joyless duty, for Augusta liked her neighbours: 'It is the best part of living in Ireland that they are always bright, intelligent and witty.' She was intrigued by their stories and observations, and began to note down incidents and phrases that appealed to her; one woman said to her, 'Aren't we very happy to have such a plain lady?' 'I hope,' Augusta added to Blunt, 'meaning a compliment.'

On some days, however, Augusta looked at her life more quizzically, wondering whether it was sufficient: 'I gave the workhouse children a day in the woods, which was my chief excitement, and I am nursing a little nephew who has a weak spine, and doing good works, and reading Gibbon's *Decline and Fall* by way of relaxation, and begin to feel rather Pharisaical,' she told Blunt.[25]

If Augusta sometimes felt crushed and over-serious at Coole she could be exuberant in London during the season, for she now delighted in the social whirl of balls, private views and dinners. At St George's Place the Gregorys held select and appreciated dinner parties – only twelve could fit round their table and they were careful to invite compatible combinations of guests – and Augusta invited people to afternoon tea.

Augusta now enjoyed the artifice of society, the challenge of making a mark in dinner-table conversation, the inherent drama of the clash of cultivated personalities and eccentric characters. She traded on her wit, her Irishness and her literariness. She knew about books, but was not intimidating, and told good stories. She liked serious conversation, but was not averse to gossip and scandal. She revelled in quirks and controversies, from earnest ladies with crackpot theories to the continual debate about Ireland, Egypt and India, the recollections of the Crimea, and the personalities of the previous generation. She was a markedly good listener. Her sparkiness is well recorded by Sir Mountstuart Grant Duff (1829–1906), an old parliamentary colleague of William's who met her in Madras in 1886 where he was Governor. His dull, slightly pompous diary was enlivened by her anecdotes. His daughter also liked Augusta, later describing her as a 'witty and friendly person, immensely fond of society with a highly developed social consciousness'.[26]

Augusta was drawn to misfits such as Robert Percy Ffrench, a former *Chargé d'Affaires* in Vienna, married to a Russian who openly deplored the superficiality of London society and was cold-shouldered by Lady Margaret Beaumont, the wife of the MP Wentworth Beaumont, both friends of the Gregorys.

She became friendly with some of William's closest friends, many members of his club, the Athenaeum. This was closed to her as a woman but, later, describing these often elderly, worldly and successful men as her 'ancestors', she expressed an identification with them. It is striking that some were writers, many had had careers that mixed an active, public life with the meditative life of an artist or a scholar, and one or two transcended different cultures; all characteristics that would define Augusta's own life.[27]

There was Alexander Kinglake, historian of the Crimea and author of *Eothen*, the eastern tales she had enjoyed as a child. Henry James, a member, became closer to the Gregorys when Blanche Lee Childe, a mutual friend, died in 1886. Lee Childe had been bringing up Paul Harvey, an orphan seventeen years younger than Augusta.[28] James and the Gregorys now collaborated as his guardians. James visited St George's Place on quiet Sunday afternoons, kissing Robert (a gesture that Augusta particularly appreciated as he was the only one to make it), discussing books and Paul

Harvey. She occasionally met the sociable and amiable Robert Browning at dinners and listened to him reading his poems in a quiet, unaffected voice. Drawn into a closer friendship with the eagerly attentive Augusta, telling her about his past, hopes and feelings, Browning also came to St George's Place for quiet Sunday teas. He was in his seventies and recognised as one of the foremost living English poets, although without the honours or financial rewards that were Tennyson's and with a touch of bitterness which he revealed to Augusta. She was flattered by his attention and enjoyed being the companion of a great poet.

Augusta could be disarmingly enthusiastic and unsophisticated. She first entered the house of the publisher John Murray as though it was a church, every corner significant – the staircase where Byron and Scott first met, the grate where Byron's manuscript was burned.[29] She admired the costly and beautiful things she found at Mentmore (Rosebery's country house). But she soon learnt how to fit in. She could be snobbish about new money, and she joined others in snubbing the independently-minded romantic novelist, Marie Louise de la Ramée Ouida, whose books were the illicit reading staples of liberal girls like Margot Tennant (later Asquith's wife). Augusta not only disliked Ouida for denouncing Arabi, but also for wilfully ignoring the niceties imposed on women in society; she did not affect humility or accept poor food unremarked, and she replied to the actor Henry Irving's polite request that she accompany him to the theatre with an imperious 'I never go to the Theatres'.[30]

In London Augusta also looked for a philanthropic role as an antidote to privilege. It was an outlet for her organisational abilities. She soon formed a connection with the parish of St George the Martyr, Holborn, and the Christmas after she returned from Egypt she arranged for a

large fir tree from Crabbet to be sent to the parish and
decorated with toys for the children, a feat of organisation
that particularly impressed William.[31] A few years later
Augusta made contact through Lady Tweeddale with the
poorer parish of St Stephen's, Southwark. With intelligent
initiative she devised her own role: as an infrequent visitor
she would be best employed helping the helpers.[32] She
relieved the Board School teachers with 'Happy Evenings' of
singing, games and food for the children, and she
accompanied a missionary on house visits to record sleeping
arrangements, occupations, levels of hygiene, household
finances and illnesses, to assess, as they saw it, whether they
were deserving of help. In the spring of 1887, after
consulting her influential friends, she decided to launch an
appeal for funds for the parish and wrote a pamphlet, *Over
the River*, which was published in 1888. It inspired
donations, some of which were put towards the rebuilding
of the church.

As Augusta shoe-horned herself into her expected roles at
Coole and in society, she experienced something of a
religious crisis. Her affair with Blunt had shaken her belief
in the dominance of the good and in a God-given moral
order. William, an unenthusiastic Protestant who tended to
omit church on Sundays if Augusta was not there to
encourage him, was not much help. The light scepticism of
London society, full of Darwin's theory of evolution, the
discoveries of archaeologists and the writings of historians
(such as W.E.H. Lecky's, *History of Rationalism*, 1865), was
not much help either. In the end Augusta was saved by the
simple expedient of maintaining the outward forms.
Persuading William to accompany her, when they were in
London, to a different church every week, ostensibly to
compare the architecture, music and sermons, Augusta
increasingly found comfort in the liturgy. 'That

"Correspondence fixed with Heaven",' she wrote in *Seventy Years*, restored her faith.[33]

This did not mean a reversion to the simple faith of her mother. She was keen to accommodate the intellectual advances of the nineteenth century, and throughout her life would read authors who tried to reconcile faith with a rational view of Biblical history. At about this time she was impressed by the controversial Hugh Haweis who preached that although Christianity was fallible it was inspired, and the Bible was still supreme in 'words and spirituality'.[34] But Augusta did not revel in the problems posed for the believer by science and archaeology. She was primarily concerned to keep her faith by finding ways of accommodating the pervasive doubts that she absorbed through her reading and dinner-table conversations. She had no difficulty stopping with a formula when she was satisfied.

With her faith restored Augusta could feel closer to her past; her former self-image was reinstated. As she got older she increasingly identified herself as a believer in a society where belief was being eroded. In 1888 when she first met the novelist, Mrs Humphrey Ward, who had no spiritual belief to back her missionary work, Augusta quickly condemned her: 'I felt I was doing wrong in rendering homage as it were to a woman who had made herself a half contemptuous judge of Christ and a wholly contemptuous one of Christianity.' In 1891 she remarked to Wilfrid Blunt, 'I notice from year to year even that unbelief in revealed religion is avowed more and more in society,' adding forcefully, 'a great pity, for why disturb the faith that remains?' She was hurt by a friend who denied the existence of a divinity, and found it preposterous in her to assert 'that this visible world is *all*'.[35]

In October 1885 the Gregorys set off for Venice to visit the Layards.[36] From there they went on an extended tour of

India and Ceylon, returning to London in May for the 1886 season. They would arrive back at Coole at the end of July having been away for ten months. It was another long separation from Robert for Augusta.

The Enid Layard who greeted Augusta in Venice on 16 October was now a friend. When the Gregorys had visited Venice in the autumn of 1882, just after Augusta had embarked on her affair with Blunt, Augusta's guard had been momentarily down. On several occasions, claiming tiredness, Augusta had failed to accompany the men to a church, and one afternoon Enid had visited 'Lady G' in her room, talking to her as she lay down.[37] They had subsequently met in London (the Layards had a house in Queen Anne Street) and Coole. Now they went to church together and shopped, Augusta sat in Enid's studio while she painted, and helped her with household duties.[38] Enid suited Augusta; she was vigorous, good tempered, practical, humorous and busy. She had recently set up a hospital in Venice. Her responses to her circumstances matched Augusta's, or at least the responses that Augusta aspired to. Was there perhaps also an element of solidarity in the face of their conjugal situation? They could surreptitiously comment on, criticise, laugh at, appreciate their elderly, self-important husbands (Layard believed he had been an indispensable Victorian). Enid was also undoubtedly discreet about anything she either knew for certain (unlikely) or guessed about Augusta's relationship with Blunt.

From Brindisi the Gregorys set sail in the *Nizam* for India, arriving in Bombay on 5 December. During the long voyage Augusta read Wilfrid Blunt's trenchantly anti-imperialist *Ideas on India*, based on his journey in 1883–4, and teased her fellow passengers, mostly British-Indian officials (as opposed to mixed race Anglo-Indians) and a British regiment, with ideas from it. Augusta, stimulated to be travelling again, thrived in the mostly male atmosphere on board the *Nizam*, where friendships were sudden and warm and there was an imperative to entertain and be entertained. It was Augusta who gave out prizes after a day of sports, with 'quips and graceful fancies' and eyes where 'fun flashes, humour dances,' as at least one admirer observed.[39] She also organised charades, writing scripts, making costumes and acting. She used the event to raise money for a sick stewardess by reciting a poem and hopping over the footlights with a new friend, Mr Trevelyan, close behind carrying the lid of her workbasket to collect the money. Trevelyan was a recent widower, whom she later made into the subject of a romantic poem. William, closely observing the proceedings, approved her verses and her success among the men.

Queen Victoria had only assumed the title of Empress of India in 1877, and although there was a secure network of administrators headed by the Viceroy, there remained a large number of Indian principalities with nominal indigenous rulers (Native Protected States), British officials, and a continuing power problem. The Gregorys, taking a similar route to the Blunts, travelled first in these principalities, staying with the Collectors and residents – the Resident of Hyderabad, Mr Cordery, was a brother of a friend from Egypt, and she had met the prime minister, Salar Jung, at a London dinner. And they were lavishly entertained by Indian princes. Ebullient, flirtatious, and above all interested in the culture and politics (though she found no one who knew much Indian history), Augusta was irresistible. She was alert to the living conditions of the Indians – she paid for the board of a 12-year-old boy, imprisoned during a recent famine, in a foster family – and later noted that the people looked happier under a measure of local rule in the Native Protected States. Like many of their contemporaries the

Gregorys favoured Muslim culture with its single deity. They bought Persian carpets, and these, together with the Arabic literature translated by friends such as *The Times* editor Thomas Chenery, would later give Coole, especially the drawing-room, the distinct oriental tone of the late Victorian period.

In January 1886 they entered the British controlled area and visited the Viceroy, the Anglo-Irish Lord Dufferin, in Calcutta. He was a ladies' man who was immediately susceptible to Augusta's blend of seriousness and flirtatiousness. As he listened carefully to her openly critical views on India at a banquet (83 to dinner, 32 servants and 250 people to the dance afterwards), she decided to use the opportunity to try to help Arabi. The nationalist Egyptian leaders were still in Ceylon living on paltry exiles' allowances. The Blunts and Gregorys had campaigned, so far unsuccessfully, to improve their conditions. Now Augusta persuaded Dufferin to look into the question of their allowance. When she later sent him a statement of their financial position he recommended the desired increase.[40]

After an emotional parting from Dufferin, who put his arm around Augusta as he took her hand, they travelled south to Madras where they stayed with Grant Duff, then in his final year as Governor. Here Augusta made another conquest, and she entered into a spirited correspondence with him soon after she left India. At the end of February they crossed to Ceylon where William still had money invested in tea plantations. They visited Arabi in Colombo, and spent a week in the interior, viewing the effects of William's reforms which had helped to revive rice cultivation and eliminate disease. Weighing the pros and cons of a Civil Service career in a letter to Paul Harvey, who was about to leave Rugby School, Augusta revealed that her support of Arabi had not turned her against imperialism; she advocated the career for the power and material success that the highest positions gave.[41] She was also enthusiastic when Dufferin suggested that he propose William as Governor of Madras.[42]

On this journey to India Augusta discovered an empathy for the unresolved lives of British-Indians, doomed to live between English and Indian cultures in a twilight of their own. She was sensitive to their sense of exile, and to the very varied, sometimes conflicting, roles they had to play. She was particularly struck by Alfred Lyall (1835–1911), Lieutenant Governor of the Western Provinces and living in the ancient Muslim city of Allahabad. As a thoughtful poet, putting final touches to 'Verses Written in India' when the Gregorys visited, he displayed an empathy for both rulers and ruled, and he discussed with her the need of the conquered Indians to retain a core of identity through their religion.[43] Yet as Lieutenant Governor he had had to perform the sometimes brutal duties of an imperial administrator; he had, she knew, put down a mutiny. One senses that these observations sharpened Augusta's awareness of her own intermediate Anglo-Irish position and helped her eventually to find a positive role for herself in the emerging independent Ireland of the twentieth century. She was also made aware of the power held by many provincial governors she met in India, a power that William had once held and which survived in the 'good name' they basked in on their visit. This, too, had its effect, enabling her, when the time came, to act with an instinctive patrician authority in the Irish cultural arena.

While she travelled Augusta sent letters to Robert. He was staying at Roxborough surrounded by a cloud of aunts who bought him boyish presents – a pistol with paper caps, a bow and arrow – and uncles who came and went. There is a torn sheet among Augusta's letters with a note proudly recording the first letter she received from him on 10 December in Poona written on lines carefully ruled by an aunt.[44] A few weeks later he announced that he could read by himself. A precocious four-and-a-half-year-old, Robert signed himself 'WRG', changing it in a later letter to 'little RG'.

There are a number of love poems scattered about Augusta's Indian diary that reveal an inner restlessness; moments of frustration with her life as a dutiful wife and mother. It is a private literary rebellion against conformity as she expresses the normally inexpressible. In one poem her darling Robert waits for her at Coole, but Blunt is now indifferent. In another she imagines she is in love with Mr Trevelyan. In 'Alas! a woman may not love!' she evokes a fear that Robert will grow away from her as her brothers had done, and bemoans the fact that conjugal love is blighted by everyday cares.[45] If a woman finds a 'kindred mind' 'too late' she must either succumb and feel remorse, or resist and grieve silently for lost love. The poem poignantly reveals that the scar of her love affair was still tender. Augusta, now 34, returned to Europe animated and handsome, and received compliments from Robert and the country people at Coole.

The Gregorys arrived in London in the early summer of 1886 to find that Gladstone, leader of the Liberals since 1867, was Prime Minister and Home Rule, now being debated in the House of Commons, the only subject of conversation. They already knew of, and had been shocked by, Gladstone's conversion to Home Rule. Coming on top of the Conservative's Land Purchase Bill of 1885, which allocated money to tenants to borrow the purchase price of their land, the Gregorys, along with many Anglo-Irish, felt their only supporters had abandoned them. They seriously considered selling the estate, but decided against it. 'The bribe is not big enough,' Augusta told Grant Duff, 'and though for peace sake one would gladly take any small sum and be sure of it, yet one has a feeling against selling one's child's birthright for a mess of hasty-pudding.'[46]

The despondent William could only think in terms of all or nothing, although their neighbour at Oranmore, Christopher Redington, had shown that selective sales to the bigger tenants on favourable terms was a workable solution.[47] Meanwhile, Dudley and Gerald at Roxborough were demonstrating what life could be like without the slightest compromise; they extracted full rents and attracted violence. However, their tenants did collect money for a salver for Algernon's forthcoming wedding (he was to marry Eleanor Gough from nearby Lough Cutra), but with the proviso that it was omitted from the present list to prevent the Land League from finding out.

Augusta was inspired by the passions of bitterness, irony, cattiness and violence that the Home Rule debate aroused. Running through her letters at this time is the presence of Gladstone, his grip on this confident and irreverent late Victorian world vicelike, his knowledge proverbial, his desire to display it gargantuan, his restraint heroic, his expression when interrupted 'diabolical', his rhetoric mesmerising, and his politics in the Gregorys' circle, profoundly distrusted. Amusing observations on the debate filled Augusta's letters and allowed her to make a splash socially.[48] She confidently told Dufferin, that, with Ireland occupying everyone, he had his chance to commit any illegal act he wished in India. Her boldness was rewarded when Dufferin quoted it in his *Life*.

The Home Rule crisis also had an impact on Augusta's emotional life, for in the spring of 1886 Wilfrid Blunt had decided to extend his sympathy for small nations by taking up the cause of the Land League. He was elected to the Irish

National League in London and travelled to Ireland to publicise the injustices of the land system. William found this outrageous, and categorically told Augusta that she must not encourage him to come to St George's Place unless he, William, was absent.[49] Augusta was piqued and uneasy, resenting Blunt's intrusion into Irish affairs where her social position prevented her from allying with him in support of the dispossessed as she had done in Egypt. Irritation was masked by the light tone she assumed in an entertaining letter to Grant Duff describing Blunt moonlighting in Ireland, depleted by his fasting as a good Catholic during Lent, refusing whiskey and pork as a good 'Mohammedan', then fleeing to Paris to restore himself in the best restaurants.[50]

The Home Rule Bill was defeated on its second hearing in July, Gladstone resigned, and a general election brought back the Conservatives with the Liberal Unionists, the anti-Home Rule Liberals whom William supported. The Land League responded to this downturn with the Plan of Campaign, implemented on 23 October 1886, which ushered in another season of violence on a small number of estates.[51] This violence, and the worrying thought that Gladstone might return and confiscate all Ascendancy property, prompted William to offer the Coole tenants the opportunity to buy their holdings at a generous price, but it was turned down.[52] The offer was for twenty years' rent. He told Layard that although he would sacrifice his income in the short term, at least the residue (the demesne) would be secure for Robert.[53]

The Plan of Campaign was vigorously supported by Blunt. Augusta, caught between William and Blunt, tried to be cautiously optimistic about the future. 'Here, we are rather at the back of the North Wind, reading exciting Irish news in the papers and living such a still, peaceful life, we are yet on most cordial terms with our people – but we mustn't boast too much till rent day comes,' she told Blunt in October. She tried to find common ground with him: 'I rather suspect we are at heart agreed, only we have never quite patience to get below the surface.'[54]

However, in November 1886 there was disagreement with the tenants about rent levels and, although it was resolved, Augusta's tone in her letter to Blunt sharpened: 'So I hope all goes well, and that we shall avoid war, which we should go into, perhaps with heavy hearts, but certainly with clear consciences.'[55] She acknowledged that he had taken his place 'in open rank with those who love me not', and she sarcastically told him that if he came to Ireland and made inflammatory speeches he had a good chance of being imprisoned.

In 1887 Lord Salisbury appointed his charming, clever nephew, Arthur Balfour, as Chief Secretary in Ireland to stamp out the Plan of Campaign. This he attempted with a draconian Crimes Act. That October, Blunt, acting for the Home Rule Union, came to Ireland to test the validity of the Act in forbidding public meetings, by speaking at a Home Rule meeting on the Clanricarde estate on 23 October 1887. The meeting was duly proscribed as illegal, and he and Anne were hustled off the platform. Four days later Blunt was sentenced to two months' imprisonment. There was an appeal and he was released on bail.

Augusta was in Venice when news arrived of Blunt's arrest on 23 October and she immediately wrote him a sympathetic, motherly letter, telling him how anxious she was and lightly encouraging him to put any prison experiences into verse.[56] To Paul Harvey she admitted that although Blunt was wrong she was sympathetic towards any 'friend being mauled by the police and marched off to a Loughrea Jail'.[57]

By December 1887 the Gregorys were in Rome. William wanted to spend the entire winter and spring in the south and return to London in May for the Season. But Augusta was despondent, feeling exiled from six-year-old Robert, now at Castle Taylor. 'I always hate this transplanting process, and have not put out any roots here yet, and Ireland and my child are very near my heart, which Rome has not touched,' she bleakly told Blunt.[58] She wrote to Robert every week and he replied with cheerful, carefully written letters in joined-up handwriting, telling her about his dog, Gip, and eating dinner with the grown-ups. By mid November he had moved to the Croft and was having regular lessons from Arabella and his cousin, Fanny Shawe-Taylor. He seemed contented, absorbed with his animals, able to relate small incidents to 'mama', confident of her interest. He would politely ask after his 'papa's' health, sometimes in a postscript. He relied on his mother's regular letters and when she missed a week, as she did in February, and again at the end of April, he was concerned; 'we were quite anxious about you', he wrote on 22 April. Meanwhile Augusta attended a Christmas party at the British Embassy in a white and gold dress and held tea parties. But she also had frequent headaches and was sick. She was preoccupied with Blunt.

Blunt was to be retried on 3 January 1888. On 28 December she wrote him a letter which showed she was now indisputably on his side, political differences forgotten.[59] Blunt was again sentenced to two months' imprisonment. Until 8 February he was an ordinary prisoner (League members were denied the status of political prisoner), required to wear prison clothes and pick oakum (unpicking old rope), but in the comparatively relaxed atmosphere of Galway Gaol he was allowed a Bible, a prayer book in which he wrote sonnets on the blank pages, and a non-regulation coat. The final weeks were spent in the harsher environment of Kilmainham. In neither place was he allowed to receive letters or personal visitors. He emerged in March a changed man – 'none the worse in body but having suffered greatly in mind'.[60]

Prisoners would always have a hold over Augusta's imagination, and she saw Blunt, the first Englishman gaoled in Ireland during the Land War, as a hero. Deeply touched by Blunt's plight and imaginatively engaged, in an echo of her behaviour in 1883, she wrote four compact, clandestine and highly personal poems in disguised handwriting in early 1888 and sent them, unsigned, to Blunt. He recorded that they were written for him while he was in prison and kept them in his diary. They were found in his personal papers.[61]

'Without and Within', a simple ballad, expressed Augusta's empathy for Blunt's experience, and her loyalty.

> Without the gate, without the gate
> I early come, I linger late,
> I wait the blessed hour when he
> Shall come and cross the bridge with me
> Without the gate, without the gate.[62]

She compared scenes within and without the prison, using effective, concrete images to describe the normal life outside, but fumbling with conventional poetic images to evoke the glorious, heroic Blunt within. The image of the vast closed doors of the gaol dividing prisoner from family stayed with her, and would be used years later as a powerful motif in her popular nationalist play, *The Gaol Gate*.

The other poems are less successful, but their messages are clear. In 'A Triumph' she reassured Blunt by reminding him of the good his act had done his daughter and the people of Ireland. 'A Lament', dated January 1888, sings,

> My heart is in a prison cell
> My own true love beside

> Where more of truth and beauty dwell
> Than in the whole world wide.[63]

In 'If-' she was critical of Blunt's disclosure of British strategy to Irish justice, suggesting that Blunt was going to suffer most from having hurt his family.[64]

She did all she could on a practical level, hampered by being in Rome, though not by being officially unsympathetic to his cause, for friendship and class were legitimately allowed to soften political differences. She appealed to her cousin, Henry Persse, a visiting magistrate in Galway, to visit Blunt, which he did (against the regulations), talking 'horseflesh' with the grateful prisoner.[65] The Roman Catholic bishop of Galway, Dr McCormack, a committed Home Ruler, promised to visit Blunt. Meanwhile the Galway Persses were fascinated by him. Robert wondered how Blunt would like his plank bed, though Augusta's mother was spiteful: 'I hope he will benefit by it, but if he walked through the country and found out the priests' pranks he might gain better information.'[66]

On Blunt's release on 6 March 1888 Augusta welcomed him to 'the free air' and, meeting him on a May morning in London, found him physically undiminished.[67] Blunt had recovered his Bible from a Galway bookseller who had labelled it 'Blunt's Bible' and charged him ten shillings.

Back in Galway in the summer, Augusta took her efforts to empathise with his experience to a curious extreme, getting herself admitted, with great difficulty, to Galway Gaol.[68] She sketched his cell and sent the sketches to him, requesting his official prison photograph. She was paying homage to her hero. She was also fetishising his prison life. Blunt participated in this, sending her a piece of oakum. In November 1888 he asked her to correct the proofs of his poem, 'In Vinculis' [Imprisonment], written on his release and dedicated 'To the Priests and Peasantry of Ireland', and their 300-year-old war 'for Faith and Freedom'. She accepted gladly, and not without humour: 'You show great confidence in me in having your prison poems entrusted to my hands. Should I not be doing a notable service to the Unionist cause by mutilating them?'[69]

In the summer of 1888 Augusta wrote a poem entitled 'The Eviction' in which she asserted her loyalty to Blunt and hinted that her own political attitude was changing.[70] She had became involved with tenants who had been arrested under the Crimes Act, so that her formerly neutral philanthropy now had a political edge: '. . . every day,' she wrote to Blunt, 'brings some of their relatives to my door appealing to my sympathy and expecting me to effect a release in some way.'[71] In June the police had arrested several suspected Land League moonlighters. Two were her tenants. Later, one who was being taken to Galway Gaol called out to his brother in the crowd to go to Lady Gregory for help. 'But I had already done what I could, for I think he is innocent and every day I hope to hear of his release.' They were side-stepping the League, and she was inching beyond the traditional bounds of Unionism.

To Blunt, in July, Augusta speculated, 'I think I am growing a little more of a land leaguer & less of a [Anti] Home Ruler – and so would you if you lived in Ireland.'[72] Her feelings for Blunt may have inspired this change, but undoubtedly her experience in Ireland (something Blunt did not have and which she still held against him), was pushing her forward. She was now becoming one of those few Anglo-Irish who could contemplate change in Ireland and the taking on of a new, less directly powerful, role. What would later be called a constructive Unionist, she wished to accommodate the angry to prevent an escalation of opposition to the status quo. It gave her a new sense of purpose and freed her from some of her residual sexual guilt;

she told Blunt in August that she was 'at present one of the happy people without a history'.[73] It is not known what William thought of her work; depressed and fearful, he was probably neither encouraging nor discouraging. She no doubt kept her views from him. His influence was waning, and Augusta was relying more on her own judgement.

FIVE

Last Years with Sir William

> . . . the last of those sheltered years.
>
> *LGJ*, I

During the last four years of her marriage Augusta began, tentatively, to develop her own interests again. Robert was often at school, and although an increasingly frail William became more emotionally dependent on her he did not exert the same intellectual or social demands.

Seventy-two in July 1888, William was dogged by minor illnesses, hypochondria and fear of ageing. His letters from London, which he still visited much more frequently than Augusta, could be self-pitying, and now often contained variations on the refrain: I long for a fortnight with my affectionate wife and enchanting son.[1] Augusta described the quiet domestic life which William was beginning to appreciate to Blunt in July 1888: 'The days slip by very quickly with housekeeping and correspondence and teaching Robert and the boys to play croquet, and attending to the poor, and seeing to the garden,' which had become her responsibility.[2] William deferred more often to her opinion at Coole, while the instructions in his letters took on an increasingly tentative note.

He was morbidly preoccupied with his legacy, making new investments to ensure an income for Robert, adding codicils to his will.[3] On his last visit to Ceylon in 1890 he sold his estate at Tangabelle. His own disposable income had dwindled: 'I am in the last stages of impecuniosity,' he wrote dramatically to Augusta on 14 July 1889, 'I greatly fear I shall have to sell some stock.' Coole income had also decreased because of the rent reductions of the past years, and, in common with other landowners, they economised by reducing the staff and their wages, especially in the house. They let the St George's Place house for short periods. William also went more frequently to the racecourse. Aware of his weakness he was tentative, unsure whether he should gamble, then only placing a small bet.[4] But on 2 June 1888 he reported that his winnings had paid the hotel bill.

Nevertheless, an irrepressible ebullience still ran through his letters; he kept up his interests in art and literature (and maintained his position as a trustee of the National Gallery in London), and he addressed Augusta, now 'duckie', more affectionately. He was still an entertaining and interesting companion, and together they had achieved a muted intellectual companionship; while Augusta read recently published poetry, Max Muller's *India*, and General Gordon's *Journals*, William was annotating Cordery's translation of *The Iliad*. Since May 1884 William had been slowly writing his autobiography, often dictating it to Augusta. Together they indulged a mild interest in Irish antiquities; nothing to differentiate them from other curious Anglo-Irish, but something which Augusta would later build on.[5] Travelling on Henry Persse's steam yacht, they visited the island of Inishmore off the Galway coast for the day on 28 June 1887, intrigued by the 'strange and elaborate' ruined forts about which, she confidently told Grant Duff, 'absolutely nothing is known'.[6]

In the summer of 1888 Augusta had discovered that her seven-year-old son had become a delightful companion, only too willing to share in her activities, and receptive to her attempts to groom him for adulthood. She taught him croquet and they joked about Blunt, they sketched in the same sketchbook, and in London he accompanied Augusta when she visited friends. She took him to the zoo, skating in St James's Park, to the National Gallery and the public gallery of the House of Commons, where she no doubt pointed out their friends and told him about his father's career. She had, since he was five, been initiating him into his role at Coole, taking him with her to the workhouse to distribute estate fruit to the children. She was tolerant of his high-spirited antics, criticising William for being angry with him and 'unjust'.[7]

When he started day school in London in November 1888 Augusta found it hard to let him go. On his first day she anxiously noted how small he looked against the mostly older boys: '. . . he could not reach the peg to hang up his little coat.'[8] But he put on a brave show, 'held up his head and put his hand on his hip and tried to look like a man!' She watched the clock until it was time to collect him. He was a quick, enthusiastic student, and Augusta was soon proud of his achievements. William's interest was finally kindled. As classics formed the basis of a gentleman's education, he began to coach him in Latin, cautiously, afraid too much new material would have an adverse effect on 'a very excitable little brain'.[9] At Christmas, when Robert complained that he was being bullied, William taught him to box.

Between times Augusta was beginning, tentatively, to concentrate some attention on her own interests. Her old bent for languages reasserted itself. 'I took up an Irish grammar by chance the other day and am puzzled over the pronunciation and growing ambitious to learn,' she told Blunt in July 1888.[10] The casual tone was deceptive for she had bought the grammar and employed a gardener to teach her. But she felt he was unconvinced by her interest and the lessons subsided. That same July she began to paint local ruins and tombs in watercolour.[11] The following spring, in Italy with William, she packed three sketchbooks, and while William watched or remained at their hotel, she drew or, using watercolours, painted towns, churches, views, discovering an unerring eye for good composition, able, occasionally, to evoke the atmosphere of a place. Robert wrote every week, his vocabulary slightly altered by school: describing defeat in cricket he wrote, 'we got awfully licked'.[12]

In London on her own in February 1890 (William was spending five months in Ceylon, Robert was in his second year at school), the independent Augusta enrolled at Heatherley's teaching studio for drawing lessons, and blossomed socially. Letters to Blunt reveal her appetite for the latest political and social gossip.[13] She wore the long fashionable dresses of the 1890s, and gave Blunt an amusing account of how she negotiated her way around dung-infested London streets: 'Your tail over your arm; a frill round your petticoat and your poultry yard round your neck, and you are in the height of fashion.'[14]

But there were days when Augusta had severe headaches and sickness. It is tempting to entertain the idea that the life she was determined to live was in some fundamental way uncongenial for her, frustrating for an intelligent and active woman. The year previously her doctor, Dobrée Chepmell, articulating a current theory, took the opposite view, blaming her (mild) intellectual pursuits for her malady: 'He says it is from a nerve connecting stomach & brain, – & that the brain has been taking the nourishment the stomach ought to have.'[15] Chepmell was replaced by Thomas Maclagan, a specialist in fevers and rheumatism, who became a family friend, and would attend William in his last illness. Undaunted by Chepmell, perhaps deliberately turning him on his head, Augusta decided to write again. In the late summer, sitting down at Coole between visitors and household duties, she wrote poetry and short stories.

She submitted 'Irene,' a poem, to *The Argosy*, a popular literary magazine which had published Trollope and Charles Kingsley. It appeared, under her own name, in the October 1890 edition. It is outwardly a humorous comment on men's double standards as regards women; they want to marry innocent, classically beautiful, inexperienced, and poised women, while they prefer to have affairs with mischievous, fun-loving women with sex appeal rather than Grecian noses. The easy flow of the poem and its implicit celebration of the wayward Irene suggests that Augusta had to some extent come to terms with her past. Instead of straining after the more conventional aspects of her own character as she had done in the sonnets, when she had set self-indulgence against conventional self-denial, she seems to be expressing an acceptance of her own past waywardness.

She wrote three short stories, two of which were published, both under the pseudonym of Angus Gray – she wanted her views but not her name known in London.[16] She found the mechanics of writing difficult, especially linking different scenes, but the finished results suggest she was inspired less by the desire to craft a good story than to explore the problem of the place of her class in Ireland in the aftermath of the Land War and Land Purchase, particularly her own possible role after William's death.[17]

All three stories deal with the relationship between English, Anglo-Irish and Irish people in a country setting. In all a challenge is implicitly presented by the Irish, resulting in a conflict for the Anglo-Irish and English. In 'A Philantropist' she considered how an Anglo-Irish woman would lose status if she married an Irish doctor with whom she had been doing philanthropic work. In 'A Gentleman' she depicted the closeness of the relationship between an Anglo-Irish landowner and his Irish gardener, mysterious to the landowner's English wife until she develops an appreciation of the gardener's moral and unmaterialistic attitude to life. In 'Peeler Astore' a Galway schoolmaster is puzzled by the love of the supercilious daughter of an English agent for a dead Irish policeman. In each case the question is asked: How close can the Anglo-Irish or the resident English come to the Irish?

There was a political dimension to each story. In 'A Philanthropist' Augusta suggested that disinterested sympathy from one with the power of class might work where the old landlord/tenant relationship had been undermined by recent political changes. If not Sir William, then Lady Gregory. 'A Gentleman' went further in implicit criticism of English policy in Ireland, as Augusta showed her English audience the often close bond between landlords and tenants in Ireland. Equally, though, she seemed to be telling the Anglo-Irish audience that their lives would be improved if they cultivated their understanding of their tenants. 'Peeler Astore', whose female protagonist secretly lamented her lost Irish love under an aloof upper-class persona, associated sympathy for the Irish with passionate love, both powerful, dangerous, forbidden emotions. This last was unpublished.

All in all, it did not amount to radical politics, but it was a creative engagement with a fluid and complex situation. It was an attempt through writing to understand that situation, an impulse that would later result in the stream of plays for the Abbey Theatre. There is one particularly significant difference between this early creative work and her later plays. At this time there is in each case a youngish female protagonist through whom Augusta tried to project her views. Later she would do this through characters that bore no outward similarity to herself. The realisation that she could act through characters with whom she did not superficially identify was the liberating realisation that allowed her to become a playwright.

There was one respect in which the stories were an apprenticeship for the plays: Augusta used stories and phrases that she had heard, and she had enough confidence to evoke the complexity of the social relationships through language.[18] There are detailed descriptions of dress and manners and, reading the stories, one is struck by Augusta's imaginative involvement with the intricacies of Irish social life before she would admit to being knowledgeable of the 'world close to me'.[19] But she does not convey an emotional involvement. However, this is evident in her diary record of the proceedings of the Parnell Commission in December 1888, where Connemara country people bore witness to rural atrocities: 'The tragedy so simply told moved me almost to tears – and it seemed cruel of the counsel to begin a pitiless cross-examination'.[20]

After years of being antagonistic to the Home Rule MP, Charles Stewart Parnell, Augusta became a passionate supporter during the winter of 1890–1 when Captain O'Shea, the husband of Parnell's mistress, filed for divorce and Parnell's party split. Sympathy for a victim, especially one whose private life was being dissected in public, overruled her aversion to his politics. Politically she was now an explicit supporter of that strand of Unionism that wanted to see Home Rule killed with kindness.[21] 'Home Rule is knocked to pieces for some time to come,' she told Blunt, 'and we whose homes are in Ireland look forward with hope to a quite unexpected horizon of peace and quietness. And Land Purchase will be growing while politics are sleeping, and by the time the Home Rule idea comes up again the peasants will be "Haves" instead of "Have-nots", and may safely look after the interests of this country as well as their own.'[22] Meanwhile, William, gloomy and pessimistic, was riveted by Gladstone as the author of the destruction of the Anglo-Irish. He told Layard that he hoped 'the Napoleon of English politics, worth 20,000 men in the field', would die, go mad or 'become effete'.[23] Yet he regularly sent him woodcock from Coole.

Politics exhilarated Augusta, but Robert's departure for Park Hill boarding school in Lyndhurst, Sussex, on 25 April 1891, upset her badly. It was made worse by the fact that he had had croup two days before: '. . . but he is all for going with the other boys – only going to bed he clung to me and said, he didn't think he wanted to go to school so much now – Oh, my child,' she wrote in her diary.[24] She and William took him to the train at Waterloo Station: 'When the bell rang, and [I] gave my last kiss and they got in, my heart failed and though I kept my veil down tears kept rolling down beneath, so that I could not take a last look at my child as the train went off.'[25] She had a raging headache. At St George's Place she missed the 'bright head at the window and quick hand at the door', and that evening she excused herself from dinner at Frank Geary's and went to the opera where she sat at the back of Lady Osborne's box hoping her tear-stained face would not be seen. Two days later she wrote in her diary that she felt sympathy for those who commit suicide, 'but I got through somehow'.

On his arrival at school Robert wrote a dutiful letter: his 'soar' throat was almost all right and he was one of the youngest. He was, however, advanced. He was put in the first class for French and the second class for Classics and Maths.[26] He had no Greek, but was inspired to master it quickly to be top of the class. He also studied English, History, Geography. After only four weeks he was writing with quiet pride of his achievement: 'I think I am rather good.' He was also pleading that his grandmother not send him religious books. He reported that a boy had been caned, but you had to do 'very bad things' to be caned. His end-of-term report stated that his 'general conduct' was 'very good'. It seemed, for the period, a fairly humane, if competitive school. It was also very small; there were only twenty boys, seven or eight in a class, four to a dormitory.

Robert arrived at Coole for the summer holidays bigger and browner, but 'his little fair face is not changed', Augusta noted anxiously. He was now mad about cricket, explaining the rules to Augusta and getting her to play. That first day home Augusta observed that he went to bed sleepy and happy, 'but no one can know how happy *I* am'.[27] Augusta was glad that he was still loving and enthusiastic, while William was pleased that he showed no sign of turning into a dissolute character; to Layard he observed that his outdoor thoughts were cricket and caterpillars, 'both harmless and cheap amusements'.[28]

William was getting weaker that summer. In early July he began to have difficulty breathing. A persistent, suffocating cough and palpitations sent him to Dr Ball who diagnosed bronchial asthma, prescribed plenty of food, only two cigars a day and port instead of champagne, and anticipated he would recover.[29] He did, but it was replaced by constantly increasing diarrhoea which made him thin and weak.[30]

Augusta tried to have a normal Christmas, entertaining the parish children, organising dinner parties and lunches, but William hardly left his room.[31] Alarmed by his loss of weight, the doctor advised Bournemouth instead of the planned journey to Algiers for spring 1892, and Augusta supervised two weeks of morning walks, afternoon drives and Sunday visits from Robert, and watched as William took to 'invalid habits' and became increasingly irritable. Just before Robert left to return to school she overheard William say, 'Goodbye my little man – mind you take good care of your mammy now, for I'm not able to do it any longer.'

Back in London William persisted in fulfilling his duties at the National Gallery and Augusta optimistically began to prepare for Algiers, but the night before their departure he finally collapsed. Dozing in the study next to the dining-room where he was sleeping, she heard his voice. '[I] found him sitting on the side of his bed, his strength gone, his mind gone, talking unintelligibly – I tore at the bell for Crouch – & with difficulty we got him back to bed, for he sank helplessly on the floor.'

This was the beginning of two weeks of illness in which Augusta never went to bed. Augusta's diary details his slow decline and records his final words in which he told her of his love for her, gave her responsibility for Robert's upbringing and asserted his belief in God. Both his ability to say such things at this moment and her desire to record them have a notable Victorian character. She was there when his breathing stopped at 3 a.m. on 6 March. She felt numb, mesmerised by the fact that he looked so peaceful after his delirium, conscious of him lying under his paintings by Velázquez and Savoldo. Mechanically she wrote letters to Robert, her mother, the Layards. She felt unable to leave the body and stayed with him until morning. Then she sent telegrams and went to bed, sleeping all day. The spell was finally broken in the evening when a telegram from her sister Eliza commiserating with her made her cry for the first time.

SIX

Coole and London

. . . had I not been widowed I should not have found the detachment of mind, the leisure for observation necessary to give insight into character, to express and interpret it. Loneliness made me rich . . .

LGJ, II

It was January 1893 before Augusta took out her diary with the intention of adding to it; ten months after William's death and what must have seemed a lifetime since that period spent with her dying husband when day had fused with night. For the next eight years she would write a much more detailed and frequent diary than she had done previously.[1] It became something of a companion during a period of anxiety and change. Many years later she would value her widowhood for the solitude and detachment it brought, as well as for the challenge it presented to make an independent social mark; such opportunities nurtured her as a writer. But it took her some time to rise to these challenges for in the immediate aftermath of William's death she was overwhelmed by sadness and dared not contemplate the empty years ahead. Instead, she clung to her duty to Robert. It helped her to execute the practical details generated by William's death with a clear-headed efficiency that she did not feel the rest of the time. This thread, grasped desperately in those initial days, would become a fundamental fibre of her being.

Augusta did not go to Coole for the burial. Thinking William would have objected to fuss she requested no wreaths, but was glad of the attention shown by four organisations, including an infant school in Holborn, London, which sent wreathes to St George's, Hanover Square, for the memorial service. She left Frank and Gerald with William's body at Euston Station. At Gort the funeral lasted two days, and the tenants showed the traditional respects, carrying the body into the church and praying by the coffin. William was buried beside his parents in a mausoleum on the estate built by his great uncle, Richard Gregory.[2]

Augusta spent the next few weeks alone at St George's Place putting her finances in order with the help of William's old friend, Sir Arthur Birch. The will, dated 18 December 1889, for which Augusta was joint executor with Frank and Algernon, had been something of a shock.[3] There was a bequest of £2,000 for a daughter of Captain Dawson of Wexford; a mistress perhaps, or the child of a mistress. More worryingly, she discovered that the mortgage advanced by William's cousin, Charles Gregory, in 1867 had been substantial and was still largely unpaid. The estate, which was in tail male (to be passed through the male line and not to be sold without legal intervention) had been left in trust for Robert.[4] She had free life tenancy of Coole, a jointure of £800 a year (equivalent income in purchasing power today in Ireland would be €53,700, or £36,856 sterling) to be paid out of the revenues of the estate and a life interest in the residue of the estate. William had left her the leasehold of St George's Place, and personal effects from other properties.

Bearing in mind the severely reduced income of Coole, and aware that if the Liberals got back into power Home Rule might again become a possibility, it was clear to her that she should ensure that Coole was paid for by the time Robert inherited, although she told Florimond de Basterot that her only plan was to 'get rid of my homes'.[5] She sold St George's Place, which was expensive to maintain, and most of its furniture. With the proceeds she offered to pay off the mortgage on Coole. Charles Gregory asked instead that the mortgage remain with a reduced interest, which she accepted as probably the more prudent course.[6] To pay this she needed to economise on her own expenses and to raise revenue by letting Coole during the winter. Already the widow, conscientiously trying to realise her husband's expectations, was creating a framework that had a better chance of success than her husband's more extravagant lifestyle had ever had.

At Easter she went to her mother at The Croft in Galway, with Robert. She visited Coole only once, for a day, 'a sad visit to the empty house & the tenanted grave'.[7] She returned reluctantly to Coole in the early summer for a month on her own to try to scale down the establishment. It was only when Robert came home, playing cricket and enjoying his first rabbit shoot, that the house and gardens came alive for her. She loved his kind, intelligent, boisterous company, and with him around the responsibilities of Coole began to feel less onerous. She realised then that they must try to spend their summers at Coole. She engaged a tutor to coach him for preparatory school exams, conscious that, lacking a formal education, she could not help him, although she had bought some books hoping that if she stimulated herself intellectually this would have a beneficial effect on him.[8]

In September she visited the Layards in their comfortable Queen Anne Street house in London. When they had heard of William's death they had written promptly, offering themselves and their home in London.[9] Her first meeting with them in June had been strained, with Augusta leaving straight after lunch, but now she enjoyed a restful month with them.[10]

She returned to Coole in October, intending to spend the autumn there, but, shortly after arriving, her brother, William Norton, appealed to her to go to Roxborough. Dudley, lonely, deluded, alcoholic, had died just seven days after William (Augusta was particularly saddened by the fact that there was no one to whom she could write to comfort) and William Norton had inherited the estate. Settled with his English wife, Rose, and five grown-up children in London, Major William had only intended to use Roxborough as a summer residence. But, enjoying the power and authority that was an Irish landlord's, he had decided to stay. Of this he had rather peremptorily informed Algernon, who had been managing the estate for fourteen years. There had been an argument and Algernon had been dismissed. Family members had taken sides, and Augusta had found herself drawn once more into the vindictive atmosphere of her family.

Now there was another crisis, for William was also an alcoholic and was drinking himself to death. Ironically, Augusta had been called upon as a calm, sensible (and available) influence, while her prompt response owed much to the fact that, confused and lifeless since her husband's death, she was hoping to find some sense of purpose in being useful.

She was empathetic to the disorientated family, taking William and Rose on a week's recuperative tour in West Clare, and moving in (temporarily). When William and Rose went back to London, Augusta stayed on as a companion for their children. She got on well with Arthur, who, at 30, was only ten years younger than her. Robert came for Christmas. Looking for new duties she seemed to be slipping back into her old supportive role in the Persse family.

However, her temporary usefulness was suspended when William Norton, increasingly convinced that she meant to replace him with Arthur, dismissed her. He also sent a letter insulting her husband. She left on a bitter New Year's Eve, sickened and angry, although when William Norton died a month later she was glad to find she bore him no hard feelings. She went to her mother's house with Robert where she wrote an account of the last year. 'Oh my husband! do you know how little I have forgotten you!' '. . . there is,' she concluded, 'a terrible difference in my life.'[11]

There were two intimately connected problems for Augusta, neither of which she could yet deal with: how should she live and where? On 29 October 1892 she admitted to Blunt that she was unable to make plans for her own future. 'I suppose some day I shall have courage & take up some line of life – but I can [at present] still do nothing but drift along, without much interest except Robert, & he is almost quite lost to me at school.'[12] Margot Tennant, one of the 'Souls', the clever, ambitious, witty group that surrounded and idealised Arthur Balfour, asked her to be a political columnist on *Tomorrow*, a journal they were considering setting up. It was an opportunity to construct an independent literary life in London. But she shrank from what she would once have wanted to embrace, using her indecision about where she would live as an excuse. 'If in London, I believe I could do what they want,' she wrote to Blunt in mid-November, 'but I am doubtful, being so far away, and my plan of life is very undecided.'[13] The Irish countryside was a powerful draw – the liveliness of the pre-election debates and the intense quiet – but she also felt she ought to live in London.[14] At present she felt strange in both places.

The Croft was no refuge. Here Protestant bigotry reigned unchecked, and Augusta endured conversation that frequently moved into a religious key without rising intellectually or morally. She was doing her duty, looking after her mother, but Mrs Persse was ageing ungraciously and demandingly. Augusta was unable to resist her melancholy thoughts, and she was hardly sleeping.

It was to London and the Layards' house (filled with treasures from Nineveh) that she looked for rest and stimulation. This time she took up the threads of her old social life with relief. She dined with Nevill Geary (now a qualified lawyer), Lord Morris, Alfred Lyall, Lady Julia Tweeddale (recently re-married), and Marc-André Raffalovich, the Russian writer and homosexual, who moved in circles dominated by Oscar Wilde where tolerance, good taste and the ability to shock were prized. The Grant Duffs at Twickenham were particularly encouraging: 'The pleasant talk & being made welcome, helped to restore my self respect which had really been shaken!'

The visit inspired her to write a political pamphlet, *A Phantom's Pilgrimage; or, Home Ruin*, published anonymously in late spring of 1893. It was a response to the fact that since the general election of July 1892 the Liberals under Gladstone, together with 71 anti-Parnellites, dominated the Commons, and Home Rule had returned to the political agenda. As William had in his pamphlet of 1881, she presented the feared consequences of Home Rule. She imagined Gladstone returning to an Ireland devastated after ten years of Home Rule – famine, unemployment, vigilante groups – intent on finding one person who had benefited, blind to the chaos. This was the Unionist message; Home Rule would be disastrous for Ireland, and Gladstone was driven by political ambition rather than an understanding of Ireland's needs. For Augusta the good of Ireland meant the good of each class, so that she described the devastating effect on everyone – farmers and labourers,

landowners, schoolchildren, the urban poor and priests –
bringing an unusually even-handed treatment to each group
and engaging the emotions of her readers.

Although her pamphlet came out too late to be part of
the Commons debate on the second Home Rule Bill, which
was passed on 21 April 1893 by 43 votes, it was available
for the Lords' deliberations.[15] They rejected the bill,
Gladstone resigned for the final time, and Home Rule
temporarily evaporated from the political agenda.
Gratifyingly, Augusta had made a mark in political circles.
Randolph Churchill, one of the few Tories who had
supported the Egyptian nationalists, now praised the
pamphlet, as did Sir William's contemporary, the journalist
William Russell, Sir Henry Layard, Frederic Burton and
Lord Wemyss, who drew a cartoon for a second edition.
The widow had stepped into her dead husband's shoes. But
further, she had developed the view of Ireland she had been
exploring in her stories. Most importantly, she had
obliquely defended Coole for Robert and so found a literary
way of fulfilling her duties in Ireland.

Although she spent Easter 1893 cheerfully at Coole with
her 'obedient & affectionate & caressing' Robert, reading
the *Iliad*, and training a puppy, she was glad to go back to
London with him after the holidays. He had started at
Elstree School just north of London. This was much bigger
than his previous school (120 boys), but Robert, eager to do
well, settled down quickly. Augusta, over anxious, visited
him twice that term and only gradually convinced herself
that he was in safe hands. Whenever she thought of Robert's
progress at school she regretted that William was not there
to see it.

In London, Augusta was faced with the problem of how
to establish herself as a widow in society; a daunting
problem, for women tended to be defined by their

relationship to men so that it was necessary to make a definite decision about remarriage or sexual availability. To be in your early forties (Augusta was 41) 'was considered the most alluring time for women', according to Anita Leslie, who has written with insight about slightly later Edwardian society. 'Edwardian hostesses did not need to worry about wrinkles and plumpness, it was their conversation that counted. Ripe figures were popular, ripe minds essential.'[16]

An alternative to association with a man as a wife or mistress was to strike out alone as a society hostess and perhaps try to make some kind of literary or artistic mark. Here Augusta had the example of Mary Kay who occasionally invited her to dine. Mary Kay had edited her husband's book on free trade after his death and had, as a young girl with her sister 'without large means or brilliance', established a distinguished social circle on the death of her father (a former Under Secretary for Ireland) with the initial help of a family friend.[17]

The protection of mourning lasted a customary two and a half years. Until the summer of 1894 some of Augusta's hesitations can be ascribed to this; she would not, for example, dine out in the first year after William's death, though she gave tea parties. Even after this period she remained reticent about dining alone and never failed to feel nervous when she arrived in London, doubtful about the reception she would get in drawing-rooms, galleries and theatres. The anger, very rare for the decorous Augusta, which she vented on Lady Robinson in 1895 when she complained about her husband's acceptance of a post in Southern Africa, indicates that the disadvantage she felt ran deep: '. . . I gave her my lecture as she left – & told her how if she knew what it wd be to lose her husband she would never vex him by a word – but follow him on her knees & do her best for him.'[18]

During the visit to London in late spring 1893, despite the restrictions of mourning, Augusta made a brave stab at the Mary Kay solution. Her Home Rule pamphlet was giving her a measure of social success, and together with Enid she gave tea parties, Enid inviting the women and Augusta the men, her own age and younger – Martin Morris, Paul Harvey, her nephew Jocelyn (a son of Major William's), Nevill Geary – as well as Sir Arthur Birch and his daughter, Una. She also permitted herself the flourish of commissioning a portrait of herself from Lisa Stillman, paid for from her literary earnings. In her diary she claimed to be motivated by the desire to leave a memento for Robert, but it was also a gesture of self-confidence.

The commission, a pastel, was modest enough; her financial resources did not stretch to an oil painting by a highly successful artist. But with Lisa Stillman, an established portraitist who exhibited at the Royal Academy, Augusta could be sure of a high standard. It is a realistic and intimate portrait of Augusta. She has a composed, serious and youthful air; she is prettier and more relaxed than she was at 28, but there is none of the worldliness she dreaded displaying. She looks out directly and thoughtfully at the viewer, and for those who never knew her it fosters the illusion of having met her at a quiet moment when her guard was down and she was admitting that she felt, though she didn't quite know why, that life alone would be good, and that there were things to do.

It was reluctantly, but with a strong sense of duty, that Augusta returned to Coole for the summer in 1893, six weeks before Robert was due. 'The arrival here is always sad and depressing, the silence, and one's responsibilities coming on again – but work is the best cure,' she wrote to Enid Layard soon after she had unpacked.[19] She was shocked to find the housemaid drinking heavily, but was lucky to find Marian McGuinness to replace her. Thirty years old, unmarried, fluent in Irish and English, literate, she would become an integral part of Coole, staying until she had a stroke 34 years later in 1927.[20] With an uncertain temper and strong feeling for right and wrong she became a formidable presence. She also had an unshakeable sense of class. Although many of the writers and artists that would come to Coole in later years could be odd and unpredictable, they were all middle or upper class. Seán O'Casey was the exception, and Marian was not welcoming: 'Great *playwright* is it? . . . I'll give him great *playwright*. What *right* at all has a man like that to come into Coole without a tie on his collar, nor a collar on his shirt.'[21] Augusta also had a cook. By 1901 this would be Norah Dooley, also fluent in Irish and English and literate. The maids wore uniforms; there was a starched apron and white cap for Marian. As Marian needed no understudy, Augusta was able to keep the establishment down to two live-in maids. This was economical compared with more prodigal Roxborough where there were six home servants.[22] Living in houses on the demesne with their families was the steward, Michael Dooley, the coachman, Murty O'Loughlin and a farm tenant, John Farrell.[23]

Augusta's attitude to the tenants had to shift slightly for it was she who was now primarily responsible for making sure that they paid their rents. In this she was helped by Algernon and Frank who were joint agents (Frank would later become sole agent), although they did not always agree with her views. Luckily, despite a drought, the tenants had potatoes and pigs, which commanded high prices.[24] She continued to respond to their requests for help, but giving piglets to recompense a tenant was, she told Enid, 'altogether . . . a much less satisfactory way of getting one's income than simply drawing dividends'.[25] Bottling fruit, the annual workhouse party, making sure Robert met 'the people' were all done with a dogged sense of future benefit: 'I am always so thankful when it is over . . . chiefly because it marks another year of being on friendly terms with our people, and I am so anxious that should last till Robert is grown up.'

Until Robert returned for the school holidays Augusta found Coole almost unbearably quiet, occasionally reading aloud to hear a human voice.[26] Robert brought noise and activity, went hunting and fishing, and she invited Arthur Birch's boys, Tony and Wyndham, to stay. Occasionally she escaped from Coole responsibilities to nearby friends for stimulation, advice and entertainment. At Duras, Florimond de Basterot, now in his late fifties, was particularly sympathetic, as well as literary and sophisticated.[27] She visited the Vere O'Briens at Newhall in County Clare, where she met the enterprising Florence who designed lace and had just set up a lace-making school in O'Connell Street in Limerick. She went to Spiddal, County Galway, in late September to visit her distant relation, Lord Morris (1826–1901). A sanguine character, who spoke in a provocatively exaggerated brogue, Morris was a Unionist Catholic who had been Lord Chief Justice of Ireland in 1887–9. His son, Martin, was preparing to enter politics as a constructive Unionist.

Of her family, Augusta was closest to Arabella. She had finally married Robert Waithman, a wealthy widower with three children, in 1891 and lived in great style at Moyne Park in Monivea, County Galway, a house that still stands. Augusta often stopped there on her journeys between Coole and London. She, like William, was not impressed by Waithman, a Galway landlord; she was contemptuous of his money-making schemes and sceptical of his forays into amateur photography and art dealing. His saving grace was a sporadic kindliness. Augusta thought Arabella too passive and idle. Three years later, after walking 5 miles to Moyne Park from the station, Augusta was particularly struck by her sister's unrewarding life, '. . . shut up nearly all the winter with bronchitis – no money no interests or power of helping anyone outside – just skinning the rats for the W[aithmans]'s benefit.'[28]

Roxborough was, as usual, dispiriting. Rose, her sister-in-law, was jealous of Eliza's daughter, Fanny, about to be married to the wealthy Honourable William Trench, second son of Baron Ashtown. Augusta found Rose and her daughters narrow-minded, trivial and 'common' compared to the people she knew in London. Meanwhile, Eliza at Castle Taylor, the dominant Persse spirit, was ignoring her relations in the flurry of Fanny's wedding. Augusta was much more sympathetic towards her brother, Gerald and nephew, Arthur, who were initiating Robert in male pursuits. 'Gerald and Arthur very kind, & dogs & rats & guns & a carpenter's shop & forge at hand.'

Once she had sorted out the domestic problems at Coole in early July 1893, Augusta began to write. She had already installed William's writing table and cabinet, salvaged from St George's Place, in the drawing-room. Here she had placed a few inherited treasures on the table, including an ivory jewel box that had belonged to the last Queen of Kandy, and made a book stand of two ebony elephants for Browning's love poems. She wanted to edit and publish William's autobiography, something he had never intended. Typically and wisely she had first sought approval from one of William's friends, George William Russell, currently Under Secretary of State for India. Her debilitating sadness had lifted and she found the work interesting, if difficult.[29] Her first task was to take out the boring, repetitive, potentially scandalous or merely upsetting passages. She was also concerned that Sir William's image should be admirable.

Sending the edited manuscript to be typed in September, she turned with considerably less enthusiasm to the problem of how to deal with the unwritten final ten years, the ones she was most qualified to write but felt least able to do; '. . . his loss is still so fresh.'[30] But when she found William's personal and opinionated weekly letters to Sir Henry Layard, full of details about Ceylon, Coole, Egypt, the National Gallery in London, Robert, herself, she realised she could continue her editing work, writing only a short bridging piece. This was done in London in the late autumn of 1893.

In her short connecting piece she deliberately underplayed her role in his life, while she presented William as a dedicated landowner who had responded positively to the changes brought about by the Land War, especially Land Purchase. This was astute. Anticipating the direction of political change in Ireland, she wanted to place the Gregory family in the right light to ensure their future in the country. It also reflected her growing conviction that this constructive, open-minded approach, which William had come to reluctantly, was what was needed in Ireland. Blunt, though moved by her 'simple' contribution, felt that, like many, she was too self-effacing.[31] However, she had gone far beyond the aim stated in her diary of keeping the Gregory name in the public domain in order to help Robert's career, and begun to construct a myth of Coole, associated with herself, which is still felt today.[32]

Before leaving Ireland for London in the autumn of 1893 Augusta had been quietly pursuing another interest. She was reading Jane Barlow's recently published *Irish Idylls*, a book of stories about the hard life of country people in the west of Ireland written in dialect, and *Grania* (1892) by Emily Lawless (1845–1913). When she was a girl Augusta had met the aristocratic, athletic and outspoken Lawless and found her unfeminine.[33] *Grania*, set on an Aran Island, traced the tragic story of a passionate woman, linking, as many popular romantic Victorian novels did, love, character and place. Under the influence of these books, and with the idea that the more elemental life of these rocky islands would be reinvigorating, Augusta set out alone early in October 1893 to visit the islands.[34]

She took a steamer to Inishmore, and from there travelled to Inishmaan and on to the smallest island, Inishere by currach, the light, open, canvas-covered rowing boat with a rising brow which was used by the islanders for fishing. It was a daring way for a solitary woman of her class to travel. There was a storm, and Augusta was forced to stay in a cottage on Inishere for five days, with only the tiny stone-walled fields and the wild sea to look at, the local people who spoke little English for company, and potatoes to eat. She felt completely cut off from the world, exposed to a life she had only glimpsed before. Used to dealing with people who could switch from Irish to English, Augusta was for the first time fully exposed to Irish – Irish conversation, Irish songs, Irish stories. It was an unforgettable and formative experience. Back on Inishmaan, writing to Grant Duff, she already had the feeling that Inishere was significantly removed from contemporary existence: 'At Inishere there is a thorn tree, bowed with age and supposed to be dying – but such an exotic is not to be found here.'[35]

Unlike J.M. Synge and W.B. Yeats, who also visited the islands in the 1890s, Augusta's imagination was not captured by the idea that she was in touch with a primordial civilisation that had miraculously survived into the late nineteenth century, although in her letters she did note the survival of old traditions. Like earlier nineteenth-century antiquarians she was interested in the artefacts ('relics') of the past – 'Druid altars', beehive huts, churches 'built by the saints of the early centuries', 'the most splendid of all Cyclopean forts, Dun Aengas, crowning the cliffs, and beds of saints and giants . . . scattered through the fields' – all today much as it was then.[36] She compared Lawless's islanders with those she encountered, quickly realising that the novelist had been simplistically romantic. 'The people are not so tragically sad as in *Grania*; I could hear low ripples of laughter from the evening fireside at Inisheer, but neither are they *merry*; a potato and fish diet, and the battle with the stones and the sea, settles this,' she wrote to Grant Duff. She came home with notes for a magazine article, which was never written, or never published and lost.

Three months later she read W.B. Yeats's recently published *The Celtic Twilight*, a disarmingly simple collection of vignettes of people he knew from Sligo and stories he had been told.[37] Here was someone approaching Ireland with a much lighter and more artistically purposeful foot than realistic Jane Barlow, romantic Emily Lawless or herself, preoccupied with status, landscape and history. 'I have desired, like every artist, to create a little world out of the beautiful, pleasant, and significant things of this marred and clumsy world, and to show in a vision something of the face of Ireland to any of my own people who would look where I bid them.'[38] Augusta read on of fairies and banshees in anecdotes from people for whom they were as real as the mountains and sea, and was introduced to the beliefs of the country people. From then on an interest in people and their stories and songs would displace their artefacts for Augusta. Folklore would replace archaeology. In November 1894, when Augusta met the American writer Bret Harte, recently settled in London and complaining that California was 'too civilised now for romance', she told him about the Aran Islands and gave him a copy of *The Celtic Twilight*, in that gesture bringing together her own experience of the west of Ireland with the book that had been a revelation.[39]

After Aran she went to Enid's house in London, rejuvenated. It was a productive visit in which she worked hard at William's autobiography, visited Robert at Elstree, dined out and entertained. 'It gives me a feel of independence & power being able to give a dinner,' she confided ebulliently to her diary. To tea she invited Emily Lawless and Henry James.

Enid was now Augusta's close friend. Enid's diary (though not Augusta's; she valued these things less) gives a vivid picture of the two women ordering muslin dresses at Regals and bonnets in Sloane Street, setting off after lunch in Enid's carriage to pay afternoon calls and leave cards, attending private views and visiting artists' studios (especially G.F. Watts's, whose portraits were particularly popular), then returning to decorate the Queen Anne Street house with flowers for tea parties. They supported each other during crises. When Robert needed a doctor Enid was there with her carriage, when Henry fell ill Augusta regularly spent the evening sitting with him.

Displaying a talent for diplomacy and the dogged ability to reach a satisfactory conclusion, Augusta secured an agreement which finally ended Adelaide's long drawn-out divorce case. It was an unusual step for a cleryman's wife to seek divorce, but Adelaide, with six children in 1884, had by then little sympathy for her intellectual, assertive husband and no patience with their continuing poverty and social insignificance. Helped financially by her family, she had escaped by travelling with her children to towns along the south coast, and had spent a year in Paris. She was finding it almost impossible to conclude negotiations for the divorce. Told to 'bestir' herself by her mother, Augusta accepted the role of arbitrator between Adelaide and her husband's solicitor. She went to great lengths to reach a compromise, bringing the two sides together, working out details, and finally contributing £125 (which she could ill afford) towards Adelaide's debts. She also acquired a bundle of letters from a woman that James Lane had been writing to, and managed, by handing them over to his solicitor, to retrieve her sister's dowry of £2,000.

A few months later Augusta dutifully used her social contacts to secure a placement with Martin Colnaghi, then the most prominent art dealer in London, for Hugh, Adelaide's third son, who was nearing his 18th birthday and the end of his father's financial support. Augusta had never felt very sympathetic towards the delicate Hugh, and had been impatient with his unboyish dislike of ferrets and guns when Adelaide had brought him to Coole as a child.[40] He had remained reserved and sensitive, but he had obtained some informal training in the cleaning and restoring of paintings, so that when the question arose about how he was to earn a living Augusta approached her friend the Keeper of the Queen's Pictures, Sir John Robinson, to ask for a reference for Colnaghi.

Coole was let for the Christmas shooting season, so Augusta spent a frustrating winter at Roxborough and The Croft, relieved for part of the time by Robert. Augusta worried about his health (especially when he dropped out of a cross-country run after 10 miles, wheezing), and was heavy-hearted when he left for school. At The Croft she depended on being able to create a world apart with him, drawing, and reading Walter Scott to him. Robert, an affectionate child, was amenable to her tuition. He was also sensitive enough to her anxious attempts to entertain him and show him off on afternoons out from school, to cry a little when they parted. But he did not cling to her as she did to him. Augusta escaped to Coole on Shrove Tuesday. 'In spite of stormy weather I [am] enjoying the free & silent life here, have elbow room to write, & liberty of thought which is denied one at The Croft'.[41] Finally, she had been able to turn to Coole as the place where she could be herself.

This personal identification with Coole inspired her to think about improving the estate. Her first priority was trees. The growing of trees had a potent significance for Ascendancy families, who viewed them as an investment for future generations. But as each generation was thinking of future ones, where trees were concerned it was never quite right to fell. For Augusta, the planting of trees was a gesture of intent to stay. During her life, when she felt optimistic she would plant trees joyfully; when she felt pessimistic she would plant trees defiantly. Now, she planted larch and silver birch in bare patches in the nutwood. Reluctantly taking Frank's advice, she marked 40 spruce for cutting for the tenants' buildings and firewood, replacing them with 50 scotch pines, 30 spruce, 25 silver birches and 25 larch, in a hollow near the middle avenue. This tension between cutting trees to help tenants and not cutting trees would resurface repeatedly. The following year (April 1895) she engaged a gamekeeper, Mike John Dooley, calculating that the extra expense was worth the full-time eye and daily attention. She was instantly cheered by the sight of him with his two dogs and gun, and he stayed at Coole for the rest of Augusta's life. He, along with John Diveney, the groom and later the driver who also made hay and did other farm jobs, would later be important personalities in the lives of Augusta's grandchildren, people who could be relied on to protect them.

Augusta was also busy responding to tenants' requests, giving presents to supplement incomes after an illness or funeral, acting as an informal arbiter in disputes, providing the £10 needed to buy a son out of the army, refusing the appeals she thought unwarranted. Her empathy with the tenants grew and she would record news of their families, and make comparisons between them.

A turning point in this still slightly uncertain toing and froing between London and Coole came in April 1894, when, returning to London to find Sir Henry seriously ill with cancer, Augusta realised that now was the time to find an apartment and establish herself there permanently, if periodically. Robert was her priority. She had convinced herself that she could afford to spend £100 a year (€7,980, £5,477 sterling) on accommodation, calculating that in eight or nine years' time Robert would need the connections she had inherited from William, and that these friendships needed to be kept 'in constant repair' by her performance in the cut and thrust of dinner-table talk. If she was absent too long she was afraid she would 'become dull in society, whereas now I have the name of brightness & agreeability'. Against this she placed the long, solitary winter evenings at Coole 'when it grows dark at 5 or 6 . . . & both appetite & sleep desert me'. London was congenial to herself, too.

Enid accompanied her to view a third-floor apartment in Queen Anne's Gate, a quiet enclave of late seventeenth-century houses lying between the domestic prettiness of St James's Park and the towering authority of Westminster Abbey and the Houses of Parliament. Politicians found it useful as a base when the House was sitting, and there was a smattering of writers including Mrs Lynn Lynton, explorers such as H.H. Johnston, and John Cross, the widower of George Eliot. The apartment in Queen Anne's Mansions (Qmansions) was small, cost £95 a year and needed no servant. There was a restaurant, a public drawing-room on the sixth floor, a lift and electricity.[42] It was perfect for that rare thing, a solitary fashionable or busy woman, and Enid advised her to take it. Together they spent the next week buying wallpaper, furniture and pictures. Enid gave her a Chippendale chair for her writing table, and there was a framed print of Sir Henry Layard's portrait, curtains from St George's Place, and Giuseppe Longhi's *A lady renouncing her worldly goods*, which had been sold at Christie's for £21 after William's death and, ironically, given the title, re-acquired by Augusta for £28 after she had caught sight of it in a dealer's window from an omnibus. 'And so I set up house, & liked the independence, & the absence of housekeeping & servant troubles'.[43]

Enid sent her there in her carriage on 1 May with a heavy heart. Augusta stayed on and off for eight years, moving to a serviced flat on the seventh floor in 1902. She was occasionally frustrated by its small size, but used the restaurant for entertaining, and attended Westminster Abbey. She embarked on the pattern of spending term-time in London (though spring was sometimes spent at Coole or The Croft), and holidays at Coole.

In London, she spent mornings writing or attending drawing classes, borrowing books from Mudie's or shopping, lunches with friends, made calls in the afternoon or visits to Southwark, then teas, and dinners in the evening with perhaps a play afterwards. Whereas William alone in London in the 1880s had tended towards extravagance, Augusta had little problem being careful. Although she dined with aristocrats and met Alexandria, the Princess of Wales, she walked, took omnibuses, ate sandwiches in stations, and rarely bought anything other than food. When she gave dinners in the Qmansions restaurant they were strictly limited to 3s 6d per head. It was a life in which duties and concern for others were balanced by the pleasures of solitary writing and socialising. Nervous and busy, she was also plagued by bouts of illness and lethargy. She had struck out on her own, for Robert, and William would not, she felt, have found fault.

This was the season that she was due to take off her mourning black. On 19 April 1894, while her decision about the mourning was still pending, she attended the wedding of Mary Cole, a distant relative, who was remarrying, this time a much younger man. Augusta, appalled when she heard the bridegroom contradict 'some little order' of Mary's to her daughter, later noted in her diary, 'I would not like to put any man in that position over Robert!' The possibility of remarriage had, of course, occurred to her, but everything about the way she had set up her life in London – her apartment, her fledgling literary reputation – suggests that she had decided against. Perhaps to underline her unavailability and promise herself to maintain her independent and intellectual momentum, she decided to remain in black – black dresses, mantillas, shawls, coats, hats, sometimes decorated with glinting old fashioned jet beads, fine lace, or pleats – with at the most a white scarf at her neck, a string of pearls and, habitually, two bracelets – one of twisted gold from Egypt, the other with two stones – and a sapphire ring.[44] Remaining a conspicuous widow also allowed her to indulge in her love of conversation and witty repartee without her friends receiving the wrong messages. It was a convenient foil.

This spring of 1894 was one of her most fulfilled in London. Less intimate with high society than Enid, but with more contacts among Bohemians such as Raffalovich, Augusta also made new friends among the colonial administrators and politicians of William's generation and among poets and politicians of her own. She still wrote regular, newsy letters to Wilfrid Blunt. She had had a recuperative visit to Crabbet at Whitsun 1893, otherwise it was the odd luncheon or dinner if he was not abroad.

Henry Layard's illness, during which she was an almost daily visitor to Queen Anne Street, and his death in July 1894, brought her even closer to Enid. Meeting a dry-eyed Enid an hour after his death, she was instantly reminded of William's death and burst into tears, so that Enid, who felt turned to stone, had to comfort her.[45] When she had recovered her composure Augusta's emotion was converted into solicitous empathy and practical help. She slept in Enid's room until the funeral. In the autumn of 1895 she helped her move house, then took her on a tour of the west of England. In London, watching her formerly well-motivated friend sinking towards self-pity and 'querulousness', she characteristically diagnosed lack of occupation and encouraged her to become involved in Southwark.[46] But Enid was more concerned about her appearance, and instead persuaded a reluctant Augusta to embark on expensive teeth straightening. Augusta begrudged the money, but reasoned that she would soon have had tusks '& I don't think I ought to let myself grow repulsive'.[47]

Augusta tried, with her 'three & sixpennies' in the Qmansions restaurant, to bring unusual combinations of people together. One evening the dyer and silk manufacturer, Thomas Wardle, 'a novelty', was invited to talk embroidery silks 'to the ladies', and Indian silk worms to Sir Arthur Clay, while Augusta and Enid teased the elderly, dyspeptic Sir Frederic Burton 'to say which of us he liked the best'.[48] She remained critical of the ambitious and socially insecure Hugh Lane whom she dutifully invited to lunches and teas, irritated by his 'second rate fashionable talk & vulgarity of mind'.[49]

She met two poets during this busy early summer in London: Coventry Patmore, partly responsible for the mid-century definition of the ideal of womanhood evoked in

'The Angel of the House', and 'Yates'.[50] This was the 29-year-old W.B. Yeats. When Augusta met him two years later they would embark on a friendship that would be of crucial importance to both of them. This meeting, in summer 1894, was no more than a social encounter at Lord Morris's house. Yeats, fashionably interested in Continental Symbolist literature and attempting to make his own contribution to 'unpopular theatre', was to be seen about London in a long black cloak, soft black sombrero, and voluminous black silk tie, and was perhaps similarly attired when Augusta met him. She considered that he looked 'every inch a poet, though', she added, 'I think his prose "Celtic Twilight" is the best thing he has done'.[51] Yeats seems to have forgotten the encounter.

Edward Martyn (1859–1923), rich, Catholic, devout (though anti-clerical), literary, and physically and socially awkward, frequented her social circle in London. Seven years younger than Augusta, he lived near Coole in Tulira, where in 1882, his formidable mother, hoping he would attract a wealthy and well-connected wife, had persuaded him to demolish a modest Georgian house and add a richly decorated Gothic Revival mansion designed by George Ashlin to an existing Norman tower. But once it was completed Edward had taken up residence in the still spartan Norman tower and showed no inclination to marry. Bulky and self-absorbed he had been closer to William than Augusta in the 1880s.[52] After William's death Augusta successfully, and surprisingly, given his freely expressed misogyny, inherited him.[53] They had a mutual friend in Neville Geary, and the shared problem of Galway tenants.[54] Martyn was consistently kind to Robert, giving him a new gun after William's death and allowing him to shoot on his land.[55] She addressed Martyn with neighbourly formality as 'Mr Martyn' in her letters, but in her diary he appears as a reliable friend, unremarked on, available to make up the numbers at a dinner party. That summer he and Geary re-introduced her to George Moore.

George Moore was an art critic and writer with an estate in County Mayo. Augusta's exact contemporary, the fair, floppy-haired Moore had a reputation for making extravagant pronouncements liberally peppered with sex and scatology, and had written a string of novels and a memoir about his Bohemian life in Paris which the circulating libraries refused to stock as immoral. For many he epitomised the 1890s. He had just published *Esther Waters*, a novel about a servant who had to give up her illegitimate baby to a callous baby-farmer to earn money as a wet nurse. Augusta read it and welcomed his articulation of hardship and injustice.[56]

She, too, infused criticism of conventional morality into fiction in a short story she wrote this spring.[57] *Dies Iræ* tells the story of a woman punished by her Harley Street doctor husband for a week-long love affair. Convinced of her guilt, she accepts his punishment as long as her children remain innocent of her transgression. But when he tells them she rebels, denounces him as cruel and feels vindicated. Asserting the woman's perspective Augusta indicated that, newly independent as she had become, she felt distanced (or desired to be distanced) from the prevailing sexual politics of the time. She was not interested in sexual licence, but in freedom from an ethos that induced such a heavy burden of guilt on those who transgressed. There is in the story an implicit criticism of that authoritative group in Victorian society which she had so far tended to look up to unquestioningly. Although she still went to her husband's generation for approval, particularly for Robert, she was, at dinner parties and social events, increasingly focused on younger men with different social values. Dissatisfaction with the double standards of her husband's generation would only be one reaction against British society; its politics towards Ireland would begin to pall for her in the coming years.

At Coole for the summer of 1894, she was preoccupied with her family, glad to see Robert transformed into a plump and hearty boy playing with his friends, under strain when 'The Mrs' came for ten days in a whirlwind of ill humour and disruptive servants.

William's autobiography was published in October to some acclaim.[58] Frank Lawley, a friend well-briefed by Augusta, acknowledged her role and wrote in *The Daily Telegraph* that it was one of the most 'entertaining and instructive' books of recent years. Pre-publication, Augusta, now in London, was very nervous, unable to eat or sleep, anxiously distributing advance copies to, among others, Robert's prospective headmaster at Harrow. It was her most significant literary achievement to date, but she was deeply ambivalent about promoting herself; she wanted recognition, but felt it was not a woman's role to court public success. She would not admit to literary satisfaction – when asked if she felt three inches taller she countered, 'no, but ten years younger'.[59] Seven months later, however, she was not above slipping the book into conversation; when Lady Haliburton congratulated her on Robert's successful entry into Harrow, saying that 'it was his *mother*'s talent coming out', Augusta replied, 'I said no, it was like the book, I took no credit, I had only edited both'.[60]

Unfortunately there were too many people around who were connected with the events described in the autobiography, and during that autumn the objections piled up. At first Augusta was bewildered and upset, but, with a second edition decided on for December, she quickly gained a sense of purpose, sifting the trivial complaints from the significant, diligently rewriting or omitting as requested. She vented her frustration in private, complaining in her diary of the publisher's ineptitude and, unfairly, of the dullness of her female friends, Ladies Lyall, Hart and Grant Duff. 'I don't think I will have more than 6 again that I may keep them all in hand myself!'[61] Thus she gained a reputation of being feared by women, a fact that would be related by Mrs Martyn to Yeats two years later.[62] As usual she was kinder to men even though they had served her badly; they were influential and she bent over backwards not to antagonise them. She was puzzled that Sir Henry Layard had not warned her about the most controversial story, which involved Lord Dufferin's aunt, Caroline Norton. Dufferin was particularly antagonistic, and she went out of her way to ask his forgiveness for including it.

Despite this burst of activity and self-assertion, the autumn visit to London was curiously lacking in a sense of purpose. Augusta was not writing and felt frustrated with the triviality of her life, wistfully recording the odd occasion when she felt she was in touch with the larger world of ideas. Her frustration occasionally showed and she could be found to be reserved. She left in December, dispirited and gritting her teeth for a winter in Galway. Yet when she arrived at Coole she was aware of an inner buoyancy, 'but I feel it my right place, & must try to stay on & do my best by it.'[63] It was a decisive moment, as the balance, poised between Galway and London, slowly began to descend towards Ireland.

At the fulcrum of this balancing act was Augusta's sense of herself as having personal priorities and ambitions and, unhappily cooped up in The Croft in the early spring of 1895, her independent spirit burst out in a splendid and varied array of artistic and intellectual projects. Taking out a new sketchbook she drew old Galway buildings, which she called 'The Stones of Galway'. She read Arthur Balfour's *The Foundations of Belief*, critical that he did not find a place for science in a life lived in faith. And she wrote a short account of her memories of William's old friends, Abraham Hayward, Thomas Chenery and Alexander Kinglake, '"Eothen" and the Athenaeum Club'. There was nostalgia for their wit and panache, an easy assimilation of history, politics, autobiography, and the issues of the day, and plenty of humour and anecdote in the piece; it was the literary equivalent of dinner conversation. On one level it was written in homage to engaging literary figures of the previous generation, but there was also a sly debunking of the Athenaeum as she revealed their eccentricities.[64]

'Eothen' was an interesting stab at biography, in which Augusta showed (though it was not her intention to make this point directly) that if written from a woman's perspective, biography might be incomplete, partly subjective, based on oral sources; quite different from the authoritative portraits being incorporated in *The National Dictionary of Biography*. It reveals Augusta's sense of being an outsider, and the way she felt she could creatively overcome it. English intellectual society and Irish peasant society both appealed to her, and yet both were closed to her; in the latter case because of her class, in both cases because of her sex. Affection and friendship and female diplomacy were her entrance tickets. Increasingly she would direct her capacity for these towards the Irish rather than the English. The light tone and nostalgic manner of 'Eothen' effectively summed up her growing attitude to London society. Gradually the suspicion that it was ephemeral and unimportant for her would grow as Ireland took precedence in her affections.

SEVEN

New Directions

E. Martyn had also poets with him, Symonds [*sic*] &
Yeats – the latter full of charm & interest & the Celtic
revival –

August 1896, diary

'Ifeel that this Land Bill is the last of "Dobson's Three
Warnings",' Augusta wrote in her diary later in that
vibrant spring of 1895, '& am thankful that we landowners
have been given even a little time to prepare & to work
while it is day – It is necessary that as democracy gains
power our power should go – & God knows many of our
ancestors & forerunners have eaten or planted sour grapes
& we must not repine if our teeth are set on edge – I would
like to leave a good memory & not a "monument of
Champagne bottles".'[1]

The Liberals' new Land Bill would become another Land
Act in 1896, providing more Exchequer money and
encouragement for tenants to purchase land. This diary entry
of Augusta's was the first time that she had acknowledged
that power as well as land would and should be devolved to
the tenants. That did not mean she was anxious to relinquish
her role at Coole completely. Quite the reverse: '. . . & with
all that, I hope to save the *home* – the house & woods at least
for Robert.' She appreciated the presents that the tenants

bought for Robert with their rents in the summer of 1895, well aware that it was a result of the long tradition of Gregory negotiation, sympathy and kindness. Her Galway neighbour Edward Martyn, still intransigent and uninterested in tenant welfare, now had tenants who were disgruntled to the point of violence; his steward was shot at near the gate lodge at Coole, and Martyn was under police protection.[2]

Her open-mindedness to change deepened her sense of responsibility, for she was aware that her contribution to Gregory tradition might well be the last. She also hoped to salvage as much as possible. There was something else, too. As Augusta was becoming increasingly interested in Ireland, she was beginning to consider how she might contribute to its regeneration.

Augusta had been provoked into thinking about the need for a greater degree of justice in Irish politics by reading J.M. Froude's *The History of the English in Ireland in the Eighteenth Century* (1873–4). Froude was a Unionist who had no doubts that Ireland should be ruled by the English; in a fair but autocratic rather than democratic manner: 'Rule him [the Irishman] resolutely, and he will not rebel. Rule him justly, and he will follow you to the world's end.' But his research revealed the incompetence and injustice of much of British rule in the eighteenth century. '[It] has opened my eyes to the failings of the landlords,' Augusta acknowledged, '& I may say of all classes in Ireland in the past, & makes me anxious to do my duty & to bring Robert up to do his.' Froude also viewed Catholic Emancipation as a moral rights issue, arguing that the majority of the population of any country should not be permanently disqualified by their religion under a parliamentary government. This, which had also been William's opinion, Augusta, too, assimilated.

It was at this time that Augusta became more interested in the beliefs of her tenants and people in Gort. She later claimed that Yeats's recording of Sligo stories in *The Celtic Twilight* provoked her to do something similar for Galway.[3] However, she did not yet set out purposely to collect folklore, but she recorded any anecdotes she was given in her diary. On 16 April she made a note, without comment or judgement in the style of her later folklore, which inadvertently revealed her alertness to the imaginative and spiritual world of her tenants: 'Mrs Grubb called – Says a woman in George St Gort who had married a widower was at last induced to lay the ghost of his first wife who kept troubling her by appearing by killing a cock & sprinkling her pillow with it – but it was not successful – she died'.[4]

Augusta was also aware of the current debate on the persistence of superstition, and interested enough to contribute a letter to *The Spectator*. Reporting from 'the West' to an educated English audience as she did at London dinners, Augusta retold several stories in the Hiberno-English idiom they had been related to her, and made a few authoritative generalisations.[5] Although Douglas Hyde, the Gaelic scholar and folklorist, had already published several collections of folk stories and songs by this date, Augusta gave no indication that she had read them, nor of an awareness that an interest in folk stories might be associated with a revival of Gaelic culture.[6] But she was beginning to write the sort of folklore that Hyde was advocating: orally based and sensitive to the speaker. In October 1895 she met the folklorist Edward Clodd in London, and confident in her new interest, she discussed folklore and superstition with him.

Augusta had no doubts that Robert should follow Gregory tradition and go to Harrow School. In his autobiography William, who had excelled at school, had written that Harrow, although educationally narrow in his day, was a 'fine manly place', and that fagging (whereby younger boys acted as servants for older ones) compensated for spoiling at home.[7] In early April 1895, just before Robert's 14th birthday, Augusta worried whether her clever but scatty son should take what she regarded as a gruelling two-day scholarship exam. She wanted him to excel, but feared that prolonged work and concentration would make him ill.[8] Robert arrived home after the ordeal rosy, and with a classical scholarship (on the strength of his Latin verses), 'a great feather in his little cap, and £80 a year in his pocket, which will be a great help in his school bills', she told Enid. 'It seems so cruel his father could not have seen this,' she added. 'I don't think anything could have given so much pleasure and it would have been new life to him to watch R's progress at Harrow.'[9]

Robert started at Harrow in May. Visiting him a week later Augusta found him apprehensive; he was the only new boy in his house and nobody was telling him what was expected of him. Augusta found Harrow daunting. This made her an empathetic mother for the subdued Robert, and a new note of camaraderie entered her diary as she helped him to shop for supplies and settle down. Later she would appreciate the Harrow influence which kept boys 'silent and orderly . . . disciplined into conventionality less by the masters' influence than that of the school traditions'. She felt this repression was good for an Irish boy, but not for 'Saxons, [who] are already over-disciplined in that way'.[10]

In London, Augusta took up her usual activities, but her interest in social life was waning. The summer at Coole also ran along established lines. This year Edward Persse's children came. As usual Augusta found the boys appealing: the active, amenable and straightforward Richard, two years older than Robert; Standish, who had a deformed back, and whose interest in taxidermy she encouraged. She criticised the girls: Ethel for being sleepy, and Gwin for being withdrawn and watchful; both reluctant to display the feminine qualities she valued.

Her health was still intermittently poor. In the autumn of 1895 she had a persistent rash, no appetite, headaches, insomnia and crying 'from weakness'. Dr Maclagan blamed her poor eating and prescribed strychnine. The symptoms suggest stress. The 43-year-old Augusta had constructed what seemed to her to be a good life: diligent, involved and useful at Coole, sociable in London, thinking first of Robert, but with sufficient writing and editing to keep her busy. Still dominated by dutiful self-restraint, it was not a life which engaged her energies and expanded her interests to a significant degree. The Victorian ideal of womanhood, which had sustained her when William was alive, could no longer cover all areas of her life, but there was no obvious alternative. In the end she would be saved by her intellectual curiosity and an ability to take an opportunity swiftly when, the following summer, it was handed to her. However, she would continue to suffer periodically from headaches, especially when she was under pressure. She would never be one to indulge herself when she was alone. Determined to spend the minimum and resist the pressure to obtain a larger flat and servant (she refused to break into Robert's legacy or 'stop my charities & grow selfish'), she continued to be frugal; it was 'bread & butter for breakfast & 6 oysters [cheap then] for lunch', and the dogged intoning of, 'it is better to keep going & not to drop out until Robert starts in life'.[11]

Despite her ennui in London, Augusta was gripped by one thing: Ireland. She was still politically anti-Home Rule, but was willing to exchange ideas with interesting and diplomatic men like the writer and nationalist, Barry O'Brien. At Mary Kay's party on 5 December 1895 the two found common ground in a pragmatic assessment of the way politics worked in Ireland, agreeing that experience of Ireland counted for more than political credentials, and that current politicians of all hues were inadequate.

The alternative was for change in Ireland to bypass politics. The Irish would help themselves. Self-help lay behind Horace Plunkett's recently established Irish Agricultural Organisation Society (IAOS). A Unionist MP and owner of a large estate, Dunsany in County Meath, Plunkett was keen to encourage self-reliance, self-respect and optimism by bringing a measure of prosperity to small farmers. He aimed to avert the need for Home Rule, on the assumption that an educated and prosperous population would value a close connection to England.[12] The IAOS presided over thirty-three co-operative creameries and agricultural societies, through which farmers combined to sell and process milk and buy good quality seeds, manures and agricultural implements.

Although Plunkett had written on his work and attracted the support of several liberal landowners, Augusta did not make contact with him at this point. Instead, at Coole in February 1896, she tentatively ordered 1 ton of improved 'Wonder' seed potatoes in the hope that the tenants would buy them.[13] She tried to improve life for the inmates of Gort Workhouse by proposing they manufacture nets and start carpentry training. This had to be shelved due to the opposition of the local parish priest, Father Jerome Fahey who had considerable power in the workhouse.[14] Finally, she stimulated the linen-weaving workshop at Gort Convent industrial school by teaching the nuns to embroider on linen, supplying designs and making orders for sale at Irish Industries in London, an organisation set up by Lady Aberdeen, the wife of a viceroy, in 1886 to sell the products of Irish cottage industries.[15] Augusta had taken Enid's place at one of their London bazaars in 1894 and was a presence – 'for the sake of Gort' – at these St Patrick's Day events until 1900. But she disliked the talking and fuss of the other ladies, and never warmed to the whole process of selling the laboriously produced items to wealthy fashionable women for competitive prices.[16]

On 22 March 1896 Augusta's mother died. Augusta was at Coole, writing. A few weeks earlier she had reluctantly visited The Croft where Arabella was too ill to look after Mrs Persse. She observed again how her 80-year-old mother had twisted herself into disagreeable old age, volubly preoccupied with her will, dividing her family into poor unfortunates and the wickedly undeserving. Her greatest asset was Lime Park, a 530-acre estate adjacent to Roxborough, which she repeatedly dangled before her children, and as repeatedly withdrew. Augusta was determined to retain her decorum and had the satisfaction of hearing her mother say her visit was her 'annual treat'.[17] Looking back at her mother on the platform as she settled down into the train at Galway, Augusta suddenly saw her as a pale and 'languid' woman and knew she would never see her again. She nevertheless failed to respond to signs soon afterwards that she was dying, and was not present at her death. The funeral, on the following Thursday, predictably brought out the Galway Ascendancy crowd in their carriages and cars. Less predictable were the pedestrians of 'all creeds and classes', and the approving *Galway Express* which noted Mrs Persse's 'amiable and charitable disposition'. This is substantiated by records of her generosity in her last years in the local press.[18] This aspect of her mother's character was not appreciated by Augusta.

Augusta had never been close to her mother, and she could perhaps feel some satisfaction that she had given her the dutiful kindness and consideration that she felt she owed her in her dependent old age; more thoughtful care, perhaps, than her mother had ever given her. She was no doubt relieved that her mother had been released from what had become a crabbed and uncomfortable life, and that the burden of looking after her had been lifted from Augusta and the rest of her family.

The extent of Augusta's detachment from her mother is evident in the short, unfinished piece describing her mother's life that she wrote two weeks after the funeral. 'It is strange to think of her long life being over – I can hardly say if it was a very happy one,' she began.[19] In careful phrases she indicated her mother's weaknesses, but apportioned no blame, and the extreme evangelical creed that Augusta disliked, and which she regarded as having had such an immoral effect on her father, she merely described as 'unfortunate'. This biographical account was also a meditation on the uselessness of her mother's life, ineffectual with her father, nothing achieved (her many children were unmentioned). This was something that Augusta was determined, increasingly, not to repeat, and her mother's death may have subtly freed her from that familial example.[20]

One of the most disturbing facets of her mother's belief was her intolerance of Catholics; the atmosphere at The Croft had been blighted by the absurd ideas it fed. Augusta shared her mother's distaste for the Catholic creed. Eight years earlier, after attending Papal masses in Rome with William, she had written in her diary, 'a mummery as usual, the rites looking altogether pagan', 'feel more indignantly Protestant than ever.'[21] She also thought the Catholic Church imposed intolerable restrictions on thought, though she did not judge individuals on the basis of their religion. When her friend Mary Studd, her children grown, converted to Catholicism in 1921, Augusta told her that she had no objections, but would have had if the children had still been at home: 'I, knowing what the bondage of the mind imposed by the R.C. Church is especially in Ireland, I should have blamed her had she, who was free born, put the children into that bondage.'[22] But Augusta did not, as her mother crudely did, enlarge this distaste into an antagonism towards ordinary Catholics. It is possible that Augusta felt constrained in her more constructive attitude to the problems of Ireland while her mother was still alive – she had been a constant reminder of where she came from – and that her death was a release. A year later she was writing about the importance of the Act of Catholic Emancipation.

The sense of release from the past would be compounded in August when her eldest sister, Eliza, another virulent anti-Catholic, died. 'So strange that she & our mother should pass away in the same year – It seems as if a whole generation had gone,' Augusta mused in her diary. But this death brought greater responsibilities to Augusta. Eliza's family seemed to disintegrate in the absence of her strong personality. Walter, her husband, was soon committed to a mental asylum for a short period, his hold on life temporarily damaged. Her daughter, Fanny, unable, Augusta had previously observed, even to choose a servant without her mother's help, was also 'rudderless'.[23] It was Augusta who was called upon to devise distractions and deal with the practicalities. She stayed with Fanny for two weeks at her large Gothic Revival castle, Clonodfy (Castle Oliver) in County Limerick, and then went on to her mother's family home in County Cork where she found the sort of chronic disorder and disrepair that Maria Edgeworth had described in *Castle Rackrent*.

This came hard upon months of worry about Robert's health – measles, then whooping cough and confinement to the school sanatorium – and Augusta rushing from his bedside to the dinners and garden parties she still felt she should attend. He was 15 in May. As Robert got older Augusta's helpless anxiety for the child's welfare was gradually turning to a fear that he would grow away from her. In February, when he had failed to send a letter, she had worried about his inevitable bid for independence: 'Robert has not written this week – which saddens me a little, as if he was beginning to think less of me.' But on his 15th birthday Augusta allowed herself to hope that he would become a friend; '15 years old! I have looked forward rather to this birthday as an epoch, because my first *real* recollections of myself are at 15 – & because I first knew Paul at that age, & know how well we have got on ever since – & that I have not *bored* him but been always on terms of warm friendship – so I hope it may be the same with my little son.'[24]

There was an interval of respite ('rest at last for body – if not for mind') in a visit to Enid in Venice during May and June. Back in Ireland, Augusta was immediately overwhelmed by the demands of her family. Then, on Monday 27 July, visiting Florimond de Basterot at a cottage on his estate to meet the poet Paul Bourget, she encountered Edward Martyn and his two guests, the poets Arthur Symons and W.B. Yeats.[25] This time the meeting between Yeats and Augusta was to be the beginning of their long friendship.

W.B. Yeats and the Irish literary revival were the equivalent of Horace Plunkett and cooperation: both were home grown, predicated on a belief in indigenous Irish ability, and both aimed at a form of self-determination outside the political arena. Augusta did not mention the literary revival in her diary or letters before she met Yeats although, growing since the mid-1880s, it was no doubt familiar to her. Yeats and the Irish scholar Douglas Hyde were aware of the importance of publicity and had published articles in many newspapers and journals. One of the most lively issues was Hyde's distinguishing between the Irish language studied by scholars in manuscripts, and the surviving, though threatened, living language, 'vast, varied, very opulent', which he saw as a key to instilling national self-esteem and creating a sense of identity in Ireland. In his lecture, 'The Necessity for De-Anglicising Ireland', he argued that the Irish language and Gaelic culture should be revived and cultivated as a matter of urgency, though not at the expense of English, something that Augusta would have appreciated.[26] She would also have valued his insistence that such cultural issues were the concerns of both nationalists and unionists. Hyde was president of the avowedly non-political Gaelic League, set up in July 1893 to keep Irish as a spoken language.

Yeats had been publishing his poems and folk tales, as well as commenting critically in journal articles on historic and contemporary Irish literature.[27] He was particularly drawn to myths as a national art, familiar to everyone not just the educated few. In a letter in March 1895 to *United Ireland* he listed six Irish books of 'strong political feeling', which included the *History of Ireland in the Eighteenth Century* by Unionist historian, W.E.H. Lecky, the autobiography of United Irishman, Wolfe Tone and the *Jail Journal* of the revolutionary John Mitchel. Such a heterogeneous list would have appealed to Augusta. These articles, and the Irish literary societies he had set up in London and Dublin, had established Yeats as the conscience of the movement. If one entertained an idea of becoming involved, he was the obvious person to address.[28]

The appeal of the Irish Literary Revival for Augusta is obvious. It sought the regeneration of Ireland in an arena relatively untouched by political divisions. It was literary. It championed the vernacular and accessible rather than the scholarly and exclusive. It involved a group of dedicated, free-thinking young men, attractive to someone who was becoming disillusioned with the staid society of an older generation in London. There was in every initiative a sense of purpose; a collaborative working together towards what was so obviously needed. And much of what she had begun to touch on – the potency of the Irish language, the value of oral culture, the distinguishing of Irish history and culture from British traditions, the role of the Anglo-Irish in rejuvenating Ireland – was an integral part of the revival. One can imagine that Augusta felt excited by what she read and had begun to think how she might contribute. Whether or not she had got as far as planning to approach Yeats, when she was brought face to face with him she acted without hesitation.

Yeats was 31, intense, volatile and an incessant talker who spilled his plans and ideas with liberal abandon. His voice, with its 'hushed, musical, eerie tone' seemed to emanate from the 'faery world' that he so often evoked, while his dark looks, floppy hair, soft clothes and dreamy, haunted expression conjured the poet.[29] Yeats seemed to personify the imaginative, fantastical realm that he wrote about. He was an adventurer in the world of myth and imagination, a member of a secret society of mystics, The Hermetic Order of the Students of the Golden Dawn, a (sceptical) follower of the theosophist Madame Blavatsky, an avid reader of the poet William Blake and occult literature, as well as the Victorian poets and Irish writers. He was searching for archetypes and subjects for his poetry, and for what he regarded as the lost secrets once known to man, now obscured by materialism. He had met, fallen in love with and been rejected by Maud Gonne, but he was sympathetic to her nationalist politics and could be summoned by her in an instant.

Some of this was on display as the poets bantered with de Basterot at Duras that July afternoon. Yeats, inspired by his idea of an unbroken connection between Tulira and Martyn and the Middle Ages, talked rapidly of visions and invocations, as if, de Basterot, considered, he was a sorcerer.[30] Augusta was quiet, contented to observe. Her verdict was concisely summed up in her diary: she found Yeats 'full of charm & interest & the Celtic revival'.[31] Before she left Duras she had invited him to Coole.

She received him with her credentials ready: a letter from Bret Harte acknowledging the copy of *The Celtic Twilight* she had sent him, and folklore she had collected since she had last seen him.[32] Once her mind was made up to court Yeats she worked single-mindedly at her project. Yeats's friend, Symons, who felt displaced, was right in one sense when he observed that 'La Strega' (Italian for witch) put her 'terrible eye' on him; with almost supernatural intuition she seemed to understand that they, so superficially different, could work to mutual benefit together. She began by offering folklore.

Yeats, full of the medievalism of Tulira and a recent vision, found Coole too classical: 'I did not like the gold frames, some deep and full of ornament, round the pictures in the drawing-room; years were to pass before I came to understand the earlier nineteenth century and later eighteenth century, and to love that house more than all other houses,' he wrote in *Dramatis Personae*.[33] He gave the impression of being cautious about his middle-aged hostess; his subsequent *Dramatis Personae* description of his early impressions of Augusta carefully evoked a woman without beauty, vivacity or sexual appeal: 'Lady Gregory, as I first knew her, was a plainly dressed woman of forty-five, without obvious good looks, except the charm that comes from strength, intelligence and kindness.'[34] In an earlier draft he gave a warmer and less polished account of her, writing that her face had 'all the charm a vivid character can give by expression & with every charm of character'.[35] He was beguiled by the offer of folklore, for he was only too aware that, mystically inclined, subjective poet that he was, he was in danger of being cut off from the reality of Ireland. He wanted to find that reality through folklore and had come to the west to search for it. Augusta's *Spectator* article was waved aside, but her suggestion that she introduce him to some tenants who could give him fairy stories, and her offer that she collect for him, were accepted.

And taken up. One day during that August Yeats walked to the foot of a lane at Lissatunna to meet Augusta who had driven over, and she introduced him to an elderly man, Diviney, who had been plagued and harassed by 'them'.[36] It was on the way back that Augusta, having waited no doubt for a suitable moment, remembered asking Yeats what she could do to 'help Ireland', to which the discouraging reply was 'Buy Irish books'.[37] In fact, the sharply focused collecting that she was soon doing for Yeats was a revelation to Augusta; '[I] am surprised to find how full of [fairy lore] are the minds of the people – & how strong the belief in the invisible world around us'; systematic folklore collection was opening up a new world for her.[38] Thus began an association that would change both their lives. For Yeats it would be the stability that he lacked, the 'life of order and of labour, where all outward things were the image of an inward life', that he would find at Coole.[39] For Augusta it would be the discovery of a protégé whose genius she would nurture, and who would (to some extent inadvertently) guide her towards her life's work.

Augusta returned to London in the early spring of 1897 in a more purposeful and optimistic frame of mind. She learnt to ride a bicycle at the Queen's Club. She typed her folklore on a typewriter borrowed from Enid, and showed the stories to Lyall and Frederic Burton who expressed interest in their simplicity. She was provocatively pro-Irish in the current financial debate.[40] But, behind her more radically formulated defence of Ireland and her improved spirits, was the magnetic presence and promise of Yeats, 'my young countryman'.

Augusta was charmed by Yeats, dazzled by his conversation. Society watched as she enthusiastically issued invitations to her friends to meet Yeats, her 'interesting Celt' as Henry James cynically remarked. Jaded eyes might have judged him to be a new project, adopted to give herself a more interesting literary profile. In fact, it was Yeats, not society, that she was courting. She held dinners to introduce him to her friends. At one, half the conversation revolved around memories of Gladstone, while the other half featured Yeats giving an account of the mystic poet and painter George Russell; the old culture of recycled anecdotes versus the new more spontaneous culture that Yeats represented. She introduced him to Lyall, confident that Lyall would like 'his simple, modest, enthusiastic way', although few others have commented on Yeats's modesty or simplicity. Yeats stayed after Lyall had gone, and Augusta encouraged him to talk about his writing and plans to build a theatre.

On 16 March Augusta was finally introduced to the Unionist MP Horace Plunkett, a stooping figure (he suffered from recurrent bouts of dysentery) with a burning purpose. Two days later she was offering to make notes from Froude to give him an historical background on Irish grievances as a preparation for the debate on the Financial Bill.

Three days later she brought Plunkett, Barry O'Brien and Yeats together for dinner at Qmansions. The atmosphere was charged as, motivated by their hostess, O'Brien and Yeats tried to galvanise the quiet, modest Plunkett to take a strong line in his speech and attempt to unite the nationalists. After dinner, 'we come down & have coffee, & I give them cigarettes' and together they defined their shared political culture. Plunkett advanced the contentious idea that Parnell had been so dominant that he had 'crush[ed] national life instead of developing it'.[41] This idea would take root for Augusta and Yeats; a vigorous cultural life could be an alternative to politics, able to flourish at a time when politicians seemed emasculated, and divisive political issues were no longer so absorbing. It would strengthen their growing conviction of the importance of focusing on Irish culture.[42] At the end of the evening Augusta handed out her folklore to Yeats, Froude notes to Plunkett, Plunkett's agricultural pamphlet to O'Brien: '. . . so I think I did my best for them all – But whether any good to Ireland will come from the meeting is another question,' she concluded in a diary entry written in the present tense, conveying an excitement that she had not felt since the Arabi years. She had combined the roles of hostess and patron and made a bid to become involved. Next day a note from Plunkett assured her that her evening had been novel and beneficial.

Augusta was often with Enid this spring, dining, lunching, driving and helping her to prepare Henry Layard's memoirs. But she did not introduce her to Yeats. Presaging possible disaster when she did was Enid's meeting with George Moore on 28 March: Enid was one of Augusta's 'two ladies' who did not 'quite mak[e] out G. Moore – who is,' Augusta wrote, 'as enthusiastic as I am about Yeats.'

On 11 April 1897 Augusta presided over her final dinner of the season in which she invited her younger friends – Nevill Geary, Milly Childers, the barrister Arthur Du Cane, George Moore and Yeats – to celebrate the publication of Yeats's poems, *The Secret Rose* and in which Augusta confidently read out and dismissed a review of the collection in *The Saturday Review*. At lunch with Lord Morris the following day, Augusta pragmatically concealed the fact that she had just been elected to the Irish Literary Society, while he decried its members as a 'set of schemers'. No doubt aware of Augusta's friendship with Yeats and Plunkett, Lord Morris was vociferous in condemnation. Equally critical, she found both father and son snobbishly excited by their well-connected friends. 'I think my poor literary society friends know more of "the things that are more excellent",' she concluded somewhat priggishly. This tense encounter in a Unionist heartland was a fitting finale to a season in which Augusta had absorbed much of the ethos of Yeats's movement, had found its members receptive to her practical gestures and, most importantly, had established comfortable, loosely collaborative and friendly relations with its mercurial star.

EIGHT

Yeats Comes to Coole

No time to possess my soul . . .
1 January 1899, diary

Yeats's first extended visit to Coole in the summer of 1897 was a pivotal moment in Augusta's life, for the relationship that would sustain them both until her death 35 years later was set on a deep and secure footing. In the succeeding year Augusta would be irrevocably drawn into Yeats's world, forming an immediate rapport with each new person that she met – George Russell, John Synge, Yeats's father, John Butler – and identifying a useful role in each new project that they discussed – the theatre, folklore. There was an element of enchantment in the ease with which she seemed to be able to make an immediate difference. But she was also working hard at her own literary work. Meanwhile, the problem of maintaining a benevolent Gregory interest at Coole in changing times continued to press.

Augusta had two potentially conflicting and passionately held aims for Coole. On the one hand she wanted to hand Robert an unencumbered estate that would make no demands on his capital (from Gregory investments and the proceeds of future land sales) and would release him from dependence on a well-paid job, especially in exile abroad.[1] On the other hand she did not, under any circumstances, want to alienate the tenants. To realise the first ambition she needed rents to stay at their existing level. To realise the second she had to give in to tenants' demands. When she did her accounts in April 1897 she calculated that she could pay off the mortgage on the estate by putting away £500 a year for the next six years, although she wanted to do it in five, for Robert's coming of age.[2] But a week later she returned to Coole and Frank reminded her that the tenants would probably, within the next two years, appeal their rents in the Land Courts where both they and Augusta knew they could get a 25 per cent reduction. Although she was aware that this would reduce the chances of paying off the mortgage before Robert came of age, she responded stoically: '. . . if they ought to have it [the reduction], better so.'

Schooling Robert in the responsibilities and pleasures of the country gentleman, she hoped he would take on his inherited role. She had maintained the tradition of inviting friends and relatives to Coole for the annual shoot at Christmas, and when 15-year-old Robert shot his first woodcock, pheasant and snipe in January 1896 she felt a traditional pride.[3] She also tried to ensure there was sufficient land for shooting, buying land in Robert's name at Lisheen Crannagh across the lake in 1901.[4] To ensure that the tenants remained friendly she persisted in the old patronage, what she called 'gracious things': the giving of fire wood, medicines, clothes, advice. The majority of Coole tenants were still receptive to this. Augusta was constantly reminded of the influence of such gestures by Edward Martyn's neglect of them and consequent unpopularity with his tenants.[5] It was an irony that one way to work for a better future was to doggedly maintain the old relations.

Another tactic was to give the tenants a good start as independent farmers (and potentially prosperous and contented neighbours) by introducing efficient farming practices. She encouraged them to embrace Co-operation, which they did after Horace Plunkett addressed them in September 1897 outside the hall door at Coole, and the subsequent setting up of the Kiltartan Co-operative Society to buy wholesale quality seed and manure.[6]

Earlier that summer Augusta had made her first carefully worded gesture against Unionism. Queen Victoria's Diamond Jubilee had fallen on 21 June 1897. Galway loyalty was orchestrated from Lough Cutra by George Gough, who asked the local landowners to light bonfires. 'I refused, saying that after the long & marked neglect shown by the Queen to Ireland I thought it right to preserve an attitude of respectful disapproval.'[7] Gough responded with an emotional letter ('a sort of wail over a lost soul'), but in the event only those with English wives lit bonfires. Augusta noted that on the following night, St John's Eve, traditionally observed by the country people, the mountains were alive with bonfires.

Yeats spent the early summer not at Coole, but with Edward Martyn at Tulira. Taking fish to Mrs Martyn at the end of June, Augusta found Yeats 'white, haggard, voiceless'. It was her first vision of Yeats wasted in his fruitless pursuit of Maud Gonne. This time he had followed her into the nationalist demonstration against the Jubilee in Dublin and, alarmed by the latent violence of the crowds, had forcefully prevented her from addressing them and been scornfully chastised. The dignified Augusta had no time for Gonne's rabble-rousing, and she got Yeats to admit (or she intuited) that he too had found the proceedings tasteless and inappropriately directed from above. Even as Augusta felt sympathy for Yeats's physical plight, she was fighting the hold of Maud Gonne, convinced already that her own influence on the poet would be the better.

Yeats arrived at Coole for his first two-month visit on 27 July. He was accompanied by the 30-year-old George Russell (1867–1935), published poet, visionary, theosophist and painter, known by the pseudonym 'AE', whom Yeats had described to Augusta as a wild man; like his fictive character Michael Robartes, 'something between a peasant, a saint & a debauchee'.[8] Before his arrival Augusta, intimidated by this account, was anxious, but the minute Russell held out his hand she was reassured; he was a 'gentle quiet man – apparently "more in dread of me than I of him"'.

Yeats, exhausted and ill, was close to a nervous collapse, but, as was his habit, he rose to his audience with a stream of brilliant stories, 'pouring out his ideas in rapid succession – hair splitting – fanciful – full of wit & poetry, deep & subtle thought,' story after story of drunken publishers and fellow artists, that made Augusta laugh till she cried, impressed, delighted, indulgent. Russell by contrast was subdued, unbrushed rather than wild, unobtrusive in thick rural tweeds, his expression thoughtful and slightly speculative behind pince-nez. There was more of the shabby clerk (he was working as a cashier in a drapery shop) or the lower middle-class Church of Ireland northerner (his origins) than the mystic in his appearance. His occult pronouncements were abrupt and his explanations obscure; any exoticism about him seemed to be Yeats's creation, and his bald philosophy only served to show how the brilliant Yeats was able to mould such things to his own ends. But Augusta warmed to Russell, and she noted down the details of his life that he revealed in conversation. He had a self-restraint which mirrored her own self-control, and his ambition to remain obscure was close to the reticence that she cultivated, though for her it was not nearly such an attractive feature in a man as the ambition, and genius, which Yeats showed. Augusta appreciated the camaraderie of the poets and their keenness to pursue mystical experiences, taking them across the lake to a megalithic tomb and waiting patiently until they both saw a purple-clad Druid.

When Russell had gone Yeats was less inclined to conceal his inner turmoil. Instead, in the quiet evenings in the library, he found himself taking the attentive, sympathetic and tactful Lady Gregory into his confidence. Not fully. He did not mention his affair with the married Olivia Shakespear and its recent falling apart, nor the dreams and visions that were plaguing him night and day, and the sexual frustration that was leading to exhausting, defeating masturbation.[9] Instead, he told her about his early life and Maud Gonne. Augusta was deeply concerned. 'Poor boy he has had a hard struggle – For some time, when he was working at his "Usheen" & at the Blake book he had hardly enough to eat, & not enough for decent boots or clothes – & he says the bitter feeling of degradation haunted him for a long time.'[10] He described the devastation of his infatuation with Maud Gonne, which for a few years '"broke up his life" – he did nothing but write to her & see her & think of her – Then he grew stronger . . . But lately, at the Jubilee riots it all came back to him – & he suffers tortures of hope & fear'. Realising that he needed some light companionable work Augusta invited him to accompany her when she went out to collect folklore.

Augusta had become far more adventurous and adept in her folklore collecting since the previous summer. In the spring of 1897 she had rented a police barracks at Burren on the Galway Coast with Enid Layard.[11] There she had pragmatically questioned the household staff, searched for wells and gone into a souterrain within the circular earthen ramparts of a ring fort, popularly believed to be places where fairies gathered. The decorous Enid, who had not followed Augusta, observed that their 'gossoon' 'did not know of more than 3 people who had ever ventured inside & evidently thought Augusta very adventurous'. Augusta's apparent daring was, for a down-to-earth woman who 'never met anything worse than myself' in the haunted woods of Coole, not daring at all; she knew she would be impervious to the invisible world.[12] And, unlike Yeats, she was not personally drawn to the beliefs she described.

She had soon discovered that her notebook was an impediment when she asked people for stories. Instead she consciously trained her memory, writing the stories down afterwards. Later she claimed that she consequently lost 'in some measure that useful and practical side of memory that is concerned with names and dates and the multiplication table'. She was also inspired to remember the stories because she was attracted to the language: 'Even when I began to gather these stories,' she wrote in 1920, 'I cared less for the evidence given in them than for the beautiful rhythmic sentences in which they were told.'[13] Her memory for the words was remarkable, and it would allow her to use the rhythms, expressions and grammatical structures in her own creative work later.[14] There was, however, a significant barrier to her communication with the country people. In 1897 she had no Irish and, although many of the people were bilingual, it was a disadvantage.[15] Even when she had learnt Irish and could translate with ease she tended to rely on an interpreter if she met someone with limited English. She also translated the stories into English when she wrote them out.[16]

Augusta had discovered the need to cultivate a more personal relationship than questioner and respondent to encourage people to open up. Around Coole she relied on her local knowledge, exchanging news about her tenants. She was in the habit of coaxing stories from itinerant beggars, basket-makers, chicken-sellers, fishwomen and farmers who came to Coole, many on a regular basis – Curley the Piper, Power the Basketmaker, Mary the Dance – so that eventually they would come equipped with stories for her. The writer Signe Toksvig, a young guest at Coole in 1921, impressed by Augusta's kind enquiry about her work, has given us an insight into the profound charm Augusta could exercise on others. 'I felt – as farmers, stone cutters . . . beggars must have felt – that here was a woman without mockery, a human being without mockery, a human being in whom there was the safety of kindness and a keen simplicity of interest that warranted understanding.'[17]

Although Augusta was conscious that the storytellers were aware of her status as a well-born lady, she did not fully allow for the fact that telling their stories to Lady Gregory gave them a different context – and therefore subtly different meaning – from telling them around a fire at the end of a day's work to family and friends. Instead, she saw herself as holding up a 'clean mirror to tradition', a transparent medium between the people and the literary world. She was here comparing herself to Yeats who approached the stories with theories and, above all, his poetry in mind, whereas she had no theories. The awareness of context would be something that later folklorists would be more attuned to.

Augusta quickly realised that some tellers were more susceptible to visions, others were sceptical. She became fascinated by Biddy Early, a wise woman variously described as a healer or a witch. She was reputed to have had numerous husbands and her power was said to have the same source as that of the enchanters and magicians of the mythic past, introducing Augusta to the idea of an unbroken tradition with pagan roots.[18] Augusta collected stories about her, but, keen to piece together some biographical facts, she drove over Slieve Echtge and found her thatched cottage near Feakle, and discovered that she had been dead for twenty years.

Temporarily forgetting Yeats – she had promised to collect material for him – she wrote an article in the Burren and later sent it, to be published anonymously, to *The Spectator*. 'Irish Visions' reveals that she was enchanted by the revelation that the country people she had lived among for 45 years inhabited a world of belief of which she had had very little awareness. Her imagination was caught by the fact that the Burren landscape, the lives of the people, their beliefs and the words they used to describe their beliefs and experiences, seemed to be of a piece. Folklore was an intrinsic part of their lives, as natural as the landscape and an inevitable result of its airy blueness: 'Shadows of cloud and rock by day, shadows of thoughts, of dreams, of the dead, by night.'

So, the experienced and confident Augusta took a passive and dependent Yeats – dazed from illness and drugs that were being sent by friends – collecting stories in the summer of 1897. Ever alert to ways of downplaying her role, Augusta would later reverse this relationship, implying that she had been Yeats's assistant.[19] He was more of an outsider than Augusta and, in his black clothes and soft black hat, had the appearance and authority of a priest, an image that had to be altered. He often stayed outside the cottages that Augusta hurried into. George Moore would later paint a malicious picture of jackdaw Yeats, perched on a wall, waiting to pounce on whatever titbits Lady Gregory had garnered. In the autumn they collected stories in Spiddal, west of Galway City, and here Augusta might devise a more active role for him. On one occasion he asked for a cure for eye pain from a cautious healer. The strategy did not elicit information, but Augusta was impressed by the fear of both the healer and his wife as they fended off questions about the *sidhe* (fairies, pronounced shee).[20]

When they got back to Coole Augusta would write down and then type up the stories, a task that she found trying, '. . . very good training if I ever want to be private secretary!' she observed dryly in her diary. Yet she was determined to put her new-found techniques at Yeats's service, for he had decided to write a series of folklore articles to earn some much-needed money. She also gave him stories she had collected before his arrival. This helping of Yeats was particularly generous, for, as we have seen, Augusta was herself formulating her own vision of the meaning and value of folklore, which had the stories, collected and unanalysed, at the centre. Passing these precious stories to Yeats, she was aware that he regarded them merely as raw material to be hammered into shape by his poetic insight.

Augusta was initiating herself into the role of Yeats's patron. He was given a desk in the library from which he could see the Burren mountains – blue on days of cloud and sun, grey when it rained. Augusta was next door in the drawing-room, available for interruption: '. . . if I was typing in the drawing-room [there he would be] suddenly bursting in with some great new idea – & when it was expounded laughing & saying "I treat you, as my father says, as an anvil, to beat out my ideas on".'[21] They often discussed the meaning of the stories, concluding provocatively 'that Ireland is Pagan, not Xtian'.

During his two months' visit Augusta found Yeats to be a delightful friend, and exactly the sort of person she enjoyed seeing first thing in the morning and last thing at night: '. . . a most brilliant charming & loveable companion – never out of humour, simple, gentle – interested in all that went on', she wrote warmly in her diary. To have found Yeats so delightful on a daily basis had involved an intensive ministering to his physical, intellectual and emotional needs. Six years earlier the young poet Katherine Tynan had written on Yeats's departure after a few weeks' stay: 'He thinks all the rest of the world created to minister to him, and there is no rebuffing of him possible. I did nothing while he was here, nor should I if he was here a twelvemonth.'[22] But, having put Yeats centre stage, Augusta would discover there was ample room for herself and her work. For the time being she supplied information, acted as secretary and demonstrated interest and intelligence in her discussion of folklore. It was a form of collaboration. Disappointingly, Yeats did not do much writing on this visit, but the work cure that Augusta had prescribed had been successful; Yeats left physically improved and restored by the 'dream of peace' that had been his at Coole.[23]

The foundations of the relationship that would last for the next 35 years had been established. Lady Gregory, now 45, had indicated how she could become patron, mother figure, collaborator and confidante for Yeats. In Yeats and all that he represented she had found the vital spark of interest and passion that would lessen her reliance on the Victorian ideal of being a good mother. From now on she had a focus for the intellectual and emotional life that had been tentatively coming alive within her. It is notable that in her role as patron, confidante and assistant, she still subscribed to the broader Victorian ideal of service, making herself available to another, and it nicely complemented her role as custodian of Coole.

It is debatable whether Augusta's passionate concern for Yeats's well-being had a sexual rather than a maternal source, and biographers such as Foster and Frazier have speculated that Augusta might have fallen in love with a flirtatious but unattainable Yeats. Although it is not inconceivable there is much that is against this interpretation. Augusta had two loves that we know of, both with men – Wilfrid Blunt and John Quinn – who had a more practised sexuality and more confident treatment of women than Yeats displayed at this time. Although he was 33 in August 1897, Yeats, with his poverty, newly awakened sexuality (he had only recently lost his virginity), his intellectual hunger, his poetry, his reliance on his charm and conversation, his egotism and ambition, had the presence of a much younger man. It is much more likely that he appealed to Augusta as a son or young relative rather than as a lover. Then there is the fact that from this time Yeats addressed his letters to 'Dear Lady Gregory' while Augusta wrote to 'Dear Willie'. The difference seems today to reflect an imbalance in the relationship. But Yeats's more formal address was only normal for a man addressing a woman, especially an older woman; to use her first name would have been to put the relationship on a more sexual footing.[24] The less circumspect, emotionally open tone in Augusta's address could easily have come from a favourite, involved aunt to a vulnerable, interesting, delightful nephew. If she had fallen in love it is more likely that she would have tried to mask it with a more formal form of address.

It was in July 1897, while Yeats was staying with Martyn, that he and Augusta had the talk in the estate office at Duras which led to the founding of the Irish Literary Theatre, later to be the Abbey Theatre, the national theatre of Ireland. Since its detailed description in Augusta's book *Our Irish Theatre* this meeting has acquired the patina of myth; it was such an informal, contingent start, and fragile beginning to something that was to have such solid importance in Irish life.

Augusta was not particularly interested in the commercial theatre that she had experienced in London. She had sat through numerous dull comedies, finding amusement only by laughing at them. She had sampled the alternatives that were beginning to appear – the serious-minded realism of Ibsen, the protracted spectacle of Wagner – but without great enthusiasm.

Meanwhile, Yeats was impatient of contemporary commercial theatre and beginning to write plays. Impressed by theatrical experiments in England and France, he was interested in creating a literary theatre in Ireland in which the writer would direct rather than a principal actor manage. Such a theatre would perform plays that reflected contemporary ideas and mythological Irish themes. He had written such a play, *The Countess Kathleen*. He imagined Florence Farr, the beautiful, sexually liberated amateur actress with whom he had briefly collaborated in 1894, as his starring actress, intoning his verses as he directed.[25] Edward Martyn had written two plays with Irish themes: *The Heather Field*, set in the west of Ireland, was about a landlord with a passion to reclaim his land; *Maeve*, completed in June 1897, was based on folklore stories of Queen Maeve, and attempted to bring the psychological intricacy of Ibsen's dramas to Irish subjects.

Augusta knew of Yeats's ideas from their frequent talks earlier that year, but in the summer of 1897 he was on the point of letting them go because of the difficulty of raising money in Ireland. She had read the manuscript of *Maeve* and felt it would be a pity to stage such an Irish play in Germany, as Martyn was expecting to do. It was then that the visit to Duras where they were at leisure to talk, the wet day which confined them indoors, and the particular trust and sense of intellectual adventure that Yeats and Augusta shared, came into play. Augusta took Yeats into the estate office and, with tea set between them, encouraged him to expound his vision of an Irish theatre: '. . . & we talked until we saw Dublin as the Mecca of the Celt,' she wrote with gentle exaggeration later.[26] '. . . things seemed to grow possible as we talked,' she wrote in *Our Irish Theatre*, echoing a theme that would feature in many of her plays, 'and before the end of the afternoon we had made our plan.'[27] Yeats's ideas were grounded within the comfortable setting of Augusta's practical, patrician and optimistic sense of the possible – she was suggesting ways of raising money, making use of her well-born contacts – and within their shared ambition to move the Irish Literary Revival forward.

Yeats went to Coole a few days later to work out the practical details of finance, programme and venue with her. They decided to try to find guarantors to supply the £300[28] needed for an initial three years, and Augusta gave the first guarantee. She was the secretary for the provisional committee. Sitting down at William Gregory's elegant writing table in the drawing-room and pulling Enid's typewriter towards her, while Yeats paced about selecting the phrases to dictate for the manifesto (signed by herself, Yeats and Martyn) to be sent to the potential guarantors, they unconsciously set in motion a working relationship that would have a profound effect on both of them.

At this point there was little dissent from the secretary who typed sentences that she would later find pompous. And indeed orotund phrases such as 'to find in Ireland an uncorrupted and imaginative audience trained to listen by its passion for oratory', would never come naturally to Augusta, although she did believe that the Irish would take to high drama once they were presented with it.[29] She was also dubious about the title, Celtic Theatre, not having much insight into Yeats's involvement in the pan-Celtic movement. But she understood precisely the aim to turn the tables on the reputation of the Irish; Yeats's phrase that Ireland 'is not the home of buffoonery and of easy sentiment, as it has been represented, but the home of an ancient idealism' became a theme in a later article.[30] She believed the audience would materialise, and that Yeats was right to look for one that would respond to poetry and good writing rather than for commercial success. In their aim to cut loose from a mannered and superficial theatrical tradition, they echoed ideas that were being propounded from Moscow to Paris in the 1890s.

It was perhaps with some private misgivings that Augusta asked her Anglo-Irish friends to be guarantors; she was pitting loyalty to herself against distrust for projects tinged with Irish nationalism. But, having secured Aubrey de Vere's support she used his name to attract others and acquired a list which included the Lord Chancellor of Ireland, Lord and Lady Ardilaun, Emily Lawless, Jane Barlow and the Duchess of St Albans, Irish nationalist politicians such as T.M. Healy, John Dillon and John Redmond and those like Douglas Hyde and Horace Plunkett who were already involved in the movement. It was more difficult to find a building as the three licensed theatres in Dublin were too big and expensive. In the end they succeeded, with the help of Plunkett and their nationalist political supporters, Healy and Dillon, in changing the law (by inserting a clause in the Local Government (Ireland) Act) to bring Dublin into line with London, where special licences could be obtained for smaller halls. Their project was delayed for a year and the first spring season opened in 1899.

Augusta was excited by the activities of the summer, and wrote on 15 July to Blunt that there was now 'a Celtic revival going on in Ireland which is beginning to be very important.' 'Can't you find enough Irish blood in your veins to join it?' she added.[31] She half believed that he might get involved, and repeated the invitation in the same light vein six months later. But Blunt was not to be diverted from the orient (though he would write a play, *Fand*, for the Abbey), and Augusta's literary progress was largely managed without his help.

While Augusta was bound up with Yeats in the summer of 1897, Robert had two cousins to amuse him: Augusta's sister Gertrude's daughter, Geraldine Beauchamp, and Edward's son, Henry. Augusta felt sorry for the motherless Geraldine and her two sisters, and had first invited them to Coole the year before. Geraldine, who got on well with Robert, had returned for Christmas. So Robert was happily and conveniently occupied shooting, cycling, boating and playing cricket. But, 16 that May, he was also stimulated by his mother's new-found involvement in things that were by-passing him, and observed that he was keen to learn Irish. Augusta needed no second prompting and, after failing to find a teacher among her tenants ('all speak but none know the grammar'), like any new recruits to the Gaelic League they acquired Father O'Growney's *Simple Lessons in Irish* and began to work steadily through the exercises, checking the pronunciation with Mike Dooley, a tenant. Robert's commitment was challenged by his first partridge shoot at the end of August, but Augusta was launched as a serious student of Irish, and when she went to London in the autumn she made contact with Norma Borthwick of the Southwark Irish Literary Society, a pioneering Gaelic group, and arranged for a series of lessons.

Her great supporter in this project to learn Irish was Douglas Hyde. By 1897 both An Craoibhin, the author of Gaelic poems, and Douglas Hyde, the scholar, were well-known to be the same person. A courteous Anglo-Irishman dressed in tweeds, with an inner vitality conveyed by piercing eyes, he was, in the summer of 1897, a prominent figure in the language movement. As president of the Gaelic League he was busy touring the country to set up branches and appoint teachers of Irish. Augusta met him one day in the early autumn of 1897 when she was at Tulira. He was wheeling a broken bicycle up the drive after an exhausting day searching for evidence of the early nineteenth-century itinerant poet, Anthony Raftery (1779–1835).[32] She was immediately attracted to his enthusiasm, his sensitivity to the nuances of the language and the way he was haunted by the fragility of the dying oral culture. She invited him to Coole, showed him the local antiquities and introduced him to tenants who had stories of mythical Irish heroes. He would become a frequent visitor, both in the summer and for the winter shooting when he was impressively and enviably at ease, bagging pheasant and woodcock on the bogs with Robert and talking easily in Irish with people he met.[33]

Before leaving for London that autumn, Augusta visited the Morrises at Spiddal with Yeats. They collected folklore, and she encouraged two Irish-speaking schoolmasters to collect stories. She also searched for a manuscript of poems for Hyde. Sending him the manuscript she began the accompanying letter with a lightly flirtatious, 'Now don't you think I deserve credit as a detective?' It continued in an ebullient vein, full of enthusiasm and flattery.[34] He became her Irish teacher, sending stories and anecdotes in Irish, supplemented with encouraging comments.[35] She progressed steadily, quickly finding that reading was much easier than speaking, dismayed when her tenants failed to understand her Irish.

In London in early November 1897, Augusta's motherly concern for Yeats's health and well-being were very much in evidence. She was anxious about his domestic arrangements in Woburn Place – no one to wait on him, food to be bought and cooked himself. She sent bottled fruit, wine and biscuits, and a request to measure his windows for curtains. 'I do not know that I should have measured the window at all,' Yeats wrote with the measurements on 10 December. He was uncertain about whether the debt being incurred was a good thing, but he was glad of the attention.

Augusta registered the latter, and the food transmuted into money. Yeats later recalled in his autobiography how he had found twenty pounds behind his clock one evening after his guests had left. Refusing to take it back Augusta said he was to give up journalism and concentrate on his poetry. After that she occasionally gave him money. He was not, she told him, to consider it a loan, though he could return it some day if he became well off.[36]

This was not the casual gift of a wealthy woman who could just as easily have spent the money on a hat. Subsidising Yeats had been a serious decision, pitted directly against Robert: the paying off of the mortgage and the upkeep of the estate. There was no surplus. Any earnings were immediately earmarked – the £13 13*s* for an article received in May 1900 was set aside for the building of a chimney at Coole.[37] That Yeats's need should have been allowed to make a dent in Robert's provision, up to now her strict priority and almost her main reason for living, indicates that although her commitment was new, it was deep. Seventeen years later, replying to Yeats's offer to repay the money, she told him that she would have probably invested it for 'my children, if I had not thought it a better investment to help you to health & leisure, both as a service to Ireland & to creative literature – That is what my conscience said, apart from personal impulse & affection'.[38] Scrupulously putting him in the picture, she was recalling two feelings; the strong desire to help her new friend and the belief that he would be a great poet who should be helped. She knew the exact sum. 'Five hundred' (€39,903, £27,387 sterling), Yeats wrote in his autobiography, 'it was a shock to find I owed so much.'[39]

During the rest of 1897 and 1898 Augusta put herself at Yeats's service in a variety of ways, gradually establishing herself more securely as his patron. Patronage, second cousin to the landlord-tenant relationship, was something that Augusta instinctively understood. The patron, like the landlord, gives generously and requests carefully. Power should never press, unless debts are not being repaid. The patron, like the landlord, relies on others for a sense of achievement and self-worth. This would not be sufficient for Augusta, for she wanted to make her own mark. But she was resourceful and clever enough to exploit the role of patron; she instinctively knew that her service would be repaid, and that she could use her patronage to lay a foundation for her own work. The inherent danger was that her contemporaries would view her primarily as a patron, and this has been the lens through which Lady Gregory's achievement has often been viewed.

When Augusta gave Yeats her folklore material she did not anticipate that she was giving away an opportunity to publish under her own name. But in autumn 1897 James Knowles, the editor of the prestigious journal, *The Nineteenth Century*, asked her to write a folklore article. Unable to say that Yeats had her material, she procrastinated. But when Yeats's second article was turned down by *The New Review* she offered it to Knowles instead of hers, and he took it. 'So all was for the best,' here was an income for Yeats, entry for him into an influential literary circle, and, 'He is pleased.'

Augusta was happy to sacrifice her folklore material if Yeats spent his money pursuing his poetry. So she was angry when she learnt that he had spent the £15 from the second article, 'The Prisoners of the Gods', on a journey made at the bidding of Maud Gonne. Fifteen years later it still rankled. She told her friend John Quinn: 'There I had let him take my article to make the fifteen pounds to keep him in change, and he had gone off and spent it and "no purpose served, no object to be gained, no work to do".[40] Quinn, who admired Augusta's sense of purpose, could also see its limitations. 'These three phrases sum up Lady Gregory – work to be done, purpose to be served, object to be gained,' he noted privately. 'She didn't seem to understand that Yeats went off to Belfast because he was in love with Maud Gonne and wanted to be with her.'

Apart from feeling that her generosity had incurred a debt Augusta felt that, because she had given him the stories, the article was substantially hers. Yeats, however, because he had analysed and 'shaped' the material, felt it was his. Each felt that their contribution was the more important because they each had a different view of what made good folklore. So it was probably wise of Augusta to refuse Yeats's notably ambiguous offer in December 1898 to collaborate formally on what he called the 'big book of folklore' of which the articles were intended as the beginning. He claimed to be offering collaboration, but he carefully defined their roles, giving himself the more important task of structuring and writing, and Augusta the passages to be written in dialect. He was also reluctant to give her equal acknowledgement, suggesting he could add her name to future essays or include a note acknowledging an anonymous friend.[41] She replied, asking only that he acknowledge her as an anonymous friend in what would be his work, and give her a dedication: 'You know you meant to dedicate it to me, and I shall feel more pride in that than I could do in any success of my own,' she wrote with apparent self-abnegation.[42] The dedication would give her the prominence of a separate, inspirational identity. They were well matched; Yeats's letter showed him wanting to both repay debts and remain in control, while in her reply Augusta showed that she was able to give Yeats precedence while retaining her own initiative to work independently if she wished. She had also kept him vaguely, and so more securely, indebted to her. In the end, Augusta wrote the book, *Visions and Beliefs*, and Yeats contributed supplementary essays, but it was not finished until 1920.

It was in London at the meetings of the Irish Literary Society that Yeats and Augusta first began to operate in public as a pair, critical of the standards of debate, a certain defensiveness in argument and of a prevailing sense of inferiority. They were no doubt disconcerting, Yeats inattentive, then demolishing the opposition with a stream of well-chosen phrases while Augusta watched, calmly appreciative.[43] Augusta was occasionally called on to intervene when a diplomatic voice was needed. Appealing to the snobbishness of William Sharp, inclined to foppishness, she ousted him as chairman when Yeats was to speak on folklore. Afterwards she organised a party at the Metropole, the first of the many social events she would host for the movement. Although manipulation and arranging came easily to Augusta, this early effort for the Irish movement was recorded at length in her diary, suggesting that like most successful first attempts it was done self-consciously and with a sense of achievement.

Augusta continued to see old friends, but Yeats and her new interests were slowly driving a wedge between them and Augusta. Her new concerns even made her less sensitive to Enid. The following February she would be glad of Enid's company when she arrived in London suffering from a severe headache after her journey from Ireland. But she would be impatient when Enid reappeared unexpectedly at Qmansions later that evening where she was entertaining Yeats. Her annoyance was well concealed as Enid later recorded in her diary that Augusta invited her to dine to meet Yeats. And it is clear that the two women still confided in each other as each remarked in their diaries that Yeats's exuberant talk was above Enid's head.[44] But both knew that Augusta's poet was coming between them.

In November 1897 Yeats introduced Augusta to his father, John Butler, and his sisters, Susan (known as Lily) and Elizabeth (known as Lollie), at his family home in Bedford Park, Chiswick. Tall, bearded John Butler was loquacious and charming, a central figure in the artistic community at Bedford Park, a failed barrister and a painter. He was a very good artist, but he worked slowly and was financially unsuccessful. Augusta, who had seen enough of his work to realise that he could produce fresh, speaking portraits in a soft pencil – a cheap and relatively quick medium – commissioned him to produce a series of drawings of people involved in the literary movement.[45]

Although Augusta's relationship with John Butler would be productive, it was not immediately warm. Augusta would soon adopt his son's tone of mildly unsympathetic exasperation when referring to him and, after he tried to provoke her by declaring both the Church and the British Empire to be 'shams', she labelled him, not indulgently, an '*enfant terrible*'.[46] Augusta, sensitive to John Butler's financial problems, paid promptly for the drawings, but the artist felt ambiguous about this. Notorious for undercharging, he wrote uneasily to her, 'I have charged you a top price . . . I can only say it is very kind of you thus to deal with me on other than business principles.'[47] Gradually they would develop a mutual respect, and a fertile correspondence based on the ready interest each had for the details of the other's activities. But John Butler, who had a good insight into character, could, as late as 1912, write to his daughter Lily:

On the whole I am very glad that Lady Gregory 'got' Willie. Arthur Symons never speaks of her except as the

'Strega' which is the Italian for witch. I don't regret her witchcraft, though it is not easy personally to like her. They are all so prejudiced that they think her plays are put into shape by 'Willie' . . . which of course is nonsense. I for one won't turn against Lady Gregory. She is perfectly disinterested. She shows this disinterestedness. That is one of the reasons why she is so infernally haughty to lesser mortals – or whom she thinks lesser mortals.[48]

There is a sincere dislike of Augusta in that, despite the effort to be fair. It suggests he viewed Augusta through the prism of class, which kept him distant and made him particularly sensitive to the reserve in her that others also noted.

Augusta had developed a closer bond with George Russell since his visit to Coole the previous summer. It was rooted in their shared desire to see Yeats fulfil his potential, and their faith in Augusta's ability to make sure he did.[49] They affectionately mocked Yeats's obsession with prophesies and enthusiasm for unproductive '98 meetings, and agreed that Gonne was more desirable as a muse than a wife. Beyond this Augusta was not untouched by Russell's oblique outlook, and his desire to search for understanding rather than to grasp ready-made solutions. When she listed the pluses of 1898 in a diary entry of January 1899 she included their friendship: 'a great good . . . & has lead [sic] me to think less of the things that are seen & more of those that are unseen'.[50]

In November 1897 Yeats had encouraged Russell to set up co-operative banks in the West of Ireland for the IAOS. Yeats revelled in the unlikeliness of engaging a poet to do prosaic work, but convinced Russell and Plunkett that he had the necessary business acumen, idealism and charisma. But in the spring of 1898 Russell wrote from Mayo that he was depressed, and worried that his spiritual life was slipping away from him. Yeats was at a loss and turned to Augusta: 'Poor W. – he finds what a responsibility there is in trying to help others!' she wrote indulgently in her diary, and dispatched a copy of Thoreau's *Walden*, a literary model for the lonely life in adverse conditions, to Russell.

After that Russell confided his doubts and ambitions to her, and she encouraged him to persist in his work. Their essential differences were revealed when Augusta recommended that he read William Henley's poem, 'Invictus'. Augusta was encouraged by its rousing expression of the poet's faith in himself, but Russell was characteristically wary: 'I generally dally with an intellectual despair before I take up that condition of inflexible resistance,' he told her.[51]

For the last three and a half years Augusta had been editing the correspondence of William's grandfather, Under Secretary to Ireland 1813–35. *Mr Gregory's Letter-Box* was published in March 1898. Augusta had been encouraged by the Irish historian William Lecky and by the thought that she was discharging her duty to Robert by keeping the name of Gregory in the public mind. She had arranged the letters into chapters, which she had introduced. Inspired by her folklore collecting, she had supplemented the letters with interviews from relatives of Gregory's political associates and tenants to bring the period to life.

Before she began the work she had known little of the early nineteenth-century personalities involved: '. . . it was extraordinarily interesting,' she wrote to Blunt, 'to find their characters forming themselves by degrees until they seemed alive and talking to me.'[52] She focused on the Act of Catholic Emancipation as central to the period, writing sympathetically about the Catholic interest, while not criticising Gregory who had opposed it. Working on the book was an apprenticeship in nationalism as she articulated a pro-Catholic position and called on the perceptions of ordinary Irish people in her support. Her political views were refined and she had deepened her awareness of oral Irish culture. It was more than the family history she had originally intended and marked a transition for Augusta in which her feeling for the autobiographical, anecdotal and domestic was gradually shifting from being used in the service of the Gregorys to the service of Ireland. But this experience did not set Augusta against the Ascendancy whose work and achievement she valued: '. . . they were all, all honourable men . . . and truly anxious for the welfare of the country.' Manifestly she had a foot in each camp, and it was not particularly uncomfortable for her.

There were two different perceptions of the author when the book was published. Some saw her as a female aristocrat with literary leanings who had produced 'a delightful volume', while Irish friends such as Barry O'Brien and Lecky realised it was a serious piece of Irish history. It raised her literary profile, and for the first time associated her with nationalist views. Frederic Burton observed, 'I see a tendency to Home Rule in your own part.' She quickly refuted this suggestion, 'No, not to Home Rule, but I defy anyone to study Irish politics history without getting a dislike & distrust of England!'[53]

That spring Augusta's family delivered two shocks. On 15 March – her birthday – a letter from his tutor, Mr Bowen, at Harrow informed her that Robert, now 17, was bottom of his class through 'idleness', all chance that he might be head of school (as his father and grandfather had been) lost, the possibility of a glittering career receding. She received a good review of *Letter-Box* on the same day: 'A splendid review of *me* & my book in the World [*The World*] . . . but my heart is heavy all the time, I wd rather my book had failed & my boy done well.'

She had been totally unprepared for the bad news. Two months previously she had told Blunt: 'My own life is happy now and I *almost* say to the passing moment "stay". Robert is doing well, is in the VIth at Harrow; is shooting well at home,' inadvertently revealing the extent to which her personal happiness was welded to Robert's ability to perform well.[54] Only five days before Mr Bowen's letter she had been at Harrow and found nothing amiss. Her first reaction was to blame Robert for negligence and to self-pityingly compare herself with William's mother, whom she imagined had been consistently proud of her boy. It was only when Robert wrote her a despairing letter about having irrevocably lost his good position in the class that she realised how he had been hurt, and she began to blame the school for giving no warning that he was to be punished.

Two weeks later, on 26 March, she received a telegram from Rose telling her that her brother Gerald had died. Five years younger than Augusta, he had grown up with her. He had never married and, an alcoholic, he had spent a sad, unfulfilled life oscillating between Roxborough, The Croft and Frank's house at Ashfield near Gort. Augusta was shocked: she found herself retching and unable to eat; she became weak and lethargic. She got through Easter at Coole with Robert. But on 5 May, alone again, she set off for Inishere to recuperate. She imagined she would collect folklore for Yeats and learn Irish for Robert, but instead the visit would result in a lengthy and significant article published under her own name.

She walked about the sunken paths between the high stone walls of the island, sketched and collected stories and songs, and she heard accounts of how the Irish language was brutally beaten out of children with parents pressurised to collude. She was acutely aware of herself as an outsider, and when she heard there was another, John Synge, she failed to make contact, preferring to hug her privileged position to herself, a solitary explorer in an unknown land, although, she noted, he was in no hurry to salute her either.[55]

Reading *Don Quixote* and thinking about how Quixote and Sancho appeared to their hosts, she began to meditate on the way the Irish appeared to the English who look 'with half-tolerant, half-impatient patronage . . . [seeing in us] one part boastful quarrelsome adventurer, one part vulgar rollicking buffoon.'[56] She wrote an article, 'Ireland, Real and Ideal', to present the Irish as she now saw them to the English – one part bent on practical improvement as shown by the IAOS and Gaelic League, one part dreaming poet, as represented by the love songs and laments collected by Hyde and the fairy stories collected by 'Mr W.B. Yeats'. It was her first long article on Irish culture, and, in its definition of what might be called the self-help movements, and her identification of them as characteristic of contemporary Ireland and the main hope for the foreseeable future, it was a substantial contribution to the Revival. Typically, she was also thinking of people she wished to help and impress: Plunkett, Hyde and Yeats.[57]

Even before this article came out Augusta had had a measure of success in establishing herself as a patron at the heart of the Irish literary movement. Gratifyingly for her, her supporters emphasised her feminine qualities. In February 1898 her friend, the Unionist Gaelic League supporting editor of the *Kilkenny Moderator*, Standish O'Grady had evoked what the Edwardians regarded as the best sort of woman: prudent, wise, sympathetic, encouraging, providing personal friendship and good counsel. He described her sympathies as broad and amateur.[58] A year later, the gallant and patronising John Pentland Mahaffy, who put up a sustained fight against the study of the Irish language in the

National University and was an enemy of Hyde, noted that she had retained her sense of humour 'which will protect her from the absurdities into which the advocates of her project continually stray'.[59]

With her concern to appear to be playing the traditional female role, albeit on a non-domestic stage, it is not surprising that Lady Gregory's sense of personal independence did not translate into support for the growing suffragist movement. Instead, she avoided the movement and ran from domineering female aristocrats who espoused the cause: 'Called, in an incautious moment, on Lady Cork – who expressed gr joy at seeing me – & attacked me to help her in her crusade for women's rights – I tried to escape after a time – but she held me with cold fingers & a glittering eye – a regular lunatic.'

In Galway some of her Anglo-Irish neighbours regarded her as mad for supporting the Gaelic League, but, appreciated as 'an admirable woman of business' by local nationalists, her name was put forward in the election for members of the Board of Guardians for the Poor Law Union.[60] She was also gaining credit among her tenants for a sympathy that went beyond a concern for their physical welfare. One tenant said, 'I hope your Ladyship will have a high place in heaven & that when you get to heaven the blessed Virgin will come to meet you – for she was the highest lady that ever lived in the world, & was always meek & mild – & you are the same yourself.'[61] She was entering their mythology.

On 29 May 1898, the *Independent* cited Coole as the centre of the Revival: 'Coole is a rendezvous for the members of the rising Irish school. To those acquainted with the rollicking tradition of the neighbourhood in the old days, when duels and elopements, hunts and dances were the chief joy of existence, it seems almost incongruous to picture

"the feast of reason and the flow of soul" in those parts.'
This too, which seems to modern ears to undermine what it
purports to praise, would no doubt have pleased Lady
Gregory.

   In fact, Coole in the summer of 1898 did not yet have the
Revival atmosphere that it would become famous for.
Decoratively, little had changed in the tall, dark rich rooms,
lit in the evenings by fluttering candles, since the days of
William Gregory; Burton's sketches of the west of Ireland
that would later line the staircase, and Jack Yeats's drawings
and watercolours that would bring the horses, stones and
the harshly lined faces of the poor to the lofty rooms, were
not yet in place.[62] Now, as ever, there was the undercurrent
of Ascendancy life with the constant coming and going of
Robert, Geraldine Beauchamp and her sister, and Augusta's
13-year-old nephew, Henry Persse. And there was cricket.
Cricket had become an institution at Coole. It was one of
those English pastimes which was only haphazardly
translated to Ireland, open to reinterpretation by people
used to playing such games as burnt ball, or by those, such
as the competitive Charles Stewart Parnell, who imposed
their own character on the game. Robert's school-inspired
enthusiasm soon led to regular matches on the front lawn at
Coole in which a Coole team, composed of tenants and
employees captained by Robert, took on teams from nearby
Lough Cutra and a Galway Grammar School.[63] In the
summer of 1896 Augusta recorded; 'Robert very keen about
cricket – challenged Gort who beat us – & then return
match in which they beat him again.' Crossing out the 'him'
and replacing it with 'us' she revealed a certain slowness in
adopting the collective mentality of competitive games. That
summer the highlight was a match between Ennis and
Kiltartan, in which certain elderly onlookers could not
understand why Kiltartan beat Ennis 'when they had come

so far', while Augusta admired Robert's 'composure and style'.

Yeats came from late June to September, and this year worked harder, writing a novel and trying to learn Irish from Augusta. Russell came in September and saw visions with Yeats. In June, John Millington Synge (1871–1909) visited for two days fresh from Aran. This was Augusta's first meeting with the man who would briefly and brilliantly carry their theatre. A young man of 27 brought up in middle-class Dublin by an evangelical mother, Synge had the reflective, questioning manner that could have been mistaken as the temporary character of the student he then was, but was in fact his fundamental nature. He was keenly interested in making his own discoveries, watching and listening carefully and making what the English poet John Masefield called his 'deductions'. In Aran, where he had gone on Yeats's suggestion, Synge had encountered what he believed to be a still ancient and primitive culture. It was a place where he felt at home and which, capturing his imagination, he would put to literary use.[64] Lady Gregory was welcoming at Coole, though with the slightly stiff dignity of the upper classes, quite different from the mobile grace of the islanders.

Augusta and Synge had several common reference points. Both had evangelical mothers, and both had found Darwin a help in extricating themselves from evangelical dogma when they were young. But whereas Augusta still believed in God, Synge had long abandoned religion. He was also free from Augusta's sense of duty and need to observe conventions, except that he was unfailingly polite and morally scrupulous. In Synge, Augusta was presented with another creative artist, like Yeats, who lived according to the dictates of his imagination. Unlike Yeats, he had renounced poetic black for tweeds that harmonised with nature; he was not self-consciously the artist. Where Augusta was free with quotations, Synge preferred to coin his own phrases. Augusta perceived his integrity, but was irritated when he did not play his part in general conversation: 'He was quite direct, sincere and simple, not only a good listener, but too good a one, not speaking much in general society,' she wrote in 1912.[65]

There was, however, an immediate rapport between Yeats, Synge and Augusta as they described singers and storytellers they had met, and recounted stories they had heard on the Aran Islands.[66] Synge would leave Coole with a bundle of articles and Augusta would later record that they became friends at once.[67] But Synge, self-contained, did not need Augusta as Yeats did, so that, with her need to be needed, there would remain a distance, subtle but definite, between them.

It had been an enjoyable and productive summer for Augusta. There is a photograph of her sitting on an elegant garden bench on the lawn with Yeats and another person, which could have been taken during this time. As befits a woman of her period, she is sitting upright, her hands together in her lap, while Yeats leans back, his legs outstretched, one arm casually flung over the back of the bench. Augusta looks at the camera from underneath the spreading black hat that she habitually wore at this time. She is smiling.

NINE

Patron of the Revival

... we are not working for Home Rule, we are preparing for it.

24 February 1900, diary

The next two years were important for Augusta as the Irish Literary Theatre was launched and, more informally, Coole became established as a place of literary activity which fed the Revival. In both of these Augusta's presence was crucial. It was also a time for learning. Augusta developed a familiarity with the culture of her country neighbours, which would underpin her subsequent creative work, and she devised a political stance derived from the ambiguities of her personal situation, which would have a profound effect on the voice of the theatre. She also discovered that there were several people with designs on Yeats who subtly threatened her position as patron.

Maud Gonne had, since Augusta's first companionable summer in Coole with Yeats, remained a potent presence. Yeats was, more than ever, Gonne's creature, prepared to do almost anything for her; he hoped that one day she would marry him. She in return was vacillatory and ambivalent. Augusta was anxious that Gonne might eventually carry him away from her influence. But she was more immediately concerned by the way Maud's behaviour threw Yeats into despondency, distracted him from writing and dragged him into the frustratingly petty infighting of her political activities for the anniversary of 1798. There were compensations. Yeats would periodically tell Augusta where he stood with Maud. On 3 October 1897 he wrote, 'She is very kind & friendly, but whether more than that I cannot tell.' Augusta, careful to remain a sympathetic friend, tried not to voice her scepticism that Maud was thinking primarily of herself. On the other hand, convinced that Yeats needed what she, Augusta, could give, she did not want to encourage him to rely on Maud. In February 1898 she counselled caution – 'I advised him not to press her while she is so taken up with '98' – while keeping her distrust for her diary. After reporting that Yeats was wondering whether Maud was keeping him to fall back on in old age, Augusta added a tart, 'which is quite likely'.[1]

The political styles of Lady Gregory and Maud Gonne could not have been more different. Where Augusta was cautious in coming to the nationalist view, and reticent in the public expression of her opinions, Gonne was one of the loudest of the loud and reckless nationalist voices that rang out in 1898. Yeats, whose political taste inclined towards Lady Gregory, allowed himself to get drawn into the more radical movement on Gonne's behalf. Here again, Augusta was put into a difficult position: she could never follow Yeats in support of Gonne, but she did not want momentary political differences to come between herself and Yeats. As a solution she distinguished between the admirable intention in 1798 ('an attempt for national freedom') and regrettable execution ('a massacre of Protestants'). 'I have no idea of celebrating that [the latter], but if he likes to celebrate the intention, well & good.'[2]

Her diplomacy was tested in February 1898, for she was scandalised by Gonne's proposal to incite the country people to kill the landlords' cattle for food in order to force the government to fire on the people to draw political attention to their case. It struck at the root of her carefully nurtured landlord–tenant relationship and confirmed Augusta's suspicion that Maud Gonne was essentially self-seeking. She abandoned caution and angrily condemned Gonne to Yeats:

> I was aghast, & spoke very strongly, telling him first that the famine itself is problematic, that if it exists there are other ways of meeting it, that we who are above the people in means & education, ought, were it a real famine, to be ready to share all we have with them, but that even supposing starvation was before them it wd be for us to teach them to die with courage [rather] than to live by robbery – that the attempt would end in arrests – Miss Gonne would, if she suffered by imprisonment also gain by it the notoriety she wants – but the poor people sent to prison would have no such consolation – In all the crimes that have been condoned in Ireland, sheepstealing has been held in horror by the people, & it wd be a terrible responsibility to blunt their moral sensitiveness by leading them to it –.[3]

Augusta convinced Yeats to try to dissuade Gonne from these arguments. He had initially told Gonne that her proposed actions would be a political mistake, but that he was prepared to support her: '. . . he had only thought of the matter as it wd affect her – not as it would affect the people (which I fancy is her point of view also).' Augusta did not criticise Yeats's misplaced loyalties, instead she pitied him and allowed her mistrust for Gonne to deepen: 'Poor boy, she is for the second time breaking up his life –'. 'Some Hermetic seer has had a vision in which he has been given a message to "tell Maud Gonne to light the seven stars" – This will set her off on a new war path –'.

Augusta went to visit Enid Layard in Venice for two months in the autumn of 1898. While she was there Yeats and Maud drew closer together in an atmosphere charged by occult preoccupations and powerfully suggestive dreams. But when Maud told him about her affair with Lucien Millevoye and the two children she had had it was to Augusta – the calm, sympathetic, detached person he needed – that Yeats turned, 'my most true friend'. He wrote her several contradictory, vague, deeply felt letters, telling her as much as he could without giving away any of Gonne's secrets.

Augusta left Venice for London on 13 December. Waiting for her at Qmansions were more distracted letters from Yeats, asking her to go to Dublin. There she found Yeats hopeful that Maud Gonne would marry him: '. . . it seems to be all for good – if marriage with her will be good', she noted in her diary. But when she saw Gonne she could not suppress within herself a personal horror at the prospect. A year previously she had seen a photograph of Gonne and concurred in her beauty, but now she was shocked: '. . . instead of beauty I saw a death's head'. Despite this, and the constraint imposed by the fact that Augusta knew more than Gonne realised, they were amicable, as befitted two society ladies. Knowing that marriage was Yeats's deep desire and committed to supporting him, Augusta took it upon herself in the succeeding months to encourage him to pursue Gonne. At New Year she wrote advocating that he look for 'peace and happiness'; 'I believe that suffering has done all it can do for your soul . . .'[4] Yeats followed Gonne to Paris, but returned to London in February depressed by her coldness and her own depression, and Augusta was confirmed in her suspicion that Gonne was merely playing with him, expressing her disgust to Enid by quoting a tenant: 'I don't wish her any harm, but God is unjust if she dies a quiet death!'[5]

In January 1899, after an uproarious Punch and Judy show in Irish for the workhouse in which the English-speaking policeman was abused to loud appreciation, the Kiltartan branch of the Gaelic League was inaugurated. Although most people in the area were bilingual, those in positions of responsibility rarely spoke Irish. The branch would try to reinstate Irish as a respected form of communication, and provide the lessons in basic reading and writing which the national school ignored.[6]

Augusta valued the Gaelic League as a non-political organisation. She became more personally involved at this time, attending the annual Galway Feis – a festival of Irish singing liberally sprinkled with Gaelic League speechifying – in September 1898 with Yeats, and, one of the few involved from the upper classes, she had allowed herself to be put on the national committee in November 1898, though she was privately reluctant to be associated with men such as the two anti-Parnellite nationalists, Michael Davitt and Archbishop Walsh, whom she described as 'ruffians' in a letter to Yeats.[7] Norma Borthwick was installed in the Coole gate lodge to give Irish classes, Augusta's workmen were encouraged to bind themselves to speak only Irish, and that summer Hyde and Yeats gave lectures at Gort Courthouse, which Augusta reported in the Gaelic League paper, *An Claidheamh Soluis*.[8]

The first county council elections were held in 1899. Kiltartan had four candidates: three local men including a Gort publican and Augusta's brother-in-law, Walter Shawe Taylor. Augusta paternalistically welcomed the chance it gave for the (limited) exercise of power: 'The people have kept the power in their own hands [Shawe Taylor was not voted in] & this is best, they will learn by responsibility.'[9]

Robert, however, was, not unexpectedly, moving in a different direction politically. Once in the VIth form at Harrow he had begun to reveal a sympathy for imperialism;

he particularly wanted to see the navy augmented and had helped to form a Navy League. In the summer of 1898 Augusta, who had been talking to him about the Irish Revival, was not unduly troubled, telling Blunt, 'I don't much mind what he takes up so that he is enthusiastic about it.'[10] Then in January 1899 he showed a more direct sympathy for the Unionists. They had been discussing the possibility of a general election and she had said that as the Conservatives still seemed to have support they may last their full seven years, adding, probingly, '"& perhaps the election won't come until you are able to support, as I hope, the Liberal side?" – He grew a little red & said "I would not do that – They will never spend as much money on the navy as the Conservatives".'[11] Augusta, now that she was being tested, was tolerant: 'This is rather an epoch, for he has assented to my opinions until now – He must work out his own salvation & anyhow I think he will always be fond of Ireland & the people.'

Far from shielding Robert from the politics she increasingly despised, she had exposed him fully to the Anglo-Irish culture – Persses, Harrow – that he had been born into, realising that censorship and denial would be counter-productive, and hopeful that even if he became a Unionist he would have a sense of duty as a landlord. A letter from Lord Gough to Augusta, written just after Robert's coming of age, indicates that she made no secret of her attitude.[12] But, now that it looked likely, she could not entertain the idea that they might end up on different sides of the political divide with equanimity. In her worst moments she was afraid that she had not even convinced him on the need to care for the tenants. Meeting the imperialist Lord Westmeath a few months after that January conversation with Robert, she listened with distaste to his diatribe against the Irish: 'The people have no common

sense, no energy – no industry'. When she got home she
wrote with feeling in her diary, 'I hope Robert will never
grow like that!' She, meanwhile, had no wish to alienate
him, or his prospective patrons in London, by the
articulation of her increasingly nationalist sympathies. It
was part of the deeper fear that he would grow apart from
her and one day perhaps stop loving her.

But in 1899, Robert, 18 that May, was still very much an
unformed and dreamy boy. A photograph taken for his
coming of age three years later shows him dutifully
immaculate.[13] He was all she wanted: open, gentle,
affectionate, respectful, without the arrogance and distance
that the public school system could inculcate. He was also
good fun. She took him to Rome for Easter 1900, keen to
show him something of her former life with his father. They
strolled in the formal Pincio gardens overlooking the city,
had tea with old friends in lavishly decorated villas and
urban palaces, visited the churches and museums. She was
proud to show off 'my fair little sonnikin' at an Embassy
ball, touched that his first 'great party' should be at the same
place as hers had been: '. . . he did his mamma very nicely,'
she noted with satisfaction.[14] They were light-hearted
companions, amused by a 'flock' of Cooks tourists in the
forum, entertained by the extravagant hats at the show-
jumping in the Villa Borghese gardens. She took him on a
pilgrimage to the graves of Tyrconnell and Hugh O'Neill,
two of the Catholic Gaelic leaders who had fled Ireland after
the battle of Kinsale in 1601. After Rome they toured Italy,
companionably taking out their sketchbooks, Robert to
draw people, Augusta scenes.

Her responsibility to get Robert established in a career
also weighed heavily, and in February 1899 Augusta
consulted Paul Harvey and Willie Peel. With Robert's
agreement she had decided to investigate the possibility of a

political career, starting with a clerkship at the House of Commons. Through Willie Peel's father (a Speaker and the son of Sir Robert Peel, Sir William's political patron in the 1840s) she was put in touch with the clerk assistant, Archibald Milman. The outcome was disappointing as Milman refused to nominate the still too young Robert as a clerk. He tried for Oxford instead, and in the autumn of 1899 went up to New College to read Classics.

The Irish Literary Theatre planned to begin its three-year experiment with performances of Yeats's *The Countess Kathleen* and Edward Martyn's *The Heather Field* on 8 and 9 May 1899 at the Antient [*sic*] Concert Rooms (on what is now Pearse Street) in Dublin. Yeats publicised it by generating controversy in Plunkett's sympathetic *Daily Express*. George Moore, full of confidence, and convinced that the new theatre was part of a vital Irish renaissance with which he wanted to be involved, had made contact with them. Unlike Yeats, Augusta and Martyn, he had some experience of the theatre, having successfully rewritten a play and become a notable critic in London, championing Ibsen. Yeats secured Florence Farr as stage manager. Augusta was a reliable, if background presence, only too aware of the clashing egos, and potentially conflicting agendas of the organisers and their potential audience.

Her diplomatic skills were required as soon as the plays went into rehearsal for George Moore sacked Florence Farr after dinner in Qmansions on 5 March.[15] Augusta saw that he was right, but that Yeats and Farr would need careful treatment. Her peacekeeping was made more difficult by the fact that Yeats, in his efforts to woo neither Unionists nor nationalists, was in danger of alienating both. Unionist supporters were particularly valuable as some were guarantors, so when Yeats refused to help the Chief

Secretary's wife, Betty Balfour, and Daisy Fingall stage *tableaux vivants* based on *The Countess Kathleen* in January at the Chief Secretary's Lodge in Phoenix Park, Augusta made sure she maintained cordial relations with these women through the Irish Industries sales of work.

Meanwhile, Yeats's play, *The Countess Kathleen*, seemed designed to offend nationalists. An experimental verse play, it was regarded as too highbrow for the majority by nationalists such as Arthur Griffith, the editor of the *United Irishman*. Worse, set during the famine it featured a countess who, in a bid to save her starving people who were selling their souls, offered her own soul in exchange for their salvation, and was thus a direct challenge to Catholics. This was particularly provocative at a time when advanced nationalists were beginning to raise the sceptre of religious (i.e. Catholic) and sexual purity as the mainspring of Irish national identity.[16]

Augusta was called to act when Edward Martyn, alarmed by priestly pronouncements that the play was heretical, withdrew his (considerable) financial and artistic support. She immediately appreciated that it was a bad example for the other guarantors and feared it would reflect badly on Ireland.[17] Confident that she could convince Martyn of the religious orthodoxy of the play and, one suspects, relishing the challenge, she invited him to lunch with enlightened Catholics, Moore and T.P. Gill, who '[made] little of Ed.'s objections', and Martyn agreed to submit the play to two priests who, fortunately, passed it, securing Martyn's continued support for the time being.

There was heckling during the first performance, inspired by a nationalist pamphlet denouncing the play.[18] It was their first experience of the volatility of Dublin audiences. While Moore was disdainful of the audience's lack of sophistication, Yeats oscillated between alarm and appreciation of how controversy promoted, and Augusta quietly noted the pitfall of introducing divisive issues such as religion or politics into plays. Augusta was given the job of setting the record straight, a task she was well suited to, for, despite her delight in verbal debate, her instinct was that arguments should be won and that this was done by clearly setting out the case in writing. She was no George Bernard Shaw, who used controversy as a creative adjunct to his plays, while Russell and Yeats had a better grasp of the value of publicity per se than she did. She had an independent aura; she was a valued supporter of the Gaelic League, on friendly terms with the Establishment and detached from public controversy. In an article for the February 1900 issue of *Beltaine*, an occasional journal set up by Yeats for the theatre, she diplomatically quoted from newspaper articles and systematically demolished each objection.[19]

In the summer of 1899, while Yeats was at Coole writing *The Shadowy Waters* and articles on the literary movement, and as Hyde discussed and collected folklore, Augusta reported on a Gaelic League meeting in Gort, and wrote a one-act play for children. The idea had come to her the previous December on the train back from Venice, when, drowsily listening to the sound of the engine, she had found herself intoning the words of the legend of the birth of St Colman, a Kiltartan saint.[20] *Colman and Guaire*, based on local legend, was written in verse – 'gentle doggerel', she later judged – in standard English, and, in its depicting of miraculous occurrences in a strongly defined romantic landscape, suggests that Tennyson's *Morte d'Arthur* had been her inspiration.[21] But, instead of discussing its performance with the parish priest Father Fahey as she had planned, she put it away. It was a false start. Victorian poetry was the wrong template and standard English the wrong medium. But she was happy in her instinct to go to folklore for her subject, and when her guests left in October she went in search of Raftery.

Anthony Raftery, who died in 1835, blind and reliant on the hospitality of the poor, had travelled the undulating, boulder-strewn East Galway countryside before the famine, playing his fiddle and singing songs. Some of these were confessional, some sparked by people he met – he eulogised his friends, cursed those who had thwarted him, evoked feasts, death, love and sex – and some were political, reflecting popular anti-English sentiments during the Tithe War or counselling pragmatism and good sense. He was a character that was still vividly remembered, and he represented the Irish oral tradition that had been significantly damaged by the famine.

For Augusta, Raftery had the lure of the local and the pertinent. He was also her quarry, elusive but knowable. 'As I heard of him in many thatched houses his image grew,' she wrote later in *Seventy Years*. 'It was almost like Browning's excitement, "Ah, did you once see Shelley plain?"'[22] She followed him persistently, cunningly, independently, not to trump her erstwhile collaborators, but from some instinct that he would be her mentor. She posed as his patron, but she was in fact his student, learning from knowledge of him about the workings of the society that was to become the subject of her plays.

Hyde and Yeats were both interested in Raftery's verse.[23] Hyde had found the house where Raftery had died and Thomas Concannon had written in the Gaelic League journal, *An Claideamh Soluis*, about Raftery's unmarked grave. Augusta, setting off in her phaeton to the nearby village of Craughwell one hazy October day, went to look for the grave.[24] She found it outside the village, at the ruined medieval church of Killeeneen, surrounded by tall trees and

Victorian high crosses, and overlooked by a substantial thatched cottage. Here, miraculously, she met two men who had been at Raftery's funeral, who could show her the grave and add to the myths she had heard about his death. She commissioned a local stonemason to make a headstone, and was, unexpectedly, given a hand-written book of Raftery's poems by a woman living nearby. As she walked to her phaeton in Craughwell the silence of the road was broken by the hounds and horses of the Galway hunt which soon surrounded her. When the master and his wife overtook her she savoured the fact that she was privy to knowledge of a poet who had once trodden this road, honoured by the people and unheard of by the landowners. From now on she was vividly aware of a world adjacent but parallel to the one she had known since childhood; where she had travelled in phaeton or carriage between Roxborough, Castle Taylor, Moyne Park and Lough Cutra, Raftery had trodden the boreens between Ballylee, Athenry, Kiltartan Cross and Kinvara.

She returned to Coole in great excitement with the manuscript, and immediately sat down to write to Hyde, and *An Claidheamh Soluis*, announcing that she had found the grave and was opening a subscription. She did not send the manuscript to Hyde straightaway, unable to resist the challenge of trying to translate the poems herself, going each moonlit evening to the gate lodge to go through her work with a tenant farmer, Pat Mulkair.[25] 'I had no idea that you had translated anything like so many, or that you would have been able to translate them anything like so well,' Hyde wrote, not concealing his surprise, on 5 June 1900, after she had sent the translations to him for approval.[26] She visited Gort Workhouse to gather more reminiscences and poems and, inspired by her discoveries, wrote an article on the poet, incorporating her translations, and revealing that she was intrigued by the way Raftery interacted with the people he met, reflecting their values and in turn influencing them. In the process, Augusta discovered a society of unsuspected distinctiveness and variation in which the prosaic and the fantastic coexisted with ease, which was, despite appearances, stratified, and where poets were central and reputation was crucial.[27]

Meanwhile, in her role as patron she chose the single word 'Raifteirí' for the headstone, in imitation of 'Homer' (also a blind wanderer in touch with older dreams and songs). It was unveiled at a Gaelic League meeting on 26 August 1900, in which the small black-clad Augusta left the speechmaking to her male companions, Yeats, Martyn, Hyde, the local priest and schoolmaster.

Another transforming experience for Augusta in the autumn of 1899 and early spring of 1900 was the Boer War, which broke out on 11 October 1899. Sympathising with the Boer farmers whom she associated with the Irish as victims of imperial aggression and injustice, she took the broadly nationalist position. More advanced nationalists, applying John Mitchel's idea, regarded it as a case of England's difficulty being Ireland's opportunity. This Augusta did not hope for, although she obliquely articulated this view in a letter she sent to *The Spectator* in early November, recounting the Irish vernacular prophesy that the apocalyptic battle of the Black Pig in Ireland would be triggered by England's defeat.

Arriving in London on 19 January she found the war all-pervasive, the inevitable subject at dinner parties, its progress announced on daily placards, support for it expressed in ubiquitous Union Jacks. She was alarmed to find many of her old friends in a 'frenzy of rage' with the Boers, and immediately realised that she must keep silent about her sympathies for them, fearing she would be taken as a die-hard nationalist.[28] It was alienating. She was coldly critical of Enid's naive support for British soldiers as her friend excitedly organised the making of safety pins decorated with Union Jacks, and she had to make a determined effort to stay on friendly terms with her. It was easier to talk to old civil servants such as Haliburton and Birch and their establishment friends, but the more she learned of cynical behind-the-scenes politicking, inefficiency and the susceptibility of British generals to 'petticoat influence', the more her dislike of British imperialism deepened.

However, three of Augusta's nephews (Edward's sons) were fighting on the British side in South Africa, and Augusta had plenty of sympathy for them and a lively appreciation of their experiences. When, in January 1901, Alec and Richard Persse, just back from South Africa, met the openly pro-Boer George Russell at Coole, Augusta was in her element, privy to both sides, herself the calm, reconciling fulcrum: '. . . he [Russell] was delighted with Richard, who has hedged by saying he tried to join the Boers first,' and she enjoyed the irony of Aubrey's experience of being fired on by the British who mistook his ambulance wagon for a Boer ambulance.[29]

During the winter of 1899–1900, George Moore presented himself as a more serious rival, asking Yeats to collaborate with him on a play based on the Grania legend. Yeats, who admired Moore's spirit and absorbing love of literature, was willing, but Augusta tried to prevent it, showing Moore what a conscientious and, now that Yeats had finally finished *The Wind among the Reeds*, successful patron she was and hinting that whereas Yeats had genius Moore only had talent.[30] Eighteen months later she would yield her own talent to Yeats's genius, indicating that it was probably not Moore's inferiority that she objected to, but his assumption of equality. She could be relied on to recognise that she was not Yeats's literary equal, but Moore could not. This was important for Yeats and for the theatre. She was proved right, for the collaboration between Yeats and Moore was stormy and unspectacular. However, it inadvertently gave Augusta an opportunity to discover how to proceed herself.

She did not, in October 1899, try to prevent Moore and Yeats from rewriting Edward Martyn's satire on recent Irish politics, *The Tale of a Town*. But she did not share their callous disregard for Martyn's feelings. She felt for him as a friend, and remembered his threat to withdraw his guarantee. Her worst fears were confirmed when she visited him in late November 1899 and found him 'depressed and mortified'.[31] Diplomatically, she criticised Moore's rewriting and tried to get Martyn to sign the finished play. But she was to be disappointed by the depth of ill-will that lined the complex Martyn/Moore relationship. On 21 January 1900 Moore announced that he had retitled the play *The Bending of the Bough* and now claimed sole authorship. Soon after that the play went into rehearsal in London.

Augusta was privately critical of the play which Yeats thought Moore had successfully reformed. Yeats sensed her independent judgement uneasily, especially her championship of Martyn, with whom she sat in rehearsals, a tolerant recipient of his whispered criticisms. This accumulated uneasiness and jealousy about Martyn and Moore spilled out into an argument between them three days later when Yeats dined with her at Qmansions. It began with Augusta's objection to Yeats's high-handed editing of *Beltaine*, but soon escalated. 'Moore claims that no one can have more than one conscience' and I, Yeats told her, have an intellectual conscience, '& no one with that can forgive Martyn's want of intelligence'.[32] This was too much for Augusta. 'I say if I have but one conscience it is a conscience of friendship.' The words were torn from her as she felt the weight of bitterness and selfishness that seemed to be threatening the young theatre. But Yeats was not convinced. He went on to state that Moore was the superior playwright, while Augusta angrily and silently noted his inconsistency: 'Then he declares that Moore wrote most of "The Heather Field" & a gr part of "Maeve" – (a new story) – says Moore told him so & he believes him – (all very well, but he doesn't believe him when he attacks Miss Gonne's morality)'. She was with Martyn against Moore and Yeats, but profoundly uncomfortable.

When Martyn visited her the following afternoon she successfully persuaded him not to publish his original play on the grounds that it could not hold its own. She had shifted to Yeats's side and the principle of quality first. But she was not ready to abandon Martyn. Yeats, too, was keen to make amends. In a letter to Augusta on 31 January he tried to accommodate Martyn: '. . . I shall do all I can to keep Martyn, but make plain that what is indispensible [sic] is the good work he may yet do & not the money which another may give as well as he & that if he goes nothing is changed except that his place is empty.'[33] Augusta's rift with Yeats was finally mended when he came to dinner at Qmansions on 15 February and he agreed with her about Moore's play. Although it would have to be performed as advertised he concurred that, with its emphasis on current politics, it was too potentially divisive for Dublin audiences: '. . . it is not really a good play, & we feel that a play we produce ought not to depend on political allusions for its success,' Augusta wrote with a note of triumph as she inscribed the vital word 'we' in her diary. Augusta was not on the theatre committee with Yeats, Martyn and Moore, but from now on the fundamental decisions would be made when Yeats and Augusta were alone together.

Moore's influence with Yeats was finally broken in May. Yeats was tempted to accompany Moore on a lecture tour of America, but Russell and Augusta, who distrusted Moore and wanted Yeats to write, joined forces in trying to dissuade him. Secure in the knowledge that Augusta had his interests at heart and appreciating that she combined an understanding of people with good judgement (he wrote a long disquisition of these things as they related to himself and Russell to Augusta), Yeats allowed himself to be persuaded by her.[34] He may not have realised that she was also keen to minimise Moore's influence. When Yeats decided not to go, Moore's jealousy of Augusta uncoiled and he attacked. 'He said, as he frequently says,' Yeats reported to Augusta, '"she is a very clever woman, I did not find out until lately how clever. She is really very wise" & he added "I think I will ask her advice myself & do just what she tells me about America."'[35] It was a spiteful, defeated response.

Moore's *The Bending of the Bough*, Martyn's *Maeve* and Alice Milligan's *The Last Feast of the Fianna* were the offerings for the second season of the Irish Literary Theatre in February 1900 at the Gaiety Theatre in Dublin. Augusta, diminutive but commanding, was an indefatigable hostess, holding 'teas' in Leinster Hall to which she invited journalists, critics, and theatre people to generate publicity and steer opinion. She was often with Yeats during the week, and it was surely symptomatic of a growing closeness that on 18 February Augusta first nominated Yeats as 'Willie' in her diary. Meanwhile, she remained sympathetic to Martyn when *Bending* was a triumph. 'Poor Edward . . . bears it very well – with no sign of irritation or bitterness – There his real goodness comes out,' she wrote, glad to find good qualities in him.[36] His magnanimity did not last and a few days later he was abusing *Bending* and declaring he would only guarantee the theatre against financial loss if one of his plays was being produced. Gaelic League support for the theatre was in evidence during the performances as the audience sang Irish songs between the acts and shouted for 'An Craoibhin'. Thus was inaugurated a brief romance between the Gaelic League and the Literary Theatre.

Augusta, who had engaged her niece, Ruth Shine (Hugh Lane's sister), as bookkeeper, was also involved with hosting an exhibition of paintings by Yeats's brother, Jack, at Leinster Hall. Excited by Jack Yeats's *Sketches of Life in the West of Ireland* at the Walker Art Gallery the year before, Augusta had written an appreciative article for the *Daily Express*, and in April 1899 she had invited Jack and his wife Cottie (Mary Cottenham) to visit Coole.[37] She considered that he was burying his talent in Devon where he had settled, and hoped that visits to Ireland would encourage him to develop Irish themes in his painting.[38] Jack, independent and a more relaxed, introverted person than his brother, liked Devon for being remote, but he was interested in building on his Sligo roots in summer sketching visits to Ireland and came away from Coole with, his father thought, expanded horizons.[39]

When she came to sum up the February season (she had started a cuttings file of reviews), Augusta recorded surprise at the Dublin audience's interpretation of *Maeve* as a nationalist play, applauding the allegories so vigorously that it was boycotted by the Castle Establishment. It was an education in the political mentality of the Dublin audience. Overall, she was content: 'The week over, & well over, for tho' there is financial loss we have gained rather than lost credit, have justified our existence & come into touch with national feeling on its best side, the side one wants to develop.'[40] This for her was decidedly non-party political. When, after the last performance, Yeats had stood up in their box and fulsomely promised the audience more plays 'equally patriotic in intention' next year Augusta, who feared controversy that provoked either nationalists or Unionists to feel alienated, had silently added, 'There will I am afraid be a disappointment, for we must try & keep politics out of plays in future.'

Sensing that Moore and Martyn might fall in behind Yeats's literary patriotism, she gave them her aphoristic response to the problem of where they stood in terms of party politics: '. . . I tell him [Moore] & Edward "we are not working for Home Rule, we are preparing for it".' It was a very useful piece of equivocation, putting them in the nationalist camp without committing them to the potential violence and unpredictability of nationalist politics and so alienating them from sympathetic conservatives. It became a well-used maxim for her. It was scribbled with others on the inside cover and back page of her 1900 diary. 'To learn to love your enemy, do him a kindness, & love will come of itself,' she also wrote, distilling her Christian belief. She was trying to bring people together at a time when politics tended to divide them and in an artistic milieu where people celebrated the making of enemies. The keeping of politics and culture apart was a political strategy based on the idea that the theatre should influence thought and not encourage polarisation of ideology, so that when political change finally took place it would be peaceful.

When Yeats and Augusta returned to London in March they heard the announcement that the Queen intended to visit Ireland, ostensibly non-politically, but in fact to rouse support for the war. 'If I were in politics, which I try to keep out of,' Augusta confided in her diary, 'I wd certainly show no welcome either to the head of the English state, or to a woman who has been callous to the failing & the famines in Ireland during a long reign.'

The projected visit injected another confrontational issue into overwrought social gatherings. The shamrock had been adopted as a safe gesture of solidarity with Ireland – it was the emblem of Irish regiments in the British army – and her London friends all wore shamrocks on 17 March, St Patrick's Day. Augusta, who had pinned an ivy leaf, Parnell's symbol, to her mantle as she set off to lunch with Enid, had at last been forced to show her colours. Tension with Enid had tightened with the threat of the Queen's visit, but now she welcomed Augusta, proudly wearing a shamrock and saying, 'so kind of us'. Augusta's response was ungenerous: 'I said I cd not wear one for fear of being mistaken for a Cockney – gr indignation on her part . . .' But after lunch, realising that Enid was deeply distressed by her stance, Augusta relented and hid her ivy leaf under her mantle. When Enid died in 1913 Augusta would recall that this was the one time that they – both scrupulous in respecting the other's feelings – had argued.[41]

In Ireland, Yeats and Moore wrote letters to the press objecting to the Queen's visit. Aware that the visit could cause riots, Augusta advised Yeats to denounce the Union, passed exactly 100 years previously; this would recognise the visit as essentially political and introduce an issue that would be less likely to incite violence than the emotive one of a personal visit. She had the satisfaction of seeing her idea taken up by constitutionalist nationalists in Dublin Corporation, which passed a resolution denouncing the Union.

Augusta's more overt and self-conscious nationalism had resulted in a growing distrust between herself and her Unionist friends. She needled Horace Plunkett about his lack of public support for the Boers (difficult for a Unionist MP), and quarrelled with Lecky, who withdrew his support from the Irish Literary Theatre. The exception was the dying Frederic Burton whom she visited daily while she was in

London in the spring of 1900. He recalled the patriotism of his youth and expressed his quasi-mystical notion of a pan-Celtic empire. When he died Augusta wrote a profile of him in *The Leader*, claiming him for the Revival.[42]

It was in the ionising atmosphere of the Boer War that Augusta wrote an essay on popular ballads, 'The Felons of Our Land', published by *The Cornhill Magazine* in May 1900, which was the most overtly political piece she ever wrote. The ballads, written in English, often jaunty in tone regardless of the content, pertly and predictably rhyming, are considerably inferior to the personal voice of Raftery's poetry. Yeats had publicly expressed his dislike of rhetorical ballads even when written by a poet of the calibre of Thomas Davis, although he conceded that some had the merit of spontaneity.[43] 'Art should only be used for its own sake,' he had declared at the Irish Literary Society in February 1898, it should not be a vehicle for politics.[44] Augusta, while not disagreeing with this in principle, allowed her more radicalised politics to shape her appreciation of the ballads of rebel Ireland.

In the article she hinted at Irish scorn for the jingoism spawned by the Boer War and, provocatively for an English audience, compared the Irish desire to sing of defeat and prison with the English tendency to celebrate victories, to the advantage of the former. She signalled her sympathy by associating Irish experience with Christ's life, and, although she admitted that many of the ballads were doggeral, she found deep emotion and power behind the stilted words, and declared that the ballads written by the felons themselves 'stand outside criticism, sweat-drops of the worker, blood-drops of the fighter shed as he passed along the hard highway'.

Augusta was in Paris staying with de Basterot when the article was published. He was critical; it was well written, but had she not departed from the opinions of William and Robert? William would have agreed with her, she told him confidently, but added that she would never publish anything so nationalist again. She had been shaken by re-reading the article and it became a watershed for her, less because it expressed her growing nationalism than because, once written, its radicalism convinced her that she must separate private belief and public pronouncements, '. . . partly,' she told de Basterot, 'because I wish to keep out of politics & work only for literature, & partly because if Robert is Imperialist I don't want to separate myself from him.' The last was a particularly powerful incentive. Her success in keeping her resolve can be measured by the fact that she was convinced that her family never knew the extent of her nationalist views.

Augusta, more than her other Protestant contemporaries, faced the dilemma of being a nationalist landowner: Plunkett was a Unionist; Moore had relinquished and Martyn tried not to face his landowning responsibilities; Yeats and Russell had no land. For some the dilemma would have been overwhelming. Augusta worked conscientiously to retain Gregory standing in Galway while also working persistently towards the creation of a distinctive and independent Irish state. Her polarised objectives influenced her profoundly; she aimed for harmony and the avoidance of controversy in all her activities, she kept her political views to herself and she emphasised cultural activity as a temporary replacement for politics and preparation for independence.

Yeats settled into his third full summer at Coole in July, and Augusta, more than ever secure in her position as his patron and the linchpin of the Revival, eased herself into extended hospitality as writers, artists and their wives migrated from

London and Dublin, bringing an invigorating combination of effervescent lightheartedness and purposeful, often collaborative, work. Amusingly irreverent sketches by Jack Yeats release a flavour of wry self-awareness. On Augusta's copy of the April *Beltaine* he drew a patrician Moore leading an ermine-clad Queen Victoria up a flight of stairs, both 'returning to Ireland', a question mark implicitly set over the depth of Moore's nationalism.

While Yeats and Russell set a mystical tone, Robert sketched with Jack Yeats who, he had discovered the previous summer, enjoyed riding and cricket. Jack was glad of Robert for he was not entirely in sympathy with the more esoteric concerns of his brother and his friends. There were other friends for Robert, too. Arnold Harvey, three years older than Robert, who had tutored him in classics the previous year, had returned, their friendship cemented by a shared passion for cricket.[45] His cousin Geraldine, now a close companion, visiting him at Oxford in the winter with Augusta, also came. Augusta may have thought she was a good match. There has been speculation that there was a romantic interest between Yeats and Geraldine, which Augusta may have tried to quash. Two years previously she had had a tête-à-tête with Geraldine before Yeats's arrival and the relationship had not developed.[46] When Augusta described her plans for the summer to Blunt she wrote archly that she intended to temper poets with cricketers and young ladies.[47] However, she was also concerned that Robert be involved in her activities, and she encouraged him to accompany her to the Galway Feis on 27 August.

Generally, Coole life was split between Robert's younger set who were active outside during the day and played music in the evening, and the older artists who worked alone in the mornings, walked or fished in the afternoons (Yeats often went out in a boat to catch fish) and gathered around the fire in the library in the evening where the fruits of the day's work were discussed and conversational wit was prized. They all came together at dinner when Yeats or Russell would dominate the conversation. Occasionally both groups sailed on the lake, one year the two Yeatses racing Robert, Arnold and Robert's cousin, Richard, in boats with home-made sails.

It is difficult to know how Robert got on with Yeats at this time. Robert may have felt that the poet, a prime focus of Augusta's concerns, had usurped his role and resented him. Yeats was notoriously aloof with people who did not share his interests, and may have only managed an absent-minded politeness for Lady Gregory's 19-year-old son. The sailing escapades suggest that there were light-hearted communal activities to bring them together. Robert was busy and self-contained, and Augusta's enthusiastic descriptions of cricket suggest that she was careful to give Robert attention.

Hyde came with his fashionable and rather distant wife, Lucy, at the end of August, in time to attend the Galway Feis, and on the following Sunday they drove to Killeeneen to the unveiling of Raftery's headstone. Committed to producing a play in Irish, Augusta and Yeats had been petitioning Hyde, a poet in Irish, but not so far a playwright, to write an Irish play, and on 28 August they finally persuaded him to cloister himself in a quiet room at Coole and write a play using a scenario based on an Irish folktale written by Yeats.[48] He wrote the dialogue of *Casadh an tSúgáin* (The Twisting of the Rope), a one-act comedy, in two days, emerging tired and unwell, to be rewarded with a bottle of champagne at dinner. Augusta was relieved by his achievement and pronounced the play 'splendid'. The next day he dictated it to her.[49]

The departure of the difficult Lucy was welcomed by Augusta. Augusta had also been annoyed by George

Russell's scholarly and unconventional wife, Violet, who preferred leafing through manuscripts to looking after her baby. Augusta accused her of untidiness and dirtiness and took it upon herself to mind the baby, working while it slept. 'I should be content to have Jack Yeats and Douglas Hyde here for six months of the year, but a few weeks of their wives makes me hide in the woods! and I have felt the same with AE and his wife. It is not that they are particularly undesirable as guests, but one is not in sympathy with them or their attitude towards various things, and it makes a constant slight strain trying to find common grounds of sympathy,' she wrote to her friend, John Quinn, six years later.[50] Augusta's defence was that the women were uninvolved in the literary and scholarly preoccupations of the men. But Violet Russell was neglecting her baby for study. The simple truth was that Augusta had little time for women; it was the men's world that she looked to.

Moore arrived in mid-September with a scenario of *Diarmuid and Grania* for Yeats and himself to develop. Augusta typed Yeats's dialogue and found that her suggestions for words and phrases in Hiberno-English were often acceptable.[51] Martyn came to dine one evening. He had withdrawn his guarantee for all plays except his own, and Augusta tried to persuade him to reconsider. He refused point blank. His obstinacy was disheartening, and Augusta was sad that he was cutting himself off from what he had helped to start. She felt he would regret it, but she knew there was no point in arguing further with him.[52]

The bustling and ever-courteous figure of Augusta, at the centre of this literary activity, but also finding first communion dresses and boots for families in Ballylee, entertaining her nieces, the Beauchamp sisters, keeping conversation to a high standard, looking out for Robert, was formidable. She was the voice and presence which kept the disparate groups if not always comfortable, at least occupied and often productive. She was undoubtedly the social cement of the Coole summer and maybe, at moments, seemed to be the binding intellectual spirit of the Revival. It was a role that suited her temperament and came easily to one of her social class. But it is no surprise that, rather than overtly revelling in her powers, she posed as a Martha, 'careful & cumbered with much serving'.[53]

Her confidence in her influence was expressed in her editing of essays on Irish culture, *Ideals in Ireland*, by a heterogeneous group of writers – Hyde, Russell and Moore were moderate nationalists, Yeats was associated with Gonne's extreme nationalism, Standish O'Grady was an unapologetic Unionist, while D.P. Moran was in the vanguard of 'Irish Ireland' nationalism and a strong, but occasional critic of Yeats; Martyn was not included. Her aim was to draw together disparate Irish voices to demonstrate the wealth and versatility of ideas about the distinctiveness of Irish culture and to present this as nationalism which could bypass the political demand for Home Rule. She wanted to inspire the Irish further. 'I am . . . trying,' she told Blunt with disarming naivety, 'to help every movement that brings back dignity to the country,' while 'politicians . . . do their forty years wandering in the wilderness.'[54] 'Bringing back dignity to Ireland' would be another of her catch-phrases. The essays would be published in January 1901 and be well reviewed; it would strengthen her name, but not extend her reputation.

In October, when the majority of her guests had gone, she immediately got on with her work editing articles, translating a Gaelic poem for *The Leader* and altering phrases in *Diarmuid and Grania*. It was good, useful work, but was it enough?

TEN

Cathleen ni Houlihan

So this was another thread to weave into the web . . .
Seventy Years

'I dreamed that I had been writing some article & that W.B.Y. said "It's not your business to write – Your business is to make an atmosphere" –'.[1]

This dream, scribbled on the back cover of Augusta's 1900 diary, tells of an ambition behind her article writing, and an accompanying guilt that she was stepping outside her allotted role. It portends a significant beginning. A few months after writing this Augusta had embarked on the translation and rearrangement of the Cuchulain myth which, published as *Cuchulain of Muirthemne* in April 1902, brought her recognition as a writer and prime influence in the Irish Revival. It would be followed by a translation of the legends of Finn and the Fianna, *Gods and Fighting Men*. In 1901 she also began her career as a playwright, collaborating with Yeats on *Cathleen ni Houlihan*. Eventually her plays would eclipse the legends in popularity, but today the legends can be read with more enjoyment. Mainly because of its timeliness and influence, though not ignoring its literary merits, the literary scholar Declan Kiberd has pronounced *Cuchulain of Muirthemne* an Irish classic.

Yeats later remembered that the folklorist Alfred Nutt had suggested to him that he paraphrase translations of Irish legends, selecting the best to do what Thomas Malory had done in *Le Morte d'Arthur*, and that he had told Augusta he was too busy to attempt such a project.[2] Maybe this gave her the idea, although she did not acknowledge it in her diary entry where she wrote on 20 November 1900: 'I have had an idea floating in my mind for some time that I might put together the Irish legends, into a sort of *Morte d'Arthur*, choosing only the most beautiful or striking.'

For Augusta it was a bold idea. The legends, referred to as the Ulster cycle, related the activities of a powerful prehistoric Ulster people. They centred on Cuchulain but also featured other mythic figures such as Deirdre. They were originally transmitted orally, but had survived in a number of manuscripts written by monks in Old Irish from the seventh century onwards. These manuscripts and various later translations in Irish, English, French and German often contained slightly different versions of the stories. Augusta was taking upon herself the responsibility of judging, selecting and rejecting; a creative act, quite different from the more usual scholarly task in this field of collating and including. The project also rested heavily on her writing style. Nutt had chosen Yeats, a prose stylist of proven quality, but Augusta was not confident about her writing style. The scope of the project was incalculable; Augusta originally thought she had work for the rest of her life.

This sudden boldness after the more modest efforts involved in editing and writing short articles suggests that Augusta, proposing to put her stamp on the legends, felt she too could take on the challenge proposed by Yeats to shake life into Irish literature. Yeats's support was vital for her. She only formulated the idea in her diary in November 1900 after she had consulted him: '. . . after a short hesitation, he thinks the idea very good, so I will try & carry it out,' she wrote stoically. Yeats himself had the poetic ambition to find the kernel of imagination in the old stories, and part of Augusta's aim was to assist Yeats in doing this by providing him with the raw material: 'I look on the book as a storehouse for poets who can take such bits as they like and make them immortal,' she told Blunt.[3]

Integral to their shared crusade for Irish literature was their ambition to formulate a reply to the attack on Gaelic literature by the two Trinity professors, Mahaffy and Atkinson. John Pentland Mahaffy had said unforgettably, referring (it was clear to Hyde and Augusta) to his colleague, the professor of languages, Robert Atkinson, 'I am told by a much better authority than any of them in Irish that it is almost impossible to get hold of a text in Irish which is not religious or which is not silly or indecent.'[4] Augusta's political instincts made her determined to turn the tables on the professors. 'It was partly that venomous attack of Atkinson's that set me to working to show there is imagination and idealism and beauty in the old Irish literature', she told Blunt.[5] 'Perhaps you might quote Mahaffy & Atkinson (no, I think better not) as having terrorised me,' she wrote to Yeats on 28 March 1902, when they were discussing her alterations to the texts. The professors' anticipated criticisms would operate as a form of self-censorship for Augusta.

Another explanation for Augusta's intention to be creatively cavalier with the legends may derive from hearing the country people speaking with familiarity of legendary heroes and giving their own views and interpretations.[6] There was manifestly no right version. 'Some say Grania was handsome and some say she was ugly,' Curly the Piper told her. But the basket-maker said, 'Many would tell you Grania slept under the *cromlechs* [megalithic tombs], but I don't believe that, and she a king's daughter. And I don't believe she was handsome either. If she was, why would she have run away?'[7]

Her first preoccupation was with style. There had been several popular published translations of Irish legends written since the late 1870s. There were awkward, literal translations, but some writers aimed for an artistic retelling, selecting tales to give a good story, embellishing with impunity. Many could not resist a certain bowdlerising to fit Victorian morality. Standish O'Grady's two-volume *History of Ireland: Heroic Period*, published in 1878–80, was the most highly regarded because his heroes were particularly noble, the action unremittingly exciting, the accoutrements rich and beautiful, his style highly charged and punctuated with superlatives. Like Daniel Maclise, the painter of great historic events in Irish history whose canvases had large casts and liberal sprinklings of harps, chalices, elaborately carved high crosses and semi-naked maidens, O'Grady gave a satisfyingly sumptuous interpretation of ancient Ireland. He had also set a standard; legends called for heroics, especially in language.

When Augusta looked to Malory's *Le Morte d'Arthur* as an ideal she was appreciating that his fifteenth-century translation of the tales of Arthur and the Knights of the Round Table from French had used a direct, fast-paced English, flavoured, to nineteenth-century ears, with the odd archaic word. Augusta's girlhood enjoyment of these had continued. Thinking of the new recruits to the Gaelic League – the poorly educated shopkeepers and shop assistants, schoolteachers, clerks, tenant farmers for whom she had set up a library in Kiltartan in January 1898 – believing that they would be 'the book-buyers of the future', and of 'our young men' – writers, painters, designers, students – she wanted to produce an accessible translation, with a clear, consecutive, readable story, 'a book with sap and pleasure in it'.[8] She decided to use the Hiberno-English of her tenants to give the legends the immediacy of folklore.

Although Augusta had been taking down folklore stories verbatim for four years she did not feel confident to reproduce the phrases and similes of the country people for this book straight out of her head. Reasoning that they were translating from Gaelic to English, she would do the same. As an experiment she asked Sean Connolly, an Irish language speaker from Aran who came to Kiltartan at the end of November to teach Irish, to translate 'Death of Cuchullin' into spoken Irish. She then translated it literally back into English. It convinced her that the Hiberno-English of her tenants was close to the Irish and perhaps gave her a technique to fall back on if she was stuck for a phrase. She would regard herself as the first to use a genuine Hiberno-English, explaining to Blunt that Hyde came near it in his love songs and folk tales but 'he does not as I do choose only the words used by the people and their *tournure de phrase*.'[9]

When Douglas Hyde came for the shooting at Christmas 1900 she showed him her translations. He subscribed to O'Grady's grandiose standards for myths, and categorically stated that the colloquial style was inappropriate.[10] He thought it was a job for a scholar and disliked her idea of amalgamating different versions into a single narrative. However, she had only wanted his consent, which he gave, and was not put out by his reservations.[11] He continued to be doubtful and vaguely discouraging: 'I do think you are plucky to tackle the great cycle . . . It is more difficult than it seems at first sight,' he wrote in March. But by May he was won over and enthusiastic: 'I am rejoiced to hear you have progressed so far with your Tain series. You are really wonderful. I shall be ever so curious to know and see what you have done.'[12] After that he give her manuscripts, information on other scholars' work, and helped her with some of the translation.[13]

Before going to London in October 1900, Augusta had gone to stay with the Morrises in Spiddal. As soon as she arrived she was handed a telegram from Robert telling her that he had been sent down from New College, Oxford, until 1 November for failing a divinity exam, and asking her to go back to Coole. Robert, who had just embarked on his second year, was not a keen student. His dutiful, rather opaque letters had inadvertently revealed that cricket and boxing had more appeal than his unfocused academic work. But this was a shock, and she was disappointed that he had lost his chance of gaining a first. However, cold ambition softened when she met him in London – she had no intention of letting her Galway neighbours speculate about his behaviour – and she found him gentle and affectionate. 'I feel that is better than having my pride satisfied by his success,' she reassured herself, though she added, 'I must give my mind to what is best for his future'.[14]

His Oxford tutor wrote saying that he had originality and power; a creative rather than scholarly talent. Thinking of his interest in art, Augusta enrolled him for drawing lessons in Newman Street, and wondered if he might eventually join his cousin, Hugh Lane (six years older than Robert), whom she had watched gain the expertise and experience to set up a successful business as an art dealer without the benefit of a university education. Although Robert worked hard when he returned to Oxford in November he still aimed for effortless achievement, so that when he passed his exam easily he immediately regretted the effort: 'I feel my time rather wasted now,' he wrote to his mother, 'as I could have got through with much less knowledge apparently.'[15]

They were alone for Christmas for the first time – Augusta

working, Robert shooting: '. . . we are very good friends . . .
I don't think R. has been lonely – & it has been quite a treat
to me'.[16] She anxiously noted that he was taking an
intelligent interest in his work for Mods (Greek sculpture
and plays). The news of Queen Victoria's death penetrated
the quiet. 'Poor old Queen, good in England – very callous
to Ireland,' she noted with a sense of balance that would
have eluded her in London, adding, 'I won't go to London
until the funeral festivities are over.'

Once in London, Augusta embarked on the translation of
'The Fate of the Sons of Usnach', reading it on 11 February
to Yeats. She summarised his reaction unemotionally in her
diary, '& he was enthusiastic – says I must go on, & that it
will be a great book – So I am encouraged'. But when she
recalled this episode in her autobiography she categorised it
as a turning point: 'He was slow in coming to believe I had
any gift for writing, and he would not encourage me to it,
thinking he made better use of my folk-lore gatherings that
I could do. It was only when I had read him . . . my chapter
the "Death of Cuchulain" that he came to look on me as a
fellow writer.'[17] Yeats himself remembered having a sudden
revelation of her as 'the founder of modern Irish dialect
literature'.[18]

Yeats was beguiled by the language, which he found
simple, dignified and lyric, 'a musical caressing English'. He
valued it as a living language whose vocabulary and rhythm
had roots in the sixteenth-century English of the translators
of the Authorised Version of the Bible. 'How could one be
interested in a hero who "ascended to the apex of an
eminence" unless one had reminded oneself that he had but
climbed a hill?' he asked rhetorically several years later. It
was also an Irish version of English and, despite brief
rhetorical support for Irish literature in Irish, Yeats was
committed to Irish literature in English.[19]

Armed with her British Museum reader's ticket (for which knowing the director had been a help in persuading the sceptical clerks), and with the conviction that she had a worthwhile project, Augusta, for the first time in her life, joined the ranks of scholars and writers in a place of work. It was a happy period for her. She was translating a Scottish version of the Deirdre story, one of the tragic stories of the Ulster cycle in which Deirdre, whose lover has been killed by a jealous rival, stabs herself, and found the work, despite its subject, pleasant and interesting.[20] She often dined in a nearby Austrian restaurant and then returned to the museum until nine or ten at night.[21] Back in her flat she would pick up *Bleak House*, surprised at her sudden enjoyment of Dickens's humour and detailed depiction of human foibles. It was a relief after the austere, heroic world of myth, and perhaps helped her to introduce the novelistic aspects of character and narrative to the legends. The novel may also have served as a warning, for neither did she want to cut the heroes down (even to Dickens's larger-than-life size) to fit into Edwardian drawing-rooms.

She summarised this solitary lifestyle in *Seventy Years*, but her diary extracts point to a much more convivial time. Yeats was researching an essay on magic at the British Museum, and they often met for lunch or tea to discuss their work. When Augusta had finished each chapter she read it to him, eager for any criticisms, taking confidence when there was none.[22]

Just before she left London for Venice with Robert she gave up her yearly lease in Qmansions. She would take short-term rents in the 'hotel' apartments on the seventh floor for the next two years until Robert had finished at New College.[23] After that she did not imagine that she would need a London base. She never did, but she remained a frequent visitor.

In Venice, Augusta was bored by the trivia emanating from their fellow guests at Ca' Capello and, although pleased that Enid admired Robert's looks and manners, could not agree that his reticence was undesirable. When they left, Augusta and Robert felt a shared sense of release, and set off adventurously for Trieste, Istra and Montenegro where Augusta bought Yeats a single-stringed lute. They returned to London, and Augusta went on to Coole. By mid-May Robert had taken his second-year exams and got a disappointing third; he had not worked hard enough. Unsympathetic, Frank told her that his laziness was due to overwork at school and she should never expect him to do well.

Frank sneered against the Revival, and his political opinions differed from Augusta's, but so far they had not argued significantly about how to run the estate. In one way estate problems seemed solved by the spring of 1901. Helped by a legacy of £1,200 (€95,769, £65,730 sterling) from her half-sister, Katherine Wale, Augusta was able to pay off Charles Gregory's mortgage and could reassure herself that she would be able to keep the house and woods 'whatever happens'.[24] However, the previous November the tenants had finally started to challenge rent levels in the land courts and join the agitation for compulsory purchase.[25] Frank's attitude was, in line with many other landowners and agents, punitive: the tenants should be forced to pay 'the hanging gall' (usually 'gale', the six-month credit that had been given to tenants when they took up their tenancies, and which a landowner had a right to extract at any moment), as a disincentive. Augusta, aware that the majority were bent on exercising their rights, and allowing that the poorer tenants could have a case, disagreed. The argument escalated, with Frank stating that it was his business to get the most out of the property, and Augusta countering that, although they needed to keep up the value of the estate,

Robert should be handed a Coole that enjoyed good relations with its neighbours, 'calling up the hanging gall might irritate them'. But she let Frank have the last word. Four years later she would write regretfully to Yeats that Frank had unwisely made the tenants who had gone to court pay the hanging gale.[26]

In the summer of 1901 Augusta, responding to requests from Hyde and Yeats, and in moments taken from her legends, found that she was engaged in play-writing. Hyde asked her to translate *The Twisting of the Rope*, and she sent it to him with a number of suggested alterations.[27] She was beginning to relish the playwright's power to dictate the action. And her translation, published in *Samhain* in October, demonstrated (to her, Hyde, Yeats) that her Hiberno-English could make for vigorous, racy, authentic-sounding dialogue.

This language could also have a haunting quality. In June, Augusta sent Yeats her translation of an Irish love poem, 'The Grief of a Girl's Heart' (sometimes titled 'Donal Og'), which he thought extremely beautiful and would subsequently quote in lectures on the Irish Revival.[28] It ends:

> You have taken the east from me; you have taken the
>   west from me;
> you have taken what is before me and what is behind
>   me;
> you have taken the moon, you have taken the sun
>   from me;
> and my fear is great that you have taken God from
>   me!

So in the summer at Coole, when Yeats had a vivid dream which he wanted to turn into a play but could not formulate into a realistic dialogue, he turned to Augusta.

Yeats's plays until this point were poetic and obscure, with symbolic characters and plots driven by ideas rather than action. They were an extension of his poetry and were not written to attract large audiences. Responding to the criticism levelled by D.P. Moran (and others) of Yeats's esoteric writing, Augusta had bluntly characterised Yeats's work and his audience to him in May 1901:

Clearly, just now your work is not directly with the masses – which would be the most directly interesting work – but that matters less as the Gaelic movement has taken up their education, & any of the beautiful work you do, besides having a direct influence on the best minds, is there ready for the time when your own countrymen will dare to praise it.[29]

There was a challenge here, although Augusta, aiming to reassure, had not intended one, and when Yeats tried to write dialogue as it might be spoken (and a play with a nationalist message) he could be seen to be rising to the challenge to appeal to a broader audience.

He had dreamt of a cottage, 'where there was well-being and firelight and talk of a marriage, and into the midst of that cottage there came an old woman in a long cloak'.[30] She was to reveal herself as Mother Ireland – Cathleen ni Houlihan – and persuade the young man in the cottage who was to be married to abandon his bride and support the French who (it was 1789) had landed in Mayo to support the United Irishmen. His idea was the old Irish theme of the call to arms for the sake of Ireland's freedom. It was like an abstract painting in blocks of colour, containing within itself the inspirational sweep of politics. But it needed someone to imagine the dialogue of the family before Cathleen enters and how exactly, for example, they would discuss an impending marriage.

This Augusta did, writing proudly in pencil under what became the first part of the play, *Cathleen ni Houlihan*, ending just after the old woman enters the cottage, 'All this mine alone A.G.'[31] What Yeats did not anticipate was that, having given Augusta free rein with this, it would be almost impossible to institute the more poetic, rhetorical tone that he wanted his Cathleen, even in disguise, to take with the Gillane family. Instead, when she enters, the play takes on a folk tale formula; the family ask the stranger, who they take to be a poor wandering woman, questions, and their suspicions, and those of the audience, that she is not what she seems grow with her enigmatic answers.

Augusta headed this section with 'This with W.B.Y.', and the strong impression from the surviving manuscripts and a style which fuses the realistic and symbolic is that they worked closely together on this. The uncertainty about the identity of the old woman is only resolved when Cathleen is allowed her final rousing speech. Was this also a joint effort? It has something of the varied rhythm of the last verse of 'The Grief of a Girl's Heart', the syntax of the Kiltartan dialect, and the imagery of the country people, but it rises effortlessly over the more prosaic speech of the Gillane family:

It is a hard service they take that help me. Many that are red-cheeked now will be pale-cheeked; many that have been free to walk the hills and the bogs and the rushes will be sent to walk hard streets in far countries; many a good plan will be broken.

Augusta's naturalistic image of peasant life was thus integrated with Yeats's symbolic intentions, so that the play avoided the unrooted poetic gesturing of his earlier plays. Collaboration had allowed Yeats and Augusta to produce a far better play than either of them were yet capable of independently.

As it stands the play is no straightforward call to arms, for the audience is too aware of the disruption to the family that the boy's desertion will bring. Martyrdom, as Cathleen eloquently exhorts, involves catastrophic loss, accepted by Michael Gillane who follows Cathleen, and the price is vividly before the audience. Augusta was not immune to the siren call of sacrifice for Ireland as her article, 'The Felons of our Land' shows. But she knew resistance to it, too, in herself and the country people. An awareness of the tragedy of their situation had been expressed most recently for her in a ballad, 'Fair-haired Donough' in which a sister voiced her anguish at the hanging of her brother for a political crime, and regretted that he had ever been drawn into political defiance.[32] As the translator of *Cuchulain*, Augusta revelled in heroism, but as the guardian of Coole she understood the need for domestic security. In the grounding of the play in the perspective of settled peasants an ambiguity to martyrdom was allowed to surface and a dramatic tension achieved.

That *Cathleen ni Houlihan* became associated with an uncomplicated radical nationalism was due in no small part to Maud Gonne's inspirational performance as Cathleen on 2 April 1902. She was playing before an audience largely composed of her radical *Inghinidhe na hÉireann* (The Daughters of Erin) in thrall to their founder and the ideal of women playing active political roles. The play was directed by the Fay brothers, amateur Dublin players who had formed the National Dramatic Society to bring theatre, preferably Irish nationalist theatre, to Dublin. Yeats had met them that summer, and their company took the remaining roles. Maud Gonne had agreed to take the part as a political duty and, not someone to ignore the potential of a figure with whom she half identified, contravened theatrical protocol by arriving at St Teresa's Hall dressed in her costume. She strode purposefully through the theatre and onto the stage minutes before the performance. The audience was spell-bound by her pale beauty, burning eyes and 'weird power'.[33] Yeats was enchanted. Gonne had projected the 'tragic meaning' of Cathleen and reinstated her as the central figure with an urgent call to arms.

Later productions with Sara Allgood as Cathleen aroused the thought that its message might be taken too seriously: 'It is enough,' George Bernard Shaw declared in 1909, 'to make a man do something foolish.'[34] That Augusta saw the part differently is clear when, in 1919, she played Cathleen on the understanding that all that was needed was 'a hag and a voice', and she played an ambiguous old woman whose time would come off-stage in the uncharted future.[35]

Augusta's scribbled pencil notes on the manuscript reveal a new author amazed and happy with her first creation. Privately to Yeats she referred freely to '*our* Cathleen'.[36] But when it was performed it was billed as Yeats's play and it was published under his name. People knew this was not the full story. 'The odd thing is that Fay told me Lady Gregory wrote the whole of it except the part of "Cathleen",' William Boyle told Joseph Holloway six years later.[37] Yeats acknowledged her help when he dedicated *Plays for An Irish Theatre* to her in 1903, but only in supplying the 'country speech'.[38] He did not suggest how this had fundamentally affected the play, and the implication was that it had been an uncreative and subordinate role. Some critics even interpreted Yeats to mean that Augusta had merely translated his dialogue. Augusta played an active part in this deception. Two years after the play was written she told a critic requesting that she articulate her role that it was as Yeats had described, and she quoted Yeats's dedication without comment in her book on the theatre, *Our Irish Theatre*.[39] She even altered the proofs of the ending so that the published version would reflect the way it was acted.

It was not hard for Augusta at this point to pose as Yeats's helper and allow him to take the credit. His work was her explicit priority and she had not yet become a playwright. She also felt indebted to him for his help with *Cuchulain*.[40] She may also have intuited that to assert her rights would be to damage the trust that was developing between them. Augusta was deeply conventional where sexual politics was concerned. So was Yeats. *Autobiographies* is punctuated by observations which suggest that Yeats thought women were emotionally driven, not fully engaged with their work, and incapable of being objective: 'Women, because the main event of their lives has been a giving of themselves and giving birth, give all to an opinion as if it were some terrible stone doll.'[41] In the summer of 1901 Augusta had not proved that she was substantially different. Yeats had also accepted Augusta as his patron with influence over his literary output at Coole. As the years went by Yeats increasingly maintained that he alone was responsible for the play. He was unenthusiastic about Augusta's 1919 performance of Cathleen. Gonne had restored his original vision to him, allowing him to imagine that the play was his, so that in 1938 he could pick it up again, and, referring to the Easter Rising in 1916, ask,

> Did that play of mine send out
> Certain men the English shot?[42]

Yet, of course, they retained the knowledge of who had written what. Twenty-four years later, in May 1925, they found themselves discussing Yeats's plays, and he observed, 'I have never made one in sympathy with my audience except *Cathleen ni Houlihan*. And that was you and a dream,' an observation that Augusta immediately wrote down in her journal.[43] So it was doubly bitter when, two months later, she read a list of Yeats's plays; '. . . *Unicorn* as before and *Pot of Broth* [also written in 1901] now – put as "written with Lady Gregory". Rather hard on me not giving my name with *Cathleen ni Houlihan* that I wrote all but all of.'[44] The misconception continued until very recently when her contribution was carefully unravelled in a scholarly paper.[45]

Meanwhile, at the end of 1901, it was the Irish language rather than rebellion which most concerned the fledgling theatre. When *Diarmuid and Grania* and Hyde's *The Twisting of the Rope* were staged on 21 October 1901 for the final season of the Irish Literary Theatre at the Gaiety Theatre it was, for Catholic nationalist Dublin, a fashionable event.[46] Synge sensed this and disliked it, picking rather unfairly on 'the beautiful Irish girls of the Gaelic League who jabbered in extremely bad Irish with young clerks pale with enthusiasm'.[47] But the critic Stephen Gwynn, anticipating a detached urban response to Hyde's play, was surprised by the spontaneity of the audience, reminiscent of fireside listeners.[48]

The Fays, who emphasised nationalist politics, indigenous actors and the Irish language, were keen to pursue an Irish language theatre, and Yeats and Moore briefly flirted with the idea.[49] But Yeats privately regarded the insistence on the Irish language as a form of propaganda. He was encouraging the Fays not because of their politics, but for their particular style of acting. Whereas English actors tended to indulge in exaggerated gestures, and to feel that everyone on stage should be moving regardless of whether they were important or not, the Fays, influenced by French traditions, encouraged their actors to remain still unless they were speaking. When they did move they aimed to appear natural and spontaneous.[50] However, Yeats and Augusta continued to encourage Hyde to write Irish plays, and Augusta wrote a scenario based on the Raftery song from

which Hyde wrote *The Marriage*. Yeats, disappointed with
Hyde's *Twisting*, encouraged Augusta, hoping that she could
provide a better structure and evoke a poet-figure who was
as concerned with the spiritual and imaginative as with the
material welfare of the people.[51]

Cuchulain was published in April 1902 shortly after the first
performance of *Cathleen ni Houlihan*. In the run up to the
publication Augusta almost fell out with Yeats over her
bowdlerising of the original texts. She had not discussed this
aspect with him so that when reading the manuscript in late
March 1902, he came across a scene in 'Boy Deeds' where
the women, usually described as being nude, were, in her
version, only partially undressed, he was surprised and
disappointed. He thought it was the only instance, and
wrote suggesting she change it or explain that she had done
it to prevent it being censored in rural Ireland.

In fact Augusta had made many alterations, modifying the
grotesque, particularly descriptions of Cuchulain – his gullet
exposed during convulsions prior to heroic deeds, the
spouting of blood – which she regarded as childish
exaggerations, and removing several accounts of
supernatural help.[52] Haunted by the Trinity professors, she
felt that a simple description would convey the meaning for
modern minds without further damaging the reputation of
the ancient Irish. It was also part of her aim to made the
book more accessible, with Cuchulain more human and the
story more like a novel with dramatised conflicts, interaction
between people, and explanations for behaviour change. She
was keen, too, that children read the book at school, and
worried that it would be kept from them if judged
'improper'.

She acknowledged her censorship by claiming that she
had written the book from the perspective of the 'People of

Kiltartan'.[53] Today, her dedication written in Hiberno-English and addressed to the 'people of Kiltartan', in which she declares that she has left out 'a good deal I thought you would not care about for one reason or another', has a patronising and disingenuous tone, especially as we know that she knew that these people still shared the fantastical imagination that revelled in the grotesque and supernatural.

Replying to Yeats on 27 March from Florence, where she was on holiday with Robert, she was abrupt and defensive, but the next day she wrote a more conciliatory letter, explaining her view, admitting that there were many such modifications, and acknowledging that if he had objected earlier she would have altered the text. Coyness was not her personal preference for, as the need to keep the text respectable lessened with time, she altered the wording of the incident in 'Boy Deeds' in subsequent editions – the women were 'uncovered' in the 1902 edition, and 'red-naked' by 1907. But in March 1902, with the proofs about to be returned to the publisher, John Murray, there was no time to make major changes. With disarming trust she left it to Yeats who was writing a preface 'to show . . . that it is not rubbishy amateur work'; he could blame or justify her as he pleased. He, who had been instrumental in finding a publisher, delicately side-stepped the issue by describing her 'work of compression and selection' as done 'firmly' and 'reverently'.[54]

Cuchulain of Muirthemne was a triumph. Many reviewers quibbled with Yeats's introductory flourish – 'I think this book is the best that has come out of Ireland in my time. Perhaps I should say that it is the best book that has ever come out of Ireland'. But the Academy chose it as most important book of 1902; the *United Irishman* (George Russell) anticipated that it would shape the imagination of the next generation; John Yeats, expecting oddness, was delighted by naturalness; Maud Gonne quoted from it; Eoin MacNeill, ideologically pro-Irish, was seduced; Synge consumed it (he told her it was part of his 'daily bread'); the American President, Theodore Roosevelt, enjoyed it and learned her name; and John Eglinton pronounced that it would become the 'authorised version' of the 'Irish Old Testament'.[55]

Why were the stories so appealing? For the modern reader there is still enough formality and rhetoric, the listing of names and places, a lack of sustained psychological insight, unusual words ('close-handed', 'geasa' explained vaguely as 'bonds'), unexplained customs, casual references to unusual size and freak occurrences, to deter. Slowly the more familiar formulas, such as the repetition of phrases so effective in fairy tales, the sure pace, and the quirkiness of the characters, take a hold. The language, too, gradually works its magic: 'And Deirdre grew straight and clean like a rush on the bog'; '. . . Naoise . . . made a fair throw over his shoulder at the young man, that put the eye out of his head.'

But the 1902 readers were immediately enthusiastic. They were enchanted by the evocation of the energy of a daring and youthful hero from the dawn of the world, told in a way that seemed to reconnect the early twentieth century directly to that world.[56] Augusta had also tapped into another literary preoccupation of the time; like Hans Christian Andersen, whose fairy stories were republished in the early years of the twentieth century, she was taking myths and legends out of a rarefied atmosphere and putting them back into common currency.

Of course, there were detractors: Martyn most notably. He came to Coole one day in May embarrassed but determined to tell her that he found the dialect vulgar. Augusta mercilessly reported their exchange to Yeats. Why could she not rewrite it in the style that Lady Charlotte Guest (Enid's mother) had written *The Mabinogion?* he asked. She replied that she liked the people and the dialect. 'I hate the country people, & I hate the way they talk,' he answered, 'which is logical at all events,' Augusta added dryly. 'He again begged me to give up the vulgarity. His face shone with kindness and benevolence.' Self-absorbed, almost ridiculous, he could safely be laughed at.[57]

Augusta had launched the book with confidence and, forgetting her usual ambiguity, she revelled in her success, whether the accolades were from London, America or from Mr Bagot in Gort. Privately, the whole exercise had been a revelation, for she had stepped beyond the Gregorys and beyond herself, delineating a male character of wilfulness, confidence and strength, and speaking directly in the idiom of her neighbours. She had found several masks that would fit comfortably for later creative work.

Before publishing *Cuchulain* she had already embarked on a sequel based on the stories of the mythical warrior hero and leader of the Fianna, Fionn Mac Cumhaill, an older figure 'nearer to the spirit world' and one frequently evoked by her country neighbours.[58] Yeats would be delighted with the exposure of a more archaic spirit. 'The men who imagined the Fianna had the imagination of children, and as soon as they had invented one wonder, heaped another on top of it.'[59] Privately he judged that Augusta, with her 'semi-feudal' upbringing in Roxborough, had privileged access to the mind-set of her heroic and aristocratic subjects.[60] Augusta herself particularly enjoyed the digressions in the original Finn texts celebrating the character of places and the beauty of nature in vivid language, and the fact that the legends still lived in the imagination of her country neighbours. Her own imagination was fired; she felt she was seeing for herself how the ancient pagan spirit had survived into the twentieth century.

While she had been doing her scholarly work the desire to

gather folklore was unsuppressible. Whenever she set out to ask people about Finn and the Fianna unexpected themes and stories would emerge and give her new insights into the lives of the country people. At Oughterard Workhouse in May 1902 she sat, a comfortable but patrician figure, in a bare gravelled yard relieved only by a few budding sycamore trees, surrounded by old men in round grey caps sitting on wooden benches. She had promised them tobacco for Finn stories, but they also told her long fantastic fairy stories. She was half impatient, 'I had never cared much for this particular kind of tale. But as I listened, I was moved by the strange contrast between the poverty of the tellers and the splendour of the tales.'[61] On other occasions she was given herbal cures by women and was interested to hear Munster songs praising the Stuart kings, routinely despised by Raftery.

Having assembled her findings and articulated her thoughts in a few short essays, she published *Poets and Dreamers* in March 1903.[62] It was a development of her Raftery work. 'There was more of my own writing in *Poets and Dreamers* than in anything I had yet published. I felt it more my own,' she wrote later in *Seventy Years*. In her essays on poems and songs she emerges as a gentle intelligent critic, applying what she had learnt from years of reading, alert to the artificial, charming and wild, to the use of formula, symbol, and the cry of passion and individuality. Where people had stories or advice she let them talk uninterrupted. She appreciated the marginal among the marginal – 'tinkers', herbalists, Aran islanders, workhouse inmates, old women who 'sit in wide chimney-nooks by turf fires'. She had an ear for the contemporary twist, which prevented the book from being a purely nostalgic enterprise, and she often sketched in the circumstances in which she heard stories and songs, suggesting that she was beginning to appreciate the dynamics of the situation and its possible bearing on the story. It was for this that she had kept her distance from Yeats's folklore in 1898. In the book there was an implicit homage to Douglas Hyde, whom she saw as 'the apostle of the Irish language'; she included her translations of his plays and poems and *Poets and Dreamers* was her contribution to his project to keep the country imagination alive. The next step was to consider how she might use this material for her own creative ends.

ELEVEN

An Awakening Imagination

> ... but desire for experiment is like fire in the blood ...
> *Our Irish Theatre*

In June 1902, Augusta invited Yeats to Coole for the ceremony to be held on Tuesday 24th at which Robert, 21 that May, would formally assume the mastership of Coole. This date had been requested by the tenants who were anxious that their celebrations not coincide with the coronation of Edward VII and be misinterpreted.[1] As Robert, now in his third year at New College, showed an interest in his mother's work and the Irish Revival, Yeats began to show an interest in him, lunching with him when he lectured at St John's College, Oxford, on the Irish Literary Theatre on 18 May.[2]

Augusta was busy before the ceremony, preparing to entertain more than 200 people to a dinner and dance. The tenants arranged bonfires, flags on the road from Gort to Coole, torches, and the presentation of plate and a formal document of welcome which, brightly decorated with popular and local symbols of nationalism, reminded Robert in Irish and English of his father's care for the tenants' well-being, interests and rights, and of the 'goodwill and kindly sympathy' of his 'cultured and gifted mother'.[3] Yeats reported to Blunt that Robert made a 'very good speech, very simple very sincere'.[4]

In her diary, Augusta expressed profound relief: 'Thank God he is so well received & on such good terms with his people & has so good a name.'[5] She was glad that her formal period of running Coole in trust for Robert had ended and that he was old enough to take over should he wish. There was every reason to be confident that he would eventually do the right thing at Coole. But, as she told Blunt, 'to Robert himself, the pleasure and profit of becoming an Irish landlord is not very great. It means for him a facing of hard questions and responsibility.'[6] To keep his spirits up she gave him a horse, Sarsfield (named after the Jacobite military commander). She also remained in charge while Robert concentrated on finishing at Oxford and deciding on a profession. Her sense of responsibility for the immediate future of Coole itself was, in fact, undiminished; it was from ultimate responsibility that she was released.

Perhaps a sense of achievement and release where Robert was concerned led her to write her first play (not counting *Colman and Guire*) later in the summer.[7] The Fays needed plays, and there was not an over-abundance of writers, though James Cousins and Frederick Ryan had recently contributed work. Writing a play was also a way of pushing the theatre in a direction that she wanted it to go: non-confrontational or non-divisive, rooted in the culture of the people, broadly nationalist.

The idea for *Twenty Five* (a one-act comedy) came directly from an emigration song in *Poets and Dreamers* ('West Irish Ballads'). Augusta asked herself what would happen if a young man, returning wealthy from America to wed his former lover, finds that she is now married? They meet and the girl shows no signs of wanting to leave her husband. Augusta used the device of a card game to allow the young man to surreptitiously give the girl his wealth by losing to the husband. This conformed to her observation in

'West Irish Ballads' that 'constancy and affection in marriage are the rule; yet marriage "for love" is all but unknown'. But it failed to adhere to another of her observations: 'Love of country, *tirgradh*, is I think the real passion; and bound up with it are love of home, of family, love of God.' By suggesting that the young man would relinquish his fortune on a hopeless love, Augusta realised she was not representing the people's values accurately and charged herself with sentimentality; she would rework the theme several times.[8]

There is an autobiographical thread to *Twenty Five*: the girl, morally unreproachable, has nevertheless kept her former admirer a secret from her husband. One can see the appeal of this theme for Augusta, remembering Blunt, and it perhaps helped her to engage with the story.

Unfortunately, the Fays, who admired the Hiberno-English dialogue, refused to perform the play. They did not want to see the Irish in what might be interpreted as a negative light (playing cards for money), or to stage plays that might encourage undesirable behaviour (emigration in order to make money).[9] So Augusta revised the play, strengthening the characters and tightening the drama. She left the emigration and card game in but, bowing to Fay pressure, developed the girl's opposition to the game and omitted the young emigrant's rhetorical revelling in his wealth. It was performed the following year.[10] 'We have the pleasure of knowing that our little Irish Theatre has found our work useful,' Yeats had written the previous September.[11] Augusta, who delighted in this image, had begun her service.

There was a steady stream of guests for the summer at Coole in 1902. This year there were many young Persses, invited to celebrate Robert's coming of age. They included Richard, Edward's son from Southampton, two years younger than Robert and a frequent visitor over the years; his older brother Peyton who had been living in Africa; Standish who had last visited seven years previously; and 18-year-old Tom. Augusta also invited Frank's daughter, May; Hugh Lane's brother, Harold and her brother, Algernon, from Ardrahan (where he lived with his wife, Eleanor Gough) with his 10-year old son, Rodolph, and 13-year old daughter, Daphne. Yeats came with Edmund Spenser's *Faerie Queene*, which she read to him in the evenings, and the Hydes were there, too. Coole now had a reputation as the workshop of Ireland and Augusta as a slave-driver, 'but the truth is there is so much to be done we can use all hands,' Augusta told Blunt, uncharacteristically missing an opportunity for humorous self-deprecation.

On 20 August they went to the Connaught Feis in Galway where Hyde had to step in at the last moment to play Raftery in a scratch performance of *The Marriage*. When they returned to Coole, Hyde was put under pressure to produce more Irish plays, using scenarios by Yeats and Augusta.[12] Augusta, intrigued by the idea of an estranged husband and wife meeting in a workhouse, wrote an extended scenario and, on Yeats's insistence, handed it regretfully to Hyde, who wrote *The Poorhouse*.[13]

On 31 August 1902, the Hydes, W.B. Yeats, Augusta and Jack Yeats got into two side cars and drove to Killeeneen for the Raftery Feis. Here, by the grey sea on the 'edge of the world' where dreams 'are real things', they found several hundred people, many in traditional white (men) and red (women), making their way to a large field where a banner decorated with a picture of Raftery had been erected over a platform.[14] In the audience, recently arrived from New York, was John Quinn (1870–1924). A lawyer and would-be patron of the Irish Revival, a realiser of dreams, he was on his first visit to Ireland.

Quinn was an impressive man. At 32, he was a rising star in New York's business life. Tall, good looking, he had a concentration of interest, even passion, that made his avowed commitment to Irish culture ring true. Perhaps, given the brittle nature of so many friendships in the Dublin literary scene, his most appealing quality was that he was an outsider with an outsider's detachment. He promised an unbiased commitment, backed by American largesse and energy. He had been drawn to Irish culture by the paintings of Jack Yeats and his father, John Butler, but, at the feis he was soon immersed in poetry, plays and legends.[15] His quick interest was greeted with spontaneous affection, expressed in Jack Yeats's scrawls on the feis programme where Quinn's rather austere profile takes its place with Hyde, a comfortably seated Lady Gregory, a meditative W.B. Yeats, Jack and a frenetic feis dancer.

He came back to Coole that evening impressed by Augusta's dignified welcome, attracted to Hyde, mesmerised by Yeats's talk and charmed by the house.[16] Letters would follow him to New York. He ensured that *Twenty Five* was published in an American magazine while the Fays were dithering about producing it in Dublin, and he organised the copyright American publication of a sensitive play, *Where There is Nothing*. On 8 November Augusta prefaced a letter Yeats was dictating to her for Quinn with gushing gratitude for what he had done: 'I can only say "thank you" and he says "thank you", but you will know that these unsatisfactory words that one uses for every small occasion mean very deep and lasting gratitude, and a hope that some day or other we may be able in some part to make you know how truly we feel it.'[17] Excessive as it was it also seemed to thank him for being what he was, an influential and reliable outsider. They all knew they had a patron, but Augusta fervently hoped she had found an ally – an 'angel unawares' she wrote later – beyond the chaos that occasionally threatened to engulf them in Ireland.

The play, *Where There is Nothing*, was based on an idea Yeats had discussed with Moore. They had fallen out and now Yeats, with Augusta's and Hyde's help, wanted to write and publish the play and get it copyrighted by John Quinn before Moore had a chance to use the original scenario.[18] Augusta, taking dictation, was, unlike Moore, happy to take second place.[19] But she was not passive: Yeats relied on her ability to write convincing dialogue and she kept them focused.[20] Nearly two years previously Augusta had told Moore that she would always favour Yeats over him. He had confided his frustrations about collaborating with Yeats on *Diarmuid and Grania* and she, aware that both men strained to dominate, had counselled the necessity of making concessions, adding that Yeats will never make concessions about style; 'words are his religion'.[21] Now Moore, settled in Ely Place in Dublin, realised there had been a conspiracy against him. He denounced the perpetrators and would not have anything to do with Yeats and Augusta for two years. He would never threaten to dominate the theatre again. But he felt free to abuse his erstwhile collaborators in his autobiography where, a few years later, they would encounter the sharp sting of his revenge.

The play was unsatisfactory. But this was not really the point, certainly as far as Augusta was concerned. Yeats and Gregory were now an acknowledged partnership. Yeats would later tell Russell that he, Yeats, was successful because he had assembled strong people around him: '. . . I am a fairly strong and capable man and . . . I have gathered the strong and capable about me, and all who love work better than idle talk will support me . . . [T]hough you are strong and capable yourself you gather the weak and not very capable about you, and . . . I feel they are a danger to all good work.'[22]

This was true. Augusta had done what no one else in their circle had had the courage or inclination to do. She had successfully offered herself to another – her work, her money, her influence, her intellectual and material support. It was a stroke of genius. Where there were as many opinions and plans as individuals, the pairing of Yeats and Augusta would prove effective and irresistible. Together they would establish and fight for what became the national theatre. And it was from her position at Yeats's right hand that Augusta would make her own individual contribution.

Their working together was not always smooth. With *Where There is Nothing* finished in November, they immediately embarked on a Christ play, *The Travelling Man*, an idea of Augusta's.[23] Broadly, the idea of the plot was that Christ, disguised as a tramp, would rescue a homeless girl. However, once established in comfort she would reject him when he returned as a tramp and disrupted her home, playing with her son. Finally, realising that he was Christ, she would live to regret it. Having written part of the play they both stepped back to analyse its meaning, and came to different conclusions: Yeats had a pagan interpretation and Augusta a more Christian view. It was a difference of outlook and belief.[24] Nevertheless, Yeats asked Augusta to work up a sketch he had written in the light of his revised interpretation. She replied with a summary of her own view, to which Yeats restated his belief. Realising that they could not continue together, and neither wanting or able to continue alone, the play was shelved.[25]

That autumn two of Augusta's nephews unexpectedly stepped into the arena of Irish public life: John Shawe-Taylor and Hugh Lane. Nationalists were agitating against the slowness with which land was changing hands, and Shawe-Taylor, 36, a Boer War veteran and a Unionist without political experience, proposed to settle the current impasse about land sales by inviting both sides to a conference.[26] Augusta supported him publicly on 25 September with a letter to *The Irish Daily Independent and Nation*, a paper largely read by the Catholic middle classes. Privately she thought he could show more understanding of the nationalist perspective, although she shared a sense of class loyalty.[27]

The conference had a major impact on the Land Act (known as the Wyndham Act) passed in August 1903, which had the support of representatives of both landlords and tenants. There was a 12 per cent bonus to be paid directly out of the British Treasury for landowners, while tenants benefitted from selling prices fixed according to current low rents, and increased state aid.[28] Augusta was proud of her nephew's brave reconciling gesture. It was a rarity in Ireland, where people mostly felt compelled to operate within one or other political community. He entered her imagination as a visionary, with dreams 'beyond possible realisation'.

Lane, who had an instinctive rather than tutored knowledge of art, had become a wealthy dealer in old masters two years after he had set up on his own in February 1898. He was slim, restless, impeccably dressed, but he suffered from neurasthenia, a nervous condition. Believing that art, whether a great painting or a felicitous arrangement of flowers, could fundamentally enhance existence, he often expressed his affection by arranging the furniture and the decorations of his friends. He seemed to be designed to contrast with his well-rooted and flexible aunt; he had no real feeling for place as she had, and was intransigent rather than diplomatic.

Augusta found her newly successful nephew arrogant and boastful, and was outraged when Hugh encouraged his impecunious mother (she had four other children to provide for and Augusta regularly sent her fruit and meat) in her snobbery by suggesting that his sister Ruth be presented at court.[29] However, in March 1900 Augusta warmed to his insightful generosity when he gave her an oil painting by Nicolas Poussin of a blind laurel-crowned poet-fiddler – 'Raftery of course!' 'I don't know whether to scold or thank you most!' she wrote, initiating the tone something between a caring, sensible mother and a more light-hearted sister that would persist.[30]

After that she invited Hugh to Revival events, though he remained fastidiously aloof from the literature, informality and nationalist ethos. He told George Moore that with Lady Gregory as an aunt, he was compelled to think of Ireland, and after John Butler Yeats's Dublin exhibition in October 1901, Lane commissioned him, with Augusta's help, to paint portraits of Irish politicians to form the nucleus of an Irish portrait gallery.[31] Then in October 1902 he proposed that the impoverished and unfashionable Royal Hibernian Academy (RHA) be given a boost by the staging of an exhibition of old masters culled from the walls and cellars of Ireland's great houses.[32] This was met with scepticism by people who felt it was a ploy to ferret out good paintings, which he could buy cheaply and sell in London, but as Augusta worked with him and saw his enthusiasm, she began to regard him as a 'fellow-worker' dedicated, like herself, to Ireland.[33] He would develop a passionate interest in Irish art and a desire to establish an Irish School at a time when most successful Irish artists were living outside the country. But he was also ambitious for an official position in the art world, easier to obtain in Dublin than in London, and it suited him to organise exhibitions and act as a patron.

The theatre had been reorganised in August 1902 and a constitution was drafted in January 1903 with Russell's help.[34] All members had voting rights and Yeats was elected president.[35] Augusta had no place in this structure, but she was on the Reading Committee with Yeats, Russell, Fred Ryan, Padraic Colum, Arthur Griffith and Maud Gonne. As the emphasis was firmly placed on the performing of new works by emerging playwrights, the Reading Committee, charged with selecting the plays, was hugely important. The meetings came to be held in Augusta's warm and comfortable drawing-room at the Nassau Hotel, so that the centre of the theatre society shifted there from the Molesworth Hall, a fact not unnoticed by the playwright, Padraic Colum. It was significant, for in this environment Yeats, supported by Augusta, could prevail when he opposed James Cousins and championed J.M. Synge.

In a burst of creativity in the summer of 1902 Synge had written *The Shadow of the Glen* and *Riders to the Sea*. Both plays were well received at informal readings in Augusta's London apartment in the spring of 1903. However, when *The Shadow of the Glen* – a play in which an elderly husband feigns death to catch his young wife with her lover and which ends with the wife, banished by her husband and abandoned by her lover, departing with a passing tramp – was put before the Reading Committee it was immediately snagged on nationalist sensibilities. Yeats pushed it through, but Hyde and Gonne, opposed to a play that could be interpreted as reflecting badly on the morality of Irishwomen, resigned before the performance in October. Russell, disappointed that the society was not operating democratically, left a few months later. Two actors, Maire Quinn and Dudley Digges, departed to form their own company.

A gulf was appearing between Yeats and Augusta, who put quality first, and nearly everyone else, except for Synge, who from now on would become more closely involved with the two of them. Yeats articulated his argument that individual genius was far more important than the mob with its tyrannising conformity in a series of articles for *The United Irishman*. Augusta accepted the primacy of genius. But asserting it publically and realising it was for Yeats to do: 'I feel verse is more than any prose can be, the apex of the flame, the point of the diamond.'[36] She also keenly appreciated that the theatre had a base in reality and saw that as her domain – prose plays, the managing and smoothing out of controversies, the getting and keeping of support. This was her way of supporting genius, particularly Yeats's genius. 'I went into this theatre for his sake & his interests have been with me all through,' she told Quinn in 1908.[37] Even while she recognised Synge's genius and his potential value for the theatre she was thinking of Yeats, telling Quinn that now he had Synge's plays to push on the Reading Committee he could not be accused of only thinking of himself when he held out for quality.[38]

When Augusta returned to Coole for Easter in 1903 she discovered for herself the devastation wrecked by what became known as the big wind of 26 February. The large evergreen oak on the front lawn, ten lime trees between the house and stables and many thousands of spruce and larch were down. It changed the aspect of Coole.[39] Augusta was horrified at the damage. But she soon began to plan the installation of a sawmill to cut 'and make saleable' the newly available timber, and redoubled her tree planting.[40]

This was the first time Yeats had come to Coole for Easter. Augusta helped him with a scenario for *The King's Threshold* (then 'Seanchan'), and arranged folklore for him. Yeats and Augusta were growing closer as their theatre friends seemed to be falling away. Maud Gonne had married John McBride in February. Yeats had been devastated. By May she would confide to Yeats that the marriage was a disaster and she was deeply unhappy. 'I feal [sic] somehow that the Maud Gonne I have known so long has passed away,' Yeats would tell Augusta, although he still found long talks with her extremely painful.[41]

There were tensions with Russell that were not only due to his disenchantment with Yeats's dictatorial attitude to the theatre. Augusta was guilty of pushing Russell aside when he criticised Yeats in ways she found unacceptable, and when he wrote warning that Yeats should take more responsibility for his father if he did not want the moral character of his work to be damaged, she was angry; this was not Russell's territory. Yeats was also increasingly critical of Russell's aesthetic standards, his spiritualism and tendency to neglect his art for more practical matters.

Augusta had remained friendly with Hyde. Their lively and mutually supportive correspondence persisted for some time. In particular, he kept her informed of the considerable ups and downs of the Gaelic League, and she considered he had 'taken up the real grievance of the time' by concentrating on education, something she would have adopted if she had 'meddled in politics'.[42]

Yeats had, in December 1902, begun to address some of his letters to Augusta 'Dear Friend', a form he also used to Gonne. 'I need not tell you that I am always wishing for the time to pass swiftly until we are together again,' he wrote on 16 December. 'I wish I was back in Ireland & at work again there, & with you near me,' he wrote on 8 May 1903. They both punctuated their letters with anxious enquiries about each other's health, and when, in October 1903, Yeats was preparing to go to America for four months, Augusta too wore her heart on her sleeve: 'I am sad at saying goodbye to you as always'.[43]

They relied on each other for work, to exchange ideas and for the everyday talk that gives us our sense of self and place in the world. When, in 1926, Augusta read Yeats's autobiographic *Estrangement*, she confided to her journal: 'Many nice words about me, bringing back the memory of those years of close companionship. I miss it. When I am too long without a friend at hand to talk with I feel, not lonely, but insincere – never speaking my whole mind.'[44]

Robert was also at Coole for Easter 1903. He had finally decided on a career. Art. Apart from the sketches of views and caricatures that punctuated his letters, his drawing lessons and interest in Greek art, Robert had been discussing theatre design with Yeats. In the spring of 1903, either invited by Yeats or working unsolicited, Robert produced sketches for the set and costumes for *The Hour Glass* in which he struck a medieval note with dark green tapestries and a few symbolic objects. Yeats was impressed with their simplicity and gave them to Sturge Moore to realise.[45] It was perhaps this success that encouraged Robert to think of training to be an artist. Augusta was glad to find that his heart and mind were finally engaged, 'especially [for] so high a profession', though she was anxious about his ability to apply himself: 'The temptation to take work easily may beset him,' she told Arabella, 'But I believe he will succeed,' she added. 'He has imagination and love of this countryside which has not yet found its expression.' From now on she would be ambitious for him as an artist, and imagined him a painter of the Galway landscape.

Augusta's next play, *The Rising of the Moon*, finished by July 1903, is a neat, deft, enjoyable play. To Blunt she acknowledged that Yeats had helped her 'as I helped him in *Cathleen* and *The Pot of Broth*. It is wonderful in play writing how one mind seems to supplement another.'[46] The fact that the play was billed as hers suggests that Yeats provided criticisms and suggestions rather than phrases and plot ideas. Yeats was impressed with the result: 'It is much better than "25",' he told Blunt, 'more simple, more energetic, more buoyant & much more to act in it,' although he still thought she was best employed translating myths.[47]

When it was performed in March 1907 it became, almost immediately, a classic of the repertoire of the Abbey Theatre. Writing in 1974 Micheál O hAodha observed: 'To three generations of playgoers the very title *The Rising of the Moon* meant the Abbey.'[48]

It is a piece of romantic nationalism in which Augusta's personal experience is dovetailed with the life of the country people. A political prisoner from Galway Gaol has escaped. Dressed as a ballad singer, he tries to keep a rendezvous with a boatman in the presence of a sergeant who has not immediately suspected that the ballad singer (with his repertoire of patriotic and seditious songs) is the prisoner. The singer, realising the hopelessness of his position, devises the tactic of persuading the sergeant of his own nationalist leanings. The audience knows exactly what is going on and is led to believe that the ballad singer will escape; the question is how and when. The theme here is secrecy and the uncovering of secrets. Not only is this a valuable dramatic ploy, but enforced secrecy and the threat of revelation was a constant theme of Irish nationalist legend, especially as expressed in ballads.[49]

Augusta wanted to give the people a voice. For this she dug into personal memories – her nurse's stories of Rowan Hamilton's attempted disguise and escape by boat, her childhood meditation on the impregnability of Galway Gaol (both acknowledged), and Blunt's incarceration there in 1888 (unacknowledged). She cemented them with what she had learned from folklore: phrases, attitudes to the police, the songs 'The Rising of the Moon' and 'Granuaile', and most effectively the Raftery-like ability of singers to manipulate their listeners. When it was first performed there were objections from both nationalists (the policeman was treated too sympathetically) and Unionists (the policeman was 'a coward and a traitor'), which showed she had achieved a balance of sorts, but eventually its romantic charm prevailed. It is pure Lady Gregory in its nationalist tone, devoid of stridency, and in her observation of an Irishness missed by the ideologues.

To date, Augusta had, with Yeats's support, written two one-act comedies to, she would argue in *Our Irish Theatre*, complement his poetic plays: 'The listeners . . . have to give so close attention to the lines . . . that ear and mind crave ease and unbending, and so comedies were needed to give this rest.'[50] But this was not the whole story. The comedies were not mere vacuous entertainment. Augusta objected to the frequent descriptions of them as farces, because that implied that they were allied to the commercial British stage. Molière and Shakespeare, with their use of comedy to reflect seriously on life as it is lived, were her models, and her interpretation of the original injunction written by herself and Yeats to 'bring upon the stage the deeper thoughts and emotions of Ireland' was to reveal underlying rather than profound or spiritual thoughts and emotions.[51]

She also wanted to experiment – it 'is like fire in the blood'.[52] She would continually tinker with the form of the play, paring down the numbers of characters and the action, and in December 1903, ignoring Yeats's suggestion that she adapt Molière, she decided to write a historical tragedy, *Kincora*.[53] She was struck by the way history infiltrated folklore and she saw their fusion as an inherent Irish genre. Historical plays, she told Blunt, were 'an absolute necessity here if the drama is to take a grip of the people', and she wanted to tour historical plays in the hope that they might capture the imagination, especially of children.[54]

Yeats had gone to America in October 1903 to lecture and she cautiously announced her new project in a Christmas Day letter: 'I am at work at Brian Boru; I can see your face when you think of it, profound distrust, and some alarm.'[55] She felt confident, with an emotion she already recognised as the accompaniment to a first attempt: 'Of course I think at present it is going to be splendid, but probably when it is done, I shall wonder at the superiority of Cousins' dramatic method.'

A week later she had her first draft, and disillusionment: 'I actually finished my first writing of Brian yesterday, but of course must begin rewriting at once; I already look back at the first act as a miserable thing.'[56] She was desperate to talk to Yeats who, she told Blunt, 'has a terribly clarifying mind' and could tell her whether it was any good.[57]

Augusta spent the next three days unable to work out why the play was unsatisfactory, but equally unable to abandon it as hopeless. Reading it to Robert clarified its shortcomings and made her so low, 'I sat down & read your Finn Preface this morning, to restore my self respect,' she told Yeats.[58] He responded on 21 January with gratifying interest and general advice: 'I am full of curiosity to know what your "King Brian" will be like. Remember that a play, even if it is in three acts, has to seem only one action. . . . Your danger will be that having thought of Act I first your other acts will be episodes by themselves.'[59] She went back to the play in April 1904, finishing it with some help from Synge who was briefly at Coole in July.

Kincora was based on the story of Brian Boru, the High King of Ireland who defeated the Danes at Clontarf in 1014 and was a nationalist hero. Augusta was drawn to this moment in Irish history not for the bombastic success, but because of the theme of rivalry and the problem of Brian's motivation. Brian had become High King by marrying

Lady Gregory

Gormleith, the sister of the King of Leinster and the widow of the former Danish chief. Peace between the Irish kings was broken when Gormleith conspired with the Danes. Augusta had been given a glimpse of the dynamics between husband and wife as viewed by the country people: 'It was the wife brought him to his end, Gormleith. She was for war and he was all for peace.'[60] It was a beguiling idea, giving Augusta an opportunity to look behind the myth of war and victory.

She was also intrigued by the theme of lost friends, echoing her own recent experience: 'Those that serve Ireland take for their lot lasting battles, lasting quarrels . . . Those that should be most their friends turn to be most their enemies, till their heart grows dry with bitterness, dry as the heads of mountains under the summer heat.' So spoke the spirit in the prologue to *Kincora* in heartfelt images.[61]

The company was enthusiastic and when they read it Yeats praised the power of the play to Horace Plunkett who replied, 'I don't wonder at it being powerful, she is the hardest woman I know to speak up to. I have been in a controversy with her and know.'[62] But Yeats encouraged her to find richer images and develop the character of Brian to balance the formidable Gormleith.[63] It became a popular play as people appreciated Augusta's treatment of Irish legends without Yeats's obscuring poetry and symbolism.[64]

However, Yeats did not leave her in peace. On 29 June 1905 he told Quinn that he felt *Kincora* had not really passed through Augusta's imagination; she rewrote it nearly five years later. This time she allowed herself to empathise with Gormleith, who, a complex character, has palpable and conflicting loyalties as the sister of one king, married to another and with a Danish son. Her love of action becomes a fatal flaw. Her fate is hinted at in the beginning, and she is allowed bitter self-realisation of what she has done at the end. By 1909 Augusta was able to make a tragedy out of the history.

It got a lukewarm reception when it was performed and severe criticism from Sinn Féin. Yeats would write in his journal, 'The old version pleased the half-educated because of its rhetoric; the new displeases because of its literature.'[65]

TWELVE

The Abbey Theatre

I am confident of a fairly good start with the plays – the
stars are quiet and fairly favourable.
                                      WBY to AG, 27 December 1904

Augusta was 52 in March 1904. Five months later she
was named as the patentee for the newly established
Abbey Theatre. The following year she became, with W.B.
Yeats and J.M. Synge, a director. Thus she moved by degrees
into the public arena. Her style became a subject for
conversation and comment, out of which a portrait of Lady
Gregory of the Abbey emerged.

It was not, by and large, complimentary, as the actress
Máire Nic Shiubhlaigh in her memoir of the Abbey, *The
Splendid Years*, written in 1955, revealed:

I have many memories of her during these years; presiding
maternally at one of those lavish suppers she loved to hold
in the theatre on first nights; or, in different
circumstances, drawing up her short rather bulky figure,
squaring her shoulders and smiling rather grimly in a thin-
lipped manner in face of opposition. Or again in later
years, bustling with her strange, short-stepped walk
through the Abbey, meeting distinguished visitors in the
vestibule before the curtain rose on new plays, smiling her

rather fixed social smile, or talking rapidly in her odd flat-toned way.

Nic Shiubhlaigh presented an image of a woman without feminine charm, manifestly in control of both herself and the situation.[1] She also found the director condescending, as did the playwright, Padraic Colum, who, disliking what he saw as manipulation, was driven to mixing his metaphors: '. . . because her diplomacy combined resolution with an apparent artlessness, and preparation with flattery of address, it was annoying to those who could see through a millstone.'[2] Even those such as Gerard Fay who were generally positive produced a faintly dislikable image, emphasising her devotion to duty. He also noted her resemblance to the elderly Queen Victoria, although during her life the Queen Victoria image was not necessarily derogatory; it was circulating during her lecture tour in America in 1915 and Augusta was determined to be complimented by it.[3] It became a popular image; Nic Shiubhlaigh used it, and it has been repeated ad nauseam in books and articles on Lady Gregory. But perhaps the most common recollection of Lady Gregory is of feeling fear in her presence.[4]

It is not too difficult to find reasons for this distancing from Lady Gregory. Máire Nic Shiubhlaigh felt that she had been forced out of the theatre by Augusta (she resigned in early 1906) and her rather catty description of Augusta's person suggests revenge. Colum, too, felt he had been wronged. The Queen Victoria image, given substance by Yeats in 1924 when he bracketed Lady Gregory with the Queen in Phase 24 in *A Vision* (published in 1926), gained popularity partly because, in her full, old-fashioned black dresses, habitual black mantilla (to detract, her granddaughter Catherine said, from an unwelcome receding chin), diminutive height and upright bearing, she did resemble the Queen Victoria of the 1890s. Augusta's haughty aristocratic style belonged to a generation that had been superseded by the naughty nineties and the lighter grace of the Edwardian period in which women were beginning to take a slightly more forthright, outspoken, down-to-earth tone. Equally, one suspects, the Queen Victoria slot was a convenient place to put women of authority and power, especially when, as Augusta did, they tried to exercise it by retaining the feminine virtues of apparent submissiveness to men, unruffled calm, unstinting kindness.

She could appear forbidding in her treatment of people with whom she was not intimate. She would dismiss people she disliked or had no need for or who had fallen out with herself and Yeats. In 1907 the young Ben Iden Payne found her 'though not ungracious . . . somewhat standoffish, as if she might be very authoritarian when she chose'.[5] In January 1906, embedded in a long letter written to persuade Padraic Colum to stay with them, she wrote with almost chilling detachment of those who had left and were 'lost', 'all of whom had been helpful in their time. Now others are dropping off. It is always sad to lose fellow workers, but the work must go on all the same.'[6] She quoted it in *Our Irish Theatre*, seeing no harm in it; for her it expressed her passion for loyalty to the task in hand. In private, Augusta made sweeping generalisations about Catholics: 'These Papists haven't the courage of a mouse, and then wonder how it is we go ahead.'[7]

Catholicism was only ever marginal to her concerns and she failed to understand (or turned a blind eye to the fact) that for nationalist Catholics religious concerns were central. She and Yeats could thus unthinkingly offend Catholics. When they perfomed *Twenty Five* during Lent, Edward Martyn, for whom religious observation was a deeply serious issue, told her it was insulting to 'Catholic and nationalist Ireland to be having such jollities when in all other European capitals there are no general gaieties'.[8] Her biographer, Elizabeth Coxhead, noted that although Augusta had little social snobbery (she made little effort to cultivate her social equals in Galway for purely social reasons, for instance) she was capable of intellectual snobbery. We have seen how she looked down on the wives of her friends and literary collaborators.

Given that she had discovered her facility for diplomacy in Egypt in the company of Sir William Gregory, Auckland Colvin and Edward Malet, it would be surprising if her manner and methods were not tinged with their imperial certainties. She was, undoubtedly, paternalistic towards the actors for whom this attitude was undesirable. They were nationalists, and for all its dictatorial intellectual tone Irish nationalism did encourage people to think of themselves as the equal of anyone, particularly an Anglo-Irish landowner.

In her defence Augusta had no role models. There were powerful women in the theatre, but they were actresses with a licence to be flamboyant. Augusta's behaviour could fluctuate from the self-effacing to the ruthlessly assertive. This suggests uncertainty. In the absence of an approved style she fell back on an amalgam of family roles. There was the understanding aunt figure sitting quietly beside the Green Room stove while the players brewed themselves tea. There was the aristocratic magnanimity of the 2ft-diameter Gort Barnbrack, traditionally served at first nights and said to be from the family estate though in fact it came from Gort town bakery – a maternalistic or paternalistic gesture depending on your view. There was the quietly authoritative mother who could be relied on for kind and wise advice, and who acted as a moral guardian. And there was the manipulative wife, getting her own way through flattery and the apparent prioritising of others, the iron will disguised by kindly gestures. It was not until she got to America and responded to the demand for lectures and statements to journalists that Augusta discovered a purpose-built role and a style to suit.

Her most consistent inspiration was to follow her duty. This duty did not have the narrow connotations associated with the more modern usage. Yeats defined what he believed to be her view in *Autobiographies*: she 'never lost her sense of feudal responsibility, not of duty as the word is generally understood, but of burdens laid upon her by her station and her character, a choice constantly renewed in solitude'.[9] This referred to her work of keeping Coole for Robert and her self-imposed duty to the Irish Revival and to Yeats. But part of this duty was also to herself: 'I idled more than you in Italy,' she wrote to Robert (or Yeats) in 1908, 'and only wanted to exist and look at the olives. But at home one must work or die or one's mind must . . .'[10] Her commitment to purposeful work was made against a background in which women of her class were not expected to work. It was an achievement to have work; she relished her duty rather than resigned herself to it. She was aware, too, of the alternative: 'everyday babbling'.[11] One gets the feeling that she felt that men might indulge in both work and babbling; for her and her female contemporaries it was either or.

One of the more unattractive aspects of Augusta's work to the modern mind is her persistently stated deference to Yeats in regard to their collaborative literary work and in the Abbey Theatre. She never deviated from this in public. Historians of the Abbey, assuming that they can always rely on this perspective from Augusta, often adopt a slightly irritated tone. Contemporaries did not take kindly to selfless Lady Gregory, insistent for Yeats, especially when she accompanied this by telling them how much she cared for and regarded them: transparent attempts to keep them on side. Although it cannot be denied that she was loyal to Yeats, and put his work first, the simple statements of selflessness were also masks designed to deflect attention from herself. Behind the scenes with Yeats she knew how to stand up for herself; she was independent-minded.

Her strengths as a director were an intelligent and tenacious diplomacy, and tact underwritten by an emotional commitment to what she saw as the right. This had little glamour in an arena where forthrightness, particularly male forthrightness, was prized. After 1905, Yeats, for instance, deliberately cultivated a bad temper and sense of outrage as a managerial technique.[12] Privately though, Augusta was appreciated. 'I wish you had been in Dublin & then I don't really think there would have been all this upset for everyone,' Lolly Yeats wrote to Augusta in January 1906 when Máire Nic Shiubhlaigh was protesting against Yeats's treatment of her.[13] Even when relations with Russell had deteriorated he could write to Augusta: 'With you or Synge *anyone* might arrange a compromise but if W.B.Y. is to act as diplomatist then I see nothing for it but a row & publicity of the whole business'.[14]

With involvement in the theatre came familiarity with Dublin. None of the directors ever really liked Dublin, or Dubliners. 'Too much Dublin I fear would ruin anyone,' Synge wrote to Augusta in December 1906.[15] Turn-of-the-century Dublin was still experiencing the downward spiral of vitality inaugurated by the Union in 1801, when the political heart had been cut from the capital leaving it with a displaced aristocracy and a rapidly proliferating working class that was gradually turning the Georgian townhouse mansions into decrepit tenements. Yet there was a middle class, both Protestant and Catholic, with a keen cultural appetite.

Arriving by tram from Dalkey, Killiney, Dun Laoghaire or the inner suburbs of Rathmines, Rathgar and Rathfarnham, they would fill many of the seats in the new Abbey Theatre. It was from the lower echelons of this class that Yeats discovered his Irish players. That this was unusual is conveyed in the patrician tones in which Augusta described their dramatic society and the Ormonde Players actors to Blunt in September 1902: '. . . a most interesting experiment, it is got up by artisans and clerks in Dublin. They have no capital . . . but . . . are starting with great spirits'.[16]

She was referring to the brothers Frank and William Fay, both amateur actors, with whom Yeats had made contact. Frank (1871–1931) who worked as a clerk, was a perfectionist, especially in elocution, and he was the brother for whom nationalist politics meant most. William (1873–1947), an electrician, was confident, with a good opinion of himself and a belief that he could make things work when set back. He had a particular talent for comedy.

The other members of the Ormonde Players were drawn from the same class: Padraic Colum was a railway clerk, Máire Nic Shiubhlaigh was a member of Gonne's Inghinidhe na hÉireann. The Allgood sisters, Sara and Molly, were brought up on the quays where their Catholic mother worked in the family furniture business after the death of their Protestant father. The family were drawn to new nationalist groups; the girls were members of Inghinidhe na hÉireann, their brothers joined Arthur Griffith's Sinn Féin after it was formed in August 1903. Sara was aware of the potential social benefits of success and became close to Lady Gregory, though she tended to flatter while Augusta acted as patron.[17] But Molly, later Synge's beloved, retained a wilder, socially independent streak for longer. They both started their acting careers with Dublin accents, which Frank Fay patiently ironed out. These actors, together with Dudley

Digges, Arthur Sinclair, Maire Quinn, J.M. Kerrigan and George Roberts, were bound together by their love of acting and their willingness to take on what was put in front of them. Iden Payne, a young English actor, brought in as a manager by Annie Horniman in 1907 to combat what she saw as the amateurishness of the company, had great regard for them, describing them as 'fine instinctive artists', who gave the theatre its enviable vitality.[18]

Apart from Gort business people Augusta had little experience of the Catholic middle class. She approached them with slightly more tolerance than Yeats, but with far less of an open mind than Synge. When she wrote to Yeats that Robert thought the actress Marie Garvey 'embodies all that is most odious in Irish life', she did not contradict his opinion.[19] And to Yeats she remarked in January 1908 that 'class distinctions' and 'Romanism' made straightforward dealings with W.G. Fay impossible; they inevitably had different perspectives.[20] Mary Colum's observation that in Dublin Augusta behaved like a grand duchess, treating the people as if they were her subjects, suggests that she was unable to adapt to the more meritocratic artistic milieu she found herself in.[21] She was incapable of breaking down barriers with affability or courtesy, as Synge did. Instead, she tried to communicate through flattery and what Mary Colum described as 'a perfectly fearsome artificial tact', which was easily ridiculed. She remained, for most people (Sara Allgood and Seán O'Casey were the notable exceptions) aloof and condescending.

By choosing (after October 1903) the Nassau Hotel as her Dublin base, Augusta maintained her social distance from the players. It stood opposite Trinity College, near the Kildare Street Club in the Anglo-Irish district of Dublin, and her sitting-room with its heavily upholstered furniture and tapestry curtains allowed Augusta to preside over what

impressed even Máire Nic Shiubhlaigh as elegant teas.[22]
Here she met the surgeon Oliver St John Gogarty, and Maud
Gonne. Yeats stayed here, too.

In January and February 1904 Augusta, alone at Coole,
displayed none of the formidable characteristics that would
become her trademark. She missed Yeats, who was lecturing
in America from October 1903 to March 1904, and she did
not enjoy the prospect of seeing the theatre's production of
his *The Shadowy Waters* in January without him.[23] In
Dublin she was unable to persuade the Reading Committee
to accept the (negligible) one-act comedy *Head or Harps*
that she had written with Yeats.

She was also concerned about Robert who was
struggling under the intimidating Henry Tonks in his first
year at the Slade School of Art, and she went to London in
March 1904 to visit him. Here she began to cultivate
artists, no doubt with Robert's career in mind. Yeats had
previously introduced her to the portrait painter, Charles
Shannon, and his partner, Charles Ricketts, a painter and
designer with avant-garde leanings who had been involved
with theatre design for Yeats. She commissioned Shannon
to paint Robert. Completed in March 1906 while Robert
was still a student, it purported to depict him as an
established painter in a loose shirt with oils, palette and
easel, but a closer inspection reveals that the tubes of paint
are unopened and the brushes clean; it portrayed aspiration
rather than fact.[24]

She was interviewed by *The Book Monthly* as a
spokesperson for the Irish Revival, but she responded with
horror to the suggestion that she lecture to the Irish Literary
Society instead of Yeats.[25] She regarded this as Yeats's role.
When Yeats tried to get out of an important lecture in
America she lectured him in messianic language: 'It is your

business to put a flame in the heart of every young man who hears you, & a hammer in his hand with which to hammer the heads of the brazen image, & a brick in his other hand to help the building of the temple.'[26] Her attitude was going to have to change as her reputation grew and her involvement with the theatre put her in the public eye.

Back in Ireland in the spring of 1904 Augusta became more actively involved in the planning for the Irish National Theatre Society's Irish tour and first English tour.[27] She wrote to Yeats, advising him that Sara Allgood should get a pay rise, and reported that she had tried to keep the young nationalist, Padraic Pearse, on their side by assuring him that they had no desire to fight with those who wanted to focus on Irish language drama. She was discovering the need to become involved in the day-to-day issues in Yeats's absence. But she was also galvanised to act by the increasing involvement of another.

Annie Horniman (1860–1937) was now becoming a force to be reckoned with. She had known Yeats for nearly ten years; they were both members of the occult Order of the Golden Dawn, and she had financed a play of his in 1894. In the summer of 1903 she had designed and made elaborate costumes for *The King's Threshold*. They had not been a great success, but on 10 October 1903, prompted by tarot card readings and a rousing post-performance speech from Yeats about his vision for an Irish theatre, she offered financial backing to make it a reality. On 1 February 1904 Yeats reported to Augusta that Miss Horniman was negotiating the purchase of the Mechanics Institute in Abbey Street, and the adjacent morgue for a new theatre. It was a good place for a theatre, close to the quays and within the commercial heart of the city. By early April 1904 Annie Horniman could formally offer the building to the theatre society, and on 9 April Yeats went to see the Under-

Secretary, Sir Antony MacDonnell, about securing a patent. The next day Joseph Holloway, an architect and theatre enthusiast, was engaged to refurbish the buildings. They planned to open in the late autumn with a new season of plays.

Augusta was sent a copy of Miss Horniman's draft petition for a patent. She only had minor criticisms, but she adopted a decidedly superior tone in her reply: 'I pointed out that her last paragraph repeated other sentences, & I would not say the new theatre will never interfere with the old ones for I hope it may do so,' she told Yeats on 14 April. Yet caution, not uncharacteristic, would not have been unjustified. Annie Horniman, an Englishwoman, had no tolerance for Irish nationalism. She had homed in on Yeats's 1903 *Samhain* statement that his theatre was not to be the home of propaganda. This, rather worryingly, could readily translate into a rejection of any play with what might be perceived as a nationalist message. Or so Augusta might have reasoned. Here also was someone who presented herself as a rival to Augusta in championing Yeats's genius. And, by providing a subsidy, she would have significant power. As Augusta indicated to Yeats on 26 March, any decisions about payments to actresses could not be taken without consulting Annie Horniman, 'as it would fall on her'.

Augusta Gregory and Annie Horniman make an interesting comparison. Horniman, 43, English, the heiress of a successful tea merchant whose independent income was largely wrapped up in rising Hudson Bay shares, and a confirmed spinster, was sartorially more flamboyant than Augusta (large jewels, brightly coloured dresses), and much more modern. She smoked, had cycled unchaperoned across the Alps in bloomers, and had rebelled against her Quakerish background by indulging her love of theatre and tarot, both forbidden. And, just as their dress sense was equally individualistic, so they were both equally independent-minded. Neither was supportive of the suffragette movement, content to be exceptional women in a male-dominated society. They had other characteristics in common: both valued hard work, honesty, appropriate conduct according to one's position. There, though, the similarities ended. In Annie Horniman these things, derived from her Quaker background, were held as self-conscious principles, and were mixed with more commercial values – the right to get value for money, prompt payment of accounts – which seemed to define her as middle class, and English.

Plain-speaking was another often-practised virtue of Annie Horniman's; it could descend to blunt recriminations, spitefulness and cattiness (especially against Yeats), and this too put her in a different class from the habitually diplomatic and polite Augusta. Annie had a vehement intolerance of any suggestion of sex; in the summer of 1906 she would react wildly against relationships between members of the theatre. Augusta was always more balanced about such matters. Writing to Quinn, Augusta was capable of lightheartedness: 'Love affairs in the company are giving us some worry (quite proper ones!), but I think in a short time everyone will either be married or in lunatic asylums, or both.'[28]

Financing the Abbey fulfilled several needs for Annie Horniman. It enabled her to find an outlet for her interest in the arts, but, more importantly, it was a way of getting close to Yeats for whom she had a passion which she knew he did not reciprocate. Giving him money gave her the occasion to write copiously and forthrightly, eliciting advances and rejections from the alternatively beholden and elusive Yeats. How soon did Augusta perceive this vulnerability? John Butler Yeats hinted at it in his oil painting of 1904 which hangs in the lobby of the Abbey Theatre. It shows a tall middle-aged woman, ethereal in a gorgeously rich dress, with pale hands resting on the arms of the chair in which she is sitting. There is purposefulness there, but she is also too tense.

Augusta was confined to Coole for Easter 1904 because Robert had chicken pox. She received a kind and thoughtful letter from Edward Martyn reassuring her that chicken pox was not dangerous, and congratulating Robert on going to art school: 'It is a great thing to have an intellectual interest in life. I think if a person has a great wish to do a work of art he will one day succeed in doing it.'[29] Unfortunately for poor Edward Martyn this was not the case; he wrote plays almost to the end of his life but none of them were very good or a great success. His letter to Augusta continued with self-deprecating humour on the subject of his inability to get on with people: 'As usual I continue to narrow the circle of my acquaintances.'

She had maintained her friendship with Edward Martyn despite their differences. In 1902 she had enjoyed a performance by his early music boys' choir, the Palestrina Choir, in the Pro-Cathedral in Dublin, lunching with him afterwards and meeting the Catholic hierarchy. She tried to support his Ibsenesque plays (which she was not keen on); in 1906 the Abbey would stage *The Heather Field* 'more as a compliment to him than caring very much for realistic work,' she told Quinn.[30] Martyn in his turn would support the Abbey from a regular first-night front row seat and praise Augusta's plays though, aspiring as he did to a 'drama of ideas', he thought 'peasant plays' too narrowly Irish.[31]

The impending realisation of the Abbey Theatre dominated hearts and minds in the summer. The patent application was challenged by the three established Dublin theatres, which meant a court hearing in early August. Yeats

A studio photo of Augusta Persse at about 28, when she married Sir William Gregory. *(Courtesy of Colin Smythe)*

Roxborough House with Slieve Echtge behind. The vast complex of stables is not shown. The house was burnt in spring 1924. *(Courtesy of Colin Smythe)*

Top: A studio photograph of Sir William Gregory at about 63, taken after his marriage to Augusta Persse. *(Courtesy of Colin Smythe)*

Below left: A photograph of Wilfrid Scawen Blunt at about 40 when he first met Lady Gregory (from her collection). *(Courtesy of Colin Smythe)*

Below right: Photograph of Ahmed Arabi from William Gregory's *carte de visite* album. *(Courtesy of Colin Smythe)*

Photograph of W.B. Yeats, *c.* 1905, at about 40, by Alvin Langdon Coburn. Yeats first went to Coole in July 1897. *(Royal Photographic Society National Museum of Photography, Film and Television, Science and Society Picture Library)*

The front of Coole Park, *c.* 1887, with Robert, Lady Gregory seated and Sir William Gregory far right. Photograph taken by Mrs Ernest Hart. *(Courtesy of Colin Smythe)*

Cover of Lady Gregory's copy of *Beltaine*, April 1900, with impromptu sketches by Jack Yeats of George Moore 'return[ing] to Ireland' with Queen Victoria, also Edward Martyn, Lady Daisy Fingall and W.B. Yeats. *(A.P. Wyatt Ltd on behalf of Michael B. Yeats)*

Douglas Hyde and Miss O'Kennedy in *The Twisting of the Rope*, written in Irish by Hyde to a scenario by W.B. Yeats, translated by Lady Gregory and performed in Irish in October 1901 at the Gaiety Theatre, Dublin. Hyde played the wandering poet based on Raftery. *(Courtesy of Colin Smythe)*

Augusta Gregory, *c.* 1912 wearing the diamond Maltese cross inherited from her mother, a discreet badge of aristocracy which she promised Hugh Lane in 1911 she would wear 'on all occasions as a set off' in America. *(Courtesy of Colin Smythe)*

Above: J.M. Synge photographed in 1906 at 35 on tour in Edinburgh. A director of the Abbey, he was recognised as a genius by Yeats and Lady Gregory. He would die three years later. *(Courtesy of Colin Smythe)*

Right: Pencil drawing of John Quinn by Augustus John dated 27 August 1909. Quinn, in John Butler Yeats's words, 'the crossest man in the world, and the kindest', was by then an established patron of the Abbey and Lady Gregory's close friend. *(Courtesy of the estate of Augustus John, Bridgeman Art Library)*

Annie Horniman, *c.* 1912–13. A wealthy English heiress, she subsidised the Abbey Theatre from 1904–10. *(National Portrait Gallery, London)*

The Abbey Theatre, built in 1904 to be a restrained setting for the spoken word. *(Failte Ireland Photographic Library)*

Above: Margaret Gregory at Coole with Richard Graham Gregory, born 6 January 1909. *(Courtesy of Colin Smythe)*

Left: Robert in the flying kit of the Royal Flying Corps. He was at the front from August 1916 to 26 January 1918 when he was accidentally shot down. *(Courtesy of Colin Smythe)*

Augusta Gregory seated at her writing table in the drawing-room, taken by George Bernard Shaw in *c.* 1915. The room also contained treasured copies of books by friends including Alexander Kinglake, Sir Alfred Lyall, J.G. Cordery, W.S. Blunt, William Sharp, Kuno Meyer, Edward Martyn, George Russell, W.B. Yeats, Somerville and Ross, Emily Lawless, Douglas Hyde, J.M. Synge. *(The Society of Authors on behalf of the Bernard Shaw Estate)*

A studio photograph of Hugh Lane, *c*. 1912, at about the time of the controversy over the Municipal Gallery of Modern Art in Dublin. *(Courtesy of Colin Smythe)*

Signed photograph of Sean O'Casey given to Lady Gregory. He was 43 and on the brink of success when he first got to know Lady Gregory in 1923. *(Courtesy of Colin Smythe)*

George Bernard Shaw and Lady Gregory at Coole, 1915, watching Richard in the car while Anne and Catherine with their nurse look out from an upstairs window. Photograph taken by W.F. Bailey. *(Courtesy of Colin Smythe)*

wired, asking Augusta to be the patentee because she was a 'resident of good standing' in Ireland. Annie Horniman would take the financial risk.

Synge and Russell visited Coole in July, and Yeats wrote a memo about the theatre in which he claimed the non-politically partisan theatre as a significant intellectual influence in the country. Historians of the Abbey inevitably emphasise Yeats's vision and, of course, without his trenchant views, his overbearing and irresistible judgement, and his poetic ideals there would have been no Abbey. Much of what he represented was distilled into the '*Samhain* principles' enunciated for the controversial 1903 season: art must override propaganda, speech must have the vitality of poetry, acting and scenery should be simplified.

Although Augusta followed this agenda with loyalty and passion, she approached the theatre from a different angle, valuing it as a conduit for retransmitting the voice of the people who had traditionally been either ignored or patronised. Much of this would be articulated in 1911 and 1912, in lectures for her American audience.[32] She depicted folk culture as a river whose overwhelming current had swept the theatre into its wake. With this she even, subtly, marginalised Yeats's 'beautiful verse plays'. These, she wrote, were sparked by folklore, but grew out of his free interpretation of it and so were not part of the mainstream. Synge, who had 'collaborated with the people,' deriving his 'fable, emotion, style' from them to give them back works that would change their perception of themselves, she characterised as completely caught in the current. She did not, of course, explicitly refer to her plays, but she obviously saw them as an important part of this mainstream.

She observed that the excitement of the discovery that a theatre could spring from folk culture made it 'a living thing'. A responsive audience was also vital, both in Dublin and the provinces.[33] In Dublin her broadly democratic bent was translated into a demand for sixpenny seats in the theatre (not achieved until after the departure of Annie Horniman), and a favouring of the pit over the stalls. In February 1914, when the company had left Dublin for their third tour of America, Augusta, left in charge of a second company, did a few experiments 'to go in the direction of a "People's Theatre".'[34] She enlarged the pit to entice people away from music hall, and trained a number of people new to acting.

But this was all to come. In the late summer of 1904 Augusta's contribution to the debate about the direction in which the theatre should be going was to write a one-act comedy, *Spreading the News*, the first play that was immediately satisfying both to her (she never revised it significantly) and to Yeats. Her idea was to present the losing of a good reputation. Given the fear she had experienced over 20 years previously about the loss of her own good name, it is not surprising that her first thoughts were of a young girl and tragedy. But Yeats and the Fays insisted on a comedy.[35] So she imagined a fair in a small country town plagued by a newly appointed magistrate on the lookout for illegal alcohol and agrarian crimes. Into this she put Bartley, who is observed pursuing a man with a hay fork. At each retelling of this incident his crimes multiplied until he was charged with murder. At first she could only think of Bartley as dull-witted but, after meeting a lugubrious old man on Kinvara beach, she had a character who could enjoy his misfortunes and would meekly comply with the unjust accusation of murder that she planned.[36]

With this comedy, set in a convincing evocation of everyday life, Augusta had found a theatrical voice which would carry her far. She had a comic technique based on characters that could be let loose on the plot. She had an inherently theatrical idea that relied on her formulating the necessary stories. And it was funny: 'delight' and 'joy' were the first words that Yeats used to describe it. She had also successfully removed herself, creating a fictional self-sufficient community that would in *Hyacinth Halvey* become Cloon. Further, the play had a nationalist slant without overt politics as she allowed the audience to savour the different vocabulary, syntax and assumptions of the magistrate and the villagers so that they could become aware of the clash of cultures, while the comedy precluded any heavy-handed moralising. However, to modern ears she still falls into the trap of lumping the country people together and laughing at communal characteristics rather than individual foibles. Also, producing comedy out of the inclination towards innocent exaggeration pandered to the old stereotypes and, laughing at the foolish rather than with the wise, Augusta was closer to the comic world of Samuel Lover's buffooning Paddy Whack and Handy Andy than she thought she was.

'But I'm thinking if I went to America its long ago the day I'd be dead! . . . And it's a great expense for a poor man to be buried in America.' So said Bartley within the first few minutes of the play, repeating (except 'the day' had replaced 'to-day') the words of the man at Kinvara. The rest of the dialogue ran along the current of everyday speech, reproducing the cadences, rhythms, phraseology and vocabulary of Hiberno-English. Augusta's 'Kiltartan' has been received sceptically, especially in the years after her death; in 1974 Micheál Ó hAodha claimed that her knowledge of the dialect was only superficial. But if her dialogue is translated into natural Irish and then re-translated into English the result comes very close to her Hiberno-English, only differing when the literal translation would not be readily understandable in English.[37]

Yeats thought it was a 'little masterpiece'. 'She seems to me,' he wrote to John Quinn (Augusta was typing), 'to have suddenly found herself in drama, and I foresee that the *Pot of Broth* will fade before its popularity.'[38] One who would appreciate the commercial value of her popularity, as well as the nature of her comedy, was Annie Horniman: 'Lady Gregory's work must be well treated – she is the best "draw" of the lot of you. I am so proud of her because she makes the people laugh in a witty manner, and I felt murderous when her work was treated as wickedly as at Edinburgh,' she would write to Yeats in November 1906.[39]

Finding George Bernard Shaw's long promised *John Bull's Other Island* too strange, dangerous and impractical to stage, Yeats and Augusta decided that *Spreading the News*, though maybe not the better play, was certainly right for the Abbey and for the opening night when it would be performed with *Cathleen ni Houlihan*, *In the Shadow of the Glen* and the premiere of Yeats's *On Baile's Strand*.

The theatre was ready for rehearsals by the end of October. By now John Quinn had joined an increasingly overwrought group in Dublin. Augusta was busy entertaining. She was also directing rehearsals of *Spreading the News*, her first experience of working with the actors. Before meeting them she made paper figures of her characters so that she could work out groupings and movements, and arrange their entrances and exits.[40] Sara Allgood, as Bartley's mother, was particularly responsive to her direction, and the *United Irishman*, which would find the play an 'improbable farce', would praise Allgood for living 'through every minute of her part'.[41] Augusta had found an actress who would be adept at interpreting her comedies and contribute greatly to their success.

The theatre was finally ready for 27 December. Although the Abbey was significantly less grand than the Gaiety, carpet greeted the audience as they entered, polished brass, scarlet leather and electric light defined the auditorium, and there were separate entrances for the wealthy and the not so wealthy. But there was a simplicity and artiness that was not to be found elsewhere. The stage dominated, allowing actors to perform with subdued voices and natural actions, contributing to a feeling of intimacy between actors and audience. 'Standing on the Abbey stage, the feeling, absent in so many other theatres, of being one with the audience was always present,' Máire Nic Shiubhlaigh claimed.[42]

The decorative restraint in Holloway's building expressed the new theatre's earnest emphasis on the spoken word. Where there was decoration it was to be Irish made and, preferably, Irish in theme. In the foyer the stained glass windows designed by Sarah Purser depicted uncontroversial trees (to satisfy Annie Horniman) while the walls were hung with oil paintings of the Fays, Máire Nic Shiubhlaigh and Annie Horniman by John Butler Yeats. It gave a strong impression of sincerity and spontaneity, exactly the tone Yeats and Augusta wished to set for the reception of the plays.

Neither Augusta, who was suffering from a severe bout of influenza (her first day in bed for nine years according to the housemaid), nor Annie Horniman were present for the first night.[43] But Augusta and Yeats were in close contact. With long days to contemplate the recent weeks, Augusta was overwhelmed by what they all owed to Yeats: 'But for your genius, which of us would have had the faith to do anything at all? I couldn't & you have kept in such a straight line – & you have conquered.'[44] Was Augusta staying away on purpose to give Yeats the opportunity to get the full credit? As he moved loquaciously between the many invited journalists the Abbey was indeed inaugurated as Yeats's theatre.

Before the opening Yeats's letters to Augusta were full of doubt and last-minute changes to costumes and scenery, and a nervous over-sensitiveness to the possible impact of the plays. He, too, was guiltily aware of what he owed Augusta, advocating that she take a long rest: 'You take care of everybody but yourself.'[45] At 10.50 pm on the first night he sent her a telegram: 'Your play immense success. all [*sic*] plays successfully packed house.'[46] A few days later he went through the event in detail in a letter, and his conclusion was generous: 'Our success could not have been greater.'[47]

THIRTEEN

Embroiled

> . . . crushing time out of odd moments to write play after
> play that kept life passing to and fro on the Abbey stage.
> Seán O'Casey, *Inishfallen, Fare Thee Well*

The Abbey moved courageously into the new year by staging Synge's *The Well of the Saints*, which, parodying belief in miraculous cures, endorsing despair, and with a gesturing towards extra-marital sex, seemed designed to wound Catholics at every sensitive point. Augusta went to Dublin for the opening on 4 February 1905 and stayed for the week of stressful and poorly attended performances. She found Synge disappointingly slow to take responsibility for his play, and when he arrived in the Green Room on the Saturday, having failed to appear on Friday, she shocked Joseph Holloway, who happened to be there, by saying, 'What happened to you last night? We thought you had committed suicide!'[1]

Robert, in his second year at the Slade, was sending home much happier letters. He was working on designs for the March production of *Kincora*. Yeats was sceptical about his motivation, but he encouraged him, suggesting he talk to Ricketts who was experimenting with pictorial curtains, a limited colour palette and suggestive detail rather than full-blown re-creation; innovations that would revolutionise theatre design in a few years' time. Such minimalism was attractive to Yeats, and to Augusta who did not want to see *Kincora* overwhelmed visually. Robert was inspired by it, too, and devised an unusual series of stencilled curtains in striking colours. But he was frustratingly slow. Augusta had to prod him repeatedly into action. The result was a triumph. Yeats pronounced that the set had a desirable 'high grave dignity and . . . strangeness'.[2] Augusta was delighted by Robert's success and for the next few years he was gradually drawn into the life of the Abbey at his mother's side.[3]

Augusta returned to Coole in May to be given a taste of how land sales might sour her relations with the tenants. Since the passing of the Wyndham Act in 1903, her tenants had stated their desire to buy. Augusta, too, was reconciled to the need to sell the tenanted land. She was also concerned to keep something of the broader character of the area: 'I have just written a long letter to Redmond about preservation of trees. I want to get those along Kiltartan road, for instance, vested in a rural council, that tenants when they purchase may not cut them down,' she told Arabella in May 1905.[4]

Prior to a sale it was necessary to agree satisfactory rent levels with the tenants, and in May 1905 this led to a debilitating fortnight of conflict with the grass farmers in which she was unable to leave Coole, hardly slept and worried that she had fallen out with them irrevocably. Yeats was empathetic, confiding that he had been worried for some time that purchase would bring her trouble. Aware that her desire to please could leave her in a weak position, and himself aware of the temptation to be over-yielding, he counselled forcefulness: 'A day comes in everything almost in which one has to fight, and wisdom is not in avoiding it but keeping no bitterness when the day is over. Of course, one should do all one can for peace and see that one is just, but after that – firmness and an easy mind.'[5] But any conflict was deeply disconcerting to Augusta for, after years of trying to support the tenants and of seeing their welfare as synonymous with the welfare of the estate, she was finding it difficult to realise that her interests were now effectively pitted against theirs.

In June Augusta spent a week in a sweltering Dublin overseeing the successful production of Colum's new play *The Land*, after which she travelled to Connemara in search of a newspaper-free, and English-free quiet. '"Virtue goes out" of one in company, and one wants solitude to bring it back again,' she told Blunt.[6]

Yeats, encouraged by Annie Horniman's promise of another instalment of money, arrived at Coole in the summer with a proposal that the theatre be radically overhauled. He was also intensely frustrated by the ability of the society's members (the actors, writers, the Fays) to dispute which plays should be acted and when. He wanted absolute control with the help and advice of Augusta and Synge, the only people whose opinion he valued. With Miss Horniman's money he saw his opportunity. He would give the actors salaries, but take away their society membership and voting rights; they would become employees not members of society which would become a limited liability company run by three directors. It would be, Yeats triumphantly declared, the end of democracy.[7]

During the summer of 1905 he campaigned vigorously, arguing to Augusta, who was not wholly convinced by the details, that the directors would consolidate their authority, and any malcontents could be dismissed. She, too, was frustrated by the power of people whose opinion she did not respect, describing the society as 'cumbrous and unworkable' to Blunt, and she was no doubt happy that Yeats would be in a better position to put his ideas into practice. Additionally, as director, she would have a formal position of influence for the first time, an opportunity she relished: 'This will put management into our hands and keep our decisions from being overruled.'[8] Russell, who had resigned from the society in April, and deeply disliked Yeats's undemocratic aims, reluctantly agreed to draft a new constitution, with dire effects on their relationship.

The summer was exhausting. It was hot, meat was difficult to keep, and Augusta was conscious of having four strong men to feed – Yeats, Robert, and two artist friends of Robert's. She compared herself 'serving tables' with the unfettered Synge who had left Coole in June for the Blasket Islands. Yeats had two young female aristocratic followers to stay: the married Countess Cromartie and the unmarried 25-year-old poet, Lady Margaret Sackville. Augusta was impressed by the way they seemed satisfied by the lack of social glamour at Coole. To Blunt she claimed not to be very interested in Lady Margaret 'because she is sure to marry and then her ideality will probably disappear'.[9] However, a watercolour sketch by Jack Yeats of a languid picnic beside the lake depicting Robert, the darkly handsome and ordained Arnold Harvey, Cottie, and Lady Margaret next to Robert's horse, Sarsfield, shows Robert relaxed in the company of Lady Margaret.[10] It is probable that Augusta considered the talented, beautiful, well-connected woman as a possible wife for him. The following year Augusta would play host to Dorothy Carleton, an intimate friend of Blunt's whom his relations, the Wyndhams, for Blunt's sake, hoped might fall in love with Robert. Dorothy flirted with both Robert and Yeats and returned to Blunt, preventing him from making peace with Anne from whom he had just separated.[11]

❖ ❖ ❖

Despite her serving, Augusta had buckled down to another play. Her success with *Spreading the News* had given her confidence, and in the next few years she would become the most reliable writer for the Abbey. In 1905 and 1906 the theatre produced ten new plays, five of which were Augusta's. From March 1905 to November 1909 she had plays ready for every spring and autumn season, a total of sixteen new plays (including translations and collaborations with Hyde and Yeats). She would supply two or three new plays a year until 1912, after which she averaged about one play a year until 1924. Her plays would also be performed more often than those of the other writers.[12]

The writing of the first plays, she later wrote, was 'a real joy, being the first entirely creative work I had done'. But, like many artists, she felt that her ability was a gift, which could at any moment be retracted, especially when her writing was interrupted, as it later was, by illness or bereavement. When she looked back on her first seven years of writing plays, Augusta saw that she had been driven by the realisation that each play presented a single, unrepeatable opportunity to have her say.[13] But she also knew that success depended on capturing the audience and keeping its attention. A play must have a smart pace, and tricks and devices to maintain interest. This populism was the secret of her success.

The White Cockade, a development of Hyde's *Rí Séamus*, for which she had written the scenario tells the story of the Battle of the Boyne of 1690 seen through the eyes of an innkeeper, his wife and a disinherited Gaelic aristocrat, Lady Dereen. It depicts the bravery of the Jacobite military commander, Patrick Sarsfield (a nationalist icon), Catholic King James II's cowardice, and the disillusioning effect of the defeat of the Stuart cause on ordinary lives. 'James II is the broken idol which shatters all faith and belief,' she wrote to

Blunt, suggesting that she was thinking beyond the folklore that not only influenced but defined the play.[14] She had devised it as a comedy to 'keep out rhetoric' and potential controversy. One particularly beguiling theme for Augusta was that the genuine hero was the man recognised by the people: 'He is surely the winner who gets a great tombstone, a figured monument, cherubs blowing trumpets, angels' tears in marble – or maybe he is the winner who . . . but writes his name in the book of the people. I would like my name set in clean letters in the book of the people,' declares Sarsfield.

Among the audience-wooing features was a barrel in which King James is concealed, the use of the rival songs of Lillibulero (Williamite) and The White Cockade (Stuart), and costumes, set design and lighting by Robert, all responsive to the nuances of the play. He brought out the inherent theatricality of the play: King James was comically overdressed, Lady Dereen was given a sympathetically restrained costume that prevented her from being ridiculed, and the lighting was dramatic and used to enhance the tragedy.

Hugh Lane appeared at one of the performances in a very bad humour, 'loudly abusing the wigs and the costumes . . . saying the whole thing was like a charade, and could not get it into his head that King James wasn't meant to be serious'.[15] He was confirmed in his opinion that his aunt had no visual sense. Joseph Holloway remarked in his diary that Lady Gregory 'pardonably waxed enthusiastic over her boy's artistic achievement'.[16] He had also watched Augusta in rehearsal and remarked that she had a strongly developed dramatic instinct which allowed her clearly to show the actors how she wanted a particular passage to be given.[17]

'I have sent off *White Cockade*, and my mind is already working on a little comedy,' she told Blunt on 8 August, giving him a summary of the plot of *Hyacinth Halvey*. It was set in the fictional present in Cloon, a place based on Gort, which allowed her 'to get a translation rather than a tracing'.[18]

There was plenty to tie Lady Gregory to Gort, the little town with its cliff-like array of plain, stone, early nineteenth-century buildings, a mile beyond the gates of Coole, much of which still survives. She sat in the Gregory gallery of the Protestant church opposite Lord Gort's family on Sundays. Whenever she visited the convent or the workhouse she would pass through the town. Her journeys to London and Dublin began and ended at Gort station. Coole acquired its provisions from Gort, paying the bills at regular intervals.[19] Her solicitor lived in Gort. Her bank was the National Bank in Gort, and she was friendly with the manager, Mr Grubb and his wife. Through her neighbours' requests for letters to relieve them of fines or support them in disputes she was familiar with the proceedings of the court. She exchanged presents and advice with the police and soldiers. In all of this Augusta could not hope to transcend her social role and to disentangle Coole from Gort; but she must have kept a careful watch as she played her part, for she had a very good idea of how life flowed back into its accustomed course once she had gone.

Augusta made great efforts to give the illusion of reality in *Hyacinth Halvey*, sketching the geography and atmosphere of the town through the dialogue. Hyacinth is the new sub-sanitary inspector to Cloon. Arriving with good testimonials, he is instantly endowed with an impossibly respectable reputation. Committing a crime and confessing it to disabuse people and show his true, fallible nature only reinforces their view as they assume he is protecting the true criminal. The humour often relies on social detail: the postmistress and the priest's housekeeper know exactly what they mean by an exemplary man: he would spend his evenings learning O'Growney's exercises and reading the *Catholic Young Man*. Hyacinth the outsider has a comparatively blander, more anglicised vocabulary than the other characters, though he speaks within a similar grammatical framework.

Augusta had vividly caught one aspect of the contemporary spirit by depicting modernising, small-town Ireland at one remove from the rural life. It was, with the historic palaces, inns and rural fairs of her other plays, another way of avoiding the big house/landlord-and-tenants scenario. With Cloon she hit on a formula that she knew well and from which she could easily exclude herself.[20]

Augusta's appreciation of the role of comedy had sharpened for she had finally taken Yeats's advice and was studying Molière that summer.[21] They had decided to perform one of his plays but, unable to find a suitable translation that would 'go across the footlights' she did her own in the Kiltartan dialect.[22] *The Doctor in Spite of Himself* dealt with a theme close to Augusta's heart, the making and destroying of false reputations. It was more knock-about than any of Lady Gregory's other comedies. She had picked up some techniques from Molière, most notably the use of two monologues posing as a dialogue between two people who fail to listen to each other which she immediately applied to *Hyacinth Halvey*.[23]

Final decisions about reorganising the theatre were set for September. Synge was peremptorily summoned from the Blasket Islands. After an intensive policy meeting at Coole the constitutional changes proposed by Russell were accepted, and on 22 September 1905 Yeats, Synge and Lady Gregory became the directors.

Despite her compliance with the changes and Yeats's

assurance that Horniman's financial contribution would be liberating, Augusta was deeply unsure about accepting more of Horniman's money. She mistrusted her conditions, and wrote to Yeats carefully on 8 January 1906 emphasising that they must get Annie Horniman to clarify what exactly was to be involved in 'turning our theatre from an "Irish toy" to a "really public object"'. A letter to Synge reveals that Augusta considered advising Yeats to say 'before or in accepting' Miss Horniman's guarantee of £400 (€31,923, £21,910 sterling) that 'we must be left absolutely free as to actors and writers. She is developing such a virulence against members of the Gaelic League, and against Colum in particular, that she may interfere some time against them, for she has been I think inclined to interfere more of late.'[24] However, Augusta tore this letter up, finally deciding they should accept the money and 'chance it, but just keep a watch that we dont get into bonds'.

Just before Christmas, Augusta, still glad she was 'first with him', held a dance for her 24-year-old son. Fifty wax candles transformed the drawing-room, cleared for dancing which lasted until three in the morning. Supper was served on 20 silver dishes, and there was Coole table silver and flowers everywhere.[25] She invited 30 people – all young, 'no chaperones or non-dancers' – including Robert's cousins and their officer friends, the Goughs, Lady Emily Nugent (a sister of Lord Westmeath), 'a very pretty Miss Waithman', 'a pretty Australian girl', and 'all that is eligible in Gort'. Augusta, who had hoped to be the only non-dancer, was dragged to the floor three times by her nephew Arthur (from Roxborough) and thoroughly enjoyed herself. 'It was the merriest dance I ever saw (my experience has not been great, Buckingham Palace & Viceregal & Embassy balls chiefly),' she told Yeats, who may have thought the list was at least impressive, 'so many youngsters laughing and light-hearted.'

She was not displeased with the idea that her local reputation had improved, and was glad that Algernon's wife was inspired to reciprocate the following night at Ardrahan, though she herself was busy holding a tea party for the old women in the workhouse.[26]

These festivities temporarily put what had become a theatre crisis in the shade. The actors had been dissatisfied with the shake up, feeling that the salaries were no compensation for loss of power, and only too aware that their single share each did not match the 100 each owned by the directors. Resentment had escalated and gathered an anti-nationalist bias. Máire Nic Shiubhlaigh dithered about signing her contract. She finally snapped when Yeats threw in an extra clause outlining costume duties. She resigned on 31 December and fled to Lily and Lolly Yeats.

There was a general feeling that Yeats's persistent insensitivity to people's feelings had exacerbated the situation. Russell wrote a long letter to Augusta, smouldering with anger: 'He would wreck anything he is concerned with by his utter incompetence to understand the feelings or character of anybody he is dealing with.'[27] Lolly too, harbouring Máire, wrote to understanding Lady Gregory of her wilful, dominating brother.[28]

Augusta did not want to alienate Máire. Although she privately thought Máire a weak woman, she was the only actress who could play Gormleith or Lady Dereen.[29] But, extremely reluctant to oppose Yeats in public, Augusta tried to engineer a return that would save face by making sure Máire came back on the directors' terms. This strategy was soon upset by Yeats's call for legal action against the actress. It put Augusta in a difficult position, for she could not agree to the over-strong legal recourse and the bullying spectacle that it would present, especially as the directors were known to have financial backing and their opponents were penniless.[30] She wrote to Yeats carefully implying that outside pressure rather than her own judgement had forced her to differ with him: 'What distressed me so much was Synge and Fay being so much against the legal action . . . & I could not bear taking sides as it were against you – & yet I feel it impossible for your sake & that of the theatre.'[31] Yeats backed down, and admitted he had been in the wrong. In her relief Augusta confided to Synge that she was 'rather tired of acting as drag on his impetuosity, but am comforted,' she added on a more positive note, 'by the thought that it means vigorous health.'[32] But the damage was done. A few days later several key actors walked out and declared their intention of setting up a new theatre under the Irish National Theatre Society name.

Augusta was not happy. In a letter written on 10 January to Synge she was vindictive and bitter, blaming Fay for the demand that Máire Nic Shiubhlaigh look after the men's wardrobe, and attacking Russell, blaming his constitution for the secession. She ended, 'I don't think Russell will be of any use to help us now, but if we find he would be of use, I would not let him off to save him trouble'; small words spat out in anger and frustration. This unreasonableness effectively exonerated Yeats, and this was surely her purpose. If it meant demonising others, so be it. It underlined to Synge that although Lady Gregory might act according to her conscience she would do anything afterwards to reinstate her partnership with Yeats.

Once the theatre season was over Augusta returned to Coole for the summer and started writing for the next season. She began with *The Jackdaw*, a rewriting of *Twenty Five* according to her now successful one-act comedy formula set in Cloon.

Yeats wanted her to write a three-act comedy, but she was

reluctant.[33] Instead, she experimented with a one-act tragedy. Armed with a story, three characters, a tragic theme (the idea of being in the grip of Fate), and the 'driving power' of the centuries-old Irish feeling against informers, she settled on a pared-down scenario of three brief lines, and wrote *The Gaol Gate* in two concentrated days.[34] This seemed too easy and she dismissed it to Quinn as 'an unconsidered trifle'.[35] But she did not alter it, and five years later when she came to put together a lecture on play-writing for her American audience, it was this minimalist play that sprang to mind as her quintessential tragedy writing experience.[36]

The play centred on two illiterate country women, the mother and the wife of a prisoner, Denis Cahel, arriving at Galway Gaol. He has been unjustly accused of a crime and the women expect him to be released. They are told he is dead and, assuming he has died of natural causes, the wife falls into a keen, a formal lament. They then learn that the prisoner has been hanged as the culprit, while the others (whom he is locally believed to have informed on, having been arrested first) have walked free. 'Did they ever hear in Galway such a thing to be done, a man to die for his neighbour?' So the mother converts tragedy into triumph.

Reading the play today one is struck by its dramatic deficiencies. There is little sense of individual character or emotional interaction between the women, and the dialogue is too regular; each phrase and reply have the same rhythm. But it is striking for the strong sense of Augusta's understanding of the society she is writing about; confidently referring to the nationalist crime without judging it, focusing on people's attitude to the informer and the felon. She demonstrates her sympathy for a broad humane nationalism that side-stepped the active, politicised nationalists' ever narrowing concerns with religion and race.

The two set speeches – the wife's keen and the mother's triumphalist pæan – have the formal, idiosyncratic texture of Irish poems she had heard and translated and are a strong authentic presence in the play.

The play was put into rehearsal as a stop-gap in October. The writer, Austin Clarke, seeing *The Gaol Gate* on his first visit to the Abbey, was overwhelmed by the sense of ancient tragedy that it presented.[37] It became an Abbey staple.

On 24 July, after she had sent *The Jackdaw* to be typed, Augusta wrote a long letter to Quinn, sympathising with him about the death of his brother. It was more confiding than her previous letters, indicating that she had drawn closer to him. However, she was still reticent on the subject of Yeats, voluble in his defence against accusations that he had abused Hyde and was alienating a timid and inert Dublin, but silent about their differences over the theatre. She was particularly forthcoming about her work. For some years she had categorised her folklore as she wrote it down – a brown 'copy book' for visions, terracotta for history and legend – and in the spring of 1905 she had put together a collection of stories about three locally venerated saints – Brigit, Columcille and Patrick – fascinated by the 'wild pagan' character of the details (she 'lopped off' any 'Romish and Jewish additions'), valuing them as indigenous.[38] *A Book of Saints and Wonders* would be published in Arts and Crafts splendour – thick paper with clear typography and an assured colophon depicting a bell, waterfall and fish by Robert – in September 1906, by the Yeats sisters' Dun Emer Press.

Now Augusta planned to write a book of Irish children's fairy stories from oral and written sources, 'so that our own children could first read the great wonderstories of the world – Cinderella and the like in versions that belong to and have grown up in Ireland, instead of starting with the

German versions. They would go on naturally then to Finn and Cuchulain.' 'Yeats does not altogether approve of this,' she added, 'because he hates children and thinks I am better employed on plays. But I am not sure that folkloring is not the best work one can do, as the old tales are vanishing so quickly.'

She would gradually publish a number of 'Kiltartan Books' of folklore. In the innovative *Kiltartan History Book* (1909 and 1926) Augusta's neighbours speak out in clear, but to us surprising voices of the flood, the Jews, the Danes, Cromwell, Elizabeth I, the Union, O'Connell, the Famine, Parnell and, in the later edition, the wars of 1914 to 1922. 'O'Connell wore his hat in the English House of Commons, what no man but the King can do. He wore it for three days because he had a sore head, and at the end of that they bade him put it off, and he said he would not, where he had worn it three days.' The sketches are alive with political and social implications, and many reveal people in the act of constructing myths and applying seventeenth- and eighteenth-century prophecies to contemporary situations.[39] *The Kiltartan Wonder Book* (1910), featured the fairy stories she started collecting in 1905, that would be a source of later plays.[40] *The Kiltartan Poetry Book* (1918) was a collection of poems and songs, some based on legends.

Augusta would not prioritise folklore. In January 1909, struggling with *The Image*, she would confess to Quinn, 'It would be much easier to sit down and collect folklore, which I never quite give up, but I don't like to give up original work as long as I can do it and get the audience to like it.'[41]

But folklore retained its importance for Augusta. She was recording and conserving that which was being forgotten. The books and articles were a source of money.[42] The material collected kept her in touch with the sources of her plays; as the people she spoke to visited springs for water or cures so she went to the epigrammatic, tight, many-layered folk stories for language, insights and themes. And the writing of folklore gave Augusta a paradigm for the theatre, for she perceived folklore as a continuous tradition to which she was contributing, just as she and others were contributing to the cultural life of theatre audiences.

In September Augusta wrote a three-act satiric comedy, *The Canavans*, not so much according to a plan but in a 'moment of lightheartedness'.[43] Set during the Munster Rebellion of Elizabeth I's reign when Spanish and Italian soldiers supported the rebels, it told the story of a miller obsessed with safety, who switches to whichever side he perceives to be the strongest. Augusta was on dangerous ground, parodying nationalist issues by coating them in burlesque, but she managed to avoid controversy, perhaps because Queen Elizabeth is not only depicted as the Fairy Queen of English mythology, but also as the grotesque monster of Irish stories. Augusta consciously restrained herself in her writing, but felt it was no hardship. 'I don't complain of bonds myself. I don't think one's writing suffers from having to keep a certain roadway any more than from having to write in one language,' she had observed to Blunt on 15 April 1905. Compared to Synge's language, Augusta's vocabulary was tame, though there are set pieces: 'WIDOW GREELY. Have we no curses do you think? . . . WIDOW GREELY. A gapped shaving to you! And a Monday hair-cutting! And the blood of your body to be in the bosom of your shirt!'[44]

Augusta spent November and December in Dublin working long days rehearsing Yeats's *Deirdre* and *The Canavans* and overseeing the organisation of the theatre. She was taking the responsibilities of her new role as director seriously: '. . . the theatre has become a big business with the daily bread of a good many depending on it, players, stage carpenters, stage hands,' she wrote to Blunt. 'And of the three writers who manage it, I, who am shaky in the multiplication table, am the most practical, so that with the writing and rehearsing of plays and the looking after figures and details I was working twelve to fourteen hours a day.'[45]

A new crisis had also arisen. This sprang from Yeats's dissatisfaction with the ability of Abbey actresses to perform tragedy and interpret the roles in his poetic plays. In the summer of 1906 he had met the flamboyant Florence Laetitia Darragh, an ambitious actress who specialised in passion and tragedy. Augusta, who had invited her to Coole to discuss possible roles in Abbey plays, had not taken to her, suspecting that this English woman, disdainful about the company, planned to take over the theatre – something that Yeats vigorously denied. Further, once Miss Darragh began to rehearse in Dublin Augusta realised that her exaggerated acting style was out of character with the Irish tradition they were trying to establish. However, she was prepared to let Yeats have his experiment.[46]

Meanwhile, Yeats was thinking strategically about the development of the theatre, and on 2 December he dictated a programme to Augusta.[47] The Abbey, he proclaimed, should be more European in scope, performing Shakespeare, Greek tragedies and other great works. They needed someone to train actors in tragic parts, something that Willie Fay was not qualified to do. They needed a paid managing director, a job now done inefficiently by Willie Fay as stage manager. This proposal was not uninfluenced by Annie Horniman's dislike of the Fays, and her promise of £500 a year for a new manager. Augusta had been anxiously aware of Horniman's blinkered opposition to the Fays since March when, after a long talk with Synge, she warned Yeats that

'the whole theatre relies on him and his brother William, &
if one or other of them failed, the whole movement would
be thrown back for a long time'.[48] However, W.G. Fay did
present problems for he was overworked and was often
called from rehearsals to attend to business; he could also be
sharp and alienate actors.

On 6 December Augusta sent a curious bundle of papers
to Synge, including Yeats's memorandum, her objections,
Miss Darragh's proposals, along with the tentative message
that she and Yeats had come to a 'practical agreement, at
least I think we have done so'.[49] It amounted to overt
resistance to Miss Darragh, scepticism about bringing in an
English manager, and an articulation of her view that they
should limit the type of foreign plays to those that were
compatible with their theatre (like Molière). In his reply,
Synge demonstrated that he agreed substantially with her.

It is at this moment, when Augusta, supported by Synge,
was fighting for a distinctive Irish theatre, that her
fundamental view of the Abbey is revealed. She was keeping
faith with the original idea first spoken of at Duras, an idea
that had developed with the production of Yeats's plays and
the 'peasant' plays of Synge, Colum and herself, and whose
potential she now realised they could achieve.

In December, as her letters to Yeats returned constantly to
the threat of Miss Darragh, Augusta tried to wean him from
the actress. In one she stated her case directly, but she also
applied emotional pressure:

> This is my difficulty – Ought I through personal
> friendship and affection for you & for my own ease to
> accept an action which I look on as you do in Farqueson
> [an actor Augusta had tried to engage for Kincora in
> opposition to Yeats] & which I believe will lead to the
> deterioration of all our work & our idea? On the other
> hand, ought I . . . drive you to make experiments in

London to the great loss of Ireland. Ought I to thwart you & have you always believe you had lost a great opportunity? . . . There must be a right and a wrong – What I want you to do is not to give up your own way to please me – that I wont hear of [at] all – but to help me to find the right – You need not answer this at once, but keep it in mind. I will show Robert your letter.[50]

'. . . to the great loss of Ireland'; but also her loss. Augusta was desperate not to lose Yeats. There was a deep fear here, not without grounds, for Annie Horniman had offered Yeats a leading role in her proposed new Manchester theatre in a letter dated 13 July 1906, an offer Augusta most probably knew about. Augusta could not imagine working without Yeats. He gave that part of her life its meaning. She effectively told him this in a letter on 29 December: 'I was thinking last night how much you have done for me. Without you I shd be a useful helper of Agricultural Organisations, a writer of the rank of Stephen Gwynn (at best). You gave me faith in myself (following faith in you) and you have done much (very much) towards making these years past very full & very happy ones.'[51] Augusta was also an instinctive and experienced strategist. As well as displaying her personal need she had given Yeats the responsibility of choosing what she considered to be the right way to serve Ireland.

Against her fear was her faith that Yeats would come round; that he was still with her and for Ireland, rather than with Miss Horniman and England. Referring to another Darragh idea in December, she expressed this airily to Synge: 'Yeats was dazzled by the new idea of a "fountain of tragedy" & the widening of the work, but he always rights himself in the end.'[52]

But her faith was severely tested when Yeats's idea that Willie Fay concentrate on his comedy work and lose his position as stage manager while they look for a new, salaried, English managing director was formally proposed by Annie Horniman. Augusta worried that Fay would threaten to leave altogether. Augusta and Synge replied to Miss Horniman with carefully stated conditions. Augusta was determined that the Fays 'shall not be shoved out either by force or gentler means'.[53] If they did have to choose between Fay and Annie Horniman Augusta was clear to Synge that Fay was preferable: 'We must just work on as best we can without Miss Horniman's further help, or goodwill.' But, aware that an effective 'no' to Miss Horniman would open up the possibility of Yeats's defection, she was more careful with Yeats, debating the pros and cons of losing Annie Horniman's subsidy, and giving him the responsibility of informing Fay.

It did not quite work as she imagined; Yeats's ideas prevailed, but Fay stayed. Letters were exchanged on an almost daily basis before and after Christmas as Synge and Augusta bowed considerably to Yeats and Horniman, accepting a new manager, but asking for conditions to curtail his power and to protect Fay, while Yeats told them that he had tried to persuade Horniman that the conditions were acceptable. When they were almost at an agreement Augusta learnt about a 'secret treaty' that Yeats had made with Horniman giving her rights to the plays he had written with Augusta when the patent expired. She felt betrayed to a woman whom she now saw as the enemy. She wrote to Yeats directly, angrily, and with a full heart:

> You will have given Miss Horniman one of our strongest possessions or weapons. She can take your plays from Ireland altogether or force you to put them into some movement opposd [sic] to your views. You will have betrayed those who have been working for you. You will yourself be in a humiliating position, seeing your friends

and comrades dictated to and not being able to take their side.

Synge and I have a right to protest because we were never told of this supposed bargain at the same time we accepted the subsidy. I certainly should not have done so at that price . . . I am taking it to heart very much – Those plays were our own children, I was so proud of them, & loved them, & now I cannot think of them without the greatest pain . . . If you agree with me you might perhaps send a line, for I am wretched.[54]

It was a highly emotional call to order. But Augusta did not really believe that Yeats had deliberately betrayed her. On the same day she wrote to Synge: 'We always said she has the theatre, Patent & money – we have the plays & players – & Yeats never had given this promise consciously I am sure of that – & I want by being very firm to give him the chance of getting free (I have given him a good excuse as well).'[55] Her ploy worked. The Horniman spell was broken for Yeats. He denied any such promise, and he finally persuaded Horniman to accept Synge and Augusta's generous counter-proposals. Fay agreed to step down as stage manager and Miss Darragh's role was limited to odd performances. A young, inexperienced English (Synge and Augusta tried to resist this detail to the last) manager, Ben Iden Payne, was appointed early in 1907. He had not been told that the company and two of the directors had not wanted him, but, finding it hard to communicate with what was a demoralised company, (the Fays, he found, were violent to each other and the actors, and the actors were regularly late for rehearsal), he resigned after six months.

Augusta had fought skilfully from the moral high ground, but, artist that she also was, these were not the things that touched her. Instead, as she sat down at Coole over Christmas to write another history play, she was haunted by Yeats's temporary forgetfulness of Ireland, the spectacle of Annie Horniman's compromised gifts, but most painfully by her own complicity in appointing the English manager. Several times in her letters to Synge she revealed that she felt very deeply about the Irishness of the Abbey and that to bring in an English manager was a betrayal, the equivalent 'of calling the Normans into Ireland'. 'I felt as if I should be spoken of some day as one who had betrayed her country's trust.'[56] *Dervorgilla*, wrought from current experience, was written out of regret.

The Norman analogy had particularly caught her imagination, for Dervorgilla, the wife of O'Rourke, King of Breffny, was either taken by or willingly went to Diarmuid McMurrough, King of Leinster, precipitating a war that escalated when McMurrough appealed to Henry II of England for help. Thus were the Normans first brought to Ireland. In folklore Dervorgilla's guilt in bringing the Normans to Ireland was unambiguous: 'As to Dervorgilla, she was not brought away by force, she went to MacMurrough herself.'[57] It was not in Augusta to resist the sexism of folklore; in fact it resonated only too well with her own well-nursed sexual guilt, and guilt is the driving force of the play. Dervorgilla tries to atone with gifts, but cannot lose her sense of culpability, and when her identity is revealed at the end, her gifts are returned.

The play can be read as an analogy of the Anglo-Irish role in Ireland: they must bear the guilt for their actions over the centuries which their 'gifts', the good that they have done, can never quite assuage.[58] Or Dervorgilla is Augusta, with her good works and guilty secret, giving that (folklore, plays) which might not be acceptable to a new generation of radical nationalists to assuage her own guilt as a member of the privileged Anglo-Irish. At the end Dervorgilla is forced to recognise 'the lasting trouble my unfaithfulness has brought upon you and your children for ever'. But there is salvation in the recognising of this bleak truth: 'There is kindness in your unkindness, not leaving me to go and face Michael and the Scales of Judgement wrapped in comfortable words, and the praises of the poor, and the lulling of psalms, but from the swift, unflinching, terrible judgement of the young!' she tells those who return her gifts. So Dervorgilla faced reality; a political and economic reality that was presented to the Anglo-Irish in the early twentieth century, and that Augusta would try hard to confront in all its complexity.

FOURTEEN

Crisis and Resolution

... in Ireland of all places one must keep straight beyond
suspicion.

AG to WBY, 22 January [1914]

In the autumn of 1906 Synge presented the theatre with *The Playboy of the Western World*, the play that would become a hallmark of the national theatre, but which would be vociferously abused by nationalists at the first performance a few months later. Synge, now ill and weak, had not quite completed it on 9 November: '. . . we were both immensely impressed & delighted with the play,' Augusta wrote encouragingly on 16 November. She thought it a powerful play.[1] Yeats immediately defined it as a work of genius. It was going to upset nationalists, but there was no question about not performing it.

Augusta was concerned, and had been for some time, that Synge's dramatic genius and the associated self-absorption were a subtle threat to Yeats. After their battle with the Fays she had, in a letter to John Butler Yeats, privately reasserted her mission to see off any opposition to Yeats and characterised Synge as 'something between a ghoul and a Voltaire'.[2] She particularly mistrusted Synge to make what she regarded as reliable decisions. 'All I was determined was that Synge should not set fire to your house to roast his own pig,' she had told Yeats in December 1906.[3] Now, on 14 January, she was blunt with Synge, revealing that even as she acknowledged the power of *Playboy* she was thinking first of Yeats; '*Pot of Broth* wouldn't do with *Playboy*. It would be an injustice to Yeats to put a slight thin peasant farce with your elaborate peasant work.' Her bias was obviously a subject of conversation between Synge and Molly Allgood. Describing a dinner where his work was being repeatedly praised, 'It was,' he told Molly, 'amusing to see Lady G dashing in at once with praise of Yeats's work.'[4]

Synge's comedy tells the story of Christy Mahon who, having run away from an arranged marriage to an older woman, arrives at a rough Mayo shebeen (public house) boasting that he has killed his father. Pegeen Mike, a proud, high-spirited girl, about to be married to a lacklustre boy, is enthralled by Christy. In the end, the father appears, Christy tries and fails to kill him and, having lost all glamour, is taken home. The play crackles with Synge's dialect, which freely employed the curses and blasphemies that he had heard in Aran and Kerry.

Depicting the materially and spiritually narrow and hopeless lives that Synge had encountered in the West, there was a dangerous bedrock of realism to the play. But it was the characters' exuberant defiance of their circumstances – their entertaining of parricide, their glorifying of violence, their flirting with sex – that would inflame nationalists. In an attempt at damage limitation Yeats and Augusta tried to cut out some of the bad language in the rehearsals, but Synge was resistant to revisions and the changes were minimal.[5]

It was clear that the nationalists were becoming less tolerant of criticisms, implied or direct, of what they were defining as the Irish character, although it was not obvious that any deviation from a depiction of the ideal would be regarded as defamation. Under the banner of Sinn Féin Arthur Griffith had, in November 1905, outlined a new nationalist policy aimed at amalgamating radical nationalist groups. Catholic dogmatism, idealisation of the Irish peasant, propaganda in art, were all securely embedded in a programme that also stressed self-reliance. Griffith could be interpreted as bowing to the lowest common denominator, and it might be supposed that in a conflict his supporters would be dogmatic, boorish, mob-like. Yeats, perceiving this, was spoiling for a fight over artistic freedom.[6] Perhaps he expected a battle of wits which he would easily win, thereby demonstrating the theatre's independence from any political ties. Instead it veered nearer to tragedy, with the emotions engaged as well and victory elusive.

Augusta shared his view. She would fight longer and harder than anyone for the play, taking it to America four years later. By then, though, she detested it.[7] But she detested bowing to the pressure of political dogmatists far more. She was fighting for freedom of speech and the separation of art and political propaganda. She was formidable, and did not suffer greatly from publicly championing that which she privately abhorred, able to keep the two separate. In fact there may have been an element of enjoyment as she argued scrupulously and vigorously for the play, for in her biography of Lane she revealed her true feelings to the public, as stated in a letter to Lane: 'If you knew how I hate Playboy that I go out fighting for! And all for the sake of this unfortunate country that doesn't think it possible for anyone to walk in a straight line.'[8] It was the enjoyment of an actor and, like an actor, she looked for praise, even if it was long after the event.

Her conviction (which had also dominated her desire to honour the sensibilities of the audience), together with a certain class-derived arrogance, made her a tenacious fighter

and a good partner for the more flamboyantly pugnacious
Yeats. Writing to Yeats much later she remarked with
satisfaction: 'We were not political at any time, we have
never put down the red carpet or put up the green flag; as to
our independent action as to Playboy and Blanco, we did not
consult anyone at any time as to our attitude.' The fight for
an independent voice was important for a person who had
struggled as a child to define herself against her family. 'It is
with political parties as with our relations, they don't mind
one's opinions, only one's independence,' she wrote with
feeling to Yeats a few years later.[9]

Augusta never clearly stated why she came to detest
Playboy. In a letter to Yeats written during the American tour
in 1912 she said that the painful experiences of the tour had
turned her against the play. But she also hinted that she
disliked the content.[10] The play had the moral foundations
she would have wanted – Christy is not revered when he
attacks his father – but, bearing her own self-censorship in
mind, it is likely that the spectacle of the violence and lust
that lurks beneath the surface grated with her, and she readily
acknowledged that she disliked the repeatedly coarse
language.[11] In this she was in tune with the audience, whose
nationalist objections to any slight on the Irish character
were underlain by an Edwardian conviction that the poor
could not be presented without idealising labour or heroic
effort, or without finding them picturesque. The sculptures
of Sir William Thornycroft (1850–1925) come to mind, and
this idea is expressed in Ellen Duncan's question in the letters
page of *The Irish Times* on 29 January 1907: 'Is unrelieved
peasant human nature a legitimate subject for drama?' In her
own plays Augusta never plunged the depths that Synge did;
she was far more interested in the workings of Irish society
and less able to create powerful, emblematic characters.
Augusta trailed Yeats, Synge and the avant-garde in

challenging traditional assumptions about how to represent the poor. She recognised this. Whatever hesitation stopped her hand when she wrote her own plays was carefully laid aside as she realised that the theatre must be the place where any voice could be heard. So, when it was presented to her that *Playboy* may mean a fight she was prepared: 'I feel we are beginning the fight of our lives, and we must make no mistakes,' she wrote to Synge on 14 January 1907. Did she even betray some relish in the anticipation of a fight? She was certainly convinced they could win.

When *Playboy* opened on Saturday 26 January for a week's run Yeats was in Scotland, Synge was paralysed with nerves and flu and the audience was substantial. Augusta bore the brunt of the initial audience reaction. After an event-free first act Augusta, relieved, sent a telegram to Yeats: 'Play great success.'[12] But, as the second act progressed, resistance began to creep from its cover; murmurs from the stalls, faint calls, a hiss from the pit. As each individual objection reinforced its predecessor an accumulated opposition mounted, riding over the word 'shift' in the second act, gathering momentum during the love scene in the third act and finally erupting in unison. Augusta despatched another telegram: 'Audience broke up in disorder at the word "shift".' It was almost inexplicable. Although a shift (slip) is underwear and so hinted at indecency, there were many more obviously objectionable words in the play. However, 'shift' did have a nationalist resonance; the disgraced Parnell had had a shift thrown at him. The coalescing of opposition around that word could not have been anticipated, and the directors now knew that releasing *Playboy* was not to be a controlled experiment, but the opening of a Pandora's Box.

On Monday *The Freeman's Journal* categorically declared that the play did not represent the Irish. That evening the audience made the play inaudible almost from the start and the disturbances were so great for most of the week that later historians have frequently referred to the *Playboy* riots.[13] Augusta tried several tactics. She had made some judicious cuts and, suspecting an organised disturbance, she had the police in reserve, though she was reluctant to use them because she knew their association with the British government would further inflame the nationalists. Most successfully she went backstage during the performance and urged the players to continue 'even if not a word could be heard', while William Fay pleaded from the footlights.[14] She was less effective front-of-house where in interviews she adopted, like Synge, an airy patrician tone, 'The public are quite at liberty to stay away, but if they come in they must take what is provided for them.'[15] Yeats, an experienced and enthusiastic spin doctor, was the one who engaged in arguments at the footlights.

The week continued eventfully. Augusta foolishly invited a nephew, Geoffrey Gough, a student at Trinity, to pack the stalls with his friends who sang 'God Save the King' to the delight of the pit. After this the police seemed inevitable, and Yeats rose to the task of pointing out noisy culprits. Hugh Lane also helped, and attracted the attention of a caricaturist who depicted him, elongated, suave, in unruffled evening dress, holding two lumpen characters by the scruff of the neck, 'The Amateur Chucker-Out'.

Nationalist opposition was not mitigated by Establishment support. Mild-mannered Unionist champions of the Abbey, such as Francis Sheehy-Skeffington, were outraged that the directors should ignore the hostility of the audience, and magistrates failed to find the disturbances premeditated and therefore criminal; the audience had not overstepped the permitted bounds.[16] However, there were a few arrests and fines. But the week ended on Saturday with the audience tamed – attentive and orderly – emitting only a few non-disruptive cries. The cuts and the policy of dogged performance had paid off. Augusta was quick to assert victory, reporting it as such to Wilfrid Blunt.[17]

Yeats, determined that they should win the argument conspicuously, organised a public debate on 'The Freedom of the Theatre'. It was marred by hostile interruptions and lack of vocal support from people like Russell, as Augusta had foreseen. But Yeats, although unable to resist anti-Catholic jibes about those with 'pliant bones' and 'suppliant knee', forcefully outlined his nationalist credentials (especially as the author of *Cathleen ni Houlihan*) and argued their case for a broad, humane nationalism. The following day Augusta could see the positive side: 'I think it was spirited,' she told Synge, who had been too ill to go, 'and showed we were not repenting or apologising,' though she added, 'It is a mercy today to think the whole thing is over.'[18] Two years later she would distil her disdain for their opponents in an imperious aside to Yeats: 'It is the old battle between those who use a toothbrush and those who don't.'[19]

Although freedom of expression had been asserted they had, in the short term, lost the nationalist argument. The ideological divergence between the theatre and popular nationalist groups had been spelt out and the 'mob' remained sceptical of their nationalist credentials for some time. The Unionists were welcoming: Judge Ross told Augusta, 'You have earned the gratitude of the whole community – you are the only people who have had the pluck to stand up against this organised intimidation in Dublin.'[20] This was a mixed blessing: they had refused help from the Unionists and had no desire to be associated with the other camp.

For Augusta personally there were dreadful repercussions at Coole. So far theatre problems in Dublin had not threatened Lady Gregory, the independent-minded Galway landowner and patron of Gort Workhouse. Now, almost immediately, provincial branch members of the Gaelic League (many of those arrested were Gaelic Leaguers) passed resolutions objecting to the directors' actions in disregarding the protests, while Gort District Council, under the influence of its chairman, a butcher whom Augusta had crossed in the Burren the previous summer, resolved to stop the workhouse children from going on their annual visit to Coole.[21] She was being boycotted as a pernicious influence, and she was devastated.[22]

Five months later, as the time approached for the workhouse children to come to Coole, Augusta grovelled to the Guardians, but Father Fahey, the local priest who had welcomed this opportunity to stand up to her, refused to lift the ban.[23] 'I am still suffering from the Playboy run,' she wrote to John Quinn on 17 August. 'The embargo has not been taken off the workhouse children, & a feeling is being nourished against me by a Sinn Féin or G[aelic] L[eague] curate in Gort that I am not to be trusted even that I am "souperizing"! It is like all Irish life, a comedy to those who think, a tragedy to those who feel.' However, she was not averse to an open rift with the priests for she felt she had compromised herself in small things to secure the children's visits in the past.

Augusta's uncontroversial plays were the obvious balm to apply to the audience in Dublin. *The Jackdaw* was premiered on 24 February 1907. Although it was dismissed as 'a trifle' by the usually positive *Freeman's Journal*, the audience, small but determined to enjoy itself, laughed consistently, and boisterously demanded that Augusta go onto the stage. 'I daresay it was partly to show we were forgiven for Playboy,' she observed dryly in a letter to Robert.[24] Two weeks later, *The Rising of the Moon*, which had the virtue of a strong nationalist theme, was finally performed. Augusta's writing was appreciated unreservedly: 'There isn't a word wasted, and interest, excitement, and uncertainty are worked into a climax which is exceptionally clever and telling,' the *Freeman's Journal* enthused. The play would become a nationalist text.[25]

It was about this time that Joseph Holloway noticed a strengthening of Augusta's confidence as director. She would emerge in the mythology of the theatre as the pre-eminent director before whom even Yeats would affect meekness. Commenting that *The Jackdaw* was really a farce rather than a comedy as Lady Gregory described it, Holloway remarked acidly in his diary, 'As one of the Directors of the company, she calls the tune, and you have to dance to it, or police will be called in.'[26]

In early April Augusta escaped for a holiday in Italy with Robert and Yeats, who was travelling to Italy for the first time. Augusta had been reading Baldassare Castiglione's *The Book of the Courtier* to Yeats, so they drove over the Apennines to the palace in Urbino where the conversations of the book had taken place. These had been presided over by Duchess Elisabetta Gonzago, and for Yeats, who was cultivating ideas about the aristocratic ideal, Augusta began to slip on the mantle of Elisabetta. Augusta would become Yeats's quintessential aristocratic patron, and the idea would inspire some marvellous poems. The downside for Augusta was that this shadowed his perception of her as a writer. The patron flourished within the aristocratic code; the writer was compromised.

Yeats would articulate these ideas more fully in *A Vision* (1926), in which he defined twenty-eight personality types and assigned each to a phase of the moon. Augusta was Phase 24 with Queen Victoria, 'at the end of ambition'. For such people a code of personal conduct formed from social and historical tradition is paramount. He described their great moral strength and humility existing with an 'impersonal pride'. They do not ignore philosophy and science, but they have no intellectual curiosity. They cannot tolerate those who break the code, but, having little involvement beyond the code, can tolerate all manner of evils there. They are adept at self-examination, but are without self-knowledge or self-created standard. They can stand alone against criticism, not because they have found themselves, 'but that they have been found faithful'. As artists they are restricted to creating an art where individuals act as a conduit to express a historical code or 'tradition of action and of feeling, things written in what Raftery called the Book of the People'.

It is a fascinating account of Augusta's character, and captures the hauteur that some people felt, and her calm, unquestioned sense of duty. He had noticed that she was almost indiscriminatingly tolerant, and attributed this to being uninvolved. This could be the case, but towards the end of her life she would make some heartfelt alliances with those whom Yeats would only ever tolerate. Underlying the whole description is the idea that Lady Gregory lacked passion, had no interior life of consequence and was unable to devise a 'self-created standard'. She is depicted as the antithesis of the romantic poet in both her life and art, living not as a voyaging individual, but in the shadow of her class, and producing art that deals with social mores rather than with the thoughts and feelings that cause joy or misery.

While it is true that Lady Gregory did not seek to live such a life and that she did not focus on the passions in her art, she was not without a strong sense of forging an individual path in the world. Much of this resulted from finding herself at odds with the expectations of her class. She had harboured subversive political ideas of some form since she was a young person and, instead of avoiding the problem of finding some way to reconcile her social position with the evolving circumstances in Ireland as most of her contemporaries did (in the end a good proportion would leave), she never stopped trying. She suffered greatly as a consequence. It is telling that although Yeats knew Augusta well – so much time spent working and talking together, so many Abbey issues and crises – she managed to conceal her passionate nature from him. Since the morning when she had given the sonnets to Wilfrid Blunt she, in Elizabeth Bowen's phrase, lived 'life with the lid on'.[27] She would allow herself one other passionate love, and there is no doubt that she was fiercely attached to Robert and later her grandchildren and to Coole. But she had decided that it was her lot to rein herself in. Some of her feeling emerged in her plays, inspiring her themes, but only very occasionally infecting the characters. Yeats was right in his description of her as controlled and detached, but he missed her passion, partly because she concealed it from him, partly because he was blinded by his poetic vision.

Dynastic concerns were in fact not far from Augusta's mind that spring, for Robert was thinking of marriage. He had graduated from the Slade in the summer of 1906 and spent June in the Burren with Augusta who had rented a house. While Augusta enjoyed the remoteness, Robert was inspired by the crystalline character of the bare terraced limestone hills and the clear light along the rocky coast, and he painted from morning till night.[28] He then went to Paris for the winter. Unsure whether he was doing the right thing, he was determined that he would not fail from lack of effort. 'I hope I shall get going this year at my painting – If I don't this year its doubtful if I shall afterwards – but I think I shall be able to,' he wrote in one of his letters from a hotel on the

Boulevard Raspail. He worked hard, not always with hope, on figure painting, but increasingly his heart was in landscape.[29] There was no mention of Margaret, a woman he had met at the Slade and whom he was to marry in September; she seems to have stayed in London.

Lily Margaret Graham Parry, three years younger than Robert, was not the suitable Anglo-Irish girl with sympathies for Ireland that Augusta may have hoped for. However, her future mother-in-law approved of her pedigree and nationality. 'Robert is going to be married to a very charming girl, Margaret Parry, clever, pretty and very bright and good,' she told John Quinn enthusiastically in August.[30] 'She is Welsh, with a Spanish grandmother, French great-grandmother, and has no English blood, and that I am just as glad of.' Her father had money, and her family had, for generations, produced barristers and army officers often with colonial postings. Later Augusta drew up a genealogy of her family.[31] Robert had not chosen Margaret for her lack of English blood nor for her social position, though he was probably too sensible to marry beneath him. He had fallen in love, sufficiently influenced by his milieu at the Slade to allow sex and shared interests to dictate. They were 'lovers and comrades both', Augusta later told Quinn.[32]

Augusta was delighted that Robert had found someone to love. She was also glad that Margaret, well bred, displayed the grace and refinement that Augusta thought desirable in a woman of their class. 'Robert is [?] beaming – & I am very content with Margaret – she has a great deal of dignity – & I think will hold her own very well,' she wrote to Hugh Lane, who had supplied the ring which she gave to Margaret as an engagement present with her best sapphire brooch. A week later, she observed the effect Margaret produced at a dance: 'I am really proud of him.'[33]

Yeats, too, responded to Margaret's glamour; 'I sometimes think that the combination of joyous youthfulness with the simplicity and conscious dignity that make up what we call the great lady is the most beautiful thing in the world.'[34] But Augusta soon found she also liked Margaret as a person. Four days before the wedding she wrote, 'how differently I should feel now if I did not care for you and trust you . . . I did my best for him, but now the time has come when you can do more for him than I do, & I can feel happy in giving him into your hands. Take care of him!'[35]

Margaret was a threat to Augusta. 'A slight nervousness, about the advent of Margaret, happy as I am about her it must make a difference, I had been so free and unquestioned,' she admitted.[36] Here was Augusta conscious that her writing and involvement in the theatre had diverted her from the behaviour proper for a woman in her position; a daughter-in-law would set up new expectations of what she should be doing which might limit her activities.

There was also the question of where she should be living. When Robert married, Coole should pass smoothly to him. 'I shall for the present stay here to look after things for them,' she told Quinn, 'but will fade away by degrees so they can be here more, for young people should have their own chance. I am glad for Robert, for he had only me and would have been very lonely in time if he hadn't married.' It is not clear exactly what happened, but this suggests that Augusta did offer to relinquish Coole. However, she stayed, probably at Robert's behest though he may have felt he had no alternative. He and Margaret had decided to divide their time between Paris, where they rented an apartment, London, where they bought a house in Chelsea, and Coole. Apart from not needing Coole in the short term, by allowing his mother to remain in charge of the family estate Robert demonstrated his love for her. One suspects that she need not have worried, as she did, that she might lose this love.

Augusta ensured that the young couple had whatever financial security she could offer. She transferred her rights to the income from a number of bonds and stocks to Robert and gave Margaret her shares in Lanka Plantations, a company that held several thousand acres of tea land in Ceylon.[37] Under indentures of 1841 and 1867 Robert could not be the outright owner of Coole unless, when he came of age, he broke the entail. Now Augusta made the legal arrangements for the breaking of the entail. The trouble with this gesture was that she no longer had the right, as given to her by Sir William's will, to reside rent-free at Coole during her lifetime, a change she did not appreciate. This did not matter in 1907, but the seeds had been sown for later friction.

Robert and Margaret were married on Thursday 26 September in St Mary Magdalene's, Paddington (London) at 8 am. Augustus John was the best man. Although only three years older than Robert, the flamboyant, bohemian John was already establishing himself as the leading portrait painter of his generation. Robert, attracted by his lively appreciation of the figure and drawn to his other disciples (Henry Lamb, James Innes), had studied under him at the Chelsea Art School in January 1906 and they had become friends. Fourteen John sketches would later line the Coole staircase. Augusta was not present at the wedding.[38]

For Augusta, imagining a future away from Coole took courage. The question of where she was to live was at this particular moment intertwined with whether she still had a place in Ireland. When Quinn wrote an empathetic letter about the treachery and mendacity of Irish life she replied with a heartfelt, 'My dear Quinn, I am not sentimental, yet your letter just received has made me feel very like crying, it is so understanding & so sympathetic.' She felt that individual expression and opinion were being swamped by 'the packs and flocks in full cry' and told him that she thought her time was up: 'I have done what I can at home'. To Blunt, combining biblical and Arabic allusions, she spoke of 'getting warning to fold up my tents'.[39] But it was only a momentary wavering. Her stoicism was far deeper than any feelings of despair. 'I don't believe, after all, any of us would live away from Ireland if we could. We are like the old man in the workhouse & would miss the quarrelling!' she wrote to Quinn, referring to the plot of *The Poorhouse* in which an elderly man rejects an offer to set up home with his sister to stay in the workhouse with the friend he argues with incessantly.

The feeling of not being appreciated in Ireland, also experienced very strongly by Yeats and Hyde at this time, was further strengthened in late August when Hugh Lane failed to get the directorship of the National Museum because he was not resident in Ireland. 'How is anyone to do anything in this impossible country?' she wrote to Lane. 'One has just to go ploughing on, ploughing on – knowing that some day or other our work will be recognised – though not probably in my lifetime.'[40]

Lane had formally proposed the idea of a gallery of contemporary art for Dublin in January 1903 and organised an exhibition of pictures owned by James Staats Forbes and his own Impressionists (Lane was one of the first outside France to collect Impressionists) to start a purchase fund. He had promised to donate his collection of modern paintings when a suitable building was found, and Dublin Corporation had voted £500 a year for maintenance. No premises had materialised and Hugh, angry and impatient, had begun to consider lending some of his pictures to

London galleries. Augusta had been careful not to forget her nephew's touchiness, tactfully encouraging him to stand firm: 'You need to fight with a sort of vehement patience, if you surrender, the whole cause of artistic intellect in Ireland is damaged for a generation. If you give up and scatter the pictures there is no man can blame you, but we in the times to come shall be the poorer for it.'[41]

On 11 January 1907, Lane's generosity and energy in promoting modern art in Ireland had been acknowledged when the Earl of Mayo, William Hutcheson Pöe, George Russell and others presented him with his portrait painted by the great Edwardian portraitist, John Singer Sargent. It depicted Hugh as an elegant man-about-town and would become one of his favourite paintings. In reply to the speeches Hugh had burst into tears.[42]

Now, in December, Clonmell House, a substantial late eighteenth-century terraced house in Harcourt Street, was finally agreed on as temporary premises for the gallery. Augusta immediately encouraged Lane to push for its opening whether or not money was available for its upkeep and on 20 January 1908 the Municipal Gallery of Modern Art was officially opened at a packed reception.[43] The following evening Augusta held a supper party to celebrate Hugh's success. Hugh had assembled a unique collection of nineteenth-century art of different styles for the eight elegant rooms. Irish artists such as George Russell, Jack Yeats and Walter Osbourne were well represented, and there were French Impressionists, Rodin bronzes and a collection of drawings and water-colours. 'You can't think what a joy the Dublin gallery is!' Augusta told Quinn on 26 February. 'I will have a catalogue sent to you. It makes such a difference being able to walk into a beautiful house and spend an hour among beautiful things at will. The working people are flocking to it, and Hugh Lane is to receive the Freedom of the City, the Sinn Féiners and Nationalists contending who should have the honour of first proposing it, and Mahaffy making a speech at the opening . . . It just shows how right it is to continue on one's own lines, & others come to you in the end.'

Apart from the gallery, another issue that had squatted sourly on her had lifted. On St Stephen's Day she was finally allowed back into Gort Workhouse with toys for the children and tobacco for the old people; gratifyingly she was received with 'great glee'.[44] Her renewed optimism was expressed in the planting of young larch in the mild spring weather, the first time she had been out planting for many years. She told Quinn that theatre business had kept her from it in recent years, but the action also spoke of a renewed confidence in her role at Coole.

Part of a gathering uncertainty about the theatre had also been resolved by the early spring of 1908. The theatre had, on many accounts, been a great cause of worry during 1907. The riots had taken their toll; audiences had remained small, the English tour had been curtailed because of the threat of disruption, and profits were non-existent.[45] Then in June its financial foundation was rocked when Annie Horniman announced that she would cease her subsidy when the patent ran out at the end of 1910.[46]

Annie Horniman, who regarded the battles of January over *Playboy* as a fight against a despised enemy (Irish nationalism) that had finally come from its cover, was disappointed that the directors did not exploit the notoriety of *Playboy* on their English tour (even with the promise that she would cover likely losses), and began to accuse them of capitulating to the nationalists. She was further incensed by her failure to net Yeats as manager for her Manchester theatre or to persuade him to assign his plays to her, writing accusingly, 'The vampire Cathleen ni Houlihan has touched you'. She knew Augusta had won and, scrabbling around for pernicious images with which to wound Augusta in Yeats's eyes, wrote vindictively, 'You are under the nets again. The poor little strawberries will soon be eaten and you will starve amongst the leaves & the gardeners won't come to let you out when they understand that nothing more is to be got out of me.' Capricious and infuriating, she was determined that they should continue to feel her presence, and concluded her June statement menacingly, 'It must never be forgotten that if the theatre be used politically I am free to close it at once and to stop the subsidy.'

'She is a terror!' Augusta exclaimed to Synge. 'I wonder how soon we shall commit some political crime!' Although Augusta was worried that they might not be able to continue without Horniman's subsidy, part of her was relieved that in two years they would be free of her demands.[47] Complaining to Quinn that Horniman was trying to make the theatre crassly popular, Augusta failed now – and in *Our Irish Theatre* – to appreciate that it was Horniman's money that had allowed them to stage risky plays such as *Playboy* and Yeats's poetic drama. As the theatre began to consolidate an identity that excluded Annie Horniman, the largely latent antipathy between the two women would emerge more strongly.

Distressing though their financial prospects were, it was Ben Iden Payne's resignation as manager and W.G. Fay's reappointment to that post which caused the greatest upheaval in the latter part of 1907. Fay was dictatorial and increasingly resented by the actors but, 'The real danger ahead is the way Fay & Yeats irritate each other,' Augusta predicted, accurately, to Synge.[48] In early December, Fay, complaining of lack of discipline in the company, imperiously outlined a series of proposals giving him enhanced responsibility – to negotiate contracts, engage special actors and have power of dismissal.[49] Yeats, reasoning that the actors would surely object to this and put pressure on him to resign, immediately saw an opportunity to get rid of him without incriminating the directors. But Augusta, although she thought him an incompetent manager, was not clear who should replace him, and more cautiously hoped he would climb down. She found the situation unnerving: 'I don't think we have ever been at such a boggy place, no enemy to fight in the open, but the ground sinking under us.' She also felt pity, of the most patrician kind, for Fay: 'He is losing grip of his own ideas and his art as well. I feel very sorry for him, for I think faults of constitution & training come in.' Just before Christmas, convinced by Synge that it was a serious bid for power, she grudgingly accepted that Fay should go, but she still favoured a waiting game, supporting Yeats's uncompromising view to Synge while privately trying to restrain Yeats.[50]

This suddenly changed when she discovered that Fay had programmed *The Gaol Gate* for Galway. She was outraged. She had not been consulted, and after the horror of the Workhouse boycott she could not risk bringing anything contentious to Galway. *The Gaol Gate* might repair her reputation among nationalists, but Unionists would view a performance as being an incitement to crime and cast her as a fiery nationalist when she wanted to remain a benevolent landowner. In her anger she pulled rank: 'But Fay giving me that rebuff means I think he can't stay,' she wrote to Yeats.[51]

She now agreed that they should persuade the actors to resign on the grounds of Fay's poor management, failing that the directors should force him to go. The Fays (including Willie's wife the actor, Brigit O'Dempsey) resigned on 13 January 1908. The former strategy had worked. 'Fay is going to leave us on grounds of not being able under existing circumstances to keep discipline in the company . . . I have not asked him to stay,' Augusta informed Yeats on 10 January, conveying the coldness of their exchange at her recent meeting with him. 'I think it is probably best for him to go, but I want it to be of course in as friendly a way as possible.'[52]

It was an ignoble end to the partnership – the Fays forced to resign, and even those on close terms with the Abbey such as William Boyle thinking the quarrel had been with the company rather than the directors. It is evident that Augusta was as keen as Yeats to present an unruffled relationship between the directors and Fays. Yet she had been reluctant to break with the Fays, and her letters indicate that she was aware of what she and Yeats owed to them (although that did not prevent her from largely omitting them from *Our Irish Theatre*). She felt the shame in the parting, and her concern that it be managed in a friendly manner was not entirely cynical.

The truth was that they were now divided, and the Fays seethed with resentment at their treatment, exacerbated when they were suspended from the Irish National Theatre Society on 13 March. They went to America where they initially allowed themselves to be viewed as representatives of the Abbey. In Dublin Sara Allgood rose to the rank of manager with mixed results.

One of the last plays produced by the Fays at the Abbey was *The Unicorn from the Stars*, performed on 21 November 1907 and billed as a joint work by Yeats and Lady Gregory. It had been an uneasy collaboration, and showed for some of the audience in a clash of styles: '. . . the work of the two writers is hopelessly incongruous . . . you can separate one from the other with a clean cleavage,' the *Evening Mail* observed.

The original concept had been Yeats's. He had wanted to write a visionary play exploring the problem of revelation.[53] He had two characters: an ecstatic visionary and a hermit whose life is dictated by morals and duties. Unable to construct a convincing dialogue he turned to Augusta whom he now openly regarded as an adept: '. . . since I had last worked with her, her mastery of the stage and her knowledge of dialect had so increased that my imagination could not go neck and neck with hers.'[54] They struggled with the play during the summer, then Augusta reluctantly agreed to work at it alone.[55] She did not use his scheme. Instead, uninterested in resolving the visionary themes, she recast the play as a dialogue between idealism and pragmatism in the context of revolution, propelling the plot forward by a series of farcical misunderstandings. It became a play of peasant realism and political allegory. Awkwardly and unhappily they finished it together in the autumn.

It was the last play in which they attempted to work together in a close complementary way. Work on *Cathleen ni Houlihan* had established the unlikely collaboration between Yeats the poet and visionary and Augusta the fledgling prosaic playwright, as Augusta helped Yeats to realise his dramatic vision and enabled him to conceive a vital role for peasant realism in Irish drama. But with *Unicorn* Augusta worked against his vision to produce a play that matched the growing body of her other work, and the limitations of her technique for his vision were forcefully demonstrated to Yeats. Yeats's recognition of Augusta's play-writing talent seemed to be a victory, but it was a pyrrhic victory for he now put her into a category from which he excluded himself.

Augusta seems not to have been unduly troubled by the possibility that Yeats was redefining her. She had never aspired to equal Yeats artistically, though she regarded her work as equally important for the theatre. 'I don't put my writing beside his,' she wrote to Quinn on 3 January 1909, 'but it is very serious for us both having to give up so much working time to [the theatre's] management.' Far from feeling pigeon-holed and losing confidence to innovate as a playwright, Augusta would, in 1908, embark on a particularly prolific year producing some of her most ambitious work.

Meanwhile, she never wavered in her role as Yeats's patron. Her most conspicuous patronly act in the autumn of 1907 was to censor Augustus John's etching of Yeats for the frontispiece of one of the eight volumes of his soon-to-be-published collected works. It had been Robert's idea to commission John and invite him to Coole, partly to repay him for artistic help in London. The result was to make Yeats look like 'a tinker in the dock'. (Annie Horniman was of the same view.) It 'won't do', Augusta told Quinn, and she fell back on Shannon who would idealise Yeats as Keats. A further portrait by the Italian painter, Antonio Mancini (1852–1930), brought to Dublin by Hugh Lane, made Yeats look like an Italian bandit.

Augusta also sat for Mancini, commissioned by Hugh for the new gallery. On 11 December Augusta sent a photograph of the result to John Quinn. 'It is a wonderful picture, luminous, radiant & triumphant,' she wrote, unrestrained by modesty.[56] It is that rare thing, a portrait of a woman which bypasses her sexual presence yet still manages to allow her magnetism. Mancini had captured the innate, underlying, irrepressible confidence that had sustained Augusta through the anxieties of 1907. When Yeats revisited Lane's gallery after Augusta's death it was this portrait which inspired him to meditate on what he had perhaps always felt, but was now able to articulate, as her unique presence.

Mancini's portrait of Augusta Gregory,
'Greatest since Rembrandt,' according to John Synge;
A great ebullient portrait certainly;
But where is the brush that could show anything
Of all that pride and that humility,
And I am in despair that time may bring
Approved patterns of women or of men
But not that selfsame excellence again.[57]

FIFTEEN

Tragedies

I am glad of the illness that brought you nearer me.
                                       AG to WBY [February 1909]

In February 1908, Augusta, not for the first time, turned against friends in the interests of repairing her relationship with Yeats. The break with the Fays had not divided her from Yeats, but it had left them, or at least Augusta, feeling uneasy and guilty. She needed a scapegoat. It was Synge that she sacrificed: '[he] was really responsible for the break up, & is now not at all inclined to take his share of the burden,' she told Quinn. To Yeats she wrote purposefully two months later, 'We must keep on our dignity, & not be spiteful. I thought Synge spiteful, & concluded it is because he is timid & had never, as you & I did, spoken up to the Fays face to face.'[1]

Synge did not cause the break with the Fays. In fact, letters between the directors reveal that he was a responsible administrator, and that Yeats and Augusta relied on him, particularly to provide insight into the actors' feelings. His main crime was probably to be too much on the side of the company. Meanwhile, cancer, only a rumour among his friends and acquaintances, was growing within him. He had had a second operation in October, and on 27 April was told he would need another.[2] Suspecting he would soon die, he wrote to Yeats on 4 May from his nursing home about the posthumous printing of his papers. He never sent the letter, and Yeats would not receive it until the following year, after Synge had died. To Augusta he attempted a debonair tone, while conveying his reliance on her sympathy and good sense: 'I am sure you will do what you can for [Molly, to whom he was engaged] if anything should go wrong with me in this "gallère".'

The surgeon judged the tumour inoperable and a weak Synge stayed for two months at the Elpis Nursing Home. Augusta, learning of the seriousness of his condition, immediately empathised with him in the severely contracted life that lay before him, telling Quinn that she hoped he would be able to finish his play, *Deirdre*, and that this work would enable him to feel 'that even invalid life is worth having'. But a month later her latent hostility emerged as she complained to Quinn that Synge never put himself out for the theatre except in rehearsing his own plays.[3] Yet that spring, Synge, who liked Augusta's translations, had directed two of them – *Teja*, by the realist Hermann Sudermann, performed on 19 March, and Molière's *The Rogueries of Scarpin*, performed the following month. It was to W.A. Henderson, the secretary appointed in August 1906, that he said her translations put 'life into the dead bones of the plays'; maybe he did not convey his approval to Augusta.[4]

In January 1908 Augusta rewrote *The Poorhouse*. Recent success had sharpened her; 'it wanted something done to it, the conversations didn't climax'. With Hyde's permission she reduced the characters to three and eliminated the stage audience. Later, in *Our Irish Theatre* she wrote that this made the 'dialogue . . . of necessity more closely knit, more direct and personal, to the great advantage of the play'.[5] Minimalism continued to have great potential. When *The Workhouse Ward* was performed on 20 April 1908 her reputation as the most 'prolific . . . healthiest and most attractive of the writers' for the theatre was sealed.[6] It became another popular play.

In March Margaret became pregnant. The Gregorys had returned to their apartment in Paris after Christmas, and Robert's letters to Augusta reveal a happy man. They enjoyed companionable days, Margaret stencilling designs for curtains, Robert painting (he was at the studio of Jacques-Émile Blanche), together planning a month's tour of Italy. But absorption with Margaret did not mean that Robert had forgotten his mother. 'I do think you ought to get away from Coole for a bit . . . I'll be very miserable if you don't get away as I'll feel its just the money you've given me which is preventing it, and I see that we can live here on very little this time, for all our fees & rents are paid, so it really is the time to spend something on yourself.' Here was solicitous concern for his mother, and a guilty awareness of his drain on Coole resources, both freely expressed.

On a recent visit to the Burren Robert had begun to represent landscape in flat colour, simple planes, and patterning rather than perspective, in a manner not unlike the Post-Impressionists. From now on he would paint views of Coole Lake and the Burren, reducing the hills, trees and rocks to strong forms with clear outlines, often restricting himself to a sombre palette of browns, slate blues, subdued greens, whites and yellow ochres.[7] This style influenced the stage designs he was still doing for the Abbey. His set for *Scapin* was successful, but when he was slow to produce a design for Synge's *The Well of the Saints* Yeats, always on the lookout for more radical design, was quick to suggest Ricketts as an alternative even though Augusta sent temporary material and assured Synge of Robert's commitment.[8]

Although he was enjoying Paris, Robert missed Coole: 'One wants to be in both places at once,' he wrote in May

1908. So it was natural that he and Margaret should plan to spend the summer of Margaret's pregnancy quietly at Coole, subletting their Parisian apartment. Augusta's approval of Margaret had blossomed into a warm sympathy. She was anxious when Margaret was ill in Rome, and gave her steady support throughout the summer.[9] Margaret responded with affection. Two years later Margaret would tell her friend Beatrice Dunsany that although Coole was Robert's she accepted that Lady Gregory lived there and ran it. Lady Dunsany privately suspected that Margaret now regretted this arrangement, but 'is too fond of Lady G. to protest'.[10]

The reason why Margaret might have come to regret Augusta's position in Coole by 1910 was because Yeats inevitably spent the summer there. Her frustration can be gauged by her exaggerated account to Beatrice who recorded it in her diary: '. . . Lady G. did say when she [Margaret] married that Yeats would cease to live there most of the year.' In fact, he only ever stayed for five months at the most, usually for two or three. In 1908, a year after their marriage, Augusta could not deny Yeats his summer visit because he was ill and needed help. She was leaning hard on Robert's easy-going nature – Lady Dunsany observed that Robert was 'nice, quiet and I should say easily ruled' – and the newly-arrived Margaret's acquiescence.

The trouble with Yeats was that when he was in residence he upset the delicate domestic balance by becoming the de facto head of the household. He occupied the Master's room, the ample bay-windowed room corresponding to Lady Gregory's on the first floor that should by rights have been Robert's. And Augusta, like a concerned wife, maintained her careful coddling of the poet to whom everyone else in the house came a distinct second. Other guests noted and mocked. Ian Hamilton, a relation of Augusta's, has given us a graphic description of the lengths she was prepared to go to: 'All along the passage for some distance on either side of Yeats' door were laid thick rugs to prevent the slightest sound reaching the holy of holies – Yeats's bed. Down the passage every now and then would tiptoe a maid with a tray bearing . . . beef tea or arrowroot, though once I declare I distinctly smelt eggs and bacon. All suggestions that I could cheer him up a good deal if I went into his room and had a chat were met with horror.'[11]

Yeats worked in a spare room above the library, and Augustus John observed that Augusta kept an account of Yeats's movements. If he was not visible in a public room or the library he was writing, and she diligently took any other guests for a walk to prevent the possibility of him falling into the idle conversation that he craved as a distraction. She would also encourage him to dominate evening conversations.

Yeats's response, Margaret told Beatrice, was to behave like a spoilt son, indulging in 'petty meannesses' towards Margaret and Robert, secure in the knowledge that Augusta would readily forgive him. He could be aloof, and many years later this act was so developed that Anne Gregory, Augusta's youngest grandchild, found Yeats distant, unresponsive, and abstracted. Yeats's ascendancy put Robert and Margaret into an anomalous position, a situation which worsened as their family grew, and his visits were an annual drain on Coole resources. Their resentment simmered, and as Margaret gained confidence she began to assert herself. In 1910 Yeats was moved from the master bedroom – 'That at least [Margaret] has struck at,' Beatrice noted; by 1913 Yeats was beginning to spend summers in England with Ezra Pound, and was being asked to bring his own wine for his autumn visit.

In the summer of 1908 the incipient tension between Yeats and the young Gregorys was dissipated when Augusta took them all to a rented cottage on Galway Bay at Newquay (near the Burren) where Robert could paint, Yeats write, and Margaret's malaise could be blown away by the sea air. Augusta was relaxed, too. On 13 July she wrote a light-hearted letter to Synge, full of pithy sentences describing the lobsters, crab and bass that were delivered living to their doorstep, and the new puppies they had acquired. She invited him to visit, but he did not go.

As usual Augusta found time to write in the summer. In 1908 she turned to tragedy and the challenge of exploring the human condition. With *Dervorgilla* she had created an empathetic character, and it was now that she rewrote *Kincora*, giving depth to the main protagonists. Then, turning to the harsh, rather obtuse story of Diarmuid and Grania from *Gods and Fighting Men*, she reforged it into a modern play in which she explored the relationships of Grania who loves Diarmuid who loves Finn who loves Grania; three people, each seeking the love they will never get.

Augusta saw Grania, the daughter of a high king, as a strong woman who, in first loving the young Diarmuid and then in marrying the elderly Finn, the chief of the Fianna, twice shaped her own life. She compared her to sorrowful Deirdre whom Yeats and Synge were writing about. She was held by the conundrum of Grania's final act: Grania blames Finn for Diarmuid's death and then marries him. She had heard explanations around Gort: 'And some said the change had come on her because the mind of a woman changes like the water of a running stream; but some said it was Finn that had put enchantment on her.'[12] But, after writing several drafts, Augusta devised her own, more psychologically insightful, explanation. As Diarmuid dies Grania speaks of her love for him, but Diarmuid, delirious, is only aware of Finn and his debt to him. Instantly the scales fall from

Grania's eyes and she sees that neither man has ever loved her for herself. In an ecstasy of revenge she takes control and crowns herself queen. Her final defiance leaves one with an image of a woman who by her own strength has risen above the social conventions and precedents devised by men. This success has replaced love for Grania.

Grania's final act was very different from the way Lady Gregory used her female status to manoeuvre herself in the world. Perhaps she herself strained against the limitations imposed by her sex more than her measured performance and conventional actions suggest.

In *Grania*, Augusta modernised the myth, her own past still haunting her. She animated the first act by analogy with her own life: the elderly Finn, the young, fearless, plain and innocent Grania, and the dashing Diarmuid recall Sir William, Augusta and Blunt. Finn and Grania, neither of them passionately in love, discuss love in a stilted way. Then there is a wonderful, if melodramatic, moment when, just as the complacent Finn anticipates years of quiet love, they hear a peal of mocking laughter and Diarmuid enters, and the essence of Augusta's experience with Gregory and Blunt seems set before us.

Although Augusta's Grania took the initiative in falling in love she is quick to anticipate guilt. The Victorian Grania, more moral than the Celtic Grania, is less assertive and very much the young Augusta. Diarmuid, the protective Victorian male, defends her against the now jealous Finn and takes her away, but with the promise to Finn that there will be no sex. Diarmuid's promise to Finn, based on what Augusta knew of Celtic Fianna ties, is unprocessed mythology; formal, archaic, and unconvincing emotionally, not a homoerotic bond as some modern commentators have argued.[13] Diarmuid initiates their love-making, spurred by jealousy when he sees she is being courted by 'the King of

Foreign'. Grania, worrying that a man who needed rousing by jealousy will fall out of love if they remain alone, now craves society. Age, jealousy, male bonding and now anxiety about keeping love alive are all shown to threaten romantic love, as Augusta needled away at the problem of whether such love can ever be fulfilling.

Grania is remarkable for the intensity (three acts, three characters) of Augusta's concentrated attention on the failures of love. But her passion is not always evident in dialogue where the characters too often explain themselves, and motives rather than individual character have the upper hand. It is an ambitious, but flawed play and her last tragedy. It was never performed during her lifetime. Elizabeth Coxhead speculated that Augusta felt it was too autobiographical to be released in public, although surviving correspondence with Yeats from spring 1912 suggests that Augusta was not opposed to its performance on tour. Yeats, who felt the play had emotional depth, opposed its performance anywhere because he thought Sara Allgood did not have the necessary emotional power. As Richard Allen Cave has suggested, it seems possible that both directors judged that Dublin was not ready for an exploration of sexual jealousy and obsession written by a woman.[14]

In the late autumn of 1908 Augusta returned to comedy. Still feeling versatile and confident, she produced a play that was more ambitious than her earlier comedies. It was in three acts and there were several layers to it. Like her other comedies, *The Image* was based on 'the talk', and the plot ran on the misconceptions resulting from the ebullient inventiveness of the characters and their reluctance to listen to explanations. Three years later in New York, Augusta would give a disarmingly simplistic account of the origins of this comic method: 'What makes Ireland inclined toward the drama is that it's a great country for conversation . . . Have you ever listened to Irish servants talking? . . . They never cease; I have often envied them their gift of conversation. Take a house in Ireland at the end of a rainy week; the supply of conversation is quite inexhaustible, though nothing has happened. And, of course, drama is conversation arranged.'[15] The implication was that she merely restructured what she had heard. This was patently inaccurate, but she may well have viewed her work as deriving from the dialogue, and certainly dialogue drove the action of her comedies. The *coup de théâtre* with *The Image* was that action was only anticipated and discussed; there was, in fact, nothing but talk. The achievement was that she managed drama and avoided a conversation piece.

Behind the talk was a palpable theme: dreams and the impossibility of realising them. When two whales are beached near a village in the west of Ireland the local community decide to use the revenue to raise a statue. They have no difficulty dreaming up a subject, but when it comes to the practicalities the project is exposed as a mirage. Each character is shown to have a personal dream which, when revealed, is ridiculed and so shrivels. The crumbling of the central project at the need to give it concrete form is a metaphor for these private dreams. All that is left is another story to be told, something the people will relish.

It is an interesting theme for someone enmeshed in the difficulties of making the dream of an Irish national theatre a reality, and may reflect Augusta's current attitude to that project. In satirising the useless wrangling that can prevail at the expense of action, the play points to her frustration. But the dreams, too, crumbling in the light of day, are useless, and Augusta raises the question that maybe dreams cannot, indeed, should not, be realised. Perhaps she was facing the fear that the theatre might never realise its ideals, and her comfort was that the secret dream was the important thing. She dedicated the play to John Shawe-Taylor and Hugh Lane, two men whom she valued for having seemingly impossible dreams. But the play itself deals with the dreams of ordinary people, and it is tempting to conclude that, after her experiences with *Playboy*, Augusta also wanted to evoke the personal dreams of ordinary people as an antidote to Sinn Féin's insistence on conformity to a single political ideal. The people in *The Image* may undermine each other's illusions, but as the dialogue unfolds the audience sees them thinking and acting cooperatively in a confusing modern world.

Augusta found the writing difficult and felt, when she had finished, that she had not been sufficiently in control. Later, she considered that it had a harmony lacking in her other plays and it became one of her favourites. Shaw would pick it out as one of the comedies that set her beside Molière.[16] Many have found the three acts an unsuccessful stretching of one, and Joseph Holloway observed that the characters were allowed to be garrulous in real time, although he noted that the audience did not seem bored by this.[17]

In the first week of January 1909 Augusta could not sleep. She was overworked and anxious. Her main anxiety focused on the theatre. In the autumn Annie Horniman had formally revoked the legacy that would have supported the Abbey after 1910. They needed at least £1,100 to continue when the patent expired, and with only £600 in a reserve fund the profit from each performance had become of vital importance.[18] The success of Yeats's *Deirdre* with the charismatic Mrs Pat Campbell in the title role in early November had been a great help and they had made £28 in three days. But, with Synge ill and unable to work, and Sara Allgood erratic as a stage manager, the theatre needed hours of daily work from herself and Yeats.

Augusta was worried about Synge, suspecting that his tumour was growing and knowing that another operation would probably be impossible.[19] Yeats, too, was unwell again, and she resented the time that the theatre took from his writing. She resented it, too, for herself as she struggled with *The Image*, and translated *Mirandolina* and *The Miser*. Seven of her popular one-act plays were to be published, but it was uncertain quite when, and Margaret's baby was due soon. Much of this was put into a letter to Quinn who was himself in need of a rest cure. 'Come back here and get strong and well,' she wrote, 'and put new life and courage into us.'

Some of the strain was relieved on 6 January when Margaret gave birth to Richard. Three days later Augusta proudly announced the fact to Quinn with affectionate humour: 'The young mother & her son are both doing well & Robert is very proud of the boy & has just been out & shot a dozen snipe for the mother!' Her grandchildren (there would be three) would become for Augusta as her son was. Already the odd sneeze or cough of tiny Richard, born at a time when the wind was like steel knives, had an all-encompassing physical effect on Augusta, 'as if all my bones had gone or melted'.[20]

Then, a few weeks later, Augusta was struck down. Robert described it to Yeats as a cerebral haemorrhage, but his emphasis on recent overwork, and her relatively quick recovery (five months) suggests that it was more likely a nervous collapse or breakdown. She was 57. She lay in her bed, immobile, while letters from Yeats asking her to come to Dublin to help with the latest crises in the theatre now that Synge was back in hospital accumulated at Coole, unread. Finally, on 4 February, Robert wrote to Yeats, telling him that she had nearly died. He said that excessive worry associated with the theatre had been particularly damaging, and added, with uncharacteristic finality, that Yeats and the others would have to manage alone.[21]

The news terrified Yeats: 'All day the thought of losing her is like a conflagration in the rafters. Friendship is all the house I have,' he wrote later in his journal. 'She has been to me mother, friend, sister and brother.'[22] He became aware of his utter dependence on her. Soon he was distilling the thoughts that had driven all others from his head in a poem:

> Sickness brought me this
> Thought, in that scale of his:
> Why should I be dismayed
> Though flame had burned the whole
> World, as it were a coal,
> Now I have seen it weighed
> Against a soul?[23]

He sent it to her two days later with an explanation: 'I mean by sickness and the scales that when one we love is ill we weigh them against a world without them.'[24] He felt, guiltily, that her illness had been caused by overwork: 'Keeping all [at Coole] in stately order while giving us enough plays, translated or original, often working much against the will, often with difficulties.'[25] That day he received her first communication: a pencilled note saying that she had 'very nearly slipped away'. She was still too feeble for the paraphernalia and posture associated with writing in ink, but she was over the worst.

The poem was sent 'with love'.[26] Torn from the heart of her friend, affirming her absolute worth, Augusta must have read it a hundred times and meditated on what Yeats meant to her. A letter written to Quinn a month previously in which she spoke of the need for an 'audience' for her thoughts in the long summer at Coole, hinted that there had recently been a loss of intellectual companionship with

Yeats.[27] If this was the case, the poem and the letter with their expression of the deep feelings he had for her must have made her recovery a magnified joy, for it restored their closeness. '[I am] glad of the illness that brought you nearer to me,' she told him.[28] Yeats had acknowledged her importance for him in his poem, and privately, confidently, Augusta acknowledged his importance for her: 'Yeats sometimes worried, restless, unwell, yet our friendship continues unbroken & I owe to him what I have done of late years – he gave me belief in myself'.[29] By mid February they were together at Coole, both too weak to work.

Augusta needed all her stoicism to weather her illness. A surviving fragment from a letter marked only 1909 reads: 'I am sorry to say I shan't be able to get over for the performances . . . I was just ready for plays and talk and sociability, but I must think of Finn's music (the music that is best with Finn is what happens) and keep my courage up.'[30]

It had been decided that Robert and Margaret would go back to Paris and that Augusta, still weak but determined to be useful, would look after Richard at Coole with the aid of a nurse. In offering to give Richard a home at Coole she was giving Robert the freedom to continue with his artistic training while cementing her role in Coole. She may also have been remembering how she had regretted leaving baby Robert when she had travelled abroad with Sir William and may perhaps have been atoning for that, although she would still leave Coole, regretfully, for long periods.

In March Synge's health deteriorated at the Elpis. Yeats was a constant visitor. 'Synge looked very very ill,' he reported on 6 March. Two days later he observed that although pale and thin Synge was not gloomy: 'He gives me an impression of peaceful courage . . . yet I thought he was certainly doubtful of the result.'[31] On 24 March Augusta received a telegram from the Abbey secretary, W.A. Henderson: Synge was dead. Yeats later recorded in his diary that on the morning of Synge's death Lady Gregory had experienced a wave of depression and felt it augured 'some evil', but it was Richard's health that she had feared for.[32]

On hearing the news Augusta wrote immediately to Yeats:

> I have had Henderson's wire – it is terribly terribly sad –. That sudden silence is so awful. Yesterday you could have asked him his wishes & heard his thoughts – today nothing. I wonder if the doctors told him the end was near – It is most wrong when they do not, there would always be some last word to say –.
>
> You did more than any for him, you gave him his means of expression – You have given me mine, but I wld have found something else to do, tho not anything coming near this, but I dont think Synge would have done anything but drift but for you & the theatre – I helped him far less – just feeding him when he was badly fed, & working for the staging of his plays, & in other little ways – & I am glad to think of it, for he got very little help from any other except you & myself – I wonder if he was ever offered a meal in Dublin except at the Nassau?
>
> Let me know what changes there are in programme – I am glad you were in Dublin as I couldn't be there, it seems a very lonely death indeed.[33]

Although Augusta was obviously deeply affected by Synge's death, in many ways this letter skirts around Synge. After the first expression of sadness she was more anxious to reassure Yeats and assuage his guilt. She may have intuited this because of her own feeling that she had not done enough for Synge, or Yeats may have hinted at it in an earlier letter. To this end she was prepared to subordinate the dead man: 'I dont think Synge would have done anything but drift but for you & the theatre.' It reveals the living tissue of her relationship with Yeats, onto which their feelings for Synge could only be grafted.

The letter also reveals the extent to which Augusta discounted Synge's family as an important part of his life. His brother, Robert and fiancée, Molly, were frequent visitors at the Elpis, and he would have had plenty of meals in Dublin, at his mother's home. This blind spot would not help when the problem of what to do with Synge's unpublished manuscripts surfaced.

She sent the letter to Yeats on Wednesday 24 March. Yeats's letter of the same day arrived soon after. Augusta wrote back straightaway. Now she gave expression to her feelings for Synge. There was also a hint that she had been assessing the relationship between the three of them. 'What a quiet end that was! No struggle or disturbance, just what he would have wished. . . . I feel very downhearted for it is such a break in our very very small group of understanding friends – which indeed has been little more than a triangle – One never had to re-arrange one's mind to talk to him – I had got to know him much better in his last year's illness when I was with him every day – It is I who ought to have gone first – Health is a mysterious thing.'[34]

Yeats would be preoccupied for years with Synge as the dispassionate, aloof genius of the Revival, and as a symbol of freedom of the artistic imagination against the philistinism he found in Dublin. In his writing he defined and redefined his Synge. He sent a draft of an essay to Augusta. In reply she said she would like him to give an impression of the three of them moving from Abbey to Nassau and back again, 'we three always', she wrote in a memorable phrase, '& the Fays or Colum or 2 or 3 others sometimes. I like to think that he stayed here also, I suppose the only county house in Ireland he came to.' Some of this was used by Yeats.

Augusta was adamant that Yeats not eulogise Synge; equally he could not reveal the weaknesses that they both knew only too well. She enumerated them for one last time: '[H]e was ungracious to his fellow-workers, authors & actors, ready in accepting praise, grudging in giving it – I wonder if he ever felt a moment's gratitude for all we went through fighting his battle over the Playboy? On tour he thought of his own plays only, gave no help to ours – if he repeated compliments they were to his own. I sometimes wondered if all my liking for him came from his being an appreciative listener.'[35] This last could sum up the elusive quality of their experience of Synge; the disconcerting feeling that he, who could seem to be so precisely one of them, could say or do something which made them realise that he had not really given himself, leaving them wondering whether they had projected his character on him. The distance between Synge and Augusta and Yeats had, in fact, been set by Synge himself.

Augusta spent much of the spring arguing with Synge's brother-in-law Harry Stephens over the editing of Synge's unfinished play, *Deirdre*, and the publishing of his poems.[36] She would spend the following cold winter finishing his play, developing a rheumatism that she never shook off. The conflict with Harry was not good for her nerves. On 4 April 1909 she wrote to Blunt that she found it hard to get 'quite strong. I want luxury and praises and pleasant dinners and the sight of the pomps and vanities of London'. By mid-April she had made her first reappearance at the Abbey, and shortly after that she set off to Venice for a two-month stay with Enid Layard in Ca' Capello, leaving Richard at Coole.

Venice was like a return to her old life with William.[37] There was the enchantment of entering her old state room with its ivy-trellised windows bright from the sunlight on the canal beneath, and meeting the elderly Italian housemaid who always welcomed her. There was delight in not being known as a writer, 'no character to keep up', 'very good for me'. She and Enid companionably embarked on the elaborate entertaining that Venice inevitably provoked. A request one Sunday morning from Queen Alexandra (wife of Edward VII), the Empress of Russia and Princess Victoria to come to lunch at 1 o'clock was met with an 'Impossible' from Enid, countermanded by a 'Possible' from Augusta, followed by a '2 o'clock' from Enid, amended to a '1.30' from Augusta. As she struggled to regain her old conversational wit and tolerance of trivia, Ireland and her old life began to feel insubstantial and remote: '. . . but when my courage comes back,' she told Yeats, 'I shall probably feel more ready for it.'

Meanwhile, she received good accounts of 'my little Richard' and treasured a paper sent by his nurse with very precocious scratches in his own hand. Finally, as her health improved and she was preparing to leave, the leisurely life began to pall and she found herself looking forward to returning to 'my world'.

SIXTEEN

Shaw and Horniman

I have an open mind myself, & not the timidity created by logic. Taste, like every other attribute of aristocracy, requires daring.

AG to WBY, c. 1909

L ondon, the next stage of the journey back to her old life, allowed her to re-enter that life by a new door. From the Birches' house at 1 Old Burlington Street (Sir Arthur was now a supporter of the Abbey and could be relied on for business advice, and his daughter, Una, admired Hyde) Augusta attended well-received Abbey performances at The Court Theatre, and found herself a minor celebrity, cheered at the end of her plays and courted by Herbert Trench who wanted her comedies for his repertory theatre.[1] She was bemused by the success, but tempted by the money involved in Trench's offer. When Yeats refused to let her sell the plays, her immediate reaction was annoyance, but she soon saw that the loss of her comedies or the popularising of them in England could damage the Abbey. The most unlikely source of encouragement came from George Bernard Shaw. His wife, he said, had 'howled' all through *Cathleen ni Houlihan* and he had felt its political power. 'I was as much surprised as if I had seen one of the Nelson lions scratch himself,' she wrote.

Shaw had not until that moment shown himself a fan of the Irish theatre. Born in 1856 in Dublin, to lower middle-class parents, he had escaped Ireland and a sense of social inferiority by moving to London at the age of 20. There, independent, unorthodox, outspoken, he had flourished, becoming a linchpin of the Fabian Society, a supporter of women's rights, a critic of the artificiality of London theatre (against which he set Ibsen), a celebrated lecturer and pamphleteer and a successful writer of witty intelligent plays. By 1909 many of the plays for which he subsequently became known had been performed. He had married into the Anglo-Irish Ascendancy with his marriage to Charlotte Payne-Townshend in 1898.

There had been tentative associations with the Revival. Shaw thought that in *John Bull's Other Island* he had been too clear-sighted about Ireland – 'no banshees nor leprechauns' as he put it – to appeal to Yeats. But Shaw appreciated Augusta's plays: 'They are quite out-of-the-way-good even from a mere professional point of view,' he pronounced, 'and I should like to know where they can be got on occasion. Dont give them to me: never give people books; I never read books that people give me; but when I buy them I feel I have thrown my money away unless I read them. Let this sordid truth be your golden rule through life. The real superiority of the English to the Irish lies in the fact that an Englishman will do anything for money and an Irishman will do nothing for it.'[2]

Lady Gregory and Shaw exchanged letters about an appropriate Synge memorial and, on her last day in England, Augusta took the train to Wheathampstead to visit Shaw at home in the rolling Hertfordshire countryside, which she found too domestic, to discuss the future of the Abbey Theatre.[3] It was disappointing; he could not help with finances (except to look for backers; he also thought they needed £5,000 which Augusta disagreed with) and was too tied up with an English theatre to take Synge's place as director. He was brisk, practical, and when Augusta said that Dublin had changed – they now had a gallery and a theatre – cordial, polite. As she left he gave her a copy of his play *The Shewing-up of Blanco Posnet*, which the English censor had just rejected.

By and large Lady Gregory and George Bernard Shaw did not meet on common political, artistic or philosophical ground, though they agreed that Home Rule was desirable for Ireland. Yet it is easy to imagine that there was an immediate rapport. Augusta quoted the passage about her plays and never giving books in full to John Quinn. She liked Shaw's style. She responded to his pragmatism and appreciated his contrariness and the pursuit of justice that underlay his projects. Between Shaw and Yeats, despite mutual respect and recognition of each other's particular power, there was always a barrier. Shaw disliked Yeats's dreamy otherworldly side, while Yeats thought Shaw too modern and journalistic. Augusta side-stepped this, never representing the more esoteric side of the Revival as Yeats did. Although Shaw described her blandly to the writer Norreys Connell (before he knew her) as 'sensible', 'nice', she, in fact, went some way towards his ideal woman. Admittedly she was not tall or strikingly good looking, but 'sympathetic, intelligent, tender and humorous . . . of great vitality and humanity'.[4] With her newly repaired vitality she realised the challenge of Shaw, and particularly of *Blanco*, which held her thoughts on her journey home.

Shaw had written *Blanco* with a copy of the Lord Chamberlain's list of proscribed phrases by his side. The play was part of his offensive against a state censorship that was conducted by underpaid underlings and tended towards the hypocritical and paternalistic. Its main effect was, in his view, to suppress often good new work which challenged the status quo. Shaw's strategy was to exploit obvious absurdities. So, into a play set in the violent, sexist, corrupt, wild west of America, whose broad theme was redemption through an impulsive act of kindness, he liberally inserted the blasphemies that were necessary to make the point. Blanco had stolen a horse, given it to a poor woman with a dying child and was arrested while staring at a rainbow. During his trial by a prejudiced jury, Blanco accused a female witness of having 'immoral relations' with his accuser. The censor dutifully objected to the euphemism and the blasphemies.[5] When Augusta got off the Wheathampstead train at St Pancras Station she had read the play and believed it had been unfairly censored; its moral universe was spotless.[6] By the time she got to Coole she was convinced they had a weapon that could right the wrongs of the *Playboy* riots and set the Abbey on a popular and profitable course that would enable them to survive the loss of Annie Horniman's subsidy.

The English censor's ruling did not apply to Ireland. The hope was that the Viceroy, from whom, as a representative of the Crown, the Abbey's patent derived, would want to follow the English censor and ban the play (though legally he had no power to do this).[7] The Abbey could then strut independently in Dublin, snubbing the red carpet and calling injustice just as it had refused to be drawn to the green flag. Augusta's only concern was that there was nothing in the play to upset Catholic sensibilities, for it was clear that die hard opponents or mavericks such as Edward Martyn could find fault – there were the blasphemies, and Shaw's final sermon which did not evoke an all powerful God. A 'riot' would fatally weaken their case. It was a gamble, but once taken, exhilarating: '. . . Blanco is our best cheval de bataille, and I am glad we had it first,' Augusta wrote to Shaw. 'It is great fun the respectable Lord Aberdeen [Viceroy] being responsible, especially as he can't come to see it, as vice-royalty doesn't like the colour of our carpets.'[8]

As expected, the Castle was rattled by the impending performances of *Blanco* (scheduled prominently for Horse Show week at the end of August), and it was arranged that Augusta would see the Under Secretary, Sir James Dougherty. This was the first of several interviews with the viceregal administration at Dublin Castle. Up until this point she had diligently and provocatively avoided viceregal society so as not to compromise the theatre; Beatrice Dunsany thought it an inverted snobbery, and George Wyndham was reputed to have offered a girl staying at the viceregal lodge £5 if she could persuade Augusta Gregory to dine there.[9]

Dougherty – elderly, gouty, a Home Ruler and supporter of the Abbey in other circumstances – was a threatening but not very formidable opponent to someone who was determined to stand her ground. He brushed aside Augusta's light 'Are you going to cut off our heads?' with a severe 'This is a very serious business', and used a medley of tactics to get her to withdraw the play, including an appeal to female sympathy with the viceregal position.[10] It is revealing that when, for the first time, Augusta was in a position to negotiate for the Abbey as patentee, face-to-face with an official, she had no difficulty in letting her feminine persona slip. She parried questions with questions and refused to make concessions. Only at the end did they meet on common ground, two members of the upper class observing that the English censor was only a bank manager. The next day Yeats and Augusta learned that if the Viceroy were to act it would be to revoke their patent. Gambling that it would be a bluff, Yeats immediately suggested that they accept the possible forfeiture of the patent and 'die gloriously', and Augusta agreed.[11]

After rehearsing the play Augusta, thinking of possible Catholic objections, asked Shaw to modify a passage dealing with the apparent powerlessness of God in the face of disease, which he reluctantly did, though he told them to make sure it was known that the play was the one refused by the English censor and that no concession had been made to him. They also appealed directly to D.P. Moran not to attack the play 'as it is the question of bringing Ireland under the English censor that is involved.'[12]

The Viceroy, Lord Aberdeen, a Home Ruler, sympathetic to the theatre but tied by his position as representative of the king, hesitated to threaten the withdrawal of their patent. But on Friday 20 August they finally had their enemy as the long-hoped-for official letter had in it enough of a threat to allow them to publish their statement calling attention to the extension of English censorship to Ireland, and the potential danger that posed to Irish theatrical liberty.[13]

Their success was sealed on the evening of Wednesday 25 August when a packed theatre – 'all artistic, literary and social Dublin' – found nothing shocking in the play, and the tense atmosphere broke at the end with loud cheering. They had defied official Ireland without alienating the nationalists, and they still had their patent.[14] The dubious artistic merits of the play (it is not one of Shaw's best) paled into insignificance beside the political frisson of the event. If there had been any doubts about Shaw's support – and Augusta's robust, ever informative correspondence suggests that she never worried that their slightly different perspectives were significant – all was blown away with the success. Shaw was generous with praise and money. Thereafter he became a source of sensible, knowledgeable theatrical advice, increasingly needed as they prepared for life after Annie Horniman's subsidy.[15]

❖ ❖ ❖

The performing of *Blanco* had also been intended as a gesture of independence from Annie Horniman's arbitrary censorship. Miss Horniman was gratifyingly provoked by *Blanco*, grumbling to Shaw that they were now encouraging Sinn Féin and the Gaelic League. In September 1909, finally persuaded that she had no real power over their actions, she decided to free herself from them and offered to sell the theatre buildings.

This disentangling of herself from the directors immediately set Annie Horniman on a different footing. From now on she was an outsider, a potential enemy. Augusta soon realised that Miss Horniman would be tempted to try to destroy their reputation, and her letters to Yeats were regularly punctuated with warnings about how to pre-empt her slander. She suggested that rather than tell tales (and put themselves on her level) they advertise her 'crackiness' before she had a chance of airing her grievances to their subscribers.[16] Augusta was adamant that they behave impeccably; she did not want Miss Horniman to have any legitimate grounds for complaints about them being unbusinesslike or acting illegally. She was determined that they swiftly counter Miss Horniman's assertion that it was she who had kept them out of politics.[17] It was a propaganda war and Augusta was determined to win it. She would indeed have the last word for in *Our Irish Theatre* Miss Horniman was given two small dutiful paragraphs, much to her fury.[18] In every case Augusta's tactics were coldly calculating. She fully understood her opponent and she despised her. 'I have never treated her as an equal without regretting it,' she told Yeats grandly after recommending that they take the 'most dignified course'.[19] It is in her dealings with Annie Horniman that Augusta emerges most strongly as the haughty aristocrat that Yeats memorialised.

Annie Horniman was offering a bargain. For buildings, fittings, furniture and scenery valued at £9,700, she asked for a down payment of £428 and quittance of £1,000.[20] Although she would not pay the subsidy of £800 for 1910, the total effective outlay for the directors was only £2,228 (€177,811 and £122,039 sterling). It was, however, still too much for them. Augusta was keen that they open a public subscription to raise the money, but Yeats, who candidly admitted to being driven by greed, wanted to beat Miss Horniman down first. He had the buildings valued at the extremely low rate of £2,000–£2,300 and then, subtracting the subsidy, decided they could only offer her £1,000.

It fell to Augusta to confront Miss Horniman with their offer in London in January 1910. Augusta was staying with Enid, recovering from an attack of rheumatic fever brought on by a bout of sustained hard work in the autumn at the theatre, producing Synge's *Deirdre* and *The Image*.[21] She met a woman almost consumed with pent-up fury at Yeats's final pitting of himself against her. In December she had written to him in the absurdly exaggerated language she sometimes used, accusing 'Superman' of treating his 'Nitschien [*sic*] "slave"' with 'greed & philistinism'.[22] During their meeting, Augusta, the recipient of a stream of abuse and threats, had no difficulty remaining coldly detached: 'I was not even angry, it was like looking at some malignant growth. One wondered how she came to be there, and felt a desire to be away and clear of it,' she reported to Yeats. 'I was so thankful I kept even good humour with Miss H— of course if she was sane one would have turned on her, but it was the performance of a raving lunatic.'[23]

But afterwards she felt that Miss Horniman should be answered – especially when she wrote accusing them of cheating in the accounts – and that Yeats should write the letter. The unequivocal demand that Yeats write was strikingly different from the usual conciliatory tone that she used with him. It was one of the rare occasions when she pitted her principles directly against his, regardless of the consequences, and not for any practical gain. It is a measure of how strongly she resented both Horniman's treatment of them and, even more, the fact that Yeats was not prepared to alienate Miss Horniman. Threatening to curtail his stay at Coole, she forced Yeats to dictate a reply, but did not send it immediately and, observing his unhappiness, eventually returned it to him.[24] Like Horniman she felt powerless; hence the threat to coerce Yeats into acting according to her wishes. Unlike Horniman she could accept the limits of her power; she never intended to send the letter. The episode continued to disturb her and she related it in detail to John Quinn two years later. On 18 February Annie Horniman finally agreed to pay £400 in subsidy and to accept £1,000 for the buildings, and Yeats replied to her in the old vein, 'do not think that I am not grateful for all you have done'.[25]

Augusta warmed to the project of setting the Abbey on a more secure financial footing and of searching for funds. She asked Henderson for a statement of what capital they needed – 'one feels unbusinesslike not being able to mention a definite sum' – and she formed a temporary financial committee to devise a financial plan. She hoped eventually to have a business director.[26] Shaw advised her about paying authors. Profits, mounting since *Playboy*, had been boosted by *Blanco*. Between April 1909 and April 1910 their takings were almost three times what they had been in the previous year.

The Abbey Theatre, with its pool of established actors and writers, had a secure reputation in Ireland and England, and was valued by people of diverse political allegiances for delivering high-quality plays representing Irish life and aspirations in a very specific style.[27] They had opened a public subscription and by June 1910 had donations or promises from the liberal Ascendancy – Hutcheson Poë, Lord Dunsany, the Duke of Leinster – and the supporters Augusta had been cultivating in London – Augustine Birrell, Huth Jackson, Blunt, J.M. Barrie. They had a total of £1,900, enough, Augusta told Shaw, to buy out Miss Horniman and pay for the new patent. But they were aiming at £5,000 to run the theatre for six years so they stepped up their campaign for subscribers with letters to *The Times* and At Homes at the theatre.[28] At least ninety guests, mostly Ascendancy people, attended one At Home on 21 November 1910. They were greeted by a hospitable Lady Gregory who gave them tea, and were then ushered into the auditorium where the fluent Yeats appealed for money. By then they had £2,800.

This administrative work was very time-consuming. Augusta would often spend the morning writing business letters, and felt that each hitch generated a disproportionate amount of correspondence. She was also keen to protect Yeats from the brunt of this work, only too aware that if he was distracted he found it hard to get back to his lyrics.[29] Sometimes she apologised to Yeats for her detailed letters, and in one she ended by saying that she only intended 'to map out ground in case we have to do anything by wire'.[30]

During 1909 and 1910 Robert and Margaret continued with their artistic life in Paris for the winter, and summers in Galway. Augusta was often with Richard and his nurse, and she continued to suffer whenever he fell ill. Writing to Yeats from Arabella's house in Galway in the summer of 1910 she told him the baby had had a cold, adding, 'you know what that takes out of me'. Whenever she was away and Robert was at Coole he gave her snippets of news charting Richard's progress. These letters also reveal that Robert had slipped into the role of country gentleman, hunting enthusiastically, holding Christmas shooting parties, entertaining friends, but with time to oversee building work, deal with tenants and indulge his talent for painting, for which Augusta had made a studio on top of the laundry.[31]

Robert was still working as a set designer for the Abbey. In November 1908 he had produced a stark and menacing interior for Yeats's *Deirdre*, and a year later he had a dramatically effective landscape backdrop ready for *The Image*. He painted a luminous wood scene for Synge's *Deirdre* in January 1910. Ominously, that same month Yeats informed Augusta that his hopes for injecting new force into Abbey Theatre scenery lay with the English avant-garde designer Gordon Craig whose simple abstract designs were far more radical than Robert's work.

Margaret was rarely mentioned, but she worked too, mainly drawing. In the summer of 1910 she presented her mother-in-law with a series of illustrations for her *Kiltartan Wonder Book* which Augusta pronounced 'very charming'. They have a comic book quality which lifts the tales lightly out of their Kiltartan context, broadening their appeal.

The focus of Robert's letters to Augusta from the summer of 1909 was the sale of Coole. The Land Act of 1909 had finally made land purchase compulsory, and his letters picked up a conversation he had been having with his mother about whether to sell Coole to the Congested Districts Board. Established to improve the conditions in many western and northern areas where the land, too poor and divided into tiny, often scattered holdings, was unable to successfully sustain the population that lived on it, the Congested Districts Board was keen to buy whole estates. It would consolidate and enlarge holdings where possible, build roads, fences and drains, repair buildings and resell to the tenants under Land Purchase terms. Augusta, alert to the fact that this would benefit the poorer tenants and so secure a lasting peace in the area, was in favour of selling to the Board.[32] Robert was more interested in securing a good price, weighing up in one letter whether this would come from the tenants or the Board.[33] Frank, meanwhile, was against selling to the Board.

Under Robert's influence the Gregorys began by offering small areas for sale to individual tenants. But when the Congested Districts Board refused to buy a half share in a farm Robert finally came round to the idea of offering it the entire estate on condition it guaranteed purchase once the offer had been made.[34] By late October 1910 the Gregorys had approached the Board with rental sheets to establish that it was a congested district, and had paid for a survey. The Board then had cold feet, eliciting an uncharacteristically emotional letter from Robert to his mother: 'I'm disgusted about the CDB.' He had been assured that the Board would take any estate that had established it was congested. Further, the Board's intervention had prevented the tenants making an offer.[35] Meanwhile, the tenants had been applying to the Land Courts for rent reductions and on 30 July 1909 fifteen of them had been given a 20 per cent reduction.[36]

When they first put the machinery of a sale into operation in 1909 Augusta did not seem to be thinking about the emotional implications of losing the estate. But Yeats was disturbed. On 7 August 1909 he wrote down ideas for a poem: '"A Shaken House". How should the world gain if this house failed, even though a hundred little houses were the better for it, for here power [has] gone forth or lingered, giving energy, precision . . . ?'[37] It would become 'Upon a House Shaken by the Land Agitation', a celebration of aristocracy, and a challenge to nationalists.

It was the following year, as the Gregorys began to sell parcels of land, that Augusta began to engage imaginatively with life after the sale, but her feelings, as expressed in the play, *The Deliverer*, written in the autumn of 1910, were more ambivalent than Yeats's. Ostensibly referring to Moses and the leading of the Israelites out of Egypt, the play is really about Parnell, the great leader who, like Moses, felt his kinship with the people despite his different upbringing, and who, betrayed by them, was still secretly revered by them. With a bleak ending – the King's Nursling (Moses/Parnell) dead and the people still in captivity – the people only have their dreams: 'Look at what came to me from my father and he dying. The key of the housedoor in my own village. It is here in the bosom of my dress. I have but to turn it going in, and to sit down beside the hearth,' says one woman.[38] So Augusta stepped inside the hundred little houses and effectively argued for their existence. After twelve years of indirectly demonising Parnell for suffocating intellectual and imaginative life in Ireland, Augusta had returned to something of her old hero worship, and the play, with its celebration of the leader, suggested that Augusta was also trying to imagine a continued role for the Ascendancy in the new Ireland of peasant proprietors.[39]

Late on Friday 6 May 1910 King Edward VII died. Yeats was in France and Augusta at Coole so it was left to the new young manager, Lennox Robinson, to decide whether the theatre should shut on Saturday. Robinson (who thought the 58-year-old Augusta an old lady, but who would find her 'hardly a day older' 20 years later) was Yeats's protégé.[40] He was one of a batch of up-and-coming Cork playwrights who were pioneering a stark realism in Irish drama.[41] Yeats thought he had the makings of a great dramatist. It was a style Augusta was learning to appreciate, though she would never warm to it. Robinson was independent-minded and Augusta, less willing to delegate than Yeats, did not find this initially attractive.[42] She would never entirely trust

Robinson's judgement despite the fact that he became a stalwart supporter of her later plays when Yeats was no longer encouraging. On 7 May 1910 Robinson reasoned that remaining open would be the least politically charged gesture, but, in reply to his telegraph asking what he should do, Augusta advised 'should close through courtesy'.[43] It came too late. Robinson had proceeded with the matinee; he went ahead with the evening show.

Annie Horniman immediately interpreted the performances as a defiant political act, and publicly – in the *Freeman's Journal* – threatened to withdraw their subsidy if they did not apologise. Augusta replied to her civilly. She also tried to circumvent a political row by claiming publicly that the theatre had remained open merely 'owing to accident'. But she privately expressed disgust at Miss Horniman's crudity to Yeats: 'I think she was quite justified in being annoyed at the Theatre not being shut, it belongs to her, and "these are your gods oh Israel!" they are all snobs at heart over there, at least all of her class. Her telegram was too strongly worded for politeness but she has never been taught mannerly ways.'[44]

In words that draw on her experiences with Arabi she also condemned Horniman for not waiting for Augusta's reply before writing to the press: 'This is the unpardonable thing. It is considered low dealing in politics or any ordinary affair to publish your demand before your correspondent has had the opportunity of replying . . . it puts her off the list of civilised enemies.'

Unimpressed by their printed apology, Annie Horniman demanded the dismissal of Robinson. When this was not forthcoming she withdrew the remaining subsidy. Augusta was happy to forfeit the subsidy; she preferred them to be perceived as overthrowing Horniman rather than as having been forced to apologise.[45] Yeats did not want to do either.

So when Augusta discovered that Horniman was legally bound to pay the subsidy he wanted to take her to court. Augusta considered such an action would show them in a bad light, but Yeats prevailed, and the case went to arbitration where, a year later, it was decided in their favour. There was a farcical coda in which Yeats and Augusta, having won the principle, nobly declined to accept the subsidy, whereupon Annie Horniman promptly paid. She sent a bitter telegram to Yeats: 'You have shown me I do not matter in your eyes'.[46]

The final act of the emergence of the new Abbey Theatre was the application for a new patent. This was a protracted process because it was contested by Edward Martyn's Theatre of Ireland. The directors fought a legal battle from 17 February 1910 to 25 December 1912. It was eventually settled by the Home Secretary, Winston Churchill, who granted sole patent to Lady Gregory and W.B. Yeats for 21 years.

In the summer of 1910 Yeats and Augusta had another quarrel which was oddly reminiscent of their disagreement in January when Augusta had forced Yeats to reply to Annie Horniman's accusations. This time it went deeper; Augusta felt it more strongly, and Yeats perceived it as their only real quarrel, resting on fundamentally different, irreconcilable attitudes.

In early December 1909 Yeats heard that the writer Edmund Gosse, dubbed 'official British man of letters' by H.G. Wells and someone who had helped Yeats by lending him money and introducing him to the right people in London, wanted to propose him for a Civil List pension. Yeats had recently been elected to the Academic Committee of English Letters, and the pension, which was in the gift of the King, was another recognition of his stature as a poet.

The £150 a year would double his annual income, but Yeats and Augusta were cautious about whether there were any political strings attached, such as abstaining from objecting to royal visits. Satisfied that there were not, Yeats agreed to let Gosse go ahead.

With Gosse Augusta had met another rival patron. At first there seems to have been no conflict as they worked in their separate fields of influence. While Gosse prepared a petition in London for the Prime Minister in the summer of 1910, Augusta drafted a petition to gain support in Dublin, corresponding with the Chief Secretary, Augustine Birrell. She sent her petition to Gosse for comment, and he added a sentence on Yeats's position on the Academic Committee of English Letters. On 23 July Gosse sent Augusta a draft of his petition. In her reply, now lost, she asked him for signatures for her petition.[47] On 25 July this courteous correspondence was interrupted:

> Dear Madam,
> I cannot express my surprise at the tone of your letter. If this is your attitude, I wish to have no more to do with the matter, and I am lost in wonder at what can have induced you to interfere in an affair when your opinion was not asked, and when you seem to intend neither to give any help nor to take any trouble.[48]

The image of her as merely an interfering busybody when the opposite was so well known to be the case was deeply wounding, and no doubt intended to be. It seems that, oversensitive as he was, Gosse now considered Lady Gregory with her separate petition to be acting independently. Augusta may have regarded herself as performing the Irish part of a joint operation, though her comment to Birrell on 29 July that she was sending Gosse her documentation to keep him in the picture out of politeness, because he had first proposed the pension, suggests otherwise. Anyway, once she had received his letter of 25 July she did not hesitate to act alone, and she would tell John Quinn that she had 'arranged Yeats's pension with Birrell in a box at the Court Theatre in fifteen minutes'.[49] Gosse would also claim to have been solely responsible. On 10 August the Prime Minister granted Yeats a pension.

Augusta, at the Burren with Robert, Margaret and Yeats, had been deeply insulted by Gosse's letter of 25 July and, with Robert's support, demanded that Yeats defend her honour and write to Gosse. After a long delay he gave Augusta the reply, but he had not, as she feared, sufficiently distanced himself from Gosse. She told him that 'if he hadn't any sense of dignity or self-respect he should remember that he was her guest', and she insisted on a stronger reply, which he produced and, which, after two weeks, she returned to him.

Yeats knew he had not adequately supported his friend. He had wanted to remonstrate with Gosse, but was reluctant to capitulate to what he regarded as the Gregorys' (not his) social code. In a lengthy journal entry he justified his behaviour to himself by addressing Robert: 'You have always lived among defined social relations and I only among defined ideas.'[50] Yeats felt he had maintained his personal integrity. But in doing so he unfairly condemned Lady Gregory: 'Being a writer of comedy, her life as an artist has not shaken in her, as tragic art would have done, the conventional standards. Besides, she has never been part of the artist's world, she has belonged to a political world, or to one that is merely social.'[51] Augusta did not appreciate that Yeats's reluctance to defend her sprang from a defined difference in attitudes. Robert realised that her feelings ran far deeper than a reaction against a social faux pas, for when Gosse sent an inadequate response to his insulting letter in the first week of August Robert conspired with Yeats not to show it to her and fan her anger. In the end Augusta was most concerned to remain friends with Yeats and she forgave him.

There was no question that Yeats had stopped valuing his friendship with Augusta but he was revising its significance to him. In January 1911 he wrote a poem about the three women – Olivia Shakespear, Maud Gonne and Augusta Gregory – whom he felt had made him what he was. The lines referring to Augusta, while sexually charged and for long taken to depict Shakespear, evoke her as the person who showed how work could restore him to a love of life. In the draft he sent to her in January there is an implicit doubt that he had been able to adequately respond to her standards –

> . . . & would give
> Every good gift that may be
> Could I copy her & live
> In a laborious reverie.[52]

This doubt had gone in the finished poem, 'Friends':

> . . . till she
> So changed me that I live
> Labouring in ecstasy.

Three years later, when the poem was published in *Responsibilities*, Augusta told Yeats that she disliked it: 'I don't like being catalogued.'[53] So their friendship continued in its elliptical way. But with fewer opportunities for quiet companionship the easy trust and mutual help sometimes seemed a precious thing of the past. On 2 February 1911 he wrote a little plaintively to her from Dublin: 'I was greatly disappointed to find you had only stayed one day. I had thought you would be here for some days and had even decided what book you would read out to me. I wanted to get a few hours of life free from business, a little of our old tranquil friendship.'[54]

That summer and autumn of 1910 Augusta was busy writing, but not very successfully. Apart from *The Deliverer* she wrote two slight plays: *Coats*, a comedy, and *The Full Moon*, Augusta's first focused foray into fantasy, with 'Cracked Mary', based on a real woman in Gort, criticising 'the talk' and values of Cloon in exuberant language.

For the moment Augusta could sustain these failures because her reputation had been made in the summer and autumn of 1909 with the publication of *Seven Short Plays*. The continued performance of such plays as *Spreading the News*, *The Rising of the Moon* and *The Gaol Gate* in Dublin and on tour had made them Abbey classics to theatregoers. Now, published with *Hyacinth Halvey*, *The Travelling Man*, *The Jackdaw* and *The Workhouse Ward*, these one-act plays, both comedies and tragedies, were available to a wider audience. *The Athenaeum* reviewer defined her as Synge's successor, displaying an analogous flexibility, artistic integrity, and control in her dialogue and structure.[55] He particularly appreciated her ability to render what he called the Irish character. Her plays do adhere to national stereotypes, more than she perceived. But crucially they did not evoke negative stereotypes and this greatly contributed to their popularity. Lennox Robinson, who described her in his autobiography as 'our most important playwright' greatly admired the artistry and economy of these plays and he would encourage her in later life when she tried new things.[56]

There was nothing about the spring and summer of 1911 which hinted that Augusta's life was about to change, although she had had warning that it would. In one of her periodic references to horoscopes in her correspondence with Blunt and Yeats she mentioned in December 1908 that in 1911 she was to have real prosperity and 'to blossom like the rose', by which time she reckoned she would be 'without power of enjoying it'.[57] Facing into the first theatre year freed from Annie Horniman, Augusta was inclined towards celebration and on 1 March 1911 she enthused to John Quinn about the recent success of the Abbey in Manchester. At Coole she was planting ebulliently for the future.

In the summer of 1911 peaceful separation for Ireland inched forward when a new Liberal government, dependent on Irish Parliamentary Party support, passed the Parliament Act which removed the Lord's veto, the obstruction that had so far scuppered all Liberal attempts to pass a Home Rule bill. Augusta had for several years been convinced that, as the police and the government showed increasing reluctance to get involved in local disputes, landowners would turn to Home Rule as an antidote to 'mob rule'.[58] She was reading books on American independence thinking about the possible style and quality of a Home Rule government in Dublin, impressed by the way the Americans had purposefully forged their own identity. To Quinn she compared it favourably with the limping constitutional steps being taken towards Home Rule in Ireland: 'What a wonderful making of a nation! A peaceful separation or "limited home rule" would never have hardened dependants into rulers as those battles did. The creeping in, little by little, of self-government here, though better than leaving things as they are, will not excite the imagination either as battles do, or as a tremendous scheme like Parnell's would have done.'[59] It was a romantic attitude but it was not out of sympathy with latent Irish views.

On 25 May Algernon died. He was only 66. He had been neighbourly, though not particularly close in recent years.

His children were frequent visitors at Coole; Daphne was there just before his death. He had been gravely ill for some time, and when Augusta saw him several months earlier she knew it was for the last time: '. . . & it was so,' she told Yeats, 'I was never allowed to see him again.'[60] His death, she said, was a break with her early life. The next generation had also taken over at Roxborough, for two years previously Augusta's sister-in-law, the querulous Rose, had died (23 May 1909), leaving Arthur, now 46, an army officer with two young children, in charge. Adelaide, too, had died, aged 69, on 8 February 1909. Ill and unhappy, her children all grown, her death had been something of a relief.

When Augusta went to London in June 1911, she stayed at Lindsey House, Lane's newly acquired seventeenth-century home in Cheyne Walk, by the River Thames in Chelsea. He had allocated Augusta a bedroom, and a sitting-room for entertaining guests. Shortly after this Hugh broke off an engagement to Lady Clare Annesley, the 18-year-old daughter of an Irish peer, which greatly disappointed Augusta.[61] A month later he had a nervous breakdown and was confined to a rest home where Augusta was one of the few people to have regular contact with him.[62] She encouraged him with her own experience, telling him that St Mark's health resort, which she had visited after her own breakdown, was 'the most oppressive and deadly place while there, but from the moment I left I began getting stronger and stronger and went on doing so until now I think!'[63]

Meanwhile, Margaret was pregnant again, the baby due in early September. By 10 September she was overdue, the nurse was anxious and Augusta's nerves were on edge. But, apart from concern about Margaret, Augusta had another reason for wanting the baby to arrive quickly. She had promised to go with the Abbey on their first tour of America.

SEVENTEEN

America

. . . it is a great excitement seeing a new country at my
time of life, and since Philadelphia I feel any romantic
adventure possible!

AG to GBS, 23 January [1912]

When the White Star liner, the SS *Cymric*, left
Queenstown (now Cobh) for Boston on 21
September 1911 Augusta Gregory was comfortably settled
in a cabin. She was to join the Abbey players who had left
the week previously with Yeats for their first tour of the
United States. She would make four visits to America in the
next four years. Augusta was 59, not a time of life when one
would expect to discover new talents or have a love affair;
yet both happened in a country which then, as now, can
have a liberating effect on the newcomer.

Augusta had not originally planned to go to America.
Two weeks previously Yeats had unexpectedly asked her to
take his place on the ship which was to leave on 12
September.[1] She told him that this was impossible because
she wanted to be there when Margaret had her baby. But she
booked a passage for the following week. Anne Gregory was
born on 13 September. Augusta was delighted with the girl
but, writing to Ruth Shine the next day, she revealed her
assumption that girls should take second place in the family:

'I think it is a good thing having a girl, it will make the home more homey for Richard than if he had a brother going to school with him and no one to receive them at home.'[2] The following year Augusta wrote on a similar theme to Hugh: 'Richard [is] a little bundle of life and fire; Anne very much in the background, as a girl should be (in our family).'[3] Her mind had also flown to Anne's marriage prospects: 'And the difference of age will be so nice, he will be 21 when she is 18 and coming out; and his friends wont be too young for her.'[4] She obviously did not intend herself to be a role model for succeeding generations.

She left Coole on 19 September, reluctant to embark on such a long sea journey and separate herself from the convalescing Hugh, Margaret and the new baby. She was eight days on the ship. Undistracted by the many elaborate social occasions that such ships prided themselves on supplying, she wrote a play, scribbling the scenario on a menu and writing the dialogue in pencil in the quiet of her cabin.[5] It was a love story, more wholeheartedly so than *Grania*. It was, perhaps, triggered by observing the closeness of Margaret and Robert as they waited for the birth of their second child. The play broke a rule, for the poor peasant couple of the story had married for love. When the husband, a piper named McDonough, returns from a sheep-shearing to find his wife dead after having a miscarriage he is distraught. Without money for a funeral and disdaining a pauper's burial, he entices people to the funeral with his pipes to ensure that 'the story of the burying of McDonough's wife will be written in the book of the people!'[6] It is, as the critic Edward Kopper has written, 'a hymn of praise to the power of music', and the pride of the artist.

Augusta incorporated several autobiographical elements: her fear for Margaret's safety, memories of Roxborough, and a portrait of Corley, a travelling piper who had played at Roxborough and now visited her at Coole, bringing news, stories and tunes. *McDonough's Wife* skilfully combines these with her feeling for the folk fable. Typed and printed in Boston, she would give manuscripts, published copy and a letter to John Quinn as an 'offering'; a gesture faintly reminiscent of the gift of sonnets to Wilfrid Scawen Blunt in 1883.[7]

When the *Cymric* docked in Boston on 29 September Augusta felt like Columbus, separated from the old world by a sterile ocean, eagerly observing the strange life before her.[8] She was arriving with a strengthened literary identity and sense of financial worth. In April 1910 she had begun to feel that she could, with a 'quiet conscience', start to make some money from her marketable plays, and had written to Shaw asking him to advise her whether Curtis Brown, an American, 'a new type' that she was drawn to, would make a good literary agent.[9]

Once he was engaged, she began to receive intermittent payments for Abbey and amateur performances of her plays.[10] On 14 September she reported to Ruth Shine that she had just received a cheque for 13*s* 11*d* for *The Rising of the Moon*. While she was in America she set up a trust fund at the Guaranty Trust Company in New York for Richard's education.[11] In it she deposited her royalties for the performances of her plays and payments for articles. Quinn, authorised to invest the money, acted as trustee with Robert. Augusta's prioritising of boys is again evident in the details of the agreement: six-month-old baby Anne was not named.

Curtis Brown advised her to get Shaw to type out the speech he had made in February 1910 about the Abbey which had been particularly insightful and complimentary about Augusta.[12] Shaw's seal of approval had involved comparing her genius to that of Molière: the 'double command of the world of fancy, and the world of the vividest, funniest fact'. He had taken her line that her plays were a response to need, but, wiping away the aura of duty, had replaced it with the shine of instinct: her unique ability was to respond to 'anything in the air' in the theatre and to be unusually sensitive to public demand. In his first draft, Shaw had expressed her versatility by describing her as 'the charwoman of the Abbey', a phrase which he left out of the final text, perhaps because of the conflation of class. Augusta herself liked it (it suggested the duty that she relished) and would quote it to American journalists. It was used in her obituaries, and for subsequent commentators it has been a favourite image, frequently pulled out to conjure the atmosphere of drudgery that has clouded Lady Gregory's posthumous reputation.

When the newspaper reporters came aboard the *Cymric* in Boston Augusta got her first taste of the American cult of personality and celebrity. Their questions were immediately personal – what exactly had her journey been like? – and she was profiled in the *Boston Transcript* that evening with the other celebrity on board, Charles Dickens's son.[13] Reporters followed her about Boston, intercepting her and Yeats as they paced the lobby of their hotel, arranging interviews.

Yeats had been combative since he had arrived so that reporters fell on Lady Gregory as a safe icon whose appearance and manner conformed to American ideas of womanhood and aristocracy. They commented on her kind eyes, quizzical expression, readiness to laugh and grandmotherly appearance; she seemed to epitomise the spirit of her comedies. They described her as having the grace and beauty of a 'true gentlewoman', but without an inhibiting formality. They were ready to be impressed by benevolent aristocracy, but were either blind to the code of exclusivity, or uninhibited by it. They saw her vitality first and foremost. This was new, and Augusta responded with humour and astute answers in which she descibed herself as 'quite a working woman', gave a mildly nationalist version of her life story and represented herself as an incarnation of the literary Revival.[14] She was also the beneficiary of the more egalitarian attitude towards the sexes in America. The *Boston Evening Transcript* reporter was quick to pick up on her folklore and legends as well as her plays, and presented her work separately from Yeats.

Later, when Augusta had become embroiled in the *Playboy* fight, John Butler Yeats, who had been living in New York since December 1907 looking for patrons and an income, eloquently explained Augusta's appeal to the Americans: '. . . I think the people have "caught on" to a great interest in your personality. You have only to show yourself as much as possible. *Personality* fascinates the American mind, it is the result of their boss system of politics. Your look breathes courage and honesty. It is honesty against dishonesty, and life against death and courage against vicious and venomous poltroonery and free men against slaves.'[15] And so it is today, on both sides of the Atlantic. All in all there seemed to be a slightly bigger space for her in America and Augusta found herself prepared to fill it.

This making of a favourable image of Lady Gregory was a sideshow to the main performance: the conflict between Irish-America and the Abbey. The Abbey had long considered a potentially lucrative American tour, but it had only become a reality when theatre agents Liebler & Co made them a generous offer of all expenses and 35 per cent of the profits, allowing the 'stars' £10 a week and the others £4.[16] The condition was that they perform *Playboy*. Liebler knew the value of controversy, and Yeats was told they must 'fight it out & win that fight again'.[17] Everyone knew that the expatriate political organisation, Clan na Gael, would cause trouble, but how much? Before Augusta arrived, Yeats had tried to pre-empt opposition with a series of oratorical salvos, explaining the Abbey's artistic mission to present an essential rather than literal reality and to challenge conventional patriotism. The hardened Irish-Americans were not much interested in this. Augusta's initial instinct was to neutrally declare that the plays should be allowed to speak for themselves; she was not prepared to engage in debate until absolutely necessary.[18]

The first attack on the company came from the *Boston Post* on 4 October, denigrating *Hyacinth Halvey* and *Birthright* (a bleak view of Irish life by T.C. Murray) as un-Irish. It used fearsome prose of a moral intensity that is more often associated with the seventeenth century: 'My soul cried out for a thousand tongues to voice my unutterable horror and disgust . . . I never saw anything so vulgar, vile, beastly, and unnatural, so calculated to calumniate, degrade, and defame a people and all they hold sacred and dear.'[19] Here was a version of the traditional patriotism that had never existed in Ireland.

Ten days later, the United Irish American Societies, representing 75 groups, printed a resolution in *The Gaelic American* to 'drive the vile thing [*Playboy*] from the stage'.[20] They claimed that they feared the plays were damaging the Home Rule cause by suggesting that the Irish were unfit to govern themselves, while the forcefully articulated moral tone gave their indignation a strong American flavour – they were, after all, one of a number of cultural groups that were fighting for recognition in American society.

The accusation that the plays represented a false Ireland would be repeated ad nauseam. Before he left America on 14

October, Yeats was already reciprocating with accusations that the Irish-Americans were ignorant of Irish life. Augusta's response was more guarded. When she was asked whether the plays were an accurate representation, she replied, 'I think it quite natural that some should misunderstand our intentions . . . We are simply giving plays.'[21] It was too disengaged to be satisfactory. The person who understood the polemic was Shaw. From the safety of London he descended straight to the level of people who by early December were accusing the Abbey actresses of not being Irish because their feet were too big, clumsy and flat, by calling their Irish credentials into question: 'You would suppose that all of these Murphys, Doolans, etc., that call themselves romantic names like Clan na Gael are Irishmen.'[22]

But Augusta's purposeful effort to be amiable and discreet was the best foil for someone who would find practical ways of defeating the enemy. She satisfied Liebler not by encouraging controversy, but by fighting. When *Playboy* was finally performed in Boston on 16 October there had been only mild interruptions; the opposition had not amounted to much and Augusta had ensured that favourable reports by the mayor and the censor had helped their cause.

Augusta liked Boston. She had arranged for introductions 'to give a start in good society', and taken Lane's advice about her wardrobe, particularly his insistence that she wear her diamond Maltese Cross on all occasions.[23] She discovered connections in less good society: people she had known at Roxborough and had subsequently emigrated. She was touchingly ambivalent about American affluence, delighted by the luxury, but unwilling to be sucked into profligacy. 'The hotel is very luxurious endless reception rooms & very good food,' she told Robert, 'but so dear one feels it a pity to eat it even at other people's expense.'[24] She and Yeats shared portions, and she bought herself a spirit lamp to make tea in her room. She described a vacuum cleaner to Robert: 'There is not much for the housemaid to do, there is a brush attached to a hose that sucks up the dust in no time.' She listed meals – a lunch of cold tongue, hot oyster stew, ices and cheese served simultaneously – and observed, 'Iced water at every meal.'[25]

It was not long before she met the 'tip top leader of fashion', the ebullient, diminutive, vigorous 71-year-old Isabella Gardner, always referred to as Mrs Jack Gardner. A well-travelled heiress, she had designed her Boston house, Fenway Court, around a courtyard to resemble a Renaissance Venetian palace, and filled it with her valuable, and beautifully hung eclectic art collection for the benefit of the public, which had been admitted since 1903.[26] She came to Augusta's box one evening at the Plymouth Theatre and seized her hand, 'you are a darling, a darling, a darling!' she enthused.[27] Augusta was drawn to her spirit and power – she later described her as one of the few 'great' ladies she had ever known – and, great lady that she also was, immediately enrolled her in the Abbey's service, asking her to use her influence with the theatre management to sort out a satisfactory programme for what had become an extended stay in Boston.

She also asked Mrs Gardner if she could give a lecture in her music room to an invited audience. Augusta was being besieged by invitations from clubs and societies to give speeches. In Ireland she had shrunk from public speaking, but now, realising it was inevitable, and aware that a formal prepared lecture in which she could control the content was preferable to off-the-cuff remarks, she decided that she must steel herself to speak. Fenway Court would be an experiment. A few days later, Augusta, standing in the medieval splendour of the music room, nervously began her lecture on playwriting, but soon found that she hardly needed her notes, never hesitated for a word or missed points and kept to her allotted time. She also read from *McDonough's Wife* as a woman played music behind an arras. Mrs Gardner pronounced it 'a screaming success', while Augusta reported in a more level tone to Yeats, 'It is a great relief to me and the discovery of a new faculty. I shan't feel nervous again; that is a great thing.'[28] She earned $40 (100 people had paid $2 each).[29] Told that her voice dropped as she read, she took a few elocution lessons.

Thus was inaugurated a parallel tour to the Abbey in which Augusta would depart for a day or two to visit university campuses or adjacent towns and cities to give her growing repertoire of lectures. She *was* nervous again, but she found she had a rapport with her audiences and the invitations kept coming in. Smith College was a particular success – 1,500 in the audience, no notes, many compliments afterwards, £10 earned.[30]

Augusta was open to America, tailoring her lectures to a nascent interest in indigenous culture and a newly developing writers' theatre. She was immediately championed by the many enthusiastic professional women's clubs and colleges who invited her to speak and spoke warmly of her achievements. She responded with flattery, showing interest in a game of football at Vassar, and promising that she would send her granddaughter to Smith.[31] This brush with so many high-achieving, ambitious and independent women did not alter her view of women's potential and she returned to Ireland without any plans for change in that direction.

The lectures gave her an opportunity to see something of America, and she enjoyed the journeys in which she passed through the villages and woods of New England and later the isolated towns of Ohio and Indiana. Recalling her experiences the following year in *Our Irish Theatre* she wrote, 'Dozing in midnight trains, I would remember, as in a dream, "the flight of a bird through a lighted hall," the old parable of human life.' It has the ring of happiness.

Above everything, the American tour was hard work for Augusta. Apart from devising ways of overcoming the Irish-American opposition, lecturing and giving interviews, arranging programmes and liaising with theatre managers, Augusta was in constant demand by the players. Lennox Robinson as manager was officially in charge, but Augusta soon discovered that he was significantly unreliable, negligent, and reluctant to take Augusta's advice:[32] '. . . his judgement always seems to fail at the moment it is wanted,' she wrote diplomatically to Yeats about his protégé. She was determined that he would never take another tour to America.

Augusta also had difficulties with Sara Allgood who was aware that she could make more money elsewhere. Many have described Augusta as snobbish with the actors, but, as her reports to Yeats reveal, she often took their feelings and opinions into account. In November, when she was negotiating a three-month extension to the tour, she consulted the players who refused to stay unless their salary was doubled.[33] She secured a Green Room for the company in their New York theatre because she knew they felt disorientated without one. Despite all the demands on her, Augusta found the time and energy to write home in great detail, though she did duplicate letters to Yeats and Coole. She was constantly tired, unable to sleep, but buoyed by the work.[34]

Augusta succeeded in winning the *Playboy* fight because she refused to believe that the opposition was as well-organised, informed or committed as rumours suggested. She also believed that the Abbey could rely on the support of those in authority. On both counts she was right. This practical assessment of the situation allowed her to remain calm and composed, an attitude which both impressed and baffled her contemporaries who found the threats and accusations of the Irish-Americans disturbing. In Boston and Providence, Rhode Island, she found the opposition friable and the authorities staunch. Informed that the Catholic Church was opposing them in Washington, she discovered it was only a few priests. But the threat from New York looked more serious.

Augusta arrived in New York on 18 November. She was met at the station by John Quinn. Since his visit to Coole in 1902 Quinn had become the reliable friend that Augusta had hoped he might be. Not only had he been indefatigable in copyrighting most of her plays in America and securing American publishers for her folklore but, as we have seen, she had been able to write to him about her work, her problems with other people, her efforts at Coole, Robert's activities, her feelings about Ireland, the delight of her discovery of Shaw, confident that he had her interests at heart. She fantasised about talking to him: 'I fancy that when you and I meet we shall be able to have a little sympathetic chat about our friends and their wives,' she had written on 24 July 1906, conjuring a cosy intimacy that was part woman-to-woman, part man-to-man. She tried not to bore him with Byzantine theatre details and she never complained, but she allowed emotion to enter her letters.

Augusta could not believe her good fortune in this friendship, and felt periodically guilty that she could not reciprocate sufficiently. 'I must certainly have some paper stamped "Grateful thanks to John Quinn", for my letters always have to begin in that way,' she wrote on 20 June 1908. One way to repay his kindness was to worry about his health, for Quinn, who had set up on his own as a financial lawyer in August 1907 and was intermittently involved in political campaigns as well as work for the Irish Revival in America, was a compulsive worker, reluctant to take holidays, enduring the symptoms of stress as an integral part of his life.

Quinn, 41, was very well respected in New York and beyond, but not always well understood. He was, John Butler Yeats pronounced, articulating the unease, 'the crossest man in the world, and the kindest'.[35] Photographs of him show a tight-lipped, steely-eyed determination, but with something humorous about the eyes. An Irish-American himself, shocked and disillusioned by aggressive Irish-American support for the *Playboy* protesters in Dublin in 1907, Quinn had no sympathy for Clan na Gael and the 'pathriots' as he called the opposition, mocking the self-conscious Irish accents of those who had never had them.[36] With a lawyer's ready acknowledgement of an adversary, Quinn was convinced they were waiting to stage a New York version of the Dublin riots and he was prepared to fight. This was quite different from Augusta's more elliptical approach. But Quinn had great respect for Augusta's judgement and he could see that her methods were having an effect. He was prepared to wait and see whether his adversarial skills would be necessary.

Meanwhile, Quinn was at Augusta's service, finding her doctors, putting his office and staff at her disposal, inviting her to tea in his luxurious Central Park apartment (58 Central Park West, 9th floor) decorated with the work of both Yeatses and contemporary European art, introducing her to the New York elite. He seemed to know exactly what she needed and, in a situation where so many appeared to be against her or providing some sort of difficulty, it must have been an incalculable relief to be with him. 'I feel his presence here a great help to me,' she told Yeats in a level tone, 'there has not been much for him to do, but I know there is little he would not do at need.'[37] Although their individual styles were different, their shared sense of moral purpose and confidence made them good partners.

The Abbey performed off-Broadway at the Maxine Elliott Theatre, where Augusta was given a little room by the stage to hold informal salons, give interviews (eight people immediately demanded interviews when she arrived) and work during performances. She stayed at the Algonquin Hotel on 44th Street, a few blocks from the theatre – 'a modern fireproof building' according to the hotel letterhead, with 225 rooms and 150 baths. The lobby, currently decorated with dark pillars and a scattering of high backed chairs and informal tables, perhaps echoing its early twentieth-century ambience, is perfect for the discreet, informal meetings called to deal with the series of crises that the New York visit would bring. 'I . . . grew fond of the little corner of the city,' she wrote, describing the 'dangerous excitement' of crossing 6th Avenue, 'with motors dashing in all directions, and railway trains [the first subway, opened in 1904, taking 425,000 passengers a day] thundering overhead.'[38] It was a pivotal time to be in New York, for much of the infrastructure and many of the landmarks which define it today were being built; the foundations of New York Public Library, which now houses many of her manuscripts, were being laid that year.

Playboy was scheduled for four nights beginning Monday 27 November. Since their arrival the newspaper campaign against them had intensified and there were predictions of possible riots. Quinn was convinced that their enemy would throw things, and *The Gaelic American* had called on its supporters not to spare Augusta because she was a woman. Máire Nic Shiubhlaigh, staying with her aunt in Brooklyn, was alarmed, and felt that the angry New York Irish 'had better be taken seriously', even though they were ignorant of the play. She begged Augusta to speak to the Gaelic League, and Quinn suggested she make a pre-emptive statement.[39] But Augusta, after astutely announcing that any dispute was between Liebler & Co and the mob, effectively declaring that the dispute was an American issue, was confident that the riot would not amount to much and that they would prevail.

In fact, there was a spectacular riot on the Monday night in which people yelled, missiles were thrown – stink bombs, rosaries, potatoes – panic spread about the auditorium and the police were called in to eject the troublemakers. At one point there was a danger that the audience would mount the stage, and Augusta found herself adopting Yeats's role and haranguing them from before the curtain, a moment that she omitted from *Our Irish Theatre*, probably because she felt it was not appropriate behaviour in a woman.[40] 'We had a confused impression of ducking figures, a glimpse of Lady Gregory, rotund, thin-lipped and very determined looking; her voice crying (rather unreasonably): "Keep playing!" to those on the stage,' Máire Nic Shiubhlaigh later recalled.[41] Augusta's strategy was identical to her Dublin strategy; they would keep performing the play until it was heard. When the police had made their arrests the players started again from act one and disturbances were minimal.

Augusta was able to write home of a victory. Giving an interview during the worst of the disturbance, Augusta cast doubt on the judgement of the rioters by saying it was the worst first night they had ever experienced with the play. John Butler Yeats congratulated her on her interview the following day: 'You gave the giant Stupidity a mortal thrust with a courteous smile.' This projected a more womanly image, and was included in *Seventy Years*.[42]

Augusta's trump card was Theodore Roosevelt, President of America until two years previously. She had first met him in London in 1910 and now visited him in Oyster Bay the day before *Playboy* was performed. He admired *Cuchulain* and *Gods* while she appreciated him as a great man of prodigious vitality, and both, tempering intellectual interests by a down-to-earth practicality, shared a passion for indigenous culture. Augusta was conscious that where her great-grandfather had known George Washington, she knew Roosevelt; she had taken the actors to Washington's house, Mount Vernon, and she told Quinn she hoped that whereas Washington had given her ancestor stuffed birds, Roosevelt would give her a bear's paw.[43] Roosevelt agreed to attend the theatre for the Wednesday performance. His presence immediately quelled any serious thoughts of protest. The audience applauded him (he drew an unresisting, smiling Augusta up with him to acknowledge it) and his enthusiasm for the humour in the play infected the crowd.[44]

The Abbey had prevailed. But Augusta was not allowed to relax. 'I seen ye where [*sic*] got slated in New York. How is the Pensioner? Yours, Mike.'[45] It was her first anonymous abusive letter. Quinn hired private detectives and instructed the Federal postal authority to trace the letter, but her correspondent was not discovered. The delinquent element in the opposition finally penetrated Augusta's calm, though only in private. She angrily denounced a delegation of Catholic women to Yeats as 'the stupidest set I ever met', and, when Yeats was accused of running from the fight, robustly told him that 'it doesn't take a man to fight a few priests and potatoes, a woman is good enough for that,' adding, 'I have not however said this to the interviewers.'[46] It was vintage Lady Gregory, denigrating the opposition, belittling her own role and letting Yeats off the hook in one sentence. But she was tolerant about the *World*'s claim (with a photograph of her at dinner) that she was often to be seen at the Petitpas, John Butler's not very reputable boarding house, a claim that Quinn was keen to contradict.[47] Elsewhere, the American press still regarded her as a gutsy fighter who yet managed to retain her feminine equanimity.

At this difficult time circumstances put a barrier between herself and Hyde. Although Augusta had been careful not to ally the Abbey players too closely with the Gaelic League, knowing that it would compromise the League's nationalist credentials, John Devoy, editor of *The Gaelic American*, asked Hyde to give an official denial that the League was associated with the Abbey. Hyde duly cabled the message to New York. Quinn was furious, only too aware that the withdrawing of League support would strengthen their enemies. Augusta however, did not doubt Hyde's personal support, speculating to Yeats that Devoy must have lied to him to make him repudiate them; in fact, he had not distanced the Gaelic League enough for Devoy.[48]

Augusta wrote to Hyde sadly, tactfully, in the cadences of folklore: 'Oh Craoibhin, what are these wounds with which we are wounded in the house of our friends?' She conveyed the damage done and expressed her solidarity with him: 'We are fighting your battle if you did but know it, and the battle of all who want to live and breathe.'[49] Yet undeniably the Gaelic League was forcing Hyde into a different set of allegiances and the episode remained an issue between them for some time.

Christmas was approaching and Augusta was constantly in the company of John Quinn. Perhaps it was at this time that Augusta fell in love with him. 'Why do I love you so much? It ought to be from all that piled up goodness of the years. Yet it is not that – it is some call that came in a moment – something impetuous & masterful about you that satisfies me – that gives me perfect rest.'[50] Augusta wrote this letter to a man who was eighteen years her junior on 2 April 1912, not long after she returned to Coole from America. There are a number of these handwritten love letters surviving, all written in the first two months back at Coole, some inserted into envelopes with less emotional typed letters. Quinn did the same, but, whereas he did not burn her letters as arranged, Augusta did – 'Your dear letter goes into the fire tonight. I must keep it till then', she wrote on 2 April – so it is difficult to assess his feelings.[51] Sometimes her letters seem to be articulating what she had not had the time to say in the final week she had spent with him in New York before setting sail on 6 March. Sometimes she admits that she is repeating what she has already said, not so long ago – 'Everything I ever said to you I say over again'; and, 'Where is the use of writing? You know all this do you not?'[52] It seems that it was not until the first week in March that they acknowledged their love and perhaps became lovers.

Quinn would never marry. His biographer, B.L. Reid, felt that Quinn was a natural bachelor who valued his freedom and, plagued by nerves and hypochondria, believed he was a physical risk for a woman. This did not prevent entanglements; he was known as a man who had success with women. He had a long affair with the sexually liberated American 'bachelor girl', Dorothy Coates. This had caused a rift with Yeats in 1909 when Yeats met Coates and Quinn accused him of trying to seduce her.[53] The men broke off communication after an argument in August, and were still estranged in 1911. Quinn had met May Morris, the daughter of William Morris in 1910. Reid asserts that Quinn was only platonically attracted to May whom he admired as an embodiment of her father's ideals. May was more smitten, and in 1911 was still writing hopeful, affectionate letters.

But Christmas 1911 was for Augusta. She was Quinn's consort at New York gatherings. They went shopping together. He bought her an expensive gold watch. Guiltily she told Robert the price – $180 – and that she would have the monogram A.G. engraved on it so that Anne could inherit it.[54] Quinn was frank about his increasingly profitable work: a recent fee of $10,000 in shares; a retaining fee of $2,000 a year.

On several occasions Augusta tried to encourage Quinn to talk about his argument with Yeats.

> One or two evenings ago I said to Quinn 'Will you ever be quite friends with Yeats again?' He said 'I don't know, I don't think about it, I feel no bitterness towards him.' I said 'I know you cannot or you cd not write so nicely of him as you do. It is not a thing I want to talk about, but Yeats said the other day "It is a strange thing that Quinn who knows me so well and I have lived with so much should think me capable of what he does."' He said 'When women get mixed up with things there are always quarrels' and changed the topic. I feel sure it is all right and that when you meet him again you can just talk as if nothing had happened.[55]

Something of Quinn's detachment emerges in this exchange, as well as Augusta's concern that Quinn and Yeats overcome their estrangement.

The company was now getting large sympathetic audiences, and the feeling was that they could run for weeks. However, the theatre was booked for another group so they left New York on 31 December for Philadelphia. Here they met very determined opposition. After two nights of protests, arrests and releases, the local Clan na Gael leader brought an injunction against further performances of the Abbey and the players were arrested. Augusta had been warned and, after alerting Quinn and the theatre lawyer, bail bonds were organised binding the players to appear in court the following day so that the performance could proceed.

As usual Augusta was determined to resist. She told them she would rather be arrested than withdraw *Playboy*, and she would later publicly assert that she 'wouldn't mind going to prison. Bunyan wrote some magnificent stuff while in prison. So did Oscar Wilde.'[56] But privately she was more fastidious and told Robert that she would like to avoid arrest, 'because of the publicity, one would feel like a suffragette'. She was now embroiled in the American legal system and was frankly confused. This was the moment Quinn had been waiting for and, appointed to cross question the witnesses when the players appeared before the judge, he decisively, and, particularly for Augusta, impressively, turned the tables on their accusers.

In a letter to Shaw expressing her impatience with 'pompous' Philadelphia she added, '. . . since Philadelphia I feel any romantic adventure possible!' It was not the only time she hinted at private feelings to Shaw, secure perhaps that even the perceptive playwright would never guess their truth, or enjoying the frisson that he might entertain the possibility of what she suggested, and then dismiss it as impossible.[57] Meanwhile, Dublin was revelling in the notoriety of the arrest, and the Abbey gained significantly in popularity in Ireland.

As the tour proceeded to its final destinations in the snowy landscapes of Pittsburgh, Richmond (Indiana), Indianapolis and Chicago, Augusta wrote long letters to Quinn. In a novel or play Philadelphia would have been the dramatic climax, but in real life the company limped on, harried and threatened. The accusations became risible; *Playboy* became '*Cowboy* of the Western World'.[58] In Chicago Augusta received a death threat. On a sheet bearing a rough drawing of a coffin, hammer, nails and pistol, was written 'your fate is sealed never again shall you gase [*sic*] on the barren hilltops of Connemara'.[59] But she continued to walk to the theatre every night, remarking with genuine bravery and her trademark wit, 'I don't feel anxious, for I don't think from the drawing that the sender has much practical knowledge of firearms.'[60]

She was exhausted and often thought of home. Since the New Year she had earmarked her lecture earnings for improvements at Coole. On 16 February she wrote to Quinn from Chicago that she only needed £50 to make a total of £300, 'a sum of which I should be very proud'. 'It makes a real difference in my life being able to add a little to the general stock instead of taking from it, though neither Robert or Margaret would ever let this thought into their mind, still one must have it.'[61]

Finally, the passage home was booked. They were due to sail on 6 March from Boston and, after a final performance in which Augusta graciously, with a few 'simple-hearted' words, received the warm appreciation of the audience, she returned to New York and Quinn.[62] Now that her performance was over she revelled in that 'call that came in a moment'. She had entered a different realm; she was passionate, candid, joyous. The woman who was habitually so measured and discreet laid bare her feelings with a rhythmic incantation that was sexually charged: 'My John, my dear John, my own John, not other peoples John, I love you, I care for you, I know, I want you, I believe in you, I see you always,' she wrote from Coole on 22 March, a week after she returned.[63] There was no room for Dorothy Coates or May Morris in her passionate claiming of Quinn. Eleven days later she wrote, 'Oh my darling, am I now lonely after you? do I not awake looking for you – & long to be alone sometimes that I may think only of you.'[64]

Augusta had found a refuge, complete, engulfing and perfectly satisfying, in Quinn. 'How good you were to me!' she wrote. On 2 March they had shopped by telephone, 'you encompassed me with thought & care . . . "Wonderful" yes! quite as wonderful', she wrote a month later.[65] For a person who usually found herself looking after other people this was no doubt a deeply satisfying reversal. It is tempting to observe that the way she fell in love was not entirely surprising. After five months of threats and controversy, the need to make decisions and keep constant vigilance, there was nothing more natural than to fall with relief into the arms of the one person who had shadowed her with anxious and effective care. In the same letter she added a poignant line, 'more wonderful to me than to you'. She was also back on familiar territory, loving more than she was loved. But, as before, she was defiant in her happiness: 'Dont think I am fretting, I am proud, I am glad, you are nearer to me than anything, everything else a little far off.'[66]

When she got back to Coole she constantly relived their time together. On the last day of March she recalled that she had begun the month 'under your roof! What a long month it always is; & always will be.'[67] It was the month of her birthday – she was 60 that year – the month of her wedding, Sir William's death and her mother's death. She felt she loved Quinn better every day.

Four weeks later, on 6 May, she sent a quite different letter, which only alluded indirectly to the affair. 'Just two months today since I said good-bye to America and you! Oh, I have worked so hard in that time yet I seem to have done very little. And these last days I have been going through what is unusual with me a fit of depression. I have felt more profound loneliness than I had felt for many a year.'[68]

Augusta seems to have decided that she must not indulge her feelings for Quinn any longer and give him up as her beloved. There is no trace of recrimination to suggest that he had initiated this. But he had not written for some time, and it may have been during that interminable time when the next letter did not arrive that she began to see more clearly that he did not love her as she loved him.

She had also begun to think of Robert. Should she not be satisfied with him and the rest of her family as she had been before she went to America? She felt guilty, and to temper the guilt she clung to Montaigne's observation that friendship between parents and children can never be entirely satisfactory as neither can fully confide in the other: '. . . and I am but too glad to see Robert and his wife wrapped up in each other. "I also once lived in Arcady",' she told Quinn.[69]

Gradually she began to see that her infatuation with Quinn was bordering on the ridiculous. In her effort to distance herself from her passion she now described the affair as 'a rapture of friendship', and put it in the past tense: 'I know that [I am] just paying for past happiness, that rapture of friendship that so possessed and satisfied me.'

At the end of this letter she wrote, 'I am afraid the seal ring is certainly gone with the *Titanic*. I felt as if it was a gloomy omen, but I try and remember our folklore and how the loss of such a thing means the sparing of a harder loss.'[70] Yet the loss of her gift seemed to set its stamp on an ending. Quinn received this news with something like relief. 'Perhaps I am as well off without the ring,' he wrote airily to Augustus John. To Augusta he wrote more gently, 'the ring that you so generously gave me and the Joseph Conrad MS of "Karain" which were on the way to me were real personal losses.'[71]

EIGHTEEN

Theatre and Gallery

To influence people, appeal to whatever is best in their
nature –

March 1900, diary

When Augusta returned to Coole in March 1912 it was the estate that first claimed her attention, for purchase had still not been resolved. Although the Congested District Board had not committed itself in November 1910, a year later, as Augusta had left for America, Board Commissioners had been back to inspect the land.[1] The tenants, too, had begun to prepare their own offer. Robert had tried to pressurise the Board by telling it that the tenants were prepared to give a good price. In fact, in May, the tenants, suffering from low agricultural prices and trying to establish a lower purchase price, refused to pay their half-yearly rents unless they were reduced by nearly a third (a 6*s* in the pound reduction). Frank responded by offering a 2*s* reduction, which was scorned. With agreement elusive, Frank planned to seize cattle.

This was anathema to Augusta, who saw it as laying the groundwork of a possibly lasting bitterness and jeopardising peace.[2] She persuaded Frank to offer a 3*s* in the pound reduction, proffering the extra shilling herself, and this was presented to the tenants at a meeting arranged by Mike John

Dooley in Father Fahey's house (he often mediated between the tenants and Gregorys), Augusta ensconced upstairs while negotiations proceeded below. The tenants accepted the 3s, although Augusta refused to apply this to the arrears. 'I hope you think I have done right – I did what I thought best . . . dear child – God bless you . . .' she wrote to Robert after a detailed description of what had been a nerve-racking episode. But, just as the estate provoked, so it consoled: 'Woods are a great solace, and all my animosities turn upon bindweed, rabbits and squirrels,' she later told Quinn.[3]

Almost immediately on her return from America Augusta began to write. Her great fear was that in the six months since she had written *McDonough's Wife* she had lost her creative touch, for the American interlude had been an unusual hiatus in her flow and she was not sure what damage falling in love might have done. A flimsy one-act comedy, *The Bogie Men*, seemed to confirm her fears.[4]

Writing the two-act comedy, *Damer's Gold*, was a more satisfying experience. Damer, a miser, Augusta found as she wrote, had an independent will, entering the play when she thought he would be a background figure and monopolising the dialogue. However, when she had finished writing she was unsure whether the play was complete. This less planned way of writing had deprived her of the confidence to judge her work. She could not trust Robert and Margaret's opinion either for, as she told Quinn, 'respect comes in; they would not give me any real criticism'.[5] Her confidence returned after the first performance in November when she rearranged the play, clear that she must let Damer loose to do as he would. Later in 1913, in America again, she wrote a lecture on playwriting using this experience to illustrate comedy writing, and gave a vivid description of Damer taking 'his own way'.[6]

While she was struggling with her first version of *Damer's*

Gold in the months after her return from America, Augusta
was also tormenting herself with an article on *Playboy*. The
idea was that on the next tour, when faced with the
troublesome 'Please tell me the exact reasons for the
objections to the Playboy', she could produce a polished
statement.[7] The difficulty was that any presentation of the
objectors' arguments and aggressive acts put the Irish in a
bad light. 'I don't want to make an indictment of my
countrymen and it seems like one when the matter is
focused,' she explained to Quinn on 6 May. During a brief
visit to London she had received an offer of a £100 advance
from the publisher, Grant Richards, for a book on the
American tour and the theatre. She had originally rejected
the idea of writing a mere record, but then it occurred to her
that such a book might be the way to present their case.[8]

Her idea for the *Playboy* section of *Our Irish Theatre* was
to use the long letters she had written from America to Yeats
and Robert, which tended to be factual without being
judgmental, for 'I just took each event as part of the business
of the day'. It would give the book a strongly personal
character. This was important. Yeats, aware that Moore was
writing his autobiography, had in May 1911 encouraged
Augusta to write on the theatre and, thinking it was
imperative that they present their version of events, had
urged 'the more you make it a personal narrative the
better'.[9] A self-confessedly personal perspective was also
disarming, for no one could argue with it; a polemic could
be more easily criticised as biased. So Augusta strengthened
the autobiographical element in her commentary by adding
reminiscences and anecdotes, and she admitted as much
material as she dared that told against her primary interests
(unfriendly priests were matched by friendly ones for
instance), to impose her own view without presenting a one-
sided argument.

She avoided being personal in the modern sense of confessional. She did not reveal her view of *Playboy*, her attitude to the audience during the riots, her feelings for Yeats and Synge or the differences between them, and the tensions with the Fays and the actors are largely absent. And she did not rise to Moore's challenge to redefine the line habitually drawn between the public and the private. He had published the first volume of his maverick and entertaining autobiography in autumn 1911 and had freely evoked his victims' personal lives. Instead, she assiduously maintained an old-fashioned respect for privacy; she did not want to alienate people from the theatre, and her humiliating experience with Sir William's autobiography was no doubt still with her.[10] In the end her victims – the Fays and Annie Horniman – were mainly invisible.[11]

Our Irish Theatre might also be viewed as Augusta's contribution to a current political debate. With Home Rule on the agenda in 1912 the issue of whether Catholics and Protestants would be able and willing to share power and influence in a post-Home Rule Ireland was becoming acute. In April 1912 Yeats was confident of Catholic tolerance of Protestants, but by November he was not so optimistic about Catholic liberalism. Augusta felt that Catholic intolerance was an inevitable, but not insurmountable problem. On 30 November she wrote calmly to Shaw, 'One is not afraid of R.C. intolerance, for as I quote from Cuchulain "Good as the attack is the defence will be as good", but one might as well say there will be no whiskey.'[12]

In *Our Irish Theatre*, Augusta presented a vision of a multicultural Ireland, by including an account of early Unionist support for the theatre, and carefully balancing the directors' resistance to nationalists in the *Playboy* riots with their resistance to Dublin Castle over *Blanco*. She made much of her Gregory background, addressing the book to her grandson and drawing the reader into the texture of Ascendancy life with the naming of plants that were rarely found beyond demesne walls.[13] *Inter alia*, her depictions of Coole and the Gregorys evoke a family of mixed background and sympathies; antagonistic to the Whiteboys, sympathetic to famine victims, displaying pictures of members of one of Sir William's London clubs, the Grillon Club, next to Burton's idealised peasants.

Overall, Augusta demonstrated that the Anglo-Irish continued to have a role in Irish life. She dared her readers to share her concern for the privileged child, Richard – '*So think a long time before you choose your road, little Richard, but when you have chosen it follow it on to the end*' – and so accept his class as they accepted the work of the theatre.[14] It was a continuation of the project begun with William's autobiography in which she had put the Gregory family in an appealing light. Now she seemed to be hoping to use the family's established credentials as part of an assertion that Ireland did not have to choose definitively between Catholics or Protestants, Ascendancy or any other class.

Her surviving letters to Quinn during this time reveal that she had succeeded in subduing her feelings for him, and that her passion had transmuted into a wifely concern for his safety and health. This theme had haunted earlier letters, but now her solicitude had a new intensity and an imaginative engagement. During a high wind at Coole she wrote that she was glad he was not on the ocean.[15] She empathised with him when his business partnership broke up and she advised him repeatedly to take an extended break. He sent her a washing machine, and they exchanged books; he gave her Meredith's letters, she sent him Blunt's *Irish Experiences*, 'the gaol part very interesting'.[16] In November Shaw sent a light-hearted account of falling in love with Mrs Patrick

Campbell: 'I scorned the danger; thought I was more dangerous than she; and went in head over ears before I had been thirty seconds in her presence. And this at fifty-six . . . Is there no age limit?'[17] It concealed a real infatuation.

Less amusing was a poem Yeats handed to her a few weeks later with the line, referring to Augusta, 'If you, that have grown old, are the first dead'.[18] It went on to evoke their companionable ghosts walking the house and gardens of Coole. Augusta, too, had often imagined that their ghosts would haunt Coole together: 'It is good to have a meeting place anyhow, in this place where so many children of our minds were born,' she told him.[19] But she did not like the image of herself as old; it underlined the gulf between her secret self (most definitely not grown old) and those around her at Coole. She wrote with some force to Yeats, 'You won't publish it just now will you? I think not.' He did not publish it for another ten years.

Augusta accompanied the main company on its second American tour which began in December 1912 in Chicago and took in Montreal, Pittsburgh, New York, Boston and Philadelphia, as well as smaller places. She wrote regular, detailed letters to Quinn, laced with concern for his welfare and betraying some excitement at the thought of seeing him again. 'If you must be ill wait till I am near, I could read & do messages for you on the telephone,' she added in pen at the foot of a typed letter from Chicago on 9 January.[20] On 1 February from Montreal she wrote, '& perhaps after a week and a day I am going to see you & have a long talk & so I am going to bed happy tonight'.[21]

Letters from Augusta to Quinn written after her stay in his apartment suggest that they had resumed a cosy, mutually solicitous intimacy, but that the love affair of the previous year was over. Something of their relationship can be gleaned from a breakfast conversation in which Augusta confided her frustrations with Yeats to Quinn and which Quinn, appreciating the momentousness of her revelations, afterwards summarised, adding a few of his own comments.[22] In a breaking of a taboo (in her letters at least), she criticised Yeats's actions in the Gonne episode of 1898 (when he had spent folklore money visiting her), the Annie Horniman letter of January 1910, and the Gosse incident of July 1910.

It could be said that the indignant Augusta was simply jealous of Horniman, Gosse and Gonne; on all three occasions Yeats had put them before Augusta. But the underlying theme of her complaints was that Yeats had let her down by failing to respond adequately to insults, or reneging on spoken or unspoken pacts. It was not merely a personal disappointment, for she also complained that Yeats had refused an invitation to have Christmas dinner with Agnes Toibin, a writer and friend. 'Yeats dined solitary and alone rather than give the evening up to her.' Augusta was disturbed and affronted by this show of male independence. She hated it for herself, but equally she hated it for this other woman who had put herself out for Yeats, as Augusta had so often done. She had harboured her resentments partly because of her emotional response at the time, but also because she disapproved of his actions from the depths of her being. The 'Statement' strongly evokes Lady Gregory of *The Vision*, with her traditional code of personal conduct. Telling Quinn was a way of relieving herself of a psychological burden, but it also points to her emotional reliance on him, and perhaps also a desire to maintain an intimacy with her old lover.

A month later Augusta suffered a minor nervous and physical collapse because of the pressures of the tour. She immediately summoned Quinn for comfort and reassurance. 'Dear John, Just a line to post tomorrow to tell you I love and thank you for this dear day of rest which did me more good than you can think,' she wrote from Philadelphia one evening in April.[23] She thought that it had probably saved her from a longer period of illness. She had felt shaky that day but lectured to 400 people. She continued, 'Oh! I am tired! I'm afraid I was a trouble to you. I must get well by Friday – and not be a cripple on your hands. You are so wonderfully patient and kind. I do care very much for you. Good Night!' It is only to Quinn that we see her admitting to weakness and searching for help; in her other relationships it was she who had to be the strong one. On the ship returning to London a heavy iron door slammed onto her hand as the ship lurched, crushing it. The pain was excruciating, and she felt faint every time her hand was dressed.[24] She told Quinn that she thought constantly of the care he would have taken if he had been there, and back at Coole she fantasised about lying on his sofa free of troubles.[25]

One of Augusta's missions during this second American tour was to campaign for money for Hugh Lane's gallery which, since summer 1912, had become a live issue again. His primary act – the proffering of a gift of inestimable value – and Dublin Corporation's effective rejection of that gift is the stuff of legend. In an Ireland rapidly bifurcating under the promise of Home Rule such princely patronage was problematic for nationalists. And the prince himself, nervous, touchy, and undiplomatic, was unable to respond effectively to their reservations. Both sides proved tragically inflexible as they performed the first act of a drama that would go on for the next 47 years. Augusta was locked onto Hugh's side, even when she judged his behaviour wrong-headed. Although the nationalists managed to cast Hugh as a villain, Augusta continuously asserted that the gallery was a nationalist project, done for the good of Ireland.[26]

A significant proportion of Hugh Lane's original gift of pictures to a Municipal Gallery of Modern Art in Dublin in January 1906 was conditional on the acquisition of a permanent structure. He had set his heart on St Stephen's Green as the site, but when Lord Ardilaun, who had presented the square to Dublin and still had the final say, refused it, Lane, frustrated and bitter, divided the pictures earmarked for Dublin into two groups. He formally presented the 'Lane gift' (Irish, British, American and some European works), but he declared that 39 paintings, the 'Lane Collection', would be withdrawn at the end of January 1913 if a 'new and suitable' gallery was not decided on. This collection included the works of French Impressionists, some of which, such as Renoir's *Les Parapluies*, Manet's *Madame Eva Gonzalés*, and Degas's *Sur la Plage*, would become icons of the genre. However, before Augusta left in December for America, Dublin Corporation had allocated money for the building. It was, Augusta assured Lane, very encouraging.[27]

Augusta's money-raising in America was a triumph. Conscientiously informing journalists, making speeches before matinee performances (proceeds from ticket sales of which went to the gallery), and appealing to business and political contacts to save Dublin from the disgrace of losing Lane's pictures, Augusta raised $20,750, enough to acquire an appropriate site.[28] But when she returned to Ireland in April she found that the gallery was now opposed by nationalists. In a city with a severe slum problem it was being derided as superfluous.

During the next six months Lane, although backed by Augusta, gradually but inexorably lost the campaign for the gallery. When the idea, initially backed by the corporation, for an elegant classical building designed by Edwin Lutyens on a bridge over the Liffey was condemned in the press, Lane abused his critics who redoubled their attack on him.

Augusta deplored the low value given to art by the nationalists. On 23 July she wrote to Yeats: 'Of course the ungraciousness to Hugh and the vulgarity of the opposition and the contempt shown towards art makes one ashamed as one so often is of Dublin.'[29] Nevertheless, she tried to steer Lane diplomatically towards a cheaper site (the Mansion House) but was rewarded with his 'bitter tongue' turned on her as he accused her of lacking aesthetic standards. Meanwhile, in the press she was bracketed with Lane as an interfering Unionist.[30] Finally, on 19 September, with a tramway strike and housing crisis putting the gallery at the bottom of the Corporation's agenda, a motion declaring the bridge site unsuitable and requiring Lane to leave the site and design of the gallery to the Corporation was passed by 32 votes to 25.[31]

It was now that Augusta expressed her resentment for those who had opposed Lane. A Biblical phrase lodged itself in her head; 'He came unto His own and His own received him not.'[32] Revenge seemed attractive: 'I hope with all my heart you will sell the collection at Christie's – it will be the best object lesson,' she told him. But she also tried to persuade him not to give up. 'You are one of my "Image-makers" & you have done more for the future than anyone else. Our Theatre will pass away before your pictures,' she told him.[33] Disillusioned with the workings of democracy, she herself tried to initiate a private scheme. When that failed she tried political string-pulling and approached John Redmond. That too failed.[34]

Meanwhile, Lane had withdrawn from the fray. Before the September vote he had arranged with the National Gallery in London that his conditional gift of 39 pictures to Dublin would be on loan to them. After the vote, his bitterness unbounded, he remade his will, leaving the 39 pictures to London to found a collection of Modern

Continental Art. He expressed his antagonism baldly to his aunt: 'You give me too much credit for my intentions towards Dublin.'[35] But he added that he was still interested in forming a new collection for Dublin after Ireland had gained Home Rule.

Dublin, too, was not entirely antagonistic. On 25 February 1914 Lane was appointed Director of the National Gallery of Ireland. He had finally achieved an official post, thanks partly to Augusta's intensive lobbying of the trustees. He would design himself a smart, be-braided uniform, and persuade his employers to let him work part-time while he maintained his picture dealing business in London.

NINETEEN

The Arrival of War

The Wrenboys today instead of bringing a dead wren brought one of their number dressed as a German soldier and drove him off in triumph . . . But afterwards they sang a song about the Volunteers, and how we'll fight Carson's men and turn them upside down.

26 December 1914, *Seventy Years*

Coole, to which Augusta returned during and after her bruising fight for the Municipal Gallery, must have seemed a sanctuary. Increasingly it was her grandchildren who made it beneficent: 'The children are splendid. What would life be without them?' she asked Quinn rhetorically in October.[1]

There was also much to worry her at Coole in the summer of 1913. Margaret was expecting her third child in early August, and was seriously ill. By 1 July she was on the mend, 'But one must be watchful still,' Augusta wrote to Yeats.[2] 'She is dreadfully weak, not allowed to get up at all . . . She has only this month to gain strength for her next trial.' A few months previously Augusta had bought an elegant two-storey dower house near Newquay on the Finvarra peninsula in Galway Bay and given it to Margaret.[3] Earnings from her books and plays which had previously gone into Richard's trust fund were now to be used to pay for the house.[4]

Augusta enjoyed Margaret's delight in 'something of her own', but it was the quality of the children's summers that preoccupied her. 'It was an almost necessary extravagance,' she told Yeats, 'for the Burren Lodges are now so dirty and tumbledown we couldn't have gone there again, and it is a fine place for the children, no smells, or drains going into the sea.'[5] The children would stay at Mount Vernon (named after George Washington's house) every summer. Augusta also realised that Robert, who a year previously, in June 1912, had had his first exhibition, at the Baillie Gallery in London, got most of his inspiration in the clear, crystalline atmosphere that gathers at the point where the rocky Burren hills slope down to the watery wastes of Galway Bay.[6]

Augusta took Richard and Anne to the new house on 3 July by pony carriage. Playing with them on the beach was a welcome escape from Coole where building work was disrupting the daily routine and where, with Marian, the housemaid, away, she had been feeling overworked.[7] She engaged a 'char' to cook, and carefully prepared the house for Margaret who stayed for most of July. Margaret finally gave birth to Catherine at Coole on 21 August. Probably prompted by Augusta, she asked Shaw to be Catherine's godfather. 'Never,' came the reply on 6 September. 'How do you know that she will not abhor my opinions, or that I may not be hanged yet? . . . Besides, if I undertook at the font to see to her religious education, I should do it; and then where would she be?'[8]

The usual tension between Yeats and the young Gregorys had been exacerbated by Margaret's prolonged confinement. Yeats was not welcome at Coole in August, and when he announced that he would come in October Robert rather stiffly asked him to bring his own wine – two or three dozen bottles of sherry – and a decanter.[9] A temporary coolness had also descended between Augusta and Yeats. There had been a few strained letters that summer about money, on the theme that Augusta felt she was contributing too much to the theatre while her plays brought in a substantial share of the revenue.[10] She was indignant in May when Yeats asked her to give half of her earnings to the theatre, adding witheringly, 'However I don't mind, I have given so much already it doesn't make much difference.'[11] When he disagreed with her about how to deal with the money raised by the Abbey for the gallery she reminded him that he himself owed her £500.[12]

After a few weeks at Mount Vernon Augusta had returned alone to Coole. With that ability to turn her back on disappointment and anxiety which Quinn admired, she had sat down to write her first fantasy play, immersing herself in a surreal world of witches and giants and, for the first time in about four years, attacking her writing with experimental vigour and some elan.[13]

Augusta had had ambitions to write for children since her first play, but it was only now, writing for Richard, that she drew imaginatively on Irish fairy tales from *The Kiltartan Wonder Book* to write a play of magic and enchantment.[14] In it a prince, after many adventures, restores his father to health with a golden apple from a garden guarded by a witch and, by marrying the King of Spain's daughter, breaks the enchantment the witch had cast on her. Irish fairy tales, with their unattended magic gardens and weak spells, are far less frightening than German tales with their evil characters vanquished only by death. So Augusta, respecting the spirit of her sources, invented a feeble witch, added humour, showed an exuberant awareness of the theatrical possibilities of her story and revelled in the magic. *The Golden Apple* is, above all, playful.[15]

The enchanted garden which, released from the old witch's spell, becomes an Eden for the young, suggests Coole, and there are some beguiling parallels between her immediate family and the characters in her story.[16] The idea that Augusta was retreating not only to her writing, but to a vision of Coole inhabited by her young family as a place beyond the pain and distress of the real world is not improbable. When she came to correct proofs of the play in September 1915 she wanted to dedicate it to Shaw and the playful friendship he had developed with her grandchildren on his recent visit. Shaw insisted she 'leave the infants out', so she celebrated his goodness instead, 'the gentlest of my friends'.[17] The play encompassed her version of the myth of the golden summer before the cataclysm of war; a war, and, as this was Ireland, a succession of wars, which would penetrate to the heart of Coole.

Augusta worked hard at *The Golden Apple* in the early autumn. 'I have nothing to ask you for, nothing much to say, but I am just thinking of you and want to say "Good morning!"' she wrote to Quinn on 11 October with a freshly typed copy of the play before her. In November she reverted to folklore. One morning she received the news that Enid Layard had died. Her response as expressed to Yeats was curiously muted and distant: 'I am sad at hearing of poor Lady Layard's death, for half my life she had been a close friend, and though that one outbreak over the Queen's letter was a little shaking, she had begun to understand my work a little, at least her last letter was the most appreciative I had ever had from her. And I felt the Venice house and indeed the London one were always open, and that I was always welcome.'[18]

This detachment is probably explained by the fact that Yeats and Enid inhabited different worlds, so that Augusta felt she had to explain the friendship to him. Yet the letter, outlining Enid's reaction to Augusta's work, is unusually self-centred for Augusta, suggesting that she was trying to justify a relationship she no longer valued as she once had. In a summary written several years later in *Seventy Years* Augusta defined the differences between them: Enid was childless, had sufficient wealth and never broadened her interests.[19] This was a significant barrier between them. It had been bridged by a shared social manner underpinning a shared social outlook. In *Seventy Years*, Augusta wrote admiringly of Enid's 'simple kindliness' and her 'dignity and stateliness', qualities she herself successfully cultivated. Enid's new interest in Augusta's work would have been a welcome strengthening of connections that had grown tenuous.

By 19 December, Augusta, having sent her grandchildren toys and fireworks, was at Lindsey House, stoically anticipating Christmas alone among Lane's beautiful things, leaving Robert and Margaret free to entertain their friends at Coole.[20] The previous year she had been in America, and Robert had written enthusiastically about their house party: 'The bag was fairly good. 1st day 80 pheasants & 24 woodcock, 2nd day 9 pheasants, 39 cock . . . Guy Gough [the heir to Lough Cutra] shot quite ⅓ of the bag.'[21]

Christmas Day was convivial for Augusta; she saw Charlotte Shaw, her brothers, Harry and Louvaine came for lunch, and she had dinner with Mrs Carstairs whose figure-hugging pink silk dress – no petticoat, and cross-gartered stockings showing – she described to her niece Ruth.[22] On 27 December she went with the Carstairs to visit Yeats who was staying with the young American poet Ezra Pound in Stone Cottage, Sussex. Pound, who was acting as his amanuensis, and the cottage were new acquisitions, which Augusta was regretfully aware were intended to replace Coole where relations with Robert and Margaret had further deteriorated.[23]

Pound had attached himself to Yeats as a disciple and was not afraid to exercise the power he had as a fellow poet. 'To talk over a poem with him is like getting you to put a sentence into dialect. All becomes clear and natural', Yeats had written carefully to Augusta in January 1913.[24] Pound was a serious threat; he was hard-working and slowly but surely would redirect Yeats back to esoteric drama by introducing him to the Japanese Noh play. But Augusta banished any jealousy as she and the Carstairs bought cold beef and cakes with them to Stone Cottage and they had a 'merry lunch'.

The following day she went to visit Blunt, who now lived, without Anne, in the venerable and beautiful Newbuildings in Sussex. He was still cutting a romantic figure as a lover of women and lost causes, with a reputation as a gossip, 'gossip, of course, of a high kind – imperial gossip', Mary Colum observed.[25] His literary contribution to the Abbey, the Cuchulain play in Alexandrines, *Fand*, had been a disaster, but he was ripe for rediscovery as a Victorian romantic poet.[26] Ezra Pound had conceived the idea that a coterie of young (male) poets led by Yeats, who valued him as a poet writing from experience when poetry was becoming abstract, might honour him. Augusta brokered the event, arranging for them to go to Newbuildings for Blunt's 74th birthday on 18 January, and for peacock from Blunt's flock to be on the menu. Blunt, who thought it was Augusta's idea (she did not correct him), was flattered, though he managed a deflationary tone in his post-prandial speech, claiming that his poetry was merely a by-product of his life, never an end in itself.

Augusta was excited by this youthful recognition of Blunt, dubbing it a 'cult' to Quinn, and she exploited it by arranging for his poetry to be republished.[27] This attempt to secure his lasting reputation inadvertently marked her own success, underlining how far she had come since the days when she had relied on his help. Valuing her mentor ('the whole collection will be extraordinarily rich & vivid') was an indirect way of valuing herself.[28]

George Moore, meanwhile, was doing his best to damage her reputation in the January and February issue of *English Review*, which contained an incendiary extract from *Vale* (the third part of his autobiography) titled 'Yeats, Lady Gregory and Synge'. In *Ave*, the first part, published in 1911, Augusta had got off relatively lightly, and she had even found 'some charm' in his description of her solicitous handling of Yeats.[29] Although Yeats had been spitefully attacked as a snob, and Augusta resented Moore's description of Hyde, she had laughed (particularly at his portrait of Martyn) and forgiven him. *Salve*, the following year, was disappointingly reticent about her contribution to the Revival.[30] He had saved himself for *Vale*, where he accused her of plagiarism in *Cuchulain*, mocked her plays as merely amusing, feminine anecdotes, and dismissed her Hiberno-English as a peppering of incorrectly used idiomatic turns of speech.[31] Worse, he insinuated that her relationship with her husband had been less than satisfactory. But most seriously, he accused her of proselytising at Roxborough as a young woman.

Although it was untrue, her initial reaction was an acquiescent, 'there is no answering such things'.[32] Quinn and Yeats, fearful of the damage that a proselytising director would do to the Abbey's reputation – especially as people were already whispering to this effect – encouraged her to object.[33] She responded with a mild letter to the publisher which, as Moore pointed out, seemed to imply that she had given practical support (tea and sugar) while her mother and sisters preached the Word. With further pressure from Yeats, Augusta finally threatened legal action, and the offending passage was altered in the published book. Her diffidence and reluctance to protect herself is notable in one who was so sensitive to the making of false reputations, although in Abbey crises Yeats was always quicker to go to lawyers than Augusta, who preferred to keep bad publicity to a minimum.

Yeats spent a gruelling February and March in America on a lecture tour, but returned confident and flush with money. He repaid Augusta her £500, glad to discharge what he now regarded as a shamefully overdue repayment.[34] She sent him a gracious reply, telling him how much happier she had been in giving it than getting it back, and how touched she was by his hard work 'for it & for me. I don't pretend that it is not of importance to me, it will straighten out some difficulties'.[35] Then the letter slipped into a minor key leaving, as Yeats's biographer R.F. Foster has observed, 'a subtle aftertaste of moral blackmail': 'It was money I should have in all likelihood have invested, & have for my children if I had not thought it a better investment'.[36] But there was something else too: 'I cd not have taken the money at some later time, when you might yourself have others depending on you – & even now, if you have any feeling at all that the payment would cloud our friendship or your thoughts of me – remember that no one knows or will ever know anything of the matter – & I would far rather keep that friendship & affection that have meant so much to me.' Their friendship had rested for so long on Yeats's dependence she feared that by freeing himself financially he might be disengaging himself emotionally. The economic and social balance between them was, irretrievably, altering, but their friendship was intact.

In early June Robert had a successful exhibition at the Chenil Gallery in London in which his painting, much improved, was appreciated for its melancholy air and originality.[37] Augusta, who began a cuttings file for his work, was delighted, for she had long hoped that Robert would do for the landscape what she was trying to do for folklore.[38]

In the summer of 1913 the political situation was dominating all their lives. That July Ireland was hovering on the brink of

Home Rule. By late 1913 the political situation had evolved to the point where the Home Rule Bill proposed by Asquith's Liberal government in April 1912 was commonly accepted outside Ulster as the probable future of Ireland. It was unsatisfactory. It only gave limited power to an Irish Parliament, amounting to jurisdiction over internal affairs but not defence, war, relations with the crown, control of the police or even effective control of revenue. Redmond, the leader of the Irish Parliamentary Party (IPP), assumed it was provisional and that fuller powers would be gained eventually.

Meanwhile, in Ulster, where the Ulster Volunteer Force (UVF) had been formed in January 1913 to coordinate Unionist paramilitary activities, the Ulster Unionists were successfully pressurising the government to allow up to six counties to opt out of the Home Rule area. Elsewhere, the clandestine, separatist, non-constitutionalist Irish Republican Brotherhood (IRB) had recently been revived. When the moderate Eoin MacNeill, a scholar and a founder-member of the Gaelic League, began to articulate the idea that Irish nationalists needed to bypass Westminster if their aspirations for independence were to be met, the IRB realised that if a paramilitary group was formed in response to the UVF it could act as a front for their separatist ambitions. The Irish Volunteers was duly set up in November 1913.

Augusta's response to the greater probability of Home Rule was to meditate on whether politics had a significant role to play in the lives of ordinary people. *The Wrens*, first produced, not in Dublin, where it might have been too contentious, but in London on 1 June 1914, revolved around the intriguing fact that the Act of Union had been passed by a majority of one. She imagined that this was due to a servant forgetting to tell his master to go to the Houses of Parliament for the vote; a small detail that set the country on the path of political union with Britain.[39] The servant had been distracted by the argument of a vagabond couple. Their allegiances are shown not to be influenced by ideological conviction – he, an alcoholic, is persuaded to pledge that he could only drink again if the bill is defeated, converting him from a pro- to anti-Unionist, and his wife from an anti- to a pro-Unionist. On the other hand, the play shows that political circumstances can profoundly influence people's lives. The bill is passed; the wife is happy, the husband miserable. The play goes some way to explaining how Augusta's political ideas evolved. In 1914 she was still largely antagonistic to Griffith's quietly growing radical Sinn Féin, in part because of his opposition to the *Playboy*.[40] In the years after the rising, when Sinn Féin was in the ascendant, Augusta could support it, not because she was suddenly converted to Griffith's narrow conception of nationalism, but because she had faith that Sinn Féin would produce the right political circumstances for change.

Augusta spent three weeks in late June and early July in London, staying at Lindsey House. She dealt with recalcitrant actresses at the Abbey, staged *The Wrens*, attended smart parties, visited Blunt and lunched at 10 Downing Street where she sat next to the Prime Minister, H.H. Asquith, who was disappointingly unforthcoming about Ulster.[41] She was back in Coole when Britain declared war on Germany on 4 August.

War had been brewing since 28 June when Archduke Franz Ferdinand had been assassinated in Sarajevo, but for Augusta and her contemporaries there was relatively little warning. On 6 September Augusta wrote Quinn a letter heavy with her intense dislike of being, once again, in a state of war (the Boer War had only finished 12 years previously). Unable to share the avid interest of people who spent all day poring over newspapers, she resented the way the war seeped into her waking and sleeping hours, made people belligerent and desensitised them to art.

Blunt had 'declared neutrality': 'I . . . keep my front door locked with a notice that belligerents are to go round to the kitchen.'[42] Augusta, however, could not be neutral: Robert, 33, wanted a commission.[43] She observed to Quinn that Belgium (a small nation like Ireland) was a respectable cause for which England could declare war. But she refused to make red flannel jackets for the wounded, and, Home Ruler that she was, she hoped Redmond would not support the war until Home Rule made the statute books. Deeply ambiguous about the war, she already understood the futility of battle in which soldiers would inevitably die, an understanding that many in Britain, blinded by patriotism and an idealist desire to play their part, would not have until thousands had been slaughtered in the trenches.

One sleepless night, tormented by the fact that formerly peaceable people could feel unrestrained anger towards individual German soldiers, she wrote a poem, 'Pat and Fritz', which imagined an Irish and German soldier killing each other simultaneously, and asked rhetorically, which one is right?[44]

Written in a jaunty ballad style, the poem evoked the absurdity rather than the tragedy of war. Both Robert and Yeats liked it, and *The Nation* printed it on 19 September. This happened to be the day after Home Rule had become law (though its enactment was postponed for the duration of the war). The following day Redmond made a speech in Wicklow in which he pledged the Irish Volunteers to support the war effort. But a radical IRB-dominated minority of the Volunteers (which retained the name, Irish Volunteers; Redmond's supporters became the National Volunteers) led by, among others, Eoin MacNeill, immediately declared their opposition to the war.[45] Thus

Augusta's poem in *The Nation* with its implied antipathy to war now had a radical nationalist edge that had not originally been intended. Meanwhile, Augusta was ready to put down a red carpet at the Abbey and sing 'God Save the King' as a gesture of solidarity with the government now that Home Rule was passed.[46]

The Persses would tie Augusta to the war. Eleven of her nephews fought, some already in the army, others joining up. Frank's son, Dudley, joined the Royal Navy and wrote her light-hearted, unrevealing letters from his ship.[47] He died in action in 1918 aged 26. Frank's other son, Geoffrey, whose schooling Augusta had financed, joined the Australian forces and died, aged 31, at Gallipoli in 1915. Algernon's son, Rodolph, a frequent visitor to Coole, was killed at Ypres on 1 January 1915. Augusta was in America when she heard this news, and commented to Blunt that the leaders were wasted in the trenches.[48] She also noted that he was an only son. Her brother Edward, who lived in Southampton and had been a colonel in the Indian army, had five sons in the war, the youngest 23. Four survived, but one, Edward, died in August 1918 in action. Henry's son, Reginald, survived to fight in the Second World War. The war hung heavily over the family.

Robert was prevented from joining up in the autumn of 1914 because they were at a delicate stage in the negotiations for the sale of Coole, and Augusta was due to leave for America in January 1915. Two years previously, in December 1912 (the day after Augusta left Coole for her second visit to America), the Congested Districts Board (CDB) had finally sent Robert an offer to purchase the estate.[49] The Board would buy the tenanted land (3,277 acres) for 20 years purchase (£27,509). They offered what Robert considered a poor price of £4,653 for untenanted land of which Coole had 1,653 acres, and a good price (£11,102) for the 1,353-acre demesne and house.[50] The Gregorys would receive it in 3 per cent government stock, which meant that the £43,264 offered would be worth about £35,044 in cash. On 22 January 1913 the Gregorys' solicitor wrote outlining what they would gain from the sale when all the payments (Quit Rent, Augusta's Jointure, Board of Works charges, etc.) had been made: £13,638.[51] They decided not to accept.

Now, in December 1914, the Gregorys accepted a less attractive offer from the CDB, pressurised by the fact that, as their solicitors dryly pointed out to them, the tenants had not paid rents since May.[52] The demesne lands and house were no longer included. The offer was in cash, and on the face of it seemed to be worth £4,034 more. However, the Board could not undertake to pay immediately and feared it might have to postpone it indefinitely. It would pay interest at 3.5 per cent on the purchase price. This would bring in just over £1,000 a year leaving them short of £227 when outgoings had been deducted. This bleak picture would be relieved by the income from farming the demesne lands, which had been grazed for the last 40 years and might now be converted to more productive tillage. They still had the demesne and house, but Robert was uncomfortably aware that if rates and taxes increased, keeping it would not be viable and they would be forced to sell.

In September 1914, before terms had been concluded with the CDB and as the war began to sink into her life, Augusta, making a huge effort of will, began to write *Shanwalla*, a play whose plot turned on the relationship between the Anglo-Irish Darcy, owner of the horse Shanwalla (named after a Coole wood), and his groom, Lawrence Scarry.[53] It is interesting for two things. Augusta restated her old belief about the mutual trust and respect that underlay the relationship of man and master in Ireland, regardless of the tensions (and the play was full of those). And it is a ghost story.

❖ ❖ ❖

Still collecting folklore that dealt with the *sidhe* for *Visions and Beliefs in the West of Ireland* (begun in 1897) to be published with Yeats, she was continually involved with the supernatural. She was also drawn in a very limited way into Yeats's occult activities. She resisted mediums, but invited occult news from him. She had her horoscope read, commenting cautiously, 'All I can say so far is that a few of the foretellings have come curiously true.'[54] She read Swedenborg and Blake, on Yeats's recommendation.[55] She was keenly aware that the Society for Psychical Research (of which Yeats was a member) studied the paranormal in as objective a way as possible and set standards in urban society. Realising that her audience for plays and folklore would probably scorn unmediated superstition she favoured a more intellectual assessment of supernatural beliefs.

In an article published in April 1912 on folklore for the American magazine *The Outlook*, Augusta had stated that she hoped readers would find that the beliefs described could be related to psychic phenomenon. But she had little understanding or interest in psychical research, and her vague references to 'learned men of Paris . . . now working at psychic science', possibly intended to spare her audience too much detail, strongly suggest that she herself had no command of the detail; she was merely falling in behind Yeats. He was busy that summer on two essays, one on witches and wizards, and another on Swedenborg and psychic phenomena, in which he related the belief in the supernatural found in Ireland to the spiritualist beliefs he encountered in mediums' London parlours and the mysticism he was discovering in scholarly works and contemporary experiments into psychic phenomena. It was to be a metaphysical strand in *Visions and Beliefs*.

Yeats's work probably encouraged Augusta to write a ghost play, but in her notes to the play she claimed that it was

Robert who persuaded her that a metropolitan audience, aware of the limits of reason as a means of understanding the world, would not scoff at the irrational.[56] However, when the play was performed on 8 April 1915, although the audience was appreciative and insisted that she appear on the stage at the end of the performance, most of the critics were scathing, some finding it 'preposterous'.[57]

When *Visions and Beliefs in the West of Ireland* was published in New York in April 1920 (London, September 1920) it was immediately recognised as a significant contribution to folklore, although it was dismissed in some quarters as superstition. Augusta consoled herself that the book was 'made with reverence; this will be felt by those who understand'.[58] It is now regarded as her great achievement in folklore.[59]

Fairylore was a well established genre, but whereas most (often male) folklorists showed more interest in often-told folk tales of the *sidhe*, usually related by men, Augusta preferred to record spontaneous personal accounts – experiences, beliefs, recollections and confidences – regardless of how fragmentary and shapeless they might seem. Many of these came from women. The result was an array of beliefs, many previously unrecorded. She arranged them into themes – sea stories, the evil eye, banshees and warnings, the unquiet dead, seers and healers, 'away' (the fairies' propensity to take people and perhaps replace them with changelings) – and showed how people expressed love, grief, pain and loss through them.

Augusta's great strength in this as in her other folklore was her desire that the stories speak for themselves without comment from her. In her preface she announced: 'This is the news I have been given of the people of the Sidhe by many who have seen them and some who have known their power.' She valued them romantically as an expression of an aboriginal understanding of the human condition: 'The impress left by the world-mind or memory upon minds that are not blurred with questions or with the talk of the towns.'[60]

In her folklore Augusta betrayed no impression that she shared the beliefs which she recorded. But, although she kept her distance, she had always felt that they were valid: '. . . one day Lady Gregory said to me when we had passed an old man in the wood: "That old man may know the secret of the ages",' Yeats recalled.[61] Together, Yeats and Augusta sensed they were journeying towards a fuller knowledge as 'that ancient system of belief unfolded before us'.

When Augusta came to write notes for *Shanwalla* in 1922, she gave a halting account of her own attitude to belief in the supernatural:

> I believe that what they feel and relate is perhaps of as great importance to that in us which is lasting, as the tested results of men of science examining into psychic things. For none have yet been certainly aware of much more than shadows upon a veil, vague, intangible, yet making the certainty clearer every day that when the veil is rent for us at our passing . . . it is not death but life that is to be discovered beyond it.[62]

The hesitations in this may be due to constraint; she did not want to appear ridiculous. Or it may express, as her reference to life after death suggests, a slowly growing appreciation that the supernatural beliefs she encountered in the countryside could be grafted onto her still strong religious belief.

Yeats was probably right (maybe a little harsh) when in *The Vision* he described Augusta as having no philosophical capacity or intellectual curiosity. Like the country people she relied on intuition. She had a way of putting the spiritual, supernatural, idealistic and altruistic together under the heading 'unseen'. Or she spoke about the 'cloud of witnesses' or 'that mountain top where things visible and invisible meet'; catch-all phrases produced in many different circumstances. Strikingly for a faithful member of the Church of Ireland, pagan ideas colour what might otherwise be assumed to be references to Heaven and its inhabitants.[63] She came to trust that the folk stories could be fused with Christian beliefs as part of her personal theology. She was prepared not to understand the significance. As she got older in the uncertain circumstances heralded by the war she became adept at finding comfort from a number of sources.

In January Robert showed *The Island*, a painting inspired by Coole lake, at the New English Art Club, a prestigious venue where well-regarded realist painters such as William Orpen and Augustus John exhibited. In a letter to his mother Robert was self-deprecating about his success. He also still seemed unsure about his ability: 'I have just been to the N[ew] English. They have hung my picture in a good place – supposed to be the place of honour in the small room . . . It is in a much lower key than the pictures round it & looks rather cloudy. However people liked it I think.'[64] Yeats in particular, who told Quinn that he was 'as much moved by Gregory's work as by anything else', admired it, finding it 'full of airy distinction'.[65] Robert's letter to Augusta proceeded slightly wistfully: 'We dined with Hutchesons last night – H. very important going off to the Admiralty roof to man a gun against the Zeppelins. Most people have got some job or other of the sort.' Robert's diffidence about his painting, underlain, perhaps, by the doubt that he would be unable to develop it any further, was overshadowed by his intense preoccupation with the war.

Augusta, writing to Quinn on 3 April as her ship neared Cobh at the end of her third American lecture tour, was excited by his exhibition: 'I am going home with a pretty light heart. I am out of debt, and have a few dollars to keep things going; I did my work well; and I have that hope of showing Robert's pictures, which is what I care about more than all the rest. And your encompassing kindness gives me a pleasant feeling, as if of having lived in summer time, even if I shrink a little from cold winds afterwards.'[66]

She landed on Easter Monday and went to Dublin to oversee the premiere of *Shanwalla* on Thursday. She stayed with Rt Hon W.F. Bailey, an Estates Commissioner with the CDB, a board member of the National Gallery and an advisor for the Abbey. When Lane heard she had arrived he invited her to the gallery and showed her around. It was a happy visit, Augusta impressed by his plans and commitment, proud that he had achieved his ambition. He gave her a copy of the new gallery catalogue, writing an inscription that suggested an almost childish delight in his position: 'To Aunt Augusta from the Director! April 8th 1915.'[67] 'I like to remember him there, in authority, in love with his work, in harmony with all that was about him,' she wrote later.[68] On Friday he left for New York on business. He stayed with Quinn and would write to Augusta, 'I feel better than I have done for years.'[69]

By 13 April, when Shaw and his wife Charlotte came on a month's visit, Augusta was back in Coole. It was a turning point for all three; they got on extremely well, Augusta's letters to 'my dear G.B.S.' (previously 'Dear Mr Shaw) were much fuller and more personal thereafter, and Mrs Shaw became 'dear Charlotte'. Shaw was entertaining and undemanding, he played with the grandchildren and praised *Shanwalla* as the best ghost play he had ever seen: '. . . he is so extraordinarily light in hand, a sort of kindly joyousness about him,' Augusta wrote appreciatively to Yeats on 16 April.[70]

Shaw photographed Augusta (either during this or a later visit) seated at her desk in front of the central window in the drawing-room, writing, not a play, but a letter engaging a kitchen maid. What is not visible is the shaky table in the right hand window on which stood her typewriter, used for letters and typed drafts.[71] Bailey visited and took a number of photographs in which the now plump figure of Augusta is encased in black, her fluttering mantilla an eccentric appendage. In one photograph she stands behind the 6-year-old Richard looking down while he confronts the camera. Another photograph shows Augusta and Shaw standing separately watching young Richard at the wheel of Shaw's car, individually amused. It reveals something of their kinship: two diminutive white-haired figures in plain, dark, thick, idiosyncratic clothes (Shaw wore knickerbockers); two obdurate, strong-minded people.

Discovering that Charlotte wanted a good artist to paint Shaw, Augusta invited Augustus John, who came and painted maniacally, even when Shaw was asleep.[72] This left John feeling he had not had time to carry his work through.[73] She persuaded John to do an oil sketch of Richard, even though, according to Anne in Me and Nu, he preferred to paint her.[74] Augusta later hung Richard's portrait in her drawing-room positioned so that his 'little brown head' was lit up by the last rays of the setting sun.

Then on 7 May the British-registered Lusitania was torpedoed off the County Cork coast and sank almost immediately. The next day Augusta received a telegram from John Quinn informing her that Hugh Lane had been on board.[75] Since the outbreak of war it was known that British-registered vessels were vulnerable to attack by German submarines. Augusta had taken Quinn's advice in

April and sailed on an American ship. Lane had ignored all warnings. Augusta's first reaction to the news was a howl of despair; it was almost as if her own child had gone.[76] When Shaw offered help, 'I said,' she wrote in her memoir, 'I longed to be alone, to cry, to mourn, to scream if I wished. I wanted to be out of hearing and sight.'[77] Her grief alarmed Robert, 'he had been so used to my composure'.[78] At the same time she knew that until she heard otherwise there was the possibility that Hugh had survived. Next morning there were no telegrams and she lost hope, 'at least I believe so'.[79] That night she had to travel to London to put on Abbey plays. She wrote to Quinn before she left, telling him she dreaded talking to people in London but was prepared to go through the necessary business. She half looked forward to the long journey alone when she would be able to cry and grieve.

She stayed at the Hotel Gwalia in Upper Woburn Place, visiting no one, stoically doing her work. Hugh's sister, Ruth Shine, had failed to recover Hugh's body at Queenstown where both the dead and the survivors were brought to shore, but she had learnt that he had faced his death calmly, without wearing a life belt.[80] Augusta did not tell Quinn about the rumour spread by an American survivor that Lane had courted death by wedging himself into the companion ladder.[81] There may have been some truth in this for all first class passengers had life belts; he might have welcomed death when he saw it coming.[82] He died within sight of his birthplace.

By the end of May Augusta, still shocked and numb, was frantically trying to find Hugh's most recent will.[83] He had told several people before he left for America that he had altered his will to leave his Continental collection to Dublin. On the strength of this Augusta instigated a search in his Dublin club. A few days later, lying in an upstairs room of

Lindsey House, desperate to find a document that would overwrite the antipathy to Dublin expressed in his 1913 will, Augusta imagined it in his desk at the National Gallery.

And that is where they found the codicil, leaving the 39 pictures, then at the National Gallery in London, to Dublin, and naming Augusta as sole trustee.[84] It was signed but, crucially, unwitnessed, and therefore not legal in England, although it would have been valid in Scotland or in the trenches. Augusta dubbed it the codicil of forgiveness, and from then on part of her life was dedicated to the almost prohibitively difficult task of persuading the British Establishment that the codicil expressed Lane's final intention and was therefore as valid as any legal document.

TWENTY

Robert's Death

My grief to tell it! he to be laid low; the man that did not
bring grief or trouble on any heart, that would give help
to those that were down.

'His Lament for O'Kelly', *The Kiltartan Poetry Book*

'I am not very light-hearted, for Robert is carrying out his
desire of this time last year, and is going to the war,'
Augusta wrote to Shaw on 19 September 1915.[1] Robert had
gone to London in early September and obtained a
commission in the 4th Battalion of the Connaught Rangers,
joining the Royal Flying Corps on 16 September.[2] 'Whether
he is right to go I don't know,' Augusta continued in her
letter to Shaw. 'I daresay I should go if I were in his place,
but I feel just now and since the *Lusitania* I should like to
kill Germans, and I don't think he is so ferocious. The only
thing I [am] sure of is that he ought to make up his own
mind about it, and so I would say nothing. But when I look
at Margaret and the little things and think in what an
unsettled state Ireland still is, my heart breaks.' This was the
severest test of her long-held conviction that she should not
try to influence Robert.

Augusta's assessment of her distress hid its complexity, for
Robert had been having an affair and, callously, had tried to
force a still loving Margaret to accept it.[3] Nora Summers

was, with her husband Gerald, a friend from the New English Arts Club. Margaret had been told in January. The couple stayed at Mount Vernon in the summer where Robert and Nora were, despite the attempts by all four at normality, unrestrained. Margaret was humiliated, patted on the back for her attempts at tolerance. Robert was indifferent to her distress and in an emotional scene, hit Gerald. Enlisting gained the added appeal of escape for Robert and Margaret found herself half confiding in Augusta. For Augusta it was agony but she emerged on 27 August, from what had probably been a sleepless night, able to judge a bullying, unprincipled son whose self-gratifying behaviour contrasted so strongly with the moral scruples she had felt so strongly in similar circumstances: 'That I should have lived to know my son was a cad,' she told Margaret, using a word which then condemned. When she left Coole for her fourth lecture tour of America on 1 October, she asked that Robert not come to the station to see her off. He was going to war, she might never see him again but at that moment, her sadness was such that she could not bear to say a public goodbye.

This experience exacerbated the distress of Hugh Lane's death that had stayed with her all summer: 'I had some very dark days, and seemed to have lost all courage,' she wrote to Yeats in August.[4] But, suddenly serene in September, she had begun a play, *Hanrahan's Oath* in which she took her comedy idea of 'the talk' to the extreme of silence.[5] She was also writing lectures for her fourth (and final) American tour. 'I feel glad to have done even a scrap of creative work, and feel my mind hasn't quite gone,' she confided to Shaw.

The Abbey was ailing. Even before the war the theatre was accused of decline in Dublin (9 May 1913) and monotony in London (11 August 1913). This confirmed the directors' uneasy feeling that they were losing their way artistically, as realistic plays increasingly outweighed poetic ones, and they were under pressure to stage music hall versions of their repertoire. Augusta proposed a series of public lectures to associate the theatre with 'things invisible' again.[6] They needed a strategy to survive the war, and in September 1915, before she left for America, Augusta outlined her plans, approved by Yeats, to Shaw.[7] They would keep the Abbey alive by staying solvent and preventing the company from scattering until the end of the war and beginning of Home Rule when they would give it to the nation. In October St John Ervine, a Unionist admirer of Shaw's irreverence and an eloquent supporter of the troubled Abbey, was appointed manager. He reformed their finances. Shaw also stepped in with a play, *O'Flaherty VC*, conceived at Coole in April and set outside the entrance porch at Coole. However, having described the simple stage set, he continued:

> Unfortunately I cannot be so reassuring about the play itself . . . The picture of the Irish character will make the Playboy seem a patriotic rhapsody by comparison. The ending is cynical to the last possible degree. The idea is that O'Flaherty's experience in the trenches has induced in him a terrible realism and an unbearable candour. He sees Ireland as it is, his mother as she is, his sweetheart as she is; and he goes back to the dreaded trenches joyfully for the sake of peace and quietness. Sinclair must be prepared for brickbats.[8]

It was an attack on Irish nationalism and without a scrap of idealism for the war. Ultimately it could not be staged, despite its oblique support for the soldiers and Shaw's insistence that it was a recruitment play. Augusta, able, under the spell of GBS, to laugh at her *Playboy* experiences, and to set aside her worries about Robert, appreciated Shaw's empathy with the soldiers and was delighted with his irreverence: 'Oh my dear G.B.S. your letter was a great cheer up.' The Abbey would survive; many English repertory theatres would be killed by the war.

It took courage to set sail for America that October in submarine-infested waters, not knowing if she would see her family again. 'Poor darlings,' Augusta wrote of her grandchildren, 'I don't know how I shall leave them.'[9] She bolstered herself by the thought that her earnings would support them. But she worried constantly about Robert: 'Sir F. Donaldson says fourteen are killed out of every thirty aviators who go out,' she wrote to Yeats. But even with this she found a way to allay her fears: 'If I get through America well I shall have new courage,' she wrote, implying that increased self-confidence would give her strength to face Robert's dangerous situation.[10]

Augusta's courageousness was appreciated by John Butler Yeats: 'In time of crisis and national peril there is no counsellor like courage – courage with you is a gift of nature – timidity is like the dust and dimness that gathers on the glass on one's spectacles (mine for instance when I paint); courage keeps the glass clean.'[11] Augusta decided that once she returned from her American tour she would stay at Coole with her grandchildren so that Margaret would be free to visit Robert at a moment's notice.

She set sail from New York, after an extensive tour of the mid-west and California and an intense schedule of lectures, in late January 1916, and arrived in London on 5 February where she stayed a few days before leaving for Ireland.[12] She saw Robert in his new Royal Flying Corps uniform. 'The khaki suits his fair hair & makes him look pathetically young,' she told Blunt, proud and anxious, and she was surprised to find Yeats (who had recently refused a knighthood) 'quite a man of fashion', and dined at Lady Cunard's with him.[13] She went on to Dublin to assess Ervine as a manager (the best in the circumstances though probably unable to judge the actors) and, finally arriving at Coole, was greeted with exuberant joy by 7-year-old Richard. In April Robert was sent to Swingate Down near Dover where he was charged with patrolling the coast on the lookout for German aircraft. Their letters to each other were interrupted, however, by the Easter Rising. Robert found that he could not even contact Augusta at Coole by telegram. 'It is extraordinary,' he wrote (unsure she would receive the letter), 'Ireland had seemed to be the one safe place'.[14]

Everyone was surprised by the rising on Easter Monday 1916. The Irish Volunteers initially organised a countrywide rising to coincide with the arrival of arms from Germany at Limerick. When the arms failed to land because of government foreknowledge, and with the arrest of Sir Roger Casement (who had been trying to gain German support for Irish independence) on Banna Strand in Kerry, it was set for Easter Sunday. This was called off by Eoin MacNeill. However, a rump of the Volunteers led by Patrick Pearse, Thomas MacDonagh, Joseph Plunkett, Sean MacDermott and others decided to go ahead on Monday 24 April in Dublin. They occupied a few buildings, including the Four Courts and the General Post Office. Here Pearse read out a proclamation declaring a republic.

Five days later they were overwhelmed by the British army, and surrendered. About 500 people died, of which 300 were civilians and 76 insurgents. Many of the leaders were captured, and between 3 and 12 May all except Casement were executed. He was hanged on 3 August. For the army it was, in the context of the war, a relatively minor incident. For Ireland it was cataclysmic, for the old tradition of violence and martyrdom, which was thought to be buried, had erupted again, and its lava quickly smothered the compromised and suspended Home Rule of the constitutionalists. The political terrain would never look the same again.

Augusta's experience was probably typical of many in Ireland, but it is one that rarely reaches the history books. For six days there were barricades on the road to Galway, the railway lines were torn up, telegraph poles were down and she, Margaret, the children, the house and demesne servants were cut off from the outside world with nothing but rumours and a few local observations from occasional visitors to go on.[15] It was wonderfully calm, she wrote to Blunt.[16] Probably because she believed that Coole would be safer from attack if she was there (her good reputation with nationalists) she did not stir from the demesne, refusing to go to Lough Cutra for male protection. There were rumours of armed men, assumed to be Sinn Féiners, camped near Athenry, requisitioning motor cars, taking cattle, besieging police stations and raiding big houses. A police inspector told her they had arrested a man with a well-organised plan to attack the police barracks at Gort. The suspension of peaceful authority had also encouraged a group of armed disaffected men, 'village tyrants', who had been periodically intimidating people for two years, to resume their terror.[17]

All these reports were alarming. They brought back memories of the Land War and the old fear that the tenants, frightened and politicised, would become alienated from the Gregorys, looking to an antagonistic group for leadership. 'It is terrible to think of the executions or killings that are sure to come, yet it must be so – we had been at the mercy of a rabble for a long time, both here and in Dublin, with no apparent policy, but ready to take any opportunity of helping on mischief,' she wrote to Yeats.[18] Such a perspective tended to make Lady Gregory of Coole less of a nationalist than Lady Gregory of the Abbey.

On Tuesday 25 April they heard rumours that the General

Post Office had been blown up in Dublin. When Margaret, determined not to be intimidated, set off in the victoria to Athenry for the Dublin train she discovered that, indeed, authority had disintegrated and there were no trains or telegraph. In the afternoon Amy Shawe-Taylor drove over from Castle Taylor with the alarming (and inaccurate) rumour that arms had been landed at Kinvara and a German invasion was imminent.[19] 'We were a little anxious but tired and I slept well,' Augusta noted in her diary. On 30 April, she received the *Clare Champion* of 29 April and found that the rumours of a rising in Dublin had not been exaggerated, but her predominant feeling was resentment that their week's siege had been virtually ignored.[20]

Before the executions Augusta was taken up with the effort to discover what exactly was going on. As was the case for nearly everyone else, it was the executions which jolted her into a greater awareness of the significance of what had happened. However, on 7 May, when she received two-weeks' worth of newspapers, she was initially overwhelmed by the slaughter in France and her reaction to the executions was relatively lukewarm: 'I am sorry for Pearse and MacDonnough [*sic*], the only ones I knew among the leaders – they were enthusiastic,' she wrote to Yeats. 'The looting and brutality were by the rank and file, I fancy,' she added, distinguishing immediately between leaders and men.[21] The execution of John McBride was different: '. . . what a release for her!' she wrote, expressing empathy for Maud, while gesturing towards Yeats's probable revival of hope to marry her. Most of all, Augusta was saddened by the fact that the Irish were fighting each other.

On 11 May Yeats wrote to Augusta describing his reactions. The revival of violence appalled him; he felt that their literary work, especially trying to free art from politics, was irrevocably overturned. Then, talking to Gonne, he had begun to see the rising as a transforming event. Gonne's view was the romantic one of the return of 'tragic dignity' to Ireland. Yeats expressed it as 'terrible beauty has been born again'. Confused and deeply touched – 'I had no idea that any public event could so deeply move me' – he was writing a poem.[22]

Augusta replied on 13 May. Her sadness at the deaths of the leaders had deepened; 'my mind is filled with sorrow at the Dublin tragedy'. She now mourned Pearse, a former critic of the theatre, whose play, *An Rí* had been performed by the Abbey in May 1913, and MacDonagh, also an Abbey playwright.[23] She felt particularly bereft by the death of Seán Connolly, a gentle, charming man whom she liked and whose acting ability she had discovered at the classes she had held in the winter of 1913–14 when the Abbey was in America.[24] She was challenged by their bravery and idealism, and inspired by their fearless act in defying authority: 'It seems as if the leaders were what is wanted in Ireland – & will be even more wanted in the future – a fearless & imaginative opposition to the conventional & opportunist parliamentarians, who have never helped our work even by intelligent opposition.'[25] She could not help regretting that these people had not ultimately been on the side of intellectual freedom, their side: '. . . I keep wondering whether we could not have brought them into that intellectual movement.' Those brief, fiercely burning lives had in a stroke put the intellectual movement into shadow.

The next day she elaborated her thoughts. She had been reading Shelley, and she now saw that the young men who had died in Dublin could have been the founders of the nation; they had the personal qualities necessary and were now martyrs:

> . . . Persons of energetic character, in whom . . . there is a large mixture of enterprise and fortitude &

disinterestedness, and the elements, though misguided &
disarranged, by which the strength & happiness of a
nation might have been cemented, die in such a manner as
to make death appear not evil but good – the death of
what is called a traitor, that is, a person who, from
whatever motive would abolish the government of the
day, is as often a triumphant exhibition of suffering virtue
as the warning of a culprit.[26]

In contrast, Ervine's opportunistic plan to stage *Playboy*
seemed a 'mean triumph' to Augusta, 'just as those who
might have attacked it are dead or in prison'. She herself, as
a survivor, felt tarred, writing to Blunt, 'Beside them we
seem a little insincere, we have all given in to compromise.'[27]

Over the next two days Augusta developed the idea that the
deaths of the young idealists could still have a revolutionary
effect on government. She saw that they challenged those left
behind to formulate a fuller manifesto than the narrow
nationalism of Sinn Féin.[28] This was expressed in an
unpublished essay, 'What was their Utopia?'[29] 'One would so
gladly hear [their plans for the better governance of Ireland],
for these men who proclaimed their promise to all the citizens
of Ireland of "religious and civil liberty, equal rights and equal
opportunities"; who promised "to pursue the happiness and
prosperity of the whole nation equally", must certainly have
shaped some scheme in detail by which to work out these
general principles.' The formulation of plans was the next
vital step, and she put the onus on Eoin MacNeill, the most
important surviving leader, to 'give full testimony'. Writing
this she also powerfully evoked the poet-soldiers with their
intense but unknowable vision (far more intense, she
declared, than any mere politician could hope to aspire to),
which had been lost with their deaths.

It was the evocation of this idealism and its unknowable

quality which arrested Yeats when he read the essay, and
these things found their way into his poem, 'Easter, 1916'.
One of the most powerful political poems of the twentieth
century, 'Easter, 1916' is full of humanity and doubt:

> enough
> To know they dreamed and are dead;
> And what if excess of love
> Bewildered them till they died?

At its heart is the irrevocable alteration of things, the idea
derived from his early reactions to the rising, expressed now in
his incantatory, 'Transformed utterly: A terrible beauty is born.'
He included a litany of names – MacDonagh, MacBride,
Connolly, Pearse. They are reminiscent of nineteenth-century
ballads and of Augusta's appreciation of them, and Blunt, when
he saw the poem after reading Augusta's essay, thought that
Augusta might have written it.[30]

Maud Gonne thought the poem too politically ambivalent,
but Augusta found it 'extraordinarily impressive' when Yeats
read it to a group at Lindsey House in December. However,
she asked him not to publish it straight away. By then she and
Yeats had embarked on their protracted campaign for the
Lane pictures, and Augusta was concerned that its republican
overtones would set the British Establishment against them.[31]
Such was the irony of their situation that as they turned
cautiously towards the republicans in Ireland they were
restrained from expressing it because of their increasing
reliance on British goodwill.

For nationalists the executions led to the transformation
of Sinn Féin. Martial law was maintained in Ireland
throughout 1916, a constant reminder of the rising. In the
next few years Sinn Féin gained considerable support,
winning two significant by-elections and quickly emerging

as the only realistic alternative to the Irish Parliamentary Party. Yeats and Augusta would never recapture the sense of mission for their intellectual movement after the rising. Augusta admitted to Quinn in September that a broader vision now eluded her: 'We are proud, all of us, of being "loyal" – but to an idea, a vision, perhaps a king if he by chance is the outward sign of it. And in this jumble and confusion in Ireland it is hard to keep the idea, the vision of the perfect, always before one.'[32] With the return of conviction politics and the allure of ideology in the country their plea for a non-political coming together could never now be popular and would have to be revised. The Literary Revival had been superseded as a cutting edge movement. They both knew this, but Augusta, not wanting to leave Ireland for any length of time, would feel the strain of their situation more acutely than the freer-moving Yeats.

In August she tried to persuade Yeats, who had gone to France, that he still had a role: 'I believe there is a great deal you can do, all is unrest and discontent – there is nowhere for the imagination to rest – but there must be some spiritual building possible just as after Parnell's fall, but perhaps more intense, & you have a big name among the young men.' But it was unconvincing, and she admitted that her own ambitions were vague: 'I don't exactly know what I want, except that Debating Society; and that I want the Theatre to at least interest the restless minds rather than amuse the dull ones.'[33]

Of those thrown into fumbling confusion by the rising, Edward Martyn presented much the most dismal spectacle. He felt betrayed by his co-directors in the Irish Theatre, Plunkett and MacDonagh, whom he had tried to dissuade from 'folly' and he was saddened by their deaths. He seemed rudderless, without hope. Augusta quoted part of his letter in one to Yeats, ending, 'Poor Edward.'[34] Many of her

Anglo-Irish neighbours were leaving, and by 21 May Augusta observed to Blunt that she was about the only occupant of a country house in south Galway.

Once communication was re-established with the outside world in May 1916 Augusta received a steady stream of letters from Robert. He expected to go to France any day; they were now hearing rumours that pilots were being sent with only a few hours' flying experience.[35] Now began the time of constant anxiety for Augusta. At the end of the war she described her fear of receiving the telegram announcing his death to Yeats:

> Often I had wondered, or there had been speculation in the background of my mind, for I tried to put away the thought, as to how one would hear, would bear the news that had become possible from the day Robert joined the Flying Corps. Every evening I had been thankful that no such news had come, every morning I had prayed for the safety of my child.[36]

In her letters to Yeats Augusta made no connection between Robert's bravery and that of the rising leaders, but it is not improbable that her appreciation of the sacrifice of the young Irishmen sprang from her fear for and admiration of Robert.

Yeats was still in London at the end of May, but finally indicating that he might come to Ireland. Augusta did not hide her relief: 'I shall be very glad indeed to see you if you come over. I had felt quite a sinking of heart to think I might not see you for a long time if you go to France [to see Maud] – for I feel the need of a talk with you, a new beginning as it were.'[37]

She was worried they might have to close the theatre as the third American tour of 1914 had not yielded the hoped-for profits. On 29 May, the players rebelled against the dictatorial (and Unionist) Ervine and left to form another company. It was not clear when the Abbey would reopen. Yeats was disappointingly detached; seven months later he would tell her that he wanted to reduce his management responsibility. So it was Augusta, determined to get the theatre going by the autumn, who tried to find a replacement for Ervine and source new actors.[38] Within a week she had engaged Augustus Keogh for six months and by mid-August she had set her heart on an autumn season of Shaw, 'our Irish Shakespeare', asking him for *John Bull's Other Island*.

Augusta continued to worry about Yeats that summer, for after his brief visit to Ireland he went to France to propose marriage to Maud. She refused him, and Augusta, thinking of both Yeats and herself, was glad: 'I was growing more & more doubtful of the possibility of its going well – it sometimes seemed as if it wd separate you from the Ireland you want to work for [rather] than bringing you nearer.'[39]

As his letters began to describe his ambiguous and strengthening feelings for Maud's beautiful, but troubled 21-year-old daughter, Iseult, Augusta encouraged him, happier with the idea of Yeats united to a young and relatively unthreatening person: 'I dont think the difference of age an objection [Iseult was 30 years younger than Yeats; Augusta had been 35 years younger than William], you are young in appearance & in mind & spirit – she may look on you as but a family friend – but I have always thought it possible another feeling might awake & in that case I see no reason why happiness might not come of it.'[40] But after his next self-indulgent letter she wrote back forcefully, telling him to return to Ireland.

In June Augusta was proud to hear that Robert had been appointed a flying officer, a month after his 35th birthday.[41] Robert Loraine, a friend of Shaw's – Loraine named Shaw as his next-of-kin – was Robert's commanding officer. Shaw told Augusta that '[Loraine] has been looking after your Robert, whom he declares a man of merit, personally and professionally.'[42] She quoted from Loraine's confidential report to Yeats: 'Everything good . . . flying very good. Exceptionally able pilot; should make a good "pusher" scout pilot.'[43]

By July Robert was with the flying scouts at Gosport where 40 Squadron was being formed under Loraine.[44] They were being supplied with the new, improved F.E.8 aircraft, equipped with a Lewis gun.[45] Robert had been designated to patrol the lines as part of the preparation for the army attack at the Somme planned for July. He did not tell his mother that this would involve encountering enemy aircraft and one-to-one combat with German pilots to the death. By the end of August Robert was in Bruay, northern France, near the Ypres and Somme battlefields.

Robert's letters, shorter now, the writing untidy, continued in their direct, never cynical, often stoical tone, with their obvious efforts not to alarm. As the autumn progressed Augusta needed to read between the lines for information about his engagements with the Germans: they were 'pretty busy' and the enemy was 'being very lively'. 'The Huns have been suffering very heavily in the air lately, so have we, but [we] have more to fall back on – & I am inclined to think that his efforts in the air will die away very soon.'[46]

She spent August at Mount Vernon with the children. Yeats finally tore himself away from Maud and Iseult and came to Dublin for the first night of *John Bull*. On the 16 September he went to Coole with Augusta for a few weeks. They were both glad to re-establish their old companionship. In late August Yeats had written to her: 'I had a gloomy night of it, thinking that for the first time for nearly twenty years I am not at Coole at the end of August.'

In mid-October Augusta went to London to campaign for the return of Hugh Lane's thirty-nine continental pictures to Dublin. Four months after Hugh's death Augusta had been optimistic.[47] The Trustees of the London National Gallery, declaring the codicil illegal, claimed that the pictures still belonged to them. But Augusta felt she had a good case. Lane's 1913 will had been made in anger. Since then his commitment to Dublin was obvious. Apart from the codicil he had told several people – including Quinn, his sister, Ruth Shine, and Ellen Duncan, the director of the Municipal Gallery – that he had always wanted to bring the pictures back to Dublin.[48] His intention was clear. The problem was to persuade the British authorities that this was a legitimate ground for acting on the codicil rather than the will. She hoped that if the Trustees could not be persuaded to drop their claim, a bill could be brought before Parliament to make the codicil legal.

A year later she realised that if any of this was to be achieved she herself needed to act. She went to London in mid-October 1916 and began an intensive lobbying campaign. She recorded her meetings, letters, casual encounters and actions in a letter that became a journal, which, more consistently detailed than any previous diary, she maintained for the rest of her life.[49] It is not an intimate diary. Reading the published text, one is conscious of Lady Gregory giving her considered, quotable opinion for posterity on many issues, in both the sphere of her private life and Irish politics, as well as making an attempt to present the record as she saw it. She consistently covered certain subjects: Yeats's work, Yeats's opinions, her work, the Lane pictures, the Abbey, O'Casey, the selling of Coole. With its daily reports of conversations, the arrival of letters, records of meals, notes on the weather and many of her activities, it gives the impression of being comprehensive.

But she missed out much; she did not describe the appearance of the people she met or what she felt about them; there are few impressions. She rarely gave details about her habitual acts of kindness to local people which emerge elsewhere. Often there is a feeling of distance, derived from the finished sentences rather than from a lack of information.

The details of her autumn in London make dizzying reading. We see Augusta in action, meticulous, thorough, prone to headaches, carefully using her contacts and forming new ones. Sometimes she excites admiration for her ability to operate among politicians, journalists and administrators, in a sphere that she knew well. At other times she seems overzealous and too fussy.

Yeats was a reliable and hard-working ally from the start. Like Augusta he had been bitterly disappointed in Dublin's rejection of Lane's gift in 1913, and both of them had expressed their disgust at the shortsighted materialism of Dublin, Yeats in two emotional poems.[50] For him, more than Augusta, the rejection damned the nationalists. He was convinced that Lane intended the pictures to go to Ireland – he consulted mediums in 1915 to find out whether Lane had made another, more complete will since his unwitnessed codicil – and as soon as the campaign became an exercise in lobbying British politicians and pressurising the press he took it on as a political crusade.[51]

George Bernard Shaw, on the other hand, thought Augusta was fighting a lost cause: '. . . your campaign has been like the Hundred Days campaign of Napoleon; but it will end the same way, I am afraid,' he told her in January 1917.[52] Mercilessly he argued that if the will had favoured Dublin they would have not let the pictures go. If Augusta was hurt she never showed it. She attracted much practical support, and in 1924 the Irish artist, Sarah Purser, formed the Society of the Friends of the National Collections of Ireland whose main purpose was to secure the return of the Lane pictures. Nevertheless, the campaign was like pushing an impossibly heavy, frequently slipping load uphill and it consumed much of Augusta's energy for the last sixteen years of her life.

Her first disappointment, in December 1916, was that the Trustees, still taking the view that the codicil was illegal, continued to refuse to return the pictures. They were taking the legalistic rather than the moral line.[53] By July 1919 she had the support of the Chief Secretary for Ireland, James MacPherson, who drew up a bill for Cabinet, but there it immediately fell victim to her enemy among the trustees, Lord Curzon, who blocked debate.[54] She spent the next year compiling Lane's biography in which she depicted Lane as a great Irishman.[55] She could not leave out the recent, well-publicised account of the controversy over the site for the gallery, and Lane's not always creditable performance. But she revealed her anxious support for her nephew and thereby served him most effectively, for if she, with her reputation for serving Ireland, was so involved and supportive, then Hugh Lane must indeed be worthy of praise.[56]

By January 1918 Dublin Corporation had publicly recognised the moral legitimacy of the codicil and in May 1923, after independence and the civil war, the Senate and the Dáil asserted that the Irish government would press for the return of the pictures. In July 1924, with the help of the Governor-General, T.M. Healy, she approached their long-term supporter, the Unionist leader, Edward Carson, who, through the Colonial Office, organised a committee to investigate the case. Although they found that Lane believed he was making a legal disposition when he wrote the codicil, they advised against legislation to give the codicil legal validity. This was supported by Cabinet.

Augusta, who had high hopes of the committee, was deeply

and angrily disappointed and, after all her wooing of British officials, she felt betrayed; she would always characterise their decision as 'the broken promise'. Her underlying nationalist agenda also emerged: '. . . we are back to the old story – English interests must have ours sacrificed to them.'[57] Her only comfort was that the Irish head of government, W.T. Cosgrave, had rejected their offer of a partial loan.

Her final effort was to persuade the Irish government to support the building of a municipal gallery in Dublin to house the existing collection and to strengthen their claim to the thirty-nine pictures. This was achieved, after a public hearing in September 1928 at which Augusta was an important witness. Charlemont House in Parnell Square was restored for the purpose and she visited the site on one of her last trips to Dublin. It opened after her death. But London had still not returned the pictures, and although there was an agreement about lending the pictures it is still the case as, Lane's biographer writes, that 'while one country has legal claim to the Lane bequest, the other has moral right.'[58]

In January 1917 Augusta saw Robert in London for a few days, and found him looking 'well and in good heart'. He was now a Flight Commander in charge of three aircraft.[59] She told Blunt that he was well regarded. Margaret was there, now permanently in London working 10 am to 6 pm every day in munitions. She arranged for her leave to coincide with Robert's and they spent a few days seeing their friends.[60] Robert left for the front, and wrote to Augusta from Treizennes, in Belgium, on 14 January telling her that the bad weather in Belgium only permitted practice flights, and they were amusing themselves putting on plays. He asked Augusta for copies of *The Workhouse Ward*, and told her they were rehearsing *O'Flaherty VC*; Robert Loraine was O'Flaherty and Robert Gregory the maid, Tessie. Shaw was due to visit them on 28 January for the dress rehearsal. The play was performed on 17 February.

Just before he arrived, Shaw told Augusta of his confidence in Robert. It was based on his knowledge of Robert's background rather than close acquaintance with his character: 'Robert was of course inevitably an officer from the first. Men accustomed to that position and able to assume it with any grace are so scarce that they will presently make him a field marshal.'[61] When he met Robert, now one of the most experienced pilots in the flying corps, frequently engaging in mortal combat with German pilots, Shaw was deeply impressed by the fact that he was enjoying life at the front despite the terrible conditions.[62] After Robert's death, Shaw, with his habitual lack of sentimentality, described his impressions to Augusta, giving what strikes as a particularly accurate insight into Robert's character:

> When I met Robert at the flying station on the west front, in abominably cold weather, with a frostbite on his face hardly healed, he told me that the six months he had been there had been the happiest of his life. An amazing thing to say considering his exceptionally fortunate and happy circumstances at home, but he evidently meant it. To a man with his power of standing up to danger – which must mean enjoying it – war must have intensified his life as nothing else could; he got a grip of it that he could not through art or love. I suppose that is what makes the soldier.[63]

Augusta was willing to concede some truth in this, but, she could not relinquish the idea of Robert as a painter despite his moral failings. To Quinn, to whom she quoted Shaw's observations in February 1918, she added, 'This is interesting, and has some truth. Yet Robert was many-sided. His painting was getting more joyous. He could have found happiness in more paths than one.' In February 1917 Shaw merely told Augusta that Robert was full of his work and doing well.[64]

Augusta was however, she told Yeats, worn down with anxiety;

> I am really suffering from the long strain of anxiety about Robert, and his ever-increasing danger. He is kept very hard at work now leading patrols and his squadron in these air-fights, his promised leave has been twice withdrawn, and there is no doubt the German machines are ahead of ours. I try to do what work comes my way as well as I can, and not to be a nuisance, but my mind is not free for a new task. I sometimes awake feeling as if some part of me was crying in another place. And all the war seems horrible and interminable.[65]

The winter and spring were cold and quiet for Augusta. With Margaret in London she was effectively tied to Coole, except for visits to Galway to see Arabella and occasional journeys to Dublin to look after the theatre. Richard and Anne went to a local school in the mornings while Augusta attended to the housekeeping, worked in the woods, oversaw the workmen engaged on ongoing repairs and worried constantly about Robert. 'I think my mind is going into dust,' she wrote to Blunt in February, 'but I am making every effort to work at a play I began last summer.'[66] This was *The Dragon*, started after Hugh's death. She worked at it on and off until early September, turning a serious idea into a comedy; a light-hearted look at marriage which also had an element of fantasy. In her notes she remarked that the 'gay-coloured comedy' seemed to come through 'some unseen inevitable kick of the swing' from 'the shadow of tragedy.'[67]

In April Robert came to Coole on a brief visit, and managed to be 'well and cheery', optimistically declaring that the Germans were beaten in the air. They could, he allowed, still inflict damage on British aeroplanes, but they would not be able to penetrate British lines. Yeats was with her in May, benefiting from the 'order and labour' that prevailed at Coole, although, in the aftermath of a review of Coole accounts overseen by Margaret, he had been tentatively requested to pay for his food.[68] He was, Augusta observed several times in letters to Blunt, the least affected by the war of anyone she knew, immersed in plans for the restoration of a nearby tower house at Ballylee,[69] and, to Augusta's relief, finally committing himself to Ireland.

Robert moved further south in the late spring. Now a squadron commander, calm, down-to-earth, and past the usual age for flying, he inspired admiration and affection from the men.[70] He seemed to have an unshakeable grasp on life, allowing him to run the daily affairs of the squadron efficiently, and to advise the chaplain. 'I can't tell you how much he helped me and encouraged me in my rather difficult "job"', the chaplain confided to Augusta after Robert's death, hinting at a crisis of faith that had been restored by Robert's broader outlook.

Augusta's anxieties were partially relieved when he returned to Coole at the beginning of June, not with extended leave but with the prospect of spending three months in England teaching at a flying school in Wiltshire[71] '. . . I may not see much more of him,' she wrote to Yeats, 'but he seems much nearer and it will be a relief for a while.'[72] The day after he got home a telegram arrived announcing that he had been awarded the Legion of Honour.[73] 'He is of course pleased and all the people here are much impressed.'[74] In July he was awarded the Military Cross for bravery.

During the summer, Yeats and Augusta were particularly close, as he confided in her his concerns about marriage, for he was approaching October 1917 burdened by the belief that this was the most astrologically auspicious time for him to marry. He now asked her whether he should propose to Iseult. Augusta was encouraging, but when he proposed Iseult refused him though in such a way that she kept him emotionally entangled.

However, there was another, Bertha George Hyde-Lees, 24, wealthy, English, upper class and with an almost obsessive interest in astrology and magic. Yeats had met her in London six or seven years previously and they were both members of the Hermetic Order of the Golden Dawn. Where Iseult inspired a febrile excitement in Yeats, once George became a possibility he began to write more calmly of a desire for a 'friendly servisable' [*sic*] quiet woman, '& with me,' he added, 'quiet and habit create great affection.'[75] But on 18 September Yeats wrote desperately to Augusta, deeply undecided, oscillating between George and Iseult.[76] She rose to the challenge. Ignoring the psychological complexities, she gave him a countrywoman's advice: 'You are certainly in a muddle, but "it's well to be off with the old love before you are on with the new" and I don't feel as if you could go straight off and engage yourself to another in the present state of affairs. You could not do so with a quiet mind, & that would be a bad beginning.'[77]

In the end he did propose to George, who accepted. When her mother, alarmed that Yeats did not love her sufficiently, appealed to Augusta to call it off, Augusta, appreciating that George was likely to provide the domestic atmosphere that Yeats craved, and prepared to foster the tacit agreement that the girl was to be kept ignorant of Yeats's feelings, wrote to reassure her and encourage George.[78]

Yeats and Augusta both knew that the marriage would

mean that Augusta would be supplanted as Yeats's main confidante. She was not a person to refuse to face this. Instead, she generously told Yeats that it eased her mind, for she had recently felt remorse at having less time for him physically and psychologically, tied up as she was with the children, and Robert: '. . . there is only half of me here while Robert is in danger.'[79] She wrote him a letter which reads like a blessing on his marriage: 'I believe the new life you are about to begin is almost a new birth,' arising out of his recent pain.[80]

To Blunt Augusta revealed that she considered marriage had become a practical necessity to Yeats: his failing eyesight, her inability to look after him as she had done, his plans to live in rural seclusion at Ballylee. George, young, well-to-do, amiable and interested in astrology, would make a good wife.[81] It is a dispiriting view, allowing George no allure of her own, and reveals that Augusta still felt proprietorial towards her friend. To Quinn, after the wedding on 20 October, Augusta allowed herself a little waspishness: 'His wife has money, though perhaps not so much as he was led to believe, and they live in extreme comfort and ease.'[82] From the start Yeats tried to prepare the way for a friendship between the two women. He likened George to Augusta: '[She] has your own moral genius,' he told her. 'My wife is a perfect wife, kind, wise, and unselfish. I think you were such another young girl once.'[83]

On 16 October Robert was suddenly ordered to France to take command of 66 Squadron. There was no time for leave, and he wrote regretting that he had not seen the children.[84] He was now a major. On 22 November his squadron was sent to the Italian-Austrian border in response to appeals for British assistance from the Italian Prime Minister. 'There is danger in both countries,' she wrote to Yeats, 'but Italy seems more worth fighting for.'[85] To Blunt she confided that she was glad of his new status for he would be doing less flying and fighting and there would be 'less opportunity for those "acts of conspicuous bravery".'[86]

By 4 December he was at Grossa, in the mountains, surrounded by snow, and wrote patronisingly about the inexperienced Italians, reassuring Augusta that the Hun was disinclined to fight.[87] However, in December there was a determined Austrian offensive, which the allies counter-attacked. Robert's job was to oversee the departure and arrival of patrols. He was officially confined to base, but, contrary to Augusta's expectations, he would often go across the lines to support fighter pilots who might loose their nerve and come down.[88] On 18 December he wrote about his hopes of getting to Venice. 'If I get leave, it's possible it may be long enough to let me get home, but everything is very uncertain at present.'

On 26 January 1918 Augusta left Coole for Dublin, stopping off in Galway to see her grandchildren who, with Margaret, were staying with Arabella, their godmother. About to attend a public meeting at the Mansion House to call on the government to restore Lane's thirty-nine pictures to Dublin, she wrote optimistically to Robert: 'Oh what a happy world it might be with you back and the war at an end!' She later included the letter in her journal and underneath, in brackets, wrote the sad sequel, 'But that letter was sent back to me unopened.'[89]

Robert had been killed in action on 23 January 1918. Augusta was later told he had fainted at the controls and never regained consciousness, but War Office records state that he was accidentally killed during a practice flight.[90]

Augusta heard the news on 1 February after she returned to Coole. She was writing letters in the drawing-room when Marian, the housemaid, came in with the telegram addressed to Mrs Gregory. After reading it she felt she could not stand up, but knew she had to go to Galway to tell Margaret.[91] Her whole effort was concentrated on that one task. When she finally got to her sister's house she asked to be shown into Arabella's room and waited for Margaret. 'I stood there, and Margaret came in. She cried at once, "Is he dead?" . . . Then I sat down on the floor and cried.'

The next day Augusta sent a telegram to Yeats: 'Dear Willie – the long dreaded telegram has come – Robert has been killed in action. I came here to tell Margaret – I will go home in a day or two – It is very hard to bear.' There was a postscript: 'If you feel like it sometime – write something down that we may keep – you understood him better than many.'[92] Here, in the first shock of grief, is Augusta's overwhelming sense of loss.

But there is something more. Robert was unknown. He had not achieved that which she had long felt it was in him to achieve. In requesting something from Yeats who 'understood him better than many' (she was relying on Yeats's poetic insight and his experience of Robert in several areas of life, rather than his personal relationship with him), Augusta was also hoping to counteract the fear that his life had amounted to relatively little compared to her ambition for him.

It was only to Yeats that she communicated this fear. To her other correspondents she described the anguish of her loss. 'It was such a happy home,' she wrote to Blunt on 2 February, ironing out the misery of Robert's affair, 'now happiness seems to have been put out for ever. If he had not been so brave he might have lived – he asked and got leave to do more than was asked of him.' To Shaw she acknowledged his idea that Robert fulfilled himself doing dangerous things: 'Danger and authority and the sense of power to do more than he had ever done – intensified his life.'[93] But she ended this letter with a heartbroken account of her dead son: 'My heart is very sore for my fair haired child who to me never seemed greatly changed, gentle and affectionate as at the first. But I have missed already these two or three years his right judgement and clear thinking and intellectual grip. I am maimed without him.' She was, however, as stoical as ever. To Shaw, Quinn, Blunt and Yeats she described an almost automatic transferring of her efforts at Coole from Robert to Richard: 'The mechanics of my life do not much change – I had to see work done in the woods yesterday – for Richard instead of for Robert.'[94]

There was comfort. Robert's fellow officers soon wrote, telling her of his bravery and how much he was loved and esteemed. Galway farmers came with their memories of Robert as a fearless hunter, enthusiastic cricketer and generous landlord, all carefully recorded by her.[95] She meditated on his last moments, and was reassured that his death was quick, his face uninjured.

Some of her own grief was laid aside in worry about Margaret who had barely recovered from a debilitating miscarriage before Christmas, and was so broken and distracted that Augusta feared she might lose her mind.[96] The Gregory children stayed in Galway city for a few weeks, and Augusta concentrated on showing strength for Margaret's sake, answering the letters (at least 140) and encouraging her to keep going, until she was well enough to see to Robert's affairs in London and Italy.

Despair could intrude at any time. From the moment she woke up in the morning she set herself tasks to prevent herself remembering, but, she told Quinn, 'one gets on well for a while, and then something – his palette hanging in the studio or his coat in the hall – does away with all reasoning . . .'[97] Quinn had had an operation for cancer (Augusta had written a long letter to him on 10 February – her first after

Robert's death – unaware of his operation) and cabled her that it had been a success. It had been a profound shock to him (he was in hospital for five weeks). His news, she wrote, 'roused me from a sort of lethargy of sorrow, making me feel fear and hope were still in my life'.[98]

Robert's body was found, and he was buried in the military cemetery in Padua, where his squadron marked his grave with a cross made from wood salvaged from aeroplanes. Margaret went, but Augusta never visited the grave. In 1923 she learnt that the government had replaced the wooden cross 'made with love' with a stone 'just the same as every other stone, made by contract'. It severed a link with those winter months in 1918 in the immediate aftermath of Robert's death. 'That grave at Padua is constantly in my mind; but I have no desire to see it,' she told Quinn.[99]

Periodically during that spring and summer Augusta encouraged Yeats to write a poem to celebrate Robert. It was not an easy assignment for Yeats who, although he admired Robert's last paintings and thought him supremely accomplished, knew there was no obvious achievement or focused ambition to celebrate.[100] Augusta's idea was that it should be his many talents that were celebrated. She typed notes for Yeats on 10 February 'not to use but to waken your memory to different sides of him'. It became a theme of a short article that Yeats wrote for *The Observer*, although it was overshadowed by Yeats's appreciation of him as a painter.[101]

On 25 February she suggested another theme; the idea of a fated early death. She described how Margaret was struck by his lack of material possessions – 'he never thought of money – or worried about it – & . . . she noticed how very few personal possessions he had' – and her own feeling that he had left nothing substantial except 'those few beautiful pictures – & a good name'. She put his personal ties to one side – 'In spite of wife & children & his love for them & for me & for Coole' – and evoked a disembodied spirit aware of its likely early death, 'I keep thinking of the "birds flight from tree to tree".'[102] It was a romantic image of doom.

Yeats's first poem, 'Shepherd and Goatherd', finished by 19 March, empathised with Augusta's grief. Yeats had told Quinn that he was moved by Robert's death more for his mother's sake than Robert's, and in the poem he evoked her grief and tried to give her the means of bearing it: '. . . I thought of rhyme alone, For rhyme can beat a measure out of trouble.'

But 'Shepherd and Goatherd' only made oblique references to what Robert had done. Soon after he arrived at Coole in April Yeats started 'In Memory of Major Robert Gregory'. Augusta was on hand with advice; it was a far cry from earlier collaborations. 'I have done nothing but . . . discuss with Lady Gregory the new stanza that is to commend Robert's courage in the hunting field,' he complained to George. 'It has been a little thorny but we have settled a compromise.' He took down 'musical place-names', which one would have expected him to be familiar with, and resisted all 'eloquence about . . . "the blue Italian sky". It is pathetic for Lady Gregory constantly says it is his monument – "all that remains".'[103] The poem made an icon of Robert as a renaissance man, 'Soldier, scholar, horseman, he'. Yet Yeats held back from endowing Robert with specific achievements. He was a renaissance man in embryo. And delicate subtexts suggested that the physical had trumped creativity: the poem restored memories of his behaviour to Margaret in its shying from the ultimate accolade that Augusta sought.

Yeats finally disentangled himself from Augusta's explicit agenda in his third poem, the now celebrated 'An Irish

Airman Foresees his Death'. In this tightly compact, neatly rhyming, finely focused poem, in which the subject speaks from beyond the grave, Yeats divorced Robert from all war ties – he neither hates the Germans nor loves the British – and evoked a reckless hero, accountable only to himself:

> Nor law, nor duty bade me fight,
> Nor public men, nor cheering crowds,
> A lonely impulse of delight
> Drove to this tumult in the clouds;

It was an engagement with Shaw's Robert, a soldier who can face danger. But Yeats, omitting the desperation and despair of battle or the comforting thoughts of leave, gave no concrete sense of what that danger was. Instead he imagined a disembodied mind, welcoming death:

> I balanced all, brought all to mind,
> The years to come seemed waste of breath,
> A waste of breath the years behind
> In balance with this life, this death.

We do not know what Augusta thought of the poem and whether she finally had what she wanted. There is something complete and unalloyed about it that gives it the authority she craved, and has ensured its popularity. The doomed disembodied spirit, the bird flitting from tree to tree, that she evoked in February is there in a new form. She would have appreciated that the Robert of the poem was only connected to Kiltartan's poor, though not the failure to mention his role as a landlord. By claiming that Robert had no attachment to the cause he fought for, 'An Irish Airman' solved the problem, felt by both Yeats and Augusta, of how to honour Robert without dragging in the British empire. But there is a too-strong current of nihilism that cancelled out the past and looked blankly at the future. Rooted in the dream of a plane crash experienced by Robert just after he enlisted and told to Yeats who had recorded it in his occult diary, it would have resonated uncomfortably with Augusta's memories of the despairing frame of mind in which Robert had gone to war.[104] Yet Yeats's anonymous airman with his cool calculations had an existence beyond his death and surely that was what she was looking for.[105]

In May 1918 Augusta wrote one of those diary summaries she usually wrote in the new year, partly gesturing to the past, purposefully strengthening herself for the future.[105] She listed those things that had been expelled from her life since Robert's death: interest in politics except in Ireland; personal ambition; the coveting of money (she was sanguine that her grandchildren had enough). She enumerated her remaining passions: the children's love and their happiness; the return of Hugh's pictures; the government of Ireland in the hands of Ireland; improvement to the Abbey. And finally she wrote, 'With all the anguish of Robert's death I have lost my one great fear of losing his affection. Now there is nothing that could hurt me so much to dread.'

TWENTY-ONE

Augusta and Margaret

I live in a poor little town, remaining there willingly lest it should become less.

Plutarch, quoted in LGJ, I

Robert's brief serviceman's will made, according to Lily Yeats, in a train in an emotional moment on the way to the front, dated 14 September 1916, could not have been clearer or more straightforward. It seemed to pose no problems.[1] But it was almost impossible to apply to the complex situation at Coole.

> I WISH to leave everything I have to my wife Margaret Gregory. I wish her to have the fullest freedom in the upbringing of my children and the management of my house and estate.[2]

It was Robert's attempt to assert his authority against Augusta's entrenched position in Coole, her misconceptions and the habits that the family had fallen into. Augusta had lived at Coole for 38 years, effectively run it for 26 years, spent significant amounts of her own money on it and was deeply attached to it. She had a moral right to live at Coole. But Margaret and Augusta had long differed in their assessment of whether Augusta had a legal right to reside at Coole. Augusta believed that her husband's will still gave her the right to live there, whereas Margaret considered (rightly) that Augusta had forfeited that right when Robert became absolute owner. Margaret believed that as she and Robert had generously allowed Augusta to continue living at Coole rent free she should show some appreciation. Much later she wrote, 'I always imagined in her hard pride that she could not bear to <u>show</u> gratitude or appreciation for being allowed to use Coole and its contents as her own house. (She was very little there during her married life.) But that she had grown to think it hers.'³ Augusta probably failed to show due gratitude because of her significant financial contributions, using income from investments and living frugally in the early years after William's death to pay off the mortgage, and in latter years using her royalties and fees to pay for repairs and improvements.

Then there were the children. With Margaret and Robert living part of the year in Paris and London and then with Robert at war, the children, still young, had spent six or seven months at Coole and Newquay each year. They had developed strong bonds with their grandmother, Coole and their nearby relatives, particularly Arabella. Augusta, as we have seen, now had an unshakeable belief that Richard was the new heir and that her role was to maintain Coole for him.

It is possible that Robert had been prompted to assert his authority by Margaret. If it was something that he himself had planned he would no doubt have made provision for his mother, recognising her long-standing role at Coole and the fact that her own income was not large. However, whatever she had felt previously, once Margaret held the will, giving her the power to act according to her own values and judgements, she had no immediate desire to assert her rights and make changes. She was overwhelmed by Robert's death, and she and Augusta were drawn together in their grief. 'You are the only one,' she told Augusta, 'who knows or can know that two thirds of me must be companionless for ever.'[4] Additionally, if she was behind the will, she had miscalculated the degree to which she could feel powerless in the presence of Lady Gregory. When, nearly two years later, she did try to assert herself, she found herself immediately considering a compromise and murmured hopelessly to Augusta, 'I know I would not have courage to do what I think right.'[5]

The status quo was also convenient for her. She herself had little interest in Galway beyond the Goughs at Lough Cutra and a few other landowning families, and had no desire to run an estate. She found it hard to distinguish between individual country people and she had no strong attachment to the place.

Lily Yeats's unkind and snobbish judgement on Margaret gives an impression of Margaret's urban roots and values: 'Just a little suburban minx who has been to a school of art and gathered a little knowledge there, and in the suburbs they like to move every three years and have no feeling or understanding of anyone not their generation.'[6] But Margaret was happy to leave her children with their affectionate grandmother during the extensive Christmas and Easter holidays and for the summer and often the autumn in an Ireland which, although it faced an uncertain future, had not yet entered the nightmare that would start to penetrate daily life in 1919.

There is no evidence that Augusta was discomforted by the will, suggesting that she was left to assume, or had been reassured – Margaret did recall that within two weeks of Robert's death Augusta offered to leave Coole immediately – that the status quo was acceptable to Margaret.[7] Altogether the implications of Robert's legacy seemed to be ignored. But it set an alternative standard and created a tension between the two women as they emerged from their initial period of mourning and began to think of the future.

Looking back on her childhood in her memoir, *Me and Nu*, Anne Gregory painted a far more vivid picture of her ever-present grandmother than of her distant mother. Not only was Margaret often away, but when she returned she was 'an astral being', remote and beautiful, someone to be admired, largely unsullied as she was by the day-to-day care of her children. Augusta empathised with Margaret, remembering that when she had been left with a young child she had felt inadequate as an influence on him; in comparison she thought Margaret was well equipped, with 'a very clear and original mind'.[8] But Margaret was not as dedicated as Augusta to being an everyday influence in their lives.

Augusta's involvement with the children grew considerably after Robert's death, and she willingly took on increased responsibility for them. Stray comments in her journals about her delight at seeing the children reveal how her passion for her 'chicks' grew. *Me and Nu* reveals that the girls in particular relied on their grandmother's well-intentioned discipline and carefully meted-out forgiveness. She was an ally, and never advertised accidents and naughtiness where they might cause further misery to the girls. When Margaret let the girls smoke cigarettes, expecting them to be sick and discouraged, Augusta was anxious and agitated. (They were not discouraged and Catherine smoked heavily until her death.) Most importantly, she could be relied on for comfort, advice and a story before bed.

A letter written to Quinn on 7 December 1918 describing a typical day from the last two years shows how closely Augusta's everyday existence was bound to the girls. Richard, 9 in January 1918, was away at preparatory school, Wilton House in Winchester. The girls, whose unsatisfactory governess had been dismissed, were taught by Augusta, though not very intensively; she preferred to see them occupied in the woods.[9]

After breakfast she would go to the kitchens to give the day's orders, often with the girls. While they played she wrote her letters – theatre, estate and picture business, a daily letter to Arabella, letters to Richard. For a brief hour at 11.30 she taught 7-year-old Anne French and encouraged her to memorise poetry. Five-year-old Catherine (Cat) was learning to read. Then she worked on her memoirs and did estate business. After lunch she revised her *Kiltartan History Book*. Then she went out to the woods with the children, Augusta dressed in galoshes and cotton gloves to rout weeds with a spud, the girls running and hiding; she also let them go there by themselves. They had tea together at five, and spent a companionable hour in the library, playing draughts and reading stories until 'they are called to bed', when Augusta read and ate a frugal supper of bread and milk.

She had modest treats for special days: Coole fruit and imaginatively decorated cakes for the girls' birthdays and, in poignant contrast to her own childhood when Sundays had been unbearably prim, a very wet Sunday would find Augusta sitting on the floor with the children poring over pictures in an enormous Bible. She took them to Gort Convent to learn Irish dancing. Gradually she came to rely on them. During the violence in the early 1920s the girls were a source of comfort to her as she read to them, looked at their treasures, and relished their ability to be happy in woods and fields. When they went to school in Galway in spring 1921 she wrote to them about the animals at Coole, sent them flowers and told them how much she missed them.[10] She was greatly loved in return. In *Me and Nu* Anne often writes, 'dear, dear grandmother', when recalling her acts, and Catherine spoke with fierce loyalty seventy years after her grandmother's death.

For some time after Robert's death Augusta felt that she would never want to do creative work again. She tried to be positive: 'I have probably done enough. It is better than falling off and weakening,' she told Quinn.[11] She had started to assemble poems for *The Kiltartan Poetry Book* before Robert's death in January, and continued stoically, taking comfort in the fact that so many of them were laments. With 'sheer strength of will' she wrote the introduction in May, but once finished she realised that work was a necessity, 'something that makes a background for the mind'.[12]

The trauma of Robert's death had left her with a greater desire to write her memoirs, which she had started in July 1914.[13] She was 66 and, feeling that her life was, or should be, almost over, she identified with the woman in Browning's poem 'Flight of the Duchess', who at the end of her life had been given a vision of her entire past.[14] She told Blunt that she was pre-empting a 'scribbler' who, because she was 'just well-known enough' might, after her death, 'make a little book of me, full of stupidities', which puts her biographer in her place.[15] However, where a biographer will err through ignorance, an autobiographer might mislead deliberately, and Augusta was not one to shy away from that. But for the time being she wrote down memories and typed extracts from her diaries. In the autumn she began to go through Yeats's letters and to discuss their contents with him. She asked Blunt for his letters. She felt she was only working with fragments while the overview eluded her, except for the feeling that the experiences of her early years had fitted her for later life.

Augusta's quiet life was briefly interrupted in early April 1918 when Yeats and 'Mrs Yeats' (Augusta found it hard to call her George) came to Coole.[16] Yeats had told Augusta that on their honeymoon George had discovered an ability to do automatic writing and that this had enabled him to overcome the misery and guilt that had surrounded his marriage.[17] George, in response to Yeats's questions, would write not what was in her thoughts but what she felt she was being told. The results were regarded by herself and Yeats as messages. George was very familiar with psychic research and astrology and almost immediately the messages thrown up by her automatic writing were not only used in their personal life but were put at the service of his work, and would eventually help him to write some of his greatest poetry. Despite knowing some of this, the reality of Yeats's marriage only struck Augusta in January when Yeats's philosophical *Per Amica Silentia Lunae* arrived not in Yeats's usual makeshift packaging, but in a well-organised parcel from the publisher. 'I liked the untidy parcel better – but I don't mean that I like the married man less!' she wrote in reply.[18] She also betrayed a fear that the husband and wife would form a united front against her, chiding Yeats for making a 'gorgon' of her.

George, handsome with her high colour, animated face, penetrating eyes and vivid dresses, was intelligent, level-headed, sensible and practical and would not in the long run pose a problem for Augusta. She knew how to handle Yeats's friend and she responded well to Augusta's handling of her. John Butler Yeats never saw the two women together, but he had a lively idea of their relationship, imagining them being carefully and warily friendly: 'George is the only woman I have met who is not scared of Lady Gregory,' he wrote to his brother after he had first met George.[19] 'I fancy Lady Gregory is extra-civil with her – naturally.' While to Lolly he wrote, 'I could see that [George] was always on the watch with Lady Gregory, too intelligent not to see her great merit, but yet alive to the necessities of self-defence.'[20]

George's championing of her poet husband, instead of being a barrier, would become a bond with Augusta, and both acknowledged that Yeats needed each of them. They would develop a neighbourly goodwill towards each other: Augusta ready with advice about local tradespeople, craftsmen and niceties, considerate and welcoming to the Yeats children; George willing to run messages for Augusta, especially as she got older. But there was not to be a warm friendship.

Unfortunately, they had a bad start. During the winter Augusta had fussed unnecessarily over the restoration work at Ballylee, which the efficient George had taken on, while George was uncharacteristically over-sensitive when she arrived at Coole. She was uncomfortably aware that Augusta had apparently forgotten that they had met previously, and quick to judge her snobbish and puritanical.[21] The atmosphere of mourning and the latent tensions between Margaret and Yeats also made that Easter visit fraught. The latter erupted one evening at dinner when Yeats, desisting in his good-mannered ignoring of Margaret's ceaseless contradictions, retaliated. Three days later the couple, united in the face of Coole difficulties, left for Galway. In May they returned to Ballinamantane House, a dower house situated opposite the road entrance to Coole, decorated by Margaret and Augusta. The Yeatses stayed for the summer, George and Augusta gradually coming to terms with each other, and moved into their tower on 21 September.

The First World War ended on 11 November 1918. In the general election a month later Sinn Féin won a landslide victory in Ireland. In January 1919 these elected MPs, turning their backs on Westminster and declaring themselves members of Dáil Éireann, set up an alternative government in Dublin and an alternative administrative presence throughout the country. At the same time, the Irish Volunteers, increasingly known as the IRA, began the attacks on the police that would lead to the brutalities of the Anglo-Irish War, which dominated the next three years. It was a time of chronic uncertainty and fear.

Augusta met Sinn Féin's political challenge more than half way. She valued its idealistic element, and, aware of its popularity, welcomed its elected members' responsibility to the electorate. 'If they have any grit,' she wrote to Quinn, '[they will] form a clear policy.'[22] But she could be snobbish about the individual MPs and their families, remarking to Blunt that they were 'most common and vulgar'. She was also anxiously aware that the promise of Sinn Féin had unleashed an iconoclastic tendency among 'bad characters'. These people, she thought, were increasingly getting away with petty crimes, intimidation and even murder in the countryside, hiding under the umbrella of Sinn Féin and aided by the passive support of people who thought that to report them to the police would be to help the British government.

Augusta's hope was for a self-government scheme 'large enough to put responsibility on the people themselves, and spectacular enough to excite the imagination, or rather to turn the already excited imagination of the young to building instead of breaking.'[23] As Irish violence escalated during 1919, debate centred on whether the British government, which was responding with some displays of military force, would offer a settlement or retaliate with official reprisals. Augusta, keen for a settlement so that the rebuilding of Ireland could proceed, was afraid Sinn Féin might not accept the proffered Dominion Home Rule as a first step. She herself, ever the pragmatist, believed that Ireland should become what she regarded as an undesirable dominion ('a territory, region, district') in the expectation that it would eventually become a republic (a 'high and noble tradition').[24]

During January 1919, before any of this had materialised, Augusta wrote *The Jester* for Richard.[25] Inspired by the magnificent susceptibility of children's imaginations, their humour and her own thoughts about education, she imagined five pampered princes living in the perfect security and luxury of a crystal palace and cared for by a solicitous dowager, changing places with five poverty-stricken wrenboys bullied by a wicked ogre. A jester, the Great Disturber, often a beneficent influence in Irish myths, orchestrates the change.[26] Augusta's preoccupations abound in the play; her perennial theatrical theme that the first shall be last and the last first, and her idea that a rigorous classical education (such as Sir William had advocated) needed to be complemented by the freedom to discover nature and indulge the imagination. Most beguilingly, the play seems to be an allegory of what she feared would happen at Coole. Here they were, cosseted within their privileges, while the great unwashed prepared to batter on their door, threatening to replace them. Yet if it expressed fear of a violent uprising the play also looked beyond this. It is only when they change places that the wrenboys and the princes learn the advantages to be had in each others' lives. Augusta the playwright was part prophet (not for the first time) and part idealist, hoping for good to come of the changes.

On 10 February Augusta left Ireland for London and Lane picture meetings. On 21 February she visited Newbuildings, and was shocked to find the 79-year-old Blunt in bed, weak, pain-ridden and breathing badly, although she knew he had been ill since February 1917.[27] His lover, Dorothy Carleton, now his adopted niece, was in attendance. Apart from her he was alone, to some extent reaping the rewards of a selfish life in which he had loved little beyond the 'mad minute'.[28] Of his family, Anne had never ceased to love him, but she was dead, and his daughter, Judith, had been irrevocably alienated; in 1896 he had planned to elope to Paris with her closest friend.

Now, after years of dispute about the Newbuildings stud, Judith was threatening a law suit, contesting his ownership. Augusta knew something about this issue, and in May 1916 had written with some insight but much naivety, unable to comprehend the ruthlessness that Judith experienced in him: 'I do hope you will recognise that Judith's waywardness comes in fact from you, & will not let it be a real break.'[29] Judging by Augusta's response to Anne's death, she had little idea of Blunt's lack of feeling towards her either. Augusta had known that there had been a partial reconciliation between them two years before Anne had died and, in her letter written to Blunt after Anne's death, Augusta, putting aside her criticisms of Anne (such as her inevitable support of Blunt), praised her courtesy and 'grande dame' character. She continued, 'you will miss terribly the new friendship that had begun between you . . . what a noble poem you may now write about her, she deserves this "elegie & friend's passion" from you'.[30] She seemed to be both reassuring him, and directing him towards his duty. Far from penning a noble poem, Blunt found he no longer wanted to write anything. However, the solid fact of Augusta and Blunt's friendship based on work and shared experiences was undisturbed and proved therapeutic during this spring visit. After a few days talk and writing and mutual admiration – Augusta approved his 1889–1900 memoir, he liked *The Jester* – Augusta left Blunt in good spirits.

A few days later she went to Ayot to see Shaw who attacked her about her plans to send Richard to Harrow.[31] A few weeks later he wrote, describing Harrow as 'that obsolete and thrice accursed boy farm', and recommending the more modern, open-minded Oundle where the boys mended cars and did classics for fun.[32] 'Richard's mother has not the Harrovian psychology,' he argued. 'You must develop the new tradition, which is a healthy one; for Robert was just on the verge of being overbred: one more generation as fine drawn as that would have produced something that might have been pretty and would certainly have been effete.' It was just over a year since Robert's death. Shaw's obvious concern for Richard, whom he knew to be inclined towards things mechanical, appears to have made such criticism acceptable for there is no evidence that Augusta was affronted. Shaw was right; a year later Richard told the family that he wanted to be an engineer. Augusta was glad the 'darling child' wanted to be 'a worker'.[33] Margaret entered him for Oundle in January 1920, but he went to Harrow in 1923.

The Abbey Theatre had not only survived the war, but had maintained its tradition of staging new plays: there had been two from Lady Gregory and three from Lennox Robinson, and it had produced five plays by Shaw as Augusta had hoped. Augusta was in Dublin at the end of January to attend rehearsals for a revival of Yeats's poetic *On Baile's Strand*, and one of the Sunday evening theatre lectures she had helped to set up.

Back in Dublin again on 16 March, Augusta discovered that Máire nic Shiubhlaigh, who was to play Cathleen in *Cathleen ni Houlihan*, was unable to get to Dublin for the performances on St Patrick's weekend. Determined not to alter the programme she offered to play the part herself.[34] Over the years some of the Abbey actresses had noticed that Augusta seemed to harbour a desire to act.[35] She all but admitted it in her diary when she remarked that if it was a success she would have been glad to have done it. Even though it was a small part she was very nervous about remembering the lines. She was also fitting in rehearsals between tense meetings about the Lane pictures.

On the night of the first performance she submitted without enthusiasm to the make-up artist who painted her face white with black under the eyes and red inside the lids. On stage she spoke, according to Joseph Holloway, clearly and with assurance, but without passion; she refused to chant the last speech as Yeats would have liked, subtly reducing the nationalistic thrill of Cathleen. But the patriotic St Patrick's Day audience applauded enthusiastically, and she recorded with satisfaction that she had two curtain calls. She went back to her hotel tired and hungry and ate stale bread and butter and drank a glass of milk, as was her habit when alone.

Yeats, who came the following night, was unimpressed. 'Yeats came up to the gallery afterwards and said coldly it was "very nice, but if I had rehearsed you it would have been much better".' Maud Gonne was there to remind them both of Yeats's original vision for the part. On 21 April *The Dragon* opened at the Abbey. It produced more favourable reviews than any other play in recent years, and was the first in a series of fantasy or 'wonder' plays that would add another dimension to Lady Gregory's reputation as a playwright. Yeats, listless and negative during the performance, did not see its potential.

Augusta in her turn was detached from Yeats's work. On 3 August she told Blunt that Yeats had not done much work since his marriage, when in fact he had been writing many lyrical poems later included in *The Wild Swans at Coole*.[36] George had given birth to Anne in February, and was keen to return to Ballylee for the summer where two adjacent cottages had been restored for the family to live in – the tower was mainly used by Yeats for writing. It was the only place in their currently unsettled life that she felt promised permanency.

Yeats was still disengaged from the theatre. He told Augusta privately that he felt standards were dropping, and suggested that Robinson take on his role as director.[37] Lady Gregory, now covertly referred to as 'The Old Lady', was left as the dominant influence on the actors' lives. The young Gabriel Fallon recalled her formidable decisiveness – her yes YES and her no NO – and the fact that the actors performed better when they knew she was in the audience.[38] She would act as intermediary between a distant Yeats and the actors on his infrequent visits, introducing him and talking volubly, while he merely inclined his head. He was, however, still keen to use the theatre for his own experimental work. In one of the Abbey lectures he was publicly critical. He tried to tone this down in a published essay, 'A People's Theatre: A Letter to Lady Gregory', but he still distanced himself from the Abbey, a people's theatre, successful because of Lady Gregory's plays and 'anxious and laborious' supervision.[39] It was the first time Yeats had publicly dissociated himself from Augusta's work. She could have felt betrayed; instead she was pleased that he acknowledged her.[40] It was a measure of Augusta's acceptance of Yeats's detachment from the running of the theatre. He remained director, and Robinson, whose case was pressed by Yeats in several letters to Augusta, became manager for the second time.

Coole was not exempt from the violence that was breaking out in Ireland during 1919. When Augusta returned at the end of April she heard that Florimund Quinn, a relatively well-to-do ex-tenant, had been shot and wounded in the demesne by a group that coveted his land. In May the old steward's house was burnt down, and in August fleeces and rugs were stolen from the harness room at Coole.[41] Augusta was keen to see these incidents as isolated troubles rather than politically motivated violence. For Margaret, unhindered by loyalty or love, these events struck like warnings of a cataclysm to come.

Augusta was at Coole with Catherine and Anne by the end of November. Margaret returned on 20 December with Richard. That evening she told Augusta that she wanted to sell the remains of the Coole estate:[42] '. . . there is no society for the children here, and it is not fair to let them grow up without it.' Augusta was shocked, it was such a sudden and brutal announcement. Even so, she assumed that Margaret would keep the house. No, Margaret told her next morning, she did not want the expense of caretakers. Augusta offered to be a caretaker. Margaret suddenly felt that she would be unable to continue to oppose Augusta, and she mumbled bitterly, 'we can stay here – and the children will marry peasants', while Augusta's reaction betrayed her own uncertainty in the face of Margaret's opposition: 'Oh, what can I do?'

Margaret's desire to sell Coole had been sharpened by the deteriorating situation in Ireland. She knew that Amy Shawe-Taylor had let Castle Taylor and gone to England, that Lord Morris had dismissed all his servants and moved to London, and that the Goughs were planning to shut up Lough Cutra. She was concerned that an independent Ireland would be a difficult place to be a landowner; there was no guarantee that people would be willing to work for the big house, and rates and taxes, already high, might increase. She was a person who was capable of keeping the financial equations before her.

Augusta wanted to keep Coole for her grandchildren, convinced that it was legally Richard's and that a Coole childhood would give them the best possible start in life. In the subsequent discussions and negotiations with Margaret,

Augusta often woke in the night haunted by the idea that she was depriving them of Coole. There was also her personal identification with Coole, which she tried to suppress: 'I will stay here I hope till my life's end, or rather I hope it will be kept open by Margaret for the children and I shall be content anywhere,' she wrote on 22 January 1920.[43] Most fundamentally she felt that if she gave up Coole she was jettisoning her responsibilities as the custodian of a national institution that had weathered the Famine, Land League, land sales and was significant as a place of peace and culture. 'If there is trouble now, and it is dismantled and left to ruin, that will be the whole country's loss. I pray, pray, pray,' she wrote in April 1920.[44] Margaret could not understand her motives and struggles, and interpreted her efforts to keep Coole as mere selfishness.

Despite their differences, Augusta and Margaret were both anxious not to alienate the other. Augusta, as ever, did what she could to avoid open confrontation. Yeats later observed that he never heard them argue. 'It was impossible to be excitable, & unrestrained in Lady Gregorys [sic] presence, & Mrs. Gregory herself had been remoulded by her and by the house.'[45] Margaret was sometimes brusque with her demands, and given to bitter and hurtful comments in writing, but at Coole she allowed herself to be drawn into lengthy discussions with Augusta. Both were convinced that their desire for Coole was best for the family and for themselves, so that the discussions would be repeated and the issues gone over, again and again. But by mid-January they had agreed to sell the demesne fields – 'it is what Robert approved,' Augusta reported tersely – and they had engaged an agent, Scott Kerr, to negotiate the sale.

TWENTY-TWO

Violence at Gort

I pray for a settlement and peace. 'Thy Kingdom come, Thy will be done – here in Coole – in Kiltartan – in Ireland.'
3 October 1920, *LGJ*, I

There had been sporadic violence in the country throughout 1919; in the early spring of 1920 it began to approach Coole. Frank Persse's house, Ashfield, was raided in February by men looking for guns. Forewarned, he had taken his to the barracks. Meanwhile, the police advised Augusta to hand over Richard's gun (he now shot rabbits and squirrels). On 3 March Augusta's nephew, Frank Shawe-Taylor (the brother of John), was shot dead as he was driving to a fair. The week previously he had refused to sell part of his estate to some local farmers.[1]

This scenario encouraged further acts of intimidation. By the end of the month there were reports that people were demanding land at Lough Cutra and that cattle drives were threatened at Castle Taylor. Despite all this Augusta's journal and her letters to Margaret betray no fear; instead she clung to the belief that the local Sinn Féin committees would be able to contain what she regarded as the latest outbreak of agrarian lawlessness. On 1 June 1920 she voted for the Sinn Féin candidate, an ex-tenant's son, Martin Cahill, in the district council elections.

In her fantasy play, *Aristotle's Bellows*, which she wrote that summer, Augusta cast doubt on the efficacy of violent revolution.[2] Conan, educated and frustrated, who discovers a magic bellows which, through its blasts, has the power of changing reality, squanders the opportunity it provides to make significant changes. Parallels with Ireland in 1920 are not left to the imagination – 'There is another two blasts in it that will bring sense and knowledge into Ireland yet!' – and the contemporary power struggle is alluded to when Conan arrogantly declares, 'There's no doubt but I'll make a better use of it than him, because I am a better man than himself.'[3] The implied message is that Ireland should be left to itself to find a peaceful course. In her journals Augusta used the image of putting clothes on a growing child to describe changes which responded to evolving circumstances.

At Coole the elements of possible tragedy were being assembled. A group of young ex-tenants led by the aggressive Regan had combined to offer an unacceptably low price (under £7,000; the Gregorys' minimum was £12,600) for the demesne land, and to prevent other offers.[4] Margaret wanted to bypass potentially dangerous confrontation by holding an auction in Dublin. But she left Augusta alone to investigate ways of selling the land. Augusta, thinking that the Congested Districts Board (CDB) might pay more, and confident that once in ownership they would be able to resist pressures from the group, went to see Sir Henry Doran at his offices in Mountjoy Square in April. But, adept though she was with officials, she was no match for the wily Sir Henry, who held out possibilities during their interview only to curtly reject her offer in a letter on 2 May. Emotionally, it was exhausting. She had left the meeting full of an exhilarating hope – 'peace and joy and relief seemed to rush into me' – to endure nine days of anxiety which terminated in dumb disappointment. This last was registered matter-of-factly in her journal; disappointment had become an integral part of her life and the prelude to more effort.

Frank and his niece were eventually forced to abandon Ashfield. Another maverick group, disowned by Sinn Féin, claimed Frank was a spy on the strength of navy envelopes headed 'On His Majesty's Service' left by his son Dudley (killed in 1918) and, arriving with guns, fired through doors and windows. After that Frank began to support Augusta in her campaign to keep the house at Coole.

Margaret wrote aggressively in early July, blaming Augusta for keeping Coole, but not arranging how to pay for it.[5] This gave Augusta a sleepless night in which she began to consider that she herself might be able to buy the house and a reduced demesne and pay the running costs on the income from her plays and books, supplemented by the sale of a few pictures. This was a turning point, for it raised the possibility of keeping Coole without unduly impairing Margaret's income. The children would have Margaret's new, well-regulated home (when she acquired it) and the freedom of Coole. Augusta wrote a rather confused letter to Margaret on 13 July displaying a lack of the business acumen that Margaret would have liked – she could be definite about neither the costs involved nor her income – but conveying all her obsessive love and care for Coole and Gregory continuity with irresistible, heroic disregard for herself, and a new, almost humble note, 'Do you think this is a possible way out of the difficulty? I hope so.'[6]

Meanwhile, Frank arranged a sale of the demesne land. It went to the Regan group for £9,000 (about €718,268, £492,977 sterling) in early October. Now places quite near the house where Augusta habitually went for firewood and earth for her garden were out of bounds.[7] It was a curiously apposite moment for the sale, for by the autumn the British had finally conceded that the conflict in Ireland was war and had dispatched the Black and Tans. This undisciplined, independently acting, auxiliary unit, composed largely of ex-soldiers dressed in a hybrid uniform of army khaki and dark police belts and caps, immediately initiated the brutal reprisals to IRA attacks on the police, which were to cause unprecedented grief and destruction in and around Gort, as well as elsewhere in Ireland.

It was on the journey home from the Burren on 27 September 1920 that Augusta first witnessed the results of the violence she had been hearing about.

> I had been told that Feeney's house in Kinvara had been burned in the night . . . and we passed by the ruined walls in the town. A little farther, at the cross roads, there was another ruin, McMerney's the smith. His house had also been burned down in the night by soldiers and police. He and his family had found shelter in the cart shed. It seemed so silent, we had always heard the hammer in the smithy and seen the glow of the fire.[8]

Three days later she wrote, 'I was quite ill, could not sleep or eat after the homecoming – the desolation of that burnt forge, and all one hears.' That same day two lorries of soldiers had driven into Gort firing and shouting, searching people, raiding houses, going through letters at the post office. At least one house was burnt. People were in terror of their lives.

Augusta, as was her habit, carefully recorded all she heard, but this time she decided to act. In order to balance the copious reporting of IRA atrocities in the British press, and apply pressure for a settlement, she sent edited extracts from her diaries anonymously to the nationalist weekly, *The Nation*. The first 'Week in Ireland' was published on 16 October. She sent six in all, the last published on 1 January

1921.[9] It was an exceptionally brave act, for the Black and Tans repeatedly rifled through letters in Gort post office and she was, if discovered, clearly a target. Until the violence broke out around her, Augusta would often indicate in her journal if she felt anxious or fearful. But now she mentioned no such emotions.

The Nation accounts were more than a list of atrocities, for Augusta reported events as they were told to her, or experienced by her. They are a jigsaw puzzle of acts, interpretations and explanations, and the reader is left to piece together what exactly had happened, while the impression of the confusion and horror is there in the raw. It would take an assiduous reader to make all the connections because Augusta only used initials for people and places, and because one episode may appear in several different articles over a number of weeks. Augusta, for example, later discovered what had happened at the smith's forge, so that the details for this appeared in the second week with only an 'M' to identify the smith.[10] It was not political propaganda like Erskine Childers's *Irish Bulletin* accounts intended, with generalisations and exaggeration, to bolster the republican cause whatever the consequences. Its aim was to expose the violence and bring it to an end.

A particularly horrifying incident was the killing of the young, pregnant wife of Augusta's ex-tenant, Malachi Quinn. She was standing in front of her house, her baby in her arms, when a lorry of Black and Tans passed close to her, shooting. 'When I pray "God save Ireland" the words come thrusting through "Gott strafe England" in spite of my desire not to give in to hatred.'[11] These bitter words did not get into the report, but the incident did. She tried to get compensation for Malachi, pressurising the authorities to take his case seriously.

A markedly sinister episode was the disappearance of two boys from their house at Shanaglish. Unusually, there was an attempt to cover up the murders, and as local people were afraid to make public enquiries about what had happened it took time before the bodies were found in a pond and the work of the Black and Tans proved. Augusta returned, as her informants did, day after day to this incident, which dominates the 18 December report. 'F [Marian] hears the Loughnane boys could not be recognised – that "the bodies looked as if they had been dragged after the lorry". When the men bringing them away in the lorry came to R [Coen's] shop for the rope they took a bottle of whiskey, too, and when he asked for payment all they did was to point a revolver at him. The bodies were brought home last night, when they passed through G- [Gort] at 6 o'clock the dead bells were ringing.' 'K. says: "It would break your heart to see that funeral, the two hearses and the poor mother between them".'[12]

One recurrent theme in her journals is the way certain phrases and situations from Abbey plays, which had previously seemed extreme or been unacceptable to nationalists, were now, horribly, vindicated. *Playboy* was recalled when she heard of a man in gaol for killing his mother, and King Brian's words in *Kincora* came back to her with force as reprisals became the theme of people's conversation: 'Death answering to Death like the clerks answering one another at the Mass.'[13] She noted with concern that shame could be mixed with anger when people reported atrocities to her.

Augusta's religion and social position did not, on occasions, fail to pull her towards the other side. She still attended the Church of Ireland church at Gort, now dominated by the military who, to her disgust, insisted on 'God Save the King' and a radically truncated service so that they would not be late for dinner. When the IRA killed 11 unarmed British officers in Dublin on 21 November at the Gresham Hotel, shooting them in bed or as they came down for breakfast, she was horrified and sickened.[14] She included the event and her revulsion in her *Nation* report, speculating that her extreme reaction had an element of class loyalty.

On 20 November the war correspondent Henry Nevinson came to Coole. He was particularly welcome as Shaw had refused her request to visit and report on the violence on the grounds that it was hopeless to try to counter British propaganda.[15] She discovered from Nevinson that she was known as the author of *The Nation* articles. Later she found out that Sinn Féin also knew. On 28 November she received 'Reprisals', a poem Yeats had recently written about the Black and Tans and sent to *The Nation*. In the poem he evoked the Robert that Shaw had seen at the front in 1917 and the belief that the First World War had been a noble cause. Then, associating the Black and Tans, now murdering Gregory tenants, with Robert's fellow soldiers, he cast doubt on the cause that Robert had fought for. It ends on a highly emotional note:

> Then close your ears with dust and lie
> Among the other cheated dead.

Augusta recoiled from the poem, which seemed to be using Robert to make a political point using second-hand information, for Yeats had not been to Ireland since the summer of 1919, and Augusta felt he had no idea about what they were going through. For those at Coole who were suffering losses from both the First World War and the current assassinations and reprisals it was unthinkable to use the war as he was doing. She had not told him about her *Nation* articles, and when he had heard a rumour that she was the author he had dismissed it unhesitatingly.[16] 'I cannot bear the dragging of R. from his grave to make what I think a not very sincere poem – for Yeats only knows by hearsay while our troubles go on – and he quoted words G.B.S. told him and did not mean him to repeat – and which will give pain – I hardly know why it gives me extraordinary pain and it seems too late to stop it,' she wrote in her journal.[17]

She immediately sent a telegram, followed by a letter telling him she disliked the poem and asking him not to publish it, not on the grounds of her dislike but because the officers' killings made it a 'bad moment to appeal to *emotion* in England'. Yeats managed to stop its publication, though his reply to her telegram shows that he failed to register her personal objection.[18] Yeats persisted in misunderstanding the horror of the situation in Gort. At the end of December Augusta was astounded that Yeats could imagine that trouble at Ballylee might be dealt with by the urbane, peacetime tactic of George's solicitor writing to the commanding officer in Gort.[19]

Out of her journal notes and articles a more radicalised Augusta emerges. Train strikes meant that she received few letters or visitors and so, alone with the terrible stream of stories from Mike John, John Diveney and other Coole people, and without the subtle restraint of her literary friends, she developed a growing empathy for the victims. This was reinforced by her reading of G.M. Trevelyan's *Garibaldi's Defence of the Roman Republic 1848–49*. In this she found many parallels with IRA activity in Gort, especially the Italian struggle against the French in Italy.[20] On 17 September 1921 she wrote out the Shelley passage that had inspired her during the 1916 rising, and concluded, 'If war can ever be justified these surprises and ambushes called murder were justified to break the government by England that has been destroying both body and soul, and my heart goes out to those who have taken that responsibility and have risked their own lives – or lost them, while I have been but "the hurler sitting on the wall".'[21]

Black and Tan atrocities and the plight of republican prisoners in 1920 were radicalising many vague sympathisers. On 9 December Lily Yeats wrote to her father in New York that a year ago she was no Sinn Féiner, just a mild nationalist, '– but – now –'.[22] The turning point for many was the death on 25 October 1920 of the Lord Mayor of Cork, Terence MacSwiney, a playwright and republican, after a hunger strike of 74 days in protest against the violence of the Black and Tans.

The news of his death was brought to Augusta, who had been reading the Prayer Book 'Service for a Sick Person' for him during his strike, by an unsympathetic local Protestant who snobbishly observed that his sister was rather 'rowdy'. Augusta coldly stood up and the woman was forced to leave. As she contemplated MacSwiney's death a phrase from *The Gaol Gate* came to Augusta: 'It is not a little thing a man to die, and he protecting his neighbour.'[23] She instructed the Abbey to close as a mark of respect, and in February 1921 supported Robinson's idea to perform MacSwiney's radical drama, *The Revolutionist*. After the performance on 25 February she told MacSwiney's widow that 'we felt we were laying a wreath upon the grave'.

Much as Augusta might support the republicans she could not deny that there were local people, especially the sons of ex-tenants, who would be happy to see her go, paradoxically supporting Margaret. One Sunday afternoon in late November 1920 Augusta, walking in the woods, was distraught to find a number of boys trapping rabbits who refused to come when she called to them.[24] Her grandchildren were with her, but she expressed no fear for their welfare. It was the 'peasants making themselves free of the woods', as in the French Revolution or Russia, that haunted her. 'I felt so helpless; the police are out of the running, and the Volunteers are being chased by the Black and Tans. It seemed as if I must give in and consent to give up Coole.'

When she calmed down she wrote a letter to Regan, requesting him to tell his associates to respect boundaries, and assuring him that she had nothing but goodwill for those who had bought their land. But two months later a similar incident drew from her the conclusion that if she could not 'mind' (an Irish phrase, unusual for her journals) the woods she was reconciled to losing them.[25] Such thoughts made her susceptible to Margaret's pressure to relinquish the house – perhaps she could not afford £800 a year. Then these doubts would be fought in night-long vigils – perhaps she could keep a truncated Coole, say 350 acres (large by modern standards) at £300 a year, selling the rest of the woods to the Forestry Commission.

In the spring of 1921 Augusta was in Dublin on theatre business, and from there she went to London. On the morning of Sunday 17 May at Shaw's house in Ayot, Augusta read in the newspaper of an ambush near Coole. Margaret, who habitually socialised with army officers and their wives, was in a car leaving a tennis party at Ballyturn near Gort (the house of the Bagots). When they got to the gates the car was attacked and all the other four occupants (three army officers, including the notorious Captain Blake, the main target, a District Royal Irish Constabulary (RIC) Inspector whom even Margaret accused of presiding over licensed murder, and his wife) were shot dead. Margaret was the sole survivor. The *Irish Independent* version of the event was that the officer who had got out of the car to open the gates had been shot instantly. The car had then been surrounded and the women ordered to get out. Mrs Blake refused to leave her husband, and when Margaret had left the car the three still inside were shot.[26] Margaret, however, told Beatrice Dunsany that she had not got out. 'As she crouched on the floor among the bleeding bodies of her friends a boy came up and asked, in the gentlest voice I ever heard, "Are you all right?"' Beatrice wrote in her diary.[27] There was a telegram from Margaret for Augusta: 'Sole survivor of five murdered in ambushed motor.'

Augusta's reaction was complex. She was shocked: '– the thought of the possibilities . . .' But she also realised that such an experience would hardly reconcile Margaret to Ireland: 'And then, though she is safe thank God, it is impossible to know how it will affect her outlook and the life of the children, and through them mine. I was quite broken up.'[28] Anxiously she sent a telegram asking whether she should come back to Coole, but Margaret preferred her to stay away. Almost immediately Margaret sent a 'harsh' letter to Augusta about Coole, presumably saying she wanted to sell it immediately, followed by one asking for forgiveness.

Augusta left London in early June, revived by the kindness of her friends, but in Ireland she was immediately engulfed by the war: soldiers filling the trains, roads shaking with lorries, low-flying aircraft, a military search on her train near Athenry, and reports of shouting and firing all night in Gort. At Coole Margaret was still shaken by her experiences, but Augusta was relieved to find her tranquil and able to talk about the ambush. The children she described as well and happy, as though they had been successfully shielded from the horror. In fact, having discovered from John Diveney, the groom, driver and farm servant and someone who frequently engaged in their games and concerns, that their mother had not been involved in an accident as they had been told, they pestered the housemaid,

Ellen, until she told them the story. But, protected as some children are by a cool innocence, they were not shaken, and Anne, not quite 10, later recalled that what most disturbed them was having to sleep with their mother.

Margaret, who was proud (she had forbidden the girls to be sick on their first boat journey to England), was primarily concerned not to appear disturbed or intimidated. She also failed to understand her mother-in-law's position locally, for she did not immediately show her a note from the IRA received the day after the ambush telling her that she was in no danger because she was a Gregory.[29] Augusta, now, no longer pretended that she was unafraid. 'So she was [afraid] and so was I, and we'd have been superhuman if we had not been,' she wrote in her journal.

Throughout the summer Augusta's doubts about whether she should press for the retention of Coole returned. An incident in June reveals a moment when she was convinced that it was still possible for her to live in the neighbourhood. 'Looking back on the day, my mind dwells with happiness on a few friendly words with Hanlon and Coppinger who I met by the lake; grateful to me for my advice about old Mrs. C's pension. It is to these people I am drawn, it startled me to find how much. G. and O. and even R. seem shadowy beside them. I would, as in early days, wish to serve them, wish to have them for my friends.'[30] The passage contains the familiar element of patronage, bestowed by her, gratefully received by them, but the new emotional connection which she was surprised and comforted to feel for these men also suggests that Augusta was beginning to see them as neighbours.

On 9 July a truce had been declared. Although relieved, Augusta at first could hardly allow herself to hope that it would be lasting peace. Returning to Coole on a crowded train, gazing at the fires blazing from mountain tops celebrating the peace, she thought of writing a poem about past Irish rebellions. 'The Old Woman Remembers', a monologue, in which Cathleen ni Houlihan lights candles to the memory of Donall O'Brien, Art MacMurrough, Phelim O'Connor, Shane O'Neill, Patrick Sarsfield, the United Irishmen, those who died in 1916 and Terence MacSwiney taps into Augusta's old interest in radical Irish history for a contemporary purpose.[31] Its most surprising feature is the Catholic imagery. Here was a woman who still habitually spoke out (in private) against the clergy and Catholic dogma writing a 'rosary of praise', counting the 700 years of Irish history on 'silver beads upon the thread'.[32] But, spontaneous public sayings of the Rosary, with independence imminent, had become popular – during the conference just after the truce Augusta had observed a large crowd outside the Mansion House saying the Rosary for peace. Augusta's seven candles empathised with this, taking the new tradition onto the stage.[33]

Anticipating scorn from Yeats for what she regarded as doggerel, she was relieved when he found some charm in it.[34] A slightly revised version taking in the civil war would be performed by Sara Allgood on 31 December 1923 at the Abbey when Augusta hoped it would be 'a little paving stone on the road to peace'.[35] Augusta's words, the simple format, and Sara Allgood's clear and passionate delivery struck a chord with the audience which, the *Dublin Magazine* recorded, was profoundly moved.[36]

In August Margaret decided to bid for a house in Celbridge; the children would move to a new home and there was no need to keep Coole. Augusta's first feeling was relief, especially from the financial burden, but it was only a momentary weakness. Margaret too was friable, stating that Coole was a financial burden, but allowing that Augusta had her uses as a custodian of Gregory furniture. Finally, in

November they had an agreement: Augusta would rent the house, garden and remaining demesne from Margaret for a nominal amount (£5 a year) and pay all expenses, taxes and rates. Margaret would let Augusta have the stock (it had originally been left to Augusta who had given it to the estate). This agreement would be renewed yearly and there was an understanding that Augusta could not be told to go at any moment. Thus Augusta became a tenant at Coole.[37]

The traumas and uncertainty of their private arrangements that autumn were inadvertently mirrored at national level. The British offer of dominion status was rejected by the Dáil headed by Eamon de Valera, but an Irish team, headed by Michael Collins, was sent to Westminster to negotiate a treaty in October. By 6 December the Anglo-Irish Treaty was signed, giving full independence on the domestic front with some restrictions in foreign affairs and requiring an oath of fidelity to the Crown that linked the new Free State to the British Commonwealth of Nations. This did not apply to the whole island of Ireland, for the Government of Ireland Act in 1920 had provided the constitutional framework for six Ulster counties to maintain close domestic links with Britain.

It was peace, and a joyful Augusta said the General Thanksgiving in church with a full heart.[38] It also, in Michael Collins's words, offered Ireland 'freedom to achieve freedom'. This idea that the Treaty would be an umbrella under which negotiators would continue to work towards a fuller independence was something that Augusta espoused. But de Valera, claiming that it '[would give] away the Republic', advised the Dáil to reject the Treaty. There had been intimations of this in Galway as early as 4 December when de Valera had addressed a gathering of Volunteers outside Coole to warn of war, all witnessed by the grandchildren through a gap in the wall.[39] So Christmas was spent anxiously waiting to hear the result of Dáil deliberations. They voted, on 7 January, to ratify the Treaty, but by a tiny majority of seven. Before relief gave way to further worry about the possible consequences, Augusta rejoiced at the departure of the soldiers from Gort. 'The army in retreat,' she observed provocatively to her Unionist neighbour, Margaret's friend, Guy Gough, a regular visitor to Coole now, and she went to the barracks to retrieve Richard's gun and cartridges.[40] Some semblance of normality was flowing back into Coole.

TWENTY-THREE

Redemption

Santayana says . . . 'A man's feet must be planted in his country, but his eyes should survey the world'.

3 August 1921, *LGJ*, I

For optimists and supporters of the Treaty the first months of 1922 were the start of nation building. Arthur Griffith was elected president of the Dáil. He formed a caretaker government without de Valera's opposition party, which had refused to take the Oath of Allegiance and enter the Dáil, and began the painstaking process of taking over from the British. Augusta relished the opportunity to put her 'hand to the rebuilding of Ireland' and went to Dublin to see if she could revive the pre-war idea of handing over the Abbey Theatre to the new state.[1]

Dublin was *en fête* in January 1922, the crowds out to see off the Black and Tans and welcome released prisoners. Augusta was confronted by a long line of the latter when she entered the hall of the Gresham Hotel. Her response was to question one – she discovered they had not been tried – and to buy them cigarettes. Despite the celebrations it was impossible to ignore the rumble of gathering opposition. Augusta, despite all her support for the Treaty, was transfixed by the republicans. She was unable to demonise de Valera whom she thought honest and idealistic. She was also critical of the Treaty, telling Yeats 'I feel tilted towards the republican side by those clauses that must be swallowed – the oath that will be taken insincerely by all but the two Trinity TDs, & that preposterous Governor-General who will be but a fly-paper for the vulgar.'[2] She would eventually characterise the alternatives, both aiming at a republic, as passion (republicans) versus patience (Free State).[3] She saw clearly that it was means rather than ends that were at issue, something that became obscured as the two sides rapidly acquired conflicting political identities.

She visited Edward Martyn, now crippled with rheumatism. His village hall had been burnt down in October 1920, and both Tulira and his Dublin flat had been raided by the Black and Tans because of his connections with Sinn Féin. Now he supported the Treaty and abused de Valera.[4] On a brief visit to London, Augusta entertained Richard to a Charlie Chaplin film, lunched with Shaw who firmly and humorously refused to visit Ireland, declaring he would be treated as the common enemy, and saw Blunt who told her she had done more for Ireland than anyone else. Unknown to them it was to be their last meeting.[5]

Augusta was back at Coole by the end of January, and on 27 March Yeats arrived. It was his first visit since the summer of 1919, and something of their former companionship was revived, even though for much of the time he was staying in a finally inhabitable Ballylee, and George and the children (Michael was born in August 1921) were there, too. Yeats was prospering. The literary successes of recent years had been cemented by a successful tour of America in 1920. Roles were subtly reversed with Augusta, at least when they were in Dublin or London. He was now indisputably the stronger of the two. Literary success had brought financial buoyancy, and Yeats enjoyed the opportunity this presented to live well. He wore well-tailored three-piece suits in soft greys, often with a bow tie and, with his head of grey hair and tall figure now fuller and weightier, his physical presence matched his growing literary stature. His conversation still dazzled, and he found that he could increasingly command the attention of the vivacious and more liberated young women that were appearing in the shorter and skimpier garments of the 1920s. He regularly used the Savile Club as his London base, and when Augusta visited Dublin he entertained her in the commodious and elegant, 82 Merrion Square, whose lease George bought in spring 1922. In the next years it would become a latter-day Ca' Capello for Augusta.

In December 1922 Yeats, who was far less ambiguous about the Treaty than Augusta and frankly desirous of playing a role in the new government, would accept an invitation to join the Irish Senate, putting him in the unusual position of being both an artist and patron of artists, and setting him firmly on the side of the new establishment. The intense spiritualist sessions with George had been sustained (they ceased in the summer of 1922) and, apart from quickening his work, had helped, according to his biographer, Brenda Maddox, to produce his children. But at Coole Yeats seemed to revert to his old self as he found it still to be a quiet and peaceful haven (he wrote a new song for their play, *Pot of Broth*), and as Augusta slipped into her customary habits of typing for him and reading to him in the evenings.[6]

Their rapprochement was helped by the fact that they were both working on autobiographies.[7] Augusta, working intermittently on hers since 1918, had been spurred on since making her agreement with Margaret in the summer of 1921, hoping its publication would help to pay the rents, rates and taxes at Coole. She was finding it a very difficult and dispiriting project. As she had done with other non-fiction works she selected and typed extracts from letters and journal entries, concerned to give an accurate impression of the past.[8]

Augusta's autobiography is in many ways a highly unsatisfactory account of her life. With the extracts cut, spliced, reassembled, and not fully (sometimes not even) identified (she did not reference them), the result could be misleading. Further, as political events, the role and status of friends and even jokes are often merely alluded to without explanation the reader is admitted into a bewildering, multifaceted world, by turns diverted and bored. Augusta also exercised considerable self-censorship. She protected her privacy, most obviously by making no mention of her affair with Blunt, and she underplayed her own role for the usual motives: she did not want to be seen to be putting herself forward; she tried to prioritise Yeats; she tried to practice selflessness. Obsessed with the idea that she should have a unifying theme, she had decided that her work and life had drawn significance from being dedicated to Ireland. Although she included much material which did not directly relate to Ireland such as her London life with William, her nationalist perspective encouraged her to exclude details which told against the story she wanted to convey. Her attitude to Catholics, for example, is missing.[9]

Yeats's memoirs were almost the opposite of Augusta's; he was discussing personal relationships and was even frank about sexual matters (he expected the memoirs to be published posthumously), and he was reworking his material to give an account of Irish history in which he played a central role.[10] Both of these elements in his memoirs draw attention to the deficiencies in Augusta's which she felt. She was typing out his 'The Trembling of the Veil', and wrote wistfully to Quinn: 'I am discouraged by reading Yeats's Memories, for he is making a wonderful piece of tapestry, of homogeneous work, that will stand with his other work. Mine is in lumps, in patches. It can't be helped. To do this in his method, even if I could do it well, I should have to sacrifice too many documents, bits of diaries, of letters, that have some value and vividness and even some historical interest.'[11] Her inability to create an integrated account of her life is an interesting comment on that life; as an Anglo-Irish nationalist with connections in both the British Establishment and the Irish literary scene, her experience had been unusually disjointed and at times apparently contradictory. Making sense of this herself without a distancing perspective was an almost impossible task.

It was the rich encyclopaedic quality of her life and its moments of historical importance that interested Yeats, and, from 8 to 18 June, alone at Coole with Augusta, he listened carefully as she regularly read her manuscript to him. She was eager for any encouragement, while also regarding Yeats as a mediator with a younger generation, and many of his criticisms were immediately incorporated chorus-like into her text.[12]

Initiatives and optimism were difficult to sustain in 1922 when the newspapers were reporting a persistent instability which constantly threatened to topple over into civil war. In April IRA Irregulars seized the Four Courts in Dublin while at Coole, although people had trenchant opinions about the Treaty, it was struggles over land which posed the greatest threat. On the evening of 10 April Augusta interviewed a particularly bitter man, angry about land he wanted that had been sold to another. In an attempt to shame him, she calmly showed how easy it would be to shoot her through the unshuttered window as she sat writing at her lighted table in the evening.[13] Sixteen years later Yeats included this in his poem, 'Beautiful Lofty Things', adding ten years to her age, evoking her quiet, instinctive courage and making it a defining incident of the period, 'a thing never known again'.

In Gort the polarisation of the army was manifest by 18 April, with Free State soldiers occupying the workhouse and the Irregulars the barracks. On 7 May Guy Gough, lunching at Coole, told Augusta that Roxborough had been requisitioned for refugees from Belfast and her nephew, Arthur (a survivor of the First World War; he had recently surprised Augusta by expressing his faith in the new Dáil) and his daughter, Kathie, had been forced out.[14] A week later one of the soldiers, at Coole about another theft from her harness room, had a polite conversation with Augusta in which he said Arthur, a freemason (news to Augusta) who could pressurise the government, had been victimised as a result of random selection; his name had been picked out of a bag. The soldier, distancing his men from the previous raiders, promised they would hand the house back. Augusta prided herself on being on good terms with both sides.[15] 'All one is afraid of is the thieving gang that takes advantage of the political split to benefit themselves,' she stressed to Quinn. The soldiers left in mid-June.

On 12 May Augusta was woken in the middle of the night by men hammering on the hall door at Coole.[16] As she waited at the foot of the stairs expecting them to break through the unshuttered window, she reassured herself that it was right that she should suffer as so many others had done. She later discovered that the men were the two accused of the harness room robbery, one of whom was the son of the gamekeeper, Mike John. Mike John was old and faithful – he was accustomed to sleeping in the house when Lady Gregory was alone, and had been with her that night – but his sons were rebelling against the traditional hold of Coole, and had for two weeks prevented their father from entering his own house.[17]

Augusta was nervous of these men. When she told Yeats about the incident the following day (he was sitting for Theodore Spicer Simson who was doing a portrait medal of him; Simson also did one of Augusta) he arranged for Free State soldiers to sleep in the house. It was a turning point for her. Although she had admitted to fear after Margaret's ambush, this was the first time she had sought protection. A year later Augusta would still be lying in bed listening for a knock on the door even though she knew one of the men was in gaol and the other in the civic guard.

The civil war was finally precipitated by the attack on the Four Courts by the Free State army with the aid of British guns on 28 June. On 2 July Augusta could see smoke over Gort from the barracks, burnt out and abandoned by the Irregulars. Then came the horribly familiar isolation: blocked roads, and lack of newspapers or post, the losing count of time, terrible news coming by word of mouth. After Michael Collins was shot in an ambush in County Cork on 22 August a new wave of cruelty was unleashed, and ambushes and reprisals held everyone in their grip for the winter and spring of 1923. There were bombs in Gort and houses burnt. Kiltartan Bridge was blown up, and so, on 19 August, was the bridge by Yeats's tower. He had been warned, and the family had time to take shelter in a distant room.

Terrible for Augusta was Margaret's decision to keep the children in England for the summer of 1922. 'I did not know I should feel it so much. I had been hoping against hope they could come. My strength gave way, I had to lie down for a while, trying to realise it and not to break down. Then I wrote to M. making the best of it,' she wrote on receiving the letter.[18] Afterwards she went outside and heard that a man had been shot because of some division of land and felt, sadly, that Margaret was vindicated.

Wilfrid Scawen Blunt died on 10 September. Augusta did not reveal her emotional reaction in her correspondence, merely telling Quinn in December that Blunt's death broke a forty-year friendship, but that she could not have wished him to linger on in pain.[19] It was a momentous thing. There would be no more letters in his familiar hand, no more writing to that particular source of sympathy, no more opportunities to share her thoughts and activities with her old friend who knew so much about her.

There were a few details from his last days to comfort her. Dorothy wrote that he had been thinking of Ireland, and Augusta inherited his prison Bible which may have come as a welcome symbol of resilience for her during the civil war.[20] When she visited the silent Newbuildings in May 1923 to look through his diaries prior to publication, Dorothy told her that he, a Catholic, had asked for a priest near the end, and Augusta recalled Sir William's observation when Blunt was renouncing Christianity: 'You will see Wilfrid will die with the wafer in his mouth.' 'And so it has happened', she added, not without a hint of feeling betrayed.[21]

The children finally returned to Coole a week before Christmas, 'well and bright, happy and simple as ever', she noted with joy in her journal. In January and February 1923 the houses of several of Augusta's Anglo-Irish friends were burnt, including Horace Plunkett's, Kilteragh, and George Moore's Moore Hall. The Connemara home of the surgeon, Oliver St John Gogarty (1878–1957), a friend who had contributed plays to the Abbey, was burnt on 19 February. He was later kidnapped, but escaped by jumping into the Liffey. In late March the Abbey, which had been closed because of curfews for much of 1920 and 1921, received a letter from the Irregulars ordering it to close. After Robinson rang the government there was a guard during performances.

Augusta longed for peace. She was reading the Spanish-American philosopher, George Santayana, on war and peace and, as usual, the Bible. On 3 December 1922 she woke with a strong impression of the divinity of Christ – 'Whatever the Church's faults, there is no such manifestation of the Divine as Christ' – and of his life as an exemplar for people to follow.[22] This conviction, which had always been an important part of her life, now had an intensified meaning for her. Her spiritual antennae had become more sensitive and she also became more receptive to Yeats's beliefs.

In their times together in the next few years the conversation would often turn to things spiritual. In November 1923 she recorded a random thought which resonates with Yeats's theology: '. . . if there is in us all some atom of the Divine flame, that must be imperishable – must unite again sooner or later with that flame. And what does it matter if the atom keeps its individuality for a while after death from the world or goes back to the Divine soul?'[23] The shock and profound disappointment of the civil war – the hellish return to violence – undoubtedly inspired this spiritualism in Augusta. It allowed her to retain the optimism that was her lifeblood and to continue to imagine a bright future for Ireland. With such beliefs she could bypass the either/or of the civil war and focus on the soul of Ireland. Two things, Ireland's fate and the divinity in man, dwelt within her, and out of them she would produce her two last, not great, but extraordinary plays.

On the other hand, true to her ambition to effect practical changes, Augusta could not ignore the political choice that proclaimed itself in every action of the civil war. In January 1923 she wrote to Russell suggesting an ideological solution to the deadlock of conflict: Republicans '*Gan molais*', 'without malice' could lead Ireland out of the bind of civil war. The idea, from old Irish poetry, and inspired, too, by

Christ's command to Love Thy Neighbour, could, she thought, be adopted by both sides, nullify the need to fight and form the basis for a peaceful state. She regarded it as a practical proposition, presenting it at an evening gathering at Russell's house in Dublin, where it was lightly dismissed as a good idea.[24] By the time of the August elections she had begun to hope that de Valera would be the apostle of '*gan molais*'. She criticised the government for preventing de Valera from declaring his policy and for continuing to support the 'insincere' oath, and did not vote for either side.[25]

There was one bright light in the gloom of the spring of 1923. On 12 April the Abbey opened with a new play, *The Shadow of a Gunman*. A tragedy set in a Dublin tenement in May 1920 during the Anglo-Irish War, it was a welcome satire on the cult of violence, 'a play of disillusion for people who have been disillusioned', as the *Irish Statesman* remarked.[26] With its cast of Dublin characters from subtly different social and political backgrounds, its snatches of republican song and phraseology, its local dialogue, it was in some ways an up-to-date urban version of Augusta's plays. Augusta was there, and the author, Seán O'Casey (1880–1964), more used to the company of labourers than theatre people, was in the wings. On the second and third night, the auditorium fuller, Augusta made him sit in the stalls. On the fourth night, when the queue wound round the block, she swept him up to look at the crowds, and as they watched they talked, easily and fluently. Thus began a new friendship.

O'Casey was 43 and this was his first successful play. Socially and culturally he (always referred to as Casey by Augusta) was far removed from Lady Gregory. He had been brought up in a large, poor, lower middle-class family that had suffered financially and socially after the death of his father, but had been kept afloat by his hard-working, resilient mother. Literature, discovered alone, was a passion pursued in the evening after earning his living as a labourer. He was involved in James Larkin's Irish Transport and General Workers' Union and the Gaelic League, and put his nationalism after his class loyalty. A poor Protestant in a country where the majority of Protestants were wealthy, he was on many counts an outsider. Photographs from this period, taken without his glasses, show an intense and worried young man with uncertain, watchful eyes under dark eyebrows, thin purposeful lips, sparse hair. There is an impression of coiled energy.

Augusta had recognised O'Casey's potential eighteen months earlier when she read *The Crimson in the Tri-colour*. It was one of hundreds of manuscript plays that had come to her over the years, which she read, commented on and passed on to the other directors.[27] O'Casey had accepted Abbey rejection of two earlier plays, but when *Crimson* was returned with comments he, harbouring sufficient pride and anger to support his work, refused to alter it. It was his first clash with the Abbey system. Augusta had been the director who most wanted to encourage O'Casey, and on 10 November 1921 had told him she thought he could write. He also remembered her saying that his strength was characterisation. From then on he treasured a memory of empathetic Lady Gregory.

In the chapter 'Blessed Bridget O'Coole' of the *Inishfallen, Fare Thee Well* volume of his autobiography, O'Casey has given a new insight into Augusta. Instead of focusing on the heavy black of her clothes he noticed the 'gay . . . touch of something white under a long, soft, black silk veil', and the accent of a 'shy' brooch; rich textures and colours that others seemed to miss. He observed with delight the apparent contradictions in her: the rugged, peasant face that emerged from aristocratic clothes, the unexpected humour about her eyes. 'She looked like an old, elegant nun of a new order, a blend of the Lord Jesus Christ and of Puck, an order that Ireland had never known before, and wasn't likely to know again for a long time to come.'[28] This is reminiscent of Yeats in 'Beautiful Lofty Things', although Yeats always saw her as a relic of an old order that was dying out.

For her part Augusta was inspired by O'Casey. While he registered the achievement of *The Shadow of the Gunman* with detachment, Lady Gregory was brimful of exuberance and, enjoying her enjoyment, he responded loquaciously. In an excited journal paragraph of questions and quoted answers she recorded their conversation: he had lost his religion; he was a socialist; they both loved the beauty of biblical language; they concurred on the importance of a self-directed education. They flattered each other. She reiterated her belief in his writing, and he replied, 'All the thought in Ireland for years past has come through the Abbey. You have no idea what an education it has been to the country.'[29] O'Casey was in fact the embodiment of the theatre's success to date, just the person that Yeats and Augusta had set out to produce in 1897. Now the success of his play was averting a financial crisis. No wonder Augusta was jubilant.

On 24 May de Valera ordered a ceasefire. It held, and marked the end of the war. However, the bitterness and fear of those months persisted, only very, very gradually loosening their hold in the country. The day after the ceasefire Augusta discovered a hard lump under her left breast.[30] On 2 May she had gone to London to stay with Margaret at her new house, River Court, on the Thames at

Hammersmith, bringing Richard whom she took to Harrow School. Now she consulted two doctors who told her it was not malignant and to wait six weeks. Instead, she went to her friend, the surgeon Oliver St John Gogarty. Although he, too, considered it benign his advice was 'Get it out'. She went straight to Dublin with Gogarty and booked herself into 96 Lower Leeson Street, a Georgian house near St Stephen's Green then converted into a private hospital, referred to as a nursing home. There she was put into the care of Dr Slattery, a surgeon at the Richmond Hospital, who, the same age as Robert, had served in the army medical corps during the war. He was a gentle, considerate man, whom she would come to know well.[31] He told her that her whole breast would need to be removed. She was shocked, but controlled herself. 'I think I have no dread at all of death, but I don't want to be cut up and become a nuisance,' she wrote calmly in her journal. The next day, after being refused tea and offered a priest, it was '"Theatre" and scaffold'. The mastectomy was performed with only a local anaesthetic. 'I was able to keep a face of courage and ask Gogarty about his feelings when being kidnapped,' she reported: '. . . some pain and at the last I fainted.' Afterwards she felt the exhilaration of having survived before she endured a slow recovery.

The first days were spent in the nursing home listening, through the traffic, to the dying sounds of the civil war: an explosion somewhere in the distance, firing in the streets nearby, news of the hunt for de Valera. Yeats was a daily visitor, bringing accounts of Senate meetings. Once Slattery had removed the stitches from her arm she was able to move to 82 Merrion Square and luxuriate in the quiet. By 12 June she was embarking on short walks with Yeats. On the 15th she signed a letter from the Abbey written by Robinson asking the government for a subsidy.

Back at Coole with Yeats she wrote letters and watered seedlings. By 22 June she was alone, apart from the servants. She was still easily tired, but 'My mind is turning again towards a Passion Play . . . to do it I must be . . . moved by invisible hands,' she wrote in her journal.[32]

It was an old idea, first presented to her by Yeats in the early days of her playwriting. No doubt her conversations with Shaw about how to write a religious play – he was writing *Saint Joan* – during a visit just before her operation had had its effect.[33] Now the subject claimed her. There was no element of duty or commission in the writing of this play; she was not even sure the Abbey would mount a religious play. It was written out of conviction, artistic compulsion, and with growing reverence for the subject.[34]

It took more than two months to write, and even in early September after the elections, when she had finished, her mind was still full of the play: 'I keep wondering what Christ would do were he here now, and it all seems to go back to "love worketh no ill to his neighbour" and the forgiveness of your brother's trespasses.'[35]

That Augusta's mind was on Ireland as she wrote out the story of the betrayal and crucifixion of Jesus is evident from her inclusion of the character Joel, an idealistic and largely ignorant young Jewish boy from the mountains who supports Christ because he interprets his revolutionary message as an appeal for a political uprising against the Roman occupation of Judea.[36]

At the first performance on 15 April 1924 Maud Gonne readily perceived a republican sympathy in the play. But Augusta intended no straightforward support for the idealists. Joel, disillusioned when he learns that Christ in fact respected Ceasar, is the first to shout 'crucify him'. Then, as Jesus goes to his death, Joel repents of his betrayal: 'That's the way of it! All the generations looking for him and praying for him. We wanted him, and we got him, and what we did with him was to kill him. And that is the way it will be ever and always, so long as leaves grow upon the trees!'[37] Here is the bitterness Augusta experienced during the civil war. In a letter to John Quinn written on 5 October 1923 she told him that the play was a study of Christ's enemies, 'of the rabble, and of the various interests that brought Him to His death'. If Christ was analogous to Ireland, then she was expressing her great disillusionment that no one had had Ireland's interest at heart.

There is, however, a redemptive element in the play. A chorus of three unnamed, politically uninvolved women steadily express their belief in Christ's goodness. They are joined by St Brigit, the Irish saint, described in Irish folklore as the Celtic Mary who fostered Christ. St Brigit articulates Augusta's hope: 'He is clean gold. Surely, there will never be any man east or west will refuse to forgive another, where our Lord gave forgiveness to his enemies.'[38] Augusta called the play *The Story Brought by Brigit*, expressing the idea that the redemption of Christ's death is being related specifically to the Irish at a needful moment in their history.

The play did not alter Augusta's reputation as a gifted writer of comedy, but it struck a chord with her contemporaries in the theatre. Yeats, who told her it showed great intellectual power, thought it was the best thing she had done. 'This is a real compliment to be thankful for at my three score years!' she told Quinn, knocking ten years off her age.[39] Robinson, given to a certain theatrical loviness, came up to her afterwards with outstretched arms saying, 'Thank you, thank you' with, she noted, 'real emotion'.[40]

The critics were far more cautious. Reading the reviews one feels that they were constrained by the fact that it was a religious play, but that they saw that the subject did not bring out the best in Lady Gregory. However, the *Times Literary Supplement* observed that Lady Gregory had refined the Kiltartan dialect so that it could be 'strange like poetry and useful like plain speech,' and for Augusta it was a moment of profound peace and contentment.

TWENTY-FOUR

Last Years

Planting roses against the house and in borders today – as if I were going to live for ever!

17 December 1929, *LGJ*, II

Augusta was 71 when the civil war ended. She would see nine years of peaceful independent Ireland. Her health would gradually fail and her contemporaries die, but there would be several years of vigour in which she responded wholeheartedly to the challenges posed by new circumstances. Then there would be the final years of stoicism made bearable by the presence of Yeats.

With the end of the civil war came a second chance to rebuild Ireland. W.T. Cosgrave had launched Cumann na nGaedheal in the spring of 1923 as a rallying point for supporters of the Treaty. Gaining 63 seats in the August elections the party was able to dominate in the absence of Sinn Féin, which had refused to take its seats. The fledgling state was governed by the Catholic upper middle classes who were not averse to maintaining many of the institutions and much of the style (with prestigious social events and the quasi-viceregal Governor General) of the British administration, while applying a strongly Catholic stamp. The Anglo-Irish still had a role: many of the 16 senators nominated by the government were drawn from that class, but the Senate had no real power. The Free State government maintained an intransigent intolerance of the republican opposition which still claimed to be the legitimate government. The result was continued official wariness in the face of continued violence. With the draconian Public Safety Act of 1923 prisoners captured during the civil war remained behind bars without trial, and suspects continued to be arrested in the interest of public safety.

Senator Yeats was an enthusiastic player in this. Although he found himself opposed to the government on particular issues (most famously over divorce), overall he agreed with the government's aims and was prepared to be involved in realpolitik. Augusta's commitment was to the resolution of differences between the Free State government and the republicans. She disliked what she called angry voices raised against republicans, and hoped, without a clear idea how it could be achieved, for an amendment to the oath that would allow the republicans to take it with a clear conscience and enter government.

In June 1925 the chairman of the Senate, Lord Glenavy, impressed by Augusta's diligence, string-pulling and stamina in conjunction with her campaign for the Lane pictures, suggested that she stand for the Senate. She disliked the idea, still resistant to becoming involved in politics, but was tempted by the prospect of being of use, by the salary and by the contact with her contemporaries. She stood, but unfortunately Yeats's mishandling of the details prevented her from getting a seat, and in the end she felt she had been rebuffed.[1]

The political differences between Augusta and Yeats emerged in November 1923 when the condition of more than 400 republican prisoners, who had gone on hunger strike in October, suddenly worsened.[2] Yeats, taking the government's line that the republicans should be opposed whatever the cost, and accepting that the government's accusations should remain secret, was vehemently against any outside intervention. Augusta thought this an irresponsible use of power. She wrote to the Irish press with Lennox Robinson, appealing to the Christian conscience of the government and asking for concessions from both sides. Diplomatically she offered to leave Yeats's house where she was staying, but he was adamant that she remain, even telling her that he thought she had perhaps acted rightly. The letter was printed on 13 November. On 20 November the first prisoner died, but after the second death on 23 November the strike was called off. Augusta's stance seems naive next to Yeats's more realistic appraisal of the situation, but one can admire the way she held tenaciously to her hope that differences could be resolved, and her faith that she could appeal to this latent belief in others, knowing that she might alienate both sides. It was the more traditional role of the artist.

That November Yeats was awarded the Nobel Prize for Literature. Augusta, glad and proud, observed with some amusement to Quinn that it had greatly improved her reputation among the remaining County Galway Anglo-Irish. All those years of entertaining 'revolutionaries' and mere writers instead of having regular country-house parties seemed worthwhile in their eyes now that one had achieved fame and fortune.[3] Augusta was not one to insist on her rights, but she was alarmed when, in March, she read in the text of his acceptance speech that he had described her as 'An old woman sinking into the infirmities of age'. 'Not even fighting against them,' she complained in her journal.[4] In a month's time *The Story Told by Brigit* was to open at the Abbey, and Lennox Robinson agreed with her that the description implied she 'had gone silly' and would lower her market value. Yeats consented to take the phrase out, but it was too late. It was a not uncharacteristic failure of Yeats to consider Lady Gregory's feelings.

Edward Martyn died on 6 December 1923. Unable to visit him at Tulira since early June 1922 because of a broken bridge, Augusta was unprepared for the immobile figure she saw through the library window as she drew up in a chauffeured car on 8 September on her way home from visiting Arabella in Galway.[5] He was severely crippled with arthritis, disabled after a paralysing stroke and had sunk into himself, hardly registering her presence when she came into the bare room (he had given his books to the Carmelites in Dublin). Full of pity that there was no one to care enough to arrange for medical attention in a nursing home, she wrote to Lady Hemphill (the wife of his heir) who got a priest and a doctor. It was her last neighbourly act. He died three months later after an operation. His death prompted Augusta to meditate on the way their lives had been linked over the last 40 years, for, despite their differences, their links had remained strong.[6]

There were still long stretches at Coole for Augusta. She kept herself busy with Lane and theatre correspondence, wrote long letters to Quinn, and diligently typed out her memoirs. She was always glad when the children were at home. They were now rumbustious 14, 12 and 10-year-olds – the girls at school in Folkestone – who climbed trees to dizzy heights, took boats onto the lake, tormented the gardeners, rode their own ponies. Anne was allowed to hitch up a barely broken-in pony to a trap to take a neighbour to Mass; it shied at the first car, throwing the woman and destroying the trap.[7] Their wildness was on display when they first encountered Yeats's pale, well-dressed, bookish, children at Ballylee. Michael and Anne attracted taunts from the Gregory girls who crowned their jibing by stuffing mud into the horrified Michael's puck-like ears, procuring a banning from Ballylee.

It was not all childish fun: Richard shot woodcock, Anne shot pheasants and rabbits. When she was still quite young (about 12, she claimed in *Me and Nu*), Anne applied for a driving licence under her own name, Augusta Anne Gregory, conscious that it could be confused with her grandmother's, and drove Coole's Model T Ford into County Clare, on which journey Augusta, sitting in the back, received a broken nose and several broken teeth when she was thrown onto the bar of the hood. But she did not insist that Anne have lessons, partly out of ignorance of their necessity, partly from her desire not to restrain the children.

On 7 March 1924, after two months alone at Coole, Augusta went to a performance of O'Casey's *Juno and the Paycock*. The theatre was packed, there was a long queue at the door, and the play, set during the Anglo-Irish war with its message that there is something ('the teaching of Christ,' she whispered to O'Casey, 'Of humanity,' he replied) beyond the 'murderous hatred', seemed a perfect expression of her own beliefs. All this made her say to Yeats, 'This is one of the evenings at the Abbey that makes me glad to have been born.'[8]

Afterwards, finding O'Casey in the Green Room, they talked about his literary progress, his daytime labouring and his single room. Two days later O'Casey went with her to one of Yeats's recently revived Monday evening gatherings in Merrion Square where they found Gogarty and George Russell. Augusta enjoyed the political arguments, but when the conversation turned to hashish she encouraged O'Casey, nervous in this unfamiliar sophisticated company, to tell her about his experience during the Easter Rising. She felt close to O'Casey, but she was also consciously choosing to be with a young writer and an outsider, rather than cultivating the politicians and administrators that Yeats would have introduced her to.

O'Casey made his first visit to Coole in June. She met him at Athenry station, and they travelled together to Gort. Their accounts – Augusta's journal, O'Casey's autobiography – indicate how their unlikely friendship developed.[9] Each, acutely aware of the other's social position, and wishing to penetrate the respective citadel, was willing to suspend habitual class-based judgements and allow a certain self-deception where the other was concerned. So O'Casey, usually intolerant of aristocratic privilege and behaviour, allowed himself to be charmed by her ability to sit elegantly at ease in a third-class train compartment, while Augusta swallowed several unlikely stories from O'Casey, including the tale that he had not learnt to read until he was in his teens.

Once at Coole the need for subtle changes became apparent. O'Casey, an object of fascination for Catherine and Anne who marvelled at his Dublin accent, had to learn how to use the cutlery at dinner, and relax on sofas while she read to him. Their conversation lapped about the routine at Coole and continued in letters and meetings that autumn. Augusta was curious about communism. O'Casey was emerging from a more radical period and was critical of the destructiveness of a workers' revolution, and Augusta often found she could agree with him. He told her that the republican Liam Mellow was a communist, and that the trade union leader, Jim Larkin, was to him the embodiment of a humane socialism. Augusta sometimes tried too hard to please. When she praised Upton Sinclair's *Singing Jailbirds*, a sentimental play about the working class, O'Casey put her in her place, telling her that working-class misery is far more prevalent among those at home, isolated and unemployed, than among the jailed.[10] He himself wanted to write a Labour play inspired, Augusta noted with satisfaction, by 'my *Brigit* the idea of one man giving himself for the people'.[11]

There was a remarkable flow of confidences. It was unusual for Augusta to open herself up to someone she hardly knew, while O'Casey spoke of his mother and his feelings in a way that was probably unprecedented for him, and not repeated until he met his future wife two years later. Over this time they gradually defined their shared interests, and discovered a shared sense of humour, although as O'Casey's letters reveal he maintained a respectful tone towards her.[12] Like Yeats and Synge, O'Casey wandered the Coole woods at will; unlike Yeats, O'Casey noticed the people who worked at Coole and his letters often ended by sending them his best wishes.One hot afternoon at Coole O'Casey found a heath covered in shimmering blue butterflies. It was a spot and a vision he felt sure Yeats had never seen, and one suspects that they symbolised for him his sense of a unique access to Lady Gregory.

Arabella died in March. The burden of dealing with the will and funeral arrangements fell on Augusta. Reading a poem by Katherine Tynan she was aware of feeling not sadness, but a calm assurance that Arabella had sailed from her Galway house by the quays to meet her dead relatives in heaven. This image of the sentient dead and the family united in heaven recalls the sonnets she wrote for Blunt in 1883 in which she evoked her dead sister, Gertrude, troubled by Augusta's love affair.

When Augusta was taken to see Arabella's grave in Galway's Protestant graveyard, with its view of the silver sea and distant Burren and Connemara hills, she decided that if she died at Coole she would be buried there.[13] She did not appear to entertain the idea of joining Sir William in the Coole mausoleum, even though it was traditional for a wife to be buried with her husband, as her mother had been in the family burial place at Roxborough. This was possibly because the monument was no longer part of the estate, but had been vested in the church in Gort and fenced off during the sale of lands in 1920.[14] Roxborough, reoccupied by soldiers, was not an option. Her body was, in a sense, homeless. The problem might have symbolised the tragedy of her position to a more melancholy person. But Augusta, wishing for an open motor rather than a gloomy hearse to carry her to the Galway graveyard, saw an opportunity for a new expression of herself. She spent the following month dismantling Arabella's house and arranging an auction, which took place just six months after the auctioning of the contents of Castle Taylor.

That summer John Quinn died; he was 54. Augusta had no idea he was near death. On 28 November 1923, referring to his eye trouble and a fall (there had been no recurrence of the cancer operated on in early 1918), she had written: 'Fifty-three seems very young to me, and you must keep yourself in "the youth of middle age" by regular rests and change of scene.'

Quinn was still unmarried, but was now the constant companion of Mrs Jeanne Robert Foster, his secretary and mistress. Mrs Foster noted his constant tiredness and weight loss, while he worked doggedly, increasingly ill and frightened. On 10 May he wrote to Augusta vaguely hinting at a liver tumour, but assuring her it was benign.[15] As his health declined rapidly in May and June, and Mrs Foster knew the cancer had reasserted itself, Augusta was still sending him detailed letters about her activities. On 11 July, when he was barely acknowledging the presence of Jeanne Foster let alone able to read letters, Augusta ended her letter innocently, 'Keep well and let me have a line sometimes.' She wrote again on 27 July giving legal details about the Lane pictures, 'as you will be interested in the legal aspect'.[16] He never received it. He died on 28 July. Augusta got a telegram from his clerk the following day. 'A great blow . . . America will seem very distant now without that warm ready sympathy and interest. The children will miss their Christmas apples. So my day and night have been sad and I am heavy hearted.' She had lost a stabilising influence on her life and the presence of someone whom she could rely on to be, in every case, on her side. A few days later she learnt that Isabella Gardner had died; another connection with America severed.

Augusta was in London in July as a guest of PEN, an international association of writers set up three years previously. As usual, although nervous in anticipation, she enjoyed the event, sitting next to the president, the novelist John Galsworthy, whom she had met the previous day at Harrow Speech Day. He told the 175 assembled writers that Lady Gregory '*is* Lady Gregory – that is the best thing I can say'.[17]

Augusta found it hard to settle to any work that summer. She typed her diaries joylessly and rummaged through old notes with an idea for a play, but it came to nothing. She read regular issues of *Sinn Féin*, and embarked on *War and Peace* which distracted her from worry about the Lane pictures. In October she went to see the ruins of Roxborough with her grand niece, Kathie.[18] Arthur and Kathie had returned to Roxborough after their stay at the Shelbourne Hotel in May 1922, but had been forced out by armed Irregulars. Later, the Free State government pressurised the Irregulars to go. Augusta and the steward's wife suspected that if Arthur had returned then the house might still be there. But Arthur and Kathie had not gone back and, by April 1924, the house had been pillaged and burnt, probably, they speculated, by a destructive breakaway group.[19] Augusta was struck by the silence that hung about the vast array of buildings: 'All silent that had been so full of life and stir in my childhood, and never deserted until now.' The land outside the walls had been sold, and she knew as she stood there that the ruined house would never be rebuilt. Some phloxes were flowering gaily in the weed-choked garden and she took them for Coole.

Augusta's passion for the Abbey never waned, despite having less feeling for the plays of the later Abbey than the earlier 'folk theatre'. 'She loved the Abbey more than I could to the very last, & always went there straight from the train,' Yeats wrote after her death.[20] She oversaw the mortgaging of the buildings and furniture and she campaigned with Yeats to receive a government subsidy, although her first thought after independence in 1922 had been to hand over the theatre to the state.[21] In early 1925 Ernest Blythe, Minister for Finance, finally offered the directors £850 a year towards performances, and the Abbey became the first state-endowed theatre in the English-speaking world. The price was the appointment of a new director, George O'Brien, a staunch Catholic and an economist, there, at least in Augusta's view, to strengthen their financial side.[22]

Inevitably, given her age and less frequent attendance in Dublin, Augusta's artistic influence slipped and, in the autumn of 1924, there was a humiliating argument with Yeats (supported by Robinson) who thought that *The Image* was too long and slow for a revival. 'And what of the losses on his plays, even outside the staging, that did not fall on the Theatre or him, but on me,' she grumbled in her journal. She was, however, placated by the manager, and the play was staged.

O'Casey, the young poet Lyle Donaghy, and Jack Yeats were allies. Jack, now a well-regarded painter, had come to Coole the previous October after an absence of many years, and Augusta had discovered his republican sympathies; her politics were now closer to his than to Willie's. Augusta occasionally met the three younger men in a café near the theatre to read their plays and poems and talk politics. She enjoyed their vivacity and involvement. On 30 November 1924 she compared them to the dispossessed aristocrats she met at Lady Ardilaun's post-matinee party at 42 St Stephen's Green. Augusta admired Lady Ardilaun, 'a "grande dame" all through', now a wealthy childless widow whose childhood home had been burnt and whose friends had left Ireland, but who had translated her despair into artistic patronage, especially of the Abbey, and help for the poor. But her Anglo-Irish guests complained that there were no jobs for their sons, that their houses were ruined and that it was futile to rebuild them in the absence of Society: '. . . it was like a change of plays at the Abbey, from my intercourse with what I may call progressives, Jack and the others last night, and the actors in the greenroom, all living in a world that is alive, and these in a decaying one. A sort of *ancien régime* party, a lament for banished society.'[23]

During the spring of 1925 Augusta interrupted routine work on her folklore and journals to write her last original performable play, inspired by the thought of bringing heaven to earth that she had been left with after finishing *Brigit*.[24] When it was finished she was alternately discouraged by Yeats's criticisms, depressed by a tepid reception from Jack and O'Casey, then bolstered by Robinson's enthusiasm.

Dave is a compact single-act miracle play about a young orphaned servant boy, who, disparaged by his fellow servants and employer, a modestly wealthy Catholic farmer, is sullen and vindictive, but, after experiencing a vision of brotherly love, leaves the house a changed man 'to give help to – my people.' The characters are not overwhelmed by the message, and there is a poignancy and interest in the writing that sets it apart from many of her other plays. She had brought Christ to Ireland in a peasant play, something she tried to conceal from Yeats until she had finished (during May he was working away in the next room, the rhythm of his work accompanying hers, as in earlier years), such plays now being on 'the Index'.

In order to give her redemptive theme full power, Augusta set the play against the harsh tragedy of the famine, something that very few people were even beginning to confront at the time, although the vivid details that Augusta supplied must have been provided by her elderly neighbours. It is possble that Augusta returned to the famine at this late stage in her life as a dying person might return to a secret guilt, desirous of making amends at least by acknowledging the tragedy before it is too late. Her linking of the famine with her vision of a future better world suggests that she now saw the famine, rather than the Land War, as the first in the series of rural tragedies from which she hoped the Free State could finally free the Irish. For Augusta, both the problem of Coole and the problem of Ireland – that it was torn in two by the civil war – were to be met and overcome by a belief in an intrinsic goodness in man, not always manifest, but there to be discovered by those with the belief. *Dave* is an expression of this. Her belief freed her from the bitterness of many of her contemporaries, of all classes and political persuasions.

In August 1925 O'Casey submitted his four-act masterpiece set in Easter Week 1916, *The Plough and the Stars*, to the Abbey. Augusta was enthusiastic, reading it out to Jack, Cottie and O'Casey who were staying at Coole. 'It is a very fine play – very terrible, very powerful – just showing where the real cruelty of war falls – in the homes,' she wrote to T.J. Kiernan, her young tax adviser who was rapidly becoming a friend.[25]

In the best Abbey tradition it provided plenty of scope for trouble, with its prostitute, its love scene, its salty language and most especially in the way it demythologised 1916. In September the new director, George O'Brien, provoked to criticism by their manager, Michael Dolan, told them that the play needed amending. Augusta, Yeats and Robinson agreed with some of his suggestions, but when he let slip that the government subsidy was dependent on the alterations they were enraged. 'I said at once our position is clear,' Augusta reported telling Yeats, 'If we have to choose between the subsidy and our freedom, it is our freedom we choose.'[26]

At a directors' meeting on 22 September in Merrion Square, Augusta, as the appointed spokesperson, successfully undermined O'Brien's self-appointed role as censor, telling him that Blythe had made no condition when he granted the subsidy and that they (well-practised in the handling of controversial material), usually made cuts in rehearsal. 'I had mistaken my position,' O'Brien repeated after them. Cuts were made, on the understanding that they were necessary to improve the play, a fact tacitly endorsed by O'Casey who did not object to them and even rewrote material.[27] It was an episode that saw Augusta at her diplomatic best.

The Abbey's 21st birthday fell in the midst of this, on 27 December. They celebrated with performances of plays by the three original directors, speeches from government representatives and one from Augusta, the only director currently not at odds with the government. It was, Lily Yeats reported, 'a charming speech, clever. She had difficulty in controlling her tears at first, the applause was so great. Her Galway voice added to the charm. She, poor woman, has suffered much in the 21 years . . .' '"Best of all I think we love the pit," Augusta had proclaimed, pausing, and adding, '"perhaps because we have had our lovers' quarrels!"' That I think was the hit of the evening,' she confided in her journal.[28]

Augusta was not at the first performances of *The Plough and the Stars* which opened on 8 February, but as she travelled to Dublin for the fifth night she read *The Irish Times* account of men and women (the latter described memorably by Hanna Sheehy-Skeffington as 'the widows of Easter Week') invading the stage to attack the actors the night before amid an uproar of stink bombs and violence. Yeats, too, had mounted the stage to claim it as a defining moment in the history of the Abbey. 'You have disgraced yourselves again. Is this to be an ever-recurring celebration of the arrival of Irish genius?' he had asked rhetorically, referring to *Playboy*.[29] The oracular phrases (written before the event) were inaudible, but he had taken the text to *The Irish Times* once the riot had started.

Augusta, scornfully dismissing the women as trivial thrill-seekers, refused to countenance a public debate: 'In *Playboy* time our opponents were men. They had a definite objective . . . These disturbers were almost all women who have made demonstrations on Poppy Day and at elections and meetings; have made a habit of it, of the excitement,' she told Yeats.[30] In fact, their message that the Easter Week revolution was sacred and that those who purported to represent the national interest should observe this (and other hallowed moments) had a momentum that would travel well into twentieth-century Ireland, scattering Irish writers in its wake. O'Casey, burnt out in futile anger in the subsequent controversy over *Plough* in newspapers and on public platforms in which writers and journalists were almost unanimously against him, and profoundly disillusioned by the behaviour of former republican friends and Abbey actors, was an early victim. Feeling he could no longer live in Dublin he left for London.

His friendship with Augusta would now be carried on through letters, and Augusta would miss him. In May, having received the proofs of Yeats's memoir, *Estrangement*, which revived memories of their close companionship with Yeats, she remarked: 'Perhaps some day suddenly again a barrier will go down and I will have made a friend. I have felt nearer it sometimes with Sean O'C. And miss him this time in Dublin.'[31] They did meet in March 1926 in London when O'Casey was awarded the Hawthornden Prize for *Juno and the Paycock*. Unsure whether to accept, suffering from sore eyes, bamboozled by society invitations, depressed by hotel life, O'Casey came to Augusta's hotel where she offered sanctuary and encouraged him to accept the prize. She agreed to make a speech at the presentation and later rewrote it as an article.[32]

In the early years of her old age Augusta several times stated that she did not want to be a nuisance. Her independent spirit revolted against dependence and decrepitude. Yet it was her fate to slowly sink towards death, increasingly tormented by the pains of cancer and rheumatism, her hearing receding, her eyes weakening, gradually robbed of her ability to work, read or look after herself. It is from March 1925 that her journals began a regular noting of pain and the relief from pain. On her birthday that year she recorded that she was plagued by aches 'but fairly content in mind'. Nights where she could hardly turn in bed for agony might be followed by one that was untroubled. She was often tired, too, especially when faced with interminable Lane correspondence.

In June 1926 she consulted Gogarty about her painfully inflamed eyes. Two months later she found a new lump where the old had been, and underwent her second operation in 96 Leeson Street. 'I was laid on the table, no chloroform, just the local anaesthetic – it lasted about 20 minutes. I had not much pain, though feeling the knife working about made me feel queer.' She concentrated on imagining the passage of the river through the fields, past the buildings, over mud and under bridges at Roxborough and Coole to ward off thoughts of the knife: '. . . presently the flow of warm blood was stopped with straps and bandages, and I was given praise for courage . . . and there was but a slight feeling of faintness and then I was carried upstairs.' On his last visit before she was discharged Slattery told her she had cancer. She was accepting: 'Thank God, if so, that it is only now it has come when I have I think done my work.'[33] She went to Yeats's house to recover.

She was physically depleted by the operation but, perhaps more significantly, psychologically debilitated. This was apparent in her obsessive typing of her diaries – the work she still craved without the effort of thought. It was also apparent in her acquiescence to Margaret's final request in January 1927 that they sell all that remained of Coole.

Margaret had never settled comfortably to the arrangement of 1921 in which Augusta rented Coole from her. She still hoped to buy a house in Ireland, financed in part from the sale of Coole. Augusta, meanwhile, worried about money: her investments might lose value, her plays go out of fashion, her small farm income drop, and rates, taxes and labour costs rise.[34] Then there were visits to London for the Lane pictures where her hotel bill was two guineas a night, although the frugal eating habits of her early widowhood had been retained and now stretched to scooping the unused sugar from afternoon teas into a used envelope, a habit that dismayed her grandchildren. After doing her accounts she would gloomily contemplate the necessity of getting out her memoir. By 1925 the children were only coming to Coole for Christmas and parts of the summer. What she did not know, because he knew he could never tell her, was that Richard, like Margaret, feeling Coole was too remote, had no desire to eventually live there and farm the land. As an adult he would display far less feeling for Coole and did not treasure mementoes as his sisters did.[35]

Margaret was still capable of periodically lashing out at Augusta, but occasionally she articulated her dependence. On 24 February 1925 Augusta was touched by a letter from her daughter-in-law: 'Remember *always* that however unpleasant I may wax I couldn't possibly get on at all without you, so *please* hold on to life for ages and ages.' Augusta's response was a light-hearted listing of the infirmities of her 87-year-old brother, Edward, and the observation that Margaret could not wish her to grow that old.[36]

In January 1927 Margaret found a house near Oughterard, County Galway, and offered Coole to the government. Augusta was stoical. It was only when she found herself discussing the prices offered by the Forestry Department (£4,000 for woods, land and house) and how the furniture was to be divided between her and Margaret, and when Yeats told her that he and George had decided to give up Ballylee if Augusta left Coole, that she realised the irreversibility of what she was doing. She began to hope for just one more summer in Coole, and pleaded with Margaret to delay the auction until the autumn. Now, for the first time, in her weakness she was selfishly reluctant to let go, and she feared she was being portrayed to the children as 'the enemy'.

Margaret in her turn began to display the disregard for Coole which she had periodically threatened. Augusta acquiesced – with what reluctance she does not convey – to Margaret's request to take the library shelves for the new house (still not a certainty). But she dug her heels in over removing the stone steps leading to the front lawn: 'I was perhaps foolish but had a bad night thinking of it, the destruction being begun by us.'[37] (The steps remain to this day.) She watched as Margaret tactlessly put new pictures into the frames which had held the portraits of Sir William's Grillon Club friends.

Augusta's response to the final loss of Coole was to write what she called a farewell to the things around her; a series of essays on the rooms and gardens. She began it on 27 March 1927, and was still writing it a year later. It was therapeutic. 'I am writing now about the books given by Authors, in my white bookcase – pleasant work enough – Richard at the piano plays his chords and I feel harmony in the room', she wrote on Easter Sunday.[38] But she fretted that the work was too desultory.

The work is, in fact, sharply focused on the cultural heritage of Coole, for Augusta, in her anguish at the imminent loss, looked with appreciation and nostalgia at the books and pictures about her. However, even as she wrote she was sending books to Sotheby's for auction (for which she received £116). Yeats's approval boosted her confidence, and he would arrange for the essays on the library, woods and gardens to be published by Cuala Press in 1931.[39]

She was also writing an article, 'Clay People Long Famous', published in a design journal in New York in 1930.[40] Here she described and meditated on the series of Staffordshire pottery figures she had collected over the years and placed about Coole in apposite groupings, fascinated by the diminutive representations of great figures that had formed the background to her life: O'Connell and Peel, Parnell and Gladstone, Queen Victoria, Florence Nightingale, General Gordon. Her appreciation of these brightly coloured, enthusiastically, often clumsily worked figures is a sort of epitaph of her work, for as she was now miniaturising the great, so she had built up the historically insignificant; the first shall be last, and the last, first.

Patrick Hogan, the Galway Member of the Dáil (TD) and Minister for Agriculture, negotiated a price of £5,000 (about €399,038, £273,876 sterling) for the house and remaining lands with the Forestry Department in March. The deed of sale arrived on the 31st. 'I don't know if I shall realise then, I cannot now, that Coole has passed altogether away from us,' she wrote anxiously in her journal.[41] After witnessing Margaret's signature the next day, she went into the garden to plant bulbs.

In the end, Augusta did not have to leave. It was agreed that she remain as a caretaker, and on 7 November 1927 she signed an agreement allowing her to take over the house, gardens and yard for a rent of £100 and some fields for dairy cows for £17.[42] While she was waiting for the arrival of government representatives Augusta wrote to Yeats regretting the sale as a defeat: 'There are so few houses left, this house had such a fine tradition – I feel the children further impoverished'.[43] Ironically, it was when Coole was sold that Augusta received a visit from a representative of the Tourist Association wanting photographs of Lady Gregory, and interested in anything connected to her writing.

There were other upheavals that summer. Yeats, abroad in Spain, suffered the first of a number of serious though not satisfactorily diagnosed illnesses. January 1928 found him with George and Ezra Pound in Rapello, Italy, and with little desire to return to Ireland in the immediate future. That Christmas Augusta was consoled by her grandchildren, two of whom – Richard and Anne – had just recovered from serious operations. Richard, now 18, and still her pet ('it would set everything right if I could feel to all as I do to, say – Richard', she wrote in January 1928) had been accepted at the Royal Military Academy at Woolwich, Kent, in October.[44] Augusta, initially shocked that he was not heading for a political career, was now reconciled to his plans, reminding herself of his practical bent. He and Anne (16) drove Augusta to church in the Coole Morris-Cowley, and brought a light-hearted atmosphere to the house: 'Dancing going on as I write . . . Maurice Studdert and Anne waltzing to the music of my Christmas gramophone – very gentle dancing it looks, not so lively as the waltzes and the polkas I had sometimes watched in my youth.' When the wrenboys came on St Stephen's Day she noted that 'Kevin Barry' and other patriotic songs were missing for the first time from their repertoire: 'That may be a sign the country is settling down – yet I felt a little sad,' she told T.J. Kiernan.[45]

The year 1928 was marked by the falling out with Seán O'Casey over *The Silver Tassie*. Their correspondence reveals that Augusta and O'Casey were good at supporting each other. Augusta told him how happy she was that the popularity of *Juno and the Paycock* had remade the Abbey as 'a "People's Theatre"', and on 28 March, in reply to a despondent letter in which she had said she should retire from writing, O'Casey, beginning 'Now, now, now; you shouldn't be sad', told her how she had done more for Irish literature than Ireland would permit.[46] They were also bound by a shared sense of struggle: 'My dear Lady Gregory you can always walk on with your head up. And remember you had to fight against your birth into position & comfort as others had to fight against their birth into hardship & poverty.' She quickly acknowledged that his letter had given her courage, especially with the Lane pictures. But did it also inspire her to be blunt about her reaction to his new play which she had just read and found disappointing?[47]

O'Casey had told her on 28 February that he thought *The Silver Tassie* was his best play. It was set during the First

World War and, after the first act, showed the influence of the avant-garde that he had encountered in London. Robinson, who disliked the fourth act, and Augusta, who felt the play progressively disintegrated, considered it needed extensive revision. Yeats, more drastically, considered that O'Casey had abandoned his subject, the working-class Irish, and told him so in a letter sent first to Augusta. In a covering letter he proposed that she suggest to O'Casey that he offer to withdraw the play for revision, to save embarrassment on all sides. Augusta, anxious to stop O'Casey getting the play published before it had been altered, unwisely sent him both these letters, criticism from herself and Robinson and a short letter from her in which the theme of their recent correspondence about courage resurfaced:

> . . . I think I ought to mail it [Yeats's letter to him] to you at once though I am afraid it might hurt you – or at least disappoint you – (as his criticism did me, on my first draft of 'Sancho.') But it is right you should at once know what he – what we all – feel and think – . . . I know you will prefer this to any attempt to 'soften' things and will believe that I, that we all – feel you would rather have the exact truth than evasions.[48]

Her doubts about sending undigested criticism, and her fear that he would interpret it badly are eloquently expressed in her hesitations. She slept badly, and next morning told him in a quick note that she relied on his courage and tenacity.[49]

Her fears were realised; he was deeply and bitterly angry, interpreting the criticisms as a total rejection of the play and of himself as a playwright. Independent and successful now, O'Casey was not amenable to Abbey guidance as he had been over *Plough*. His reply to her was 'kind' but he vented his spleen on Yeats.[50] Despite her sympathy for O'Casey

Augusta aligned herself with Yeats and Robinson, and in her journal she stoically regretted the breaking of her friendship with O'Casey.

She had not, however, given him up. In her next letter, after reiterating her belief that he had valued her bluntness, she dismissed the subject and, hoping their friendship stood a better chance of survival if they ignored the whole episode, concentrated on her latest work for the Lane pictures.[51] O'Casey, too, refused to mention *Tassie*, perhaps for similar reasons.[52] Yet a sketch in his papers showing Yeats, Robinson and Gregory outside the Abbey, Augusta on her knees between Yeats's legs, her arms raised in an 'Amen' while the other two denounce a retreating, though defiant, O'Casey as a heretic, shows that he regarded Augusta as one of those arrayed against him.[53]

George Yeats considered Augusta an 'obstinate old woman [who] will never even say she is sorry', which, although harsh, was not entirely wrong. By June Augusta regarded the episode as a series of misunderstandings and bad luck and felt little guilt for her part.[54] O'Casey engaged in an orgy of retaliation, publishing his correspondence with the directors in the British press (at first excluding Augusta's letters) and vilifying many of her old friends. In the end she felt pity: 'I am sad, for it is not worthy of him as I knew him.'[55]

The Lane pictures and other shared concerns such as socialism (she was avidly reading Shaw's *Intelligent Woman's Guide to Socialism*, and would approve Labour's successes in June 1929) allowed them to remain amicable. Then in November, in a long letter full of chat about art and friends, O'Casey offered reconciliation if, he implied, she would accept his criticisms of Yeats and Robinson.[56] Augusta's reply was friendly but she ignored the *Tassie* episode and tacitly suggested that criticisms of others were out of place in their correspondence.[57] It was not enough. 'Her letters are always kind and gracious,' he would write to Gabriel Fallon, 'but never an answer to a criticism about LR, or AE, or Yeats or [Will] Shields. This may be a divine dignity, or it may be a fluttering fear.'[58] She could not now be disloyal to Yeats. She tried to avoid the either/or by pressing on with her friendly correspondence but, until just before her death, O'Casey could not accept her loyalty to Yeats. He wrote seldom and whenever he found himself bending towards reconciliation he recalled his bitterness towards Dublin.

In April 1928, during this harrowing time, Augusta's brother Frank died suddenly of bronchitis. His death immediately restored to her the wild, charismatic brother of her youth. She went to Craughwell graveyard for the funeral, but would not join the few mourners – his two daughters and a few elderly men that had worked for him – around the grave.[59] The family came back to Coole for tea.

On 14 May, alerted by her niece, Rose, she visited her last surviving brother, Henry, in a nursing home in Dundrum. Mentally unstable, he was now dying and did not recognise her. 'He is the last of my brothers, and though the only one I had not felt much affection for, it upset me, and I came away tired and sad.'[60] Ten days later he was dead. His death meant she was the last sibling still alive. It was a sad achievement and strengthened her resolve to get her papers in order.[61]

When Johnny Hehir, the young son of an ex-tenant, died in September, Augusta was told by his grief-stricken parents when she went to the house after the funeral that when he knew he was about to die he had sent his love to Lady Gregory. Unusually for his generation he had inherited his parents' respect for the Gregorys. She took on the hospital fees, but asked John Diveney 'to find out if the Health Insurance helps at all'.

On 15 June Augusta arrived for her last visit to Merrion Square. Yeats, still delicate, had decided to retire from the Senate, and was looking forward to wintering in Rapello. George wanted to sell the house and look for a smaller one. Augusta was becoming a difficult guest. She was increasingly deaf. 'In conversation I still *look* intelligent but miss a great deal,' she admitted in her diary.[62] Her memory was also fading. 'Christ how she repeats herself now,' an intolerant George wrote to Dorothy Pound two years later, 'she'll tell you the same saga quite literally three times in less than an hour, and repeat it again the next day, and the day after that too.'[63] When she was not busy with Lane and theatre business Augusta read. One week she consumed so many detective novels that she began to confuse innocents and criminals. Meanwhile there were stabs of pain under her scar, though Slattery's touch seemed to dispel them.

Yeats stayed with her at Coole in August. In October George shut down Ballylee. She sent Augusta a rare letter, expressing her gratitude for Augusta's kindness which had 'made many things easy that might otherwise have been most difficult.' 'But the kindness,' Augusta rejoined in her diary, 'has been from her rather than from me.'[64]

On 8 September Augusta was in Dublin for Margaret's marriage to Guy Gough. Guy, who had been a captain in the 60th Rifles, and was heir presumptive to the viscountcy, had been courting Margaret for several years. But the marriage was sudden, coming after a tense summer in which Guy had intermittently told Augusta of the state of his relations with a deeply undecided Margaret. When Guy came to Coole on 8 August neither he nor Augusta could speak of the possible marriage which hung heavily between them. This is not to imply that Augusta disapproved; on the contrary she believed that Robert 'would be, or is, glad'.[65] By the end of August all was resolved, but Augusta was kept in suspense about the day of the wedding until 5 September when she received a letter from Robert's old tutor, Arnold Harvey, now a rector in Blackrock and the priest who was to marry them, asking her to sign a declaration that Guy was unmarried. Still not yet invited, she reasoned wistfully, 'I think she would like to have me, and Robert would wish it.'[66] A few hours later Margaret wired an invitation.

It was a quiet wedding in the fine Gothic Revival church at Booterstown. George, Guy's brother, was best man. Nora, Guy's aunt and Augusta's sister-in-law (she had married Algernon) and Olive, her daughter, were present. Augusta gave away the bride.[67] The children were not there. 'Guy so steadfast – I felt "till death us do part" was no empty declaration.' Margaret, she noted, 'was brave'.[68] Lily Yeats would observe that Augusta emerged from the wedding, freed of Margaret, looking fifteen years younger. Lily's thumb-nail sketch of Guy is illuminating: 'Captain Gough is rich and what is known as "a very decent fellow", which I think means dull but knows how to behave.'[69] He was also a Unionist who reinforced Margaret's anti-nationalism, which did not bode well if any of Augusta's papers fell into her daughter-in-law's hands after her death.

The marriage changed her grandchildren's prospects and, subtly, their relationship with Augusta. Margaret, redecorating rooms, was making her mark on Lough Cutra. Guy's mother, Hilda Gough, wrote a kind letter to Augusta expressing her desire that the three children would look at Lough Cutra as 'a real Home'. And Guy, who knew the children well, had been acting like a father to them for some time, taking Anne to school in Paris, reporting on their well-being to Augusta. The children thus moved easily towards the Goughs. They sat in the Gough pews in the Gort church and slept at Lough Cutra. Augusta appreciated their visit to Coole for the shoot in January 1929, remarking with a lightness that no doubt concealed anxiety, 'Their belief in Coole (run down in favour of Lough Cutra) is rising again.'[70]

Augusta had her third operation for breast cancer on 28 January 1929. Her terror at the thought was undiminished, her stoicism under a local anaesthetic unchanged. This time she concentrated her thoughts on the roots of newly planted trees spreading out with relief in the damp fresh soil, but 'when a second little avenue of stabs began being made by kind wise Slattery on the old scar, it was rather the spade that came to mind'.[71] When she returned to Coole she stayed put until October.

That spring and summer was to be Augusta's last period of writing. On her 77th birthday she considered adding an entertaining chapter to her autobiography depicting a deranged Annie Horniman, but instead she wrote a series of single-act 'eclogues', light-hearted dramatic ideas each with three characters, reworking old themes, succinctly presented.[72] Yeats listened tolerantly as she read them to him, while she was glad to have written them at all.

Augusta could have concentrated on enjoying her reputation which, at the end of her life, was very good. Her one-act plays, particularly her comedies, were translated and acted all over the world, and the publication of collections of her other plays had broadened her reputation.[73] There was something of a consensus that her dialogue, described as 'rich, pleasant and real' in her obituary in *The Irish Times* on 24 May 1932, was her strong point. A year after her death the critic Andrew E. Malone wrote unhesitatingly that Lady Gregory was the most popular playwright of the Irish theatre, regarded by foreign critics as a leading playwright.[74]

Augusta was aware of her achievement. When *The Spectator*, reviewing *Three Last Plays* in 1928, asked whether there could have been an Irish Theatre without Lady Gregory, Augusta noted in brackets, 'No, there could not. That's Poz.'[75] She enjoyed reading of her technical mastery, and of her vigorous and tender imagination, while she could happily ignore bad reviews. But she had a balanced view of her achievement: 'I know I have left a sheaf that contains its quota of golden grain; I have been but the reaper, the ripened ears came from the poor, the people; the sun that ripened the harvest comes from beyond the world, I can claim diligence, and love – for the work – for the people – for the Abbey – for Ireland – that "constraineth me" to do such service as I may.'[76] This was not just practised humility. She knew her debt and she valued her hard work and enthusiasm over her creative abilities. 'I sometimes think my life has been a series of enthusiasms,' she wrote in December 1928.[77] And she was right. Her work is not shown in its best light when exaggerated claims are made for its artistic achievement. It is more valuably seen as a reflection of the culture in which she steeped herself – she did not just grasp 'the Irish character' as contemporaries most often claimed, but also the values of a society that existed alongside her own, and which has progressively faded from view since her death. As the writer of the *New York Times Book Review* put it in 1912, she stands as a 'sort of sentient light' in her understanding of the 'passionate and vital interests' of the present.

Contemporaries also valued her folklore, biography and history; her books were well reviewed when they appeared. More long-lasting than her reputation as a writer would be her image as a patron of the Irish Revival, fostered by her tours of America, by *Our Irish Theatre*, and by her role in the Abbey, all emphasised in her obituaries. But it was Yeats's words that gave this image its force. During the summer of 1929 he gave it an iconic power, rooting it irrevocably in the soil of Coole in his poem 'Coole Park, 1929', used as a dedication in *Coole*. In it he evoked a 'powerful character' that 'Could keep a swallow to its first intent', which worked not only on himself but on many others – Hyde, Synge, Shawe-Taylor, Lane. Augusta's unnamed presence in a poem that does not shy from naming names is implicitly likened to a natural force. She is an influence among defined characters, a muse. It is the traditional female role.

Throughout the autumn of 1929 Augusta was predominantly cheerful. However, while she was in London in October she saw *The Silver Tassie* and was overcome by the feeling that the Abbey should have produced it; they would have done a more faithful job.[78] She asked O'Casey to meet her, but, unable to forgive her for siding with Yeats – he referred to 'the many Artistic & Literary Shams squatting in their high places in Dublin' – he refused.[79] It was a letter that he later regretted, groaning aloud when, thirty-four years later, the editor of his collected letters read it out to him.

Augusta was not to be put off, replying humbly and emotionally: 'Your letter has grieved me – perhaps I deserve that – but I do ask you to change your mind and allow me to come and see your wife – and the boy – and the garden and the pictures and *yourself* – I do not feel that any word need be spoken on that grievous matter that has given me so much pain – I am here but a few days . . . Could go tomorrow afternoon – if you give me leave.'[80] But he would not relent. It was not until October 1931, seven months before Augusta's death, that in a warm letter that recaptured the spirit of their earlier correspondence he finally forgot his bitterness. 'It gave me,' she replied, 'very great pleasure to see your writing again.'[81]

By the middle of June 1930 she had reached the beginning of the end. She found herself sitting idle at her writing table for the first time in her life and, typing her journal, felt purposeless. She could hardly walk for rheumatic pain. She felt blank for periods. When Yeats, recovered from a severe bout of Malta Fever, arrived on 7 August he found her in agony. He took her to Dublin, and she had another operation, underplayed in her journal as 'rather a bad time'.[82] Yeats would now be with her, on and off, until her death. It was her desire for she was reassured by his presence, and especially by the concentrated work he was doing. George, with whom Yeats had developed a certain emotional detachment, was relieved to have him off her hands, and encouraged him to stay in Galway.[83] Yeats himself, although possessing a renewed exuberance and sexual vitality that was entering his poetry, needed the utter quiet of Coole. And he was haunted by the tragedy that was unfolding as his friend, 'my sole adviser for the greater part of my life, the one person who knew all that I thought and did', underwent her slow death.[84]

In the Berg Collection there is a memo in a very shaky hand dated 21 August 1930 in which Augusta agrees that when a suitable house has been acquired for the children she will give up her tenancy of Coole and allow the contents left to her for her lifetime to be removed and the surplus sold, 'not asking any share in the profits'. Margaret was negotiating the purchase of a house in Celbridge. It seems a curiously insensitive statement to extract from a dying woman. Yeats conveyed his disgust at Margaret's avariciousness to Lily, whose verdict was: 'Suburban and greedy.' '"Little girls" like her, married gaily when young, "have a way of growing up into hard greedy women without imagination".'[85] Augusta probably did not reveal to Margaret the extent to which she now dreaded the idea of leaving Coole, but to her journal she confided the relief she felt when the owner of Celbridge briefly stalled in the negotiations.

This was her last typed journal entry. What was written after early November 1930 was probably not reread, certainly unedited and never typed. Augusta's appetite for work had finally diminished. Yeats was at Coole in February. He wanted her to edit her autobiography for immediate publication, to avoid Margaret's likely censorship once Augusta was dead.[86] Although extremely reluctant to see her life story published, she bravely sent *Seventy Years* to Constant Huntington of Putnam & Co who returned it to be condensed. Gamely Augusta began the task, but soon gave up.

There was a brief visit to London, travelling in first class comfort at last, after which her health began to deteriorate more rapidly. Now, almost every week she had new or worsening symptoms: by 17 April 1931 she was hobbling with pain; on 31 May she noted 'the two Rs', rheumatic pains and ringing in her ears; there were nose bleeds at the end of June. 'Her judgement is vigorous, but her memory comes and goes,' Yeats reported to George.[87] Augusta and Yeats maintained the fiction that her pain was caused by rheumatism, and Yeats only knew that the lump remained in her breast from Margaret.

Augusta worried constantly that she would not be at Coole for the summer. A former Abbey secretary was employed to type her letters. On 22 September she resolved that Yeats should be the final editor of her journals. Worried by pain around her scar she went to Dublin in September, but Slattery told her there was no new tumour. As she was leaving he said, '"If it ever get[s] *very* bad let me know". (That I am sure means drugs – & I hope to have fortitude to avoid that. A bleak prospect, if life keeps lingering on . . .)'[88]

'WBY working well, & happy & very kind – his companionship helps me to belittle pain,' she wrote on 20 October.[89] Six days later, 'Pain increasing – night & day.' '*Agony*', 23 November. After her death Yeats recalled that he never heard her moan or sigh with pain.[90] By now Yeats was an almost constant presence; from the late summer of 1931 until her death he was living at Coole. He and Margaret had called a halt to their 'courteous, indirect war' and Margaret asked him to spend as much time at Coole as he could.[91]

In February 1932, when Yeats was in Dublin voting in the general election, Augusta experienced a faintness and ebbing of strength which made her think she was dying. She wrote him a farewell letter in blue pencil:

It may be the time has come for me to slip away . . . I have had a full life & except for the grief of parting with those who have gone, a happy one.

I do think I have been of use to the country – & for that in great part I thank you. I thank you also for these last months you have spent with me – your presence has made them pass quickly and happily in spite of bodily pain, as your friendship has made my last years – from first to last fruitful in work, in service.

All blessings to you & to George also.[92]

It was never sent and he never saw it.

Yeats returned with pain-killing drugs from Slattery without the mind-affecting morphia she dreaded. Behind the scenes he argued with Margaret who was reluctant to administer them.[93] Now Augusta lay in the room next to her bedroom during the day, except for once when she went downstairs and sat outside the hall door in the sun. She still read to Yeats after dinner. She made her last diary entry on 9 May. On the 10th she signed an agreement with Putnams giving them the right to edit her journals. A few days later, a sign of her extreme agony, she asked Yeats to feel the enlarged lump on her breast. She wanted to see Slattery, but Yeats persuaded her the journey would be too painful. The next day he went to Dublin on Abbey business and himself saw Slattery.

He was not there at the end. It was something he deeply regretted and about which he felt guilty. An unpolished account he wrote afterwards, carefully recording the details he heard from her maid Ellen Keller and Margaret, reads like an atonement for his absence.[94] Held up by her two servants Augusta made a slow and painful tour of the main rooms of the house on Wednesday 18 May. This, no doubt to Margaret's dismay, included the drawing-room where she noticed, without comment, that the curtains had gone, removed by Margaret for Celbridge Abbey.[95] On Saturday John Diveney, one of the last remaining estate servants, sent for Margaret, Guy, Yeats, Catherine and Anne. The three women were with her on Sunday the 22nd. The Canon called, not praying with her, as the High Church Margaret wished, but talking, to reassure her. In the afternoon Margaret persuaded Augusta, reluctant to give in, to go to bed. '"We are all here",' Margaret told her when Augusta was settled, convinced that she thought Richard and Yeats were present, too. Augusta had retreated within herself, saying only, 'I do not know.' Finally she asked for a prayer, and Catherine, the only one who could still speak, said the Lord's Prayer, after which Augusta lost consciousness. She died early the next morning. Yeats, having caught the first train from Dublin, arrived later that day with Guy. Augusta was buried in the Protestant graveyard in Galway, next to Arabella, neither a Roxborough Persse nor a Coole Gregory, but a singular spirit surveying the airy blue of the Galway sea and the distant Connemara mountains.

Notes

Abbreviations

AG	Augusta Gregory
AH	Annie Horniman
Berg	Berg Collection, New York Public Library
DH	Douglas Hyde
EL	Enid Layard
EM	Edward Martyn
FB	Florimond de Basterot
FF	Frank Fay
FP	Frances Persse
GR	George Russell
HL	Hugh Lane
IAOS	Irish Agricultural Organisation Society
INTS	Irish National Theatre Society
JBY	John Butler Yeats
JMS	John Millington Synge
JQ	John Quinn
LGJ	*Lady Gregory's Journals*
LY	Lily Yeats
NLI	National Library of Ireland
NYPL	New York Public Library
OIT	*Our Irish Theatre*
PH	Paul Harvey
SO'C	Seán O'Casey
TLS	*Times Literary Supplement*
TNA	The National Archives, London
WBY	W.B. Yeats
WF	William Fay
WHG	Sir William H. Gregory
WSB	Wilfred Scawen Blunt

Chapter One

1. *Seventy Years*, p. 1.
2. Married 1826, Katherine died 11 December 1829. See *Burke's Irish Family Records*.

3. She had married Commander Wale and lived in Cambridge from 1862.
4. *Sir Hugh Lane*, p. 26.
5. Yeats, *Autobiographies*, p. 391.
6. 'A Woman's Sonnets', 1883, Saddlemyer and Smythe, pp. 102–13.
7. Holograph Memoirs, vol. 2, Berg, in Saddlemyer and Smythe, p. 64.
8. *LGJ*, II, pp. 407, 249.
9. *Seventy Years*, p. 5.
10. Folklore Archives, collected 1938, University College, Dublin in Saddlemyer and Smythe, p. 56.
11. *Seventy Years*, p. 4.
12. *Ibid.*, p. 5.
13. *Coole*, p. 46.
14. Holograph Memoirs, vol. 9, Berg, in Saddlemyer and Smythe, p. 58.
15. Holograph Memoirs, vol. 10, Berg, in Saddlemyer and Smythe, p. 59.
16. *Seventy Years*, pp. 22–3.
17. *Ibid.*, pp. 4–5.
18. Pinnock's *Improved Edition of Dr. Goldsmith's History of Greece*. New books were only grudgingly added at Roxborough when the girls could answer all the questions in Mrs Richmal Mangnall's *Historical & Miscellaneous Questions*, a popular nineteenth-century textbook. *Seventy Years*, p. 4.
19. AG to JQ, 6 May 1912, Berg.
20. Pethica, 1996, pp. 111–12.
21. 'An Emigrant's Notebook', Emory.
22. *Seventy Years*, p. 10.
23. 'An Emigrant's Notebook', Emory.
24. Holograph Memoirs, vol. 2, Berg, in Saddlemyer and Smythe, pp. 63–4.
25. No. iii, in Saddlemyer and Smythe, p. 104.
26. In 'The Municipal Gallery Re-visited', 1937.
27. *Hail and Farewell*, p. 547.
28. *Seventy Years*, p. 447.
29. The first Persse was Revd Robert who came to Ireland in *c.* 1602. *Burke's Irish Family Records*.
30. Fahey, pp. 320–1.
31. 'Owners of One Acre and Upwards, Co Galway', 1876.
32. Griffith's Valuation, *c.* 1850. *Seventy Years*, p. 11.
33. 1987, p. 19.
34. See Revd J. Mitchell.

35. *Mr. Gregory's Letter-Box*, p. 19. She later wrote an unpublished essay, 'The Volunteer Bridge' dated 9 April 1930, Berg.
36. *Mr. Gregory's Letter-Box*, p. 21.
37. *Autobiographies*, pp. 392–3.
38. Griffith's Valuation for *c*. 1850 records no tenants with less than two acres.
39. When she was undergoing surgery for breast cancer without a general anaesthetic in September 1926 she steadied herself by imaginatively tracing the course of the river at Roxborough, *LGJ*, II, pp. 135–6. She later wrote that she was glad to have been deprived of the novels of Walter Scott, that Scottish stimulator of romantic nationalist sentiment, so that her imagination was free to feed on her Irish experiences.
40. 'An Emigrant's Notebook,' Emory.
41. Archdeacon Persse was granted the 'mansion house' of Cregarosta in the late seventeenth century, Fahey.
42. The landscaping was probably done by Robert Persse, who inherited in 1733 and was the brother-in-law of Sir Lawrence Parsons who, in the 1740s, was employing the landscape architect Samuel Chearnley to redesign the gardens of Birr Castle and adjacent Parsonstown, now Birr. The gateway may have been in emulation of the turrets and battlements of nearby Lough Cutra which Nash and the Pain brothers were redesigning from 1811. The gateway was incongruously placed on a subsidiary drive and the 1850 map suggests that it was unused.
43. *LGJ*, II, p. 135.
44. 'An Emigrant's Notebook', Emory. Augusta often visited Margaret who she found sensitive; she gave her an engraving of Mary Magdalen at Christ's feet, and watched her savouring Christ's expression. Her experiences would be used in 'A Philanthropist'.
45. *The Kiltartan Books*, pp. 18–19.
46. *Seventy Years*, p. 13.
47. *Ibid.*, p. 14.
48. *The Kiltartan Books*, p. 19.
49. 'An Emigrant's Notebook', Emory.
50. Holograph Memoirs, vol. 3, Berg, Saddlemyer and Smythe, p. 61. See 'Our Nurse' in 'An Emigrant's Notebook', Emory, for account.
51. Pethica, 1996, p. 114.
52. *Seventy Years*, pp. 14–15.
53. By 1907, as Edmund Gosse observed, Protestantism had to 'combine with its subjective faith a strenuous labour for the good of others . . .' *Father and Son*, London, Penguin, 1979, p. 211, 1st edn 1907.

54. *Our Irish Theatre*, pp. 100, 118. She arranged for the Catholic Miss Daly to be present, but the priest remained implacable. Holograph Memoirs, vol. 10, Berg, in Saddlemyer and Smythe, p. 65.
55. He was related to AG's father's first wife. By 1853 he had published a translation of *The Adventures of Donncha Ruadh Mac Conmara* in rhyming couplets and was a founder member of the Ossianic Society.
56. *Seventy Years*, p. 17.
57. 'Where Wild Swans Nest', *Inishfallen, Fare Thee Well*.
58. Holograph Memoirs, vol. 10, Berg, in Saddlemyer and Smythe, p. 67.
59. *Sir Hugh Lane*, p. 26.
60. *Ibid.*, pp. 27–8.
61. *Seventy Years*, p. 19.
62. 'An Emigrant's Notebook', Emory.
63. Holograph Memoirs, vol. 10, Berg, in Saddlemyer and Smythe, p. 68.
64. *Seventy Years*, p. 20.
65. Holograph Memoirs, vol. 10, Berg, in Saddlemyer and Smythe, p. 68.
66. AG to WBY [26 May 1911], Berg. *Seventy Years*, pp. 26–7.
67. AG to Lennox Robinson, 3 July 1926, Carbondale, in Saddlemyer and Smythe, p. 68.
68. *Seventy Years*, p. 28.

Chapter Two

1. *Seventy Years*, p. 23. Unless otherwise stated the source for Augusta's experience in this chapter is *Seventy Years*.
2. He was born 13 July, *Sir William Gregory*, p. 11.
3. Photograph in the frontispiece of *Sir William Gregory*, signed by him and chosen by Augusta.
4. WHG to AG, 28 May 1888, Emory.
5. *Seventy Years*, pp. 23–5
6. *Ibid.*, pp. 24–5.
7. Source for information on William is *Sir William Gregory*.
8. Glendinning, p. 152.
9. Auction on 13 January 1857 he sold about half; more was sold subsequently. See Jenkins, pp. 105–8.
10. *Ibid.*, p. 72. *Sir William Gregory*, p. 133. He also proposed an amendment to encourage emigration.
11. She was the third daughter of Sir William Clay, MP, and widow of James Temple Bowdoin.

12. She also left him life interest in revenues from a trust fund worth almost £50,000 (about €3,990,380, £2,738,765 sterling). Will of Elizabeth Gregory, 11 January 1872, Emory.

13. WHG to Bess Gregory, 29 October 1873, quoted in Saddlemyer and Smythe, 1987, p. 73.

14. 'An Emigrant's Notebook', Emory.

15. Going through his journals years later she came across his entry for that day, '"To Vallauris with R. Persse". Only my brother's name given not mine.' She still had the head in her room at Coole, *LGJ*, I, p. 534.

16. *Seventy Years*, p. 25.

17. *Ibid.*, pp. 25, 27.

18. WHG to AG, 21 March [1879], Emory.

19. WHG to Henry Layard, 15 February 1880, quoted in Saddlemyer and Smythe, 1987, p. 75.

20. *Seventy Years*, p. 27.

21. WHG to AG, 25 January 1880, Emory.

22. WHG to AG, 1 February 1880, Emory.

23. Holograph Memoirs, vol. 10, Berg, quoted in Pethica, 1987.

24. *Seventy Years*, p. 28.

25. WHG to AG, 16 February 1880, Emory.

26. 'Memorandum as to property in which William Robert Gregory is interested', 1893, Emory. Equivalent income in purchasing power today in Ireland for £800 would be €53,700, £36,856 sterling, for £1,100 would be €87,788, £60,252 sterling.

27. *Sir William Gregory*, p. 359.

28. Calzolari, Colin Smythe Collection. Another image from the same studio is printed in the second edition of Elizabeth Coxhead's biography.

29. *Seventy Years*, p. 29. Certificate of Registry of Marriage, Representative Church Body Library, Dublin.

30. WHG to AG, 16 February 1880, Emory and *LGJ*, II, pp. 169–70.

31. WHG to Henry Layard, 9 March 1880, quoted in *Sir William Gregory*, p. 368.

32. *Seventy Years*, p. 30.

33. *Ibid.*, p. 139

34. *LGJ*, II, p. 170.

35. 19 March–29 March 1880, autograph diary, 1880–1882, Emory.

36. *Seventy Years*, p. 181.

37. *Ibid.*, p. 161.

38. 7 May 1880, Enid Layard's diary, British Library.

39. Quoted in G.M. Trevelyan, *English Social History*, 1978 edn, pp. 499–501.

40. *Seventy Years*, pp. 100–1.

41. *Ave*, 1911, and *Vale*, 1914, both published by William Heineman, later combined with *Salve* as *Hail and Farewell*.

42. *Hail and Farewell*, p. 548.

43. *Seventy Years*, p. 101.

44. 29 July 1880, autograph diary, Emory. It was slightly rephrased in *Seventy Years*, where she replaced the casual reference to the mob with 'goodwill everywhere'.

45. There are accounts of the history of Coole in Vere Gregory, Brian Jenkins and Lady Gregory's *Coole*. The contents of the house that had not been retained by Augusta's daughter-in-law, Margaret Gough, were sold at auction on 8–9 August 1932 by A.M. Toole of Loughrea.

46. It was subsequently enlarged to over 15,000 acres by the purchase of the Ballylee estate, holdings around the port of Kinvara on Galway Bay, and the Clooniffe estate by Lough Corrib.

47. He planned a relatively grand house with a domed hall supported by columns, see *Coole* end papers which show a cross-section of Coole House from Lewis, *Original Designs in Architecture*, London, 1797, in NLI, that was built after 1797. There are plans of the house in Smyth, 1995, constructed from information supplied by Augusta's granddaughters.

48. Arthur Young, travelling through Co. Galway in 1776, noted his walling, tree nursery, two English bailiffs, and his turnips, *A Tour of Ireland*. See 'Coole Library', C. Smythe, *The Private Library*, second series, vol. 6:2, summer 1973. His books were on Eastern art, drainage, husbandry, plants, trees. Augusta sold a few books at Sothebys in 1927. On her death more were sold locally. Many of her personal books are in the Berg Collection. For Augusta's account of the library see *Coole*, pp. 17–28.

49. Richard Gregory, a collector and scholar, only got a life interest in Coole.

50. During those years he lived in the Under Secretary's Lodge in Phoenix Park where his grandson, Sir William, spent his boyhood.

51. *Coole*, pp. 67–80.

52. In 1841–3 Robert Gregory spent £1,000 on new furniture and upholstering, curtains and carpets, and a further £500 on plate, coffee and tea services, glass, china. He also bought equipment for the household staff. See *Coole*.

53. Fowl were raised near the dairy. They also made their own butter, grew fruit, incuding grapes, and vegetables (Coole apples were later distributed liberally by Augusta) and there were glass vineries in the flower garden.

54. Census, 1901. Two derelict houses remain, and one house, which had all the bare discomfort of an old house inhabited by a

bachelor – upright chairs, cold turf fire waiting to be lit, wooden table placed against the wall – was inhabited until recently by Martin Hehir whose elder brother, John had been Augusta's driver in the 1920s.

55. Foster, 1997, pp. 169, 568.
56. WHG to Henry Layard, 26 October 1880, quoted in Jenkins, p. 264.
57. Jenkins, p. 264. WHG to AG, 9 March 1881 from London suggests that AG had been at Roxborough where she was well looked after. WHG still planned to travel to France. Emory.
58. To WBY, no date, in *Seventy Years*, p. 443.
59. WHG to Henry Layard, 26 October 1880, quoted in Jenkins, p. 265.
60. Pethica 1996, p. 260.
61. WHG to Henry Layard, 3 September 1881, quoted in *Sir William Gregory*, p. 369.
62. *LGJ*, I, p. 304.
63. See Jenkins, pp. 277–84.
64. Gregory had about 130 tenants and a yearly rental income of about £2,800. His income had increased when his mother died and he no longer paid a jointure of £1,500 from the estate, Emory Memorandum, 1864. The trust-based relationship between landlord and tenant was subtly altered with the passing of the Landlord and Tenant Act in 1870 for it gave legal force to customary tenant rights such as the right to claim compensation for improvements in the case of unjust eviction, and extended them elsewhere. Now the law began to stand between landlord and tenant.
65. WHG to AG, 9 March 1881, Emory. The pamphlet was intended to inspire debate with a dire warning of peasants in full possession of their farms, the Ascendancy powerless, and an independent Ireland uninterested in maintaining the British connection. Disappointingly, people accepted this fatalistically as a realistic prognosis. See Jenkins, pp. 280–1.
66. *Ibid.*, pp. 283–4.

Chapter Three

1. EL's diary, British Museum and AG's autograph diary 1880–1882, Emory.
2. WHG to Henry Layard, 27 November 1881, in *Sir William Gregory*, p. 371.
3. 19 November 1881, autograph diary 1880–1881, Emory. Ahmed El Arabi (*c.* 1838–1911), also known in Egypt as Orabi.

4. Holograph notebook, 2 October [1881]. Berg, in Pethica, 1987.
5. Account of Egyptian politics from Longford, 1979, and Jenkins, 1986.
6. 23 November 1881, autograph diary 1880–1882, Emory.
7. Glendinning, p. 294.
8. WHG to Henry Layard, 4 May 1881, in *Sir William Gregory*, p. 379.
9. WHG met Arabi on 9 December, autograph diary 1880–1882. For WHG's opinions also see WHG to HL, 27 November 1881, 2 January 1882, 13 March 1882, 4 May 1882, in *Sir William Gregory*, pp. 371–82.
10. Account of Blunts from Longford, 1979, Winstone, 2003.
11. Now with about £3,000 a year he was richer than Gregory, Winstone.
12. *Seventy Years*, p. 478.
13. AG to WSB, 29 August 1882, Berg, on Blunt's expectations. WHG to Henry Layard, 27 November 1881, *Sir William Gregory*, p. 371; WHG affectionately belittled her enthusiasm to Henry Layard.
14. *Alms to Oblivion*, one of Blunt's unpublished memoirs revised in his last years, Longford, p. 34, now in the Blunt papers, Fitzwilliam Museum, Cambridge, quoted in Saddlemyer and Smythe, 1987, pp. 89–90.
15. AG to WSB, 24 [July 1882]. Berg.
16. Anne Blunt's diary, British Library.
17. 26 December 1881, autograph diary 1880–1882, Emory.
18. *Ibid.*, 8 February 1882.
19. Arabi also gave Augusta a photograph of himself – a meditative profile – in October 1883 signed 'Ahmed Arabi the Egyptian'.
20. AG to WSB, 24 [July 1882], Berg. 'Lady G— thinks if the Khedive becomes impossible her dear Arabi may be recalled to govern the country.' WHG to Henry Layard, 27 June 1883, quoted in Jenkins, p. 270.
21. 26 February 1882, autograph diary 1880–1882, Emory.
22. *Ibid.*, 19 February 1882.
23. 17 May [1882], Berg, quoted in Pethica, 1987, p. 38.
24. *Ibid.*, 29 April [1882] Berg.
25. Jenkins, p. 269.
26. WHG to AG, 11 June 1886, Emory. William was asked several times to stand for Parliament in the early 1880s. C. Smythe, *The Gregorys and Egypt, 1855–6 and 1881–2*, unpublished.
27. *Seventy Years*, p. 47.
28. See AG to WSB, Monday 24 [July 1882], Berg.
29. Autograph diary, 1880–1882, Emory.

30. Quoted in Saddlemyer and Smythe, 1987, p. 90.
31. Observed by Pethica in Saddlemyer and Smythe, pp. 408–9.
32. Published in Saddlemyer and Smythe, pp. 102–12.
33. Blunt, 'Secret Memoirs', quoted in Saddlemyer and Smythe, 1987, pp. 91–2. Blunt also wrote that they 'tell all our love's history that needs the telling'. Longford, p. 194.
34. Longford, 1979, brought this knowledge to a wider audience. 'I see no reason why those twelve sonnets should not be published if you think them worth it – merely calling them 'Sonnets written by a Woman'. AG to WSB, undated [14 October 1891], Berg, quoted in Saddlemyer and Smythe, p. 99.
35. Much of what they allude to can be found in the letters Augusta wrote to Blunt and are now in the Berg Collection.
36. No. i.
37. *Seventy Years*, p. 44.
38. AG to WSB, Monday 24 [July 1882], Berg.
39. Sonnets, No. x, line 11.
40. See Leslie.
41. WSB to AG, 29 July 1882, Emory.
42. No. viii, line 11.
43. 29 July 1882, Emory. In *Seventy Years*, p. 46, Augusta self-deprecatingly suggested that someone else had given her the idea. Blunt also recorded in his diary 29 June, that Augusta had already written a paper on 'the Control in Egypt'.
44. *Seventy Years*, p. 44 and AG to WSB, 24 [July 1882], Berg.
45. See Jenkins, pp. 284–5.
46. Holograph diary, vol. 1, Berg, 2 August 1882, quoted Kohfeldt p. 62.
47. AG to WSB, Thurs [11 August 1882], and 21 August 1882, both Berg.
48. 'Secret Memoirs', Longford, p. 191.
49. Saddlemyer and Smythe, p. 89.
50. AG to WSB, 21 August 1882, Berg.
51. AG to WSB, 29 August 1882, Berg.
52. AG to WSB, 16 September [1882], and 17 September 1882, both Berg.
53. *Seventy Years*, pp. 48–54.
54. AG to WSB, 21 December 1907, Berg.
55. 'Arabi and his Household', was produced as a booklet the same year.
56. *Seventy Years*, p. 46.
57. AG to WSB, 23 April [1883] from Coimbra, Berg.
58. AG to WSB, 13 May [1883], Berg.
59. Mon [22 May 1883], Berg.

60. AG to WSB, 17 May 1883, quoted in Kohfeldt, p. 66.
61. No. viii, lines 5 and 6.
62. No. v, lines 13 and 14.
63. No. v. Blunt's version is published in Saddlemyer and Smythe, pp. 103–13.
64. Blunt was also writing 'The Wind and Whirlwind' at this time, inspired not by sexual passion but political idealism. The poems evoke the formidable legacy of Europe's treatment of Arabi; a whirlwind of resentment with the British empire at the eye of the storm. Blunt's private papers include a neat first draft of this poem transcribed by Augusta.
65. Discussed in Longford, pp. 194–7, and in Winstone, pp. 203–6.
66. AG to WSB, 21 August [1882], Berg, Augusta tells Blunt that she found three of his sonnets in William's notebook.
67. WSB to AG, August 1883 and 11 September 1883, quoted in Kohfeldt, p. 69.
68. AG to WSB, 4 October 1883, in *Seventy Years*, p. 207.
69. AG to WSB, 4 October 1883, in *Seventy Years*, p. 206. WHG to AG, 8 January 1883, Emory.
70. AG to WSB, August 1883 quoted in Kohfeldt, p. 69.
71. WHG to AG, 20 November 1883, Emory. William advises her to leave her summer room for the blue room, 'but of course you won't take my advice'.
72. AG to WSB, 4 October 1883, in *Seventy Years*, p. 207.
73. WHG to AG, 3 October [1883], Emory.
74. WHG to AG, 13 January 1884, Emory.
75. 1 March 1884, *Fortnightly Review*, 377–84. WHG to AG, 8 April 1884, Emory. 'Glimpses of the Soudan' was published as the Mahdi began a ten-month siege of Khartoum, which ended in the death of the British defender, General Gordon, and the fall of that city to the Mahdi. Her source was *Heart of Africa* by Dr Schweinfurth whom she had met in Egypt. William published an article in *The Nineteenth Century* in March 1885, advocating that Arabi would be the ideal person to negotiate with the Mahdi.
76. First draft of 'An Emigrant's Notebook', Berg, quoted in Pethica, 1987.
77. 'An Emigrant's Notebook', Emory.

Chapter Four

1. WHG to AG, undated fragment, Emory.
2. WHG to AG, 15 July 1889, Emory.
3. WHG to AG, 30 January 1890 and 2 January 1884, Emory.

4. WHG to AG, 27 May 1887, 12 January 1884, 18 August 1888, Emory.
5. AG to FB, 17 March 1892 quoted in Saddlemyer and Smythe, p. 84.
6. Information from Catherine Kennedy. Gerald Kelly painted two portraits of Augusta, one now in the National Gallery of Ireland; the other was in the possession of Catherine Kennedy until her death in 2000.
7. Holograph Memoirs, in Pethica, 1996, p. xiii.
8. *Seventy Years*, pp. 84–5.
9. *Ibid*., p. 210.
10. *Ibid*., p. 209.
11. *Ibid*., p. 206.
12. WHG to AG, 30 October 1886, 8 August 1885, Emory.
13. Holograph diary, vol. 10, 16 May 1887, in Kohfeldt, pp. 84–5. But the marriage would be unhappy.
14. Specification of materials and construction methods signed by Francis F. Persse, architect, Sycamore Lodge Loughrea. Kiltartan, in Kiltartan Museum.
15. *LGJ*, I, pp. 304–5.
16. Quoted in Kohfeldt, p. 77.
17. WHG to AG [January to April 1884], Emory.
18. WHG to AG, 4 September 1885, Emory.
19. AG to WSB, 9 September 1884 in *Seventy Years*, p. 208.
20. *Ibid*.
21. See Leslie. WHG to AG, 9 June 1888, Emory refers to an invitation from Lady Warwick to the Gregorys.
22. AG to WSB, 12 March 1885 in *Seventy Years*, p. 209.
23. Holograph diary, 16 June 1887, in Kohfeldt, p. 72.
24. AG to WSB, 14 April 1885 in *Seventy Years*, p. 209.
25. June 1885, *Seventy Years*, pp. 210–11.
26. Quoted in Kohfeldt, p. 78.
27. See '"Eothen" and the Athenaeum Club'.
28. Pethica, 1996, p. 9.
29. *Seventy Years*, p. 109.
30. 1 January 1887 in *Seventy Years*, p. 113.
31. WHG to AG, 28 December 1884, Emory.
32. See 'Among the Poor', in *Seventy Years*, pp. 80–95.
33. p. 82.
34. *Seventy Years*, p. 83.
35. *Ibid*., p. 247.
36. EL diary, 16 October–9 November 1885, British Library.
37. EL diary, 30 September 1882, British Library.
38. Enid was the eighth child in a large family. Augusta met her mother,

Lady Charlotte Guest, who had translated the medieval Welsh tales, *The Mabinogion*, which were well-regarded in literary circles. Familiarity with her may have played its part in Augusta's much later decision to translate Irish legends. In 1885 Lady Guest was collecting porcelain and antique playing cards, Kohfeldt, p. 72.

39. See Holograph diaries, November 1885–19 April 1886, Berg, for her experiences. Much is quoted in Kohfeldt, pp. 72–7. Here her admirer, Judge Brandt, wrote a poem in her honour.

40. Her helper in this was Auckland Colvin who, medals won from the British bombardment of Alexandria clinking on his chest, had introduced himself at the dance. Augusta, immediately accepting that her one-time enemy could become a friend, welcomed his company. It was not a superficial acceptance as indicated in two poems written by her. See Kohfeldt, p. 75.

41. 15 December 1885, in *Seventy Years*, p. 218.

42. Holograph diary, Kohfeldt, p. 75. William was less keen, and it was given to a more active supporter of the Liberals.

43. In *Coole*, written in 1927–8, Augusta quoted his observation that in India the people had been 'incessantly conquered politically, but never overpowered or subdued spiritually'.

44. Emory.

45. Published in McDiarmid and Waters, p. 431, see also pp. 546–7.

46. May 1886, *Seventy Years*, p. 66.

47. Christopher Redington, who lived at Kilcornan House, was a Catholic, five years older than Augusta, but with a similar background to William Gregory; his father had been Under-Secretary, Christopher had been to Oxford and travelled widely on the Continent. Christopher had known Gregory since he was a sceptical young man and criticised his support for Gladstone. See J. Murphy, p. 225.

48. In *Seventy Years* Augusta grouped them together under the heading 'Folklore in Politics: Mr. Gladstone and Ireland', commenting in the text that she had unconsciously 'begun to learn the art of a folklorist'.

49. WHG to AG, 11 June 1886, Emory.

50. 26 September 1886, in *Seventy Years*, p. 225.

51. The Plan of Campaign sought rent reductions and supported those evicted by landlords who refused to reduce rents. There was violence on the estate of the Gregorys' neighbour, the Earl of Clanricarde, an absentee, and notorious for ruthless evictions.

52. WHG to AG, 30 October 1886, Emory.

53. See Jenkins, p. 292.

54. *Seventy Years*, p. 225.

55. *Ibid.*, p. 226.

56. AG to WSB, 29 October 1887, Berg.
57. AG to PH, Fragment, '25 Thurs', Berg, Pethica, 1987.
58. AG to WSB, 10 December 1887, in *Seventy Years*, pp. 230–1.
59. 28 December [1887], Berg.
60. Quoted in James Mitchell, p. 86.
61. The poems are published in James Mitchell, pp. 90–5. Blunt's papers are in the Fitzwilliam Museum, Cambridge.
62. Verse 7, in James Mitchell.
63. *Ibid.*, Verse 1.
64. Blunt's source was Balfour who had informally outlined British strategy in an after-dinner conversation. His cousin, George Wyndham, Balfour's secretary, had been particularly distressed by his lack of loyalty.
65. *LGJ*, II, p. 531.
66. RG to AG, 2 January 1888, Emory. FP to AG, 9 January 1888, Emory.
67. March 1888, in *Seventy Years*, p. 231. Holograph diary, 11 May 1888, in Kohfeldt, p. 83.
68. Holograph diary, 21 May 1888, quoted in Pethica, 1987.
69. 24 November 1888, in *Seventy Years*, p. 232.
70. It was published with alterations by Blunt in *The Love Lyrics and Songs of Proteus*, 1892. No manuscript copy of Augusta's original poem survives, see Saddlemyer and Smythe, p. 408. Blunt's letter requesting Augusta's poem suggests that he expected her to publish her own volume of poetry sometime.
71. 5 June 1888, in *Seventy Years*, p. 231.
72. 13 [July 1888], quoted in Pethica, 1987.
73. 29 August 1888 in *Seventy Years*, p. 232.

Chapter Five

1. WHG to AG, 2 June 1887, Emory.
2. *Seventy Years*, p. 213.
3. WHG to AG, 4 July 1887, 2 June 1888, Emory.
4. WHG to AG, 31 May 1888, Emory.
5. July 1888, *Seventy Years*, p. 213.
6. Holograph diary, vol. 8, Berg, in Pethica, 1987. Inishmore is the largest of the Aran Islands off the Galway coast often referred to as Aran. The challenge of Inishmore stayed with her, and a few years later she would vivaciously debate the purpose of Irish round towers at Grant Duff's London dinner table with Frederic Burton. 17 February 1890, Duff, 1901, p. 224.
7. 27 August 1886, quoted in Kohfeldt, p. 80. About skating lessons: 'So my time and money spent in teaching him are not

thrown away', 17 January 1891, Notebook, 'Recollections of Robert Gregory', Emory.

8. 1 November 1888, *ibid*. He attended Miss Guerini's School in Sloane Street.

9. WHG to Henry Layard, 23 August 1889, in Jenkins, p. 295.

10. *Seventy Years*, p. 213.

11. Sketchbooks in National Library of Ireland, Dublin.

12. RG to AG, 20 June [1889], Emory.

13. *Seventy Years*, pp. 242–3.

14. 6 December 1891, *Seventy Years*, p. 249.

15. 1889, Berg, quoted in Pethica, 1996, p. 43.

16. Pethica, 1996, p. xxxiii.

17. AG to WSB, 20 September 1890, *Seventy Years*, p. 243.

18. The doctor in 'A Philanthropist', who replies succinctly and with the medic's slightly patronising tone, to one talkative patient – 'Well, we must try and get you a better next time' – can also slip into the syntax of his Irish patients: 'Oh, don't be giving yourself up like that.' In this story Augusta relied on speech to demonstrate how talkativeness signified social inferiority. Louise Eden, the heroine, responded to a tenant's anecdotes, speculations and rhetoric with clear, well-focused questions, while the doctor, interviewed by Louise Eden's brother, replies uneasily with increasing loquaciousness. The dialect she uses falls mid-way between the traditional way of rendering spoken Irish, which relied on transcribing the phonetics of the spoken words ('ould' for 'old') and her later Kiltartan dialect which aimed to represent spoken syntax, rhythm, figures of speech while rendering the words in standard form. Gerald Griffin, *The Collegians*, 1829, transcibes the phonetics of spoken words.

19. *The Kiltartan Poetry Book* (1919) in 1971, p. 20.

20. 11 December 1888, Holograph diary, Berg, in Pethica, 1987.

21. AG to WSB, 3 December 1890, Berg, quoted in Pethica, 1987.

22. 3 December 1890, quoted in *Seventy Years*, p. 244. There had been a Land Purchase Act in 1888 which had doubled the Exchequer money available to tenants to borrow in order to purchase their farms, making it a more realistic option for a substantial number of tenants.

23. WHG to Henry Layard, 8 January 1891, Emory.

24. Notebook, 'Recollections of Robert Gregory', 24 April 1891, Emory.

25. *Ibid*., 25 April 1891, Emory.

26. RG to AG, 30 May 1891, Emory.

27. Notebook, 'Recollections of Robert Gregory', 31 July 1891, Emory.

28. 8 September 1891, in *Sir William Gregory*, p. 398.
29. WHG to AG, 8 July 1891, Emory.
30. WHG to Henry Layard, 22 November 1891, in *Sir William Gregory*, p. 399.
31. Christmas 1891 to William's death in March 1892 was recorded a year later in her diary, Pethica, 1996, pp. 3–6. Also see *Sir William Gregory*, pp. 399–400, and AG to FB, 7 March [1892], Emory.

Chapter Six

1. Pethica, 1996. Unless otherwise stated this is the source for her activities in this chapter.
2. Pethica, 1996, pp. 6–7, *Seventy Years*, foreword, p. ix, *LGJ*, I, p. 121.
3. Pethica, 1996, pp. xiii–xiv.
4. 'Memorandum as to Property in which William Robert Gregory is Interested,' 1893, Emory.
5. 17 March 1892, Emory.
6. Pethica, 1996, pp. 24–5.
7. *Ibid.*, p. 7.
8. AG to JQ, 22 February 1918, Berg.
9. EL's diary, 9 and 10 March 1892, British Library, Henry Layard to AG, 6 October 1892, Emory.
10. 15 June 1892, EL's diary, British Library.
11. Pethica, 1996, pp. 6, 9.
12. AG to WSB, 29 October 1892, Berg, quoted in Pethica, 1996, p. xiv.
13. AG to WSB, 16 November 1892, Berg, quoted in Pethica, 1996, p. xiv.
14. AG to WSB, 1892, Berg.
15. Her diary suggests the pamphlet was brought out sometime between 22 April and 14 June.
16. Leslie, p. 103.
17. *Seventy Years*, p. 98.
18. Pethica, 1996, p. 72
19. *Seventy Years*, p. 265.
20. Census 1901.
21. Anne Gregory, p. 84.
22. The 1901 census reveals that William Norton's eldest son, Arthur, his wife, Katherine, and their three-year old daughter had a cook, two general maids, a 'servant', a nurse and a butler.
23. The names all come from the 1901 census.
24. AG to EL, summer 1893, *Seventy Years*, p. 265.

25. *Ibid.*, pp. 265–6.
26. AG to WSB, July 1893, Berg.
27. Pethica, 1996, p. 17.
28. January 1896, Pethica, 1996, p. 107.
29. AG to WSB. July 1893, Berg, quoted in Pethica, 1996, p. 17.
30. *Sir William Gregory*, p. 357.
31. WSB to AG, Berg, 24 November 1894, in Kohfeldt, p. 98, 1996, p. xix.
32. Augusta was prepared to shoulder the risk and expense of publishing the memoir for its long-term benefits, but the publisher John Murray agreed to publish the book and proposed to give her half the profits. It was a relief financially, but also a considerable boost; she could now regard herself as an independent literary figure.
33. Lawless, the daughter of Lord Cloncurry, could be 'hard and decided' and rude to men, *LGJ*, II, p. 153. Augusta told Enid that *Irish Idylls* was one of her 'sermon books', AG to EL, 6 July 1893, Berg, in Pethica, 1996, p. xx. In 1929, Augusta recalled her relief at finding writing that viewed the country people seriously, *LGJ*, II, p. 400. She visited Barlow, the daughter of a Protestant clergyman, in Rahenny, Co. Dublin, and found her serious and shy.
34. *c.* 1–6 October. See AG to WSB, 16 October 1893, Berg.
35. Duff, 1901, p. 276.
36. *Ibid.*, p. 275.
37. *The Celtic Twilight* was published in December 1893.
38. *Ibid.*, 1990, p. 1.
39. Pethica, 1996, p. 48, and Typescript diary, part 6, Berg, quoted in Pethica, 1996, p. xxxiv. Yeats had also published *Poems and Ballads of Young Ireland and Fairy and Folk Tales of the Irish Peasantry* (1888), *The Wanderings of Oisin*, a long poem based on the Fionn cycle (1889), *Irish Fairy Tales* and *The Countess Kathleen and Various Legends and Lyrics* (1892).
40. *Sir Hugh Lane*, p. 29.
41. Pethica, 1996, p. 24.
42. Wednesday 18 April 1894, EL's diary, British Library. Also note 18, Pethica, 1992, p. 89.
43. Pethica, 1996, p. 27.
44. Last will, dated 9 September 1930.
45. 5 July 1894, EL's diary, British Museum, and Pethica, 1996, p. 35.
46. Pethica, 1996, p. 92.
47. *Ibid.*, p. 86.
48. *Ibid.*, p. 28.
49. *Ibid.*, p. 34.

50. *Ibid.*, p. 32.
51. *Hail and Farewell*, p. 78. Pethica, 1996, p. 32.
52. Martyn came to William for advice about the non-payment of rents; he was afraid of as well as unsympathetic to his tenants. WHG to EM [October 1881], in Gwynn, p. 55. In 1890 Martyn published *Morgante the Lesser*, a satire, praised by William for its cleverness, and by de Basterot for its depth. Gwynn, pp. 99–100.
53. His letters are free of any criticisms of her, and in 1899 he would tell her how much her friendship meant to him. Personal communication from Madeleine Humphreys. EM to AG, December 1899, in Humphreys. He was a homosexual who had admitted his feelings privately to Moore, but did not, Moore felt, expect to fulfil them, Frazier, 2000, p. 100.
54. Geary was mildly in love with Martyn (and whom in the autumn of 1895 Augusta helped, through her contact with the Governor of the Gold Coast, Lord Maxwell, to get a post as Attorney-General for the Gold Coast, Pethica, 1996, p. 82); Geary's letters to Augusta after Martyn's death in 1923 revealed that he had missed Martyn whom he had not seen since 1895: 'I do wish our dear Edward had been driven out like me to fend for himself in Africa,' he wrote on 31 October 1929. Berg.
55. Letter from Augusta, 6 June 1902, Berg. Robinson, 1946, p. 30.
56. Pethica, 1996, p. 123.
57. It was published in 1896. She also wrote two unpublished articles on the Disestablished Church and 'Our boys in India', both in Berg.
58. *Sir William Gregory.*
59. Pethica, 1996, p. 42.
60. *Ibid.*, p. 71.
61. *Ibid.*, p. 50.
62. *Memoirs*, 1972, p. 102.
63. Pethica, 1996, p. 63.
64. It was published in December 1895 by *Backwoods Magazine*, then a solidly respectable literary journal, and received as good, gossipy journalism.

Chapter Seven

1. 8 April 1895, Pethica, 1996, p. 68. The reference is to Ezekiel: 'The fathers have eaten sour grapes and the children's teeth are set on edge.'
2. *Ibid.*, p. 78.
3. *Visions and Beliefs*, p. 15.
4. Pethica, 1996, p. 70.

5. 'Irish Superstitions', 20 April 1895, p. 533. She drew on stories heard over a number of years, including a chance meeting with a dispensary doctor in Clare, when she and William asked directions to a ring fort on 25 June 1889.

6. Hyde's publications before 1895: *Beside the Fire*, London, David Nutt, 1890; *Love Songs of Connacht*, Dublin, Gill, London, T. Fisher Unwin, 1893; *The Last Three Centuries of Gaelic Literature*, London, Irish Literary Society, 1894.

7. *Sir William Gregory*, p. 36.

8. Pethica, 1996, pp. 67–9, 106.

9. AG to EL, 28 April 1895, Notebook, 'Recollections of Robert Gregory', Emory.

10. AG to WSB, 1898, Berg.

11. Pethica, 1996, pp. 85–8.

12. See Trevor West, and F.S.L. Lyons, 1985, chapter 4. Plunkett published 'Agricultural Organisation', in *New Ireland Review*, June 1894, and a pamphlet in the same year. *The Irish Homestead*, the organ of the IAOS, was inaugurated in March 1895.

13. *Ibid.*, p. 108.

14. This was to be a Brabazon scheme, an idea proposed by the Earl of Meath, Pethica, 1996, p. 108.

15. Pethica, 1996. pp. 108–9. For the convent AG designed a blind incorporating Celtic features for her hall, and a cushion, decorated with her shamrocks and fleur-de-lis, was illustrated in the *Daily Graphic* in March 1898, Pethica, 1996, p. 166. She wrote 'Gort Industries,' *Erin* (an art journal), November 1896.

16. Pethica, 1996, p. 180.

17. *Ibid.*, p. 110.

18. Saturday 28 March 1996, Pethica, 1996, p. 111.

19. *Ibid.*, p. 111.

20. Robert received a £100 legacy which Augusta put in a bank, Pethica, 1996, p. 142.

21. 1 January 1888, and 26 February 1888, Holograph diary, Berg, quoted in Kohfeldt, p. 83.

22. *LGJ*, I, p. 252.

23. *Ibid.*, p. 118.

24. Pethica, 1996, p. 114.

25. FB to John Wilson-Lynch, 31 July 1896, in Gould, Kelly and Toomey, p. 49.

26. Extracts from Hyde's American speech on the state of the Irish language had been printed in Irish newspapers in the summer of 1891. He had delivered 'The Necessity . . .' as president of the newly formed National Literary Society in November 1892.

27. See *Uncollected Prose* I. He had written on Samuel Ferguson, Standish O'Grady, William Carleton, Emily Lawless, Douglas Hyde, J. Todhunter, Clarence Mangan, George Russell (AE) in *The Bookman, Leisure Hour*, and *United Ireland*.

28. He set up the Irish Literary Society in London with T.W. Rolleston in December 1891; the National Literary Society was set up in Dublin in May 1892.

29. Coote, p. 78.

30. Gould, Kelly, Toomey, p. 49.

31. Pethica, 1996, p. 118.

32. *Seventy Years*, p. 308. W.B. Yeats, *Memoirs*, p. 101. Folklore Notebook 'A', 1–24 August 1896, Pethica, 1987.

33. W.B. Yeats, *Autobiographies*, p. 389.

34. *Ibid.*, p. 391.

35. In Foster, 2003, p. 485.

36. *Seventy Years*, p. 390, Gould, Kelly and Toomey, p. 48.

37. *Seventy Years*, p. 390. Yeats recalled that she had asked him this question within minutes of taking him into her library on the day of the lunch, and that his reply had been the less blunt 'If you get our books and watch what we are doing, you will soon find your work.' *Memoirs*, p. 102.

38. Pethica, 1996, p. 118.

39. *Memoirs*, p. 101.

40. Ireland had been overtaxed since the Union in 1800, and in February 1897 an all-Ireland committee had called for Irish parliamentarians to act in the absence of a government response.

41. Pethica, 1996, p. 136.

42. It was such an influential idea that historians for some time regarded the period between the fall of Parnell and the rise of John Redmond as being politically uninteresting, dominated instead by the cultural revival. Current reassessments of the period are now much more alert to the activities of political organisations such as the Irish Republican Brotherhood, and to the political element in such avowedly cultural movements as the Gaelic League and IAOS. See Roy Foster and Mathews.

Chapter Eight

1. But she did expect him to work. In AG to WSB, January 1898, Berg, she expressed the hope that she could 'clear the property for him so that, by working himself, he need not fear losing it'.

2. Pethica, 1996, p. 142.

3. *Ibid.*, p. 106.

4. *Ibid.*, p. 295.

5. *Ibid.*, p. 298. However, after January 1898 the United Irish League was set up. It used violence and its more extreme demands for compulsory purchase became increasingly popular in the next few years. By January 1901 Coole tenants were involved.

6. *Ibid.*, p. 152. 'Ireland Real and Ideal,' p. 773. Within a few months prices for manure had fallen in Gort and the tenants were buying ammonia and superphosphates, Pethica, pp. 164, 184. Augusta contributed articles to Plunkett's *Irish Homestead* on cottages and tree planting – she advocated that newly independent farmers plant fruit trees for the income.

7. Pethica, 1996, p. 148.

8. *Ibid.*, p. 149.

9. Foster, 1997, pp. 182–3.

10. Pethica, 1996, pp. 150–1.

11. *Ibid.*, p. 147.

12. Quoted by Elizabeth Coxhead in Foreword to *Visions and Beliefs in the West of Ireland*, p. 7.

13. *Ibid.*, pp. 15–16.

14. Yeats made this connection in *Autobiographies*, p. 400.

15. Pethica, 1996, p. 293. When she started to take Irish lessons from Sean Connolly in November 1900 her written Irish was far in advance of her comprehension of the spoken word.

16. M. Murphy.

17. 'A Visit to Lady Gregory', *North American Review*, CCXIV (August 1921) 190–200 in Mikhail, 1977, p. 19.

18. *Visions and Beliefs*, pp. 31–50.

19. *Ibid.*, pp. 15–16.

20. In Yeats, 'Irish Witch Doctors', Frayne & Johnson, pp. 219–20; *Visions and Beliefs*, p. 69.

21. Pethica, 1996, p. 150.

22. In Coote, p. 98.

23. WBY to AG, 1 November 1897, Gould *et al.*, p. 137.

24. Glendinning, p. 375.

25. *Autobiographies*, p. 396.

26. Pethica, 1996, p. 153.

27. *OIT*, p. 19.

28. £300 is equivalent to €23,942 and £16,432 sterling. Augusta asked for £1.00 (€79.50 and £54.00 sterling) from each guarantor, but never drew the money as Martyn made up the losses. *OIT*, p. 21.

29. *OIT*, p. 20.

30. 'Ireland Real and Ideal.'

31. AG to WSB, 1897, Berg.

32. *Seventy Years*, p. 317. Hyde diary, 9 October 1897, in *Songs Ascribed to Raftery*, p. ix.

33. Pethica, 1996, pp. 200–1.
34. AG to DH, 23 October 1897, NLI.
35. DH to AG, 26 October 1897, in Saddlemyer and Smythe, p. 133, he sent a copy of his book of Irish stories, *An Sgeuluidhe Gaodhalach*, intended as a text book 'if you were going to really learn to read Irish'.
36. *Autobiographies*, p. 408.
37. Pethica, 1996, p. 268. Her attitude to Yeats can be compared to her attitude to Frank. When, after she had finished paying his son's schooling in January 1902, he persuaded her to give him an extra £50 she immediately altered her will 'so that Robert will be no poorer'. p. 310.
38. AG to WBY, 8 [April 1914], quoted in Pethica, 1987.
39. *Autobiographies*, pp. 408–9.
40. 'Statement by LG [Lady Gregory] to JQ', n.d. (cat. March 1913), Foster-Murphy Collection, NYPL.
41. WBY to AG, 22 December 1898, Berg.
42. [23 December 1898] Berg, in Pethica, 1992, p. 76. AG to EL [23 December 1898] *ibid.*, states that she had reasons (unspecified) for not collaborating with WBY.
43. Augusta was not impressed by Thomas Rolleston, or Alfred Graves, poet and secretary of the society, though she appreciated any support for Yeats.
44. Pethica, 1996, p. 166.
45. The drawing of Hyde is now in the National Gallery of Ireland and is illustrated in Patricia Butler, *Three Hundred Years of Irish Watercolours and Drawings*, London, Weidenfeld and Nicolson, 1990, p. 163. She wrongly states that Hugh Lane commissioned this drawing.
46. Pethica, 1996, p. 217.
47. 18 June 1898.
48. JBY to LY, 22 October 1912 in Hone, pp. 151–2.
49. GR to AG, 21 October 1897, Emory.
50. Pethica, 1996, p. 199.
51. Quoted in *Seventy Years*, p. 326. Russell would be a success with the IAOS and he edited *The Homestead* for nearly 20 years.
52. [March] 1898, Berg. She had sent the edited letters and her own introductory chapters to the publisher, John Murray, in October 1896, AG to WSB January 1898. Murray felt the period was obscure and the letters generally dull, but he liked her 'brightly written' additions and asked her to reformulate the book as a continuous historical narrative. This she could not attempt. Instead she filled gaps by acquiring 1,200 letters Gregory had written to Robert Peel, and by doing interviews. It was published by Smith Elder & Co.

53. Pethica, 1996, p. 175.
54. AG to WSB, 9 January 1898, Berg.
55. *OIT*, p. 73.
56. 'Ireland, Real and Ideal', *The Nineteenth Century* in November 1898, p. 769.
57. She argued for the recent bill to establish a government department of agriculture and technical instruction in Ireland, supported the current Gaelic League campaign to change the regulations about teaching Irish in National Schools, and alluded to the discoveries she and Yeats had made about the meeting of the pagan and the Christian in the Irish imagination. The article was eloquent of the hope expressed by Plunkett and Yeats that the ideal and the real could work side by side.
58. *Kilkenny Moderator* in February 1898.
59. *The Nineteenth Century*, quoted in Saddlemyer and Smythe, pp. 149–50.
60. AG to SO'C, 2 April 1928, in Krause p. 234. Augusta denied any interest in being a Guardian, but Frank advised her to accept her candidature, see *Tuam Herald*, 17 December 1898, p. 4, and Pethica, 1996, p. 199.
61. Pethica, 1996, p. 188.
62. Burton, who died in spring 1900, left sketches to AG. AG had spent £60 on Jack Yeats's pictures by May 1899. They included 'The Returned American', 'Playing Thimselves' [*sic*], 'The Runaway'.
63. AG to WSB, June 1901, Berg.
64. In 1907 he would publish *The Aran Islands*, in which he described the hard daily life of the islanders, work which, Synge felt, made the men and women who did it beautiful and which gave them an understanding of life that the rest of Europe had largely forgotten. Of all the folkloric writings to emerge from this period, this is by far the most direct and enjoyable.
65. In *OIT*, p. 74.
66. See JMS to AG, 1 July 1898 in Saddlemyer, 1982.
67. *Idem. OIT*, p. 74.

Chapter Nine

1. Pethica, 1996, p. 167.
2. *Ibid.*, p. 177.
3. *Ibid.*, p. 167.
4. AG to WBY, 1 January 1899, Berg, quoted in Foster, 1997, p. 204.

5. AG to EL, *c.* 17 February 1899, Berg, quoted in Pethica, 1996, p. 203.

6. Augusta also hoped (as she had with Co-operation) that by supporting the language movement the country people would discover improvement without resorting to more radical political groups such as the United Irish League. AG to WSB, 13 September [1902], 25 pp. 36–7.

7. Pethica, 1996, p. 200. AG to WBY, 23 November [1898], Berg.

8. 'Lecture at Gort', *An Claidheamh Soluis*, 12 August 1899, pp. 342–3.

9. Pethica, 1996, p. 221.

10. AG to WSB [June/July] 1898, Berg.

11. Pethica, 1996, p. 199.

12. 9 June 1902, Emory.

13. Illustrated in Smythe, 1995, p. 54.

14. Pethica, 1996, p. 262.

15. *Ibid.*, p. 213.

16. Hyde had already tried to defend the theatre to Eoin MacNeill, the editor of *An Claidheamh Soluis*, the Gaelic League newspaper, by asking him to refrain from alienating valued friends such as Lady Gregory. 'They are not enemies to us. They are a halfway house.' *An Claidheamh Soluis* had expressed its dislike of anything Irish in English in the April 1899 edition. DH to MacNeill, 7 May 1899, in Saddlemyer and Smythe, p. 134.

17. Pethica, 1996, p. 220.

18. Frank Hugh O'Donnell, an embittered nationalist, produced a denunciatory pamphlet, 'Souls for Gold', which inspired a group of young men from the Catholic University in Dublin to heckle.

19. Reprinted in *OIT*, pp. 190–3.

20. Preface, *My First Play*.

21. *LGJ*, II, p. 495. See Hill for discussion of her writing in 1899–1900.

22. p. 410.

23. Hyde, helped by Augusta's local contacts, was trying to compile an anthology of poems that people remembered or had written down, while Yeats, marvelling at the phenomenon of a blind poet who loved beautiful women, had persuaded Augusta to find someone to take them to the cottage of Raftery's most famous love, Mary Hynes, hidden in an overgrown boreen near the Norman tower at Ballylee. Augusta translated 'Mary Hynes of Ballylee' for Yeats's article 'Dust hath Closed Helen's Eye', published in *The Dome*, October 1899, and 1902 reissue of *The Celtic Twilight*. Hyde used Augusta's material in his 1903 publication on Raftery, and Augusta used his material.

24. See 'Raftery' in *Poets and Dreamers*.
25. Pethica, 1996, p. 223.
26. In Saddlemyer and Smythe, p. 135.
27. The Raftery tradition continues today in parts of Connacht, partly fed by the work of Hyde and Augusta, partly continuing the established tradition of handing down songs and poems. From Lillis O'Laoire.
28. Pethica, 1996, pp. 226–50.
29. *Ibid.*, p. 296.
30. *Ibid.*, p. 173. *Hail and Farewell*, pp. 203–7.
31. AG to WBY, 26 November–December 1899. Berg.
32. Pethica, 1996, p. 231.
33. In Gould *et al.*, pp. 492–3.
34. *Ibid.* WBY to AG [2 June 1900], pp 533–4.
35. *Ibid.* WBY to AG [*c.* 5 June 1900], p. 536.
36. Pethica, 1996, p. 243.
37. 'Ireland in Bond Street', 25 February 1899, p. 5. She found a melancholy tone in his work which she interpreted as essentially Irish: the pain of emigrating, the awkwardness of returning well-to-do. She bought 'The Returned American'.
38. See Pethica, 1996, p. 221. She no doubt concurred with Russell who hoped Yeats would 'become the Millet of our peasants', GR to AG, 28 April 1899, Emory.
39. JBY reported to Augusta that Jack came away from Coole with new ideas, ambitions and hopes, JBY to AG, 19 May 1899, quoted in Arnold, p. 86.
40. Pethica, 1996, p. 247.
41. AG to WBY, Monday 4 November [1913], Berg.
42. 'Sir Frederic Burton', *The Leader*, 8 December 1900, pp. 231–2.
43. Letter, *Freeman's Journal*, 5 April 1899. See Hill.
44. Pethica, 1996, p. 172.
45. 'Memories of Coole', *The Irish Times*, 23 and 24 November 1959, pp. 5 and 7.
46. Pethica, 1996, p. 187.
47. AG to WSB, 1 July 1900, Berg.
48. DH diary in *Poets and Dreamers*, pp. 224–5. There was no tradition of Irish language drama, but Alice Milligan had thrown down the gauntlet in January 1899 by reporting in *The Daily Express* that a living Gaelic poet had written an act in Gaelic verse for a play performed at the Letterkenny Feis, Hogan and Kilroy, 1899–1901. Augusta would unfairly airbrush Alice Milligan and the Gaelic League from her subsequent account of Irish drama in *OIT*.

49. Before he left, Hyde began another Irish play, *An Cleamhnas* (The Matchmaking), Pethica, 1996, p. 278.
50. AG to JQ, 24 July [1906], Berg.
51. Pethica, 1996, p. 288.
52. In 1918 Martyn wrote that the foundation of the ILT was 'the most significant action of my life', in Humphreys, p. 7. Martyn was, in the end, dispensable. Fourteen months later, in January 1902, he left the Irish Literary Theatre to set up his own company.
53. Pethica, 1996, p. 275.
54. AG to WSB, 22 November 1900, Berg. Letter, *All Ireland Review*, 15 December 1900.

Chapter Ten

1. Pethica, 1996, p. 259.
2. *Autobiographies*, pp. 455–6.
3. AG to WSB, 7 April 1902, Berg.
4. From Mahaffy's representation to the Intermediate Education Commission which was considering Irish as a school subject, quoted in Dunleavy and Dunleavy, p. 210.
5. AG to WSB, 7 April 1902, Berg.
6. This mostly applies to the Finn legends – the Cuchulain legends, associated with Ulster, had largely been forgotten or never existed in Galway – and resulted from tailoring the stories to the audience.
7. 'Living Legends of the Fianna', p. 77.
8. AG to WSB, January 1898, Berg. AG to Mary Hutton, 8 May 1902, NLI. AG to DH, 11 [May 1901], NLI. But, 'one cd not copy Morte d'Arthur yet they shd be in something to answer to it – Now I think of ~~copying~~ [putting] each story into [the Irish idiom of] the original ~~& putting them into~~ . . .' where [ ] indicates AG's amendments, Pethica, 1996, p. 290.
9. AG to WSB, 7 April 1902, Berg.
10. He advocated Hiberno-English for folk songs and stories so that they would not be filtered through English and reduced, but convey some of the spirit of the Gaelic. Introduction, *Beside the Fire*, p. xi. Yeats was also critical of overlaying the language of a literary, sophisticated culture onto the oral traditions of the peasants.
11. Pethica, 1996, p. 293.
12. DH to AG, 13 March 1901 and 1 May 1901, Berg, in Pethica, 1996, p. 293.
13. AG to WSB, 7 April 1902, Berg.
14. Pethica, 1996, p. 284.

15. RG to AG [December 1900] quoted in Saddlemyer and Smythe, p. 350.
16. Pethica, 1996, p. 294.
17. *Seventy Years*, p. 390.
18. *Autobiographies*, p. 455.
19. Letter to *The Daily News*, 11 May 1904, in Frayne and Johnson, p. 328. See Pethica, 2002, for discussion of how Yeats was provoked by Hyde's assertion of Irish in his 1892 speech on 'de-Anglicisation'.
20. Unable to read old Irish manuscripts, she used printed texts and referred to existing translations by, among others, Eugene O'Curry, De Jubainville, Alfred Nutt, Kuno Meyer, Hyde, Whitley Stokes and Eleanor Hull. She extracted sections, sometimes phrases, from different translations and amalgamated them. Some details and incidents she omitted, some she modified. See her notes in *Cuchulain*, and AG to WBY, 28 March 1902, Berg.
21. *Seventy Years*, pp. 393.
22. *Ibid.*, p. 390. Yeats was contemplating using Cuchulain as a poetic subject. In June, Augusta, worried that he was not writing enough poetry, wrote encouragingly that she had just worked on a piece with 'texts for half a dozen poems in it'. Soon after that he embarked on his poem 'Baile and Aillinn' and his Cuchulain play, *On Baile's Strand*; Lady Gregory's translations had, he told several people, released ideas which allowed him to write what he had long wanted to write. AG to WBY, 16 June [1901], Berg. Foster, 1997, p. 250.
23. Pethica, 1996, pp. 304, 311.
24. *Ibid.*, pp. 295, 298–300.
25. A neighbouring landowner, Mr Bagot, assured them that, although the courts often judged poor ground to be too pricey and was thus being revalued at a lower level, good ground was often under rented. In May 1901, with a branch of the United Irish League just established at Kiltartan and more tenants threatening to go to the land courts, Frank and Augusta had an argument about what they should do. *Ibid.*, p. 306.
26. AG to WBY, Friday [10 December 1905], Berg.
27. AG to DH, 11 [May 1901], NLI, and 11 October 1901, NLI.
28. *Poets and Dreamers*, pp. 54–5. In 1994 Ted Hughes chose it for the anthology *Lifelines*.
29. AG to WBY, undated and incomplete, Berg. James Pethica has dated it to 24 May 1901.
30. Yeats's notes to the play quoted in Pethica, 1988, p. 8.
31. Draft ms., Berg.
32. In *Poets and Dreamers*, pp. 44–5.

33. WBY to AG, 2 April 1902, Berg, quoted in Hogan and Kilroy, 1976, p. 15.
34. AG to JQ, 18 June 1909, Berg.
35. *LGJ*, 1, p. 55.
36. 28 December 1904, Berg.
37. 20 February 1908, quoted in Foster, 1997, p. 580.
38. Quoted in *OIT*, pp. 53–4.
39. AG to WBY, 18 April 1904, Berg.
40. WBY to JQ, 8 November 1902, Kelly and Schuchard, p. 243. Typed by Augusta and as if written by her.
41. p. 504.
42. 'Man and the Echo'.
43. *LGJ*, II, p. 13.
44. *Ibid.*, p. 28.
45. Pethica, 1988.
46. *Twisting* was performed by the Gaelic League in Irish with an enthusiastic Hyde playing the main role.
47. In Kiberd, 1979, p. 228.
48. Hogan and Kilroy, 1975, p. 114. See articles by Yeats and Synge and Gregory (AG to WBY, 26 March 1904, Berg) arguing in the face of successive challenges from people like the journalist D.P. Moran and Patrick Pearse, that an alliance between the language movement and the literary revival was inevitable and desirable.
49. Frazier, 2000, pp. 302–3.
50. Yeats at this point was attracted by the focus on the speaking actor and the attention of the rest. He felt it had potential for his verse plays. In fact, the Fays' acting methods would prove best for the comedies that Augusta, Synge and others would write for them. See O hAodha.
51. See Pethica, 2002. On 18 November 1901 she sent him her scenario, which in effect reconciled Hyde's materialism and Yeats's spiritualism, for comments.
52. See Leerssen, and Kiberd, 2000.
53. AG to WBY, 28 March 1902, Berg.
54. AG to WBY, 9 January 1902, Berg. She sent the manuscript to Murray in autumn 1901. He returned it with the message that she should rewrite it for the English market. Augusta, despairing that he had completely misunderstood her project, gave the manuscript to Yeats 'to dispose of'. By 13 December, through a combination of politeness and obstinacy, Yeats had persuaded Murray to publish it as it stood.
55. *Seventy Years*, pp. 400, 403. WBY to AG, 6 October 1902, Kelly and Schuchard, p. 234.

56. In 'Living Legends of the Fianna' Augusta referred to 'the guardians of the old unwritten lore'.
57. AG to WBY, 17 May 1902, Berg.
58. Pethica, 1996, p. 309. She was encouraged by Yeats and the Gaelic scholar, Eoin MacNeill, Hyde and Russell. *Gods and Fighting Men* was published with a preface by Yeats, *c.* 31 January 1904.
59. Preface, *Gods and Fighting Men*.
60. *Autobiographies*, p. 456.
61. *Poets and Dreamers*, p. 98.
62. Reviewers were appreciative; Martyn, won over to her work at last, wrote on 9 March, 'you have a wonderful intuition of the soul of the people'.

Chapter Eleven

1. AG to WSB, 22 June 1902, Berg.
2. RG to AG, 20 May 1902, Emory, in Kelly and Schuchard, p. 186. In a letter dated 21 May, Robert commented on *Cuchulain*: 'Everybody I have heard from about the book [Cuchulain] have [*sic*] liked it very much. Jennings our literary critic likes the idiom very much.' Emory in Saddlemyer and Smythe, p. 351.
3. The document of welcome is now in the Kiltartan Museum. See *Hearth and Home*, 24 July 1902 (570), in Kelly and Schuchard, p. 214.
4. WBY to WSB, 4 July 1902, in *ibid.*, p. 214.
5. Pethica, 1996, p. 312.
6. 22 June 1902, Berg.
7. AG to WSB, 13 September [1902], Berg.
8. *The Jackdaw* and *On the Racecourse*.
9. *The Collected Plays I*, p. 253. FF to WBY, 26 September 1902 in Robinson, 1951, pp. 28–9. WBY to AG, 6 October 1902, in Kelly and Schuchard, pp. 233–4. Published in December 1902 as 'A Losing Game', in *The Gael* (New York).
10. Yeats finally persuaded the Fays to stage *Twenty Five* with his *The Hour Glass* on 14 March 1903 in the Molesworth Hall in Camden Street.
11. 19 September 1902, in Kelly and Schuchard, p. 227.
12. He wrote *An Naomh ar Iarraid* (The Lost Saint) and *An Pléusgadh na Bulgóide* (The Bursting of the Bubble). Yeats and Augusta hammered out a scenario for *The Nativity*, which he wrote in September. *Poets and Dreamers*, pp. 137–8, 224–6, Pethica, 1996, p. 312.

13. She rewrote it six years later as *The Workhouse Ward*. *OIT*, pp. 55–7. Hyde's plays would be performed in the next few years but not by Irish language groups. Despite the rhetoric, Irish language was never an integral part of their theatre. See Hogan and Kilroy, 1976.

14. *Poets and Dreamers*, pp. 134–5.

15. AG to WBY, 16 November 1901, Berg.

16. Quinn, 1911.

17. WBY and AG to JQ, 8 November 1902, Berg, in Kelly and Schuchard, p. 243.

18. It is possible that Yeats and Augusta fell into a trap set by George Moore who had threatened a lawsuit if Yeats developed the idea independently. Frazier, 2000, pp. 320–1.

19. AG to WSB, undated, 1903, Berg. *OIT*, p. 53.

20. 'What frightens me is your joy of creation, you are like Puppy after a chicken, when you see a new idea cross the path, tho' it may but end in a mouth full of feathers after all.' [5 December 1902], Berg.

21. November 1900, Pethica, 1996, pp. 288–9.

22. 8 January 1906.

23. *OIT*, p. 64.

24. See WBY to AG, 18 November 1902, Kelly and Schuchard, p. 252, and AG to WBY, 22 November 1902, Kelly and Schuchard, p. 264.

25. WBY wrote a pagan version, 'The Black Horse', in May 1903; AG later rewrote it as *The Travelling Man* and it was published in her well-received *Seven Short Plays* in 1909.

26. See AG to WBY, 25 December [1903], Berg, for his conviction that believers, whether Catholic or Protestant, should unite against unbelievers. He was probably also inspired by his aunt. He wrote a pithy letter published in a number of Dublin newspapers on 3 September.

27. She criticised his idea that patriotic Unionists should be rewarded with honours, telling him 'that would be a very bad service to his own class, it would leave the nationalists with a monopoly of disinterestedness.' AG to WBY, 25 December [1903], Berg.

28. Purchase was still not compulsory, but if three-quarters of the tenantry of any estate agreed the sale could proceed. In Coole the new Act inspired the tenants to consider purchasing their acres, but Augusta waited for them to make an offer. On 29 December 1903 she told Blunt that no definite offer had yet been made. Berg.

29. 5 February 1900, Pethica, 1996, pp. 235, 242.

30. *Ibid.*, p. 252. AG to HL, undated [March 1900], in O'Byrne p.

30. Secretly she felt overpaid; she had only ever been a dutiful aunt. *Sir Hugh Lane*, p. 33.

31. AG to HL, 1 December 1903 [postmark], Berg.

32. See O'Byrne, pp. 42–4.

33. In her biography of Lane she would write dramatically of his conversion to Ireland and unworldliness.

34. Once the Irish Literary Theatre had completed its three-year experiment in 1901 Yeats and Augusta had identified their theatre with Fay's Irish National Dramatic Society (though, as we have seen, other groups also performed their plays). Now the reorganized theatre was named the Irish National Theatre Society.

35. Russell, Gonne and Hyde were vice-presidents, W.G. Fay the stage manager.

36. *OIT*, p. 52.

37. AG to JQ, 28 March [1908], Berg, quoted in Pethica, 2004, p. 12.

38. AG to JQ, 30 April 1903, in Pethica, 2004.

39. *Seventy Years*, p. 427.

40. AG to WSB, 26 February 1905, Berg.

41. 6 May 1903, Kelly and Schuchard, p. 359.

42. Saddlemyer and Smythe, p. 138. AG to WSB, 26 February 1905, Berg.

43. Saturday [October 1903], Berg.

44. *LGJ*, II, p. 95.

45. Saddlemyer and Smythe, pp. 353–4.

46. 26 July 1903, Berg.

47. 26 July [1903], in Kelly and Schuchard, p. 405. *Seventy Years*, p. 426.

48. Micheál O hAodha, *Theatre in Ireland*, Oxford, Basil Blackwell, 1974, p. 62.

49. Augusta too was no stranger to secrecy; apart from Blunt she perhaps looked back on her life and wondered if she had not kept her nationalist feelings a secret from herself for much of it. It is easy to imagine Augusta empathising with the sergeant's gradual discovery of his nationalist sympathies as he is pleasantly manipulated by the ballad singer.

50. *Our Irish Theatre*, pp. 52–3.

51. *Ibid.*, p. 20. But her comedies relying on situation were often farces. This could be emphasised with exaggerated acting, and in the October 1918 production Augusta noted with disappointment that Bartley in *Spreading the News* was presented as a stage Irishman. *LGJ*, I, p. 31.

52. *OIT*, p. 57.

53. WBY to AG, 9 November 1903, in Kelly and Schuchard, p. 462.

54. AG to WSB, 16 January 1905, Berg. *OIT*, pp. 57–8.

55. 25 December [1903], Berg.
56. 1 January 1904, Berg.
57. 14 February 1904, Berg.
58. 4 January 1904, Berg.
59. 21 January 1904, in Kelly and Schuchard, p. 529.
60. *The Collected Plays II*, p. 288.
61. First version of *Kincora*, *The Collected Plays II*, p. 316.
62. AG to WSB, 14 February 1904. WBY to AG, 3 August 1904, in Kelly and Schuchard, p. 630.
63. WBY to JMS, 21 August 1904, in Kelly and Schuchard, p. 637. In her assertion that bellicosity was morally superior to the quiet pursuit of peace, Gormleith was not dissimilar to Maud Gonne. Kincora was performed on the 25 March to a small audience, and made a £50 profit. Arthur Griffith admired it.
64. Máire Nic Shiubhlaigh, p. 68.
65. *Memoirs*, p. 167.

Chapter Twelve

1. Quoted in Mikhail, 1977, p. 28.
2. Quoted in Mikhail, 1988, p. 67.
3. AG to WSB, 12 March 1915, Berg.
4. A generalisation based on many interviews by James W. Flannery referred to in R.F. Foster, *Paddy and Mr Punch*, London, Penguin, Allen Lane, 1993, p. 224.
5. Payne, p. 66.
6. 7 January 1906, quoted in Saddlemyer, 1982, p. 103.
7. Fragment, *c*. 1906, in Foster, 1997, p. 568. See also AG to WBY, 15 May [1914], in Foster p. 518, 'That sentence is the long cry of the church's – give us your intellect, to save your soul.' Augusta could write flippantly to Yeats in 1901 – 'Get something from Edward to keep the church quiet', in Humphreys, p. 8.
8. EM to AG, 20 March 1903, in Humphreys, p. 8.
9. W.B. Yeats, *Autobiographies*, 1955, p. 395.
10. *Seventy Years*, p. 430.
11. AG to WBY [1909], in *ibid*., p. 443.
12. Foster, 1997, p. 342.
13. 8 January 1906, Berg, in *ibid*., p. 342.
14. n.d. Berg, in *ibid*., p. 340.
15. 1 December, in Saddlemyer, 1982, p. 162.
16. 13 September [1902], Berg.
17. See Coxhead, 1979.
18. O hAodha, p. 79.
19. Saturday [spring 1906], Berg. Yeats's awareness of class was

expressed man-to-man to Synge to whom he generalised about the actresses in August 1904: 'One of our difficulties is that women of the class of Miss Garvey and Miss Walker [Máire Nic Shiubhlaigh] have not sensitive bodies, they have a bad instrument to work with, but they have great simplicity of feeling, a readiness to accept high ideals, a certain capacity for noble feeling. Women of our own class on the other hand have far more sensitive instruments, are far more teachable in all that belongs to expression, but they lack simplicity of feeling, their minds are too full of trivial ideals, and they seldom seem capable of really noble feeling.' 21 August 1904, in Kelly and Schuchard, p. 638. Dispiritingly it suggested that women were irredeemably compromised by class. As Synge fell in love with one of the women from the former category it is unlikely that he fully agreed with Yeats on this.

20. 3 January 1908, Berg.
21. See Colum, p. 119. Mary Colum trained as an actress at the Abbey and married Padraic Colum.
22. Payne, p. 66.
23. AG to WBY, 1 January 1904, Berg.
24. The portrait is in the Hugh Lane Municipal Gallery of Modern Art. Augusta did not find the likeness convincing, but she approved the image. Saddlemyer and Smythe, p. 372.
25. 'Ireland in letters, Lady Gregory tells of an intellectual revolution' was published in April.
26. 16 February 1904, Berg.
27. AG to WBY, 26 March 1904, Berg.
28. 24 July [1906], Berg.
29. 19 April 1904, Berg.
30. 12 October 1906, Berg.
31. He praised *Spreading the News*, finding it humorous, and predicted it would become 'immensely popular'. He thought *Cathleen ni Houlihan* went to pieces after the old woman goes out. EM to AG, 28 December 1904, Berg.
32. 'The Theatre and the Return of the People' dated November 1911, NLI, printed in *OIT* as 'The Irish Theatre and the People', pp. 140–3.
33. She wrote several times about her desire to see her history plays touring to schoolchildren to ground them in the myths of their forebears, and her letters reveal that she was diligent in preparing programmes and itineraries for tours in Ireland. AG to JQ, 24 July 1906, Berg; *Book Monthly* article April 1904.
34. *Seventy Years*, p. 473.
35. AG to WBY, 18 January 1904, Berg.

36. See Notes in *The Collected Plays I*, pp. 253–5.
37. Private communication from Dr Maura Cronin. The phrases are also very similar to those spoken in parts of Ireland today.
38. 28 September 1904, in Kelly and Schuchard, p. 652.
39. 26 November 1906, in Saddlemyer, 1982, p. 162.
40. *Seventy Years*, p. 412.
41. 31 December 1904 in Hogan and Kilroy, 1976, p. 130.
42. Nic Shiubhlaigh, p. 57.
43. AG to WSB, 16 January 1905, Berg.
44. [24 December 1904], Berg.
45. 17 December 1904, in Kelly and Schuchard, p. 687.
46. *Ibid.*, p. 690.
47. Quoted in *OIT*, p. 36.

Chapter Thirteen

1. Quoted in Hogan and Kilroy, 1978, p. 22.
2. Quoted in *OIT*, p. 65
3. AG to WSB, 3 April 1905, Berg.
4. *Seventy Years*, p. 428.
5. Quoted in *ibid.*, p. 437.
6. AG to WSB, 7 May and 1 July 1905, Berg.
7. See Foster, 1997, p. 338.
8. AG to WSB, 24 September 1905, Berg.
9. 8 August 1905, Berg.
10. Reproduced in Smythe, 1995, pp. 28–9.
11. Longford, p. 365.
12. Between December 1904 and December 1907 eleven of her plays were performed in 123 performances, more than the combined total of all the other Abbey playwrights, excluding Yeats. Daniel Murphy, 'Lady Gregory, Co-Author and Sometimes Author of the Plays of W.B. Yeats', in Harrington, p. 441. In the following four years she produced ten more. Her rate dropped thereafter. From 1913 to 1927, 14 years, she wrote only nine plays. She left several unperformed plays at her death in 1932.
13. Unpublished essay, 'Making a Play', Berg.
14. 24 July 1905, Berg.
15. Friday [10 December 1905], Berg.
16. Tuesday 12 December 1905, in Hogan and O'Neill, p. 65.
17. Wednesday 25 October 1905, *ibid.*, p. 62. The play was well received on 8 December 1906, and Yeats told Symons that the play was original, 'at once merry and beautiful'. It has been appreciated by later critics: Hogan and Kilroy list it has one of her best plays and Elizabeth Coxhead as one of her two best full

length plays. Most gratifyingly for Augusta, Synge appreciated that her tragi-comedy with its serious intent, ironic humour, straightforward entertainment and folkloric themes had made historical drama possible again. Lennox Robinson would also value her ability to animate historical characters. *The Collected Plays II*, p. 303. Robinson, 1942, p. 106.

18. Cloon is the name of an estate on the road from Gort to Roxborough. She first used the name in 'A Philanthropist' in 1890.

19. *Connacht Tribune*, 22 December 1989.

20. *Hyacinth Halvey* was performed on 19 February. It cemented Augusta's reputation as a writer of comedy. The play was often revived and Augusta would marvel that people would continue to find it funny 'as if it were new'. From now on she would appreciate the commercial value of her short comedies, pushing her work for tours, advocating that they be used sparingly in Dublin otherwise they would 'use them up & we should want them later'. See AG to WBY, Sunday [24 December 1905 or January 1906], Berg.

21. AG to WBY [2 November 1905], Berg.

22. *OIT*, p. 60. *The Doctor in Spite of Himself* was performed on 16 April 1906. They applied to the Comèdie Francais for the 'business', the traditional stage directions for French actors which was used in later productions.

23. She described her Molière translations – there would be others – as 'adaptations' to ensure that they could be copyrighted as her work, though she translated the French almost verbatim and kept most of the content. See AG to JQ, 2 December [1910], Berg, and Mary FitzGerald in Saddlemyer and Smythe. Synge and Yeats welcomed her adaptations; Synge felt she put 'life into the dead bones of the plays' and Yeats preferred them to the original.

24. AG to JMS, 6 January 1906, Saddlemyer, 1982, p. 95.

25. AG to WBY, Thursday [December 1905], Berg.

26. AG to JMS [6 January 1906], Saddlemyer, 1982, p. 97.

27. n.d., quoted in Foster, 1997, p. 340.

28. 8 January 1906, quoted in Foster, 1997, p. 342.

29. AG to WBY, Thursday [December 1905], Berg. AG to JMS, 6 January 1906, Saddlemyer, 1982, p. 95.

30. AG to FF [December 1905], Berg.

31. AG to WBY, Wednesday [3 January 1906], Berg.

32. AG to JMS, Saturday [6 January 1906], Saddlemyer, 1982, p. 94.

33. AG to JQ, 24 July 1906, Berg.

34. AG to JQ, 12 October 1906, Berg.

35. AG to JQ, 12 October 1906.

36. 'Making a Play' [1911], Berg.
37. In Mikhail, 1988, p. 127.
38. 'The Continuity of Folklore', unpublished lecture, unsigned, undated, Berg. AG to WSB, 26 February 1905 and 15 April 1905, Berg.
39. Many of the prophecies deal with the replacement of the powerful by the weak, the rich by the poor, the English by the Catholic Gael. Augusta included this notion in several plays, including *The Rising of the Moon* and *The White Cockade*. See M. Murphy. She also points out that Augusta amalgamated stories on the same subject from different sources which detracts from their authenticity.
40. There were reviews including Ethel Davidson in *The New Ireland Review* in which she characterised Lady Gregory as someone who had animated 'peasant' tales with her understanding and imagination. XXXIV No 6, February (1911), 370–1.
41. 3 January 1909, Berg.
42. She also published three long articles for *Monthly Review*: 'The Haunted Islands', on Aran folklore, May 1906; 'Living Legends of the Fianna', February 1905: 'Living Legends of the Saints', November 1905.
43. AG to WSB, 26 September 1906, Berg. *OIT*, p. 59.
44. *The Collected Plays II*, p. 207. She finished it by early October. After the first performance on 8 December 1906 she rewrote what Frank Fay considered to be a weak ending, and nearly a year later she completely revised it. On 2 February 1911 Yeats would write to her, 'I cannot tell you what a joy *Canavans* has been to me. I told the audience in my speech before the curtain that of all our comedies it was my favourite.' *Seventy Years*, p. 483.
45. AG to WSB, 25 December 1906, Berg.
46. She praised her to Quinn in October, and cautiously told Synge that she was warming to her in November. AG to JQ, 12 October 1906, Berg. AG to JMS, 26 November 1906, Saddlemyer, 1982, p. 162.
47. Foster, 1997, p. 354.
48. AG to WBY [23 March 1906], Berg.
49. Saddlemyer, 1982, pp. 163–77.
50. [December 1906], Berg.
51. Quoted in Foster, 1997, p. 355.
52. Wednesday [19? December 1906], Saddlemyer, 1982, p. 181.
53. AG to JMS, Sunday [23 December 1906], *ibid.*, p. 183.
54. Probably 10 January 1907, Berg, quoted in Foster, 1997, p. 357.
55. Thursday 10 [January 1907], Berg, Saddlemyer, 1982, p. 202.

56. Wednesday [19? December 1906], Saddlemyer, 1982, p. 181. *OIT*, p. 58. She couched her support for Fay in political terms, too, referring to the Parnell split: 'We should all refuse [Horniman's scheme to oust Fay] – & not be like Dillon & Co, giving up Parnell to please an English howl.' AG to JMS, Saturday [29 December 1906], Saddlemyer, 1982, p. 191.
57. Notes in *The Collected Plays II*, pp. 293–4.
58. See Kiberd, 1996, pp. 89–93.

Chapter Fourteen

1. AG to WSB [May 1907], Berg.
2. AG to JBY, 9 January 1906, Berg, quoted in Pethica, 2004, p. 13.
3. AG to WBY, December 1906, Berg.
4. JMS to Molly Allgood, 19 November [1907], Saddlemyer, 1984, p. 81.
5. W.J. McCormack, pp. 306–7.
6. Radical elements were also surfacing in the Gaelic League, putting pressure on the more conservative Hyde to engage in nationalist gestures rather than to solve the financial crisis which had sent him to America to raise funds in 1905. See Dunleavy and Dunleavy, chs 12 and 13. Edward Martyn was president of Sinn Féin 1904–1908.
7. AG to HL, Thursday 14 [1913], Berg.
8. p. 104.
9. *Seventy Years*, pp. 421 and 447.
10. Friday 13 [December 1912], Berg, quoted in Foster, 1997, p. 449.
11. *OIT*, p. 80.
12. *Ibid.*, p. 67.
13. See particularly James Kilroy, *The Playboy Riots*.
14. *OIT*, p. 67. See Foster, 1997, pp. 359–67 and McCormack, ch. 19 on the riots.
15. *The Freeman's Journal*, 29 January 1907, p. 7. In *OIT*, p. 69, Augusta would stress that it was the violent methods that the audience used to express its opinion that the directors objected to, diplomatically leaving the issues about whether the play was right or wrong, good or bad, cloudy.
16. *The Irish Times*, 29 January 1907, p. 8.
17. 14 March 1907, Blunt, 1920.
18. AG to JMS, Tuesday [5 February 1907], Saddlemyer, 1982, p. 213.
19. Quoted in Tóibín, p. 65.
20. Robert to Hugh Viscount Gough, 3 February 1907, Berg, quoted in Foster, 1997, p. 363. Rt Hon. John Ross P.C.

21. *Clare Champion*, 9 February 1907, reported the resolution of the Kiltartan branch and *Connacht Champion*, 16 February 1907 reported the resolution of the Athenry branch.
22. 14 March 1907, Blunt, 1919, p. 166.
23. Letter from AG to WSB, September 1907, Berg.
24. *Seventy Years*, p. 419.
25. A few months later, after its performance in London, Augusta would be told, 'you have succeeded in bringing treason into the heart of London', and its performances by local groups during the 1920s was approved by republicans. AG to WSB, 17 June [1907], Berg.
26. 23 February 1907, Hogan and O'Neill, p. 88.
27. From the essay 'English Novelists', 1945, quoted in V. Glendenning, *Elizabeth Bowen, Portrait of a Writer*, 2nd edn, London, Phoenix, 1993, p. 67.
28. AG to WSB, 27 June [1906], Berg.
29. RG to AG, undated, Emory.
30. AG to JQ, 17 August 1907, Berg. Margaret was the daughter of Graham Parry of Cobham, Virginia, USA.
31. Gregory papers, Emory.
32. AG to JQ, 10 February 1918, Berg.
33. AG to HL, postmarked 18 August 1907 and Friday 23 August 1907, Berg.
34. Quoted in Read p. 54, letter dated 4 October 1907.
35. Quoted in Afterword, *LGJ*, II, p. 642. Sunday 22 [September 1907].
36. *Seventy Years*, p. 428.
37. Indenture, 28 April 1908, Emory. AG to T.J. Kiernan, 4 June 1925.
38. Telegram RG to AG sent on day of wedding, information from Colin Smythe. They had planned to be married in October – this is what Augusta expected – but it had been rearranged.
39. AG to JQ, 17 August 1907, Berg. AG to WSB, September [1907], Berg.
40. AG to HL, postmarked Friday 23 August 1907.
41. For an account of the Harcourt Street Gallery see O'Byrne, ch. 9. Letter from AG to HL, 10 January 1907, Berg.
42. O'Byrne, p. 87.
43. AG to HL, 6 December 1907, NLI, ms. 27,756, quoted in O'Byrne, p. 103.
44. *Seventy Years*, p. 418.
45. JMS to AG, 14 August 1907, Saddlemyer, 1982.
46. AG to JQ, 17 August 1907, Berg.
47. AG to JMS [20 June 1907], Saddlemyer, 1982, p. 224; AH to

WBY [19? June 1907], quoted in Frazier, 1990, p. 198; AH to WBY and AG, 28 June 1907, Saddlemyer, 1982, p. 230; AG to JMS [29 June 1907], Saddlemyer, 1982, p. 229; AG to JMS [20 June 1907], Saddlemyer, 1982, p. 225.

48. AG to JMS, Thursday [20 June 1907], Saddlemyer, 1982, p. 226.
49. Quoted in Saddlemyer, 1982, p. 245.
50. AG to WBY, 14 December 1907, Berg. AG to WBY [18 December 1907], Berg. AG to JMS, Sunday [21 December 1907], Saddlemyer, 1982, p. 258. AG to WBY [18 December 1907], Berg.
51. AG to WBY [20 or 27 December 1907], Berg.
52. Saddlemyer, 1982, p. 270.
53. *Where There is Nothing.* See Pethica, 1987.
54. Yeats, 'Unicorn from the Stars,' *Plays in Prose and Verse*, London, 1922, pp. 246–7.
55. AG to JQ, 17 August 1907, Berg.
56. AG to JQ, 11 December [1907].
57. Yeats, from 'The Municipal Gallery Re-visited', 1937. There is also another portrait by Mancini which depicts Augusta reading.

Chapter Fifteen

1. AG to JQ, 26 February [1908] Berg. AG to WBY, 19 April 1908, quoted in Foster, 1997, p. 601.
2. For details about Synge's illness see McCormack.
3. AG to JQ, 16 May [1908], Berg. AG to JQ, 6 June [1908], Berg, quoted in Pethica, 2004.
4. Saddlemyer, 1982, p. 297.
5. AG to JQ, 26 February [1908], Berg. *OIT*, p. 57.
6. *The Freeman's Journal*, 21 April 1908, p. 4.
7. See Gordon, and Smythe, 1981, for black and white reproductions.
8. AG to WBY, 11 April 1908, Saddlemyer, 1982, pp. 272–6.
9. AG to JQ, 20 June [1908], Berg.
10. Lady Dunsany's diary, 20 October 1910, quoted in Mark Amory, p. 73.
11. Letter Hamilton to Hone in Hone, 1965, p. 225.
12. *Gods and Fighting Men*, 'The Boar of Beinn Gulbain', p. 266.
13. Murray, p. 59. Linda Mizejewski, 'Patriarchy and the Female in Lady Gregory's *Grania*,' *Éire/Ireland*, 22 (1) (1987), 122–38. If Augusta had perceived it as a homoerotic bond she might have integrated it more convincingly into the dynamics of emotional and sexual attraction.
14. Cave, 1991, p. 11; R. Hogan *et al.*, 1979, p. 193.

15. *The New York Times Magazine*, December 1911, quoted in Mikhail, 1977, pp. 58–9.
16. AG to JQ, 3 January 1909, Berg. *Seventy Years*, p. 423. Notes to play, *The Collected Plays II*, p. 297. 15 July 1921, *LGJ*, I, p. 280. Laurence and Grene, p. 64.
17. Performed 11 November 1909. Hogan and O'Neill, 1967, p. 132.
18. Foster, 1997, p. 397.
19. AG to JQ, 3 January 1909, Berg.
20. AG to JQ, 9 January 1909, Berg. *Seventy Years*, p. 430.
21. Foster, 1997, p. 398.
22. *Memoirs*, pp. 160–1.
23. 'A Friend's Illness', W.B. Yeats.
24. *Seventy Years*, p. 438.
25. *Memoirs*, p. 161.
26. Quoted in Foster, 1997, p. 398
27. AG to JQ, 3 January [1909], Berg.
28. n.d., Berg, quoted in Foster, 1997, p. 398. Berg n.d.
29. Diary entry, 1909, Pethica, 1996, p. 316.
30. *Seventy Years*, p. 428.
31. *Ibid.*, p. 439.
32. *Autobiographies*, p. 508.
33. AG to WBY, Wednesday [24 March 1909], in Saddlemyer, 1982, p. 298.
34. AG to WBY [25 March 1909], Berg, Saddlemyer, 1982, pp. 298–9.
35. n.d. Berg, quoted in Foster, 1997, p. 401. Slightly different version in Pethica, 2004, and dated tentatively to 12 April 1910.
36. AG to JQ, 21 April [1909], Berg. It was another month before Yeats received his letter of 4 May 1908 which gave him and Lady Gregory power to make decisions.
37. *Seventy Years*, pp. 440–4.

Chapter Sixteen

1. *Seventy Years*, p. 44.
2. GBS to AG, 12 June 1909, in Laurence and Grene, p. 2.
3. *Seventy Years*, pp. 446–7.
4. Holroyd, vol. 2, p. 20.
5. *OIT*, pp. 212–16.
6. *Ibid.*, p. 84.
7. GBS to AG, 12 August 1909, Laurence and Grene, pp. 18–19.
8. AG to GBS, 9 August 1909, Laurence and Grene, p. 12.
9. AG to JQ, 2 July 1922, Berg. Amory, p. 68.
10. 12 August [1909], *Lady Gregory's Journal* in Laurence and Grene, pp. 14–17.

11. *Ibid.*, Friday [13 August 1909], pp. 19–20.
12. GBS to AG, 19 August 1909, Laurence and Grene, pp. 35–6. GBS to WBY, 22 August 1909, *ibid.*, pp. 43–4. AG to GBS, 17 [August 1909], *ibid.*, pp. 27–8.
13. Laurence and Grene, pp. 39–42.
14. AG to GBS, Midnight [25–26 August 1909], Laurence and Grene, p. 49.
15. AG to WBY, Wednesday night [August 1909], Berg.
16. AG to WBY, TLS, Coole, Saturday [1909], Berg.
17. AG to WBY, TLS, Galway, 7 January [1910], Berg. AG to WBY, TLS, Galway, Sunday [January 1910], Berg.
18. pp. 33–4. See Flannery.
19. AG to WBY, TLS, Galway, Sunday 22 [May 1910], Berg.
20. Frazier, 1990, pp. 230–1.
21. AG to JQ, 19 February 1909, Berg.
22. AH to WBY, 23 December 1909, in Frazier, 1990, p. 232.
23. [January 1910] in Foster, 1997, p. 414.
24. 'Statement by LG [AG] to JQ', n.d. (cat. March 1913), Foster-Murphy Collection, NYPL.
25. [February–March 1910] in Foster, 1997, p. 414.
26. AG to WBY, Thursday [1910], Berg. AG to GBS, 7 April [1910], Laurence and Grene, p. 61.
27. By 1909 the Abbey Theatre letterhead listed 12 theatres in Britain and Ireland outside Dublin where it regularly performed.
28. They also had money for an endowment to ensure the continued running of the theatre. AG to GBS, 7 April 1910, Laurence and Grene, pp. 60–1.
29. Letter AG to WBY, 3 January [1909], Berg.
30. TLS, Galway, Friday [Summer 1910] (dated by Berg to Autumn 1910).
31. RG to AG [8 February 1904], Saddlemyer and Smythe, p. 359.
32. *LGJ*, 1, p. 143.
33. Undated, Emory.
34. Undated, Emory.
35. Sunday [early November 1910], Emory.
36. Yeats, *Memoirs*, note p. 226.
37. *Ibid.*, pp. 225–6.
38. *The Collected Plays II*, p. 269.
39. Yeats, too, in 1912, would begin to re-evaluate Parnell as an Irish prophet. For both of them the fact that he was Anglo-Irish was important. *The Deliverer*, whose characters needed greater emotional depth than Augusta could manage, was not a success when it was premiered on 12 January 1911. The audience was irritated by Hebrews and Egyptians speaking in Kiltartanese,

Gordon Craig's experimental screens, which aimed at sublimity, did not match the *The Deliverer*'s bleak realism, and Yeats disliked the costumes, designed by Robert. See Hogan, Burnham and Poteet, pp. 104–9.

40. Robinson, 1942.
41. T.C. Murray's *The Wheel of Fortune*, Daniel Corkery's *The Hermit and the King* and Robinson's *The Lesson of his Life* were all performed on 2 December 1909.
42. WBY to Kiernan, 17 March 1933 in Foster, 2003, pp. 443–4.
43. *Seventy Years*, p. 448.
44. AG to WBY, Sunday 22 [May 1910], Berg.
45. AG to WBY, 6 June 1910 in Foster, 1997, p. 422.
46. 5 May 1911, in Frazier, 1990, p. 238.
47. Recounted in AG to Birrell, 29 July 1910, in Yeats, *Memoirs*, Appendix E, pp. 290–1.
48. *Ibid.*, pp. 289–90.
49. 'Statement by LG to JQ', n.d. (cat. March 1913), Foster-Murphy Collection, Berg.
50. Yeats, *Memoirs*, p. 252.
51. *Ibid.*, pp. 257–8.
52. In Foster, 1997, p. 436.
53. January 1914, in Tóibín, p. 107.
54. *Seventy Years*, p. 483.
55. *The Atheneum*, 2 October 1909, p. 403.
56. Robinson, 1942, p. 117.
57. AG to WSB, 3 December 1908, Berg.
58. AG to JQ, 26 February [1908], Berg.
59. 11 March 1911, Berg.
60. AG to WBY, 26 May 1911, Berg.
61. In a letter AG to HL, Thursday, postmarked 27 July 1911, Berg, Augusta could barely conceal the hope that he might change his mind. But Hugh had not been in love. O'Byrne, pp. 147–8.
62. *Ibid.*, pp. 154–5.
63. Wednesday [10 September 1911], Berg.

Chapter Seventeen

1. *OIT*, p. 97.
2. Thursday [14 September 1911], NLI.
3. Nassau Hotel [Autumn 1912], Berg.
4. AG to Ruth Shine, Thursday [14 September 1911], NLI.
5. Notes in *The Collected Plays II*, pp. 294–6.
6. *Ibid.*, p. 125.
7. In *The Outlook*, 16 December 1911 as *McDaragh's Wife*.

8. *OIT*, pp. 98–9.

9. 7 April [1910], Laurence and Grene, p. 60.

10. AG to HL, Sunday 27 [August 1911] Berg.

11. Trust Agreement, 11 March 1912, Emory. Statements in Emory; by 8 March 1915 the balance was $1,501.05.

12. 3 February 1910, written statement 27 September 1910, Laurence and Grene, pp. 63–4 and xxv.

13. 29 September 1911, in *OIT* pp. 160–1.

14. See Reynolds.

15. 25 November 1911, *Seventy Years*, p. 497.

16. See Robinson, 1951.

17. WBY to AG, 28 April 1911, quoted in Foster, 1997, p. 444.

18. 1 October 1911, *Sunday Herald* (Boston) in Mikhail, 1977, pp. 41–5.

19. *OIT*, p. 101.

20. 14 October, in *ibid.*, p. 222.

21. 8 October 1911, *Sunday Post* (Boston) in Mikhail, 1977, p. 47.

22. *Gaelic American*, 2 December 1911, in Laurence and Grene, p. 66.

23. AG to HL, Wednesday [10 September 1911], Berg.

24. Hotel Touraine, 3 October 1911, Berg.

25. Sunday 8 [October 1911], Berg.

26. Now The Isabella Stewart Gardner Museum.

27. AG to RG, Sunday 8 [October 1911], Berg. Robinson, 1946, p. 241.

28. *OIT*, p. 107.

29. AG to JQ, 16 February [1912], Berg. In Cleveland she would be offered $100 for a lecture.

30. AG to WBY, 12 November [1911], Berg.

31. *OIT*, p. 108. Mary Colum was sceptical of her enthusiasm.

32. See letters to WBY, 8 December [1911] and 12 November [1911], Berg.

33. AG to WBY, 21 November [1911], Berg. Liebler raised his contribution and Augusta organised their finances so that the players got what they wanted.

34. *OIT*, p. 115.

35. Reid, p. 58.

36. Quinn welcomed the fact that the Abbey, unlike the Gaelic League, was earning its money in America, and he supported it by explaining the simple naturalistic Abbey style to people accustomed to more elaborate shows.

37. Friday 1 December [1911], Berg.

38. *OIT*, p. 110.

39. *Ibid.*, p. 111.

40. AG to WBY, 27 November 1911, in Foster, 1997, p. 449.
41. Nic Shiubhlaigh, p. 129.
42. *Seventy Years*, 28 November 1911, p. 497.
43. AG to JQ, 11 March [1911], Berg.
44. See Nic Shiubhlaigh, and *Seventy Years*, pp. 460–2.
45. AG to WBY, Saturday, n.d., in Foster, 1997, p. 450.
46. AG to WBY, Tuesday 17 [December 1911], in Foster, p. 450.
47. AG to WBY, 12 November [1911], Berg.
48. AG to WBY, 8 December [1911], Berg.
49. 7 December 1911, NLI, in Saddlemyer and Smythe, p. 141.
50. Tuesday 2 [April 1912], in Saddlemyer and Smythe, p. 129.
51. Kohfeldt, p. 232.
52. Postmarked 22 March 1912, *ibid.*, p. 129.
53. Foster, 1997, pp. 407–8.
54. Christmas Day 1911, Berg.
55. AG to WBY, Christmas Day 1911, Foster, 1997, p. 611.
56. AG to RG, Laurence and Grene, p. 69–76.
57. 23 January [1912], Laurence and Grene, p. 68.
58. AG to JQ, 9 February 1912, Berg.
59. *OIT*, p. 234.
60. *Ibid.*, p. 135.
61. 16 February [1912], Berg.
62. Reynolds, p. 90.
63. Postmarked 22 March 1912, in Saddlemyer and Smythe, p. 129.
64. 2 [April 1912], *ibid.*, p. 129.
65. *Ibid*.
66. Postmarked 22 March 1912, *ibid.*, p. 129.
67. 31 March [1912], *ibid.*, p. 129.
68. *Ibid.*, p. 130.
69. 6 May 1912, Berg; TLS version is longer.
70. She later told Quinn that sending the ring had been Robert's idea, AG to JQ, 10 February 1918, Berg.
71. Kohfeldt, p. 237.

Chapter Eighteen

1. RG to AG, 8 November [1911], Emory.
2. AG to RG, Thursday 18 May [1912], Berg.
3. 9 November [1912], Berg.
4. Performed in London in July to poor reviews. Even in the revised version the idea does not stretch to a one-act play. Hogan, Burnham and Poteet, pp. 194–5.
5. 6 May 1912, Berg.
6. 'Making a Play', MS in Berg. The play became a morality tale in

which the miser is redeemed by loosing his wealth to the innocent Simon who beats him at cards to win his gold; innocence, instead of merely being celebrated, is shown to be a power for good in the world. This would be a theme in her last plays.

7. AG to GBS, 5 October [1912], Laurence and Grene, pp. 79–80.
8. AG to JQ, 6 May 1912, Berg.
9. 26 May 1911, Foster, 1997, p. 450.
10. She engaged Quinn to go through the American section, and asked all her correspondents whether they had objections to her selections.
11. George Russell objected to her misrepresentation of the Fays, and Annie Horniman is a mere shadow, although Augusta later regretted that she did not depict her 'on the war path', *LGJ*, II, p. 410. Coxhead, 1961, p. 165. She finished by early December. She wrote an epilogue in July 1913, by which time she was confident that it would be accepted as the 'authentic' history of the theatre. AG to JQ, 12 August [1913], Berg. Published November, Putnam's Sons, New York, January 1914, London.
12. 30 November [1912], Laurence and Grene, p. 84.
13. *OIT*, p. 17. She told her publisher this was to enhance the impression of intimacy, AG to Constant Huntington, 17 July 1913 in *OIT*, pp. 257–60.
14. *Ibid.*, p. 139.
15. 4 September [1912], Berg.
16. AG to JQ, 22 October 1912, 9 November [1912], Berg.
17. 18 November 1912, Laurence and Grene, p. 80.
18. In Foster, 1997, p. 477.
19. In *ibid.*, p. 477.
20. Thursday 9 [January 1913], Berg.
21. 1 February [1913], Berg.
22. 'Statement by LG to JQ', n.d. (cat. March 1913), Foster-Murphy Collection. NYPL.
23. Typed copy in Berg, undated.
24. AG to JQ, 7 May [1913], Berg.
25. 13 May [1913], Berg.
26. Yeats, in particular, saw Lane's gift as a test for about-to-be-independent Ireland.
27. 11 December 1912, Berg, in O'Byrne, p. 174.
28. A group of businessmen in Montreal pledged the dollar equivalent of £1,000. At a dinner organised by Quinn in the Ritz-Carleton in New York Alexander Cochrane gave $5,000, 'Statement by LG to JQ', Foster-Murphy Collection, NYPL. See AG to HL, 6 February [1913], Berg.
29. AG to WBY [23 July 1913], Berg.

30. O'Byrne, p. 181.
31. *Ibid*., p. 186.
32. Saturday, undated [September 1913], Berg.
33. Thursday 14 [1913], Berg.
34. AG to HL, 16 September [1913], Berg. She did not want to return the money raised by the Abbey which angered some players who sued. It went to court where Augusta and Yeats lost.
35. In O'Byrne, p. 191.

Chapter Nineteen

1. 11 October 1913, Berg.
2. Postmark 1 July 1913, Berg.
3. Bought from Ruth Skerrett; information from the late Mrs Helmore.
4. AG to JQ, 19 July [1913],and 12 August [1913], Berg.
5. AG to WBY [23 July 1913], Berg.
6. One critic praised a jug of roses as 'an exquisite piece of colour and handling'. Smythe, 1981, p. 35. Catalogue in Sir Hugh Lane papers in NLI.
7. AG to JQ [5 July 1913], Berg, AG to WBY, 1 July 1913, Berg.
8. 6 September 1913, Laurence and Grene, p. 86.
9. 'Sunday', summer 1913, in Foster, 1997, p. 503.
10. 13 April [1913], Berg.
11. 22 May [1913], Berg.
12. Foster, 1997, p. 503.
13. JQ to AG, 27 November 1913, in Kohfeldt, p. 240.
14. AG to JQ, 12 August [1913], Berg.
15. *The Golden Apple* amalgamates at least three stories; 'The Three Sons', 'The Well of Healing', 'The Seven Fishers'. Its main fault is that it is overlong, lacking the elegant clarity often found in fairy stories.
16. Mary Lou Kohfeldt, *Lady Gregory, the Woman Behind the Irish Renaissance*, New York, 1984; London, André Deutsch, pp. 241–2.
17. GBS to AG, 23 September 1915, Laurence and Grene, p. 102.
18. Monday 4 November [1913], Berg.
19. *Seventy Years*, p. 285.
20. AG to JQ, 19 December 1913, Berg.
21. [December 1912], Emory.
22. AG to Ruth Shine, Saturday [27 December 1913], NLI.
23. See Foster, 1997, p. 504.
24. 13 January 1913, Longenbach, p. 19.
25. Colum, p. 180.

26. *Fand* was performed on 20 April 1907; Synge dismissed it as 'bastard literary pantomine', JMS to AG and WBY, 7 May [1907], and Augusta was not surprised, AG to JMS, 10 [May 1907], Saddlemyer, 1982, pp. 220–1. See Lucy McDiarmid, 2004. Foster, 1997, pp. 509–10, *Seventy Years*, pp. 478–81 for accounts of the 'peacock dinner'.

27. 1 January 1914, Berg.

28. AG to WSB, 7 May 1914, in McDiarmid.

29. AG to WBY, n.d., Berg, in Foster 451.

30. AG to WBY, 15 December 1912, Berg.

31. *Hail and Farewell*, pp. 550, 552, 563.

32. AG to JQ, 1 January 1914, Berg.

33. Foster, 1997, pp. 507–9.

34. *Autobiographies*, pp. 408–9.

35. 8 [April 1914], in Pethica, 1987, pp. 259–60.

36. Foster, 1997, p. 517.

37. *Illustrated London News*, 6 June 1914. *The Sunday Times* declared that his work revealed 'a very decided and original personality', Smythe, 1995, p. 40. There were criticisms – *The Studio* thought his drawing lacked assurance – but Hugh Lane bought 'Coole Lake' for the Municipal Gallery, and at least two others were sold.

38. Cuttings file in Emory.

39. The title derives from the folklore story of the wrens picking crumbs from the Danes' drums which had alerted them to an Irish attack and so caused Ireland to be 'destroyed'.

40. AG to WBY, Tuesday 4 [May 1915], Berg.

41. AG to JQ, 12 July 1914, Berg. She negotiated another lecture tour in America for 1915 with Pond's Lyceum Bureau (which also organised tours for Yeats) reasoning, 'It is as well to use one's talent while it lasts'.

42. Related to JQ, 6 September 1914, in J. Murphy, 1961.

43. AG to GBS, 19 September 1915, Laurence and Grene, pp. 97–8.

44. Berg, dated 15 August 1914. *Seventy Years*, pp. 520–1.

45. Foster, 1988, pp. 472–3. Blunt disapproved of Redmond's action, *Seventy Years*, p. 527.

46. *Ibid.*, pp. 514–15.

47. *Ibid.*, pp. 519–20.

48. 12 March [1915], Berg.

49. RG to AG, n.d. Berg.

50. David Moore (of Whitney & Moore, now Whitney, Moore & Keller) to RG, 17 December 1912, Emory.

51. Emory.

52. David Moore to RG, 9 December 1914, Emory. AG refers to agreement in AG to HL, 25 December 1914, NLI.

53. AG to JQ, 6 September 1914, Berg.
54. 'Three Kiltartan Folk Tales', *The Outlook*, 27 April 1912, pp. 978–85.
55. AG to WSB, 17 June 1918, Berg. See references to reading in *Seventy Years*, pp. 469, 471.
56. *The Collected Plays III*, pp. 375–6.
57. Hogan, Burnham and Popeet, pp. 381–2. Yeats, to whom she had read the play and who had already advised her on the second act, sent her a long letter with Robinson's criticisms and his own carefully worded suggestions for the 'muzzy' third act, and Augusta rewrote it making it clearer.
58. *LGJ*, I, p. 178.
59. See *The Irish Book Lover* XII January–February (1921), 84; Patricia Lysaght, 'Perspectives on Narrative Communication and Gender: Lady Augusta Gregory's Visions and Beliefs in the West of Ireland (1920)', *Fabula* 39 (1998), 256–76. Lady Augusta Gregory, 'Three Kiltartan Folk Tales.' It is her longest book. Included at the end were two landscapes by Robert.
60. 'Three Kiltartan Folk Tales', p. 979.
61. *Visions and Beliefs*, p. 311.
62. *The Collected Plays III*, p. 376.
63. *Visions and Beliefs*, p. 15.
64. [January 1915], Emory.
65. WBY to JQ, 24 June 1915, in Wade, p. 596.
66. Berg. She had enjoyed exercising her gift for public speaking, particularly making her audience laugh, to WSB, 12 March 1915, Berg.
67. In O'Byrne, p. 209.
68. *Sir Hugh Lane*, p. 151.
69. Received after drowned, see AG to JQ, 18 May 1915, Berg.
70. 16 April 1915, in *Seventy Years*, p. 474.
71. Anne Gregory, p. 47.
72. A letter she wrote to Quinn eight months later reveals how Augusta managed the wayward artist: 'I think one's only chance is to seize him and get rapid work like Shaw's portrait which is really fine.' 11 February [1916], Berg.
73. AJ to AG, Tuesday [1915], Emory.
74. p. 47. In *Coole*, pp. 54–5 Augusta writes that John asked to paint Richard.
75. See JQ to AG, 11 May 1915, NLI.
76. AG to JQ, 9 May 1915, Berg, 'I was very fond of him, and he was one of the very few outside one's own children whose death would make a real difference in one's life.'

77. AG Memoirs Ms, 7 (for 8) May, Berg, in Laurence and Grene, p. 91.
78. In Tóibín, p. 91.
79. AG to JQ, 9 May 1915, Berg.
80. AG to JQ, 18 May 1915, Berg. AG to WSB, 13 May 1915, Berg.
81. B. Maddox, pp. 14–15.
82. Account of the survivor, Viscountess Rhondda in *The Spectator* 1828–2003, 175th anniversary issue, pp. 84–5.
83. AG to JQ, 27 May 1915, Berg.
84. *Sir Hugh Lane*, pp. 162–3, 11–12.

Chapter Twenty

1. Laurence and Grene, p. 97.
2. He applied for appointment to the special Reserve of Offices, Royal Flying Corps on 16 September, TNA.
3. See Pethica for discussion of Robert's affair, revealed in a diary kept by Margaret Gregory and for a reinterpretation of Yeats's poems written after Robert's death.
4. *Seventy Years*, p. 475.
5. See AG to GBS, 19 September 1915, above note. First produced 29 January 1918 to bad reviews.
6. The war had exacerbated this by restricting performances, stemming the flow of new plays, and encouraging the music hall. In April 1916 Augusta would write to Yeats, 'It seems to me that Our Theatre has from the immeasurable become concrete, has fallen from imagination to reason . . . I don't see how we can help it.' *Seventy Years*, p. 471. They had also had management problems; Lennox Robinson had resigned in June 1914, and nearly a year later his replacement, A. Patrick Wilson, left after a damaging row.
7. AG to GBS, 19 September 1915, Laurence and Grene, p. 99.
8. GBS to AG, 14 September 1915, *ibid.*, p. 94.
9. *Ibid.* AG to GBS, 19 September 1915, p. 101.
10. 10 October 1915, *Seventy Years*, p. 469.
11. *Ibid.* JBY to AG, 14 August 1920, p. 507.
12. See AG to WSB, 13 December [1915], Berg.
13. AG to WSB, 4 April [1916], Berg. Robert joined the RFC on 10 January 1916, memo 43/F.S./383, TNA.
14. 27 April [1916], Emory.
15. See ch. 28, *Seventy Years* for Augusta's diary.
16. AG to WSB, 21 May [1916], Berg.
17. AG to WBY, 13 May [1916], Berg.
18. AG to WBY, 27 April [1916], Berg, quoted in Foster, 2003, p. 47.
19. Amy was John Shawe-Taylor's widow.

20. When Vere Gregory, a second cousin of Sir William's and a District Inspector, appeared at the hall door that afternoon Augusta hesitated before admitting him, afraid to be seen to be supporting the government. He brought 'authentic' news about Dublin, and could tell her that the roads were now safe; there had only been one large group of rebels (about 400) at Moyode but, confronted by the military, they had withdrawn to the mountains.

21. 7 May [1916], Berg.

22. Thursday [11 May 1916] in Wade, pp. 612–14.

23. The king of *An Rí* accepts his own death as a sacrifice for the good of his kingdom. In MacDonagh's *When the Dawn Came* a young man impatient with compromise, realises that one day he may grow old, 'who knows? – and may see young men fighting for more than now I claim'. MacDonagh had been a founder member with Joseph Plunkett of Martyn's Irish Theatre.

24. AG to T.J. Kiernan, 29 November [1927], in D. Murphy, 1968.

25. 13 May [1916], Berg.

26. 14 May [1916], Berg. This idea that the 'traitor' might inspire those who were left behind resonated with Augusta's awareness that in Ireland 'felons' had always been heroes, *Felons*, 1900. However, looking at the situation in Galway where the Sinn Féiners seemed half-hearted and the police and military were restrained, revolution did not seem desirable or likely.

27. 23 May 1916, Berg, in Foster, 2003, p. 49.

28. She expressed her continuing dislike of Sinn Féin when she told Yeats that although she had signed the circular letter of sympathy for James Connolly she was concerned that it showed too much support for 'what he considers Sinn Féinism'. 27 May [1916] in Foster, 2003, p. 49.

29. Typescript, signed and dated 16 May, Emory.

30. Yeats wrote much of the poem in the summer in France while he was staying with Maud Gonne. But when he came to Coole in September he showed it to Augusta, and in a departure from tradition dated it specifically – 11 May–25 September 1916 – implicitly acknowledging her influence.

31. Foster, 2003, p. 64.

32. 3 September 1916, Berg.

33. 20 August 1916, Berg.

34. Saturday, Berg. Probably August 1916.

35. Early 1916 was one of the most dangerous times to join. German aircraft had recently improved, they usually outnumbered the British by two or three to one, and pilots' life expectancy at the front was about eleven days.

36. August 1918, *Seventy Years*, p. 552.

37. Thursday 25 [May 1916], Berg.
38. She rejected Yeats's suggestion of Pound as manager, and suggested they temporarily reappoint Robinson, telling Yeats on 8 July: 'We can't let the Abbey die on the verge of Home Rule, or let it die at all after all the work we have put into it.' TLS, 8 July 1916, Berg.
39. AG to WBY, 8 July [1916], in Foster, 2003, p. 56.
40. *Ibid.*
41. Memo 43/F.S./409, TNA.
42. 22 August 1916, Laurence and Grene, p. 121.
43. *Seventy Years*, p. 550. Robert had assumed that Loraine's knowledge of him through the Shaws had brought him his promotion but later discovered that an Irishman, Mullholland, in the Connaught Rangers had 'arranged it'.
44. Squadron history TNA. RG to AG, 15 July [1916], Emory.
45. In fact, the F.E.8 would be obsolete in seven months.
46. n.d. [November 1916], Emory. This letter was written in early November 1916 after an advertised air battle. In his letter he only observed that the battle had been a great success, but when they had returned that evening Robert had considerately wired to tell her he was safe. 14 November 1916, *LGJ*, I, p. 9.
47. AG to GBS, 19 September 1915, Laurence and Grene, p. 98.
48. AG Letter to *The Irish Times*, 2 October 1915 reprinted in *The Times*, 5 October 1915, p. 5.
49. She finished *Seventy Years* in 1918, and typed her journals for publication as its sequel. Lennox Robinson published selections after her death in 1946, and the whole manuscript was published in 1978.
50. 'The Gift', written December 1912, later titled 'To a Wealthy Man who promised a Second Subscription to the Dublin Municipal Gallery if it were proved the People wanted Pictures.' AG to JQ, 12 August [1913], quoted in Foster, 1997, p. 495: 'I dont mind Americans being materialistic because they work with a sort of fiery energy for what they want. But these Dubliners dont work hard or get up early or take the trouble even to keep themselves clean, and yet, cry out against any who look from things visible to things in[vi]sible.' Yeats, 'Romance in Ireland (on reading much of the correspondence against the Art Gallery),' later titled 'September 1913', sent to AG in early August and published in *The Irish Times* on 8 September.
51. Yeats also wrote a pamphlet, *Sir Hugh Lane's French Pictures*, published in February 1917, making the case for their return which was published under Augusta's name. Foster, 2003, p. 65. It is reproduced in *Sir Hugh Lane*, appendices V, VI, XI. By 1926

Yeats was lobbying Irish politicians and he made an important speech in the Senate in which he gave the issue a political resonance. Foster, 2003, p. 329.

52. 22 January 1917, Laurence and Grene, pp. 129–30.

53. She made a formal request to the Trustees of the National Gallery to return the pictures and canvassed individual members and Irish artists, advised by Augustine Birrell, no longer Chief Secretary. *LGJ*, I, pp. 1–22. Augusta and Yeats retaliated with a letter to *The Times*, 6 December 1916, in *Sir Hugh Lane*, pp. 216–18.

54. *LGJ*, I, pp. 81, 164.

55. *Ibid.*, I, p .87. D.S. MacColl, curator of the Wallace Collection in London, and Alec Martin had both failed, see O'Byrne. She described Lane as 'among the chief of our mighty men', 'whose achievements are their country's title deeds of honour', *Sir Hugh Lane*, pp. 77 and 185.

56. Martin Wood's brother refused to return the Lane archive to Augusta so she was dependent on letters she had retained, her own memories and whatever she could elicit from people who had known Hugh. She wrote much of the Lane biography in winter 1919–20. It was published on 22 January 1921 to some acclaim.

57. *LGJ*, II, p. 107. She published a reply to the original report with *Case for the Return of Sir Hugh Lane's Pictures to Dublin*, in October 1926 in *Sir Hugh Lane*, pp. 191–201.

58. O'Byrne, p. 241. In 1959 there was an agreement to divide the pictures and lend each lot for alternate five years for twenty years; a compromise suggested by MacColl in 1917. There was a second agreement which expired in 1993 when a new temporary agreement to run until 2005 allowed thirty-one pictures to stay in Ireland. The remaining eight, the most valuable Impressionists, were to be lent to Dublin, four at a time for six years.

59. AG to WSB, 25 February 1917, Berg.

60. RG to AG, 14 January 1917.

61. 22 January 1917, Laurence and Grene, p. 130.

62. A few of Robert's reports, 'Combats in the Air', are in TNA.

63. Quoted in letter to JQ, 10 February 1918.

64. AG to WSB, 25 February 1917, Berg.

65. December 1916, *Sir Hugh Lane*, p. 186.

66. 25 February 1917, Berg.

67. *The Collected Plays III*, p. 392. WBY to AG 8 September [1917], Wade, p. 631 refers to the completed play.

68. Tóibín, p. 84.

69. Robert had told him in November 1916 that the tower house, which had been sold with the rest of the outlying estate to the

Congested Districts Board, was for sale, and Yeats had begun to negotiate its purchase. By May he had possession. He had engaged William Scott, an Arts and Crafts architect.

70. See *Sunday Herald*, 29 April 1917, in AG's papers at Emory, and *Seventy Years*, pp. 555–7.

71. RG to AG, 13 June 1917, from Central Flying School, Upavon, Wiltshire, Emory.

72. AG to WBY, 2 June 1917 *Seventy Years*, p. 551.

73. 26 June 1917, he became Chevalier of the Légion d'Honneur.

74. Augusta was glad that he got it fighting for France, perhaps because this would go down better with the tenants. She personally could not avoid ambiguous feelings about the fact that Robert was in the British army. Apart from the political difficulties over Irish independence, her experience with the Lane pictures underlined for her that Irish and British interests rarely coincided. In November 1916 when, at a meeting in London about the Lane pictures, Balfour remarked that he was against giving anything to Ireland, Augusta noted caustically in her journal, 'Rather hard on me with my child at the Front.' *LGJ*, I, p. 12.

75. WBY to AG, 22 September 1917, in Foster, 2003, p. 96.

76. Wade, p. 632.

77. Thursday 20 [September 1917], Foster, 2003, p. 92.

78. Coote, p. 391.

79. *Seventy Years*, p. 551.

80. [October 1917], Berg.

81. 9 November 1917, Berg.

82. Quoted in Kohfeldt, p. 251.

83. 29 October [1917], Wade, p. 634. 16 December [1917], *ibid.*, p. 634.

84. n.d. [October 1917], Emory.

85. 3 December 1917, *Seventy Years*, p. 552.

86. 9 November 1917, Berg.

87. 18 December [1917], Emory.

88. AG to JQ, 3 March 1918.

89. *LGJ*, I, p. 23.

90. AG to JQ, 10 February 1918. Minute Sheet: ref. 110547/9, TNA. His children only learnt of this in the early 1980s. Smythe, 1981, p. 5.

91. *Seventy Years*, pp. 553–4.

92. 4 February [1918], NLI, in Foster, 2003, p. 117.

93. 8 February [1918], Laurence and Grene, p. 138.

94. AG to WBY, from letters 13 and 18 February 1918, in Saddlemyer and Smythe, p. 237.

95. *Seventy Years*, pp. 554–9. See also notes in Emory.
96. B. Maddox, p. 113. AG to WSB, 23 December [1917], Berg mentions MG's serious illness.
97. 3 March 1918, Berg.
98. AG to JQ, 22 February 1918, Berg.
99. AG to JQ, 28 November 1923, Berg.
100. WBY to JQ, 8 February 1918, Wade, pp. 645–6.
101. 17 February 1918, in Smythe, 1981, pp. 15–16.
102. 25 February 1918, in Saddlemyer and Smythe, p. 238.
103. May 1918, Saddlemyer and Smythe, pp. 239–40.
104. Pethica, 2009, pp. 20, 40–42.
105. The fact that, in her papers, there is a poem written by an Italian, Adolfo Fenelli, translated into English in her hand, which romanticises the freedom of English airmen, suggests that she shared Yeats's vision of the disattached airman. Emory.

Chapter Twenty-one

1. 'No man should make his will at an emotional moment, but with careful and much thought. Lady Gregory must have had a hard task to keep silent.' Lily Yeats to JQ, 20 June 1920, in Foster, 2003, p. 692.
2. Copy in Emory.
3. MG to Constant Huntington of Putnams, 1945 quoted in Afterword, *LGJ*, II, p. 641.
4. AG to WSB, 17 June [1918], Berg.
5. *LGJ*, I, p. 116.
6. To JQ, 2 September 1920, Foster, 2003, p. 173.
7. Afterword, *LGJ*, II, p. 640.
8. AG to JQ, 22 February 1918, Berg.
9. AG to WSB, 9 November 1917, Berg.
10. *LGJ*, I, pp. 231–2.
11. 22 February 1918, Berg.
12. AG to JQ, 7 December 1918, Berg.
13. Earliest material is dated 29 July 1914. She resumed it in June 1918, AG to WSB, 17 June [1918].
14. AG to JQ, 7 December 1918, Berg.
15. 17 June [1918], Berg.
16. B. Maddox, p. 85.
17. 29 October [1917] in Wade, p. 632.
18. Monday [January 1918], Stony Brook, in Saddlemyer, 2002, p. 168.
19. JBY to Isaac Yeats, 26 October 1920, in Saddlemyer, 2002 p. 191.
20. *Ibid.*, 7 July 1920.

21. Foster, 2003, pp. 122–3.
22. 12 January 1919, Berg.
23. AG to WSB, 27 April 1919, in Foster, 2003, pp. 140–1.
24. *LGJ*, I, p. 225. A conversation in Dublin with the Sinn Féin MP, Desmond Fitzgerald, reassured her of Sinn Féin's desire for peace, so that later, in London, finding herself in conversation with the Chief Secretary for Ireland, James MacPherson, she imperiously told him to 'Give so large a measure of Dominion Home Rule as will touch their imagination – and then bribe Ulster [with favourable taxes]', recalling her conversations with Gladstone in the 1880s. October 1919, *LGJ*, I, p. 98.
25. AG to JQ, 12 January 1919. *The Jester* was never professionally produced.
26. There were disturber figures in *Cathleen ni Houlihan* and *Twisting of the Rope*. Thoughts of Shaw gave life to the jester, Manannan, 'upsetting the order of the world and making confusion in its order and its ways'. *The Collected Plays III*, p. 206 and see Notes, pp. 379–81. As a reference to the part supposedly played by the wren in the Viking invasion of Ireland, on St Stephen's Day, wrenboys visit houses to sing and receive money or food.
27. *LGJ*, I, p. 40.
28. See Winstone.
29. 14 June [1916], Berg.
30. 23 December 1917, Berg. 'I hope she wont, like Lady Anne Blunt, spend her time in "looking for facts with which to bolster up her husband's arguments".' Monday [January 1918], in Saddlemyer, 2002, p. 168.
31. *LGJ*, I, pp. 44–5.
32. 28 April 1919, in Laurence and Grene, pp. 144–5. He mischievously suggested the aptness of Oundle: 'The headmaster is rather like Granny in respect of calmly doing everything he wants to do, however subversive of established institutions, by simply walking in his heavy amiable way through every prejudice.'
33. *LGJ*, I, p. 120.
34. *Ibid.*, pp. 55–8.
35. Nic Shiubhlaigh, p. 30.
36. Foster, 2003, p. 148.
37. *Ibid.*, pp. 153–4.
38. From unpublished 'History of the Abbey Theatre', in Saddlemyer and Smythe, pp. 30–4.
39. *Irish Statesman*, 29 November and 6 December 1919.
40. *LGJ*, I, p. 100.

41. *Ibid.*, pp. 67–72, 166, 185.
42. *Ibid.*, p. 116.
43. *Ibid.*, p. 120.
44. *Ibid.*, p. 148. She would be 'the last limpet clinging to a rock', in Martin Morris's words.
45. 'The Death of Lady Gregory', in *LGJ*, II, p. 636.

Chapter Twenty-two

1. Bence Jones, p. 193. *LGJ*, I, pp. 125, 136.
2. AG to JQ, 20 November 1920. Yeats thought the dialogue mechanical. Robinson, Augusta and her audiences, who found it a delightful interlude in the daily horrors when it was performed in March 1921, liked it. Hogan and Burnham, pp. 36–8.
3. *The Collected Plays III*, pp. 295, 293.
4. *LGJ*, I, p. 138.
5. *Ibid.*, p. 179.
6. *Ibid.*, pp. 181–3.
7. *Ibid.*, p. 193.
8. *Ibid.*, p. 188.
9. 'A Week in Ireland', 16 October 1920, 63–4; 'Another Week in Ireland', 23 October 1920, 123–4; 'Murder by the Throat', 13 November 1920, 215–16; 'A Third Week in Ireland', 4 December 1920, 333; 'A Fourth Week in Ireland', 18 December 1920, 413–14; 'A Fifth Week in Ireland', 1 January 1921, 472–3.
10. 'Another Week in Ireland', 23 October 1920, pp. 123–4.
11. *LGJ*, I, p. 197.
12. Also see *ibid.*, pp. 209–10.
13. *Ibid.*, p. 205.
14. *Ibid.*, p. 205.
15. [6 November 1920], Laurence and Grene, pp. 154–5.
16. WBY to AG, 3 December 1920 in Foster, 2003, p. 702 n. 53.
17. 28 November 1920, p. 207.
18. It was first published in 1948, well after her death.
19. *LGJ*, I, p. 216.
20. *The Nation*, 13 November 1920, p. 216.
21. *LGJ*, I, p. 293.
22. W. Murphy, p. 511.
23. *LGJ*, I, p. 196.
24. *Ibid.*, pp. 203–4.
25. *Ibid.*, p. 220.
26. *Irish Independent*, 17 May 1921.
27. Amory pp. 177–8.
28. *LGJ*, I, p. 256.

29. *Ibid.*, p. 274.

30. 15 June 1921, *ibid.*, p. 270.

31. It started as a personal lament for Séan Connolly, but Yeats confirmed her suspicion that the too personal Connolly verse should go. *Ibid.*, p. 291.

32. *The Collected Plays II*, p. 359. See conversation with Mary Studd two months earlier referred to in Chapter 9. See WBY to Ottoline Morrell, 25 July 1924, in which Yeats commented on Lady Gregory's abiding dislike of all clergy, particularly Catholic clergy in Foster, 2003, p. 715.

33. *LGJ*, I, p. 276.

34. *Ibid.*, p. 289, 291.

35. *Ibid.*, p. 477. In September 1923, after the civil war, she replaced the four final lines (The Binding) which focused on the sacrifice of Irish martyrs with 16 lines that appealed for reconciliation within Ireland. Published in *The New Republic* (New York) 20 February 1924, p. 339; *The Irish Statesman*, 22 March 1924, pp. 40–1; *The Collected Plays II*, pp. VI, 357–61, with notes. There are slightly different versions of the last eight lines in Berg, published in Coxhead.

36. Hogan and Burnham, p. 154. Yeats wanted Cuala to publish it as a broadside with illustrations by Jack, and it was listed as one of the best poems of 1924. WBY to AG, 13 January 1924, Wade, p. 702.

37. Original agreement, 19 September 1921, *LGJ*, I, p. 294. See AG to MG, 14 November 1921, Berg, for their spoken agreement. Augusta felt reassured but Margaret reneged. They argued about former agreements with Robert and rights to the contents of the house. For final agreement, similar to that made in September, see Holograph Agreement [1 November 1921], Berg.

38. *LGJ*, I, pp. 314–15. AG to JQ, 7 December 1921, Berg.

39. Phrases from Dáil debates in Conor O'Clery, *Phrases Make History Here*, Dublin, The O'Brien Press, 1986, pp. 71, 74. *LGJ*, I, pp. 312–13.

40. *Ibid.*, p. 318.

Chapter Twenty-three

1. *LGJ*, I, p. 332.

2. AG to WBY, n.d. NLI, in Foster, 2003, p. 207. She told Quinn in November 1923 that she found so much to agree with in principle and so much to disapprove in practice on both sides that she was unable to commit herself to either of them.

3. AG to JQ, 5 October 1923, Berg.

4. *LGJ*, I, pp. 295, 139, 323–4.
5. *Ibid.*, p. 328.
6. *Ibid.*, p. 336.
7. *Seventy Years* was first published posthumously in 1974.
8. She arranged them according to themes and pasted them onto more scrap paper with added introductions and connecting pieces. This was typed as a rough draft, to be revised. It was remarkably laborious work.
9. She was inspired in her nationalist perspective by reading Henry James's letters in the autumn of 1921, struck that his letters to his American family and friends had a more natural tone than those to Europeans. AG to JQ, 20 November 1920, Berg.
10. WBY to JQ, 5 June 1922, Wade, p. 684.
11. 30 May 1922.
12. WBY to JQ, 5 June 1922, Wade, p. 684. Augusta submitted *Seventy Years*, as it had become, in May 1923 to her agent. Watt, who gave the manuscript to Murray, was not keen. Six months later she asked for the manuscript back to write articles. AG to JQ, 5 October 1923, Berg.
13. *LGJ*, I, p. 337.
14. AG to JQ, 7 December 1921, Berg.
15. 30 May 1922, Berg.
16. *LGJ*, I, pp. 354–7.
17. *Ibid.*, p. 335.
18. *Ibid.*, p. 381.
19. 10 December 1922, Berg.
20. *LGJ*, I, pp. 398, 419.
21. *Ibid.*, p. 451.
22. *Ibid.*, p. 418.
23. *Ibid.*, p. 491.
24. *Ibid.*, pp. 425, 438.
25. *Ibid.*, p. 473.
26. 7 June 1924.
27. *OIT*, pp. 61–3. They could be returned as unsuitable, or with an 'Advice to Playwrights' form which outlined Abbey standards. Those which showed 'a mind behind it' were given detailed criticisms and suggestions for revision. They failed to make allowances for the arrogance and assurance of genius; despite being acquainted with genius the Abbey did not anticipate it.
28. O'Casey, pp. 102–3.
29. *LGJ*, I, p. 446.
30. *Ibid.*, pp. 459–64.
31. Medical directories. Obituaries: *The Irish Times*, 8 July 1940; *Irish Independent*, 8 July 1940.

32. *LGJ*, I, p. 467.
33. They discussed the need to capture the spiritual side of Joan and minimise the reliance on sexual attraction, and whether the end should be tragic. Shaw also praised Augusta as one of the few playwrights who had a natural gift for dialogue. *LGJ*, I, pp. 455–9.
34. AG to JQ, 5 October 1923, Berg.
35. 2 September 1923, *LGJ*, I, p. 474.
36. *Ibid.*, p. 319. He may have been modelled on Frank Gallagher, an idealistic republican journalist, imprisoned during the Anglo-Irish war, who saw the Treaty as a materialistic compromise and whom she knew of from George Russell.
37. *The Collected Plays III*, p. 339.
38. *Ibid.*, p. 337.
39. 5 October 1923, Berg.
40. *LGJ*, I, p. 522.

Chapter Twenty-four

1. *LGJ*, II, pp. 16, 22, 32.
2. *LGJ*, I, pp. 484–6.
3. AG to JQ, 28 November 1923, Berg.
4. *LGJ*, I, pp. 513–14.
5. *Ibid.*, p. 475.
6. *Ibid.*, p. 494.
7. Anne Gregory, pp. 52–3.
8. *LGJ*, I, pp. 512–13.
9. *Ibid.*, pp. 546–9. SO'C, 'Where Wild Swans Nest', *Inishfallen, Fare Thee Well*.
10. SO'C to AG, October 1924, in Krause, 1975, pp. 118–19.
11. *LGJ*, I, p. 584.
12. SO'C praised the sneeze in G.B.S.'s *St Joan* as 'particularly lovely' because he knew she had suggested it, 29 June 1925. On 12 July 1924 he referred to the Lane pictures as 'the treasures they have taken from our Temple'. 'I am looking forward to many a gentle talk with you about the things that we believe to belong unto our Country's place!' he wrote in August 1925, all in Krause, 1975, pp. 137, 112, 141.
13. *LGJ*, I, p. 517.
14. *The Galway Express*, 28 March 1896. AG to MG, 15 February [1920], Berg.
15. Reid, p. 625.
16. *LGJ*, I, p. 569.
17. *Ibid.*, p. 557.

18. *Ibid.*, pp. 588–9.
19. There was compensation; in July the Galway court awarded Arthur £14,000 (about €1,117,306, £766,854 sterling) for malicious burning and £2,400 for the looted furniture, but the two witnesses, the coachman and steward, were kidnapped on their way to court. *The Connacht Tribune*, 12 July 1924.
20. WBY to Kiernan, 17 March 1933 in Foster, 2003, pp. 443–4.
21. With the new mortgage they had paid off their old debts and had £500 in the bank, *LGJ*, I, p. 604. But they needed an annual £1,000 for better salaries, and a down payment of £1,000 for repairs. See *ibid.*, p. 317 for her hope to pass it over to the Free State government. Yeats, more concerned about possible government interference in artistic policy, preferred to go to the government for a subsidy. The government was without the resources to grant an immediate subsidy in 1922.
22. *LGJ*, II, p. 39.
23. *LGJ*, I, p. 610.
24. It was performed in May 1927 and received with respect rather than acclaim. See *The Irish Statesman*, 14 May 1927. In autumn 1925, she began a long-contemplated adaptation of Cervantes' *Don Quixote*, titled *Sancho's Master*, which opened 14 March 1927 to some good reviews including the *South Wales News* remark that she had done it 'with something very like genius'. *LGJ*, II, p. 275.
25. 17 February 1926, in D. Murphy, 1968. She wrote this after seeing a performance.
26. *LGJ*, II, p. 39.
27. *Ibid.*, p. 43. Murray, 2004, p. 168.
28. Lily Yeats to Ruth Lane-Poole, 31 December 1925, in Foster, 2003, p. 301. *LGJ*, II, p. 56. Kevin O'Higgins told Yeats it was the most beautiful speech he had ever heard.
29. Quoted in Foster, 2003, pp. 305–6.
30. *LGJ*, II, p. 62.
31. *Ibid.*, p. 96.
32. 'How Great Plays are Born: The Coming of Mr. O'Casey', *Daily News*, 27 March 1926, p. 6.
33. *LGJ*, II, pp. 135–7.
34. Her investments were all held by the Bank of England except for one of £120 held by the Free State National Loan, AG to Kiernan, 12 May 1925, D. Murphy, 1968. She received a half-yearly dividend of £2 10s from the Free State Loan. She earned £474 3s 10d (about €37,829, £25,965 sterling) in 1923–4 from book and performance royalties, and £467 3s 10d in 1924–5. She only suffered a £7 drop in literary income between 1924 and 1925. AG

to Kiernan, 26 May 1925, D. Murphy, 1968. They paid income tax of £256 12s 6d, and just over £94 on tithes, quit rent and Board of Works rates, undated notes in MG's hand in Emory. She paid rates of £142 in 1924. In 1924 her income from the selling of wool, cattle and rabbits was much less than in former years. Farming income was £69 in 1924, *LGJ*, I, p. 612. She received a legacy of £1,135 from Arabella *ibid.*, p. 615, invested for her grandchildren, and knew she could not avoid estate and household maintenance. In 1924 she paid the local carpenter, Raferty, £20 to alter the wall at the gate and repair the stable and house eaves, and she paid an upholsterer £50, *ibid.*, p. 612.

35. *LGJ*, II, Afterword, p. 641, and information from Catherine Kennedy.
36. *LGJ*, I, p. 628.
37. *LGJ*, II, p. 172.
38. *Ibid.*, p. 183.
39. *c.* 9 July. 250 copies. The essays on the Breakfast Room and Drawing Room were not published until 1971 when *Coole* was reissued, edited by C. Smythe, Dolmen Editions X.
40. *Arts and Decoration* (New York), 30 April 1930, pp. 106, 117, 133. Four of Robert's drawings were included in 1909 edition of *The Kiltartan History Book* and Smythe, 1981, p. 30.
41. *LGJ*, II, p. 180.
42. AG to Kiernan, 27 December 1927, D. Murphy, 1968. The government departments had formally taken possession on 20 October.
43. 20 October 1927, Berg.
44. *LGJ*, II, p. 225.
45. *Ibid.*, p. 226. AG to Kiernan, 27 December 1927, D. Murphy, 1968.
46. AG to SO'C, 27 November [1927], in Edwards, p. 97. SO'C to AG, 28 March 1928, in Krause, 1975, p. 232.
47. AG to SO'C, 2 April 1928, Edwards, p. 99. Entry dated 28 March 1928, *LGJ*, II, p. 247.
48. 27 April 1928, Edwards, pp. 99–100. *Ibid.*, p. 251.
49. AG to S O'C, 28 April 1928, Edwards, p. 100.
50. AG to S O'C, 10 May 1928, Edwards, p. 100.
51. AG to SO'C, 10 May 1928 and 31 May 1928, Edwards, pp. 100–1.
52. 14 May 1928, Krause, 1975, pp. 245–6.
53. Krause, 1975, p. 265.
54. She was also less critical of the play and less opposed to its performance at the Abbey than Robinson or Yeats. *LGJ*, II, pp. 273–4.

55. *Ibid.*, p. 303.
56. [7 November 1928], Krause, 1975, pp 318–20.
57. 1 December 1928, Edwards, p. 104.
58. 28 February 1929, Krause, 1975, p. 342.
59. *LGJ*, II, p. 249.
60. *Ibid.*, p. 258. Her brother Edward had died in August 1925.
61. AG to SO'C, 31 May 1928, Edwards, p. 102.
62. *LGJ*, II, p. 399.
63. In Foster, 2003, p. 408.
64. Entry dated 17 October 1928, *LGJ*, II, p. 327.
65. In Tóibín, p. 119.
66. *LGJ*, II, p. 314.
67. *The Irish Times*, 10 September 1928.
68. *LGJ*, II, p. 315.
69. Ruth Shine to Ruth Lane-Poole, 3 October 1928, in Foster, 2003, p. 730.
70. Entry dated 6 January 1929, *LGJ*, II, p. 372. In October 1928 she altered her will, leaving all her royalties to Richard instead of shared between the three, aware that Margaret was in a better position to provide for the girls. But she divided the royalties equally in her last will, 9 September 1930.
71. *LGJ*, II, p. 385.
72. They were never produced, but published in *The Collected Plays I*.
73. *Seven Short Plays* was reissued in 1922 and her comedies were translated into Dutch, Chinese, German, Italian and Japanese, and performed by professional and amateur groups in South Africa, Australia, India, Europe and regularly in America. Other collections: *Irish Folk-History Plays*, 1912; *New Comedies*, 1913; *The Image and Other Plays* and *Three Wonder Plays*, 1922, and *Three Last Plays*, 1928.
74. Saddlemyer and Smythe, p. 36. Her name was prominent in contemporary scholarly appraisals of the theatre. On 21 November 1924 the *Manchester Guardian Weekly* assessed her strengths and weaknesses in relation to Yeats and Synge.
75. *LGJ*, II, p. 291. *Sancho's Master, Dave, The Would-be Gentleman*. She thought Yeats had undervalued her creativity in *A Vision*, responding to his description in her diary, 'But I don't think she could have written *Seven Short Plays*.' *Ibid.*, p. 45.
76. Entry dated 29 July 1928, *ibid.*, p. 301.
77. *Ibid.*, p. 363.
78. AG to SO'C, 23 October 1929, Edwards, p. 108.
79. 15 October 1929, in Krause, 1975, p. 369.
80. 15 October [1929], Edwards, p. 107.

81. SO'C to AG, 25 October 1931, in Saddlemyer and Smythe, pp. 177–8. AG to SO'C, 30 October 1931, Edwards, p. 112.
82. *LGJ*, II, p. 548.
83. See Foster, 2003, p. 408.
84. Letter to the Swami Shri Purohit, 6 June 1982, in Foster, 2004, p. 120. In the February before her death he started the elegy 'Coole Park and Ballylee, 1932' in which he meditated on what Augusta and Coole had meant to him.
85. To Ruth Poole-Lane, 30 September 1930, and 8 September 1930, in Foster, 2003, p. 408.
86. Augusta feared she would censor anything critical of the British government and the Black and Tans, AG to WBY, 25 February 1930, in Foster, 2003, p. 434.
87. n.d. [August 1931], in Foster, 2003, p. 420.
88. *LGJ*, II, p. 625.
89. *Ibid.*, p. 628.
90. *Ibid.*, WBY, 'The Death of Lady Gregory', *ibid.*, p. 638.
91. Quote from WBY to Olivia Shakespear, 30 August 1931, in Foster, 2004, p. 110.
92. 18 February 1932, Berg.
93. Maddox, p. 254.
94. 'The Death of Lady Gregory', in *LGJ*, II, pp. 633–8.
95. Lily Yeats to Ruth Lane-Poole, 24 May 1932, in Foster, 2003, p. 436.

Bibliography

For unpublished sources and more articles see Notes

Published works by Lady Gregory, including selected articles

'Arabi and His Household', *The Times*, 23 October 1882, p. 4, London, Kegan Paul, Trench & Company, 1882

A Book of Saints and Wonders, Dundrum, Dun Emer Press, 1906

The Collected Plays, I, The Comedies, ed. Ann Saddlemyer, Gerrards Cross, Colin Smythe and Irish University Press, 1971

The Collected Plays, II, The Tragedies and Tragic-Comedies, ed. Ann Saddlemyer, Gerrards Cross, Colin Smythe and Irish University Press, 1971

The Collected Plays, III, The Wonder and Supernatural Plays, ed. Ann Saddlemyer, Gerrards Cross, Colin Smythe, 1979

The Collected Plays, IV, The Translations and Adaptations of Lady Gregory and Her Collaborations with Douglas Hyde and W.B. Yeats, ed. Ann Saddlemyer, Gerrards Cross, Colin Smythe, 1979

Coole, Dublin, Cuala Press, 1931

Coole, ed. Colin Smythe, Dublin, Dolmen Press, 1971

Cuchulain of Muirthemne: The Story of the Men of the Red Branch of Ulster, London, John Murray, 1902; Reed International Books, 1994

'"Eothen" and the Athenaeum Club', *Blackwood's Magazine* (December 1895), 797–804

'The Felons of Our Land', *Cornhill Magazine*, 47 (May 1900), 622–34

Gods and Fighting Men: The Story of the Tuatha de Danaan and of the Fianna of Ireland, London, John Murray, New York, Scribner, 1904, Reed International Books, 1994

'A Gentleman', *The Argosy* (July 1894), 72–81

Ideals in Ireland (ed.) London, At the Unicorn, 1901

The Images and Other Plays, New York and London, G.P. Putnam's, 1922

'Ireland, Real and Ideal', *The Nineteenth Century* (November 1898), 769–82

'Irene', *The Argosy* (October 1890), 352

'Irish Visions', *The Spectator* (10 July 1897), 46–7

'An Italian Literary Drama', *Daily Express* (8 April 1899), 3

The Kiltartan Books Comprising The Kiltartan Poetry, History and Wonder Books, Gerrards Cross, Colin Smythe, 1971 (originally published separately in 1918, 1909, 1910)

Lady Gregory's Journals, vol. I, ed. Daniel J. Murphy, Gerrards Cross, Colin Smythe, 1978

Lady Gregory's Journals, vol. II, ed. Daniel J. Murphy, Gerrards Cross, Colin Smythe, 1987

Lady Gregory's Journals: 1916–1930, ed. Lennox Robinson, Dublin and London, Putnam, 1946

'Living Legends of the Fianna', *The Monthly Review* (February 1905), 74–92

Mr Gregory's Letter-Box: 1813–1830, ed. by Lady Gregory, London, Smith, Elder & Co, 1898

My First Play, London, Elkin Mathews & Marrot, 1930

In *The Nation*, six articles from 16 October 1920 to 1 January 1921

Irish Folk History Plays, 2 vols, New York and London, G.P. Putnam's, 1912

Our Irish Theatre, A Chapter of Autobiography, Gerrards Cross, Colin Smythe, 1972, first pub. New York and London, G.P. Putnam's, 1913

'Land Conference', letter, *The Irish Daily Independent and Nation* (25 September 1902), p. 56

New Comedies, New York and London, G.P. Putnam's, 1913

The Old Woman Remembers (poem), in *Col. Plays II*

'Over the River' (pamphlet), London, Ridgeway, 1888

'Pat and Fritz' (poem), *The Nation* (19 September 1914), p. 866

A Phantom's Pilgrimage or Home Ruin (pamphlet), London, Ridgeway, 1893

'A Philantropist', *The Argosy* (June 1891), 468–83

'The Poet Raftery', *The Argosy* (January 1901), 44–58, revised version in *Poets and Dreamers*, 15–42

Poets and Dreamers: Studies and Translations from the Irish including Nine Plays by Douglas Hyde, Gerrards Cross, Colin Smythe, 1974, first pub. in smaller edition, Dublin, Hoggis Figgis; London, John Murray, 1903

'Political Prophecy' (letter), *The Spectator* (11 November 1899), 693

'Raftery, Poet of the Poor', *An Claidheamh Soluis* (14 October 1899), 488–9

[Letter about Raftery's Grave], *An Claidheamh Soluis* (2 December 1899), 605

'Raftery's Grave', *An Claidheamh Soluis* (8 September 1900), 406

Seven Short Plays, Dublin, Maunsel, 1909

Seventy Years: 1852–1922: Being the Autobiography of Lady Gregory, ed. Colin Smythe, New York, Macmillan, 1976, 1st American edition, 1st edition, 1974

'Sir Frederic Burton', *The Leader* (8 December 1900), 231–2

Sir Hugh Lane: His Life and Legacy, Gerrards Cross, Colin Smythe, 1973, first pub. as *Hugh Lane's Life and Achievement, with Some Account of the Dublin Galleries*, London, John Murray, 1921

Sir William Gregory, K.C.M.G., An Autobiography, ed. Lady Gregory, London, John Murray, 2nd edn, 1894

'Three Kiltartan Folk Tales', *The Outlook* (New York) (27 April 1912), 978–85

Three Last Plays, New York and London, G.P. Putnam's, 1928

Three Wonder Plays, New York and London, G.P. Putnam's, 1922

'Through Portugal', *Fortnightly Review*, 40 (1883), 571–80

'Tree Planting', *The Irish Homestead* (12 and 19 February 1898), 141–2, 164

Visions and Beliefs in the West of Ireland Collected and Arranged by Lady Gregory: With Two Essays and Notes by W.B. Yeats, Gerrards Cross, Colin Smythe, 1976, first pub. in 2 vols, New York and London, G.P. Putnam's, 1920

Secondary Sources

Adams, Hazard, *Lady Gregory*, Lewisburg, Bucknell University Press, 1973

Amory, Mark, *Biography of Lord Dunsany*, London, Collins, 1972

Arac, Jonathan and Ritvo, Harriet (eds), *Macropolitics of Nineteenth-Century Literature: Nationalism, Exoticism, Imperialism*, Philadelphia, University of Pennsylvania Press, 1991

Arnold, Bruce, *Jack Yeats*, New Haven and London, Yale University Press, 1998

Bence-Jones, Mark, *Twilight of the Ascendancy*, London, Constable, 1987

——, *Life in an Irish Country House*, London, Constable, 1996

Blunt, Wilfrid Scawen, *My Diaries: Being a Personal Narrative of Events, Part I, 1888–1900, Part II, 1900–1914*, London, Martin Secker, 1919 and 1920, with a foreword by Lady Gregory

Brown, John Russell (ed.), *The Oxford Illustrated History of Theatre*, Oxford, Oxford University Press, 1997

Burke's Irish Family Records, London, Burke's Peerage Limited, 1976

Cave, Richard Allen, 'The Dangers and Difficulties of Dramatising the Lives of Deirdre and Grania', in Jacqueline Genet and Richard Allen Cave (eds), *Perspectives of Irish Drama and Theatre*, Maryland, Barnes and Noble Books, 1991

Colum, Mary, *Life and the Dream*, London, Macmillan, 1947

Connolly, S.J., *The Oxford Companion to Irish History*, Oxford, Oxford University Press, 1998

Coote, Stephen, *W.B. Yeats, A Life*, London, Hodder and Stoughton, 1997

Courtney, Sister Marie-Thérèse, *Edward Martyn and the Irish Theatre*, New York, Vintage Press, 1956

Coxhead, Elizabeth, *Lady Gregory: A Literary Portrait*, New York, Harcourt, Brace & World, Inc., 1961; 2nd revised edn, London, Secker & Warburg, 1966

——, *Daughters of Erin*, Gerrards Cross, Colin Smythe, 1979

Dalsimer, Adele M., 'Players in the Western World: The Abbey Theatre's American Tours', *Eire-Ireland*, 16:4 (Winter 1981), 75–93

De Vere White, Terence, *The Anglo-Irish*, London, Gollanz, 1972

Dolan, Terence Patrick (ed.), *A Dictionary of Hiberno-English*, Dublin, Gill & Macmillan, pb. edn 1999

Dooley, Terence, *The Decline of the Big House in Ireland*, Dublin, Wolfhound Press, 2001

Duff, Sir Mountstuart Elphinstone Grant, *Notes from a Diary 1889–1891* and *1892–1895*, London, John Murray, 1901 and 1904

Dunleavy, Janet and Dunleavy, Gareth W., *Douglas Hyde, A Maker of Modern Ireland*, Berkeley, University of California Press, 1991

Edel, Leon (ed.), *Henry James, Letters*, London, Macmillan, 1982

Edwards, A.C., 'The Lady Gregory Letters to Seán O'Casey', *Modern Drama* (8 May 1965), 95–111

Ellmann, Richard (ed.), *Selected Letters of James Joyce*, London, Faber & Faber, 1975

——, *James Joyce*, Oxford, Oxford University Press, new and revised edition, 1982

Fahey, J., *The History and Antiquities of The Diocese of Kilmacduagh*, Dublin, 1893

Fay, Gerard, *The Abbey Theatre: Cradle of Genius*, Dublin, Clonmore Reynolds Ltd, 1958

Finneran, Richard J., Harper, George, Mills, Murphy, William, J. (eds), *Letters to W.B. Yeats*, vols 1 and 2, London, Macmillan, 1977

Flannery, James W., *Miss Annie Horniman and the Abbey Theatre*, Dublin, The Dolmen Press, 1970

Foster, R.F., *Modern Ireland, 1600–1972*, London, Allen Lane, 1988

——, *W.B. Yeats, A Life, 1. The Apprentice Mage*, Oxford, Oxford University Press, 1997

——, *W.B. Yeats, A Life, II. The Arch-Poet*, Oxford, Oxford University Press, 2003

——, 'Yeats and the Death of Lady Gregory', *Irish University Review*, vol. 34, no. 1 (Spring/Summer 2004), 109–21

Frayne, John P. and Johnson, Colton (eds), *Uncollected Prose by W.B. Yeats*, vol. 2, 1897–1939, London, The Macmillan Press, 1975

Frazier, Adrian, *Behind the Scenes, Yeats, Horniman, and the Struggle for the Abbey Theatre*, Berkeley, University of California Press, 1990

——, *George Moore, 1852–1933*, New Haven and London, Yale University Press, 2000

Gilbert, Martin, *First World War*, London, Weidenfeld and Nicolson, 1994

Glendinning, Victoria, *Trollope*, London, Hutchinson, 1992

Gordon, D.J. (ed.), *W.B. Yeats: Images of a Poet*, Manchester, Manchester University Press, 1961

Gould, Warwick, Kelly, John, Toomey, Deirdre (eds), *The Collected Letters of W.B. Yeats*, vol. 2, 1896–1900, Oxford, Clarendon Press, 1997

Gregory, Anne, *Me and Nu, Childhood at Coole*, Gerrards Cross, Colin Smythe, 1970

Gregory, Sir William, KCMG, *Sir William Gregory, K.C.M.G., An Autobiography*, ed. Lady Gregory, London, John Murray, 2nd edn 1894

Gwynn, Denis, *Edward Martyn and the Irish Revival*, London, Jonathan Cape, 1930, 2nd edn New York, Lemma Publishing Corporation, 1974

Harrington, John P. (ed.), *Modern Irish Drama*, New York, London, W.W. Norton & Co, 1991

Hill, Judith, 'Finding a Voice: Augusta Gregory, Raftery, and Cultural Nationalism, 1899–1900,' *Irish University Review*, vol. 34, no. 1 (Sping/Summer 2004), 21–36

——, 'Lady Gregory', in David Holderman and Ben Levit (eds), *W.B. Yeats in Context*, Cambridge, Cambridge University Press, 2010, 129–138

Hogan, Robert and O'Neill, Michael J. (eds), *Joseph Holloway's Abbey Theatre: A Selection from His Unpublished Journal*, Carbondale and Edwardsville, Southern Illinois University Press, 1967

Hogan, Robert and Kilroy, James, *The Irish Literary Theatre 1899–1901*, Dublin, The Dolmen Press, 1975

—— and ——, *Laying the Foundations 1902–1904*, Dublin, The Dolmen Press, 1976

—— and ——, *The Abbey Theatre: The Years of Synge 1905–1909*, Dublin, The Dolmen Press, 1978

Hogan, Robert, Burnham, Richard, Poteet, Daniel P., *The Abbey Theatre: The Rise of the Realists, 1910–1915*, Dublin, The Dolmen Press, 1979

Hogan, Robert and Burnham, Richard, *The Years of O'Casey 1921–1926. A Documentary History*, Gerrards Cross, Colin Smythe, 1992

Holderman, David and Levit, Ben (eds), *W.B. Yeats in Context*, Cambridge, Cambridge University Press, 2010

Holroyd, Michael, *Bernard Shaw*, vol. 2, *The Pursuit of Power*, London, Chatto & Windus, 1989

Hone, Joseph, *W.B. Yeats, 1865–1939*, London, Macmillan, 1965, 1st edn 1943

—— (ed.), *J.B. Yeats: Letters to his son W.B. Yeats and Others 1869–1922*, London, Faber & Faber, 1944

Humphreys, Madeleine, *Edward Martyn and the Irish Dramatic Movement: A Reappraisal*, unpublished

Hunt, Hugh, *The Abbey: Ireland's National Theatre, 1904–1978*, Dublin, Gill & Macmillan, 1979

Hyde, Douglas, *Love Songs of Connacht (being the fourth chapter of The Songs of Connacht)*, 1st edn London and Dublin 1893, reprint, Dublin, Irish University Press, 1987

——, *Songs Ascribed to Raftery (being the fifth chapter of The Songs of Connacht)*, 1st edn London and Dublin 1903, reprint, Shannon, Irish University Press, 1973

——, *The Religious Songs of Connacht (being the sixth and seventh chapters of The Songs of Connacht)*, 1st edn London and Dublin 1906, reprint, Shannon, Irish University Press, 1972

Jenkins, Brian, *Sir William Gregory of Coole*, Gerrards Cross, Colin Smythe, 1986

Kelly, John and Domville, Eric, *The Collected Letters of W.B. Yeats, Vol. I 1865–1895*, Oxford, Clarendon Press, 1986

Kelly, John and Schuchard, Ronald, *The Collected Letters of W.B. Yeats, Vol. III 1901–1904*, Oxford, Clarendon Press, 1994

Kiberd, Declan, *Synge and the Irish Language*, London, The Macmillan Press, 1979

——, *Inventing Ireland*, London, Jonathan Cape, 1995, 2nd edn, Vintage, 1996

——, *Irish Classics*, London, Granta Books, 2000

Kilroy, James, *The 'Playboy' Riots*, Dublin, The Dolmen Press, 1971

Knapp, 'History Against Myth: Lady Gregory and Cultural Discourse', *Éire-Ireland*, 22: 3 (1987), 30–42

Kohfeldt, Mary Lou, *Lady Gregory, the Woman behind the Irish Renaissance*, New York, 1984, London, André Deutsch, 1985

Kopper, Edward A., Jr., *Lady Isabella Persse Gregory*, Boston, Twayne Publishers, 1976

Krause, David (ed.), *The Letters of Seán O'Casey Volume 1 1910–1941*, New York, Macmillan, 1975

——, *Seán O'Casey and his World*, London, Thames & Hudson, 1976

Laurence, Dan H. and Grene, Nicholas, *Shaw, Lady Gregory and the Abbey*, Gerrards Cross, Colin Smythe, 1993

Lawless, Emily, *Grania: The Story of an Island*, London, Smith, Elder & Co., 1892

Leerssen, Joep, *Remembrance and Imagination*, Cork, Cork University Press, 1996

Leslie, Anita, *Edwardians in Love*, London, Arrow Books, 1974

Longenbach, James, *Stone Cottage, Pound, Yeats, and Modernism*, New York and Oxford, Oxford University Press, 1988

Longford, Elizabeth, *A Pilgrimage of Passion: The Life of Wilfrid Scawen Blunt*, London, Weidenfeld & Nicolson, 1979

Lyons, F.S.L., 'George Moore and Edward Martyn', *Hermathena* (1964), 9–32

——, *Ireland Since the Famine*, London, Fontana, 1985, 1st edn, 1971

McCoole, Sinéad, *A Life of Lady Lavery 1880–1935*, Dublin, Lilliput, 1996

McCormack, W.J., *Fool of the Family, A Life of J.M. Synge*, London, Weidenfeld & Nicolson, 2000

McDiarmid, Lucy and Waters, Maureen (eds), *Lady Gregory, Selected Writings*, London, Penguin, 1995

McDiarmid, Lucy, 'Lady Gregory, Wilfrid Blunt, and London Table Talk', *Irish University Review*, vol. 34, no. 1 (Spring/Summer 2004), 67–80

Maddox, Brenda, *George's Ghosts: A New Life of W.B. Yeats*, London, Picador, 1999

Mathews, P.J., *Revival: The Abbey Theatre, Sinn FÈin, The Gaelic League and the Co-operative Movement*, Cork, Cork University Press, 2003

Mikhail, E.H. (ed.), *Lady Gregory Interviews and Recollections*, London, The Macmillan Press, 1977

—— (ed.), *J.M. Synge Interviews and Recollections*, London, The Macmillan Press, 1977.

——, *Lady Gregory: an Annotated Bibliography of Criticism*, Troy, New York, The Whitston Publishing Company, 1982

—— (ed.), *The Abbey Theatre, Interviews and Recollections*, London, The Macmillan Press, 1988

Mitchell, Revd J., 'Colonel William Persse', *Galway Archaeological and Historical Society Journal*, vol. 30, nos 3, 4 (1963), 49–89

Mitchell, James, 'The Imprisonment of Wilfrid Scawen Blunt in Galway: Cause and Consequence', *Journal of the Galway Archaeological and Historical Society*, 46, 1994, 65–110

Moore, George, *Hail and Farewell, Ave, Salve, Vale*, ed. Richard Cave, Gerrards Cross, Colin Smythe, 1976

Murphy, Daniel J., 'The Letters of Lady Gregory to John Quinn'; Ph.D. Thesis, Columbia University, 1961

——, 'Letters from Lady Gregory: A Record of Her Friendship with T.J. Kiernan', *Bulletin of the New York Public Library*, LXXII, no. 1 (January 1968), 19–63, and LXXII, no. 2 (February 1968), 123–31

Murphy, Joseph, *The Redingtons of Clarenbridge: Leading Catholic Landlords in the Nineteenth Century*, Shannon, Joseph Murphy, 1999

Murphy, Maureen, 'Lady Gregory: "The Book of the People"', *Colby Quarterly*, 27 (1) (March 1991), 40–7

Murphy, William M., *Prodigal Father: The Life of John Butler Yeats (1839–1922)*, Ithaca and London, Cornell University Press, 1978

Murray, Christopher, *Twentieth-Century Irish Drama: Mirror up to Nation*, Manchester, Manchester University Press, 1997

——, *Seán O'Casey: Writer at Work, A Biography*, Dublin, Gill & Macmillan, 2004

Nic Shiubhlaigh, Máire, *The Splendid Years, as told to Edward Kenny*, Dublin, James Duffy & Co, 1955

Nolan, J.C.M., 'Edward Martyn and Guests at Tulira', *Irish Arts Review* (1994), 167–73

O'Brien, Joseph V., *"Dear Dirty Dublin", A City in Distress, 1899–1916*, Berkeley, University of California Press, 1982

O'Byrne, Robert, *Hugh Lane, 1875–1915*, Dublin, The Lilliput Press, 2000

O'Casey, Sean, *Autobiographies 2*, New York, Carroll & Graf, 1984, 1st edn of *Inishfallen, Fare Thee Well*, 1949

O'Connor, Garry, *Seán O'Casey A Life*, London, Hodder & Stoughton, 1988

O'Dwyer, Riana, '"There was a kind Lady called Gregory": James Joyce, Augusta Gregory and the Irish Literary Revival', in Tobin, Sean, *Lady Gregory Autumn Gatherings: Reflections at Coole*, Galway, Lady Gregory Autumn Gathering, 2000

O'Grady, Standish, *Selected Essays*, Dublin, Phoenix, (post-1917)

O hAodha, Micheál, *Theatre in Ireland*, Oxford, Basil Blackwell, 1974

O'Malley, S. and Torchiana, D.T., 'John Butler Yeats to Lady Gregory: New Letters', in Robin Skelton and David R. Clark (eds), *Irish Renaissance: A Gathering of Essays from The Massachusetts Review*, Dublin, The Dolmen Press, 1965

Payne, Ben Iden, *A Life in a Wooden O: Memories of the Theatre*, New Haven and London, Yale University Press, 1977

Pethica, James, 'A Dialogue of Self and Service: Lady Gregory's Emergence as an Irish Writer and Partnership with W.B. Yeats', D.Phil. dissertation, University of Oxford, 1987

——, '"Our Cathleen": Yeats's Collaboration with Lady Gregory in the writing of *Cathleen ni Houlihan*', *Yeats Annual* (1988), 3–31

——, 'Patronage and Creative Exchange: Yeats, Lady Gregory and the Economy of Indebtedness', in Deirdre Toomey (ed.), *Yeats and Women*, Basingstoke, Macmillan Press, 1992

—— and Roy, James Charles, '"Nothing but misery all round me": Henry Stratford Persse and the Galway Famine of 1822', *Galway Archaeological and Historical Society Journal*, 47 (1995), 1–35

—— (ed.), *Lady Gregory's Diaries 1892–1902*, Gerrards Cross, Colin Smythe, 1996

——, 'Claiming Raftery's Curse: Yeats, Hyde, Lady Gregory and the Writing of *The Marriage*', in Wayne K. Chapman and Warwick Gould (eds), *Yeats's Collaborations, Yeats Annual*, 15 (2002), 3–35

——, '"A Young Man's Ghost": Lady Gregory and J.M. Synge', *Irish University Review*, vol. 34, no. 1 (Spring/Summer 2004), 1–20

Pilkington, Lionel, '"Every Crossing Sweeper Thinks Himself a Moralist": The Critical Role of Audiences in Irish Theatre History', *Irish University Review* (Spring/Summer 1997), 152–65

Quinn, John, 'Lady Gregory and the Irish Theatre', *Outlook* (New York) (16 December 1911) 916–19 in Mikhail, E.H. (ed.), *Lady Gregory, Interviews and Recollections*, London, The Macmillan Press, 1977

Reid, B.L., *The Man from New York: John Quinn and his Friends*, New York, Oxford University Press, 1968

Reynolds, Paige, 'The Making of a Celebrity: Lady Gregory and the Abbey's First American Tour', *Irish University Review*, vol. 34, no. 1 (Spring/Summer 2004), 81–93

Robinson, Lennox, *Curtain Up, an Autobiography*, London, Michael Joseph, 1942

——, *Lady Gregory's Journals, 1916–1930*, London, Putnam & Company, 1946

——, *Ireland's Abbey Theatre, A History, 1899–1951*, London, Sidgwick and Jackson, 1951

Rowe, Veronica, 'Two Forgotten Talents of Limerick Lace Michael Hayes and Eileen O'Donohue,' *Irish Arts Review* (1999), 61–70

Saddlemyer, Ann, 'In Search of the Unknown Synge', in Sekine, *Irish Writers and Society at Large*, Gerrards Cross, 1985

——, *In Defense of Lady Gregory, Playwright*, Dublin, The Dolmen Press, 1966

—— (ed.), *Theatre Business*, Gerrards Cross, Colin Smythe, 1982

—— (ed.), *The Collected Letters of John Millington Synge, Vol. I 1871–1907*, Oxford, Clarendon Press, 1983; *Vol. II 1907–1909*, 1984

—— and Smythe, Colin (eds), *Lady Gregory, Fifty Years After*, Gerrards Cross, Colin Smythe, 1987

——, *Becoming George, The Life of Mrs W.B. Yeats*, Oxford, Oxford University Press, 2002

Sekine, Masaru (ed.), *Irish Writers and Society at Large*, Irish Literary Studies, 22, Gerrards Cross, Colin Smythe, 1985

Skelton, Robin, *J.M. Synge and his World*, London, Thames & Hudson, 1971

Smythe, Colin, *A Guide to Coole Park, Co. Galway*, Gerrards Cross, Colin Smythe, 3rd revised edn 1995

—— (ed.), *Robert Gregory, 1881–1918*, Gerrards Cross, Colin Smythe, 1981

——, 'Lady Gregory's Contributions to Periodicals: A checklist', in *Lady Gregory Fifty Years After*, ed. Ann Saddlemyer and Colin Smythe, Gerrards Cross, Colin Smythe, 1987

Summerfield, Henry, *Selections from the Contributions to 'The Irish Homestead' by G.W. Russell* vol. 1, Atlantic Highlands, N.J., Humanities Press, 1978, vol. 2, Gerrards Cross, Colin Smythe, 1978

Synge, J.M., *The Aran Islands*, Oxford, Oxford University Press, 1979, first published 1907

——, *Plays*, London, George Allen & Unwin Ltd, 1910

Szladits, Lola L., 'New in the Berg Collection 1962–1964', *Bulletin of the New York Public Library*, 73 (4 April 1969), 227–52

Tobin, Sean (ed.), *Lady Gregory Autumn Gatherings: Reflections at Coole*, Galway, The Lady Gregory Autumn Gathering, 2000

Tóibín, Colm, *Lady Gregory's Toothbrush*, Dublin, The Lilliput Press, 2002

Vaughan, W.E., *Landlords and Tenants in Mid-Victorian Ireland*, Oxford, Clarendon Press, 1994

Wade, Allan (ed.), *The Letters of W.B. Yeats*, London, Rupert Hart-Davis, 1954

Warwick, Gould, Kelly, John and Toomey, Deirdre (eds), *The Collected Letters of W.B. Yeats*, vol. 2, 1896–1900, Oxford, Oxford University Press, 1997

Welch, Robert (ed.), *The Oxford Companion to Irish Literature*, Oxford, Clarendon Press, 1996

——, *The Abbey Theatre 1899–1999: Form and Pressure*, Oxford, Oxford University Press, 1999

West, Trevor, *Horace Plunkett: Co-operation and Politics, An Irish Biography*, Gerrards Cross, Colin Smythe, 1986

Winstone, H.V.F., *Lady Anne Blunt: A Biography*, London, Barzan Publishing, 2003

Yeats, W.B., *The Celtic Twilight, Myth, Fantasy and Folklore*, 1st edn 1893, 2nd enlarged edn 1902, later edn, Dorset, Prism Press, 1990

——, *The Collected Plays of W.B. Yeats*, London, Macmillan, 2nd edn 1952

——, *Memoirs*, ed. Denis Donoghue, Dublin, Gill & Macmillan, 1972

——, *Autobiographies*, London, Macmillan, 1955, Papermac 1980

——, *Uncollected Prose by W.B. Yeats*, ed. John P. Frayne, vol. 1, London, Macmillan, 1970

Yeats's 'Vision' Papers, 3 vols, ed. George Harper Mills, *et al.*, London, Macmillan, 1992

Index

Abbey Theatre: buildings, 271–2, 278–9; patent, 271–2, 274–5, 357; first night, 278–9; reorganisation, 283–4, 288–9, 296–300; crisis, 290–1, 296–300; audiences, 319; and *The Playboy of the Western World*, 303–9; tours, 319, 343, 566 (n. 27); resignation of Fays, 321–2; and *The Shewing-up of Blanco Posnet*, 245–8; finances 319–20, 335, 350–2, 566 (n. 28), 585 (n. 21); reputation, 351; and King Edward VII's death, 355; American tours, 368–83, 391; pre-war difficulties, 419–20; during war 420–1, 429–30, 459, 574 (n. 6); and the new state, 479, 491; and *The Plough and the Stars*, 506–8; 21st birthday, 507; 'Advice to Playwrights', 583 (n. 27)

Aberdeen, Lord, 348

Allgood, Molly, 268, 304

Allgood, Sara, 235, 268, 269, 271, 278, 322, 333, 335, 373, 476

Anglo-Irish Treaty, 477–8, 479

Anglo-Irish War, 456, 461–2, 464–75

Arabi, see El Arabi

Ardilaun, Lady Olivia, 179, 505

Ardilaun, Lord, 179, 394

Atkinson, Robert, 224

Bailey, Rt Hon. William Frederick, 414, 415

Balfour, Arthur James, 106, 126, 148

Barlow, Jane, 134, 179, 542 (n. 33)

Beauchamp, Geraldine (AG's niece), 180, 193, 218

Beaumont, Lady Margaret, 44, 95

Beltaine, 205

Birch, Sir Arthur, 44, 123, 130, 209, 343

Blunt, Lady Anne, 60–2, 65, 81, 457–8

Blunt, Judith, 60–1, 458

Blunt, Wilfrid Scawen: appearance, 60; character and background, 60–1;

early travels, 60; in Egypt, 60–66; meets AG, 60–2; attitude to WHG, 60–2, 67–8; support for Arabi, 63–6, 67–8, 77–8; works with AG for Arabi, 67–9, 76–8; appreciation of AG, 76, 458, 480; love affair with AG, 68–82; uses 'A Woman's Sonnets', 70, 79–81; *Ideas on India*, 99; supports Land League, 104–9; in prison, 106–9; reaction to *Sir William Gregory*, 134; and *Fand*, 179; and separation from Anne, 284; and peacock dinner, 402; and First World War, 407; and 'Easter 1916', 427; ageing 457–8; response to Lady Anne's death, 458; death, 486; *The Wind and Whirlwind*, 536 (n. 64); *The Love Lyrics and Songs of Proteus*, 539 (n. 70)

Borthwick, Norma, 180, 200

Boston, 364–72

Bowdoin, Elizabeth Temple (WHG's first wife), 32–3

Boyle, William, 235, 322

Browning, Robert, 44, 96, 453

Burton, Sir Frederic, 41, 79, 128, 143, 163, 189, 193, 215–16

Carleton, Dorothy, 284, 457, 486

Carson, Edward, 434

Churchill, Lord Randolph, 128

Civil War, 483–90

Clay, Sir Arthur, 44, 143

Collins, Michael, 477, 485

Colum, Mary, 269, 402, 558 (n. 21)

Colum, Padraic, 353, 263, 264, 268, 283, 297

Colvin, Sir Auckland, 58, 59, 538 (n. 40)

Connolly, Seán, 425, 427, 582 (n. 31)

Connolly, Sean, 226

Coole Park: intellectual tradition, 30; as it is today, 46–7; history and character, 47–9, 192–3; tenants and Land League, 53–5, 75; household,